Multi-Asset Risk Modeling

Multi-Asset Risk Modeling

Techniques for a Global Economy in an Electronic and Algorithmic Trading Era

Morton Glantz

Robert Kissell

AMSTERDAM • BOSTON • HEIDELBERG • LONDON
NEW YORK • OXFORD • PARIS • SAN DIEGO
SAN FRANCISCO • SINGAPORE • SYDNEY • TOKYO
Academic Press is an imprint of Elsevier

Academic Press is an imprint of Elsevier
525 B Street, Suite 1800, San Diego CA 92101, USA
225 Wyman Street, Waltham, MA 02451, USA
The Boulevard, Langford Lane, Kidlington, Oxford, OX5 1GB, UK

Notices
Knowledge and best practice in this field are constantly changing. As new research and experience broaden our understanding, changes in research methods, professional practices, or medical treatment may become necessary.

Practitioners and researchers must always rely on their own experience and knowledge in evaluating and using any information, methods, compounds, or experiments described herein. In using such information or methods they should be mindful of their own safety and the safety of others, including parties for whom they have a professional responsibility.

To the fullest extent of the law, neither the Publisher nor the authors, contributors, or editors, assume any liability for any injury and/or damage to persons or property as a matter of products liability, negligence or otherwise, or from any use or operation of any methods, products, instructions, or ideas contained in the material herein.

Library of Congress Cataloging-in-Publication Data
Application submitted.

British Library Cataloguing-in-Publication Data
A catalogue record for this book is available from the British Library.

ISBN: 978-0-12-401690-3

For information on all Academic Press publications
visit our Web site at *www.elsevierdirect.com*

Printed in the United States
14 15 16 17 18   10 9 8 7 6 5 4 3 2 1

To my wife Maryann, an endless source of love, patience, and inspiration.
To my wife Felise, an endless source of love and encouragement.

Contents

Preface

Multi-Asset Risk Modeling: Techniques for a Global Economy in an Electronic and Algorithmic Era is written to assist readers improve their understanding financial risk and risk management practices in a new and ever volatile environment and across multiple asset classes.

The text focuses on the application of proper volatility and factor models, optimization techniques and provides insight into the evaluation of traditional and non-traditional sources of risk (for example, extreme value events, and electronic and algorithmic trading risk). Readers will learn how to properly evaluate non-traditional sources of risk, and monetize financial investment decisions in real-time.

We describe the latest and most advanced risk-modeling techniques for equities, debt, fixed income, futures and derivatives, commodities, and foreign exchange, as well as advanced algorithmic and electronic risk management. With mathematics playing a prominent role, we present standard risk-management and asset allocation models and more advanced extensions, discuss the laws in standard models that contributed to the 2008 financial crisis, and talk about current and future banking regulation. Importantly, we will also explore algorithmic trading, which currently receives sparse attention in the literature. You will study extreme value functions, explore Basel III compliance modeling specifically in areas of specialized lending, develop concepts of sustainability management, and work with risk-hedging techniques. Emphasis throughout the text will focus on applying an financial risk management framework and proper utilization of statistical analysis required for fiduciary decision making.

Primary readership includes graduate students, industry practitioners, risk managers, money managers, bankers, regulators, corporate risk officers, accountants, and CFOs.

In order to address the essential aspects of Multi-Asset Risk Modeling, the book is arranged in fourteen chapters, each providing a specific focus. A description of the chapters in the book is as follows:

In Chapter 1, *Introduction to Multi-Asset Risk Modeling — Lessons from the Debt Crisis*, we review how statistical pricing and risk-forecasting models contributed to the debt crisis. For example, many of these models provided improper insight for risk analysis, and lead to mispriced collateralized debt obligations, mortgage backed securities and credit derivatives, as well as misguide algorithmic trading instructions.

The chapter shows how risk managers can incorporate views and information sets across different asset classes to improve risk forecasts in rapid changing markets. We present an overview of different types of risk and risk management products. In particular, we discuss details inherent in credit and equity risk: price risk (volatility), operational risk, country risk, default risk, company specific risk, liquidity risk, interest rate risk, operational risk, macro-economic factor risk; how money managers, investors, and risk managers expand their understanding of risk and infer real-time information from derivatives and options, FX rates, debt markets, and macro-economic changes. Finally, we discuss components of algorithmic trading — the industry's lifeblood.

In Chapter 2, *A Primer on Risk Mathematics*, we discuss applications of risk modeling, providing an overview of the mathematics, statistics, and probability required to measure, analyze, forecast, and measure risk. We discuss probability theory and statistical analysis, unbiased estimates, time series math, linear regression, and non-linear estimation techniques including logit and probit models. The chapter also provides an overview of some of the important statistics used to evaluate regression models such as T-test, F-test, and R2 goodness of fit. We provide an overview of the linear algebra technique used to estimate model parameters and corresponding parameter errors to develop confidence intervals surrounding the estimates. The chapter concludes with an in-depth discussion of probability distribution functions and their use in finance and risk management. This include continuous distributions, discrete distributions, and extreme value functions such as Gumbel (type I), Frechet (type II), and Weibul (type III). Extreme value functions have gained recent traction in the financial industry since the financial crisis, and have become essential risk-management tools across all asset classes.

Chapter 3 preserves the quantitative focus as we learn to develop uncertainty forecast models. *A Primer on Quantitative Risk Analysis* provides the fundamentals of quantitative risk analysis that is required knowledge and a prerequisite for more advanced applications in financial services. The chapter begins with an interesting historical perspective of risk, followed by discussions of the basic characteristics of risk and the nature of risk versus returns. It then provides detailed hands-on applications of running quantitative Monte Carlo risk simulations using Real Options Valuation's Risk Simulator software. Other topics presented include correlations and precision control, setting seed values, setting run preferences (simulation properties), and creating a simulation report and forecast statistics table. Finally, the chapter wraps up with two hands-on exercises for using the software on running risk simulations and understanding the diversification effects of correlations on risk. Readers are invited to reinforce concepts presented in Chapter 3 by visiting www.realoptionsvaluation.com for free videos, case studies, and models, as well as downloadable trial versions of the software.

Chapter 4 explores, in mathematical and practical terms, *Price Volatility*. We open with an overview of price-volatility forecasting models. We describe the mathematics behind these models and provide an in-depth analysis of scaling properties. We discuss various techniques employed in the industry to forecast volatility as well as appropriate methods to calibrate these models. We expand volatility concepts by providing readers with findings and empirical evidence across time period and asset classes. We will further develop scaling properties of volatility over time. This chapter also reiterates and expands on techniques presented in the Price Volatility Chapter in The Science of Algorithmic Trading and Portfolio Management (Kissell, 2013).

Chapter 5 concentrates on defining the challenges and use of *Factor Models*. Factor models have gained increased status. Much of this is due to continued market turmoil and asset price uncertainty. Analysts are now turning to factor risk models to estimate asset returns and corresponding financial risk rather than relying on their traditional approaches that all too often have proven unreliable. Our goal using factor risk models is to determine a set of factors (e.g., explanatory variables) that explain price movement. Analysts able to successfully forecast these factors or factor returns will be in a position to successfully forecast asset returns (the ultimate goal of financial management!). Factor models have also become increasingly widespread for estimating asset volatility, especially covariance and correlation across asset returns. This chapter also reiterates and expands on techniques presented in the Price Volatility Chapter in The Science of Algorithmic Trading and Portfolio Management (Kissell, 2013).

Moving on to Chapter 6, Equity Derivatives, we introduce readers to the equities derivatives market and related financial instruments. We explore options, forwards, futures, and swaps. We show how practitioners can infer risk from the different derivatives via implied volatilities and implied correlations. The chapter begins with a focus on the various options-pricing models (Black-Scholes, binomial trees, etc.), put-call parity, and pricing call and put options. We introduce the reader to the different derivative risks: delta, vega, theta, and gamma, as well as volatility smiles and volatility skew. We then expand on these models and show how the implied volatility and implied correlation measures derived from these instruments can lead to better real-time risk metrics and risk-monitoring systems. We provide an in-depth analysis of the financial crisis period of 2008-2009, and show how these equity derivatives risk metrics provided practitioners with better metrics and more timely market insight. Readers will gain a thorough knowledge of the different risks and modeling approaches used in the equity derivatives asset class and proper methods to apply these approaches and build more efficient risk metrics.

With increased globalization comes an increased need to understand the foreign exchange markets. In Chapter 7, we present readers with an overview of the *Foreign Exchange Market and Interest Rates*, spot prices, forwards, futures, cross-currency interest rate swaps, and options. We explore the economics corresponding to exchange rates and international trades, differences between fixed and variable exchange rates, the gold standard, and provide an overview of the different currency risk metrics. We apply the mathematical models and approaches developed in Chapter 2 to develop best-in-class FX volatility and correlation risk models. The chapter concludes with practical examples and applications.

We study *Algorithmic Trading Risk* in Chapter 8. Algorithmic trading represents computerized executions of financial instruments. Currently, algorithms are being used to trade stocks, bonds, currencies, and a plethora of financial derivatives. The new era of algorithmic trading has provided investors with more efficient strategy implementation and lower transaction costs, resulting in improved portfolio performance. In addition to these advantages and savings comes a new set of algorithmic risks. Here we introduce readers to the algorithmic trading process and corresponding uncertainty. We follow the techniques presented in *The Science of Algorithmic Trading and Portfolio Management* (Kissell, 2013) and adapt these techniques for Risk Management. Readers interested in a more thorough examination of algorithms can obtain (Kissell, 2013).

In Chapter 9, *Risk Hedging Techniques*, we provide mathematics behind some of the more advanced portfolio-hedging techniques. In particular, we discuss derivation of the hedge ratio and its usage in finance to determine the optimal manner to hedge a held portfolio. We examine the hedge ratio in terms of various pricing models, such as CAPM and APT, and discuss the ratio in terms of portfolio dollars and weights. The chapter concludes with a general solution to the optimal hedging ratio problem that moves across asset class and investment instruments.

We move on to Chapter 10, *Rating Credit Risk: Current Practices, Model Design, and Applications*. The credit crisis of 2008−2009 was in many ways a credit-rating crisis. The financial crisis might not have happened without credit-ratings agencies issuing stellar ratings on toxic mortgage securities. Doubts about credit-rating agencies arose due to alleged conflicts of interest and the alleged backward-looking nature of the analytical process. Structured finance products, such as mortgage-backed securities, accounted for over 11 trillion dollars of outstanding U.S. debt. The lion's share of these securities was highly rated. For example, more than half of the structured finance securities rated by Moody's carried AAA ratings, the highest credit rating, typically reserved for near-riskless securities. Important point: Financial institutions should develop industry- and deal-specific internal risk models. Internal ratings, because they are founded on "know thy customer," provide a potent framework for assessing multi-asset portfolios. The internal risk models discussed understand client fundamentals.

We offer specialized lending risk models proposed by the Bank for International Settlements including project finance, commodity finance, real estate, and object finance. In addition, the chapter includes an industry-specific, deal-specific corporate system and the CAMELS rating, the United States supervisory rating of a bank's overall condition. Risk rating is developed further in Appendix 1 to Chapter 10, *Corporate Risk Rating: Obligor and Facility Grade Requisites*.

Chapter 11, *A Basic Credit Default Swap Model*, provides readers with an introduction to credit derivatives. The credit derivative market has emerged as one of the most dynamic and innovative sectors of the global financial system. Credit derivative contracts are financial instruments that transfer between two parties the risk and return characteristics of a credit-risky reference asset. As such, they have become an integral part of the risk management and investment strategies of global investors and intermediaries. We explore the credit derivative marketplace, examine the instruments from various different angles, including applications, valuation, and control, and demonstrate how each provides perspective on the essential elements of the marketplace. Finally, readers review the "bad" side of these assets, so-called toxic credit derivatives and their role in the recent debt crisis. The term "toxic asset" was coined during the recent financial crisis to refer to mortgage-backed securities, collateralized debt obligations, and credit-default swaps, none of which could be sold after they exposed their holders to massive losses.

Chapter 12, *Multi-Asset Corporate Restructurings and Valuations*, discusses techniques for decision making in the presence of risk, such as valuating corporate restructuring strategies under uncertainty. In particular, we discuss asset allocation and restructuring, risk budgeting, and stress testing. We present techniques based on real-world data to construct multi-asset class portfolios, and provide techniques to minimize risk, manage factor exposure, and maximize alpha. This chapter relies heavily on techniques presented above, and incorporates Monte Carlo simulations and stochastic optimization as a means to uncover potential extreme movements. An appendix to Chapter 12, *A Banker's Guide: Valuation Appraisal of Business Clients*, was developed for readers who operate as financial consultants and advisors.

Recent history tells us that it is unwise to discount the possibility of extreme events. Fat tail risk is real, and the real world does not fit neatly into a bell curve. Chapter 13, *Extreme Value Theory and Application to Market Shocks for Stress Testing and Extreme Value at Risk*, deals with extreme value functions and the role these functions play in the financial services. If credit portfolio losses were bell shaped, we could specify the likelihood of large losses by defining portfolio expected and unexpected loss. The problem is that individual debt assets have very "skewed" loss probabilities. For instance, AAA debt assets enjoy a near-zero standard deviation, while a B-rated debt asset may have a five standard deviation within its distribution. In most cases, the obligor does not default, and the loss is zero, but when default occurs, the loss is substantial. Given the positive correlation between defaults, this unevenness of loss never fully resolves. There is always a large probability of relatively small losses, and a small probability of rather large losses. We explore value at risk and extreme value functions and show derivations. The chapter concludes with a comprehensive extreme value modeling case authored by Dr. Johnathan Mun.

Tail risk is the bane of a financial institution's revenue model, and always has been. Chapter 14, *Ensuring Sustainability of an Institution as a Going Concern: An Approach to Dealing with Black Swan or Tail Risk* by Karamjeet Paul explains that despite rigorous models and risk management controls, financial institution exposure from tail risk can accumulate. For highly leveraged financial institutions, cumulative exposure from tail risk can threaten survival in a stressed environment. While traditional models normally work well in relation to portfolios, they do not address certain critical issues related to policies, governance, limits, strategies, and guidelines to manage the total risk of an institution. What should be the goal of tail risk management? How much tail risk does the institution have? How do you manage tail risk proactively?

As we begin our journey through the chapters, it might be helpful to remember that quantitative methods, such as the use of advanced models or the employment of math, do not alarm sharp professionals. Modeling tools that work are not black boxes that ignore or inhibit wisdom or that mechanize the decision-making process. The traumatic experience of the debt crisis taught us that financial institutions require fresh multi-asset risk models controlled by risk managers with, above all, good common sense.

Morton Glantz
Robert Kissell

About The Authors

Professor Morton Glantz

Professor Morton Glantz serves as a financial consultant, educator, and adviser to a broad spectrum of professionals, including corporate financial executives, government ministers, privatization managers, investment and commercial bankers, public accounting firms, members of merger and acquisition teams, strategic planning executives, management consultants, attorneys, and representatives of foreign governments and international banks. Professor Morton Glantz is a principal of Real Consulting and Real Options Valuation, firms specializing in risk consulting, training, certification, and advanced analytical software in the areas of risk quantification, analysis, and management solutions.

As a J.P. Morgan Chase (heritage bank) senior banker, Professor Glantz built a progressive career path specializing in credit analysis and credit risk management, risk grading systems, valuation models, and professional training. He was instrumental in the reorganization and development of the credit analysis module of the Bank's Management Training Program-Finance, which at the time was recognized as one of the foremost training programs in the banking industry.

Professor Glantz is on the (adjunct) finance faculty of the Fordham Graduate School of Business. He has appeared in the Harvard University International Directory of Business and Management Scholars and Research, and has earned Fordham University Deans Award for Faculty Excellence on three occasions. He is a Board Member of the International Standards Board, International Institute of Professional Education and Research (IIPER). The IIPER is a global institute with partners and offices around the world, including the United States, Switzerland, Hong Kong, Mexico, Portugal, Singapore, Nigeria, and Malaysia. Professor Glantz is widely published in financial journals and authored 8 books: *Credit Engineering for Bankers Second Edition,* Academic Press/Elsevier, 2011; *The Bankers Handbook*, Elsevier, 2008; *Credit Derivatives*, McGraw-Hill, 2006; *Optimal Trading Strategies*, AMACOM, 2003; *Managing Bank Risk*, Academic Press/Elsevier, 2002 (RISKBOOK.COM Award: Best Finance Books of 2003); *Scientific Financial Management*, AMACOM 2000; and *Loan Risk Management*, McGraw-Hill, 1995.

Dr. Robert Kissell

Dr. Robert Kissell is the president and founder of Kissell Research Group. He has over twenty years of professional experience specializing in quantitative modeling, statistical analysis, and risk management. He advises and consults portfolio managers throughout the US and Europe on appropriate risk management and portfolio management techniques.

He is author of the leading industry book "Optimal Trading Strategies," "The Science of Algorithmic Trading & Portfolio Management," and "Multi-Asset Risk Management." He has published numerous research papers on trading strategies, algorithmic trading, risk management, and best execution. His paper, "Dynamic Pre-Trade Models: Beyond the Black Box," won institutional investors prestigious paper of the year award. His latest [copy missing]

Dr. Kissell is an associate editor of Institutional Investor's Journal of Trading and Journal of Index Investing, and he is a frequent speaker in the US and abroad. He has previously been an instructor for Cornell University in their graduate program for financial engineering, and as a guest lecturer at NYU and Fordham University. He has worked with a number of Investment Banks and Investment Management companies, including UBS Securities where he was the Executive Director of Execution Strategies and Portfolio Analysis, and at J.P. Morgan Securities where he was Executive Director and Head of Quantitative Trading Strategies. He was also previously at Citigroup/Smith Barney where he was Vice President, Quantitative Research, and at Instinet where he was Director, Trading Research. He began his career as an Energy Consultant at R.J. Rudden Associated specializing in energy pricing models, risk management, and optimization.

Dr. Kissell has a Ph.D. in Economics from Fordham University, a MS in Applied Mathematics from Hofstra University, and a MS in Business Management and a BS in Applied Mathematics & Statistics from Stony Brook University.

Acknowledgements

The authors greatly appreciate the efforts of Professor Dr. Johnathan Mun who contributed important chapters and stochastic risk models. Dr. Johnathan C. Mun is the founder, Chairman and CEO of Real Options Valuation, Inc. (ROV), a consulting, training, and software development firm specializing in strategic real options, financial valuation, Monte Carlo simulation, stochastic forecasting, optimization, and risk analysis located in northern Silicon Valley, California. He is also the Chairman of the International Institute of Professional Education and Research (IIPER), an accredited global organization providing the Certified in Risk Management (CRM) designation among others, staffed by professors from named universities from around the world. Dr. Mun is widely published. We also wish to thank Karamjeet Paul for his chapter contribution. Mr. Paul is CEO of Strategic Exposure Group, an advisory firm with an exclusive focus on extreme-exposure management of financial and business interruption risks. Finally, we wish to offer a special word of thanks to Dr. J. Scott Bentley, Senior Acquisition Editor, Elsevier Inc. for his support and encouragement.

Additionally, we would like thank Dr. Roberto Malamut for his keen insight regarding proper mathematical techniques for estimating short-term and real-time risk, and for helping to structure the best in class equity risk management practices. Furthermore, Diana Muzan provided much of the research for risk modeling and risk management for Currencies and Equity Derivatives. She provided helpful direction and suggestions regarding combing asset risk across the asset classes, and assisted in developing our framework. And finally, we thank Michael Blake for all of his assistance on the data management side of this project. Mr. Blake is one of the true industry experts regarding Big Data, Cloud Computing, and Smart Technology. The data management framework he has put in place is one of the underlying reasons why investors and asset managers are now able to assess, evaluate, monitor, and manage risk across all asset classes in real-time.

Introduction to Multi-Asset Risk Modeling—Lessons from the Debt Crisis

Financial services firms suffered significant losses brought on by one of the deepest crises ever to hit the financial services industry. As a result, risk modeling and management, loan valuation methods, capital allocation, and governance structures are shaken top to bottom. Fallout from the debt crisis continues to afflict most banks. Credit is still tight at the time of this writing. Banks, particularly those with significant levels of illiquid and difficult to sell assets, were finding it difficult to raise funds from traditional capital suppliers. In response, many institutions exited capital intensive, structured deals in an effort to deleverage and, notably, move away from international operations to concentrate on domestic business.

The debt crisis began when loan incentives, coupled with the acceleration in housing prices, encouraged borrowers to assume mortgages in the belief that they could refinance at favorable terms. Once prices started to drop, refinancing became difficult. Defaults and foreclosures increased dramatically as easy terms expired, home prices failed to go up, and interest rates reset higher. Foreclosures accelerated in late 2006, triggering a global financial crisis. Loan activities at banks froze while the ability of corporations to obtain funds through commercial paper dropped sharply. The expression *a perfect storm*, a "once in a hundred years" event, found its marker. The same could be said for Hurricane Sandy, Black Monday, and the October 1987 crash.

The CEO of Lehman Brothers said the firm was also the victim of "the perfect storm"—yet Lehman did not resist the lure of profits, leveraged balance sheets, and cheap credit. At Goldman Sachs, credit swaps created four billion dollars in profits. The financial modeling that helped produce results at these two investment banks were cutting edge, yet it appears that Lehman, AIG, and other profit takers amassed scant few algorithms to preserve capital protection against unexpected macroeconomic collapse.

Two government-sponsored enterprises, Fannie Mae and Freddie Mac, encouraged home sales by convincing investors that home values would rise over the long term, and that housing investments were safe. Fannie Mae and Freddie Mac created and sold Mortgage-Backed Securities (MBS), an investment considered reliable since the two firms guaranteed interest and principal payments on these loans.

Originally, the two firms had strict rules governing their securities. However, during the 1990s, looser standards resulted in loan approvals to borrowers who had neither collateral nor financial strength to satisfy their obligations. Subprime loans encouraged the housing market initially, but later led to an uncontrollable housing expansion that ended up as the baseline of the financial crisis. Loan oversupply combined with the willingness of the borrowers to lend freely created an untenable outcome for lenders and borrowers.

On the government side, the debt crisis started with the notion that home ownership was a right. Fannie Mae was founded as part of Roosevelt's New Deal to both purchase and securitize mortgages so that cash would be available to lend to home buyers. In 1970, a Republican congress created Freddie Mac to purchase mortgages on the secondary market, and pool and sell the mortgage-backed securities. Social and political pressure expanded the pool of home owners, mostly adding low- and middle-income families. The Equal Credit Opportunity Act prohibited institutional discrimination against minorities, while the Community Investment Act addressed discrimination in lending and encouraged financial institutions to lend to all income brackets in their communities.

In the early 80s, the passage of the Alternative Mortgage Transaction Parity Act preempted state laws by prohibiting adjustable rate mortgages, balloon payments, and negative amortization while allowing lenders to make loans with terms that obscured the loan's cost. The Tax Reform Act prohibited taxpayers from deducting interest payments on consumer loans such as auto loans and credit cards, permitting them to deduct interest on mortgages, which sent homeowners in the millions to refinance mortgages and apply for home equity loans. As a result, household debt increased to 134% from 60% of disposable income. The elimination of Regulation Q was partially responsible for the Savings and Loan Crisis, resulting in a 40 billion dollar taxpayer loss. Despite the closing of hundreds of thrifts, lawmakers continued to deregulate the industry.

The Federal Housing Enterprises Financial Safety and Soundness Act of 1992 required Freddie Mac and Fannie Mae to devote a higher percentage of loans to support affordable housing. Banks were encouraged to do business across state lines, creating the mega banks we have today. Community banks, which had traditionally kept loans in neighborhoods, dwindled along with local loans. Behind the scenes, the banking lobby worked to repeal the Glass-Steagall Act of 1932 that separated commercial and investment banking. Gramm-Leach-Bliley, known also as the Financial Services Modernization Act of 1999, allowed financial institutions to operate as commercial and investment banks and insurance companies.

Many financial institutions ignored sustainability strategies[1] and credit guidelines originating at the Federal Reserve, Comptroller of the Currency, the Basel Committee, and other regulators years prior to the financial crisis. As an example, the office of the Comptroller of the Currency, Administrator of

---

[1]Discussed in Chapter 14, Ensuring Sustainability of an Institution as a Going Concern: An Approach to Dealing with Black Swan or Tail Risk.

National Banks defined nine categories of risk for bank supervision purposes ten years before the crisis. Risks identified by the OCC included credit, interest rate, liquidity, price, foreign exchange, transaction, compliance, strategic, and reputation.[2]

Types of Risk
Credit Risk

Loans are the largest source of credit risk. There are other credit risk products, undertakings, and services included here such as the investment portfolio, overdrafts, letters of credit, and derivatives, foreign exchange, and cash management services. A financial institution's credit policies and procedures define its risk profile. For example, sound credit policies and procedures deal with the following: *(1) establish an appropriate credit risk environment; (2) operate under a sound credit granting process; (3) maintain an appropriate credit administration, measurement and monitoring process; and (4) ensure adequate controls over credit risk. Although specific credit risk management practices may differ among banks depending upon the nature and complexity of their credit activities, a comprehensive credit risk management program focuses on these four areas. These practices should also be applied in conjunction with sound practices related to the assessment of asset quality, the adequacy of provisions and reserves, and the disclosure of credit risk, all of which have been addressed in other recent Basel Committee documents.*[3] While the exact approach chosen by individual supervisors depends on a host of factors, doctrines set out in Principals for the Management of Credit Risk should have formed the basis of *all* bank audits. Yet, profits took rank over sustainability.

Effective management of multi-asset, particularly loan portfolio, credit risk requires that the board and (loan) administration understand and control an institution's risk profile, and preserve credit culture and portfolio integrity. To accomplish this, bankers must have a thorough knowledge of the portfolio's composition and its inherent risks. They must understand the portfolio's product mix, industry and geographic concentrations, average risk ratings, and other aggregate characteristics. They must be sure that the policies, processes, and practices implemented to control risks of individual loans and portfolio segments are sound and that lending personnel adhere to them.[4]

---

[2]Comptroller of the Currency, Administrator of National Banks, Loan Portfolio Management Comptroller's Handbook, April 1998.

[3]Principles for the Management of Credit Risk, Basel Committee on Banking Supervision, Basel, September 2000.

[4]Comptroller of the Currency, Administrator of National Banks, Loan Portfolio Management Comptroller's Handbook, April 1998.

Interest Rate and Market Risk

Market risks arise from adverse movements in market price or rates, for instance, interest, foreign exchange rates, or equity prices. Traditionally, management and regulators concentrated strictly on credit risk. In recent years, another group of assets have come under scrutiny: assets typically traded in financial markets. The level of interest rate risk attributed to the bank's lending activities depends on the composition of its loan portfolio and the degree to which the terms of its loans expose the bank's revenue stream to changes in rates. As part of the risk management process, banks typically identify exposures with heightened sensitivity to interest rate changes, and develop strategies to mitigate the risk: interest rate swaps, for example.

Liquidity Risk

Liquidity risk embodies the likelihood that an institution will be unable to meet obligations when due because assets cannot be liquidated, required funding is unavailable, or specific exposures cannot be unwound without significantly lowering market prices because of market disruptions brought on by a macroeconomic shock. Despite rigorous models and risk management controls, financial institution exposure from tail risk can accumulate. For highly leveraged financial institutions, cumulative exposure from tail risk can threaten survival in a stressed environment, as many banks learned too late. Capital position has a direct bearing on an institution's ability to access liquidity and survive a debt crisis. Weak liquidity might cause a bank to liquefy assets or acquire liabilities to refinance maturing claims. As part of liquidity planning, a bank's overall liquidity strategy should form an important measure of sustainable management.[5]

Price Risk

Exposures originated for sale as part of a securitization or for direct placement in the secondary market carry price risk while awaiting packaging and sale. During that period, the assets should be placed in a "held-for-sale" account, where they must be repriced at the lower of cost or market.[6]

Foreign Exchange Risk

Foreign exchange risk is present when a loan or portfolio of loans is denominated in a foreign currency or funded by borrowings in another currency. In some cases, banks enter into multi-currency credit commitments that permit borrowers to

---

[5]Discussed in Chapter 14, Ensuring Sustainability of an Institution as a Going Concern: An Approach to Dealing with Black Swan or Tail Risk.

[6]Comptroller of the Currency, Administrator of National Banks, Loan Portfolio Management Comptroller's Handbook, April 1998.

select the currency they prefer to use in each rollover period. Foreign exchange risk increases if bankers do not hedge political, social, or economic developments. In addition, results can be unfavorable if one currency becomes snarled in stringent exchange controls or experiences wide exchange-rate fluctuations.

Transaction Risk

The level of transaction risk depends on the capability of information systems and controls, the quality of operating procedures, and the capability and integrity of employees. Significant losses in loan and lease portfolios have resulted when information systems failed to provide adequate statistics to identify concentrations, failed to document auditing failures, expired facilities, or when stale financial statements led to model breakdowns. *Banks have incurred losses because they failed to perfect or renew collateral liens; to obtain proper signatures on loan documents; or to disburse loan proceeds as required by the loan documents.*[7]

Compliance Risk

"Lending activities encompass a broad range of compliance responsibilities and risks. By law, a bank must observe limits on its loans to a single borrower, to insiders, and to affiliates; limits on interest rates; and the array of consumer protection and Community Reinvestment Act regulations."[8] A bank's lending activities may expose it to liability for the cleanup of environmental hazards.

Strategic Risk

Inappropriate strategic decisions about underwriting standards, loan portfolio growth, new loan products, or geographic and demographic markets will threaten a bank's sustainability in a debt crisis. It is for this reason that regulators are taught to be especially focused when auditing new business and product ventures. These ventures require significant planning and careful oversight to ensure the risks are appropriately identified and managed. As we know, many banks extended consumer loan activities to "subprime" borrowers with dire consequences. The following was written 10 years prior to the debt crisis: "*Do banks understand the unique risks associated with this market, can they price for the increased risk, and do they have the technology to service this market? Moreover, how will they compete with the nonbank companies who dominate this market? Both bankers and examiners need to decide whether the opportunities outweigh the strategic risks. If a bank is considering growing a loan product or business in a market saturated with that product or business, it should make sure that it is not overlooking other lending opportunities with more promise.*

---

[7]Comptroller of the Currency, Administrator of National Banks, Loan Portfolio Management Comptroller's Handbook, April 1998.
[8]Comptroller of the Currency, Administrator of National Banks, Loan Portfolio Management Comptroller's Handbook, April 1998.

During their evaluation of the loan portfolio management process, examiners should ensure that bankers are realistically assessing strategic risk."[9]

Reputation Risk

Negative publicity regarding business practices will cause a decline in the customer base, costly litigation, or revenue reductions. Inefficient loan delivery systems, failure to meet a community's credit needs, and lender-liability lawsuits will compromise reputations.

Faulted Risk Models

The most disastrous business failures in the 2008 financial crises arose due to unpreparedness and the lack of the imagination needed to plan for the next *inevitable* economic crisis. The Chief Financial Officer of Goldman Sachs commented to the Financial Times in August 2007: "We are seeing things that were 25-standard deviation moves, several days in a row." Putting that quote in perspective, a 7.26 sigma daily loss would emerge once in every 14 billion years: the age of the universe. The problem here is not 7.26 sigma, but rather within formula-rich, badly behaved models failing the human test: profits above strategic long-term planning, haphazard development, programming errors, and a foggy notion of systemic risk. Since the financial crisis, educators and practitioners investigated failed deals to figure out how the deal was analyzed, why it was accepted, and, sadly, what was ignored. Even if basic tenets of best practice financial modeling had been followed, models programmed to maximize short-term profit at the expense of sustainability planning self-destructed in an economic crisis.

For that reason, 2008 might well be recalled as the year stress-test modeling failed.[10] "(Modeling) failed those institutions who invested hoping it would transform risk management. Failed the authorities who had relied − perhaps over-relied − on the signal models provided about financial firms' risk management capabilities. And, perhaps most important of all, failed the financial system as a whole by contributing, first, to the decade of credit boom and, latterly, the credit bust."[11] Perhaps above all, after every major disaster stress testing addresses regulatory objectives, which are not necessarily going-concern objectives. Regulatory objectives relate to the preservation of the financial system, prevention of systemic problems, and minimizing taxpayer cost; going-concern objectives, on the other hand, must address

---

[9]Comptroller of the Currency, Administrator of National Banks, Loan Portfolio Management Comptroller's Handbook, April 1998.
[10]Rohit VM, Sudarsan Kurnar, Jitendra Kumer, Basel II to Basel III − The Way Forward, Infosys.
[11]Rohit VM, Sudarsan Kurnar, Jitendra Kumer, Basel II to Basel III − The Way Forward, Infosys.

the ongoing integrity of an institution.[12] When tested against real stress—the crisis itself—large segments of the financial system panicked, and a large number failed.

Against that backdrop, now is as good a time as any to review model failure from a regulatory perspective: "During the crisis, value-at-risk (VaR) models severely underestimated the tail events and the high loss correlations under systemic stress. VaR model workhorse for assessing risk in normal markets did not fare well in extreme stress situations. Systemic events occur far more frequently and the losses incurred during such events have been far heavier than VaR estimates have implied."[13] Value at Risk (VaR) is based on normality and linked to historical statistical relationships. Under the normality assumption, the probability of large market movements is largely underestimated and, more specifically, the probability of any deviation beyond 4 sigma is near zero. In the real world, 4-sigma events do occur, and they certainly occur more than once every 125 years, which is the supposed frequency of a 4-sigma event (at a 99.995% confidence level) under the normal distribution. Even worse, the 20-sigma event corresponding to the 1987 stock crash is supposed to happen not even once in trillions of years. VaR failures led the Basel Committee to encourage banks to focus on rigorous stress testing that captures risk beyond the normality assumption, that is, extreme tail events and the requisite sustainability strategies.

Financial Models Breaking Down in the Equity Markets

A funny thing happens when we model: things that are supposed to happen, do.

The deficiencies of financial models and frequency of the so-called extreme outliers in the financial industry have been dissected over and over. These include, for example, the 1987 Program Trading Crash, the Internet/tech bubble of 2003, the Sub-Prime and Debt Crisis of 2008–2009, and the May 2010 Flash Crash. Mathematical models have had a proven history of breaking down, especially when they were needed the most. To be fair, in some situations the reason behind modeling failures was the onset of extreme and unprecedented events: e.g., events not observable or even imaginable prior to the event. Possibility of the extreme was rarely quantified. However, in innumerable other cases, these mathematical and financial models "behaved badly" because analysts made errors within an ill-conceived model structure, measured inappropriate historical lookback periods, and applied incorrect statistics. Analysts and quants blamed model breakdowns on "regime shifts," "structural change," or a "black swan" event. After eons of financial research and empirical studies, predicting when events

---

[12]Karmjeet Paul, Chapter 14.

[13]The Basel III capital framework: a decisive breakthrough, Hervé Hannoun, Deputy General Manager, Bank for International Settlements, BoJ-BIS High Level Seminar on Financial Regulatory Reform: Implications for Asia and the Pacific Hong Kong SAR, 22 November 2010.

will take place or even uncovering them at the onset is an extremely difficult undertaking; analysts learn of these events only after they have already taken place, and harm has occurred.

Emanuel Derman[14] provided an overview of how models have broken down over the years and how incorrect application of these models helped lead to the financial crisis of 2008–2009. He traced the usage of quantitative models and corresponding improper insight beginning with the mortgage markets (2007) through the end of the financial crisis and directly questioned why bankers put so much faith in these models in the first place. The fundamental problem: We put too much reliance on models without adequate questioning and understanding.

Amir E. Khandani and Andrew Lo[15] investigated the sudden devaluation of several quantitative long/short equity hedge funds. During the first week of August, many of these funds experienced "unprecedented losses," and it has been postulated that this was due to a "coordinated deleveraging of similarly constructed portfolios" caused by a high correlation across quantitative strategies. The authors found evidence that the hedge funds began unwinding their portfolio position in July 2007 through the first week in August, after which there appeared to be a reduction in market-making activity, resulting in a liquidity crunch. One of the key takeaways from this paper is that even if the quantitative approach was properly structured with accurate model parameters, the models still broke down because the funds failed to consider the effect of using incorrect input variables in the model. That is, the strategies across many firms may have been highly correlated, with the majority of these firms selling shares at the same time, resulting in a large reduction in market liquidity. This in turn caused a drop in market price (temporary market impact) due to the liquidity discount required to offset the portfolio positions.

The models may have only considered the holdings of each individual fund and concluded that there was adequate market liquidity to offset positions during the specified timeframe. But if the models considered the effect of the aggregated sell-off, then the fund strategies may have been different. In short, the August 2007 Quant Meltdown (as it has become known) may have been caused by a gross understatement of the systematic market risk and the highly correlated strategies, e.g., inaccurate model input data. Bernard Donefer[16] noted many aspects of trading algorithms and the data that they rely on to make execution decisions. Incorrect data, either due to bad calculations, simple data errors, or even untested trade code can dramatically affect the way electronic trading algorithms will behave in the market place in real-time. Modeling errors can cause a

---

[14]Emanuel Derman, *Models Behaving Badly: Why Confusing Illusion with Reality Can Lead to Disaster on Wall Street and in Life,* Free Press (2011).
[15]Amir E. Khandani and Andrew Lo, *What Happened To The Quants In August 2007?: Evidence from Factors and Transactions Data*, 2008, web.mit.edu/alo/www/Papers/august07.pdf).
[16]Bernard Donefer published a paper in Journal of Trading (Spring 2010) titled "Algos Gone Wild: Risk in the World of Automated Trading Strategies.".

strategy to be highly profitable if we are lucky or to suffer a disastrous loss if we are unlucky. And if we are on the unlucky side of the trade, it may even threaten the funds viability and potentially force the company out of business (e.g., algorithm (algo) trading errors of August 2012).

Empirical analysis conducted over the 2008–2009 financial crisis revealed several real-world examples where models have broken down due to various reasons and have caused numerous issues. Some of these observations are described ahead. The financial crisis of 2008–2009 was accompanied by numerous unprecedented events (sub-prime defaults, company bankruptcies, etc.), and notably a large number of measured extreme price-movement days (Kissell, 2009). For example, over the 189 day period from July 2008 through March 2009, many financial professionals have reported that there were 44 days where the SP500 price index moved three standard deviations or more, i.e., 23% of the days experienced a three standard deviations move or more! However, this extreme price-movement period is highly exaggerated and was calculated using volatility computed over the period 1990 to June 2008, where volatility was 18.6% annualized and 1.17% daily. But even a short-term volatility measure, such as a 66-day rolling measure, results in a large number of calculated extreme price-movement days. For example, this model results in extreme price movements occurring 7 days or 4% of the 189 day period, which is still extremely high. A data point should only exceed a three standard deviations movement 0.27% of the time. This relates to approximately 1.5 days in a 250 trading-day year. Models that were using any historical volatility measure to gauge potential extreme price movement during the financial crisis were significantly underestimating the true potential of price swings and significantly underestimating the potential of extreme price movement and price surprises. Incorporation of the VIX volatility index into current volatility estimates, however, dramatically improves estimation accuracy, especially during periods of rapid price movement and regime shifts. Application of our VIX volatility adjustment (see Chapter 3) finds only one three standard deviations price-movement day in this period, which is consistent with statistical theory. Models that were relying on a historically based volatility measure (either long-term or short-term) during this period were significantly underestimating the likelihood of extreme price movement.

The financial crisis taught us a few things about price volatility and outliers:

- A regime shift in market volatility could come extremely quickly and swiftly (see Sept 2008).
- Short-term historically based volatility models do not provide required insight into the potential of extreme price swings and may under-predict the likelihood of surprises.
- The options market and implied volatility estimates provide a real-time volatility forecasting technique that is able to better adjust to a changing market structure and that results in fewer surprises (see Chapter 4: HMA-VIX Adjustment Model).

Table 1.1 Demystifying Extreme Outliers
Analysis Period: 7/1/2008 – 3/31/2009

	Number of Standard Deviation Moves					
	3	4	5	6	7	8
Normalized Process						
Historical Volatility:	44	25	15	6	5	3
66-day Lagged:	7	2	1	0	0	0
VIX Adj:	1	1	0	0	0	0
Percentage						
Historical Volatility:	23%	13%	8%	3%	3%	2%
66-day Lagged:	4%	1%	1%	0%	0%	0%
VIX Adj:	1%	1%	0%	0%	0%	0%
Theoretical Values						
Prob of occurrence:	0.27%	0.01%	0.0001%	0.000%	0.000%	0.000%
1 occurrence in years	1.48	63.15	>100	>100	>> 100	>>> 100
Prob at least 1 in 189 days	40.01%	1.19%	0.0108%	0.000%	0.000%	0.000%
Total Days:	189					

Period	Anualized Volatility		Daily Volatility	
1950–present:	15.3%		0.97%	
1990–present:	18.6%		1.17%	
2001–present:	22.3%		1.41%	

Table 1.1 shows the number of extreme price movement days for three volatility models: 1) Long-term historical volatility estimate over the period 1950–June 2008, 2) Short-term 66-day historical moving volatility model, and 3) a VIX-adjusted model. Actual SP500 index price change was normalized by dividing by the volatility estimate to measure the magnitude in price movement in standard deviation units. Both the long term and short term models resulted in a number of outliers much greater than predicted by theory. The VIX adjusted model, however, was consistent with theory and shows that the options market provides insight into real-time price changes.

Figures 1.1 to 1.3 illustrate the adjusted price movement for each of our volatility models. Notice the excess number of outliers encountered when relying on a long-term historical model (Figure 1.1). Additionally, even a short-term model during a period with a volatility shift could result in an

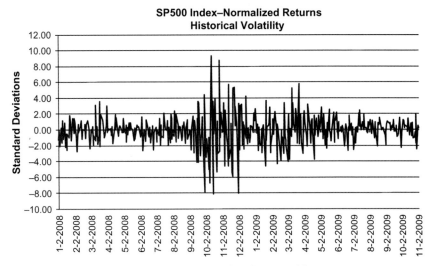

FIGURE 1.1 SP500 Index–Normalized Returns Historical Volatility

underestimation of price volatility and a much higher number of observed outliers than expected (Figure 1.2). The VIX-adjusted model (Figure 1.3) does provide the best results from our three models regarding the changing volatility structure, and it is the best predictor of the potential for extreme price movement. Analysts have to ensure that their risk models will properly adjust to changing market conditions in order to be able to accurately predict extreme price movement days.

Covariance Models

During the financial crisis, many analysts realized that long-term models were not providing accurate insight into market conditions due to changing market events. Some of these analysts even tried to make improvements to their models by using data that was more current. Some succeeded, and some failed, and some failed dramatically. One example of extreme failure was a risk management trading desk that utilized a portfolio optimizer and covariance model to determine the best way to hedge risk. Unfortunately, this risk model was constructed for the full universe of US stocks, using one month of stock-returns data (e.g., 22 trading days in a month). The issue here was that in addition to extreme price movement and unprecedented price-movement behavior, there just simply was not enough data to be able to accurately compute covariance across all pairs of stocks in the US trading universe. These data limitations and the need for factor risk models are further discussed in Chapter 5: Factor Models.

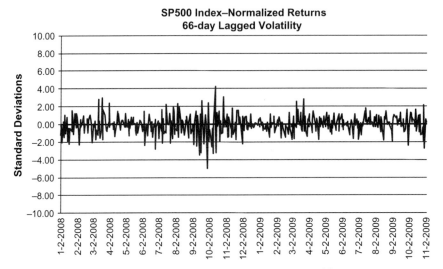

FIGURE 1.2 SP500 Index—Normalized Returns 66 Day Lagged Volatility

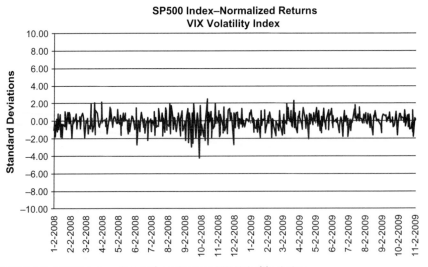

FIGURE 1.3 SP500 Index—Normalized Returns VIX Volatility Index

For example, for a 100-stock portfolio, there are 5,050 unique variance-covariance data points. But in a trading month with 22 days, there are only 2,200 data points. Therefore, we find ourselves in a situation where there are more unknowns than data points, and as any junior level statistician or mathematician will attest, there is no way we can compute accurate volatility or covariance estimates this way. And any model based on incomplete data sets will fail, especially in times of financial distress. And fail that model certainly did! This issue is further exasperated when we are trying to construct portfolios for larger groups of stocks, especially when statistical accuracy is required. For example, for an n-stock portfolio, using d-trading days, there are:

$$\text{unique parameters} = (n\hat{2} + n)/2$$
$$\text{total data points} = n \cdot d$$

In order to be able to calculate parameters we need to have:

$$d \geq (n+1)/2$$

And if we require statistical accuracy, we require an even larger number of days with historical data. Table 1.2 shows the number of days of data required to be able to estimate all unique volatility and covariance for different sizes of portfolios. For a 500-stock portfolio, we need one full year of data just to be able to solve the problem and 20 years of data if we require 20 data points for each parameter. For a 3000-stock portfolio, we require six years of data just to be able to solve our problem, and if we require statistical accuracy of 20 data points per parameter we require 120 years of data! Now imagine the data requirements and historical look-back period required if we are seeking to estimate variance and covariance parameters across all stocks!

Table 1.2 Estimating Variance & Covariance

Number Stocks	Unique Parameters	Minimum Requirement		20 Data Points Per Parameter	
		Days	Years	Days	Years
10	55	6	0.0	110	<0.5
25	325	13	0.1	260	1
100	5,050	51	0.2	1,010	4
500	125,250	251	1.0	5,010	20
1000	500,500	501	2.0	10,010	40
2000	2,001,000	1,001	4.0	20,010	80
3000	4,501,500	1,501	6.0	30,010	120

Suffice it to say that this modeling methodology did blow up a trading desk. The traders utilizing this model believed that they were hedged to market risk, but due to incorrect calculations and erroneous mathematical process the portfolio was not well hedged at all. So when things went bad, they went very bad in a hurry. Poor risk management lead to improper hedging techniques and another large market loss. To be completely fair, this type of modeling technique would also have certainly blown up any trading desk during normal conditions too.

Analysts have to *beware of type II statistical error!* Proper techniques to estimate variance and covariance for large portfolio using risk models are provided in Chapter 5: Factor Models.

Correlation Modeling

Volatility and covariance errors were not the only issues to occur during the financial crisis. There were also errors with calculated pairwise correlations due to extreme buying and selling pressure in the stock. As we know, stocks with positive correlation tend to go up and down together, and stocks with negative correlation tend to move in opposite directions. Additionally, buying and selling pressure in a stock will push the price up for buys and down for sells. When portfolio managers discuss correlation, they are most interested in how market forces affect stock prices and how stock prices move together based on market forces. Computed correlation across stocks was found to be extraordinarily high during the financial crisis; but this was not completely correct. Correlations increased, but not nearly to levels calculated.

Due to the market-wide buying and selling of equities during the financial crisis, e.g., risk-on and risk-off investing, much of the stock price movement was due to the aggregated buying and selling pressure of the market (e.g., market impact) in addition to market forces. Therefore, computed pairwise correlation during the financial crisis due to market forces was overstated.

An analysis of market correlation that adjusted for the buying and selling price movement in the stock price (Kissell, 2009), finds correlations were relatively stable during the period 11/2007−12/2009 and that price co-movement due to market forces did not increase to the levels believed. Much of the increase in correlation was due to aggregated buying and selling pressure in the stocks. Models that incorporated the higher correlation terms to develop long term buy and hold strategies found that their portfolios did not behave as expected after leaving the financial crisis. This is illustrated in Figure 1.4. Portfolio managers need to understand how and why stock prices are moving together or apart when developing risk management strategies.

Algorithm Trading Issues

Electronic trading algorithms have also suffered inferior performance due to incorrect models and modeling methodologies. Trading algorithms have blown up numerous

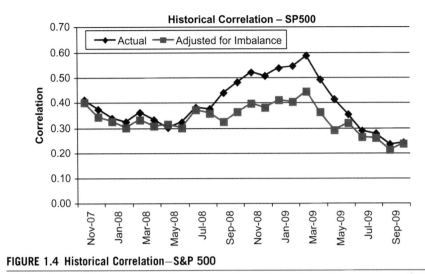

FIGURE 1.4 Historical Correlation—S&P 500

Source: Kissell, 2009, Curt Engler CQA/STA Trading Conference

times since gaining widespread acceptance for execution of an investment decision as well as for profit and loss trading via black box models. While many participants say this is due to algorithmic growing pains, we find that the reasons were often due to inadequate application of statistical models. Prior to the financial crisis, during the period of time between 2004 and 2008, volatility was at extremely low levels, and these low levels remained constant from week to week (except for the Aug 2007 period and Quant Meltdown).

Regardless of the volatility models used or historical look-back period selected, volatility forecasts were all relatively constant and similar. This was also the period when trading algorithms were gaining widespread industry acceptance and being embraced by the investment community. Since volatility was relatively stable, actual market results matched historical simulations. For simplicity during this time, many of the trading algorithms used a long-term volatility calculation (e.g., 3-month volatility) as an input into their market impact models. But when the financial crisis came, volatility spiked. The VIX index more than doubled form the middle to the end of September and then continued to spike through the end of the year. However, those trading algorithms that used volatility as an input into market impact were still calculating volatility using values in July and August 2008 where volatility was extremely low. These trading algorithms suggested that funds execute their positions in a passive manner because they did not believe that the market was sensitive or order imbalanced, and they also greatly underestimated market risk. Investors who traded in a passive manner at the beginning of the finan- cial crisis incurred market risk and suffered inferior execution quality due to trading too passively. When we emerged from the financial crisis, those algorithms with a long-term lagged volatility estimate indicated that the market was much more risky than it was and traded in a much more aggressive manner than they could have, which resulted in higher market-impact cost and, again, inferior execution quality.

In the early days of electronic trading algorithms, many of these models were reactive rather than proactive. Therefore, in many situations where there was an unanticipated market event such as a large block trade or spike in volume due to dark pool trading, the algorithms behaved in an incorrect manner and actually hurt rather than helped performance. For example, many of the early percentage of volume algorithms were tasked with following volume at a user-specified rate, e.g., 20% of volume. Thus, for every 1000 shares that was traded in the market, the algorithm would need to trade 200 shares. This worked fine in most cases. If there was increased volume on the day the algorithms traded, they traded more quickly and took advantage of the higher liquidity; when there was decreased volume on the day the algorithms traded, they traded more slowly and did not force unnecessary incremental market impact into the stock price. But when there was a one-time large block trade during the day the algorithms traded, many trading algorithms believed this higher volume was going to persist through the rest of the day. These algorithms reacted to the increased volume by trading faster and faster, causing more and more market impact. For example, if we expected 10,000 shares to trade in 10 minutes, the algorithm with a 20% rate would need to trade 2000 shares. If there was a large block of 100,000 shares, many algorithms incorrectly believed this higher volume would continue, and they set out to trade 20,000 shares in the next 10 minutes rather than only 2000 shares. So if the increased volume did not continue, the investor would find that the algorithm would be trading 10 times faster than it was requested to trade, resulting in inferior trading performance. Today, luckily, most algorithms are much better behaved and are much more proactive with regards to intraday forecast techniques. These algorithms filter large prints (public dissemination of the trade price and share quantity) that are not likely to continue throughout the rest of the day, and forecast remaining volume appropriately. But investors still need to discuss with their brokers how the trading algorithms are going to behave in times of large block prints as well as dark pool executions in order to ensure that these tactics match the investment goals of the funds.

One of the more infamous algorithmic trading tragedies to date has become known as the May 6th 2010 Flash Crash. On this day, trading algorithms caused the major indexes to fall -8% to -10% in only 20 minutes: a flash of time! Algorithms on that day, like any other day, were tasked with adhering to prescribed trading rules and trading rates. But on the Flash Crash Day, market liquidity was not at the expected levels, so many of the trading algorithms forced trades and pushed trading further downwards. This set off an unprecedented chain reaction where some algorithms knew there was an issue and pulled out of the market to wait for corrections, but other algorithms were not equipped with safety nets to realize that there was an error, and these algorithms continued to push prices down further and further. Some stocks and exchange-traded funds (ETFs) lost as much as 90% of their value in a matter of minutes before correcting. This mispricing further created statistical arbitrage opportunities, and several parties reentered the market to take advantage of price differentials. To make a long story short, regulators broke some but not all trades, resulting in some investors suffering large losses.

There have been numerous theories, academic papers, and an SEC investigation looking into the cause of the Flash Crash. But the true reasons may never be known. We only know with certainty that it was a time when algorithms did indeed go wild! Trading algorithms at that time did not have proper safety nets or criteria for pulling out of the market when faced with unknown conditions. Today, investors should have the confidence that most algorithms provided have implemented appropriate safety checks, and exchanges have further implemented circuit breakers and trading halts to protect investors from another potential Flash Crash event.

As a side note, markets almost fully recovered by the end of the day on May 6th 2010, regaining almost all of their losses. And most, if not all, algorithmic providers have implemented their own sets of circuit breakers and safety nets to protect investors from potential adverse circumstances. Investors, however, should discuss these criteria with their brokers to ensure that the sets of rules are not too strict or limiting for their trading needs, and how exactly they will be applied in times of true adverse price movement.

Risk Models Breaking Down
Deterministic Optimization

Deterministic optimization software is capable of solving linear and nonlinear problems, but actuate under the implicit assumption of certainty. Because deterministic optimization models lack random variables, they produce single-valued, simplistic results that are not much use in assessing the risk of complex loan portfolios. Some portfolio managers attempt to run different values for select uncertainty variables and see how the output changes. However, sensitivity analysis might resolve small levels of uncertainty, but the extent and range of uncertainty is often too significant for any well-reasoned amount of (sensitivity) trials, not to mention online time. On the other hand, stochastic optimization algorithms have been growing rapidly in popularity, with a number of methods now becoming "industry standard" approaches for solving challenging optimization problems. Stochastically driven optimization models provide a more realistic flow of random variables. Consider an optimization problem whereby you try to maximize an objective function over a feasible region. Suppose the problem is very large, containing tens of thousands of variables, so that it is unrealistic for you to run sensitivities. Obtaining these optimal values generally requires that you search in an iterative or ad hoc fashion. This entails running a simulation for an initial set of values, analyzing the results, changing one or more values, rerunning the simulation, and repeating this process until you find a satisfactory solution. This process can be very tedious and time consuming even for small models; it can be unclear how to adjust variables from one simulation run to the next, and so on.

Simplistic Investment Models

Simplistic real investment models popular before and during the debt crisis include net present value (NPV) and internal rate of return (IRR). NPV models disregard opportunities to alter investment game plans and consequently under-value explicitly elastic projects. NPV models tell managers to accept invest-ments where the NPV is greater than zero. However, that measure does not tell us when a positive NPV is achieved. With IRR models, computational anoma-lies can produce misleading results, particularly with regard to reinvestments. The biggest disadvantage to the calculation of NPV is its sensitivity to discount rates. NPV computations are simply a summation of multiple discounted cash flows, positive and negative, converted into present-value terms for the same point in time (usually when the cash flows begin). As such, the discount rate used in the denominators of each present value (PV) computation is crucial in determining the final NPV number. A small change in the discount rate could have a considerable effect on the final output. Net present value cannot evaluate management's ability to invest now and make follow-up investments later if the original project is a success. NPV cannot (or at best, can only inefficiently) value the management's ability to abandon a project if it is unsuccessful. Finally, deterministic NPV and IRR methods cannot value management's ability to wait and learn, resolving uncertainty before investing.

Real options steer management toward maximizing opportunity while mini-mizing obligation, encouraging it to think of every situation as an initial investment against future possibility. *"In real options, we assume that the underlying variable is the future profitability of the project, which is the future cash flow series. An implied volatility of the future free cash flow or underly-ing variable can be calculated through the results of a Monte Carlo simulation previously performed. Usually, the volatility is measured as the standard deviation of the logarithmic returns on the free cash flow stream. In addition, the present value of future cash flows for the base case discounted cash flow model is used as the initial underlying asset value in real options modeling. Using these inputs, real options analysis is performed to obtain the project's strategic option values."*[17]

---

[17]Dr. Johnathan Mun, A Layman's Primer on Quantitative Decision and Risk Analysis, Real Options, Real Options Valuation Website http://www.realoptionsvaluation.com/.

Deterministic or Static Forecasting

The deterministic model is the most common framework for business financial models. Deterministic models base projections on historical data and seek to establish a relationship between historical data and key dependent variables. Because static forecasting limits the variability of outcomes to base, optimistic, and stress cases, the methodology is not appropriate in today's uncertain and extreme value financial environment. Introducing the technique known as "Monte Carlo" simulation, an entire range of results and confidence levels are feasible for any given forecast run, and, most appropriately, at the stress level. The principles behind the Monte Carlo simulation is comprised of real world situations involving elements of uncertainty too complex to be solved with naïve methods.

References

Donefer, B., 2010. Algos Gone Wild: Risk in the World of Automated Trading Strategies. J. Trading 5 (2), 3134, Spring 2010.

Comptroller of the Currency, Administrator of National Banks, Loan Portfolio Management Comptroller's Handbook, April 1998.

Emanuel Derman, 2011. Models Behaving Badly: Why Confusing Illusion with Reality Can Lead to Disaster on Wall Street and in Life. Free Press.

Khandani A.E., Lo A., What Happened To The Quants In August 2007?: Evidence from Factors and Transactions Data, 2008, <web.mit.edu/alo/www/Papers/august07.pdf>.

Kissell, R., 2009. Volatility: Is it safe to get back into the water? CQA/SQA Trading Seminar. <http://sqa-us.org/cde.cfm?event=248380>.

Principles for the Management of Credit Risk, Basel Committee on Banking Supervision, Basel, September 2000.

Rohit, V.M., Sudarsan, K., Jitendra, K., Basel II to Basel III — The Way Forward, Infosys.

The Basel III capital framework: a decisive breakthrough, Hervé Hannoun, Deputy General Manager, Bank for International Settlements, BoJ-BIS High Level Seminar on Financial Regulatory Reform: Implications for Asia and the Pacific Hong Kong SAR, 22 November 2010.

A Primer on Risk Mathematics

INTRODUCTION

In this chapter, we provide an overview of important mathematics, statistics, and probability functions used in the financial industry to analyze, forecast, and manage risk. We discuss the mathematical processes used in regression analysis, including linear, log-linear, and non-linear analysis, as well as in probability models such as logit and probit models. We discuss the necessary mathematics to estimate model parameters and corresponding confidence intervals, and the statistical metrics to critique the model. The chapter concludes with a description of probability distributions functions to model risk and uncertainty. These distributions include discrete, continuous, and extreme value functions.

Regression Analysis

Regression analysis is a statistical technique used to determine a relationship between a dependent variable and a set of explanatory factors. The dependent variable, denoted as the y variable, is the value that we are looking to determine based on the explanatory factors. The explanatory factors, denoted as the x variables, are also referred to as the independent factors, the predictor variables, or simply the model factors. Regression analysis helps analysts uncover the sensitivity of the dependent variable to changes in the explanatory factors. These sensitivities are essential for proper risk management.

There are three types of data that are commonly used in regression analysis: time series, cross-sectional, and pooled data.

Time series: Data that are collected over a period of time. In economic and financial series these data often refer to market returns, index returns, asset prices and values, GDP, unemployment, interest rates, etc. These data points are collected at equal intervals of time such as daily, monthly, quarterly, etc.
Cross-sectional: Data that are collected for a family of variables at the same point in time. For example, in fundamental analysis we often collect

company-specific information such as price-to-earnings, price-to-book, debt-equity ratio, or average daily trading volume.

Pooled data: Data that are a combination of time series and cross-sectional data.

Linear Regression

A linear regression model is a model in which we formulate a linear relationship between the dependent variable and the explanatory factor(s).

In the case where we have a single explanatory factor, the analysis is called a simple regression model and has the form:

$$y = b_0 + b_1 x + \varepsilon$$

where y is the dependent variable (what we are looking to predict), x is the explanatory factor (what we are using to predict), and ε is random noise. The random noise component is the value of the y variable that is not explained by the explanatory factor. Additionally, the dependent variable y, the explanatory factors x, and the error term ε are column vectors of values.

In the previous equation, b_0 and b_1 are the actual model parameters that define the exact sensitivity of the dependent variable to the explanatory factors, and ε is the quantity of variability that is not explained by the model. In practice, however, these exact values are not known with certainty and must be estimated from the data. The corresponding simple regression equation used to estimate the parameters is:

$$\hat{y} = \hat{b}_0 + \hat{b}_1 x$$

where

$$E[b_0] = \hat{b}_0$$

$$E[b_1] = \hat{b}_1$$

$$E[\varepsilon] = 0$$

$$Var[\varepsilon] = \sigma_\varepsilon^2$$

In the case where we have multiple explanatory factors, the analysis is called a multiple regression model and has the form:

$$y = b_0 + b_1 x_1 + b_2 x_2 + \cdots b_k x_k + \varepsilon$$

where y is the dependent variable that we are looking to predict, $x_1, x_2, \ldots, x_k$ are the k-explanatory factors, and ε is the random noise (e.g., the value of y that is not explained by the set of explanatory factors).

Our $b_0, b_1, \ldots, b_k$ represent the actual parameter values of the model, and define the exact sensitivity of the dependent variable to the explanatory factor. In practice, however, these exact values are not known with certainty and must be estimated from the data. Thus, they are subject to uncertainty.

The corresponding multiple regression model used to estimate the parameters is:

$$\hat{y} = \hat{b}_0 + \hat{b}_1 x_1 + \hat{b}_2 x_2 + \ldots \hat{b}_k x_k$$

where

$$E[b_k] = \hat{b}_k$$

$$E[\varepsilon] = 0$$

$$Var[\varepsilon] = \sigma_\varepsilon^2$$

The goal of regression analysis is to determine the set of explanatory factors and corresponding sensitivities that explain as much of the observed dependent values as possible.

Model Evaluation Metrics

In performing regression analysis, the important metrics to analyze the analysis are:

$\hat{b}_k$ = Model parameter – estimated sensitivity of y to factor k
$Se(b_k)$ = standard error of the estimated parameter b_k
σ_y = standard error of the regression model
R^2 = goodness of fit (the percentage of overall variance explained by the model)
T-stat = critical value for the estimated parameter
F-stat = critical value for the entire model

Model Assumptions

There are six main assumptions or properties of a linear regression model. If any of these assumptions are violated, the results of the analysis could be suspect and potentially give incorrect insight into the true relationship between a dependent variable and its factors.

In these cases, analysts need to make adjustments to the data. These techniques are further explained in Gujarati (1988), Kennedy (1998), and Greene (2000).

The main assumptions of the linear regression model are:

A1) Linear relationship between dependent variable and explanatory factors.
A2) Error term mean zero—the expected value of the error term is zero.
$E(\varepsilon) = 0$
A3) Constant variance—each error term has the same variance, e.g., no heteroskedasticity.
$Var(\varepsilon_k) = \sigma^2$ for all k

A4) Uncorrelated error terms, e.g. no autocorrelation.

$E(\varepsilon_k \varepsilon_{k-t}) = 0$ for all lagged time periods t

A5) Errors are independent of explanatory factors.

$Cov(\varepsilon, x_k) = 0$ for all factors k

A6) Explanatory factors are independent.

$Cov(x_j, x_k) = 0$ for all factors j and k

Regression Analysis Statistics

In this section, we provide readers with an overview of the important statistics for performing regression analysis. Our summary is not intended to be a complete listing of the required analysis and evaluation metrics, but it will serve as an appropriate starting place for the analyses. These important statistics follow.

T-Test

The t-test is used to test the null hypothesis that a parameter value is zero. This indicates that the selected explanatory factor does not have any predictive power in our regression equation.

The corresponding t-stat for parameter k is:

$$Tstat(k) = \hat{\beta}(k)/Se(\hat{\beta})$$

where

$\hat{\beta}(k) =$ parameter k

$Se(\hat{\beta}) =$ standard error of parameter k

$Tstat(k) =$ t-statistic for parameter k

The testing hypothesis is:

$$H_0: \beta_k = 0$$
$$H_1: \beta_k \neq 0$$

Analysts could also test the alternative hypothesis that the parameter value is greater or less than zero depending on the goal of the analysis. A general rule of thumb is that if the absolute value of the t-stat is greater than two, then reject the null hypothesis. That is:

$$if\ |t| > 2\ then\ reject\ the\ null$$

F-Test

The F-test is used in regression analysis to test the hypothesis that all model parameters are zero. It is also used in statistical analysis when comparing statistical models that have been fitted using the same underlying factors and data set to determine the model with the best fit. That is,

$$H_0: B_1 = B_2 = \cdots = B_k = 0$$
$$H_1: B_j \neq 0 \text{ for at least one } j$$

The F-test was developed by Ronald A. Fisher (hence F-test with a capital F) and is a measure of the ratio of variances. The F-statistic is defined as

$$F = \frac{explained\ variance}{unexplained\ variance}$$

A general rule of thumb that is often used in regression analysis is that if $F > 2.5$ then we can reject the null hypothesis, because we can conclude that there is at least one parameter value that is non-zero.

R2 Goodness of Fit

The R2 statistic is a measure of the goodness of fit of a regression model. This statistic is also known as the coefficient of determinant. A regression model with strong explanatory power will have a high coefficient of variation R^2.

$$R^2 = 1 - \frac{Residual\ Sum\ of\ Squares}{Total\ Sum\ of\ Squares}$$

In matrix notation, the R2 statistic is computed as follows:

Step 1. Compute the M matrix (See Green, 2000):

$$M = (I - X(X'\ X)^{-1}X')$$

Step 2. Compute R^2:

$$R^2 = \frac{e'e}{y'\ My}$$

The coefficient of determination will be between 0 and 1. The closer the value to one, the better the fit of the model.

Unbiased Estimators

In statistics, we are very often concerned with deriving an unbiased estimator for a parameter. In this section, we discuss the derivation of an unbiased estimator for some of the more often used parameters.

Definition: An estimator θ^* is an unbiased estimate of θ if $E[\theta^*] = \theta$ for every possible value of θ. The difference $\delta = (E[\theta^*] - \theta)$ is called the bias of θ.

Is the average an unbiased estimator of the population mean?

$$E[\bar{x}] = E\left[\frac{1}{n}\sum_{i=1}^{n}x_i\right]$$

$$= E\left[\frac{1}{n}(x_1 + x_2 + x_3 + \cdots + x_n)\right]$$

$$= \frac{1}{n}E[(x_1 + x_2 + x_3 + \cdots + x_n)]$$

$$= \frac{1}{n}[E(x_1) + E(x_2) + \cdots + E(x_n)]$$

$$= \frac{1}{n}[\bar{x} + \bar{x} + \cdots + \bar{x}]$$

$$= \frac{1}{n}[n \cdot \bar{x}]$$

$$= \bar{x}$$

Is the standard deviation an unbiased estimator of the population standard deviation? We follow the approach illustrated by Devore (1982). Start with the following relationship (readers should verify these calculations).

$$\sum_{i=1}^{n}(x_i - \mu)^2 = \sum_{i=1}^{n}((x_i - \bar{x}) + (\bar{x} - \mu))^2$$

$$= \sum_{i=1}^{n}(x_i - \bar{x})^2 + \sum_{i=1}^{n}(x_i - \bar{x})(x - \mu) + n(\bar{x} - \mu)^2$$

$$= \sum_{i=1}^{n}(x_i - \bar{x})^2 + n(\bar{x} - \mu)^2$$

Then we have:

$$E[s^2] = E\left[\frac{1}{n}\sum_{i=1}^{n}(x_i - \bar{x})^2 + n(\bar{x} - \mu)^2\right]$$

$$= \frac{1}{n}n\sigma^2 - \frac{1}{n}\sigma^2$$

$$= \frac{n-1}{n}\sigma^2$$

Therefore,

$$E\left[\frac{n}{n-1}\right]s^2 = \sigma^2$$

and

$$s^2 = \frac{n}{n-1}\hat{s}^2 = \frac{1}{n-1}\sum_{i=1}^{n}(x_i-\bar{x})^2$$

Matrix Algebra Techniques

In matrix notation, the full regression model is written as:

$$y = X\beta + \varepsilon$$

The model used for estimation is:

$$\hat{y} = X\hat{\beta}$$

The vector of error terms (also known as vector of residuals) is then:

$$e = y - X\hat{\beta}$$

Estimate Parameters

The parameters of our regression model are estimated via ordinary least squares (OLS) as follows:

Step I. Compute the residual sum of squares:

$$e^T e = (y - X\hat{\beta})^T(y - X\hat{\beta})$$

Step II. Estimate the parameters $\hat{\beta}$ via differentiating. This yields:

$$\hat{\beta} = (X^T X)^{-1} X^T y$$

Compute standard errors of $\hat{\beta}$

This is calculated by computing the covariance matrix of $\hat{\beta}$. We follow the approach from Greene (2000) and Mittelhammer, Judge, and Miller (2000), as follows:

Step I. Start with the estimated $\hat{\beta}$ from above and substitute for y.

$$\hat{\beta} = (X^T X)^{-1} X^T y$$
$$= (X^T X)^{-1} X^T (X\beta + \varepsilon)$$
$$= (X^T X)^{-1} X^T X \beta + (X^T X)^{-1} X^T \varepsilon$$
$$= I\beta + (X^T X)^{-1} X^T \varepsilon$$
$$= \beta + (X^T X)^{-1} X^T \varepsilon$$

Therefore, our estimated parameters are:

$$\hat{\beta} = \beta + (X^T X)^{-1} X^T \varepsilon$$

Step II. Computed expected $\hat{\beta}$ as follows:

$$E(\hat{\beta}) = E(\beta + (X^T X)^{-1} X^T \varepsilon)$$
$$= E(\beta) + E((X^T X)^{-1} X^T \varepsilon)$$
$$= E(\beta) + (X^T X)^{-1} X^T E(\varepsilon)$$
$$= \beta + (X^T X)^{-1} X^T \cdot 0$$
$$= \beta$$

Therefore we have

$$E(\hat{\beta}) = \beta$$

Which states $\hat{\beta}$ is an unbiased estimate of β.

Step III. Compute the covariance matrix of $\hat{\beta}$ as follows:

$$Cov(\hat{\beta}) = E((\hat{\beta} - \beta)(\hat{\beta} - \beta)^T)$$
$$= E(((X^T X)^{-1} X^T \varepsilon)((X^T X)^{-1} X^T \varepsilon)^T)$$
$$= E((X^T X)^{-1} X^T \varepsilon \varepsilon^T X (X^T X)^{-1})$$
$$= (X^T X)^{-1} X^T E(\varepsilon \varepsilon^T) X (X^T X)^{-1}$$
$$= (X^T X)^{-1} X^T (\sigma^2 \cdot I) X (X^T X)^{-1}$$
$$= \sigma^2 \cdot (X^T X)^{-1} X^T X (X^T X)^{-1}$$
$$= \sigma^2 \cdot I (X^T X)^{-1}$$
$$= \sigma^2 (X^T X)^{-1}$$

It is important to note that if $E(\varepsilon\varepsilon^T) \neq \sigma^2 \cdot I$ then the data is heteroskedastic, e.g., it is not constant variance, and it violates one of our required regression properties.

The standard error of the parameters are computed from the above matrix:

$$Se(\hat{\beta}) = diag\left(\sqrt{\sigma^2(X^TX)^{-1}}\right)$$

Linear Regression: Graphic Example

Figure 2.1 illustrates an example of a linear regression model with a high R2 measure (R2 = 0.89). In this analysis, the choice of explanatory factors showed a very strong linear fit. Notice how close the best fit linear line is to every data point. This model provides the analyst with very accurate insight into the actual dependent variable. Figure 2.2 illustrates an example of a linear regression model with a lower R2 measure (R2 = 0.36). In this model, the best fit line could be quite different from the actual data observations. When the R2 measure of a regression is low, the analyst may not have determined the complete set of explanatory factors for the model.

Log-Linear Regression Model

A log-linear regression is a regression equation (relationship) that can be linearized via a log transformation. Once linearized, the regression parameters can be estimated following the ordinary least squares techniques discussed earlier. This

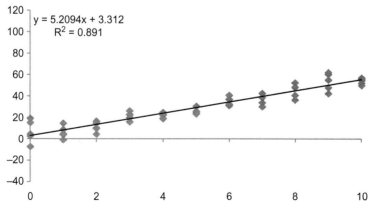

FIGURE 2.1 Linear Regression Model w/high R2

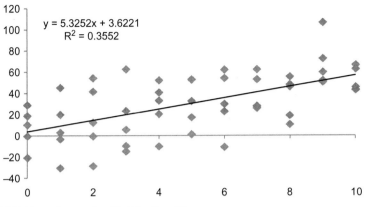

FIGURE 2.2 Linear Regression Model w/low R2

allows us to transform a complex non-linear relationship into a simpler linear model that can be easily evaluated using direct and standard techniques.

For example, let the regression equation be as follows:

$$Y = b_0 X_1^{b1} X_2^{b2} \varepsilon$$

If Y has log-normal distribution, then lnY has a normal distribution. Thus,

$$lnY = y$$
$$y = b_0 + b_1 X_1 + b_2 X_2 + \varepsilon$$

The parameters of this equation can now be estimated via the ordinary least squares estimation process shown above. If the distribution of y is

$$y \sim N((\hat{b}_0 + \hat{b}_1 \overline{X}_1 + \hat{b}_2 \overline{X}_2), \sigma_y^2)$$

Then the expected value of Y is

$$E(Y) = e^{lnY + 0.5\sigma_y^2}$$

Notice that the expected Y value now includes the variance of the linearized regression. This is a direct consequence from the log-normal distribution function.

Log-Transformation: Graphic Example

An example of a regression model that can be solved through a log-transformation of the data is shown in Figure 2.3. This has the form

$$y = b_0 \cdot x^{b1} \varepsilon$$

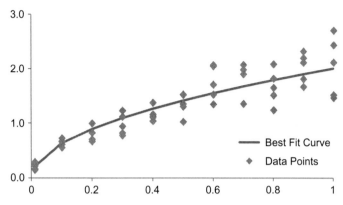

FIGURE 2.3 Log-linear Regression Model

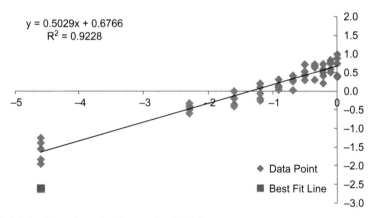

FIGURE 2.4 Log-Transfomation Regression Model

where $\ln(\varepsilon) \sim N(0, \sigma^2)$. Notice the relationship between the dependent variable y and the explanatory variable x. The sensitivities b_0 and b_1 in this case can be determined via a log-transformation regression.

Figure 2.4 illustrates the log-transformation of the model. That is,

$$\ln(y) = \ln(b_0) + b_1\ln(x) + \varepsilon$$

The parameters of this model are determined via the ordinary least squares regression technique described above, using the following formulation:

$$\ln(y) = \alpha_0 + \alpha_1\ln(x) + \varepsilon$$

Solving, we obtain:

$$\alpha_0 = 0.6766$$
$$\alpha_1 = 0.5029$$
$$\sigma_y = 0.1898$$

The original parameters are finally computed as follows:

$$b_0 = \alpha_0 + \sigma_y^2 = 0.6766 + 0.1898^2 = 1.9853$$
$$b_1 = \alpha_1 = 0.5029$$

And the best fit equation is:

$$y = 1.9853 \cdot x^{0.5029} \varepsilon$$

Non-Linear Regression Model

Now let us turn our attention to a non-linear model that cannot be linearized via a log-transformation. An example of a model of this form is the I-Star Market Impact model introduced by Kissell and Malamut (1999) for electronic and algorithmic trading. See Kissell, Glantz, and Malamut (2004), Kissell and Malamut (2006), or Kissell (2013) for an overview of this model and its applications.

The model has the form:

$$MI^* = a_1 Size^{a2} \sigma^{a3} \cdot POV^{\beta4} + (b_1 POV^{a4} + (1 - b_1)) + \varepsilon$$

where:

> MI = the market impact cost of an order. This is the price movement in the stock due to the buying and selling pressure of the order or trade. It is comprised of a temporary and permanent component.
> $Size$ = the percentage of average daily volume to trade (expressed as a decimal).
> σ = annualized volatility (expressed as a decimal).
> POV = the percentage of volume, and used to denote the underlying trading strategy (expressed as s decimal).

The parameters of the model are $a_1, a_2, a_3, a_4,$ and b_1.

A process to estimate the parameters of this model via non-linear least squares is described in Greene (2000), Fox (2002), and Zhi, Melia, and Guericiolini, et al. (1994).

We outline the parameter estimation process for a general non-linear model ahead.

Step I. Define the model:

$$y = f(x, \beta) + \varepsilon$$

where

$$\varepsilon \sim iidN(0, \sigma^2)$$

Let

$$f(x; a_1, a_2, a_3, a_4, b_1) = a_1 Size^{a_2} \sigma^{a_3} \cdot POV^{\beta_4} + (b_1 POV^{a_4} + (1 - b_1))$$

Step II. Define the likelihood function for the non-linear regression model:

$$L(\beta, \sigma^2) = \frac{1}{(2\pi\sigma^2)^{(\frac{n}{2})}} exp\left\{ -\frac{\sum_{i=1}^{n} [y_i - f(\beta, x)]^2}{2\sigma^2} \right\}$$

Step III. Maximize the likelihood function by minimizing the following:

$$S(\beta) = \sum_{i=1}^{n} [y_i - f(\beta, x)]^2$$

Step IV. Differentiate $S(\beta)$:

$$\frac{\partial S(\beta)}{\partial \beta} = -2 \sum_{i=1}^{n} [y_i - f(\beta, x)] \frac{\partial f(\beta)}{\partial \beta}$$

Step V. Solve for the model parameters.

The parameters are then estimated by setting the partial derivatives equal to zero. This is determined via maximum likelihood estimation techniques.

Figure 2.5 illustrates a non-linear regression model for different percentage of volume (POV) rates. The graph shows two different aspects of the model. It shows

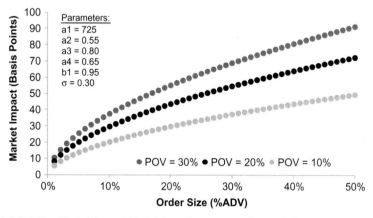

FIGURE 2.5 I-Star Market Impact Model (non-linear regression model)

how market impact cost increases with order size and how market impact cost is higher for a higher-POV strategy. A more urgent trading strategy will have a higher corresponding percentage of volume. This type of model is extremely important to develop electronic trading algorithms and in high-frequency trading applications, as well as portfolio construction.

Probability Models

A probability model is a model that maps the dependent variable y to either 1 or 0. That is, the event either happened or did not happen. Probability models have gained a great deal of attention in financial modeling over the last several years. This model is defined as follows:

$$y = \begin{cases} 1 & p \\ 0 & 1-p \end{cases}$$

where p is the probability that the event will occur.

Probability models are used in finance to estimate the probability of bond defaults or credit rating change, as well as more recently with algorithmic trading to determine the likelihood of transacting at a specified price or to estimate the likelihood of executing the order at a specified destination or dark pool.

The more common probability models in use are the logit and probit models. Both are described ahead.

Model Formulation

The probability model is written as follows:

$$y = f(\beta, x) + \varepsilon$$

The dependent variable is estimated as follows:

$$E(y) = f(\beta, x)$$

since $E(\varepsilon) = 0$.

Mean and Variance

The expected mean of the probability model is computed by definition:

$$E(y) = \sum p_i y_i = p \cdot 1 + (1 - p) \cdot 0 = p$$

Which is equivalent to:

$$f(\beta, x) = p$$

Since $E(y) = f(\beta, x)$.

The variance of the probability model is also computed by definition:

$$V(y) = E(y) = \sum p_i(y_i - E(y))^2 = p \cdot (1 - p)$$

Logit Model

The logit probability model is based on the logistic equation. The logistic model has historically been used in the social sciences and in medical fields where researchers are interested in determining the likelihood of achieving a certain outcome. But recently, the logistic model has gained momentum in finance and risk management.

The logistic function has the form:

$$f(z) = \frac{1}{1 + e^{-z}}$$

with $0 \leq f(z) \leq 1$, where z is a linear function of explanatory variables such as:

$$z = b_0 + b_1 x_1 + b_2 x_2 + \cdots + b_k x_k$$

Then the logistic regression can take on the form:

$$g(x) = \frac{1}{1 + e^{-(b_0 + b_1 x_1 + \cdots + b_k x_k)}}$$

with $0 \leq g(x) \leq 1$. Therefore, the probability that the event will occur is:

$$p = \frac{1}{1 + e^{-(b_0 + b_1 x_1 + \cdots + b_k x_k)}}$$

And the probability that the event will not occur is:

$$1 - p = 1 - \frac{1}{1 + e^{-(b_0 + b_1 x_1 + \cdots + b_k x_k)}}$$

Dividing these two expressions yields:

$$\frac{p}{1 - p} = e^{(b_0 + b_1 x_1 + \cdots + b_k x_k)}$$

Finally, taking logs of both sides yields:

$$ln\left(\frac{p}{1 - p}\right) = ln(e^{(b_0 + b_1 x_1 + \cdots + b_k x_k)})$$

Finally, the logit probability model is:

$$ln\left(\frac{p}{1-p}\right) = b_0 + b_1 x_1 + \cdots + b_k x_k$$

The parameters of this model are estimated using OLS regression techniques as described previously.

Probit Model

The probit probability model is similar to the logit model described previously, but it incorporates a normal distribution rather than the logistic distribution. The cumulative normal distribution for a random variable $z \sim N(\mu, \sigma^2)$ is

$$F(z) = \int_{-\infty}^{z} \frac{1}{\sqrt{2\pi\sigma}} \cdot \exp((z-\mu)^2/2\sigma^2)$$

with

$$-\infty \leq z \leq \infty$$
$$0 \leq F(z) \leq 1$$

Our random variable z can also be a linear function, such as

$$z = b_0 + b_1 x_1 + b_2 x_2 + \cdots + b_k x_k$$

The probability of the event y being observed is then computed from the inverse of the normal distribution. This is

$$Prob(y) = F^{-1}(z)$$

The parameters of the probit model need to be computed via a non-linear solution (e.g., optimization). It cannot be solved via OLS as can be done with the logit model.

Comparison of Logit and Probit Models

Figure 2.6 shows a comparison of the logit probability model using a cumulative logistic distribution and the probit probability model using a cumulative normal distribution. The logit probability model is similar to the probit model, but has fatter tails. Figure 2.7 illustrates how the logit probability model can be used to approximate the cumulative normal distribution curve for a specified parameter adjustment. This adjusted model is

$$\frac{1}{1 + \exp(-1.70 \cdot z)} \approx F(z)$$

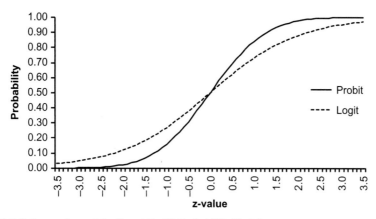

FIGURE 2.6 Comparison of Logit and Probit Probability Models

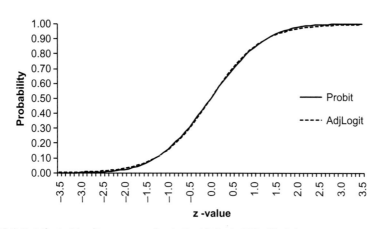

FIGURE 2.7 Adjusted Logit can approximate Probit Probability Model

Probability Distributions

Probability distributions are used throughout all of the sciences. They are used to measure and predict probabilities, and to estimate the likelihood of achieving certain outcomes. They are also used to determine confidence intervals around estimated values. There are two types of probability distributions functions: discrete and continuous.

Discrete distributions are comprised of data elements that can only take on a finite number of values within a defined interval. A probability mass function

(PMF) is a function used to provide the probability associated with the discrete variable. A cumulative mass function (CMF) is a function used to determine the probability that the observation will be less than or equal to some specified value. In general terms, these functions are as follows.

Probability Mass Function (PMF):

$$f(x) = Prob(X = x)$$

Cumulative Mass Function (CMF):

$$F(x) = Prob(X \leq x)$$

Continuous distributions are comprised of data elements that can take on any value within a defined interval. A probability density function (PDF) provides the likelihood that a random variable will fall within a specified range. In theory, the probability that a continuous value can be a specified value is zero because there are an infinite number of values for the continuous random value. The cumulative density function (CDF) is a function used to determine the probability that the random value will be less than or equal to some specified value. In general terms, these functions are as follows.

Probability Density Function (PDF):

$$Prob(a \leq X \leq b) = \int_a^b f(x)dx$$

Cumulative Density Function (CDF):

$$F(x) = Prob(X \leq x) = \int_{-\infty}^x f(x)dx$$

Going forward, we will use the terminology PDF to refer to probability density function and probability mass function, and we will use the terminology CDF to refer to cumulative density function and cumulative mass function.

Extreme Value Functions

Extreme value functions, also known as extreme value distributions (EVDs) are limiting distributions for maximums or minimums of a sample of independent and identically distributed (iid) random variables. These extreme value distributions are continuous probability functions that are intended to model the likelihood of tail probability (i.e., the extreme events). In finance, these extreme events include likelihood of a default or credit crisis, company bankruptcy, asset price drop, volatility jump, etc. Extreme value functions have gained a following in the financial industry, especially for risk management, and have been extremely useful for modeling the likelihood of low probability events.

The family of extreme value distributions (EVDs) consists of three extreme value functions. These are Gumbel (type I), Frechet (type II), and Weibull (type III).

Descriptive Statistics

Each probability distribution has a set of descriptive statistics that can be used in analysis. Important descriptive statistics for risk modeling include the following.

Mean: The arithmetic mean, also known as the simple mean or equal-weighted mean. The mean of a data series is a unique value. The mean is also known as the first moment of the data distribution.

$$\mu = \frac{1}{n} \sum_{i=1}^{n} x_i$$

Mode: The value(s) of a data series that occurs most often. The mode of a data series is not a unique value.

Median: The value of a data series such that one-half of the observations are lower or equal value, and one-half the observations are higher or equal value. The median value is not a unique number. For example, in the series 1, 2, 3, the median is the value 2. But in the series 1, 2, 3, 4, there is not a unique value. Any number $2 < x < 3$ is the median of this series since exactly 50% of the data values are lower than x, and exactly 50% of the data points are higher than x. A general rule of thumb is that if there is an odd number of data points, the middle value is the median, and if there is an even number of data points, the median is selected as the mean of the two middle points. In our example, 1, 2, 3, 4, the median would be taken as 2.5. However, any value x such that $2 < x < 3$ would also be correct.

Standard Deviation: The amount of dispersion around the mean. A small standard deviation indicates that the data are all close to the mean, and a high standard deviation indicates that the data could be far from the mean. The standard deviation $\sigma(x)$ is the square root of the variance $V[x]$ of the data. The variance is also known as the second moment about the distribution mean.

$$\sigma^2 = \frac{1}{n} \sum_{i=1}^{n} (x - \mu)^2$$

$$\sigma = \sqrt{\sigma^2} = \sqrt{\frac{1}{n} \sum_{i=1}^{n} (x - \mu)^2}$$

Coefficient of Variation: A measure of the standard deviation divided by the mean. The coefficient of variation serves as a normalization of the data for a fair comparison of data dispersion across different values (e.g., as a measure of data dispersion of daily or monthly stock trading volumes).

Skewness: A measure of the symmetry of the data distribution. A positively skewed data distribution indicates that the distribution has more data on the right tail; data is positively skewed. A negatively skewed data distribution indicates that the distribution has more data on the left tail; data is negatively skewed. A skewness measure of zero indicates that the data is symmetric. Skewness is also known as the third moment about the mean.

$$Skewness = \sqrt{\frac{1}{n}\sum_{i=1}^{n}\frac{(x-\mu)^3}{\sigma}}$$

Kurtosis: A measure of the peakedness of the data distribution. Data distributions with negative kurtosis are called platykurtic distributions, and data distributions with positive kurtosis are called leptokurtic distributions.

$$Kurtosis = \sqrt{\frac{1}{n}\sum_{i=1}^{n}\frac{(x-\mu)^3}{\sigma^2}}$$

Probability Distribution Functions

In this section, we provide a description of the important probability distribution functions that are used in finance and for risk management. Readers interested in a more thorough investigation of these distributions are referred to Meyer (1970), Dudewicz and Mishra (1988), Pfeiffer (1978), and DeGroot (1989). The summary tables of the distribution statistics and moments below are follow from www. mathworld.wolfram.com, — www.wikipedia.org/wiki/Probability_distribution_ function, www.statsoft.com/textbook, and http://www.mathwave.com/articles/ distribution_fitting.html. These are excellent references, and they are continuously being updated with practical examples. See the endnotes at the end of the chapter for further references.

Continuous Distribution Functions
Normal Distribution

A normal distribution is the workhorse of statistical analysis. It is also known as the Gaussian distribution and a bell curve (for the distribution's resemblance to a bell). It is one of the most used distributions in statistics and is used for several different applications. The normal distribution also provides insight into issues in which the data is not necessarily normal, but can be approximated by a normal distribution. Additionally, by the central limit theorem of mathematics, we find that the mean of a sufficiently large number of data points will be normally distributed. This is extremely useful for parameter estimation analysis such as with our regression models.

Normal Distribution Statistics[1]	
Notation	$N(\mu, \sigma^2)$
Parameter	$-\infty < \mu < \infty$
	$\sigma^2 > 0$
Distribution	$-\infty < x < \infty$
Pdf	$\dfrac{1}{\sqrt{2\pi}\sigma} \exp\left\{ -\dfrac{(x-\mu)^2}{2\sigma^2} \right\}$
Cdf	$\dfrac{1}{2}\left[1 + \operatorname{erf}\left(\dfrac{x-\mu}{2\sigma^2}\right)\right]$
Mean	μ
Variance	σ^2
Skewness	0
Kurtosis	0

where *erf* is the Gauss error function, that is,

$$\operatorname{erf}(x) = \frac{2}{\sqrt{\pi}} \int_0^x \exp(-t^2)$$

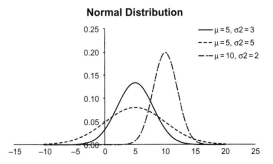

Normal Distribution

Normal Distribution Graph

Standard Normal Distribution

The standard normal distribution is a special case of the normal distribution where $\mu = 0, \sigma^2 = 1$. It is often essential to normalize data prior to analysis. A random normal variable with mean μ and standard deviation μ can be normalized via the following:

$$z = \frac{x - \mu}{\sigma}$$

Standard Normal Distribution Statistics[1]	
Notation	$N(0, 1)$
Parameter	n/a
Distribution	$-\infty < z < \infty$
Pdf	$\dfrac{1}{\sqrt{2\pi}} \exp\left\{-\dfrac{1}{2}z^2\right\}$
Cdf	$\dfrac{1}{2}\left[1 + erf\left(\dfrac{z}{2}\right)\right]$
Mean	0
Variance	1
Skewness	0
Kurtosis	0

Standard Normal Distribution

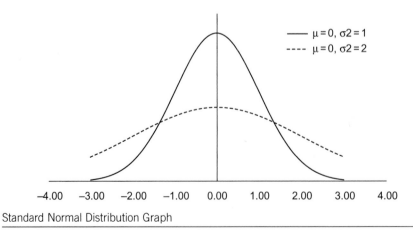

— $\mu = 0$, $\sigma2 = 1$
---- $\mu = 0$, $\sigma2 = 2$

−4.00   −3.00   −2.00   −1.00   0.00   1.00   2.00   3.00   4.00

Standard Normal Distribution Graph

Student's T-Distribution

Student's t-distribution (aka, t-distribution) is used when we are estimating the mean of normally distributed random variables for which the sample size is small and the standard deviation is unknown. It is used to perform hypothesis testing around the data to determine if the data is within a specified range. The t-distribution is used in hypothesis testing of regression parameters (e.g., when developing risk factor models). The t-distribution looks very similar to the normal distribution, but with fatter tails. However, it also converges to the normal curve as the sample size increases.

Student's t-Distribution[1]	
Notation	t-dist(ν)
Parameter	$\nu > 0$
Distribution	$-\infty < x < \infty$
Pdf	$\dfrac{\Gamma\left(\dfrac{\nu+1}{2}\right)}{\sqrt{\nu\pi}\,\Gamma\left(\dfrac{\nu}{2}\right)}\left(1+\dfrac{x^2}{\nu}\right)^{-\frac{\nu+1}{2}}$
Cdf	
Mean	$= \begin{cases} 0 & \nu > 1 \\ undefined & o.w. \end{cases}$
Variance	$= \begin{cases} \dfrac{\nu}{\nu+1} & \nu > 2 \\ \infty & 1 < \nu \leq 2 \\ undefined & o.w. \end{cases}$
Skewness	$= \begin{cases} 0 & \nu > 3 \\ undefined & o.w. \end{cases}$
Kurtosis	$= \begin{cases} \dfrac{6}{\nu-4} & \nu > 4 \\ \infty & 2 < \nu \leq 4 \\ undefined & o.w. \end{cases}$

Students t-Distribution

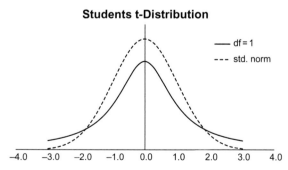

— df = 1
--- std. norm

Student's t-Distribution Graph

Student's T-Distribution: Interesting Notes

Have you ever wondered why many analysts state that you need to have at least 20 data points in order to compute statistics such as average or standard deviation? The reason is that once there are 20 data points, Student's t-distribution converges to a normal distribution. Then analysts can begin to use the simpler distribution function.

Where did the name Student's t-distribution come from? In many academic textbook examples, Student's t-distribution is used to estimate performance from class tests (e.g., mid-terms and finals, standardized tests, etc.). Therefore, the t-distribution is the appropriate distribution, since it is a small sample size, and the standard deviation is unknown. But the distribution did not arise from evaluating test scores. The Student's t-distribution was introduced to the world by William Sealy Gosset in 1908. The story behind the naming of Student's t-distribution is as follows: William was working at the Guinness Beer Brewery in Ireland and published a paper on the quality control process they were using for their brewing process. To keep their competitors from learning their processing secrets, Gosset published the test procedure he was using under the pseudonym Student. Hence, the name of the distribution was born.

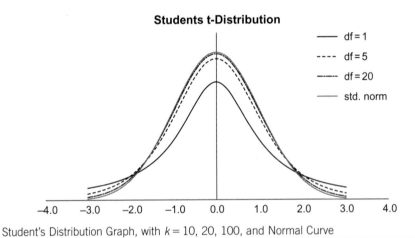

Students t-Distribution

——— df = 1
---- df = 5
—·—· df = 20
——— std. norm

-4.0   -3.0   -2.0   -1.0   0.0   1.0   2.0   3.0   4.0

Student's Distribution Graph, with $k = 10, 20, 100$, and Normal Curve

Log-Normal Distribution

A log-normal distribution is a continuous distribution of random variable y whose natural logarithm is normally distributed. For example, if random variable $y = \exp\{y\}$ has log-normal distribution, then $x = \log(y)$ has normal distribution. Log-normal distributions are most often used in finance to model stock prices, index values, and asset returns, as well as exchange rates, derivatives, etc.

Log-Normal Distribution Statistics[1]	
Notation	$lnN(\mu, \sigma^2)$
Parameter	$-\infty < \mu < \infty$ $\sigma^2 > 0$
Distribution	$x > 0$
Pdf	$\dfrac{1}{\sqrt{2\pi}\sigma x}\exp\left\{-\dfrac{(\ln(x)-\mu)^2}{2\sigma^2}\right\}$
Cdf	$\dfrac{1}{2}\left[1 + erf\left(\dfrac{\ln(x-\mu)}{\sigma}\right)\right]$
Mean	$e^{\left(\mu + \frac{1}{2}\sigma^2\right)}$
Variance	$(e^{\sigma^2} - 1)e^{2\mu + \sigma^2}$
Skewness	$(e^{\sigma^2} + 2)\sqrt{(e^{\sigma^2} - 1)}$
Kurtosis	$e^{4\sigma^2} + 2e^{3\sigma^2} + 3e^{2\sigma^2} - 6$

where *erf* is the Gaussian error function.

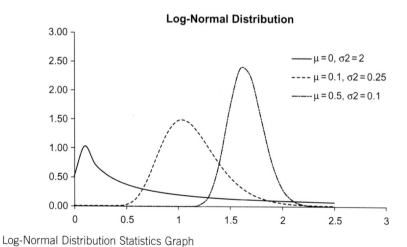

Log-Normal Distribution Statistics Graph

Uniform Distribution

The uniform distribution is used when each outcome has the same likelihood of occurring. One of the most illustrated examples of the uniform distribution is rolling a die, in which case each of the six numbers has equal likelihood of occurring, or spinning a roulette wheel, in which case (again) each number has an equal likelihood of occurring. The uniform distribution has constant probability across all values. It can be either a discrete or a continuous distribution.

Uniform Distribution Statistics[1]	
Notation	$U(a,b)$
Parameter	$-\infty < a < b < \infty$
Distribution	$a < x < b$
Pdf	$\dfrac{1}{b-a}$
Cdf	$\dfrac{x-a}{b-a}$
Mean	$\dfrac{1}{2}(a+b)$
Variance	$\dfrac{1}{12}(b-a)^2$
Skewness	0
Kurtosis	$-\dfrac{6}{5}$

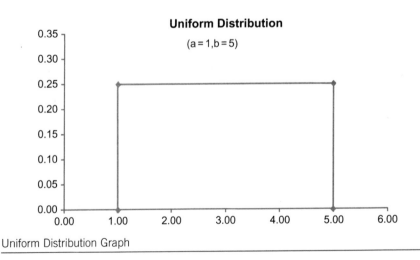

Uniform Distribution
$(a=1, b=5)$

Uniform Distribution Graph

Exponential Distribution

The exponential distribution is a continuous distribution that is commonly used to measure the expected time for an event to occur. For example, in physics it is often used to measure radioactive decay; in engineering it is used to measure the time associated with receiving a defective part on an assembly line; and in finance it is often used to measure the likelihood of the next default for a portfolio of financial assets. It can also be used to measure the likelihood of incurring a specified number of defaults within a specified time period.

Exponential Distribution Statistics[1]	
Notation	$Exponential(\lambda)$
Parameter	$\lambda > 0$
Distribution	$x > 0$
Pdf	$\lambda e^{-\lambda x}$
Cdf	$1 - e^{-\lambda x}$
Mean	$1/\lambda$
Variance	$1/\lambda^2$
Skewness	2
Kurtosis	6

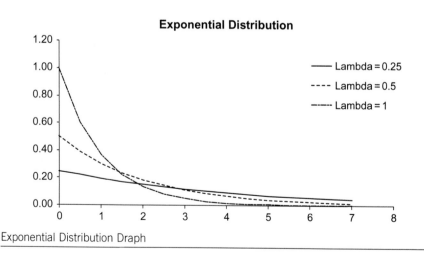

Exponential Distribution Draph

Beta Distribution

The beta distribution is a continuous distribution defined on the interval $0 \le x \le 1$. It is an important financial distribution for modeling extreme events. The beta distribution allows researchers to incorporate their prior beliefs about an event (such as the expected default rate) into the distribution via two parameters: $\alpha > 0, \beta > 0$. This is an important tool for analysts incorporating Bayesian forecasting procedures.

Beta Distribution Statistics[1]	
Notation	$B(\alpha, \beta)$
Parameter	$\alpha > 0, \beta > 0$
Distribution	$0 \le x \le 1$
Pdf	$\dfrac{\Gamma(\alpha + \beta)}{\Gamma(\alpha)\Gamma(\beta)} x^{\alpha-1}(1-x)^{\beta-1}$
Cdf	$I(x; \alpha, \beta)$
Mean	$\dfrac{\alpha}{\alpha + \beta}$
Variance	$\dfrac{\alpha\beta}{(\alpha+\beta)^2(1+\alpha+\beta)}$
Skewness	$\dfrac{2(\beta-\alpha)\sqrt{1+\alpha+\beta}}{(\alpha+\beta+2)\sqrt{\alpha\beta}}$
Kurtosis	$\dfrac{6[(\alpha-\beta)^2(1+\alpha+\beta) - \alpha\beta(\alpha+\beta+2)]}{\alpha\beta(\alpha+\beta+2)(\alpha+\beta+3)}$

where $I(x; \alpha, \beta)$ is the regularized beta function, and $\alpha, \beta > 0$

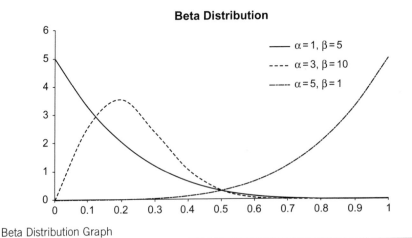

Beta Distribution

— $\alpha = 1, \beta = 5$
---- $\alpha = 3, \beta = 10$
—·— $\alpha = 5, \beta = 1$

Beta Distribution Graph

Gamma Distribution

The gamma distribution is a continuous distribution with two parameters, $\alpha > 0, \beta > 0$, and is defined for $x > 0$. It has been used to model "ruin and risk," such as with the size of insurance claims and credit defaults, as well as floods.

Gamma Distribution Statistics[1]	
Notation	$\Gamma(k)$
Parameter	$\alpha > 0, \beta > 0$
Distribution	$x \geq 0$
Pdf	$\dfrac{\beta^\alpha}{\Gamma(\alpha)} x^{\alpha-1} e^{-\beta x}$
Cdf	$\dfrac{1}{\Gamma(\alpha)} \gamma(\alpha, \beta x)$
Mean	$\dfrac{\alpha}{\alpha + \beta}$
Variance	$\dfrac{\alpha\beta}{(\alpha+\beta)^2(\alpha+\beta+1)}$
Skewness	$\dfrac{2(\beta - \alpha)\sqrt{\alpha + \beta + 1}}{(\alpha + \beta + 2)\sqrt{\alpha\beta}}$
Kurtosis	$\dfrac{6[(\alpha-\beta)^2(\alpha+\beta+1) - \alpha\beta(\alpha+\beta+2)]}{\alpha\beta(\alpha+\beta+2)(\alpha+\beta+3)}$

where $\Gamma(\alpha) = \int_0^\infty x^{\alpha-1} e^{-x} dx, \alpha > 0$, and $\gamma(\alpha, \beta x)$ is the lower incomplete gamma function.

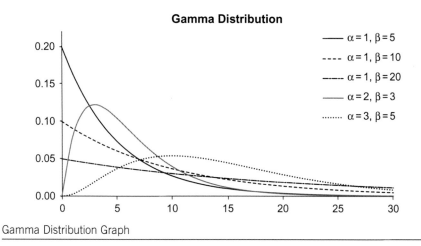

Gamma Distribution Graph

Chi Square Distribution

A chi square distribution is a continuous distribution with k degrees of freedom. It is used to describe the distribution of a sum of squared random variables. It is also used to test the goodness of fit of a distribution of data and whether data series are independent, and is used for estimating confidences surrounding variance and standard deviation for a random variable from a normal distribution. Additionally, chi square distribution is a special case of the gamma distribution.

Chi Square Distribution Statistics[1]	
Notation	$\chi(k)$
Parameter	$k = 1, 2, \ldots$
Distribution	$x \geq 0$
Pdf	$\left(x^{\frac{k}{2}-1}e^{-\frac{x}{2}}\right)/\left(2^{\frac{k}{2}}\Gamma\left(\frac{k}{2}\right)\right)$
Cdf	$\gamma\left(\frac{k}{2},\frac{x}{2}\right)/\Gamma\left(\frac{k}{2}\right)$
Mean	k
Variance	$2k$
Skewness	$\sqrt{8/k}$
Kurtosis	$12/k$

where $\gamma\left(\frac{k}{2},\frac{x}{2}\right)$ is known as the incomplete Gamma function (www.mathworld.wolfram.com).

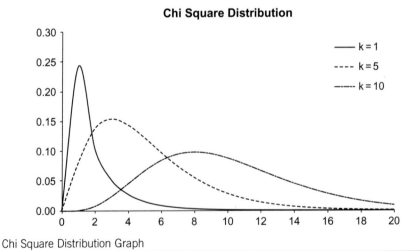

Chi Square Distribution

Chi Square Distribution Graph

Logistic Distribution

The logistic distribution is a continuous distribution function. Both its PDF and CDF functions have been used in many different areas, such as logistic regression, logit models, and neural networks. It has been used in the physical sciences and sports modeling, and has recently been used in finance. The logistic distribution has wider tails than a normal distribution, so it is more consistent with the underlying data, and it provides better insight into the likelihood of extreme events.

Logistic Distribution Statistics[1]	
Notation	$Logistic(\mu, s)$
Parameter	$0 \le \mu \le \infty$ $S > 0$
Distribution	$0 \le x \le \infty$
Pdf	$\dfrac{\exp\left(-\dfrac{x-\mu}{s}\right)}{s\left(1+\exp\left(-\dfrac{x-\mu}{s}\right)\right)^2}$
Cdf	$\dfrac{1}{1+\exp\left(-\dfrac{x-\mu}{s}\right)}$
Mean	μ
Variance	$\dfrac{1}{3}s^2\pi^2$
Skewness	0
Kurtosis	6/5

Logistic Distribution

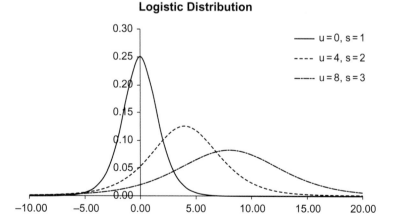

Logistic Distribution Graph

Cauchy Distribution

The Cauchy distribution is a continuous probability distribution. It is often used in physics to model differential equations describing force and in mathematics to describe the Laplace equation. If two variables have standard normal distributions, then their ratio will have a standard Cauchy distribution.

Cauchy Distribution[1]	
Notation	$\text{Cauchy}(\mu, \sigma)$
Parameter	$-\infty < \mu < \infty$
	$\sigma > 0$
Distribution	$-\infty < x < \infty$
Pdf	$\dfrac{1}{\pi\sigma\left[1 + \left(\frac{x-\mu}{\sigma}\right)^2\right]}$
Cdf	$\dfrac{1}{\pi}\arctan\left(\dfrac{x-\mu}{\sigma}\right) + \dfrac{1}{2}$
Mean	*undefined*
Variance	*undefined*
Skewness	*undefined*
Kurtosis	*undefined*

Cauchy Distribution

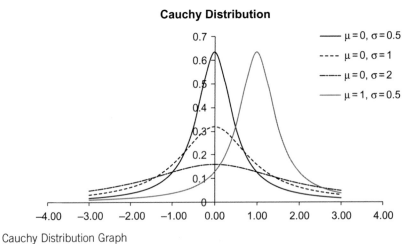

Cauchy Distribution Graph

Triangular Distribution

The triangular distribution is when there is a known relationship between the variable data, but relatively little data available to conduct a full statistical analysis. It is often used in simulations when there is very little known about the data-generating process, and it is often referred to as a "lack of knowledge" distribution. The triangular distribution is an ideal distribution when the only data on hand is the maximum and minimum values and the most likely outcome. It is often used in business decision analysis.

Triangular Distribution[1]	
Notation	Triangular(a, b, c)
Parameter	$-\infty \le a \le \infty$ $b > a$ $a < c < b$
Distribution	$a < x < b$
Pdf	$= \begin{cases} \dfrac{2(x-a)}{(b-a)(c-a)} & a \le x \le c \\[2mm] \dfrac{2(x-a)}{(b-a)(b-c)} & c \le x \le b \end{cases}$
Cdf	$= \begin{cases} \dfrac{2(x-a)^2}{(b-a)(c-a)} & a \le x \le c \\[2mm] 1 - \dfrac{(b-x)^2}{(b-a)(b-c)} & c \le x \le b \end{cases}$
Mean	$\dfrac{a+b+c}{3}$
Variance	$\dfrac{a^2 + b^2 + c^2 - ab - ac - bc}{18}$
Skewness	$\dfrac{\sqrt{2}(a+b-2c)(2a-b-c)(a-2b+c)}{5(a^2+b^2+c^2-ab-ac-bc)^{\frac{3}{2}}}$
Kurtosis	$-\dfrac{3}{5}$

Triangular Distribution

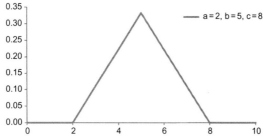

Triangular Distribution Graph

Extreme Value Functions
Gumbel Distribution

The Gumbel distribution (EVD type I) was named after Emil Gumbel. It is a continuous distribution that is used in the physical sciences to model the distribution of the maximum or minimum values of a sample of data. The Gumbel distribution has been used to model extreme events, such as the maximum level of a river in a given year, the maximum or minimum temperature (for cooling and heating planning), or to determine the likelihood of an extreme natural disaster such as a flood or earthquake. It is also used to determine the likelihood of financial disasters, such as the likelihood of default in an economic shock, extreme price movement, or volatility jumps.

Gumbel Distribution Statistics[1]	
Notation	$Gumbel(\mu, \beta)$
Parameter	$0 \le \mu \le \infty$
	$\beta > 0$
Distribution	$x \ge 0$
Cdf	$\dfrac{1}{\beta} exp\left[\dfrac{x-\mu}{\beta} - exp\left(\dfrac{x-\mu}{\beta} \right) \right]$
Pdf	$exp\left\{ -exp\left(-\dfrac{x-\mu}{\beta} \right) \right\}$
Mean	$\alpha - \gamma\beta$
Variance	$\dfrac{1}{6}\pi^2 \beta^2$
Skewness	$-\dfrac{12\sqrt{6}\xi(3)}{\pi^3}$
Kurtosis	$12/5$

where

γ = Euler-Mascheroni constant

$\xi(3)$ = Apery's constant

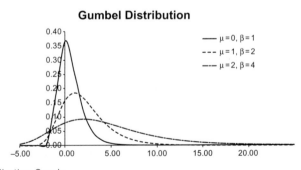

Gumbel Distribution

Gumbel Distribution Graph

Frechet Distribution

The Frechet distribution (EVD type II) is named after Maurice Frechet. It is used to model extreme value events, for example, credit defaults, bankruptcy, or volatility jumps. It is a special case of the generalized extreme value functions.

Frechet Distribution Statistics[1]	
Notation	$\text{Frechet}(\alpha, s, m)$
Parameter	$\alpha \geq 0, \beta \geq 0, -\infty \leq \gamma \leq \infty$
Distribution	$x \geq \gamma$
Pdf	$\dfrac{\alpha}{\beta}\left(\dfrac{\beta}{x-\gamma}\right)^{\alpha+1} e^{-\left(\frac{\beta}{x-\gamma}\right)^{\alpha}}$
Cdf	$e^{-\left(\frac{\beta}{x-\gamma}\right)^{\alpha}}$
Mean	$\gamma + \beta\Gamma\left(1 - \dfrac{1}{\alpha}\right) \alpha > 1$
Variance	$s^2\left(\Gamma\left(1 - \dfrac{2}{\alpha}\right) - \Gamma\left(1 - \dfrac{1}{\alpha}\right)\right)^2 \alpha > 2$
Skewness	(see www.mathworld.wolfram.com)
Kurtosis	(see www.mathworld.wolfram.com)

Frechet Distribution

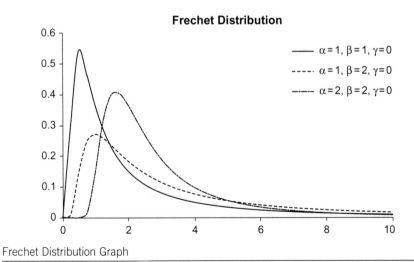

— $\alpha = 1, \beta = 1, \gamma = 0$
---- $\alpha = 1, \beta = 2, \gamma = 0$
----- $\alpha = 2, \beta = 2, \gamma = 0$

Frechet Distribution Graph

Weibull Distribution

The Weibull distribution (EVD type III) is named after Waloddi Weibull. It is a continuous distribution that is used across any of the physical sciences. It is used in survival and reliability analysis, in manufacturing and control theory, for weather forecasting of extreme temperature days, and, most recently, it has found its way into the financial sciences to model extreme value events such as default rates, asset swings, and spikes in price volatility.

Weibull Distribution Statistics[1]	
Notation	$Weibull(\lambda, k)$
Parameter	$\lambda > 0$
	$k > 0$
Distribution	$x \geq 0$
Pdf	$\dfrac{k}{\lambda}\left(\dfrac{x}{\lambda}\right)^{k-1} e^{-\left(\frac{x}{\lambda}\right)^{k}}$
Cdf	$1 - e^{-\left(\frac{x}{\lambda}\right)^{k}}$
Mean	$\lambda \Gamma\left(1 + \dfrac{1}{k}\right)$
Variance	$\lambda^{2}\Gamma\left(1 + \dfrac{2}{k}\right) - \mu^{2}$
Skewness	$\dfrac{\lambda^{3}\Gamma\left(1 + \dfrac{3}{k}\right) - 3\mu\sigma^{2} - \mu^{3}}{\sigma^{3}}$
Kurtosis	*(see www.mathworld.wolfram.com)*

Weibull Distribution

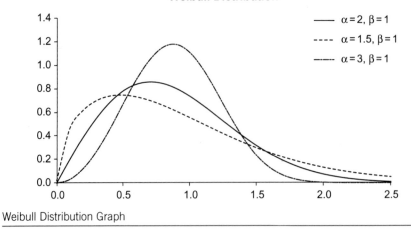

Weibull Distribution Graph

Discrete Distributions
Binomial Distribution

The binomial distribution is a discrete distribution used for sampling experiments with replacement. In this scenario, the likelihood of an element being selected remains constant throughout the data-generating process. This is an important distribution in finance for situations in which analysts are looking to model the behavior of the market participants who enter reserve orders to the market. Reserve orders are orders that will instantaneously replenish in the order book with additional shares to execute if the shares are transacted. For example, an investor who has 1000 shares to buy entered at the bid may be showing 100 shares to the market at a time. Once those shares are transacted, the order immediately replenishes with an additional 100 shares to buy at the same bid price (but the priority of the order moves to the end of the queue at that trading destination at that price). These order replenishments could occur with a reserve or iceberg type of order or via high frequency trading algorithms in which once a transaction takes place the market participant immediately submits another order at the same price and order size, thus giving the impression that the order was immediately replaced.

Binomial Distribution Statistics[1]	
Notation	Binomial(n, p)
Parameter	$n \geq 0,\ 0 \leq p \leq 1$
Distribution	$k = 1, 2, \ldots, n$
Pdf	$\binom{n}{k} p^k (1-p)^{n-k}$
Cdf	$\sum_{i=1}^{k} \binom{n}{i} p^i (1-p)^{n-i}$
Mean	np
Variance	$np(1-p)$
Skewness	$\dfrac{1-2p}{\sqrt{np(1-p)}}$
Kurtosis	$\dfrac{1 - 6p(1-p)}{np(1-p)}$

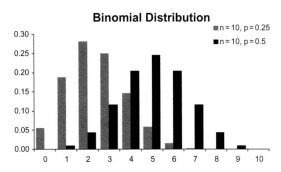

Binomial Distribution

■ n = 10, p = 0.25
■ n = 10, p = 0.5

Binomial Distribution Graph

Poisson Distribution

The Poisson distribution is a discrete distribution that measures the probability of a given number of events happening in a specified time period. In finance, the Poission distribution could be used to model the arrival of new buy or sell orders entered into the market or the expected arrival of orders at specified trading venues or dark pools. In these cases, the Poisson distribution is used to provide expectations surrounding confidence bounds around the expected order arrival rates. Poisson distributions are very useful for smart order routers and algorithmic trading.

Poisson Distribution Statistics[1]	
Notation	Poisson(λ)
Parameter	$\lambda > 0$
Distribution	$k = 1, 2, \ldots,$
Pdf	$\dfrac{\lambda^k e^{-\lambda}}{k!}$
Cdf	$\displaystyle\sum_{i=1}^{k} \dfrac{\lambda^k e^{-\lambda}}{k!}$
Mean	λ
Variance	λ
Skewness	$\lambda^{-1/2}$
Kurtosis	λ^{-1}

Poisson Distribution

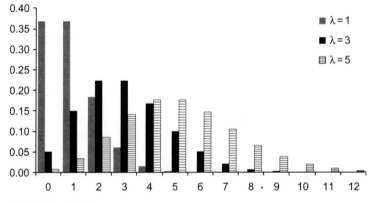

Poisson Distribution Graph

Geometric Distribution

The geometric distribution is a discrete probability function. It is used in statistics to model Bernoulli trials in which each observation is either a success or a failure. For example, if X_i represents the number of failures before the first success, the variable X_i will have a geometric distribution. The geometric distribution is an important distribution for order-routing logic and algorithmic trading. It provides insight into the likelihood of not receiving fills on a specified number of orders entered into the market.

Geometric Distribution Statistics[1]	
Notation	Geometric(λ)
Parameter	$0 \leq p \leq 1$
Distribution	$k = 1, 2, \ldots,$
Pdf	$(1-p)^{k-1}p$
Cdf	$1 - (1-p)^{k+1}$
Mean	$\dfrac{1}{p}$
Variance	$\dfrac{1-p}{p^2}$
Skewness	$\dfrac{2-p}{\sqrt{1-p}}$
Kurtosis	$6 + \dfrac{p^2}{1-p}$

Geometric Distribution

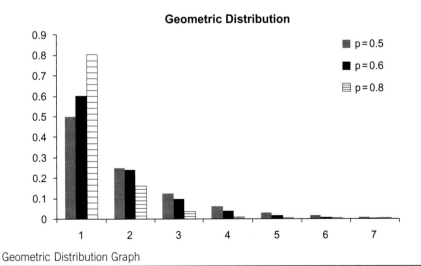

Geometric Distribution Graph

Hypergeometric Distribution

The hypergeometric distribution is used for calculating probabilities for samples drawn from small data universes without replication. In traditional experiments, this means that the elements that were not chosen have a higher probability of being selected on each subsequent draw than on the previous draw (e.g., lottery draws without replacement). In finance, the hypergeometric distribution has become useful for modeling order book depth in dark pools, as well as for smart order routing in the displayed venues.

Hypergeometric Distribution Statistics[1]	
Notation	$HyperGeometric(N, K, n)$
Parameter	$0 \leq p \leq 1$
Distribution	$x = 1, 2, \ldots,$
Pdf	$\dfrac{\dbinom{K}{k}\dbinom{N-K}{n-k}}{\dbinom{N}{n}}$
Cdf	$\displaystyle\sum_{i=1}^{k} \dfrac{\dbinom{K}{i}\dbinom{N-K}{n-i}}{\dbinom{N}{n}}$
Mean	$n\dfrac{K}{N}$
Variance	$n\dfrac{K}{N}\dfrac{(N-K)}{N}\dfrac{(N-n)}{(N-1)}$
Skewness	$\dfrac{(N-2K)(N-1)^2(N-2n)}{[nK(N-K)(N-n)]^{\frac{1}{2}}(N-2)}$
Kurtosis	(see *www.mathworld.wolfram.com*)

where N = population size, K = number of successes in the market, n = number of child orders sent, and k = number of successes.

Hypergeometric Distribution

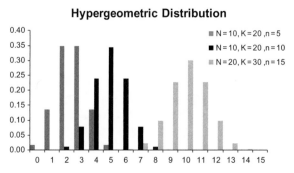

Hypergeometric Distribution Graph[1]

Endnotes

[1] The probability distribution statistics shown in the tables in this chapter can be found at:

www.mathworld.wolfram.com/topics/ProbabilityandStatistics.html
www.statsoft.com/textbook/
www.wikipedia.org/wiki/Probability_distribution_function
www.mathwave.com/articles/distribution_fitting.html
www.uah.edu/stat/special

References

De Groot, M.H., 1986. Probability and Statistic, second ed. Addison Wesley, New York.

Devore, J., 1982. Probability & Statistics for Engineering and the Sciences. Brooks/Cole Publishing.

Dudewicz, E., Mishra, S., 1988. Modern Mathematical Statistics. John Wiley & Sons.

Fox, J., 2002. Nonlinear Regression and Nonlinear Least Squares: Appendix to An R and S-Plus Companion to Applied Regression, <http://cran.r-project.org/doc/contrib/Fox-Companion/appendix-nonlinear-regression.pdf>.

Greene, W., 2000. Econometric Analysis, fourth ed. Prentice-Hall, Inc.

Gujarati, D., 1988. Basic Economics, second ed. McGraw-Hill, New York.

Kennedy, P., 1998. A Guide to Econometrics, fourth ed. The MIT Press, Cambridge, Massachusetts.

Kissell, R., 2013. The Science of Algorithmic Trading and Portfolio Management. Elsevier, New York.

Kissell, R., Glantz, M., 2003. Optimal Trading Strategies. AMACOM, Inc, New York.

Kissell, R., Malamut R., 1999. Optimal Trading Models. Instinet Working Paper.

Kissell, R., Malamut, R., 2006. Algorithmic decision making framework. J. Trading Winter 2006.

Kissell, R., Glantz, M., Malamut, R., 2004. A Practical Framework for Estimating Market Impact and Achieving Best Execution. Elsevier, Finance Research Letters 1.

Mittelhammer, R., Judge, G., Miller, D., 2000. Econometrics Foundation. Cambridge University Press.

Meyer, P., 1970. Introductory Probability and Statistical Applications, second ed. Addison-Wesley Publishing Company.

Pfeiffer, P., 1978. Concepts of Probability Theory, second Revised ed. Dover Publications, Inc.

Zhi, J., Melia, A.T., Guericiolini, R., et al., 1994. Retrospective population-based analysis of the dose-response (fecal fat excretion) relationship of orlistat in normal and obese volunteers. Clin. Pharmacol. Ther. 56, 82–85.

A Primer on Quantitative Risk Analysis

3

Dr. Johnathan Mun[1]

This chapter gets into the nuts and bolts of quantitative risk analysis as it pertains to making business decisions in a bank. As part of credit risk analysis and credit engineering, the general underlying principles of risk analysis remain the same as in general business risk. For instance, credit risk analysis may require applying a Monte Carlo simulation for forecasting and back-testing the accuracy of a credit-scoring model, testing scenarios and sensitivities on a credit portfolio, integrating and accounting for correlations in a basket of credit issues and vehicles, and so forth. Therefore, this chapter provides the fundamentals of quantitative risk analysis that are required knowledge and prerequisites for more advanced applications in banking and credit risk. The chapter starts off with an interesting historical perspective of risk, followed by discussions of the basic characteristics of risk and the nature of risk versus returns. It then provides detailed hands-on applications of running quantitative Monte Carlo risk simulations using the Risk Simulator software. Finally, the chapter wraps up with two hands-on exercises for using the software on running risk simulations and understanding the diversification effects of correlations on risk. Visit www.realoptionsvaluation.com for free videos, case studies, and models, as well as to download trial versions of the software.

A Brief History of Risk: What exactly is Risk?

Since the beginning of recorded history, games of chance have been a popular pastime. Even in Biblical accounts, Roman soldiers cast lots for Christ's robes. In earlier times, chance was something that occurred in nature, and humans were simply subjected to it as a ship is to the capricious tosses of the waves in an ocean. Even up to the time of the Renaissance, the future was thought to be

---

[1]Dr. Johnathan Mun, Chairman, is founder and CEO of Real Options Valuation, Inc., a premier software, training, and consulting firm located in California (www.realoptionsvaluation.com). The software applications presented herein include Risk Simulator, Modeling Toolkit, and others from the company. Dr. Mun holds professorships at multiple universities globally and has authored 12 books, some of which were co-authored with Morton Glantz.

simply a chance occurrence of completely random events and beyond the control of humans. However, with the advent of games of chance, human greed propelled the study of risk and chance to ever more closely mirror real-life events. Although these games were initially played with great enthusiasm, the players rarely sat down to actually figure out the odds. Of course, the individual who understood and mastered the concept of chance was bound to be in a better position to profit from such games of chance. It was not until the mid-1600s that the concept of chance was properly studied, and the first-such serious endeavor can be credited to Blaise Pascal, one of the fathers of modern choice, chance, and probability. Fortunately for us, after many centuries of mathematical and statistical innovations from pioneers such as Pascal, Bernoulli, Bayes, Gauss, LaPlace, and Fermat, our modern world of uncertainty can be explained with much more elegance through methodological applications of risk and uncertainty.

To the people who lived centuries ago, risk was simply the inevitability of chance occurrence beyond the realm of human control, though many phony soothsayers profited from their ability to convincingly profess their clairvoyance by simply stating the obvious or reading the victims' body language and telling them what they wanted to hear. We modern-day humans—ignoring for the moment the occasional seers among us—with our fancy technological achievements, are still susceptible to risk and uncertainty. We may be able to predict the orbital paths of planets in our solar system with astounding accuracy or the escape velocity required to shoot a man from the Earth to the Moon, but when it comes to predicting a firm's revenues the following year, we are at a loss. Humans have been struggling with risk our entire existence, but through trial and error, and through the evolution of human knowledge and thought, we have devised ways to describe, quantify, hedge, and take advantage of risk.

Clearly the entire realm of risk analysis is vast and would most probably be intractable within the few chapters of a book. Therefore, this book is concerned with only a small niche of risk, namely, *applied business risk modeling and analysis*. Even in the areas of applied business risk analysis, the diversity is great. For instance, business risk can be roughly divided into the areas of operational risk management and financial risk management. In financial risk, one can look at market risk, private risk, credit risk, default risk, maturity risk, liquidity risk, inflationary risk, interest rate risk, country risk, and so forth. This book focuses on the application of risk analysis in the sense of how to adequately apply the tools to identify, understand, quantify, and diversify risk such that it can be hedged and managed more effectively. These tools are generic enough that they can be applied across a whole spectrum of business conditions, industries, and needs. Finally, understanding this text together with *Modeling Risk*, Second Edition (Wiley 2010) and the associated Risk Simulator and Real Options SLS software are required for the Certified Risk Management (or CRM) certification (see www.realoptionsvaluation.com for more details).

Risky ventures are the norm in the daily business world. The mere mention of names such as George Soros, John Meriweather, Paul Reichmann, and Nicholas

Leeson, or firms such as Long Term Capital Management, Metallgesellschaft, Barings Bank, Bankers Trust, Daiwa Bank, Sumimoto Corporation, Merrill Lynch, or Citibank brings a shrug of disbelief and fear. These names are some of the biggest in the world of business and finance. Their claim to fame is not simply for being the best and brightest individuals nor being the largest and most respected firms, but for bearing the stigma of being involved in highly risky ventures that turned sour almost overnight.

George Soros was and still is one of the most respected names in high finance; he is known globally for his brilliance and exploits. Paul Reichmann was a reputable and brilliant real estate and property tycoon. Between the two of them, nothing was impossible, but when they ventured into investments in Mexican real estate, the wild fluctuations of the peso in the foreign exchange market caused nothing short of a disaster. During late 1994 and early 1995, the peso hit an all-time low and their ventures went from bad to worse, but the one thing that they did not expect was that the situation would become a lot worse before it was all over and that billions would be lost as a consequence.

Long Term Capital Management was headed by Meriweather, one of the rising stars in Wall Street, with a slew of superstars on its management team, including several Nobel laureates in finance and economics (including Robert Merton and Myron Scholes). The firm was also backed by giant investment banks. A firm that seemed indestructible blew up with billions of dollars in the red, shaking the international investment community with repercussions throughout Wall Street as individual investors started to lose faith in large hedge funds and wealth-management firms, forcing the eventual massive Federal Reserve bailout.

Barings was one of the oldest banks in England. It was so respected that even Queen Elizabeth II herself held a private account there. This multibillion dollar institution was brought down single-handedly by Nicholas Leeson, an employee halfway around the world. Leeson was a young and brilliant investment banker who headed Barings' Singapore branch. His illegally doctored track record showed significant investment profits, which gave him more leeway and trust from the home office over time. He was able to cover his losses through fancy accounting and by taking significant amounts of risk. His speculations in the Japanese yen went south, he took Barings down with him, and the top echelons in London never knew what hit them.

Had any of the managers in the boardrooms at their respective headquarters bothered to look at the risk profile of their investments, they would surely have made a very different decision much earlier on, preventing what became major embarrassments in the global investment community. If the projected returns are adjusted for risks, that is, finding what levels of risks are required to attain such seemingly extravagant returns, it would be sensible not to proceed.

Risks occur in everyday life that do not require investments in the multimillions. For instance, when would one purchase a house in a fluctuating housing market? When would it be more profitable to lock in a fixed-rate mortgage rate rather than keep a floating variable rate? What are the chances that there will be insufficient funds at retirement? What about the potential personal property losses when a hurricane hits? How much accident insurance is considered sufficient? How much is a lottery ticket actually worth?

Risk permeates all aspects of life, and we can never avoid taking or facing risks. What we can do is to understand risks better through a systematic assessment of their impacts and repercussions. This assessment framework must also be capable of measuring, monitoring, and managing risks; otherwise, simply noting that risks exist and moving on is not optimal. This book provides the tools and framework necessary to tackle risks head-on. Only with the added insights gained through a rigorous assessment of risk can we actively manage and monitor risk.

> Risks permeate every aspect of business but we do not have to be passive participants. What we can do is develop a framework to better understand risks through a systematic assessment of their impacts and repercussions. This framework must also be capable of measuring, monitoring, and managing risks.

The Basics of Risk

Risk can be simply defined as any uncertainty that affects a system in an unknown fashion whereby the ramifications are also unknown, but bear with them great fluctuation in value and outcome. In every instance, for risk to be evident, the following generalities must exist:

- Uncertainties and risks have a time horizon.
- Uncertainties exist in the future and will evolve over time.
- Uncertainties become risks if they affect the outcomes and scenarios of the system.
- These changing scenarios' effects on the system can be measured.
- The measurement has to be set against a benchmark.

Risk is never instantaneous. It has a time horizon. For instance, a firm engaged in a risky research and development venture will face significant amounts of risk, but only until the product is fully developed or has proven itself in the market. These risks are caused by uncertainties in the technology of the product under research, uncertainties about the potential market, uncertainties about the level of competitive threats and substitutes, and so forth. These uncertainties will change over the course of the company's research and marketing activities—some uncertainties will increase, while others will most likely decrease through the passage of time, actions, and events. However, only the uncertainties that affect the product directly will have any bearing on the risks of the product being successful. That is, only uncertainties that change the possible scenario outcomes will make the product risky (e.g., market and economic conditions). Finally, risk exists if it can be measured and compared against a benchmark. If no benchmark exists, then perhaps the conditions just described are the norm for research and development activities, and thus the negative results are to be expected. These benchmarks have to be measurable and tangible, for example, gross profits, success rates, market share, time to implementation, and so forth.

> Risk is any uncertainty that affects a system in an unknown fashion whereby its ramifications are unknown but may bring great fluctuation in value and outcome. Risk has a time horizon, meaning that uncertainty evolves over time, which affects measurable future outcomes and scenarios with respect to a benchmark.

The Nature of Risk and Return

Nobel Laureate Harry Markowitz's groundbreaking research into the nature of risk and return has revolutionized the world of finance. His seminal work, which is now known all over the world as the *Markowitz Efficient Frontier*, looks at the nature of risk and return. Markowitz did not look at risk as the enemy, but rather as a condition that should be embraced and balanced out through its expected returns. The concept of risk and return was then refined through later works by William Sharpe, and others, who stated that a heightened risk necessitates a higher return, as elegantly expressed through the *capital asset pricing model* (CAPM), in which the required rate of return on a marketable risky equity is equivalent to the return on an equivalent riskless asset plus a beta systematic and undiversifiable risk measure multiplied by the market risk's return premium. In essence, a higher-risk asset requires a higher return. In Markowitz's model, one could strike a balance between risk and return. Depending on the risk appetite of an investor, the optimal or best-case returns can be obtained through the efficient frontier. Should the investor require a higher level of returns, he or she would have to face a higher level of risk. Markowitz's work carried over to finding combinations of individual projects or assets in a portfolio that would provide the best *bang for the buck*, striking an elegant balance between risk and return. In order to better understand this balance, also known as *risk-adjustment* in modern risk analysis language, risks must first be measured and understood.

Uncertainty Versus Risk

Risk and uncertainty are very different-looking animals, but they are of the same species; however, the lines of demarcation are often blurred. A distinction is critical at this juncture before proceeding, and it is worthy of segue. Suppose I am senseless enough to take a skydiving trip with a good friend, and we board a plane headed for the Palm Springs desert. While airborne at 10,000 feet and watching our lives flash before our eyes, we realize that in our haste we forgot to pack our parachutes on board. However, there is an old, dusty, and dilapidated emergency parachute on the plane. At that point, both my friend and I have the same level of uncertainty—the uncertainty of whether the old parachute will open and, if it does not, whether we will fall to our deaths. However, being the risk-adverse, nice guy I am, I decide to let my buddy take the plunge. Clearly, he is the one taking the plunge and the also the one taking the risk. I bear no risk at this time, while my friend bears all the risk. However, we both have the same level of uncertainty as to whether the parachute will actually fail. In fact, we both have the same level of uncertainty as to the outcome of the day's trading on the New York Stock Exchange—which has absolutely no impact on whether we live or die that day. Only when he jumps and the parachute opens will the uncertainty become resolved through the passage of time, action, and events. However, even when the uncertainty is resolved with the opening of the parachute, the risk still exists as to whether he will land safely on the ground below.

Therefore, risk is something one bears, and it is the outcome of uncertainty. Even though there is uncertainty, there could very well be no risk. If the only thing that bothers a US-based firm's CEO is the fluctuation in the foreign exchange market of the Zambian kwacha, then I might suggest shorting some kwachas and shifting his portfolio to US-based debt. This uncertainty, if it does not affect the firm's bottom line in any way, is only uncertainty and is not risk. This book is concerned with risk known by performing uncertainty analysis—the same uncertainty that brings about risk by its mere existence as it impacts the value of a particular project. It is further assumed that the end user of this uncertainty analysis uses the results appropriately, whether the analysis is for identifying, adjusting, or selecting projects with respect to their risks, and so forth. Otherwise, running millions of fancy simulation trials and letting the results "marinate" will be useless. By running simulations on the foreign exchange market of the Zambian kwacha, an analyst sitting in a cubicle some-where in downtown San Francisco will in no way reduce the risk of the kwacha in the market or the firm's exposure to the same. Only by using the results from an uncertainty simulation analysis and finding ways to hedge or mitigate the quantified fluctuation and downside risks of the firm's foreign exchange expo-sure through the derivatives market could the analyst be construed as having performed risk analysis and risk management.

To further illustrate the differences between risk and uncertainty, suppose we are attempting to forecast the stock price of Microsoft (MSFT). Suppose MSFT is currently priced at $25 per share, and historical prices place the stock at 21.89% volatility. Now suppose that for the next five years, MSFT does not engage in any risky ventures and stays exactly the way it is, and further suppose that the entire economic and financial world remains constant. This means that the *risk* is fixed and unchanging, that is, volatility is unchanging for the next five years. However, the price uncertainty still increases over time. That is, the width of the forecast intervals will still increase over time. For instance, Year 0's forecast is known, and it is $25 per share. However, as we progress one day,

MSFT will most probably vary between $24 and $26. One year later, the uncertainty bounds may be between $20 and $30. Five years into the future, the boundaries might be between $10 and $50. So, in this example, *uncertainties increase* while *risks remain the same*. Therefore, risk is not equal to uncertainty. This idea is, of course, applicable to any forecasting approach in which it becomes more and more difficult to forecast the future even though the risk remains the same. Now, if risk changes over time, the bounds of uncertainty get more complicated (e.g., uncertainty bounds of sinusoidal waves with discrete event jumps).

In other instances, risk and uncertainty are used interchangeably. For instance, suppose you play a coin-toss game; you bet $0.50, and if heads comes up you win $1; but you lose everything if tails appears. The risk here is that you lose everything, because the risk is that tails may appear. The uncertainty here is that tails may appear. Given that tails appear, you lose everything; hence, uncertainty brings with it risk. Uncertainty is the possibility of an event occurring, and risk is the ramification of such an event occurring. People tend to mistakenly use these two terms interchangeably.

In discussing uncertainty, there are three levels of uncertainties in the world: the *known*, the *unknown*, and the *unknowable*. The known is, of course, what we know will occur and are certain of its occurrence (contractual obligations or a guaranteed event); the unknown is what we do not know and can be simulated. These events will become known through the passage of time, events, and action (the uncertainty of whether a new drug or technology can be developed successfully will become known after spending years and millions on research programs; it will either work or not, and we will know this in the future). These events carry with them risks, but these risks will be reduced or eliminated over time. However, unknowable events carry both uncertainty and risk such that the totality of the risk and uncertainty may not change through the passage of time, events, or actions. These are events such as when the next tsunami or earthquake will hit, or when another act of terrorism will occur around the world. When an event occurs, uncertainty becomes resolved, but risk still remains (another one may or may not hit tomorrow). In traditional analysis, we care about the known factors. In risk analysis, we care about the unknown and unknowable factors. The unknowable factors are easy to hedge: Get the appropriate insurance! That is, do not do business in a war-torn country, get away from politically unstable economies, buy hazard and business interruption insurance, and so forth. Risk analysis will provide the most significant amount of value for the unknown factors.

Risk Simulation Applications

This chapter continues by providing the novice risk analyst an introduction to the Risk Simulator software for performing Monte Carlo simulation, and a 30-day trial of this software is included as part of this book. To claim the necessary license, follow these instructions:

Visit www.realoptionsvaluation.com/creditenginneringbook.html or www.rov-downloads.com/creditenginneringbook.html and click on the Downloads link, scroll down to the Risk Simulator software section, review the system require-ments, then download and install the software. Make sure your system has all the required prerequisites listed on this webpage (e.g., Windows XP, Windows Vista, Windows 7, Windows 8 or later; Excel 2003, 2007, 2010, 2013, or later; and that you have administrative rights to install software). Follow the instruc-tions on this web page to install your free extended trial license of the software.

We continue the chapter by illustrating what Risk Simulator does and what steps are taken in a Monte Carlo simulation, as well as some of the more basic ele-ments in a simulation analysis. The chapter then continues with how to interpret the results from a simulation and ends with a discussion of correlating variables in a simulation, as well as applying precision and error control. As software versions with new enhancements are continually released, be sure to review the software's user manual for more up-to-date details on using the latest version of the software.

The Risk Simulator is a Monte Carlo simulation, forecasting, optimization, and risk-analytics software. It is written in Microsoft .NET C# and functions together with Excel as an add-in. When you have the software installed, simply start Excel, and you will see a new menu item called Risk Simulator. If you are using Excel 2007, Excel 2010, or Excel 2013, you will see a new tab called Risk Simulator, as well as some large icons that you can access. The examples used throughout this book use Risk Simulator version 2013 and above, with the following languages: English, Chinese, Japanese, Korean, Spanish, French, Italian, German, Russian, and Portuguese.

> Monte Carlo risk simulation is used very heavily in credit risk analysis and credit engineering. Applications may include perturbing certain input variables (e.g., interest rates and yield curves) to determine the effects on outputs (e.g., creditworthiness, credit spreads), where thousands of economic scenarios can be run and sensitivity analyses can be performed to identify the credit impact of a specific credit vehicle and so forth. The results from such risk simulations may include Value at Risk, worst-case scenarios, probability of defaults, probability of losses, exposure at default, and so forth.

This software is also compatible with and often used with the Real Options SLS (Super Lattice Solver) software, both developed by the author. The different functions or modules in both software applications are briefly described in the list that follows. Note that there are other software applications such as the ROV Basel II Modeling Toolkit, ROV Employee Stock Options Valuation Toolkit, ROV Compiler, ROV Risk Extractor and Evaluator, ROV BizStats, ROV Modeler, ROV Valuator, ROV Dashboard, and ROV Quantitative Data Mining created by Real Options Valuation, Inc., the same company that developed Risk Simulator, but these are not introduced in this book. You can get more information on these tools by visiting www.realoptionsvaluation.com, where you can also view some free modeling videos and obtain whitepapers, case studies, and other free models. In fact, it is *highly recommended* that you first watch the getting started videos on the DVD or attempt the step-by-step exercises at the end of this chapter *before* reading the text in this chapter. The videos and exercises will get you started immediately, whereas the text in this chapter focuses more on the theory and detailed explanations of the properties of simulation. You can also view the videos online at www.realoptionsvaluation.com/risksimulator.html.

- The *Simulation* module allows you to run simulations in your existing Excel-based models, generate and extract simulation forecasts (distributions of results), perform distributional fitting (automatically finding the best-fitting statistical distribution), compute correlations (maintain relationships among simulated random variables), identify sensitivities (creating tornado and sensitivity charts), test statistical hypotheses (finding statistical differences between pairs of forecasts), run bootstrap simulations (testing the robustness of result statistics), and run custom and nonparametric simulations (simulations using historical data without specifying any distributions or their parameters, for forecasting without data or applying expert opinion forecasts).
- The *Forecasting* module can be used to generate automatic time-series forecasts (with and without seasonality and trend), multivariate regressions (modeling relationships among variables), nonlinear extrapolations (curve fitting), stochastic processes (random walks, mean-reversions, jump-diffusion, and mixed processes), Box-Jenkins ARIMA (econometric forecasts), Auto ARIMA, basic econometrics and auto-econometrics (modeling relationships and generating forecasts), exponential J curves, logistic S curves, GARCH models and their multiple variations (modeling and forecasting volatility), maximum likelihood models for limited dependent variables (logit, tobit, and probit models), Markov chains, trendlines, spine curves, and others.
- The *Optimization* module is used for optimizing multiple decision variables subject to constraints to maximize or minimize an objective, and can be run either as a static optimization, as dynamic and stochastic optimization under uncertainty together with Monte Carlo simulation, or as a stochastic optimization with super-speed simulations. The software can handle linear and nonlinear optimizations with binary, integer, and continuous variables, as well as generate Markowitz efficient frontiers.
- The *Analytical Tools* module allows you to run segmentation clustering, hypothesis testing, statistical tests of raw data, data diagnostics of technical forecasting assumptions (e.g., heteroskedasticity, multicollinearity, and the like), sensitivity and scenario analyses, overlay chart analysis, spider charts, tornado charts, and many other powerful tools.
- The Real Options Super Lattice Solver is another stand-alone software that complements Risk Simulator, and it is used for solving simple to complex real options problems.

The following sections walk you through the basics of the *Simulation Module* in Risk Simulator, while subsequent chapters provide more details on the applications of other modules. To follow along, make sure you have Risk Simulator installed on your computer to proceed. Also note that there are additional hands-on exercises available at the end of certain chapters in which you can get step-by-step instructions on running sample models using Risk Simulator.

Running a Monte Carlo Simulation

Typically, to run a simulation in your existing Excel model, the following steps have to be performed:

- Start a new simulation profile or open an existing profile.
- Define input assumptions in the relevant cells.
- Define output forecasts in the relevant cells.
- Run the simulation.
- Interpret the results.

If desired, and for practice, open the example file called *Basic Simulation Model* and follow along with the examples provided here on creating a simulation. The example file can be found by first starting Excel and then clicking on *Risk Simulator | Example Models | 02 Basic Simulation Model*. Also, do not forget to visit www.realoptionsvaluation.com to watch free getting started videos and to download Excel models, case studies, whitepapers, and trial versions of the software.

Start a New Simulation Profile

To start a new simulation, you must first create a simulation profile. A simulation profile contains a complete set of instructions on how you would like to run a simulation; that is, all the assumptions, forecasts, run preferences, and so forth. Having profiles facilitates creating multiple scenarios of simulations—using the same exact model, several profiles can be created, each with its own specific simulation properties and requirements. The same person can create different test scenarios using different distributional assumptions and inputs, or multiple persons can test their own assumptions and inputs on the same model.

- Start Excel and create a new model or open an existing one (you can use the *Basic Simulation Model* example to follow along).
- Click on *Risk Simulator | New Simulation Profile*.
- Specify a title for your simulation as well as all other pertinent information (Figure 3.1).
- *Title*. Specifying a simulation title allows you to create multiple simulation profiles in a single Excel model. Using a title means that you can now save different simulation scenario profiles within the same model without having to delete existing assumptions and change them each time a new simulation

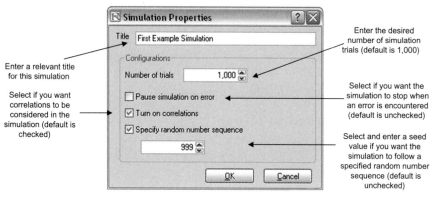

Enter a relevant title for this simulation

Enter the desired number of simulation trials (default is 1,000)

Select if you want correlations to be considered in the simulation (default is checked)

Select if you want the simulation to stop when an error is encountered (default is unchecked)

Select and enter a seed value if you want the simulation to follow a specified random number sequence (default is unchecked)

FIGURE 3.1 New Simulation Profile

scenario is required. You can always change the profile's name later (*Risk Simulator | Edit Profile*).

- *Number of trials*. This is where the number of simulation trials required is entered. That is, running 1,000 trials means that 1,000 different iterations of outcomes based on the input assumptions will be generated. You can change this number as desired, but the input has to be positive integers. The default number of runs is 1,000 trials. You can use precision and error control to automatically help determine how many simulation trials to run (see the section on precision and error control later in this chapter for details).

- *Pause simulation on error*. If checked, the simulation stops every time an error is encountered in the Excel model. That is, if your model encounters a computation error (e.g., some input values generated in a simulation trial may yield a divide by zero error in one of your spreadsheet cells), the simulation stops. This feature is important to help audit your model to make sure there are no computational errors in your Excel model. However, if you are sure the model works, then there is no need for this preference to be checked.

- *Turn on correlations*. If checked, correlations between paired input assumptions will be computed. Otherwise, correlations will all be set to zero, and a simulation is run assuming no cross-correlations between input assumptions. As an example, applying correlations will yield more accurate results, if, indeed, correlations exist, and will tend to yield a lower forecast confidence if negative correlations exist. After turning on correlations here, you can later set the relevant correlation coefficients on each assumption generated (see the section on correlations and precision control later in this chapter for more details).

- *Specify random number sequence*. Simulation, by definition, will yield slightly different results every time a simulation is run. Different results occur by virtue of the random number generation routine in Monte Carlo simulation; this characteristic is a theoretical fact in all random number generators. However, when making presentations, if you require the same results (such as, especially, when the report being presented shows one set of results and during a live presentation you would like to show the same results being generated, or when you are sharing models with others and would like the same results to be obtained every time), then check this preference and enter in an initial seed number. The seed number can be any positive integer. Using the same initial seed value, the same number of trials, and the same input assumptions, the simulation will always yield the same sequence of random numbers, guaranteeing the same final set of results.

Note that once a new simulation profile has been created, you can come back later and modify these selections. In order to do this, make sure that the current active profile is the profile you wish to modify; otherwise, click on *Risk Simulator | Change Simulation Profile*, select the profile you wish to change, and click *OK* (Figure 3.2 shows an example where there are multiple profiles and how to activate a selected profile). Then, click on *Risk Simulator | Edit Simulation Profile* and make the required changes. You can also duplicate or rename an existing profile. When creating multiple profiles in the same Excel model, make sure to provide each profile with a unique name so you can tell them apart later on. Also, these profiles are stored inside hidden sectors of the Excel *.xls file, and you do not have to save any additional files. The profiles and their contents (assumptions, forecasts, etc.) are automatically saved when you save the Excel file. Finally, the last profile that is active when you exit and save the Excel file will be the one that is opened the next time the Excel file is accessed.

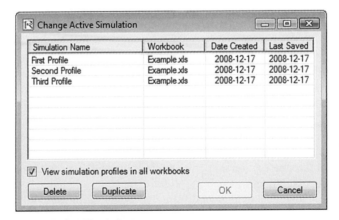

FIGURE 3.2 Change Active Simulation

Define Input Assumptions

The next step is to set input assumptions in your model. Note that assumptions can only be assigned to cells without any equations or functions (i.e., typed-in numerical values that are inputs in a model), whereas output forecasts can only be assigned to cells with equations and functions (i.e., outputs of a model). Recall that assumptions and forecasts cannot be set unless a simulation profile already exists. Do the following to set new input assumptions in your model:

- Make sure a Simulation Profile exists, open an existing profile, or start a new profile (*Risk Simulator | New Simulation Profile*).
- Select the cell you wish to set an assumption on (e.g., cell G8 in the Basic Simulation Model example).
- Click on *Risk Simulator | Set Input Assumption* or click on the set input assumption icon in the Risk Simulator icon toolbar.
- Select the relevant distribution you want, enter the relevant distribution parameters (e.g., select Triangular distribution and use 1, 2, and 2.5 as the minimum, most likely, and maximum values), and hit OK to insert the input assumption into your model (Figure 3.3).

Note that you can also set assumptions by selecting the cell you wish to set the assumption on and, using the mouse right-click, access the shortcut Risk Simulator menu to set an input assumption. In addition, for expert users, you can set input assumptions using the Risk Simulator *RS Functions*: Select the cell of choice, click on Excel's *Insert | Function*, select the *All* category, and scroll down

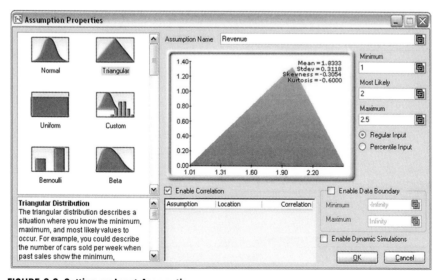

FIGURE 3.3 Setting an Input Assumption

to the *RS* functions list (we do not recommend using RS functions unless you are an expert user). For the examples going forward, we suggest following the basic instructions in accessing menus and icons.

Notice that in the Assumption Properties (see Figure 3.4), there are several key areas worthy of mention:

- *Assumption Name.* This is an optional area that allows you to enter in unique names for the assumptions to help track what each of the assumptions represents. Good modeling practice is to use short but precise assumption names.
- *Distribution Gallery.* This area to the left shows all of the different distributions available in the software. To change the views, right-click anywhere in the gallery and select large icons, small icons, or list. More than two dozen distributions are available.
- *Input Parameters.* Depending on the distribution selected, the required relevant parameters are shown. You may either enter the parameters directly or link them to specific cells in your worksheet. Hard coding or typing the parameters is useful when the assumption parameters are assumed not to change. Linking to worksheet cells is useful when the input parameters need to be visible or are allowed to be changed (click on the link icon to link an input parameter to a worksheet cell).
- *Enable Data Boundary.* This feature is typically not used by the average analyst; it exists for truncating the distributional assumptions. For instance, if a normal distribution is selected, the theoretical boundaries are between negative infinity and positive infinity. However, in practice, the simulated variable exists only within some smaller range, and this range can then be entered to truncate the distribution appropriately.

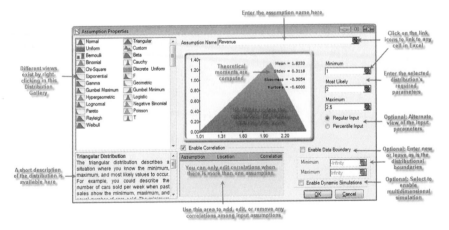

FIGURE 3.4 Assumption Properties

- *Correlations.* Pairwise correlations can be assigned to input assumptions here. If assumptions are required, remember to check the *Turn on Correlations* preference by clicking on *Risk Simulator | Edit Simulation Profile.* See the discussion on correlations later in this chapter for more details about assigning correlations and the effects correlations will have on a model. Notice that you can either truncate a distribution or correlate it to another assumption, but not both.
- *Short Descriptions.* These exist for each of the distributions in the gallery. The short descriptions explain when a certain distribution is used, as well as the input parameter requirements.
- *Regular Input and Percentile Input.* This option allows the user to perform a quick due-diligence test of the input assumption. For instance, if setting a normal distribution with some mean and standard deviation inputs, you can click on the percentile input to see what the corresponding 10th and 90th percentiles are.
- *Enable Dynamic Simulation.* This option is unchecked by default, but if you wish to run a multidimensional simulation (i.e., if you link the input parameters of the assumption to another cell that is itself an assumption, you are simulating the inputs, or simulating the simulation), then remember to check this option. Dynamic simulation will not work unless the inputs are linked to other changing input assumptions.

Note: If you are following along with the example, continue by setting another assumption on cell G9. This time use the *Uniform* distribution with a minimum value of 0.9 and a maximum value of 1.1. Then, proceed to defining the output forecasts in the next step.

Define Output Forecasts

The next step is to define output forecasts in the model. Forecasts can only be defined on output cells with equations or functions. The following describes the set forecast process:

- Select the cell you wish to set an assumption on (e.g., cell G10 in the Basic Simulation Model example).
- Click on Risk Simulator and select Set Output Forecast or click on the set output forecast icon on the Risk Simulator icon toolbar.
- Enter the relevant information and click OK.

Note that you can also set output forecasts by selecting the cell you wish to set the assumption on and, using the mouse right-click, access the shortcut Risk Simulator menu to set an output forecast.

Figure 3.5 illustrates the set forecast properties:

- *Forecast Name.* Specify the name of the forecast cell. This is important because when you have a large model with multiple forecast cells, naming the forecast cells individually allows you to access the right results quickly. Do

FIGURE 3.5 Set Output Forecast

not underestimate the importance of this simple step. Good modeling practice is to use short but precise assumption names.

- *Forecast Precision.* Instead of relying on a guesstimate of how many trials to run in your simulation, you can set up precision and error controls. When an error-precision combination has been achieved in the simulation, the simulation will pause and inform you of the precision achieved, making the number of simulation trials an automated process and eliminating guesses on the required number of trials to simulate. Review the section on precision and error control later in this chapter for more specific details.
- *Show Forecast Window.* This property allows the user to show or not show a particular forecast window. The default is to always show a forecast chart.

Run Simulation

If everything looks right, simply click on *Risk Simulator | Run Simulation* or click on the *Run* icon on the Risk Simulator toolbar and the simulation will proceed. You may also reset a simulation after it has run to rerun it (*Risk Simulator | Reset Simulation* or the reset simulation icon on the toolbar) or to pause it during a run. Also, the *step* function (*Risk Simulator | Step Simulation* or the step simulation icon on the toolbar) allows you to simulate a single trial, one at a time, useful for educating others on simulation (i.e., you can show that at each trial, all the values in the assumption cells are being replaced and the entire model is recalculated each time). You can also access the run simulation menu by right-clicking anywhere in the model and selecting *Run Simulation*.

Risk Simulator also allows you to run the simulation at extremely fast speed, called Super Speed. To do this, click on *Risk Simulator | Run Super Speed Simulation*, or use the run super speed icon. Notice how much faster the super-speed simulation runs. In fact, for practice, click on *Reset Simulation* and then

Edit Simulation Profile, change the *Number of Trials* to *100000*, and click on *Run Super Speed*. It should only take a few seconds to run. However, be aware that super-speed simulation will not run if the model has errors, VBA (Visual Basic for Applications), or links to external data sources or applications. In such situations, you will be notified and the regular speed simulation will be run instead. Regular speed simulations are always able to run, even with errors, VBA, or external links.

Interpret the Forecast Results

The final step in Monte Carlo simulation is to interpret the resulting forecast charts. Figures 3.6 through 3.13 show the forecast charts and the corresponding statistics generated after running the simulation. Typically, the following features are important in interpreting the results of a simulation:

- *Forecast Chart*. The forecast chart shown in Figure 3.6 is a probability histogram that shows the frequency counts of values occurring in the total number of trials simulated. The vertical bars show the frequency of a particular *x* value occurring out of the total number of trials, while the cumulative frequency (smooth line) shows the total probabilities of all values at and below *x* occurring in the forecast.
- *Forecast Statistics*. The forecast statistics shown in Figure 3.7 summarize the distribution of the forecast values in terms of the four moments of a distribution. You can rotate between the histogram and statistics tab by depressing the space bar.

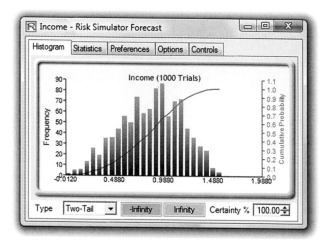

FIGURE 3.6 Forecast Chart

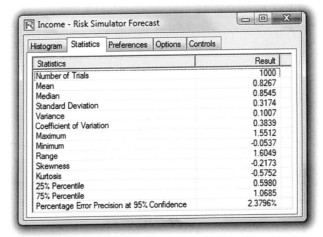

FIGURE 3.7 Forecast Statistics

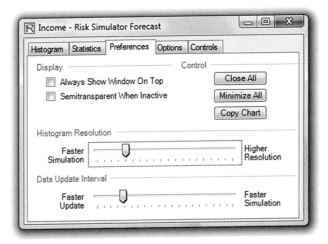

FIGURE 3.8 Forecast Chart Preferences

- *Preferences.* The preferences tab in the forecast chart (Figure 3.8) allows you to change the look and feel of the charts. For instance, if *Always Show Window On Top* is selected, the forecast charts will always be visible regardless of what other software is running on your computer. *Histogram Resolution* allows you to change the number of bins of the histogram, anywhere from 5 bins to 100 bins. Also, the *Data Update* section allows you to control how fast the simulation runs versus how often the forecast chart is updated. That is, if you wish to see the forecast chart updated at almost every trial, this feature will slow down the simulation as more memory is being allocated to updating the chart versus running the simulation. This option is merely a user preference and in no way changes the results of the simulation; it only changes the speed of completing the simulation. To further increase the speed of the simulation, you can minimize Excel while the simulation is running, thereby reducing the memory required to visibly update the Excel spreadsheet and freeing up the memory to run the simulation. The *Clear All* and *Minimize All* selections control all the open forecast charts.

- *Options.* The forecast chart options (Figure 3.9, top) for showing data allow you to show all the forecast data or to filter in/out values that fall within some specified interval you choose or within some standard deviation you choose. Also, the precision level can be set here for this specific forecast to show the error levels in the statistics view. See the section on precision and error control later in this chapter for more details. *Show the following statistic on histogram* is a user preference as to whether the mean, median, first quartile, and fourth quartile lines (25th and 75th percentiles) should be displayed on the forecast chart.

- *Controls.* This tab (Figure 3.9, bottom) has all the functionalities that allow you to change the type, color, size, zoom, tilt, 3D, and other things in the forecast chart as well as provide overlay charts (PDF, CDF) and running distributional fitting on your forecast data (see the Data Fitting sections in the user manual for more details on this methodology).

Using Forecast Charts and Confidence Intervals

In forecast charts, you can determine the probability of occurrence called *confidence intervals*. That is, given two values, what are the chances that the outcome will fall between these two values? Figure 3.10 illustrates that there is a 90% probability that the final outcome (in this case, the level of income) will be between $0.2653 and $1.3230. The two-tailed confidence interval can be obtained by first selecting *Two-Tail* as the type, entering the desired certainty value (e.g., 90) and hitting *TAB* on the keyboard. The two computed values corresponding to the certainty value will then be displayed. In this example, there is a 5% probability that income will be below $0.2653 and another 5% probability that income will be above $1.3230. That is, the two-tailed confidence interval is a symmetrical interval centered on the median or 50th percentile value. Thus, both tails will have the same probability.

Alternatively, a one-tail probability can be computed. Figure 3.11 shows a *Left-Tail* selection at 95% confidence (i.e., choose *Left-Tail* ≤ as the type, enter 95 as the certainty level, and hit *TAB* on the keyboard). This means that there is a 95% probability that the income will be at or below $1.3230 or a 5% probability

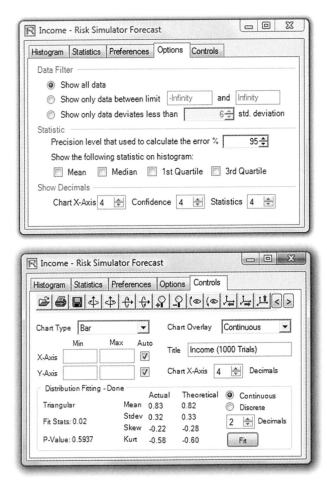

FIGURE 3.9 Forecast Chart Options and Control

that income will be above $1.3230, corresponding perfectly with the results seen in Figure 3.10.

Forecast charts and forecast statistics can be used to determine the Credit Value at Risk of your credit issue or portfolio of credit instruments (e.g., Value at Risk for a one-tail 99.95% confidence for a 10-day holding period) as well as determine the risk characteristics of your portfolio (e.g., looking at the fourth moment of the distribution or kurtosis to determine if there are extreme value events or catastrophic events that may have a high probability of occurrence, potentially wiping out the profits of your portfolio). You can also determine the probability that your engineered credit vehicle will be profitable, and compare one vehicle or instrument versus another in terms of risk and return characteristics.

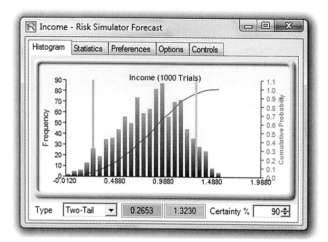

FIGURE 3.10 Forecast Chart of a Two-Tailed Confidence Interval

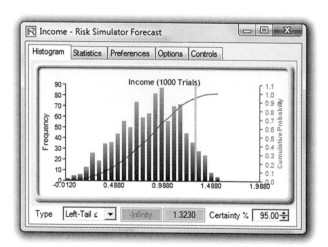

FIGURE 3.11 Forecast Chart of a One-Tailed Confidence Interval

In addition to evaluating what the confidence interval is (i.e., given a probability level, find the relevant income values), you can determine the probability of a given income value (Figure 3.12). For instance, what is the probability that income will be less than or equal to $1? To do this, select the *Left-Tail* ≤ probability type, enter 1 into the value input box, and hit *TAB*. The corresponding

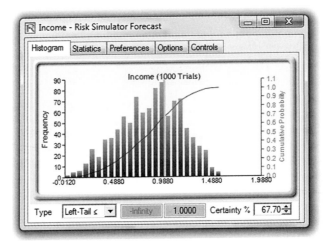

FIGURE 3.12 Forecast Chart of a Probability Evaluation

certainty will then be computed (in this case, there is a 67.70% probability income will be at or below $1).

For the sake of completeness, you can select the *Right-Tail* > probability type and enter the value 1 in the value input box, and hit *TAB* (Figure 3.13). The resulting probability indicates the right-tail probability past the value 1, that is, the probability of income exceeding $1 (in this case, we see that there is a 32.30% probability of income exceeding $1). The sum of 32.30% and 67.70% is, of course 100%, the total probability under the curve.

TIPS

- The forecast window is resizable by clicking on and dragging the bottom right corner of the forecast window. It is always advisable that before rerunning a simulation, the current simulation should be reset (*Risk Simulator | Reset Simulation*).
- Remember that you will need to hit *TAB* on the keyboard to update the chart and results when you type in the certainty values or right- and left-tail values.
- You can also hit the *spacebar* on the keyboard repeatedly to cycle among the histogram, statistics, preferences, options, and control tabs.
- In addition, if you click on *Risk Simulator | Options*, you can access several different options for Risk Simulator, including allowing Risk Simulator to start each time Excel starts or to only start when you want it to (by going to *Start | Programs | Real Options Valuation | Risk Simulator | Risk Simulator*), change the *cell colors* of assumptions and forecasts, or turn *cell comments* on and off (cell comments will allow you to see which cells are input assumptions and which are output forecasts, as well as their respective input

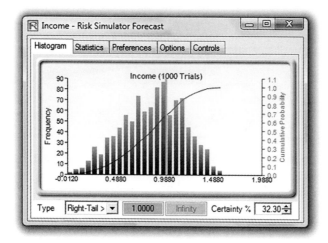

FIGURE 3.13 Forecast Chart of a Probability Evaluation

parameters and names). Do spend some time experimenting with the forecast chart outputs and the various bells and whistles, especially the *Controls* tab.

Correlations and Precision Control

The Basics of Correlations

The correlation coefficient is a measure of the strength and direction of the relationship between two variables, and it can take on any values between -1.0 and $+1.0$. That is, the correlation coefficient can be decomposed into its sign (positive or negative relationship between two variables) and the magnitude or strength of the relationship (the higher the absolute value of the correlation coefficient, the stronger the relationship).

The correlation coefficient can be computed in several ways. The first approach is to manually compute the correlation r of two variables x and y using:

$$r_{x,y} = \frac{n \sum x_i y_i - \sum x_i \sum y_i}{\sqrt{n \sum x_i^2 - \left(\sum x_i\right)^2} \sqrt{n \sum y_i^2 - \left(\sum y_i\right)^2}}$$

The second approach is to use Excel's *CORREL* function. For instance, if the 10 data points for x and y are listed in cells A1:B10, then the Excel function to use is *CORREL (A1:A10, B1:B10)*.

The third approach is to run Risk Simulator's *Multi-Fit Tool*, and the resulting correlation matrix will be computed and displayed.

It is important to note that correlation does not imply causation. Two completely unrelated random variables might display some correlation, but this does not imply any causation between the two (e.g., sunspot activity and events in the stock market are correlated, but there is no causation between the two).

> Correlations affect risk, or the second moment of the distribution, and when multiple credit instruments are placed in a portfolio, correlations are critical in determining the credit concentration or credit diversification effects that one instrument may offset another. Some credit instruments have linear correlations to other credit instruments and are nonlinearly correlated to their underlying assets (e.g., probability of default, exposure at default) and exogenous economic variables (e.g., interest rates, inflation, foreign exchange exposures).

There are two general types of correlations: parametric and nonparametric. Pearson's correlation coefficient is the most common correlation measure and is usually referred to simply as the correlation coefficient. However, Pearson's correlation is a parametric measure, which means that it requires both correlated variables to have an underlying normal distribution and that the relationship between the variables is linear. When these conditions are violated, which is often the case in Monte Carlo simulation, the nonparametric counterparts become more important. Spearman's rank correlation and Kendall's tau are the two nonparametric alternatives. The Spearman correlation is most commonly used and is most appropriate when applied in the context of Monte Carlo simulation; there is no dependence on normal distributions or linearity, meaning that correlations between different variables with different distributions can be applied. To compute the Spearman correlation, first rank all the x and y variable values and then apply the Pearson's correlation computation.

In the case of Risk Simulator, the correlation used is the more robust nonparametric Spearman's rank correlation. However, to simplify the simulation process, and to be consistent with Excel's correlation function, the correlation inputs required are the Pearson's correlation coefficients. Risk Simulator will then apply its own algorithms to convert them into Spearman's rank correlation, thereby simplifying the process. However, to simplify the user interface, we allow users to enter the more common Pearson's product-moment correlation (e.g., computed using Excel's CORREL function), while in the mathematical codes, we convert these simple correlations into Spearman's rank-based correlations for distributional simulations. See Exercise 2: Correlation Effects Model at the end of this chapter for more details on these linear parametric and nonlinear nonparametric correlations.

Applying Correlations in Risk Simulator

Correlations can be applied in Risk Simulator in several ways:

- When defining assumptions (*Risk Simulator* | *Set Input Assumption*), simply enter the correlations into the correlation matrix grid in the Distribution Gallery.
- With existing data, run the Multi-Fit Tool (*Risk Simulator* | *Tools* | *Distributional Fitting* | *Multiple Variables*) to perform distributional fitting

and to obtain the correlation matrix between pairwise variables. If a simulation profile exists, the assumptions fitted will automatically contain the relevant correlation values.

- With existing assumptions, you can click on *Risk Simulator | Tools | Edit Correlations* to enter the pairwise correlations of all the assumptions directly in one user interface.

Note that the correlation matrix must be positive definite. That is, the correlation must be mathematically valid. For instance, suppose you are trying to correlate three variables: grades of graduate students in a particular year, the number of beers they consume a week, and the number of hours they study a week. One would assume that the following correlation relationships exist:

Grades and Beer: − The more they drink, the lower the grades (no show on exams).
Grades and Study: + The more they study, the higher the grades.
Beer and Study: − The more they drink, the less they study (drunk and partying all the time).

However, if you input a negative correlation between Grades and Study, and assume that the correlation coefficients have high magnitudes, the correlation matrix will be nonpositive definite. It would defy logic, correlation requirements, and matrix mathematics. Nevertheless, smaller coefficients can sometimes still work even with bad logic. When a nonpositive or bad correlation matrix is entered, Risk Simulator will automatically inform you and offer to adjust these correlations to something that is semi-positive definite while still maintaining the overall structure of the correlation relationship (the same signs as well as the same relative strengths).

The Effects of Correlations in Monte Carlo Simulation

Although the computations required to correlate variables in a simulation are complex, the resulting effects are fairly clear. Figure 3.14 shows a simple correlation model (Correlation Effects Model in the example folder). The calculation for revenue is simply price multiplied by quantity. The same model is replicated for no correlations, positive correlation (+0.9), and negative correlation (−0.9) between price and quantity.

The resulting statistics are shown in Figure 3.15. Notice that the standard deviation of the model without correlations is 0.1450, compared to 0.1886 for the positive correlation and 0.0717 for the negative correlation. That is, for simple models, negative correlations tend to reduce the average spread of the distribution, and create a tight and more concentrated forecast distribution as compared to positive correlations with larger average spreads. However, the mean remains relatively stable. This result implies that correlations do little to change the expected value of projects, but can reduce or increase a project's risk.

	Correlation model		
	Without Correlation	Positive Correlation	Negative Correlation
Price	$2.00	$2.00	$2.00
Quantity	1.00	1.00	1.00
Revenue	$2.00	$2.00	$2.00

FIGURE 3.14 Simple Correlation Model

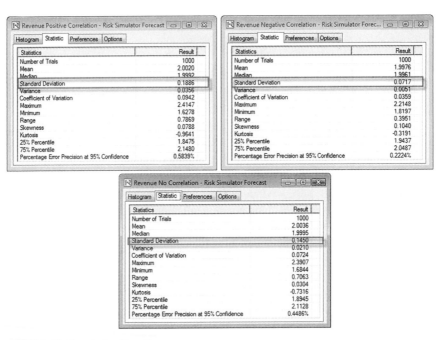

FIGURE 3.15 Correlation Results

Figure 3.16 illustrates the results after running a simulation, extracting the raw data of the assumptions, and computing the correlations between the variables. The figure shows that the input assumptions are recovered in the simulation. That is, you enter +0.9 and −0.9 correlations, and the resulting simulated values have the same correlations.

Precision and Error Control

One very powerful tool in Monte Carlo simulation is that of precision control. For instance, how many trials are considered sufficient to run in a complex

Spearman's Nonlinear Rank Correlation on Raw Data Extracted form Simulation

Price Negative Correlation	Quantity Negative Correlation	Correlation	Price Positive Correlation	Quantity Positive Correlation	Correlation
676	145	−0.90	102	158	0.89
368	452		461	515	
264	880		515	477	
235	877		874	833	
122	711		769	792	
490	641		481	471	
336	638		627	446	
495	383		82	190	
241	568		659	674	
651	571		188	286	
854	59		458	439	
66	950		981	972	
707	262		528	569	
943	186		865	812	

FIGURE 3.16 Correlations Recovered

model? Precision control takes the guesswork out of estimating the relevant number of trials by allowing the simulation to stop if the level of prespecified precision is reached.

The precision control functionality lets you set how precise you want your forecast to be. Generally speaking, as more trials are calculated, the confidence interval narrows and the statistics become more accurate. The precision control feature in Risk Simulator uses the characteristic of confidence intervals to determine when a specified accuracy of a statistic has been reached. For each forecast, you can specify the specific confidence interval for the precision level.

> Precision and errors in a credit model, as well as calibrating and stress testing a model over time, are important factors to consider as part of doing due diligence.

Make sure that you do not confuse three very different terms: error, precision, and confidence. Although they sound similar, the concepts are significantly different from one another. A simple illustration is in order. Suppose you are a taco shell manufacturer and are interested in finding out how many broken taco shells there are on average in a box of 100 shells. One way to do this is to collect a sample of prepackaged boxes of 100 taco shells, open them, and count how many of them are actually broken. You manufacture 1 million boxes a day (this is your *population*), but you randomly open only 10 boxes (this is your *sample* size, also known as your number of *trials* in a simulation). The number of broken shells in each box is as follows: 24, 22, 4, 15, 33, 32, 4, 1, 45, and 2. The calculated average number of broken shells is 18.2. Based on these 10 samples or trials, the average is 18.2 units, while based on the sample, the 80% confidence interval is between 2 and 33 units (that is, 80% of the time, the number of broken shells is between 2 and 33, *based on this sample size or number of trials run*). However, how sure are you that 18.2 is the correct average? Are 10 trials sufficient to establish this?

The confidence interval between 2 and 33 is too wide and too variable. Suppose you require a more accurate average value in which the error is ± 2 taco shells 90% of the time—this means that if you open *all* 1 million boxes manufactured in a day, 900,000 of these boxes will have broken taco shells on average at some mean unit ± 2 taco shells. How many more taco shell boxes would you then need to sample (or how many more trials run) to obtain this level of precision? Here, the 2 taco shells is the error level, while the 90% is the level of precision. If sufficient numbers of trials are run, then the 90% confidence interval will be identical to the 90% precision level, where a more precise measure of the average is obtained such that 90% of the time, the error and, hence, the confidence will be ± 2 taco shells. As an example, say the average is 20 units; then, the 90% confidence interval will be between 18 and 22 units, in which this interval is precise 90% of the time—that is to say, in opening all 1 million boxes, 900,000 of them will have between 18 and 22 broken taco shells. The number of trials required to hit this precision is based on the sampling error equation of

$$\bar{x} \pm Z \frac{s}{\sqrt{n}}$$

where

$$Z \frac{s}{\sqrt{n}}$$

is the error of 2 taco shells, $\bar{x}$ is the sample average, Z is the standard-normal Z score obtained from the 90% precision level, s is the sample standard deviation, and n is the number of trials required to hit this level of error with the specified precision.

Figures 3.17 and 3.18 illustrate how precision control can be performed on multiple simulated forecasts in Risk Simulator. This feature prevents the user from having to decide how many trials to run in a simulation and eliminates all possibilities of guesswork. Figure 3.17 illustrates the forecast chart with a 95% precision level set. This value can be changed and will be reflected in the *Statistics* tab as shown in Figure 3.18.

Exercise 1: Basic Simulation Model

This sample model illustrates how to use Risk Simulator for:

- Running a Monte Carlo Risk Simulation
- Using Forecast Charts
- Interpreting the Risk Statistics

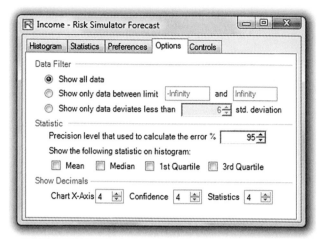

FIGURE 3.17 Setting the Forecast's Precision Level

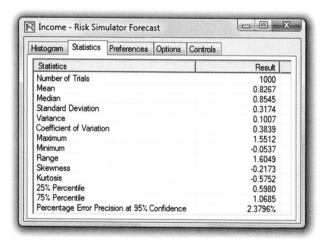

FIGURE 3.18 Computing the Error

- Setting Seed Values
- Running Super Speed Simulation
- Setting Run Preferences (Simulation Properties)
- Extracting Simulation Data
- Creating a Simulation Report and Forecast Statistics Table

- Creating Forecast Statistics Using the RS Functions
- Saving a Simulation Run's Forecast Charts
- Creating New, and Switching Among, Simulation Profiles
- Distributional Truncation and Multidimensional Simulation

Model Background

File Name: Basic Simulation Model.xls

Access: *Risk Simulator* | *Example Models* | *02 Basic Simulation Model*

The *Static and Dynamic Model* worksheet illustrates a very simple model with two input assumptions (revenue and cost) and an output forecast (income) as seen in Figure 3.19. The model on the left is a static model with single-point estimates, while the model on the right is a dynamic model on which we will set Monte Carlo input assumptions and output forecasts. After running the simulation, the results can be extracted and further analyzed. In this model we can also learn to set different simulation preferences, to run a simulation, how to set seed values, and much more. To perform these exercises, you will need to have Risk Simulator version 2013 or later installed and working.

Running a Monte Carlo Risk Simulation

To set up and run a simulation model using Risk Simulator is as simple as 1-2-3; that is, (1) create a new profile, (2) set inputs and outputs, and (3) run. To follow along, open the example Basic Simulation Model and do the following:

- Select *Risk Simulator* | *New Simulation Profile* (or click on the New Profile icon), provide it with a name (e.g., "Practice Simulation"), and leave everything else as is (we come back later and revisit some of these settings).
- Select cell G8 and click on *Risk Simulator* | *Set Input Assumption* (or click on the Set Input Assumption icon), then select Triangular Distribution and set

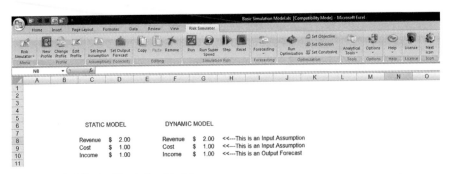

FIGURE 3.19 A Basic Simulation Model

the Min = 1.50, Most Likely = 2.00, Max = 2.25 and then hit OK (Figure 3.20).

- Select cell G9 and set another input assumption. This time use Uniform Distribution with Min = 0.85 and Max = 1.25.
- Select cell G10 and set that cell as the output forecast by clicking on *Risk Simulator | Set Output Forecast*. You can use the default name "Income" that it picked up from the model.
- Select *Risk Simulator | Run Simulation* (or click on the Run icon) to start the simulation.

Figure 3.21 shows the simulation run. At the end of the simulation, click *OK*. There are a few things to notice here. The first is that the resulting model at the end of the simulation run returns the same results as the static model. That is, two dollars minus one dollar is equal to one dollar. However, what simulation does is create thousands of possible outcomes of "around two dollars" in revenue minus thousands of possible outcomes of "around one dollar" in cost, resulting in the

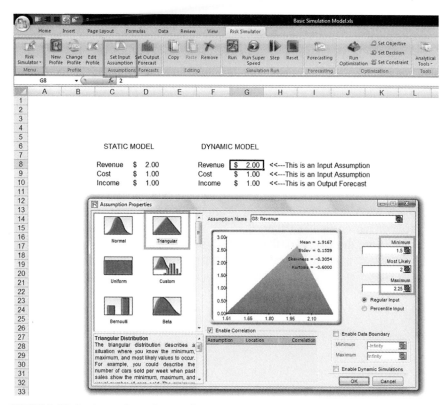

FIGURE 3.20 Setting an Input Assumption

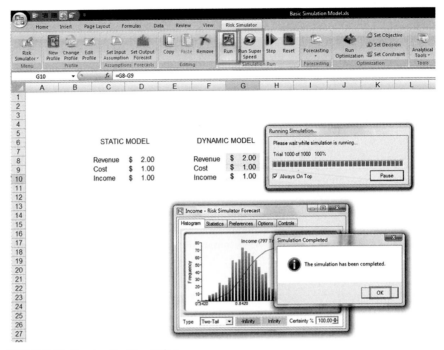

FIGURE 3.21 Running the Simulation

income of "around one dollar." The results are shown as a histogram, complete with the risk statistics, which we review later in this exercise.

Using Forecast Charts

The forecast chart (Figure 3.22) is shown when the simulation is running. Once simulation is completed, the forecast chart can be used. The forecast chart has several tabs: *Histogram, Statistics, Preferences, Options,* and *Controls.* Of particular interest are the first two, the histogram and statistics tabs. For instance, the first tab shows the output forecast's probability distribution in the form of a histogram, where the specific values can be determined using the certainty boxes.

In the *Histogram* tab, select *Two-Tail*, enter 90 in the Certainty box, and hit TAB on your keyboard. The 90% confidence interval is shown (0.5269 and 1.1712). This result means that there is a 5% chance that the income will fall below $0.5269, and another 5% chance that it will be above $1.1712. Alternatively, you can select *Left-Tail* ≤ and enter 1.0 on the input box, hit TAB, and see that the left-tail certainty is 76.30%, indicating that there is a 76.30% chance that the income will fall at or below $1.0 (or that there is a 23.70% chance that income will exceed $1.0). Note that your results will *not* be exactly the same as what we illustrate here due to the theoretical fact that we

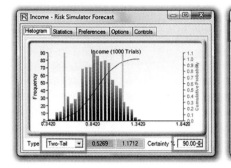 

FIGURE 3.22 Simulation Results and Forecast Charts

are running a simulation of random numbers. Do not be concerned at this point; continue on to the seed value exercise for more details on how to get the same simulation results going forward.

Interpreting the Risk Statistics

The *Statistics* tab illustrates the statistical results of the forecast variable. Refer to the earlier section on the basics of risk statistics for more details on how to interpret and use these risk profile statistics in risk analysis and risk management. Note that your results will not be exactly the same as those illustrated here because a simulation (random number generation) was run, and, by definition, the results will not be exactly the same every time. However, if a seed value is set (see later section), the results will be identical in every single run.

Optional Exercises

For additional practice, view the *Preferences, Options*, and *Controls* tabs and play with some of the settings. Specifically, try the following:

Preferences

- Try selecting and deselecting the *Always Show Windows On Top* option. Navigate around different applications that might be open, and notice the behavior of the forecast chart.
- Run a simulation with at least three forecasts, and select Semitransparent When Inactive on all three forecast charts (e.g., use your own model, or in cell G11, set it to be = G10, in G12, set it also to be = G10, set these two cells G11 and G12 as output forecasts, and then run a simulation). Then, minimize all other software applications, leaving these three forecast charts visible, overlay one chart on top of another, then click anywhere on the desktop to deactivate the forecast charts. Notice that you can now compare different forecast charts.

- Change the histogram resolution to different levels, and view the histogram to see how the shape changes.

Also, if you have multiple forecast charts up and running and you forget to reset the previous simulation (resetting the simulation will clear all the forecast charts and simulated data from temporary memory, allowing you to rerun another simulation), you can Minimize All Charts, Close All Charts, or Copy a specific chart (you can set up the chart any way you like, and then copy the chart to the clipboard and paste it into another program such as Microsoft Word or Microsoft PowerPoint) from this tab.

Options
- Play with the data filter by showing only limited data, such as only 2 standard deviations from the mean, or a specific range of values. Go back to the histogram and notice the change in the chart; go back to the Statistics tab and notice that the computed risk statistics are now based on the truncated data rather than the entire data set.
- You can also select the statistic to show or the number of Decimals to show in the histogram chart and statistics tabs. This option may come in handy if you wish to obtain higher precision of results (more decimals) or show fewer decimals for large-value results.

Controls
- From this tab, you can control how the histogram looks by changing the orientation, color, 2D and 3D aspects of the chart, background, type of overlay curve to show (CDF versus PDF), chart types, and many other chart controls. Try out several of these items, and see what happens to the histogram chart each time.
- You can also perform a distributional fitting of the forecast results, and obtain the theoretical versus empirical moments of the distribution (see the Distributional Data Fitting exercise for more details on how distribution fitting routines work), or show the fitted distribution's theoretical curve on top of the empirical histogram (first click on *Fit*, select either *Continuous* or *Discrete* from the *Chart Overlay* droplist, and then go back to the *Histogram* tab to view the resulting charts).
- Finally, you can change the chart type (bar, cylinder, pyramid, and so forth), chart title, min and max values of the chart axes, and the Decimals to show on the chart. Try out several of these items and see what happens to the histogram chart each time.

If you are using Risk Simulator 2013 or later, you can click on the *Global View* link on the top right corner of the forecast chart to view all the aforementioned tabs and functionalities in a single view, or click on the *Normal View* link to return to the tabbed view previously described.

Setting Seed Values

- Reset the simulation by selecting *Risk Simulator | Reset Simulation*.
- Select *Risk Simulator | Edit Simulation Profile* (Figure 3.23).
- Select the check box for random number sequence, enter in a seed value (e.g., 999), and click OK (Figure 3.23).
- Run the simulation and verify that the results are the same as the results obtained in Figure 3.23. In fact, run the simulation a few more times, and each time verify that the results are identical.

Note that the random number sequence, or seed number, has to be a positive integer value. Running the same model with the same assumptions and forecasts with an identical seed value and the same number of trials will always yield the same results. The number of simulation trials to run can be set in the same run properties box (Figure 3.23). Setting a seed value is important especially when you wish to obtain the same values in each simulation run. Say, for example, that you need the live model to return the same results as a printed report during a presentation. If the results in your live demonstration are slightly off compared to the printed results, questions may arise as to their validity. By having a seed value, the results are guaranteed to always be the same.

Let us now revisit the confidence interval analysis after you have run another simulation with the seed value. Figure 3.24 illustrates the results of these manipulations.

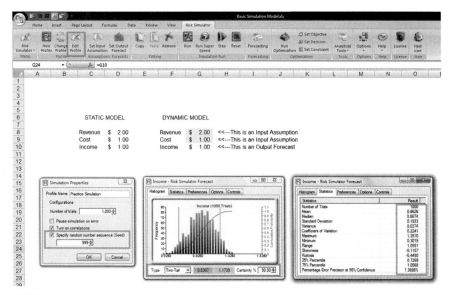

FIGURE 3.23 Using a Seed Value

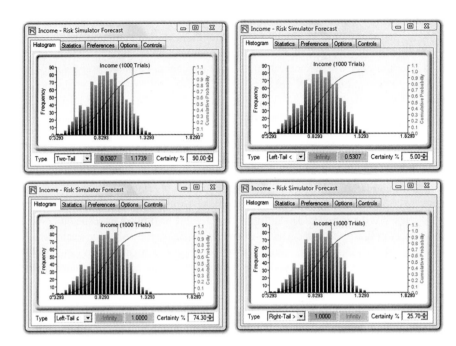

FIGURE 3.24 Left-, Right- and Two-Tail Probabilities (Simulation Results with Seed Values)

- Select *Two-Tail*, enter a certainty of 90, and hit TAB on the keyboard. You will obtain the two-tailed 90% confidence interval of 0.5307 and 1.1739, which means that 90% of the time, the income level will be between these two values, with a 5% chance it will be below 0.5307 and 5% it will be above 1.1739.

- To verify that 5% result, select *Left-Tail* <, enter a certainty of 5, and hit TAB. You will obtain the value of 0.5307, indicating that there is a 5% chance you will receive an income less than 0.5307.

- Next, select *Left-Tail* ≤, enter in the value 1, and hit TAB. This time, instead of providing a probability to receive a value, you provide a value to receive the probability. In this case, it states that you have a 74.30% chance that your income will be less than or equal to the 1.000 value that your static single-point model had predicted. In fact, in Figure 3.23, you see that the mean or average income value is 0.8626. In other words, the expected value (mean) is not the same as the value expected (in your original single-point estimate static model).

- Select *Right-Tail* >, enter in 1, and hit TAB. Here you can see the complement of the *Left-Tail* ≤ value. In other words, the value you receive, 25.70%, indicates the probability you will make more than your target of

1.000, and if you take 100% minus 25.70%, you obtain 74.30%, the *Left-Tail* $\leq$ value. When doing this exercise, make sure you select the correct inequality signs (less than, $<$, less than or equal to, $\leq$, greater than, $>$, or greater than or equal to, $\geq$).

Running Super Speed Simulation
- Reset the simulation by selecting *Risk Simulator* | *Reset Simulation*.
- Select *Risk Simulator* | *Run Super Speed Simulation* (Figure 3.21).

Notice how much faster the super-speed simulation runs. In fact, for practice, *Reset Simulation*, *Edit Simulation Profile*, change the *Number of Trials* to 100,000, and *Run Super Speed Simulation*. It should only take a few seconds to run. However, be aware that super-speed simulation will not run if the model has errors, VBA (visual basic for applications), or links to external data sources or applications. In such situations, you will be notified and the regular speed simulation will be run instead. Regular speed simulations are always able to run even with errors, VBA, or external links.

Setting Run Preferences (Simulation Properties)
The run preferences or *Simulation Properties* dialog box that came up when you first created a new profile or edited the current profile (Figure 3.23), allows you to specify the *Number of Trials* to run in a particular simulation (by default it will be 1,000 trials). In theory, the higher the number of trials, the more precise the results (try rerunning the simulation again; this time, keep an eye on the *Percentage Error Precision at 95% Confidence* value, which should decrease as you increase the number of trials). In addition, *Pause Simulation on Error* can be set up so that the simulation will stop running if a computational error in Excel is encountered (e.g., #NUM or #ERROR), which is a good tool for ascertaining if your model is set up correctly. If this option is not checked, any errors will be ignored and only the valid results will be used in the forecast charts. Correlations can also be specified between pairs of input assumptions, and if *Turn on Correlations* is selected, these specified correlations will be imputed in the simulation. See Exercise 2: Correlation Risk Effects Model for how to set up correlations and to understand how correlations affect the outcome of your results, the theory of risk diversification, portfolio effects on distributional moments, and more.

Extracting Simulation Data
The simulation's assumptions and forecast data are stored in memory until the simulation is reset or Excel is closed. If required, these raw data can be extracted into a separate Excel sheet. To extract the data, simply:

- *Edit Simulation Profile*, reset the *Number of Trials* to 1,000, and then *Run Simulation*.

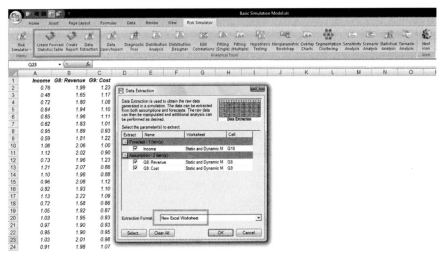

FIGURE 3.25 Extracting Simulation Data

- After the simulation is completed, select *Risk Simulator | Tools | Extract Data* (you can also access this function by clicking on the Next icon repeatedly until you get to the tools icon ribbon, and then click on the Data Extraction icon as shown in Figure 3.25).
- Choose the relevant assumptions or forecasts to extract, select New Excel Worksheet as the extraction format, and click OK.

Optional Exercises

- The 1,000 simulated revenue and cost values will be extracted, as well as the computed forecast income variable (Figure 3.25). Note that if you had not first run a simulation, the extracted data report would be empty, as there would be no values to extract. Try clicking on the Select button a few times to see what happens.
- Using the extracted data, apply Excel's functions to compute all of the risk statistics, for example, the mean, median, standard deviation, and so forth, and compare to make sure the results are identical to those obtained in Risk Simulator's Forecast Statistics tab. Hint: Use the following Excel functions for this exercise: AVERAGE(), STDEV(), VAR(), SKEW(), KURT(), MIN(), and MAX().

Creating a Simulation Report and Forecast Statistics Table

The simulation's input assumptions and output forecasts, as well as the detailed risk statistics, can also be extracted after a simulation has been run. *Assuming the simulation has already been run*, simply:

- Select *Risk Simulator* | *Tools* | *Create Report* (you can also access this function by clicking on the Next icon repeatedly until you get to the tools icon ribbon, and then click on the Create Report icon as shown in Figure 3.25). Spend some time reviewing the report that is generated.
- Select *Risk Simulator* | *Tools* | *Create Forecast Statistics Table* (you can also access this function by clicking on the Next icon repeatedly until you get to the tools icon ribbon, and then click on the Create Forecast Statistics Table icon as shown in Figure 3.25). Here you can select the forecasts you wish to show. In this simple example, we only have one forecast, but in larger models, you can select multiple forecasts at once. We suggest you try creating this statistics table with the other exercises.

Creating Forecast Statistics Using the RS Functions

You can also obtain the forecast statistics not in a report format, but in a specific cell, by using the Risk Simulator function call. For example, do the following:

- Save the example file, and then exit Excel and click on *Start* | *Programs* | *Real Options Valuation* | *Risk Simulator* | *Tools* | *Install Functions*. When the installation is complete (in a few short seconds), hit the spacebar to close the black console pad and start Excel. Note: If you are running Windows Vista, Windows 7, or Windows 8, right-click on Install Functions in the Start menu and choose Run As Administrator.
- Reopen the example at *Risk Simulator* | *Example Models* | *02 Basic Simulation Model* and run a simulation in super speed: *Risk Simulator* | *Run Super Speed Simulation*.
- Select cell G12 and click on the FX (insert function) icon in Excel, or click on and select the ALL category, and scroll down to the RS functions list. Here you see several set input assumption functions for various distributions. The last item on the RS list is RS Forecast Statistic. Select this function, or you can type this function directly into the cell. For instance, type in = RS Forecast Statistic (G10,"Average"), where G10 is the forecast output cell and "Average" is the statistic you wish to obtain. Remember to keep the quotes (""), and you can replace the Average parameter with any of the following: Average, Coefficient of Variation, Median, Maximum, Standard Deviation, Minimum, Variance, Range, Skewness, Percentile 75, Kurtosis, Certainty 1.0, or Percentile 99.9. In fact, you can use "Percentile XX.XX" and "Certainty XX.XX," and just replace the X with your own number for a left-tail < value. The Percentile parameter means that you enter the percentage and receive the value X, whereas for the Certainty parameter, you enter the value X and get the left-tail percentage.
- Just for practice, reset the simulation, and run a regular speed simulation; notice that the statistics will keep changing as you run the simulation, and that it stops at the final result when the simulation completes. You can now use this function call as part of your model. One quick note: If you run a super-

speed simulation, the function call will not be updated automatically. You will have to select the cell with the function after the simulation is run, hit F2 on the keyboard, and then hit Enter to update the function calculation.

Saving a Simulation Run's Forecast Charts

Suppose you run a large model and want to save the forecast charts. You can do so in Risk Simulator by saving the results in the Risk Sim file format. Saving the forecast charts allows you to reopen the results without having to rerun the simulation, thereby saving you some time.

- Run a simulation as usual.
- Select *Risk Simulator | Tools | Data Extraction/Export* (you can also access this function by clicking on the Next icon repeatedly until you get to the tools icon ribbon, and then click on the Data Extraction icon). Here, you select the Extraction Format to be a Risk Simulator Data (Risk Sim) file (Figure 3.26). Save the file to the desired location. You can now save and exit Excel.
- Open Excel and select Risk Simulator | Tools | Data Open/Import (you can also access this function by clicking on the Next icon repeatedly until you get to the tools icon ribbon, and click on the Data Open/Import icon). Select the Risk Sim file you saved previously, and the forecast charts will now reappear.

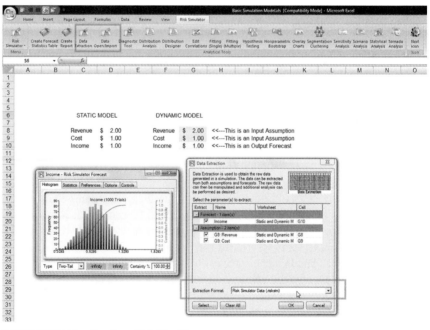

FIGURE 3.26 Extracting to a Risk Sim File

Creating New and Switching Among Simulation Profiles

The same model can have multiple Risk Simulator profiles. That is, different users of the same model can, in fact, create their own simulation input assumptions, forecasts, run preferences, and so forth. All these preferences are stored in separate simulation profiles, and each profile can be run independently. This is a powerful feature that allows multiple users to run the same model their own way, or for the same user to run the model under different simulation conditions, thereby allowing for scenario analysis in Monte Carlo simulation. To create different profiles and switch among different profiles, simply:

- Create several new profiles by clicking on *Risk Simulator | New Simulation Profile*, and provide each new profile with a unique name.
- Add the relevant assumptions and forecasts, or change the run preferences as desired in each simulation profile.
- Switch among different profiles by clicking on *Risk Simulator | Change Active Simulation*.

Note that you can create as many profiles as you wish, but each profile needs to have its own unique name. Also, you can select an existing profile and click on Duplicate (Figure 3.27) to duplicate all the input assumptions and output forecasts that are in this profile, which means you do not have to replicate all these manually. You can then change to this new profile and make any modifications as required. From this user interface, you can also delete any unwanted profiles (but note that you need to have at least one profile active in the model, which means that you can delete any profile you choose, but you cannot delete all of them, as

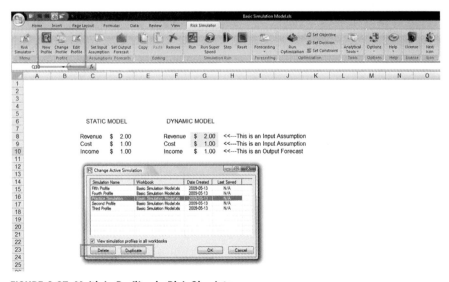

FIGURE 3.27 Multiple Profiles in Risk Simulator

one profile must be left in the model). You can also click on a profile, click again on the name of the profile, and rename the profile as required.

Finally, as you save the Excel file, you will also save these profiles in the same Excel file. Profiles are stored in a special hidden segment of the Excel file and will be available to you as you open the Excel file in the future. For further practice, try saving the Excel file and then reopening the file again; notice that all your profiles and settings are still available. Just bear in mind that if you have multiple profiles, the last profile used will be the profile that is activated by default when the Excel file is opened the next time. Depending on what you are trying to do, you may need to remember to *Change the Profile* to the one you wish to use before you start running any simulations.

Distributional Truncation, Alternate Parameters, and Multidimensional Simulation

Distributional truncation, or *data boundaries*, are typically not used by the average analyst, but they exist for truncating the distributional assumptions. For instance, if a normal distribution is selected, the theoretical boundaries are between negative infinity and positive infinity. However, in practice, the simulated variable exists only within some smaller range, and this range can then be entered to truncate the distribution appropriately. Not considering truncation is a major error users commit, especially when using the triangular distribution. The triangular distribution is very simple and intuitive. As a matter of fact, it is probably the most widely used distribution in Risk Simulator, apart from the normal and uniform distributions. Simplistically, the triangular distribution looks at the minimum value, the most probable value, and the maximum value. These three inputs are often confused with the worst-case, nominal-case, and best-case scenarios. This assumption is, indeed, incorrect.

In fact, a worst-case scenario can be translated as a highly unlikely condition that will still occur given a certain percentage of the time. For instance, one can model the economy as high, average, and low, analogous to the worst-case, nominal-case, and best-case scenarios. Thus, logic would dictate that the worst-case scenario might have, say, a 15% chance of occurrence; the nominal-case, a 50% chance of occurrence; and a 35% chance that a best-case scenario will occur. This approach is what is meant by using best-, nominal-, and worst-case scenario analyses. However, compare that to the triangular distribution, where the minimum and maximum cases will almost never occur, with a probability of occurrence set at zero!

For instance, see Figure 3.28, where the worst-, nominal-, and best-case scenarios are set as 5, 10, and 15, respectively. Note that at the extreme values, the probability of 5 or 15 occurring is virtually zero, as the areas under the curve (the measure of probability) of these extreme points are 0. In other words, 5 and 15 will almost never occur. Compare that to the economic scenario in which these extreme values have either a 15% or 35% chance of occurrence. Instead, distributional truncation should be considered here. The same applies to any other

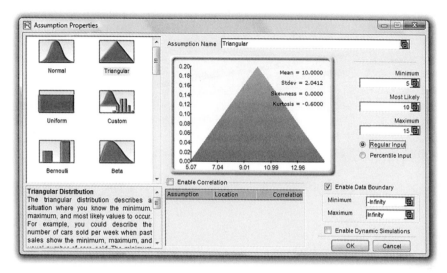

FIGURE 3.28 Sample Triangular Distribution

distribution. Figure 3.29 illustrates a truncated normal distribution where the extreme values do not extend to both positive and negative infinities, but are truncated at 7 and 13.

Another critical activity is looking at *alternate parameters*, that is, to look at the same distribution but through a different set of parameters. For instance, if a normal distribution is used in simulating market share, and the mean is set at 55% with a standard deviation of 45%, one should be extremely worried. Using Risk Simulator's Percentile Input selection in the Set Input Assumption user interface, the 10th and 90th percentiles indicate a value of −2.67% and 112.67% (Figure 3.30). Clearly these values cannot exist under actual conditions. How can a product have −2.67 or 112.67% of the market share? The alternate-parameters function is a very powerful tool to use in conditions such as these. Almost always, the first thing that should be done is to use alternate parameters to ascertain the logical upper and lower values of an input parameter. So, even if you obtained the 55% and 45% through distributional fitting (which, by the way, is correct, because the fit was probably very strong in the center of the normal distribution), but by virtue of a theoretical fitting routine, the entire normal distribution will be fitted, and the normal distribution's tails extend from negative infinity to positive infinity, (which is clearly outside the range of the norm for market share), using the alternate parameters will quickly allow you to visualize the 10th and 90th percentiles. Then you can decide to change the distribution, or still use the distribution, but apply distributional truncation as discussed previously. See the exercise on distributional analysis tools for obtaining other percentiles for any distribution, other than the default 10% and 90% as described here.

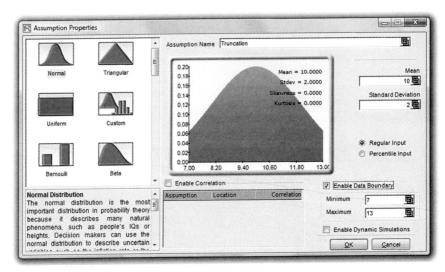

FIGURE 3.29 Truncating a Distribution

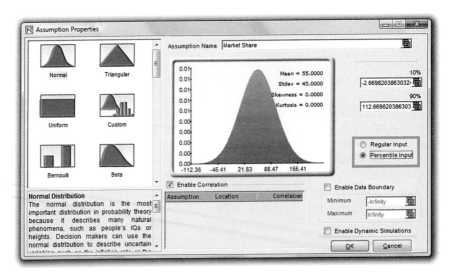

FIGURE 3.30 Alternate Parameters

Finally, Figures 3.31 and 3.32 illustrate how *multidimensional simulation*, or *dynamic simulation*, works. Suppose you have a model like the one shown in Figure 3.31. Further suppose that you have an input triangular distribution assumption in cell G5, and you used the Link icon to link its input parameters to

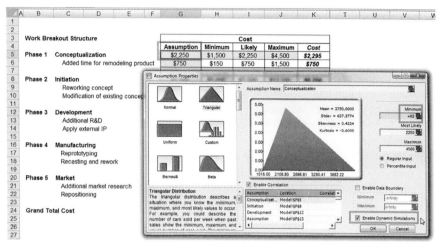

FIGURE 3.31 Dynamic or Multidimensional Simulation

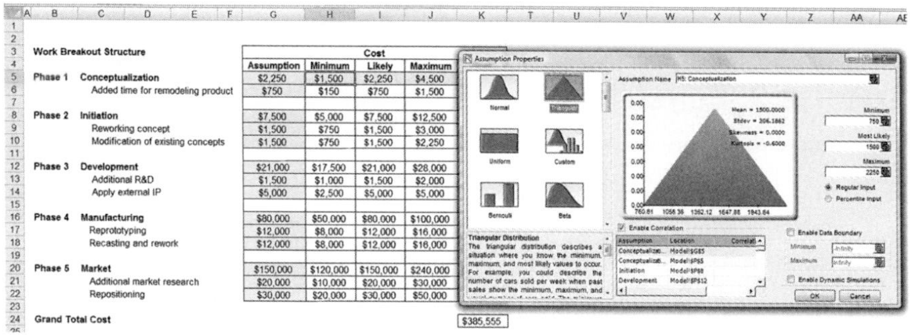

FIGURE 3.32 Input Parameter as an Assumption

other cells (H5, I5, and J5 for the minimum, most-likely, and maximum values), also as shown in Figure 3.31. Typically, this is a basic assumption, and you are all done. However, what if the minimum, most-likely, and maximum inputs are themselves uncertain? If that is the case, then you can set an input assumption for these inputs (cells H5, I5, J5). In other words, if you have an assumption that is linked to other cells, and these other cells themselves are assumptions, you have just created a two-layer simulation (of course, you can add additional layers where these input cells are again linked to other cells that are simulated and so forth, creating a multidimensional simulation model). If you do this, remember to select the *Enable Dynamic Simulation* checkbox (Figure 3.31) on the assumption that links to other assumptions. So, if you ran a 1,000-trial simulation, instead of having a single triangular distribution and picking random numbers from this single distribution, there are actually 1,000 triangular distributions, in which, at each trial, there will be new parameters for this triangular distribution, and a random number is selected from this distribution; then on the next trial, you repeat the entire process. This multidimensional simulation approach allows you to add uncertain input parameters into the simulation.

There is one little word of caution: Do not overdo the multidimensional layers. Suppose you are using a triangular distribution with min = A, most likely = B, and max = C. Further suppose A is a uniform distribution with min = D and max = E. If C is also another uniform distribution with min = F and max = G, all is well as long as E and F do not cross each other. Put another way, if you accidentally set E > F, there will be times in a random simulation where the random value E is higher than F. This result means that A will be greater than C in the original distribution, which violates the input requirements, causing the simulation to stop and creating an error (i.e., the maximum value is less than the minimum value in the triangular distribution; this cannot work and the simulation stops). So, if you are confused by distributional truncation, it might be best to avoid using it.

Exercise 2: Correlation Effects Model

This sample model illustrates how to use Risk Simulator for:

- Setting up a simulation's input assumptions and output forecasts
- Copying, pasting, and deleting simulation assumptions and forecasts
- Running correlated simulations and comparing results between correlated and uncorrelated Models
- Extracting and manually computing and verifying the assumptions' correlations
- Pearson's product moment linear correlation and Spearman's nonlinear rank correlation

Model Background

File Name: Correlation Risk Effects Model.xls
Access: *Risk Simulator | Example Models | 04 Correlation Risk Effects Model*

This model illustrates the effects of correlated simulation versus uncorrelated simulation. That is, depending on whether a pair of simulated assumptions is not correlated, positively correlated, or negatively correlated, the results can sometimes be very different. In addition, the simulated assumptions' raw data are extracted after the simulation and manual computations of their pairwise

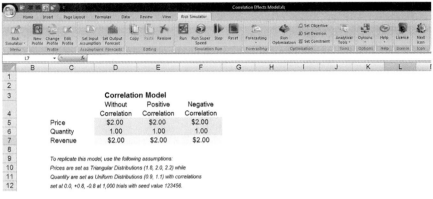

FIGURE 3.33 Correlation Model

correlations are performed. The results indicate that the input correlations hold after the simulation.

Setting Up a Simulation's Input Assumptions and Output Forecasts

Open the model *Risk Simulator | Example Models | 04 Correlation Risk Effects Model*. Go to the *Correlation Model* worksheet (Figure 3.33). Follow the instructions shown on the following pages to set up and run this model.

Copying, Pasting, and Deleting Simulation Assumptions and Forecasts

We replicate the assumptions and forecasts per the instructions on the worksheet by setting the input assumptions for price and quantity and forecast outputs for revenue. When setting up the input assumptions, you can practice by setting up one assumption at a time, or set up a single assumption, and then use the Risk Simulator copy and paste technique to replicate the assumptions across multiple cells at once. Follow these steps:

Procedures

- Create a new profile with *Risk Simulator | New Profile* (or use the New Profile icon) and give it a name.
- Select cell D5 for the price without correlation. Click on *Risk Simulator | Set Input Assumption* (or use the Set Input Assumption icon), select the Triangular distribution, and set the parameters as 1.8, 2.0, and 2.2 as instructed on the worksheet (Figure 3.34). Click OK when done.
- Select cell D5 again, after the assumption has been set, and click on *Risk Simulator | Copy Parameter* (or use the Copy icon in the Risk Simulator toolbar). Make sure you *do not* use Excel's copy, Ctrl + C, or right-click | Copy, because using Excel copy will only copy the cell contents, color,

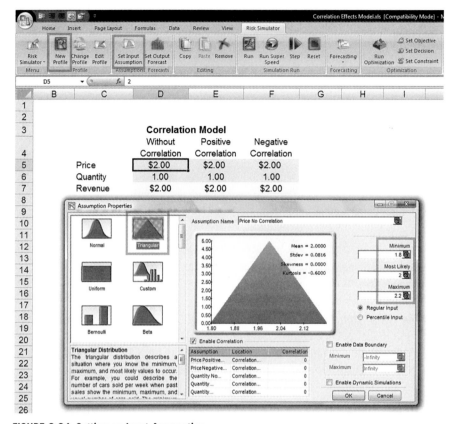

FIGURE 3.34 Setting an Input Assumption

equations, and font. Only by using Risk Simulator's copy can you copy the input assumption and its parameters.

- Select cells E5 and F5, and click on *Risk Simulator* | *Paste Parameter* (or use the Paste icon in the Risk Simulator toolbar). Again, make sure you do not hit Enter, and do not use Excel's paste function or Ctrl + V, as this will only paste the Excel cell contents, not the input assumptions (Figure 3.35).
- Select cell D6 and repeat the previous process, this time using a uniform distribution with 0.9 and 1.1 as the input parameters. Copy/paste the parameters for cells E6 and F6.
- Select cell D7 and set it as an output forecast by clicking on *Risk Simulator* | *Set Output Forecast* (or use the Set Output Forecast icon), and link the forecast name to cell D4. Then, select cell D7 again, copy the parameter, and select cells E7 and F7 to paste the parameters using Risk Simulator copy and

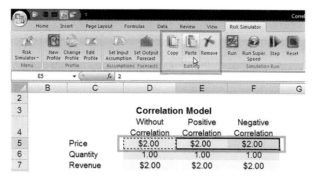

FIGURE 3.35 Simulation Parameter Copy and Paste

paste. Later, review the tip presented in the next section for an important reminder on copy and pasting.

- Next, set the correlations among the variables. There are two ways to set correlations: You can set correlations one pair of assumptions at a time or set them in a correlation matrix all at once. We explore both approaches as follows:

  - As cell E5 is supposed to be correlated to cell E6, select cell E5 and click on *Risk Simulator | Set Input Assumption* (or use the Set Input Assumption icon) once again. This time, look at the pairwise correlation section (Figure 3.36). You may click and drag to enlarge the user interface form, as well as to increase the width of the three columns for assumptions, location, and correlation. Find the input assumption for E6, enter the correlation of 0.8, and hit Enter on the keyboard (Figure 3.36). Remember to hit Enter on the keyboard when you are done entering the correlation, otherwise the software will think that you are still typing in the input box. Click OK when done. For the sake of completeness, select cell E6 and again set an input assumption, and notice that by setting the assumption in cell E5 previously and correlating it to E6, cell E6 automatically correlates back to E5. Repeat the correlation process for cell F5 and F6.

  - Click on *Risk Simulator | Tools | Edit Correlations,* and you will be provided with a correlation tool (Figure 3.37). Select the Show Cell Name checkbox and you can select the variables you wish to correlate, or click on Select All to show all of them. In the correlation matrix section, enter the correlation value (correlations have to be between −1 and 1, and zeroes are allowed, of course). Notice that the correlation matrix shown is a full-square matrix, and the upper triangle mirrors the lower triangle. So, all you need to do is enter the correlation on either the upper or lower triangle and hit Enter on the keyboard. The value will be updated in both

	Correlation Model		
	Without Correlation	Positive Correlation	Negative Correlation
Price	$2.00	$2.00	$2.00
Quantity	1.00	1.00	1.00
Revenue	$2.00	$2.00	$2.00

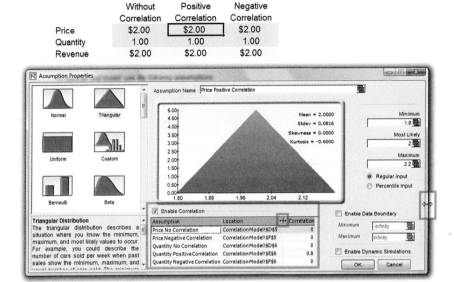

FIGURE 3.36 Pairwise Correlations (Manual)

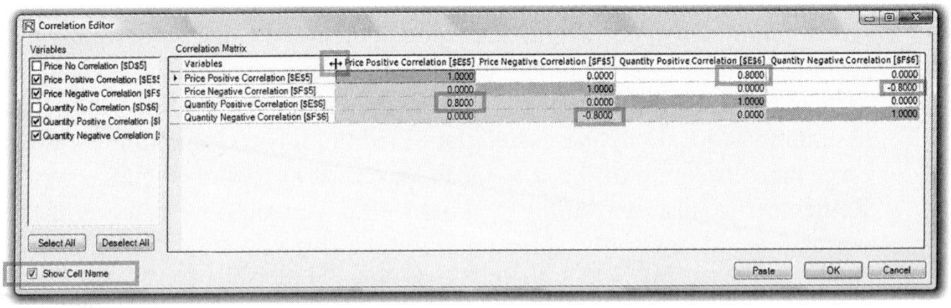

FIGURE 3.37 Pairwise Correlations (Matrix)

upper and lower triangles. Click OK when done. Also, note that the user interface allows you to paste in a correlation matrix. This tool comes in handy if you wish the correlation matrix to be visible in Excel. When you have an existing matrix in Excel, you can copy the matrix, and then paste it here (making sure the matrix you copied is square, and the upper and lower triangles have identical pairwise correlation values). You are now done with setting correlations. For the sake of completeness, you can select any one of the input assumptions, and set the assumption again to make sure that the correlations are set up correctly (Figure 3.36).

Run the simulation by clicking on *Risk Simulator | Run Simulation* (or use the Run Simulation icon) and interpret the results. Proceed to the next section for an interpretation of the results. You can also try running a super speed simulation for faster results.

Tips

For copy and paste in Risk Simulator, this quick tip will come in handy when you are setting inputs and outputs on larger models. When you select a cell and use the Risk Simulator copy function, it copies everything into the Windows clipboard, including the cell's value, equation, function, color, font, and size, as well as Risk Simulator's assumptions, forecasts, or decision variables. Then, as you apply the Risk Simulator paste function, you have two options. The first option is to apply the Risk Simulator paste directly, and all cell values, colors, fonts, equations, functions, and parameters will be pasted, akin to the preceding example. However, the second option is to first click Escape on the keyboard, and then apply the Risk Simulator paste. Escape tells Risk Simulator that you only wish to paste the Risk Simulator assumptions, forecasts, or decision variables, and *not* the cell's value, color, equation, function, font, etc. Hitting Escape before pasting allows you to maintain the target cell's values and computations, and pastes only the Risk Simulator parameters.

In Risk Simulator version 2013, you can also click on the View Correlation Charts tool to view sample representations of how different correlation levels look when variables are plotted on a scatter chart. You can also use this tool to compute correlations of your raw data.

In Risk Simulator version 2013, you can select multiple cells with assumptions and forecasts, and use Risk Simulator copy and paste functionalities.

Running Correlated Simulations and Comparing Results Between Correlated and Uncorrelated Models

The resulting simulation statistics indicate that the negatively correlated variables provide a tighter or smaller standard deviation or overall risk level on the model. This relationship exists because negative correlations provide a diversification effect on the variables and, hence, tend to make the standard deviation slightly smaller. Thus, we need to make sure to input correlations when there are, indeed, correlations between variables. Otherwise, this interacting effect will not be accounted for in the simulation.

The positive correlation model has a larger standard deviation because a positive correlation tends to make both variables travel in the same direction, making the extreme ends wider and, hence, increasing the overall risk. Therefore, the model without any correlations will have a standard deviation between the positive and negative correlation models.

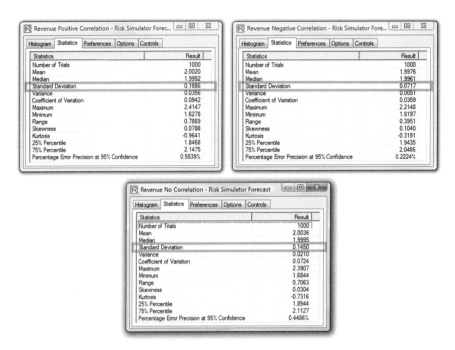

FIGURE 3.38 Risk Effects on Distributional Moments

Notice that the expected value or mean does not change much. In fact, if sufficient simulation trials are run, the theoretical and empirical values of the mean remain the same. The first moment (central tendency or expected value) does not change with correlations. Only the second moment (spread or risk and uncertainty) will change with correlations (Figure 3.38).

Note that this characteristic exists only in simple models with a positive relationship. That is, a Price×Quantity model is considered a "positive" relationship model (as is Price+Quantity), in which a negative correlation decreases the range, and a positive correlation increases the range. The opposite is true for negative relationship models. For instance, Price/Quantity or Price−Quantity would be a negative relationship model, in which a positive correlation will reduce the range of the forecast variable, and a negative correlation will increase the range. Finally, for more complex models (e.g., larger models with multiple variables interacting with positive and negative relationships and sometimes with positive and negative correlations), the results are hard to predict and cannot be determined theoretically. Only by running a simulation can the true results of the range and outcomes be determined. In such a scenario, tornado analysis and sensitivity analysis would be more appropriate.

Extracting and Manually Computing and Verifying the Assumptions' Correlations

For additional practice, run the simulation, and then extract the simulated data. Then run a correlation computation, and see if the correlations are similar to what you have entered into Risk Simulator.

Procedures

- Run the simulation with *Risk Simulator* | *Run Simulation* (or use the Run Simulation icon). Click OK when simulation is done.
- Extract the data with *Risk Simulator* | *Tools* | *Data Extraction and Export* (or use the Data Extraction icon under the Analytical Tools ribbon). Select New Excel Worksheet, and you can click the Select All... button repeatedly to select only the forecasts, only the assumptions, or all forecasts and assumptions at once (Figure 3.39). For now, select all forecasts and assumptions, and click OK to extract the data.
- Go to the extracted data worksheet and use Excel's CORREL function to compute the pairwise correlations of the simulated data. For example, Figure 3.40 illustrates that the computed correlations are +0.8 and −0.8 for the positive and negative correlation pairs, plus the uncorrelated pair is close to zero (the correlation is never exactly equal to zero because of the randomness effect, and 0.03 is statistically significantly identical to zero in this case). In other words, the correlations we inputted originally are maintained in the simulation model.

FIGURE 3.39 Data Extraction

| | Revenue Positive | Revenue Negative | Price No | Price Positive | Price Negative | Quantity No | Quantity Positive | Quantity Negative | | | | | | | |
Revenue No Correlation	Correlation	Correlation	Correlation	Correlation	Correlation	Correlation	Correlation	Correlation							
2.08	1.77	2.00	2.08	1.95	1.89	1.00	0.91	1.06							
1.83	1.83	2.08	1.89	1.92	1.98	0.97	0.95	1.05		0.03	Equation: =CORREL(D2:D1001,G2:G1001)				
2.10	2.10	2.06	2.05	2.02	1.89	1.03	1.04	1.09		0.80	Equation: =CORREL(E2:E1001,H2:H1001)				
2.19	2.09	1.95	2.04	2.04	1.88	1.08	1.03	1.04		-0.80	Equation: =CORREL(F2:F1001,I2:I1001)				
2.07	1.71	1.82	2.04	1.89	1.96	1.01	0.91	0.93							
1.92	2.07	1.89	2.09	1.98	2.02	0.92	1.05	0.93							
2.01	2.11	2.04	1.92	2.05	2.00	1.05	1.03	1.02							
2.05	1.71	1.93	2.05	1.87	1.86	1.00	0.91	1.04							
2.04	1.67	1.99	1.93	1.84	1.96	1.06	0.91	1.02							
1.95	2.13	1.94	1.95	2.06	1.90	1.00	1.03	1.02							
1.98	2.00	2.11	1.98	1.98	1.92	1.00	1.01	1.10							
1.80	1.91	2.03	1.91	1.99	2.00	0.94	0.96	1.02							
1.92	1.95	2.02	1.88	1.93	1.84	1.03	1.01	1.10							
2.11	2.04	2.01	2.17	2.01	1.83	0.98	1.02	1.09							
2.05	1.75	1.98	1.97	1.89	1.81	1.04	0.93	1.10							
2.13	2.02	2.12	1.94	2.04	2.01	1.10	0.99	1.05							
1.92	1.72	2.05	2.03	1.86	1.87	0.94	0.92	1.09							
1.79	1.79	1.94	1.92	1.94	1.98	0.93	0.92	0.98							
1.93	2.11	1.99	2.03	2.11	1.81	0.95	1.00	1.10							
2.07	2.17	1.94	2.10	2.10	2.09	0.98	1.03	0.93							
2.17	1.71	2.03	2.13	1.88	1.96	1.02	0.91	1.04							
1.84	2.38	2.11	2.05	2.17	1.95	0.90	1.10	1.08							
1.99	2.38	1.96	1.96	2.18	2.04	1.01	1.09	0.96							

FIGURE 3.40 Correlation of Simulated Values

Pearson's Product Moment Linear Correlation and Spearman's Nonlinear Rank Correlation

Typically, when we use the term *correlation*, we usually mean a linear correlation. And, of course, correlations can take on any value between −1 and +1 inclusive, which means that the correlation coefficient has a sign (direction) and magnitude (strength). The problem arises when there is nonlinearity, and we use linear correlations. Figure 3.41 illustrates a few scatter charts with pairwise X and Y variables (e.g., hours of study and school grades). If we draw an imaginary best-fitting line in the scatter diagram, we can see the approximate correlation (we show a computation of correlation in a moment, but for now, let's just visualize). Part A shows a relatively high positive correlation coefficient (R) of about 0.7 as an increase in X means an increase in Y, so there is a positive slope and, therefore, a positive correlation. Part B shows an even stronger negative correlation (negatively sloped; an increase of X means a decrease of Y and vice versa). It has slightly higher magnitude because the dots are closer to the line. In fact, when the dots are exactly on the line, as in Part D, the correlation is +1 (if positively sloped) or −1 (if negatively sloped), indicating a perfect correlation. Part C shows a situation where the curve is perfectly flat, or has zero correlation, where, regardless of the X value, Y remains unchanged, indicating that there is no relationship.

Problems arise when there are nonlinear relationships (typically the case in many real-life situations) as shown in Figure 3.42. Part E shows an exponential relationship between X and Y. If we use a nonlinear correlation, we get +0.9, but if we use a linear correlation, it is much lower at 0.6 (Part F), which means that there is information that is not picked up by the linear correlation. The situation gets a lot worse when we have a sinusoidal relationship, as in Parts G and H. The nonlinear correlation picks up the relationship very nicely with a 0.9 correlation coefficient; using a linear correlation, the best-fitting line is literally a flat

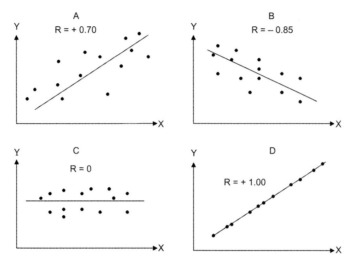

FIGURE 3.41 Correlation of Simulated Values

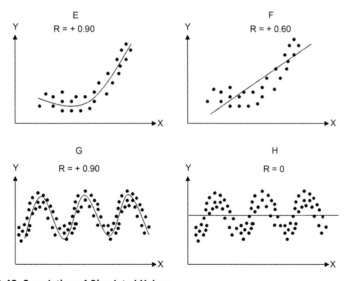

FIGURE 3.42 Correlation of Simulated Values

horizontal line, indicating zero correlation. However, just looking at the picture would tell you that there is a relationship. *So, we must therefore distinguish between linear and nonlinear correlations, because as we have seen in this exercise, correlation affects risk, and we are dealing with risk analysis!*

The linear correlation coefficient is also known as the Pearson's product moment correlation coefficient. It is computed by $R = \dfrac{\sum_{i=1}^{n}(X_i - \bar{X})(Y_i - \bar{Y})}{\sqrt{\sum_{i=1}^{n}(X_i - \bar{X})^2 (Y_i - \bar{Y})^2}}$ and assumes that the underlying distribution is normal or near-normal, such as the t-distribution. Therefore, this is a parametric correlation. You can use Excel's CORREL function to compute this effortlessly. The nonlinear correlation is the Spearman's nonparametric rank-based correlation, which does not assume any underlying distribution, making it a nonparametric measure. The approach to Spearman's nonlinear correlation is very simple. Using the original data, we first "linearize" the data, and then apply the Pearson's correlation computation to get the Spearman's correlation. Typically, whenever there is nonlinear data, we can linearize it by using either a *LOG* function (or, equivalently, an *LN* or natural log function) or a *RANK* function. The following table illustrates this effect. The original value is clearly nonlinear (it is 10^x where x is from 0 to 5). However, if you apply a log function, the data becomes linear (1, 2, 3, 4, 5), or when you apply ranks, the rank (either high to low or low to high) is also linear. Once we have linearized the data, we can apply the linear Pearson's correlation. To summarize, Spearman's nonparametric nonlinear correlation coefficient is obtained by first ranking the data and then applying Pearson's parametric linear correlation coefficient.

Table 3.1

PEARSON'S VALUE	LOG(VALUE)	RANK(VALUE)
1	0	1
10	1	2
100	2	3
1000	3	4
10000	4	5
100000	5	6

Reference

Mun, J. CEO of Real Options Valuation, Inc., premier software, training, and consulting firm located in California <www.realoptionsvaluation.com>. The software applications presented herein includes Risk Simulator, Modeling Toolkit, and others from the company.

Price Volatility

INTRODUCTION

In this chapter, we present the reader with an overview of price volatility forecasting models. We describe the mathematics behind these models, and provide an in-depth analysis of scaling properties. We discuss various techniques that are used in the industry to forecast volatility, as well as appropriate methods to calibrate these models.

This chapter further reviews and expands upon the volatility chapter from *The Science of Algorithmic Trading and Portfolio Management* (Kissell, 2013) by providing readers with findings and empirical evidence across time period and asset classes. This chapter further discusses the scaling properties of volatility over time.

What is Volatility?

Volatility is the uncertainty surrounding the potential price movement of the asset. It is calculated as the standard deviation of log price returns. This definition is a measure of the potential variation in price trend, not a measure of the actual price trend. For example, two stocks could have the same exact volatility, but very different trends. If stock A has a volatility of 10% and a price trend of 20%, its one standard deviation return will be between 10% and 30%. If stock B also has a volatility of 10% but a price trend of 5%, its one standard deviation return will be between −5% and 15%. Stock with higher volatility will have larger swings than the stock with lower volatility, resulting in either higher or lower returns.

This point is further elaborated upon using data for the SP500 large cap and R2000 small cap indexes. We analyzed return and volatility for each in 2011 and 2012. Our findings are shown in Figure 4.1 (returns as a function of volatility). For each index and each year, we plot annual return as a function of annualized volatility. Annual return was computed as the log return over the year, and annualized volatility was computed using daily log returns over the year, scaled for the year by multiplying by $\sqrt{250}$. Our data sample consisted of stocks in each index for which we had complete data over the period 2011−2012.

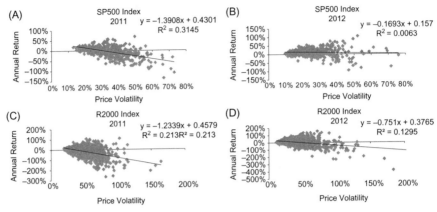

FIGURE 4.1 Returns as a Function of Volatility

Figure 4.1a shows annual returns for the SP500 index as a function of it volatility for 2011. Average return on the year was −4.9%, and average volatility was 34.5%. As shown in the figure, there is a very wide range across price returns (y-axis) for a specified volatility (x-axis). For example, stocks with volatility of 35% had returns that ranged from −50% to +50%! Overall, there was a strong negative relationship between returns and volatility, but with large variability. The best-fit equation line of returns as a function volatility was $R^2 = 0.31$, with a significant t-stat.

Figure 4.1b shows annual returns for the SP500 index as a function of its volatility for 2012. In 2012, returns were higher, and volatility was lower compared to 2011. The average return in 2011 was +11.4%, and the average volatility was 25.4%. Again, there was a very large dispersion across returns at volatility levels. For a volatility level of 35%, stock returns again ranged from −50% to +50%. But unlike in 2011, we did not find a relationship between stock returns and stock volatility. The best-fit equation line of returns as a function of volatility found $R^2 = 0.006$, and the t-stat was insignificant, thus indicating no statistical relationship between returns and volatility level.

Observations on the R2000 index were similar to the SP500 index. Figure 4.1c illustrates R2000 index returns as a function of volatility for 2011. The average return was −16.8%, and the average volatility was 50.8%. Volatility was much higher for small cap stocks than for large cap stocks, and small cap returns were much lower than for large cap stocks. The dispersion of returns at a specified volatility level was also much larger for small cap stocks. For example, for a volatility level of 60%, stock returns ranged from −95% to +70%. There was a strong negative relationship between returns and volatility, but also a very large variability. The best-fit equation line had $R^2 = 0.21$, with significant t-stat.

Figure 4.1d shows annual returns for the R2000 stocks as a function of its annualized volatility in 2012. Average return was +8.0%, and average volatility

Table 4.1 Returns as a Function of Volatility

SP500 Index	2011		2012	
	Slope	**Constant**	**Slope**	**Constant**
Est. Beta	−1.39	0.43	−0.17	0.16
Se. Beta	0.09	0.03	0.10	0.03
t-Stat	−14.95	12.83	−1.76	5.97
R2	31.5%		0.6%	
Reg. Err	21.6%		21.6%	
Number	487		487	
R2000 Index	**2011**		**2012**	
	Slope	**Constant**	**Slope**	**Constant**
Est. Beta	−1.23	0.46	−0.75	0.38
Se. Beta	0.06	0.03	0.05	0.02
t-Stat	−20.54	14.34	−15.23	17.51
R2	21%		13%	
Reg. Err	37%		36%	
Number	1559		1559	

was 39.4%. Similar to large cap stocks, small cap stocks had higher returns and lower volatility in 2012 compared to 2011. The dispersion of returns was again very large. For a volatility of 60%, we found stock returns to range from approximately −80% to +80%. The best-fit equation of returns as a function of volatility was negative with $R^2 = 0.13$, and significant t-stats. Stocks with larger volatility tended to have lower returns. Table 4.1 shows the regression results for Returns as a function of Volatility for the SP500 and R2000 indexes for 2011 and 2012.

In general, our analysis found:

- There are large variations in price returns for a specified volatility level.
- There is a negative relationship between returns and volatility.

Volatility Measures

There are two volatility measures commonly used in the financial industry: realized and implied. Realized volatility is computed from historical prices and is often referred to as historical volatility. Realized volatility uses past history to predict the future. Implied volatility, on the other hand, is computed from the market's consensus of the fair value for a derivative instrument, such as the

SP500 index option contract. Implied volatility is a "forward-looking" or "future" expectation estimate.

Historical volatility lets the data predict the future.
Implied volatility lets the market predict the future.

Practitioners utilize volatility in many different ways. For example, traders use volatility to understand potential price movement over the trading day, as input into market impact models, to compute trading costs, and to select algorithms. Algorithms use volatility to determine when it is appropriate to accelerate or decelerate trading rates in real time. Portfolio managers use volatility to evaluate overall portfolio risk, as input into optimizers, for value-at-risk calculations, as part of the stock selection process, and to develop hedging strategies. Derivatives desks use volatility to price options and other structured products. In addition, plan sponsors use volatility to understand the potential that they will or will not be able to meet their long-term liabilities and financial obligations. Volatility is a very important financial statistic.

Definitions
Price Returns/Price Change

Price returns or price change can be computed using either the "percentage" returns or "log" returns formulation. But since returns have been found to be log normally distributed, it is appropriate to use the log returns calculation. We describe these two measures here.

Percentage Price Return:

$$r_t = \frac{p_t}{p_{t-1}} - 1 \tag{4.1}$$

Log Price Return:

$$r_t = \ln\left(\frac{p_t}{p_{t-1}}\right) \tag{4.2}$$

where $\ln(\cdot)$ represents the natural log function.

Average Return

This average period price return $\bar{r}$ is calculated differently for the "percentage" and "logs" methods.

Average Return: Percentage Method:

The process for computing an n-period average return using the percentage change methodology is to start with:

$$p_n = p_0 \cdot (1 + \bar{r})^n$$

Then solving for $\bar{r}$, we have:

$$\bar{r} = \left(\frac{p_n}{p_0}\right)^{\frac{1}{n}} - 1 \tag{4.3}$$

Notice that the average return is not calculated as the simple average of all returns.

Average Return: Logarithmic Change Method:

The average return using the logs methodology, however, is determined directly from the simple average formula. This is:

$$\bar{r} = \frac{1}{n}\sum r_k \tag{4.4}$$

The average can also be computed directly from the starting and ending price as follows:

$$\bar{r} = \frac{1}{n}\cdot\ln\left(\frac{p_t}{p_0}\right) \tag{4.5}$$

How do percentage returns and log returns differ?

For small changes, there actually is not much difference between these two measures. Figure 4.2 shows a comparison percentage price change compared to log price change over the range of returns from -40% through $+40\%$. As shown in this figure, there are very small differences in calculation process between -20% to 20%, and negligible differences between -10% and $+10\%$. However, we start to see differences once we are outside of this range. For trading purposes where the daily price change is quite often less than $\pm 10\%$, either returns

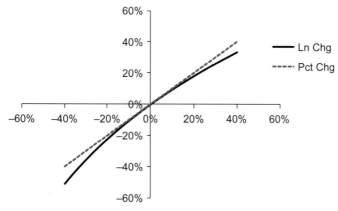

FIGURE 4.2 Comparison of Natural Log Price Change to Percentage Price Change

measure is reasonable. However, for a portfolio manager with a longer time horizon, we will start to see some differences between these two measures.

Log returns can take one any value from $-\infty$ to $+\infty$, and the distribution of returns is symmetric. However, the percentage returns can only take on values between -100% to $+\infty$. The percentage return data values have a skewed distribution, while the log returns distribution is symmetric.

The log returns method is a symmetric measure and provides mathematical simplification in many of our calculations. It is also more intuitive than the percentage change method. For example, if the price for a financial asset changes from 100 to 80, the percentage price change is -20%. However, if the price in the next period changes from 80 to 100, the percentage price change is $+25\%$. So this asset first lost -20%, then increased $+25\%$, but it is currently at its original starting value; it is not $+5\%$ overall. But using the log returns method, we do not run into this inconsistency. If the stock price changes from 100 to 80, this corresponds to a log change of -22.31%. If the price change in the next period increases 80 to 100, it corresponds to a log change of $+22.31\%$. The sum of these returns states that the current price should be the same as the starting price, since $+22.31\% - 22.31\% = 0$, which is exactly what we have.

Price returns have been found to have a log-normal distribution. Thus, using the log-returns measure is more consistent with the underlying data. Going forward we will use the log-return methodology.

Volatility:

Volatility is calculated as the standard deviation of price returns.

$$\sigma_i = \sqrt{\frac{1}{n-1}\sum_{k=1}^{n}(r_{ik}-\bar{r}_i)^2} \tag{4.6}$$

In the preceding formula, there are n-historical returns, but we divide by $(n-1)$ to ensure an unbiased estimate. This formulation is also called the sample standard deviation.

Covariance:

The covariance of returns for two stocks σ_{ij} is a measure of the co-movement of prices.

$$\sigma_{ij} = \frac{1}{n-2}\sum(r_{ik}-\bar{r}_i)(r_{jk}-\bar{r}_j) \tag{4.7}$$

Positive covariance means that the prices will move up and down together, and negative covariance means that the prices will move in opposite direction.

Correlation:

The correlation between two stocks ρ_{ij} is the covariance of the stocks divided by the volatility of each stock. This provides a correlation coefficient between 1 and -1, or $-1 \leq \rho_{xy} \leq 1$.

$$\rho_{ij} = \frac{\sigma_{ij}}{\sigma_i \cdot \sigma_j} \tag{4.8}$$

Stocks with a correlation of $\rho_{ij} = 1$ move perfectly with one another, stocks with a correlation of $\rho_{ij} = -1$ move perfectly in the opposite direction of one another, and stocks with a correlation of $\rho_{ij} = 0$ do not move together at all. Correlation provides a measure of the strength of co-movement between stocks.

Dispersion:

The dispersion of returns is computed as the standard deviation of returns for a group of stock. It is a cross-sectional measure of overall variability across stocks.

$$dispersion\ (r_p) = \sqrt{\frac{1}{n-1} \cdot \sum_{j=1}^{n} (\bar{r}_j - \bar{r}_p)^2} \qquad (4.9)$$

where $\bar{r}_j$ is the average return for the stock, and $\bar{r}_p$ is the average return across all stocks in the sample.

Dispersion is a very useful to portfolio managers because it gives a measure of the directional movement of prices and how close they are moving in conjunction with one another. A small dispersion measure indicates that the stocks are moving up and down together. A large dispersion measure indicates that the stocks are not moving close together.

Value-at-Risk:

Value-at-risk (VaR) is a summary statistic that quantifies the potential loss of a portfolio. Many companies place limits on the total value-at-risk to protect investors from potential large losses. This potential loss corresponds to a specified probability α level, or alternatively, a $(1 - \alpha)$ confidence.

If the expected return profile for a portfolio is $r \sim N(\bar{r}_p, \sigma_p^2)$, then a $\alpha\%$ VaR estimate is the value return that occurs at the $1 - \alpha$ probability level in the cumulative normal distribution. If $\alpha = 95\%$, this equation is:

$$0.05 = \int_{-\infty}^{r^*} \frac{1}{\sqrt{2\pi}\sigma_p} \exp\left\{-\frac{(r-\bar{r}_p)^2}{2\sigma_p}\right\} \qquad (4.10)$$

Implied Volatility:

Implied volatility is determined from the price of a call or put option. For example, the Black-Scholes option pricing model determined the price of a call option as follows:

$$C = S \cdot N(d_1) - X \cdot e^{-r_f T} \cdot N(d_2) \qquad (4.11)$$

where,

$$d_1 = \frac{\ln(S/X) + (r_f + \sigma^2/2)T}{\sigma\sqrt{T}}$$

$$d_2 = d_1 - \sigma\sqrt{T}$$

$$C = \text{Call Price}$$
$$X = \text{Strike Price}$$
$$S = \text{Stock Price}$$
$$\sigma = \text{Stock Volatility}$$
$$N(d) = \text{probability that actual return will be less than } d$$
$$r_f = \text{risk free rate of return}$$
$$T = \text{future time period}$$

The implied volatility is the value of the volatility in the above formula that will result in the current value of the call option. Since the call option price is determined by the market, we are able to back into the volatility terms that would provide this value, and thus, the volatility implied by the formulation. Implied volatility is most often solved via non-linear optimization techniques.

Beta:

$$\beta_k = \frac{cov(r_k, r_m)}{var(r_m)} = \frac{\sigma_{ij}}{\sigma_m^2} \tag{4.12}$$

The beta of a stock represents the stock's sensitivity to a general market index. It is determined as the covariance of returns between the stock and the market divided by the variance of the index (volatility squared). The calculation is also the slope of the regression line of stock returns (y-axis) as a function of market returns (x-axis). Stocks with a positive beta $\beta_k > 0$ move in the same direction as the market, and stocks with a negative beta $\beta_k < 0$ will move in the opposite direction of the market. Stocks with an absolute value of beta greater than one $|\beta_k| > 1$ are more variable than the market, and stocks with an absolute value of beta less than one $|\beta_k| < 1$ are less variable than the market.

Market Observations: Empirical Findings

In order that we better understand the meaning of these variability trends in the market, we evaluated volatility, correlation, and dispersion over the period January 1, 2000 through June 30, 2012. The universe used for our analysis was the SP500 index for large-cap stocks, and R2000 index for small-cap stocks. Stocks that were in each index on the last trading day in the month were included in calculations for that month.

Volatility:

Volatility was computed as the 22-day standard deviation of log returns annualized using a scaling factor of $\sqrt{250}$. We computed volatility across for all stocks in our universe on each day, and reported the cross-sectional average as our daily data point. Figure 4.3a shows the average stock volatility for large-cap stocks. In the beginning of 2000, volatility was fairly high. This was primarily due to the technology boom and increased trading volume. Volatility began the

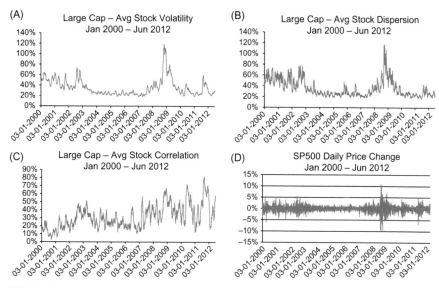

FIGURE 4.3 Market Observations: Volatility, Correlation, and Dispersion

decade around 60%, but decreased to about 20%. Volatility remained low until spring 2007, and then started to spike in August 2007 due to the quant crisis. But this was nothing compared to the financial crisis period of 2008−2009, in which volatility spiked to over 100% and reached as high as 118%. Following the financial crisis, volatility decreased to more reasonable levels of 20%−30% and these lower levels persisted until Fall 2011 due to the US debt ceiling crisis and re-emergence of macro-economic uncertainty in Europe. After the United States addressed its debt issues, volatility decreased shortly thereafter.

The average large-cap volatility during our sample period was 36%, and the average small-cap volatility was 54%. Small-cap volatility tends to be consistently higher than large-cap volatility.

Correlation:

Correlation was computed as the 22-day correlation measure across all pairs of stocks in each index. Figure 6.2b shows the average pairwise correlation across all pairs of stock on each day for large-cap stocks. For example, for a universe with 500 stocks, there are 124,500 unique two-pair combinations. Hence, we computed correlations across all 124,500 combinations of stocks and published the average value in Figure 4.3b. For an index consisting of 2000 stocks, there are just slightly less than 2 million unique combinations of stocks (1,999,000 to be exact). Computing average pairwise correlations is a very data-intensive process. The graph of average large-cap correlations over our period found relatively low correlation (less than 30%) in the beginning of the decade, but then spiked at the time of the collapse bubble. This increase in correlation was due in part to the market's re-evaluation of stock prices to lower levels and a sell-off of stock from institutions that further pushed the prices in the same direction. Since Spring 2007, correlations have been on the rise and only recently seem to have leveled off, but at much higher levels than at the beginning of the decade. An interesting finding of our historical analysis is that the market experienced the highest level of correlation following the Flash Crash (but it was very short-lived) and again during the US debt ceiling crisis. These correlation levels were even higher than the levels experienced during the financial crises, when markets experienced their highest levels of volatility.

The average large-cap pairwise correlation during our sample period was 32%, and average pairwise small-cap correlation was 23%. Opposite to the volatility relationship mentioned previously, small-cap correlation tends to be lower than large-cap correlation. This is primarily due to the smaller companies having a larger amount of company risk. However, there are periods when correlation is larger across the small-cap stocks.

Dispersion:

We measured dispersion as the standard deviation of 22-day stock returns. For example, for the SP500 we computed the 22-day price return for each of the 500 stocks in the index. We then computed the standard deviation of these returns as our dispersion. Figure 4.3c illustrates large-cap returns dispersion over our analysis period. As shown in the figure, dispersion was fairly constant in the beginning of the decade and then declined through August 2007, when it suddenly increased and spiked during the financial crisis. Dispersion decreased shortly thereafter, but began increasing again during the US debt crisis of Fall 2011. Comparison of dispersion to pairwise correlation shows a slightly negatively relationship. As correlation increases, dispersion tends to fall, and as correlation decreases, dispersion tends to increase. This inverse relationship between dispersion and correlation is more dramatic for small-cap stocks than for large-cap stocks.

Over our sample period, the average large-cap dispersion was 36%, and the average small-cap dispersion was 58%. Small-cap dispersion tends to be consistently larger for small caps than for large caps.

Volatility Clustering:

Figure 4.3d illustrates the daily price change for the SP500 index. Notice the extent of volatility clustering. This means that large price swings tend to be followed by large price swings (either positive or negative), and small price swings tend to be followed by small price swings (either positive or negative). The beginning of the decade was associated with a higher volatility regime due to the technology bubble. This was followed by relatively lower volatility through the beginning of the quant breakdown starting in Aug 2007, followed by ultra-high volatility during the Financial Crisis of 2008–2009. The graph also illustrated the higher volatility period after the Flash Crash in May 2010 and again during the US debt crisis in Fall 2011. Volatility appears to be time varying with a clustering effect. Thus, traditional models that give the same weighting to all historical observations may not be the most accurate representation of actual volatility. The volatility clustering phenomena was the driving force behind advanced volatility modeling techniques such as ARCH, GARCH, and EWMA. These models are further discussed ahead. Table 4.2 provides market statistics for volatility, correlation, and dispersion from Jan 2000 through Jun 2012.

Cross-Sectional Analysis:

We next compared volatility across stocks by index for 2011 and 2012 (Figure 4.4, Cumulative Volatility Distribution). Our sample universe consisted of all stocks for which we had complete data. In 2011, the average SP500 stock volatility was 34% and ranged from 13% (min) to 73% (max). The standard

Table 4.2 Market Observations from Jan 2000–Jun 2012

Statistic	Avg Volatility		Avg Correlation		Avg Dispersion	
	LC	SC	LC	SC	LC	SC
Avg:	36%	54%	32%	23%	36%	58%
Stdev:	16%	20%	15%	12%	16%	20%
Min:	18%	30%	3%	2%	16%	33%
Max:	119%	146%	81%	67%	118%	142%

Source: Science of Algorithmic Trading and Portfolio Management, Elsevier, 2013

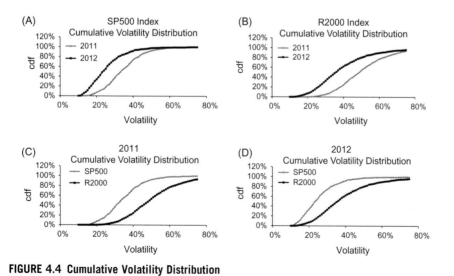

FIGURE 4.4 Cumulative Volatility Distribution

deviation of volatilities was 11%. In 2012, the average SP500 stock volatility was 25% and ranged from 10% (min) to 76% (max). The standard deviation of volatilities was 10%. The SP500 stock volatility experienced similar ranges and standard deviation across stocks for both years in our sample period, but was much lower in 2012 compared to 2011.

In 2011, the average R2000 stock volatility was 51% and ranged from 19% (min) to 165% (max). The standard deviation of volatilities was 16%. In 2012, the average R2000 stock volatility was 39% and ranged from 11% (min) to 202% (max). The standard deviation of volatilities was 19%. The standard deviation of R2000 stock volatility was similar for both years in our sample period. Volatility was lower in 2012 compared to 2011, but did experience a larger range.

Why is small-cap volatility often higher than large-cap volatility?

It is important to keep in mind that small-cap stocks such as those that comprise the R2000 index will be subject to larger price swings due to company sales and revenues and future projects. If a small-cap company procures a contract, it could result in a large percentage increase in sales, which will result in a large price jump. Similarly, if a small-cap company loses a contract, it could result in a large percentage decrease in sales which will result in a large decrease in price. Both of these situations will result in higher volatility for the small-cap company. When large-cap companies experience new sales contracts or lose sales contracts, it may result in the same revenue loss or gain to the company, but will likely represent a much smaller percentage of current sales and revenue, therefore, it will not have as large of an effect on volatility as with the small-cap companies. Another reason why small-cap volatility is often higher than large-cap volatility is due to the analyst coverage. Large-cap companies, for the most part, have more analyst coverage, so there is more market knowledge, fewer surprises, and less magnitude of surprise. Small-cap companies, for the most part, have less analyst coverage, so they will not have the same robust information base as large-cap companies, and are thus subject to more surprises and a larger magnitude of surprise. All of this could potentially result in higher volatility.

Figure 4.4a illustrates the cumulative distribution of volatility across SP500 stocks in 2011 and 2012. The cumulative distribution function (CDF) increases at a quicker rate in 2012 compared to 2011, signifying lower volatility. Figure 4.4b illustrates the cumulative distribution of volatility across R2000 stocks in 2011 and 2012. We notice the same pattern, with the CDF for 2012 increasing at a faster rate. Figure 4.4c compares the cumulative distribution function of volatility for the SP500 compared to R2000 for 2011. Figure 4.4d compares the cumulative distribution function of the SP500 to the R2000. Once again, the CDF increases at a faster rate for SP500 than R2000 due to large-cap stocks having smaller volatility. The R2000 CDF increases at a slower rate and is more spread out (larger volatilities), even in an environment in which volatility is relatively low. The reason is due to the company-specific volatility. Table 4.3 shows the computed cross sectional volatility for the SP500 and R2000 indexes for 2011 and 2012.

Table 4.3 Cross-Sectional Volatility

Statistic	SP500		R2000	
	2011	2012	2011	2012
Avg:	34%	25%	51%	39%
Stdev:	11%	10%	16%	19%
Min:	13%	10%	19%	11%
Max:	73%	76%	165%	202%

Forecasting Stock Volatility

In this section, we describe various volatility forecasting models, as well as appropriate techniques to estimate their parameters. We also introduce a new model that incorporates a historical measure coupled with insight from the derivatives market. These models are:

- Historical Moving Average (HMA)
- Exponential Weighted Moving Average (EWMA)
- Autoregressive Models (ARCH and GARCH)
- HMA-VIX Adjustment

Some of these descriptions and our empirical findings presented have been disseminated in the Journal of Trading's "Intraday Volatility Models: Methods to Improve Real-Time Forecasts," (Kissell, 2012), and have been described in *The Science of Algorithmic Trading* (Kissell, 2013). Ahead we follow the same outline and terminology as in the journal and the reference.

Volatility Models

We describe four different volatility models: the historical moving average (HMA), the exponential weighted moving average (EWMA) introduced by J.P. Morgan (1996), an auto-regressive heteroscedasticity (ARCH) model introduced by Engle (1982), a generalized autoregressive conditional heteroscedasticity (GARCH) model introduced by Bollerslev (1986), and an HMA-VIX adjustment model that combines the stock's current realized volatility with an implied volatility measure.[1]

---

[1] The HMA-VIX volatility model was presented at Curt Engler's CQA/SQA Trading Seminar (February 2009), "Volatility: Is it safe to get back in the water?" and taught as part of the volatility section in Cornell University's Graduate Financial Engineering Program, "Introduction to Algorithmic Trading" in Fall 2009 (Kissell & Malamut). The HMA-VIX Model was also published in the Journal of Trading, "Intraday Volatility Models: Methods to Improve Real-Time Forecasts," Fall 2012.

We fit the parameters of these models to the SP500 and R2000 indexes over the one-year period 7/1/2011–6/30/2012 and compared the performance of the models. Readers are encouraged to experiment with these techniques to determine which model work best for their needs.

Price Returns

Price returns for each index were computed as the natural log of close-to-close price change:

$$y_t = \log(p_t/p_{t-1}) \tag{4.13}$$

A general short-term model of price returns is:

$$y_t = C + \sigma_t \varepsilon_t \tag{4.14}$$

where C is a constant, ε_t is a random noise with distribution $\varepsilon_t \sim N(0, 1)$, and σ_t is the time-varying volatility component. In practice, the short-term constant term C is rarely known in advance, and analysts often use a simplifying assumption of $C = 0$. Then the general short-term price returns model simplifies to:

$$y_t = \sigma_t \varepsilon_t \tag{4.15}$$

Data Sample

We used the SP500 and R2000 index returns over the one-year period July 1, 2011–June 30, 2012 as our data sample. Figure 4.5a shows the daily price returns for the SP500. The standard deviation of daily returns over this period was 1.5%, and the index had price swings as high as +4.6% (8/9/2011) and as low as −6.9% (8/8/2011). These large swings occurred during the US crisis (Aug–Sept 2011). Figure 4.5b shows the price returns for the R2000 index over the same period. The R2000 index was more volatile than the SP500 index. It has a standard deviation of daily returns of 2.1% and price swings as high as +6.7% (8/9/2011) and as low as −9.3% (8/8/2011). As is evident in both figures, volatility was fairly low through the middle of August 2011, when there was a sudden spike in volatility that caused it to remain high through year end. This was then followed by a relatively low volatility period from January 2012 through the end of May 2012, when markets started to experience increasing volatility levels. The most important finding over the time period investigated is that volatility of both indexes appears to be time varying with clustering. The volatility model needs to be able to quickly adjust to these types of sudden regime shifts.

Historical Moving Average (HMA)

The historical moving average volatility measure is computed by definition:

$$\bar{\sigma}_t^2 = \frac{1}{n-1} \sum_{k=1}^{n} y_{t-k}^2 \tag{4.16}$$

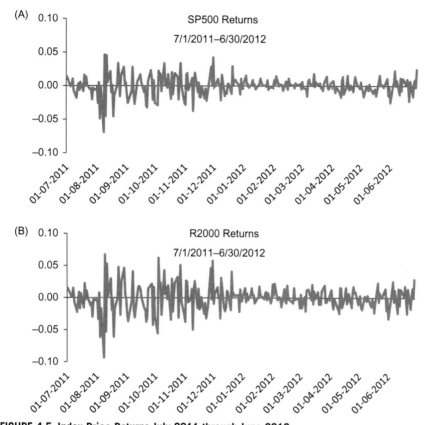

FIGURE 4.5 Index Price Returns July 2011 through June 2012

This is a simple, unbiased average of squared returns (since we are taking the trend term to be $C = 0$). The advantage of this approach is that the calculation is straightforward. The disadvantage is that the HMA assumes returns are independent and identically distributed with constant variance. However, this assumption does not seem to hold true over our period analyzed (see Figure 6.3a and b). Since this model applies an equal weighting to all historical data points, it has been found to be slow to adapt to changing volatility regimes, such as the US debt crisis (Aug–Sept 2011) and during the financial crisis (Sept 2008–Mar 2009).

Exponential Weighted Moving Average (EWMA)

The exponential weighted moving average (EWMA) is computed as follows:

$$\hat{\sigma}_t^2 = (1 - \lambda)y_{t-1}^2 + \lambda\hat{\sigma}_{t-1}^2 \tag{4.17}$$

EWMA applies weights to the historical observations following an exponential smoothing process with parameter λ in which $0 \leq \lambda \leq 1$. The value of the smoothing parameter is determined via maximum-likelihood estimation (MLE). J.P. Morgan (1996) first introduced this model in 1994 as part of their Risk Metrics offering.

The advantage of the EWMA is that it places more emphasis on recent data observations. This allows the model to quickly update in a changing volatility environment. Additionally, its forecasts only require the previous period price change and the previous volatility forecast. We do not need to recalculate the forecast using a long history of price returns.

ARCH Volatility Model

The ARCH(p) volatility model was introduced by Engle (1982) and consists of the "p" previous returns. We can formulate as follows:

$$\hat{\sigma}_t^2 = w + \sum_{i=1}^{p} \alpha_i r_{t-i}^2 \qquad (4.18)$$

where

$$w > 0, \alpha_1, \ldots, \alpha_p, \geq 0, \sum \alpha_i < 1$$

The parameters of the model are determined via ordinary least squares (OLS) regression analysis. The model differs from the HMA in that it does not apply the same weighting to all historical observations. To the extent that the more recent observations have a larger effect on current returns, the ARCH model will apply greater weight to the more recent observations. This allows the model to react quickly in a changing volatility environment.

A simple ARCH(1) model only consists of the previous day's price return. This is formulated as:

$$\hat{\sigma}_t^2 = w + \alpha_1 y_{t-i}^2 \qquad (4.19)$$

where

$$w > 0, 0 \leq \alpha_1 < 1$$

GARCH Volatility Model

The GARCH volatility model was introduced Bollerslev (1986) and is an extension of the ARCH model (Engle, 1982). A GARCH(p,q) model consists of "p" previous returns and "q" previous volatility forecasts as follows:

$$\hat{\sigma}_t^2 = w + \sum_{i=1}^{p} \alpha_i r_{t-i}^2 + \sum_{j=1}^{q} \beta_j \hat{\sigma}_{t-j}^2 \qquad (4.20)$$

where

$$\omega > 0, \alpha_1, \ldots, \alpha_p, b_1, \ldots, b_q \geq 0, \sum \alpha_i + \sum \beta_j < 1$$

The GARCH model applies more weight to the more recent observations, thus allowing the model to quickly adapt to changing volatility regimes. The parameters of the model are determined via maximum likelihood estimation.

A simple GARCH (1,1) model consists of only the previous day's price return and previous day's volatility forecast and is formulated as:

$$\hat{\sigma}_t^2 = \omega + \alpha_1 y_{t-i}^2 + \beta_1 \hat{\sigma}_{t-j}^2 \tag{4.21}$$

where

$$\omega > 0, \quad \alpha_1, b_1 \geq 0, \alpha_1 + b_1 < 1$$

HMA-VIX Adjustment Model

The HMA-VIX volatility-forecasting model (Kissell, 2012; Kissell, 2013) is an approach that combines the stock's current volatility with an implied volatility estimate. We formulate this model as:

$$\hat{\sigma}_t = \overline{\sigma}_{t-1} \cdot \frac{VIX_{t-1}}{\overline{\sigma}_{SPX,t-1}} \cdot AdjFactor \tag{4.22}$$

where $\overline{\sigma}_{t-1}$ is the HMA stock trailing volatility, $\overline{\sigma}_{SPX,t-1}$ is the SP500 index trailing volatility, VIX_{t-1} is the VIX implied volatility index, and *AdjFactor* is the adjustment factor needed to correct for the risk premium embedded in the VIX contract.

Over the years, the options market has proven to be a valuable, accurate, and timely indicator of market volatility and changing regimes. Options traders are able to adjust prices quickly based on changing volatility expectations. Analysis can easily infer these expectations through the options prices. This is known as the implied volatility. The question arises then, if implied volatility is an accurate and timely estimate of volatility, why can analysts not just use implied volatility from the options market rather than using the results from these models? The answer is simple. Unfortunately, implied volatility estimates do not exist for all stocks. The options market at the stock level is only liquid for the largest stocks. Accurate implied volatility estimates do not exist across all stocks. Fortunately, the options market still provides valuable information that could be extended to the stock level to help provide accurate forward-looking estimates (and in a more timely manner than the other historical techniques). This also provides ways for algorithms to quickly adjust to changing expectations in real-time, and provide investors with improved trading performance.

The HMA-VIX technique consists of adjusting the stock's trailing volatility by the ratio of the VIX index to the SP500 trailing volatility plus a correction factor. The ratio of the VIX to the SP500 realized shows whether the options market believes that volatility will be increasing or decreasing. However, since the VIX usually trades at a premium of 1.31 to the SP500 trailing volatility, we need to include an adjustment factor to correct for this premium. If the VIX Index/SP500 realized volatility > 1.31, then we conclude that the options market believes volatility will be increasing; if the VIX Index/SP500 realized volatility < 1.31, then we conclude that the options market believes volatility will be decreasing.

The increasing/decreasing expectation obtained from the options market is then applied to individual stocks. A comparison of the VIX implied to the SP500 trailing is shown in Figure 4.6.

The advantage of incorporating the implied expectations into our real-time volatility estimator is that if there is a sudden market event that will affect volatility, it will almost immediately be reflected in the HMA-VIX measure. The historical models (HMA, EWMA, ARCH, and GARCH) will not react to the sudden market event until after this event has affected stock prices. Thus, the historical models will always be lagging behind the event to some degree. Furthermore, if the options market is anticipating an event that has not yet occurred, and priced the uncertainty of the event into its prices, the HMA-VIX model will also reflect anticipated events and increased uncertainty prior to that event taking place. Just the worry of a potential event taking place will be reflected in the HMA-VIX model. Models updated nightly will miss this event and will not necessarily provide timely, accurate volatility estimates.

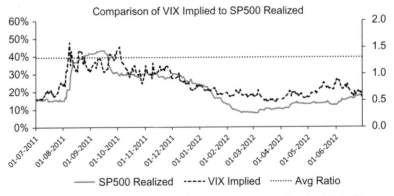

FIGURE 4.6 Comparison of VIX Implied Volatility to SP500 Index Realized Volatility

Determining Parameters via Maximum Likelihood Estimation

Parameters of the GARCH and EWMA volatility models are computed via maximum likelihood estimation (MLE). An overview of the estimation process follows.

Likelihood Function

Let log price returns be normally distributed with mean zero and time varying volatility, that is, $y_t \sim N(0, \hat{\sigma}_t^2)$. Then the probability density function (PDF) of these returns at any time is:

$$f_t(y_t; \hat{\sigma}_t) = \frac{1}{\sqrt{2\pi\hat{\sigma}_t^2}} \cdot e^{-\frac{y_t^2}{2\hat{\sigma}_t^2}} \tag{4.23}$$

The likelihood of achieving the observed series of returns is:

$$L = \prod_{t=1}^{n} \frac{1}{\sqrt{2\pi\hat{\sigma}_t^2}} \cdot e^{-\frac{y_t^2}{2\hat{\sigma}_t^2}} \tag{4.24}$$

The log-likelihood function $\ln(L)$ of achieving this sequence of returns is:

$$\ln(L) = \sum_{t=1}^{n} \left(-\frac{1}{2}\ln(2\pi) - \frac{1}{2}\ln(\hat{\sigma}_t^2) - \frac{1}{2}\frac{y_t^2}{\hat{\sigma}_t^2} \right) \tag{4.25}$$

The parameters of the EWMA and GARCH models are found by maximizing the $\ln(L)$ where $\hat{\sigma}_t^2$ is defined from the corresponding volatility models. This maximization process can be simplified as:

$$\text{Max: } \ln(L) = \sum_{i=1}^{n} -\ln(\hat{\sigma}_i^2) - \frac{y_i^2}{\hat{\sigma}_i^2} \tag{4.26}$$

Many times, optimization packages will only minimize an equation. In these situations, the parameters are found by minimizing the negative of the log-likelihood function as follows:

$$\text{Min: } -\ln(L) = \sum_{i=1}^{n} \ln(\hat{\sigma}_t^2) + \frac{y_i^2}{\hat{\sigma}_i^2} \tag{4.27}$$

Estimation Results

Our parameter estimation results are displayed in Table 4.4. For the EWMA model, we found $\lambda = 0.88$ for both SP500 and R2000. For the GARCH model, we found $\beta = 0.84$ and $\beta = 0.82$ for R2000. These findings are slightly lower than what has been previously reported for other times in which λ and β are closer to 0.95 and indicate a stronger persistence. This difference is likely due to

Table 4.4 Estimated Parameters

Index	EWMA		GARCH	
	λ	ω	α	β
SP500	0.8808	3.42E-06	0.1519	0.8420
R2000	0.8758	9.92E-06	0.1614	0.8222
Source: Science of Algorithmic Trading and Portfolio Management (Kissell, 2013)				

the cause of volatility persistence over our timeframe: a high volatility regime caused by the debt issues was followed by a lower volatility regime after the issues were resolved. The August 2011 through September 2011 debt issue in the United States was relatively short-lived and was resolved relatively quickly.

Measuring Model Performance

We compared the HMA-VIX technique to the historical moving average (HMA), exponential weighted moving average (EWMA), and generalized autoregressive conditional heteroscedasticity (GARCH) models. We evaluated the performance of the volatility models using three different criteria: root mean square error (RMSE), root mean Z-Score squared error (RMZSE), and an outlier analysis. Menchero, Wang, and Orr (2012) and Patton (2011) provide in-depth discussions of alternative volatility evaluation statistics that can be used to further critique the accuracy of these models. Our usage of these aforementioned performance statistics is to provide a point of comparison across techniques. These procedures are:

Root Mean Square Error (RMSE):

$$RMSE = \sqrt{\frac{1}{n}\sum(\hat{\sigma}_t - \sigma_t)^2} \tag{4.28}$$

The RMSE is simply the difference squared between the estimated volatility $\hat{\sigma}_t$ and realized volatility. Realized volatility was measured as the square root of squared return (e.g., absolute value of return), or $\sigma_t = \sqrt{y_t^2}$. This follows along the lines of the more traditional statistical tests such as minimizing the sum of squares used in regression analysis.

Root Mean Z-Score Squared Error (RMZSE):

$$RMZSE = \sqrt{\frac{1}{n}\sum\left(\frac{y_t^2}{\hat{\sigma}_t^2} - 1\right)^2} \tag{4.29}$$

The RMZSE is a measurement of the squared difference between our test statistic z from 1.

This test is derived as follows. Let, $z = \frac{y - \mu}{\sigma}$. Then we have $E[z] = 0$ and $Var[z] = 1$.

Since we have $y_t \sim N(0, \hat{\sigma}_t^2)$ our test statistic z can be written as $z_t = \frac{y_t}{\hat{\sigma}_t}$. And the variance of z is simply $Var[z_t] = \frac{y_t^2}{\hat{\sigma}_t^2} = 1$. The root mean Z-Score squared error is then a test of how close the test statistic is to its theoretical value.

Outlier Analysis:

The outlier analysis was used to determine the number of times actual returns exceeded a predicted three standard deviation movement. That is:

$$\text{Outlier if } \left| \frac{y_t}{\hat{\sigma}_t} \right| > 3$$

The outlier analysis consists of determining the total number of outliers observed based on the predicted volatility from each model. We choose three standard deviations as the criteria for outliers. If the absolute value of price return for the index was greater than three times the forecasted standard deviation for the index on that day, the observation was counted as an outlier. The goal of the outlier analysis was to determine which model resulted in the fewest number of surprises.

Results:

The HMA-VIX model was found to have significant improvement over the historical moving average model. It also performed better than the GARCH and EWMA models under various test statistics, and as well as the GARCH and EWMA in the other tests.

RMSE Performance Criteria:

The HMA-VIX volatility model was the best-performing model. The EWMA was the second-best model for the SP500 index, followed by the GARCH. The GARCH was the second-best model for the R2000 index, followed by the EWMA. So while the HMA-VIX was the best, there was no clear second-best. As expected, the simple HMA standard deviation model was the worst-performing model for both indexes.

RMZSE Performance Criteria:

The GARCH model was the best-performing model for both SP500 and R2000 indexes. The HMA-VIX was the second-best performing model for the R2000 index, followed by the EWMA. The EWMA was the second-best performing model for the SP500 index, followed closely by HMA-VIX. Therefore, while the GARCH was the best, there was no clear second-best. The HMA-VIX model performed as well as the EWMA, based on the RMZSE analysis.

These testing metrics for the RMSE and RMZSE are shown in Table 4.5.

Outlier Performance Criteria:

The HMA-VIX and GARCH models had the fewest number of outliers (surprises) for predicted SP500 index returns. There were two surprises with these models. The EWMA approach resulted in three outliers, and the HMA resulted in five. The GARCH and EWMA models resulted in two outliers each for the

Table 4.5 Performance Results

Model	SP500		R2000	
	RMSE	RMZSE	RMSE	RMZSE
HMA	0.0106	2.6310	0.0135	4.9373
HMA-VIX	**0.0095**	2.2965	**0.0129**	4.1787
EWMA	0.0102	2.1019	0.0131	4.1824
Garch	0.0103	**1.6825**	0.0131	**3.2585**

Source: Science of Algorithmic Trading and Portfolio Management (Kissell, 2013)

R2000 index. HMA-VIX had three outliers, and the HMA had six. Overall, the GARCH model had the fewest outliers with four total, followed by HMA-VIX and EWMA with five each. The HMA had the most outliers, with 11 total. The total number of outliers from each model is shown in Figure 4.7.

Figure 4.8 compares the GARCH volatility model to the HMA volatility model. Notice the lagged effect using the HMA model compared to actual volatility. The GARCH model updates in a timelier manner. Table 4.8 provides a mathematical comparison of the various volatility models. Figure 4.9 illustrates the ratio of price return divided by predicted HMA-VIX volatility for the SP500 index over our sample period. As shown in this figure, there were two outliers that occurred towards the end of August 2011 during the US debt ceiling crisis.

Under a conservative set of testing criteria, there appears to be compelling statistical evidence that the HMA-VIX adjustment model is as accurate as the EWMA and GARCH models. These are extremely encouraging results, since only the HMA-VIX model is capable of reacting in real-time to market events or potential market events that will impact volatility, but have not yet affected realized market prices. The historical models will not react to these events until that information is captured in the prices. This makes the HMA-VIX a potentially powerful volatility-forecasting model that for intraday trading applications and electronic trading algorithms.

Some of the advantages of the HMA-VIX volatility model over other techniques are:

- Reacts to new information sets prior to those events affecting prices. Historical models will only react to new information after it has already affected prices. There is always some degree of lag when using historical models or models based on realized prices.
- Incorporates real-time information from the options market, e.g., forward-looking implied volatility, across the full universe of stock. Implied stock volatility is only available for a very limited number of stocks.
- Provides necessary real-time volatility estimates that can be incorporated into trading applications and electronic trading algorithms.

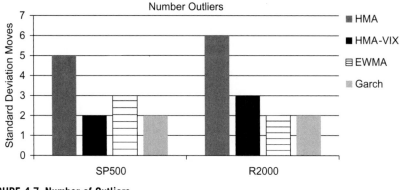

FIGURE 4.7 **Number of Outliers**

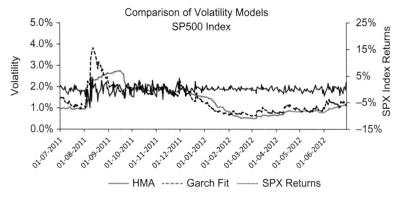

FIGURE 4.8 **Comparison of Volatility Models**

- Allows algorithms to make real-time revisions to their execution strategies, limits order models, and uses smart order-routing logic in real time.
- Performed as well as, and in some cases better than, some of the more traditional volatility-forecasting models.

As a follow-up exercise, we propose further research that combines alternative historical volatility measures with forward-looking implied volatility terms (see Table 4.6). For example, combine the GARCH or EWMA models with an implied volatility term. The implied volatility term can be based on the ratio of the VIX index to trailing SP500 index volatility (as proposed earlier), or possibly based on the net-change or log-change in the VIX index from one period to the next. It is often said that execution performance will only be as good as the models that are used to manage the executions, and that those models are only as good as the accuracy of the forecasted explanatory factors. Since real-time volatility is often a

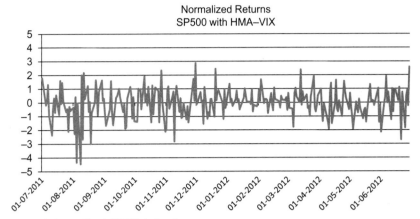

FIGURE 4.9 Normalized SP500 Index Returns

Table 4.6 Comparison of Volatility Models

Volatility Model	Formula	Parameter(s)	Calculation
HMA	$\bar{\sigma}_t^2 = \dfrac{1}{N-1}\displaystyle\sum_{t=1}^{N} r_{t-1}^2$	n/a	By Definition
EWMA	$\bar{\sigma}_t^2 = (1-\lambda)r_{t-1}^2 + \lambda\bar{\sigma}_{t-1}^2$	λ	MLE
ARCH(1)	$\bar{\sigma}_t^2 = \omega + \alpha r_{t-1}^2$	ω, α	OLS
GARCH(1,1)	$\bar{\sigma}_t^2 = \omega + \alpha r_{t-1}^2 + \beta\bar{\sigma}_{t-1}^2$	ω, α, β	MLE
VIX Adj.	$\bar{\sigma}_t^2 = \bar{\sigma}_{t-1}^2 \cdot \left(\dfrac{VIX_{t-1}}{SP_{500}\bar{\sigma}_{t-1}}\right)^2$	n/a	By Definition
	$\bar{\sigma}_t^2 = \beta_0 + \beta_1 \cdot VIX_{t-1}^2$	β_0, β_1	OLS

key explanatory factor in these models, having improved volatility forecasts on hand will likely lead to more accurate models. And having more accurate models will allow investors to better react to changing market conditions. Most importantly, this ensures consistency between trading decisions and investing objectives of the fund.

Cross-Sectional Comparison

The next step of our analysis was to perform a cross-sectional analysis of volatility model parameters across the different indexes in order to determine if the models work well and if the parameters are robust and consistent across indexes and stocks. The indexes we analyzed consisted of SP500, SP400, SP600, R1000, R2000, NYSE, and NASDAQ over the period 2011. We performed the analysis using the GARCH(1,1) model.

Table 4.7 shows the results of our GARCH, ARCH, and EWMA model analysis. The volatility parameters were pretty consistent across indexes. Notice the consistency in parameter estimates for the SP500 and R1000 indexes (both represent large-cap stocks), as well as the consistency in parameter estimates for the SP600 and R2000 indexes (both represent small-cap stocks). This provides a nice additional level of verification around our approach. Table 4.8 compares the results of these models to actual price movement in the respective indexes. Using the RMSE test procedure, we find that our HMA-VIX model consistently provides the lowest error across indexes. The GARCH and EWMA models have the next-best-fitting model. Using the MHSE test procedure, we find that the GARCH model has the lowest error, followed by the HMA-VIX model. This further supports the HMA-VIX model and insight that can be obtained from the options market.

Historical Analysis of GARCH Parameters

In this section we analyze the robustness of a GARCH model. Our sample universe consists of equities (SP500, R2000, and MSCI indexes), commodities (gold, silver, oil, and natural gas), and exchange rates (GBP, EUR, and JPY). We estimate the parameters of the GARCH volatility model using daily log price change data over a ten year period (2003−2012). The parameters were estimated for each financial asset for each year using the maximum likelihood estimation techniques described earlier in this chapter. The GARCH volatility model equation we are using is:

$$\hat{\sigma}_t^2 = \omega + \alpha \sigma_{t-1}^2 + \beta \hat{\sigma}_{t-1}^2$$

Table 4.9 shows the estimated parameters for the GARCH(1,1) model for each of our financial assets. For the most part, the estimated parameters were relatively stable from year to year. There were, however, a few years where the financial assets exhibited large and sudden change. For example, the GARCH model parameters for silver changed in 2006, but reverted back to long-term patterns in 2007. All parameters exhibited a change in 2008 due to the financial crisis, reverting back in 2009. Additionally, the parameters exhibited another change in 2011, most likely due to the US debt ceiling crisis and the ongoing macro-economic events in Europe. In most instances, the beta parameter of the GARCH model has a higher weight than the alpha parameter.

Figure 4.10 provides a graphical comparison of the parameters. Figure 4.10a illustrates the alpha parameters for the GARCH volatility model. Figure 4.11b illustrates the beta parameters for the GARCH volatility model. Notice the spike in silver in 2006, as well as the changes for both parameters in 2008 and again in 2011. This graph shows the robustness of the estimated GARCH parameters over

Table 4.7 Estimated Parameters: Jan 2011–Dec 2011

	SP500	SP400	SP600	R1000	R2000	NYSE	Nasdaq
GARCH Estimates							
K	0.00005	0.00007	0.00008	0.00005	9.13E-05	0.00007	0.00007
GARCH	0.81281	0.82498	0.82191	0.81536	0.8266	0.81416	0.84217
ARCH	0.17083	0.16216	0.16689	0.16970	0.1591	0.16911	0.13148
ARCH Estimates							
K	0.00016	0.00024	0.00030	0.00017	0.00031	0.00019	0.00020
ARCH	0.24676	0.25974	0.25939	0.24447	0.28308	0.23794	0.22860
EWMA Estimates							
Lambda	0.9039	0.8922	0.8815	0.9019	0.8902	0.9065	0.9182

Table 4.8 Performance Analysis: Jan 2011–Dec 2011

RMSE Error Analysis

Model	SP500	SP400	SP600	R1000	R2000	NYSE	NASDAQ
HMA	0.00011	0.00015	0.00018	0.00011	0.00020	0.00012	0.00012
HMA / VIX	0.00009	0.00012	0.00015	0.00009	0.00016	0.00010	0.00010
GARCH	0.00010	0.00015	0.00018	0.00011	0.00019	0.00012	0.00012
ARCH	0.00012	0.00017	0.00020	0.00013	0.00022	0.00014	0.00013
EWMA	0.00010	0.00014	0.00017	0.00010	0.00019	0.00011	0.00011

MHSE Error Analysis

Model	SP500	SP400	SP600	R1000	R2000	NYSE	NASDAQ
HMA	0.62210	0.56939	0.55618	0.61843	0.57334	0.60231	0.58633
HMA / VIX	0.57159	0.54127	0.52654	0.56880	0.52915	0.56683	0.53056
GARCH	0.46722	0.42640	0.41847	0.46341	0.42599	0.46400	0.45564
ARCH	0.59703	0.54973	0.52555	0.59694	0.53245	0.58185	0.55219
EWMA	0.54044	0.48404	0.47568	0.53481	0.48738	0.53007	0.52170

Table 4.9 GARCH Volatility Model: Estimated Parameters

	2003	2004	2005	2006	2007	2008	2009	2010	2011	2012
SP500										
K	2.00E-07	4.72E-05	5.64E-06	8.90E-07	5.48E-06	7.04E-06	7.20E-07	3.38E-06	5.45E-05	4.57E-06
ARCH	0.0357	0.0355	0.0917	0.0408	0.0754	0.1364	0.0559	0.1086	0.1708	0.0382
GARCH	0.9576	0.9328	0.7723	0.9344	0.8731	0.8578	0.9372	0.8684	0.8128	0.8910
R2000										
K	1.38E-04	2.00E-07	1.24E-05	2.90E-06	1.92E-06	1.02E-05	2.44E-06	4.02E-06	9.13E-05	4.22E-06
ARCH	0.0269	0.0206	0.0526	0.0474	0.0366	0.1547	0.0638	0.1038	0.1591	0.0369
GARCH	0.9150	0.9763	0.8261	0.9274	0.9555	0.8379	0.9275	0.8811	0.8266	0.9249
MSCI										
K	2.00E-07	4.08E-06	2.33E-05	8.98E-07	4.44E-06	3.56E-06	4.93E-07	3.77E-06	3.01E-06	1.54E-06
ARCH	0.0555	0.0873	0.0390	0.0938	0.1036	0.1654	0.0408	0.0762	0.1172	0.0272
GARCH	0.9370	0.7977	0.9054	0.8779	0.8273	0.8318	0.9530	0.8888	0.8733	0.9479
Gold										
K	9.75E-06	8.78E-06	3.50E-07	1.86E-06	1.31E-05	1.23E-05	3.25E-06	6.03E-06	5.37E-06	2.00E-07
ARCH	0.0330	0.0285	0.0160	0.0662	0.0331	0.0601	0.0586	0.0353	0.1193	0.0095
GARCH	0.8751	0.9175	0.9801	0.9241	0.8444	0.9087	0.9222	0.9019	0.8527	0.9865
Silver										
K	4.24E-05	1.08E-04	2.97E-06	8.43E-05	2.21E-04	1.79E-05	3.21E-06	1.83E-05	2.52E-04	2.00E-07
ARCH	0.0710	0.0788	0.0123	0.3385	0.1096	0.1336	0.0175	0.0895	0.2554	0.0000
GARCH	0.6478	0.6898	0.9693	0.5779	0.7658	0.8615	0.9735	0.8582	0.4217	0.9984

Oil										
K	3.13E-05	3.31E-05	1.44E-04	1.75E-05	3.31E-05	2.53E-05	4.45E-06	4.79E-05	1.65E-04	1.14E-04
ARCH	0.0432	0.0337	0.0522	0.0691	0.0237	0.1335	0.0561	0.0940	0.0537	0.0452
GARCH	0.9049	0.9062	0.6387	0.8815	0.8733	0.8262	0.9329	0.7465	0.9056	0.8760
Nat Gas										
K	5.96E-04	1.99E-05	5.59E-06	1.95E-05	6.42E-05	1.04E-05	7.97E-05	6.40E-04	4.83E-04	5.75E-05
ARCH	0.0444	0.0814	0.0492	0.0679	0.0218	0.0475	0.0630	0.0449	0.0329	0.0470
GARCH	0.8201	0.9064	0.9107	0.9111	0.9423	0.9460	0.9047	0.9022	0.8935	0.8951
GBP										
K	1.16E-06	3.33E-07	1.63E-05	2.43E-07	2.00E-07	6.18E-07	2.00E-07	2.27E-06	2.17E-05	6.59E-07
ARCH	0.0374	0.0248	0.0610	0.0190	0.0000	0.0662	0.0203	0.0218	0.0355	0.0523
GARCH	0.9154	0.9650	0.9317	0.9690	0.9914	0.9129	0.9740	0.9135	0.8995	0.9070
EUR										
K	3.53E-05	2.00E-07	2.96E-05	2.00E-07	2.00E-07	4.32E-07	2.58E-07	8.26E-07	1.77E-06	6.51E-07
ARCH	0.0029	0.0163	0.0122	0.0107	0.0172	0.0328	0.0221	0.0056	0.0144	0.0220
GARCH	0.9416	0.9767	0.9217	0.9789	0.9689	0.9462	0.9702	0.9766	0.9511	0.9540
JPY										
K	8.48E-06	5.13E-06	1.56E-05	2.00E-07	9.02E-07	1.66E-06	7.14E-05	3.79E-05	6.78E-06	7.72E-07
ARCH	0.0453	0.1009	0.0485	0.0090	0.0455	0.0743	0.0433	0.0737	0.0277	0.0308
GARCH	0.6404	0.7735	0.8596	0.9815	0.8597	0.9112	0.9015	0.8535	0.7339	0.9337

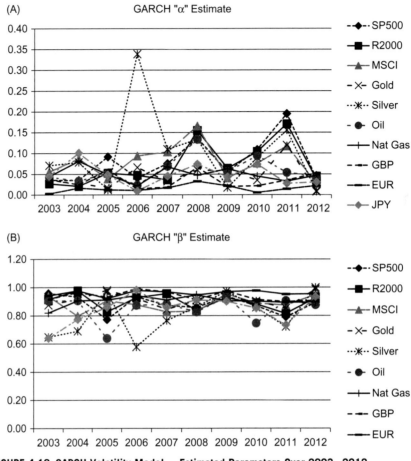

FIGURE 4.10 GARCH Volatility Model — Estimated Parameters Over 2003–2012

time and across asset classes. Readers interested in a larger understanding of the volatility structure of the financial markets are encouraged to further analyze these parameter estimates to determine if the change from one year to the next is statistically significant.

Volatility Scaling

In this section we provide techniques that can be used to evaluate long-term volatility scaling properties. The techniques are based on a field of mathematics known as fractal analysis (aka, fractal geometry) and have been developed by

Hurst (1950, 1951), Mandelbrot (1982), Peters (1991), and Hastings and Sugihara (1993).

These methodologies are extremely useful for investors to test for data independence and long-term scaling trends, such as trending persistence and/or mean reversion.

Most financial practitioners are well aware that volatility scales with the square root of time, and variance scales with time. For example, if the current daily volatility is 2%, the volatility after 1 year is $2\% \cdot \sqrt{250} = 31.62\%$. If the current daily variance is 0.04%, then the variance after one year is $0.04\% \cdot 250 = 0.1000 = 10\%$ (based on 250 trading days in a year).

Formulaically, this is written for variance and volatility as follows:

$$\sigma(t) = \sqrt{t} \cdot \sigma$$
$$\sigma^2(t) = t \cdot \sigma^2$$

From these mathematical relationships, we can write a general scaling property for growth of variance and growth of standard deviation (Hastings & Segihara, 1993) as follows:

Growth of Variance:

$$\sigma^2(\Delta t) = \Delta t^{2H} \cdot \sigma^2 \tag{4.30}$$

Growth of Standard Deviation:

$$\sigma(\Delta t) = \Delta t^{H} \cdot \sigma \tag{4.31}$$

where the exponent H is known as the Hurst Exponent (Hurst, 1950).

Analysts can infer different data trends based on the value of the Hurst exponent. For example,

$$= \begin{cases} H < 1/2 & \rightarrow mean\ reversion \\ H = 1/2 & \rightarrow independent\ data\ series \\ H > 1/2 & \rightarrow trend\ is\ persistent \end{cases}$$

These relationships are used to test for long-term data trends. If we find that $H = 1/2$, then we have statistical evidence that the data is independent. If $H < 1/2$, then there is statistical evidence that the data series is subject to mean reversion in which above-average data values tend to be followed by below-average data values, and below-average data values tend to be followed by above-average data values. If $H > 1/2$, then there is statistical evidence that the data series is subject to trend persistence in which above-average data values tend to be followed by above-average data values, and below-average data values tend to be followed by below-average data values.

Another useful property of random variables that can be used to evaluate data independence and scaling trends is based on chi-square distribution. If $x \sim N(0, 1)$ then $x^2 \sim Chi - Square(1)$ (e.g., the square of a standard normal random variable will have a chi-square distribution with one degree of freedom).

The sum of squares of random iid normal random variables $x \sim N(0, 1)$ is:

$$X = \sum_{i=1}^{t} x_i^2$$

Here, X has a chi-square distribution with t degrees of freedom with expected value and variance:

$$E[X] = t$$

$$V[X] = 2t$$

Then we can formulate a general sum of squares relationship using the Hurst Exponent as follows:

Sum of Squared Returns:

$$X = 2H \cdot t \tag{4.32}$$

where

$$= \sum_{i=1}^{t} x_i^2$$

Similar to the growth of variance and growth of standard deviation, the Hurst exponent H will provide insight into whether successive returns are independent, trending, or mean-reverting.

Long-Term Trend Analysis:

We performed an analysis of volatility scaling properties over the ten year period 2002–2011 to determine if we can uncover any long-term trends. We evaluated eight index return series: SP500, SP400, SP600, R1000, R2000, NYSE, and NASDAQ. Our analysis consisted of estimating the Hurst Exponent following the previous techniques (see Hastings & Sugihara, 1993) for time periods from 1 to 10 years.

Table 4.10 shows the estimated Hurst exponent for each of our analyses. For the growth of variance and sum of squared returns, we reported the value $2 \cdot H$ and for the growth of standard deviation, we reported the value H. Independent data series will have theoretical values for growth of variance and sum of squared returns of $2H = 1$ and for growth of standard deviation of $H = 1/2$

The analysis results find that for the shorter term (days $< 30-60$), data is scaling following a trending series, for mid-term (years 1–3 years), data is scaling following a mean-reverting pattern, and for the longer term (years 4–10), the scaling properties adhere to the expected trends of independent data series. This is consistent with empirical findings, and further justifies the usage of time-varying volatility models. Figure 4.11a–c depicts the data in Table 4.10. Figure 4.12a–c compares the Hurst exponent for shorter times for a one-day and a 10-year series.

Table 4.10 Volatility Scaling Properties

Calculated Hurst Exponent: "2 * H"

Growth of Variance

Index\Years	1	2	3	4	5	6	7	8	9	10
SP500	0.773	0.846	0.887	0.899	0.902	0.900	0.899	0.897	0.900	0.905
SP400	0.806	0.851	0.882	0.947	0.948	0.941	0.942	0.939	0.941	0.943
SP600	0.794	0.845	0.898	0.928	0.925	0.917	0.916	0.913	0.917	0.927
R1000	0.779	0.849	0.887	0.910	0.912	0.910	0.909	0.907	0.910	0.914
R2000	0.800	0.848	0.887	0.914	0.910	0.903	0.904	0.902	0.911	0.926
NYSE	0.771	0.845	0.895	0.912	0.914	0.913	0.914	0.913	0.921	0.924
NASDAQ	0.753	0.859	0.866	0.927	0.934	0.934	0.935	0.936	0.932	0.933

Growth of Stdev: "H"

Index\Years	1	2	3	4	5	6	7	8	9	10
SP500	0.387	0.423	0.444	0.450	0.451	0.450	0.449	0.449	0.450	0.452
SP400	0.403	0.425	0.441	0.473	0.474	0.470	0.471	0.469	0.470	0.472
SP600	0.397	0.423	0.449	0.464	0.462	0.458	0.458	0.457	0.459	0.464
R1000	0.390	0.424	0.443	0.455	0.456	0.455	0.454	0.454	0.455	0.457
R2000	0.400	0.424	0.444	0.457	0.455	0.451	0.452	0.451	0.456	0.463
NYSE	0.385	0.423	0.447	0.456	0.457	0.457	0.457	0.457	0.461	0.462
NASDAQ	0.377	0.430	0.433	0.464	0.467	0.467	0.468	0.468	0.466	0.466

Sum of Squared Returns: "H"

Index\Years	1	2	3	4	5	6	7	8	9	10
SP500	1.022	1.005	0.991	1.004	1.005	1.004	1.003	1.002	1.000	1.001
SP400	1.021	1.005	0.992	1.004	1.004	1.003	1.002	1.002	1.000	1.001
SP600	1.018	1.005	0.992	1.003	1.004	1.003	1.002	1.002	1.001	1.001
R1000	1.022	1.005	0.991	1.004	1.005	1.004	1.003	1.002	1.000	1.001
R2000	1.019	1.006	0.992	1.003	1.004	1.003	1.002	1.002	1.001	1.001
NYSE	1.021	1.004	0.992	1.004	1.005	1.004	1.003	1.002	1.000	1.001
NASDAQ	1.021	1.005	0.989	1.003	1.005	1.003	1.002	1.002	0.999	1.000

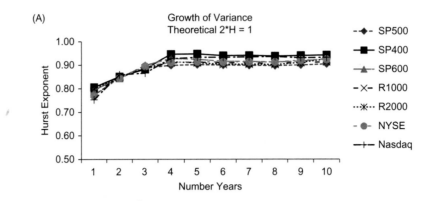

FIGURE 4.11A Growth of Variance

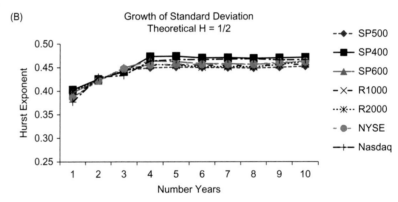

FIGURE 4.11B Growth of Standard Deviation

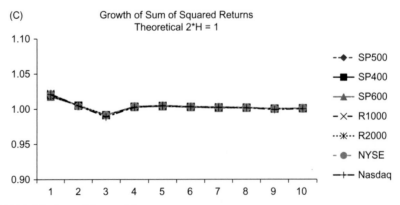

FIGURE 4.11C Sum of Squared Returns

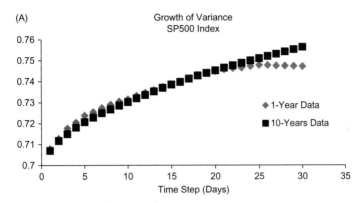

FIGURE 4.12A Variance Scaling Properties

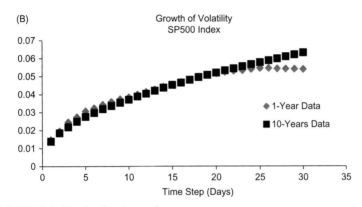

FIGURE 4.12B Volatility Scaling Properties

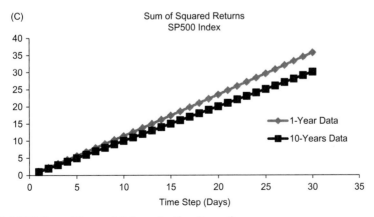

FIGURE 4.12C Sum of Squared Returns Scaling Properties

CONCLUSIONS

In this chapter we provided readers with an overview of price volatility. We provided a theoretical explanation of the different definitions of volatility, as well as empirical data and statistical evidence. We showed how the options market can provide significant insight into changing volatility structures. The advantage here is that analysts can couple a real-time volatility estimate from the options markets with an historical volatility metric to better forecast real-time volatility. The chapter concluded with an examination of the volatility parameters across stocks and across time, and an in-depth analysis of techniques that can be used to investigate long-term volatility scaling properties based on fractal analysis theory.

References

Bollerslev, T., 1986. Generalized Autoregressive Conditional Heteroskedasticity. J. Econom. 31, 307–327.

Engle, R., 1982. Autoregressive conditional heteroscedasticity with estimates of the variance of United Kingdom inflation. Econometrica., 987–1007.

Hastings, H.M., Sugihara, G., 1993. Fractals: A User's Guide for the Natural Sciences. Oxford Science Publications.

Hastings, H.M., Kissell, R., 1998. Is the Nile Outflow Fractal? Hurst's Analysis Revisited. Nat. Resour. Model. 11 (2).

Hurst, H.E., 1950. Long-term storage capacity of reservoirs. Am. Soc. Civ. Engrs. Proc v76, April 1950. Also reprinted: Transactions of the American Society of Civil Engineers 116 pp. 770–808, Sept 1951.

Morgan/Reuters, J.P., 1996. Risk Metrics™ – Technical Document, fourth ed., <http://gloria-mundi.com/UploadFile/2010-2/rmtd.pdf>.

Kissell, R., 2009. Volatility: is it safe to get back into the water? CQA/SQA Trading Seminar, <http://sqa-us.org/cde.cfm?event=248380>.

Kissell, Fall 2009. Introduction to Algorithmic Trading: Cornell University, Graduate School of Financial Engineering- Manhattan, Class Notes.

Kissell, Fall 2010. Introduction to Algorithmic Trading: Cornell University, Graduate School of Financial Engineering- Manhattan, Class Notes.

Kissell, R., 2011. Creating dynamic pretrade models: beyond the black box. J. Trading 6 (4), 8–15, Fall 2011.

Kissell, R., 2012. Intraday volatility models: methods to improve real-time forecasts. J. Trading 7 (4), 27–34, Fall 2012.

Kissell, R., 2013. The Science of Algorithmic Trading and Portfolio Management. Elsevier, New York.

Mandelbrot, B.B., 1982. The Fractal Geometry of Nature. Freeman, San Francisco, NY.

Menchero, J., Wang, J., Orr, D.J., 2012. Improving risk forecasts for optimized portfolios. Financ. Analysts J. 68 (3), 40–50.

Patton, A., 2011. Volatility forecast comparison using imperfect volatility proxies. J. Econom. 160 (1), 246–256.

Peters, E. (1989), Fractal structure in the capital markets," Financ. Analysts J., July/August 1989.

Peters, E., 1991. Chaos and Order in the Capital Markets. John Wiley & Sons.

Peters, E., 1994. Fractal Market Analysis. John Wiley & Sons.

Factor Models

5

The use of factor models in the financial industry has gained increased popularity recently. Much of this is due to the continued market turmoil and asset price uncertainty. Analysts are now turning to factor risk models to estimate asset returns and corresponding financial risk, rather than relying on their traditional approaches that all too often have proven unreliable.

The analyst's goal in using factor risk models is to determine a set of factors (e.g., explanatory variables) that will explain price movement. In these situations, analysts who are able to successfully forecast these factors or these factor returns will also be in a position to successfully forecast asset returns (the ultimate goal of financial management!). These factors models have also become increasingly popular for estimating asset volatility and (especially) covariance and correlation across asset returns. As we show ahead, the reason behind using factor risk models to estimate covariance and co-movement is that historical data alone is often unreliable and leads to incorrect estimates.

In this chapter, we focus our attention on the usage of factor risk models to estimate these covariance and correlation terms.

Data Limitations

Why do we need risk models at all when we can simply measure volatility, covariance, and correlation directly from the underlying asset returns data? Isn't it possible for analysts to use historical returns data and to determine co-movement across asset returns rather than implement a sophisticated risk modeling approach? The answer to these questions is simple and might even surprise some of the most seasoned practitioners. First, historical data is subject to a great deal of false relationships. For example, it is possible for two assets to move in the same direction (both assets increase in value or both assets decrease in value), but have a negative correlation measure, and it is possible for two assets to move in opposite directions (one asset increases in value and one asset decreases in value), but have a positive correlation measure. Second, in most situations we do not have enough historical data to determine a statistically significant correlation measure. In this case, there is a data limitation issue. Mathematicians refer to this as a degrees of freedom issue.

What effect can false relationships have in the process? Having incorrect false relationships in the data could have dire consequences on the portfolio management practices. Managers who uncover a false positive correlation relationship may implement a risk management approach to hold one asset long and short the other assets, believing that this will result in reduced risk. They believe that regardless of market movement, the gain on one asset will offset the loss on the other asset. For example, if the market increases the manager will lose on the asset they are short, but gain on the asset they are long, and thus have a net position that is unchanged (or at least a much smaller change). Similarly, if the market decreases, the manager will lose on the asset they are long, but earn a profit on the asset that they are short. Again, the net fund position will remain unchanged (or at least a much smaller change). Thus the portfolio has less potential for large price swings.

Managers who uncover a false negative correlation relationship between two assets may choose to hold both assets long in the portfolios. They would expect that regardless of market movement that loss that might be incurred in one asset will be offset by the gain in the other asset. A negative correlation is meant to imply that the stocks will move in opposite directions, but as we show ahead, this is not necessarily true. In both situations described previously, the manager could incur losses from both assets or gains from both assets, thus making their portfolio holdings much more risky then they may be led to believe.

Ahead we highlight two issues that may arise when relying on historical data for calculation of covariance and correlation across stocks using historical price returns. As explained in our examples, these issues can have dire consequences on the value of the portfolio. These are:

• False relationships
• Degrees of freedom

In the descriptions ahead we borrow from *The Science of Algorithmic Trading*, (Kissell, 2013), and we additionally provide further enhancement of these points through empirical examples and market observations.

False Relationships

It is possible for two stocks to move in same direction and have a negative calculated covariance and correlation measure, and it is possible for two stocks to move in the opposite direction and have a positive calculated covariance and correlation measure. Reliance on market data to compute covariance or correlation between stocks can result in false measures.

Following the mathematical definition of covariance and correlation we find that the covariance of price change between two stocks is really a measure of the co-movement of the "error terms" of each stock, not the co-movement of prices. For example, the statistical definition of covariance between two random variables x and y is:

$$\sigma_{xy} = E[(x - \bar{x})(y - \bar{y})]$$

It is quite possible for two stocks to have the same exact trend, but for their errors (noise term) to be on opposite sides of the trend lines. For example, if $\bar{x} = \bar{y} = z$, $x = d$, $y = -d$ and $d > z$, our covariance calculation is:

$$E[(x - \bar{x})(y - \bar{y})] = E[(d - z)(-d - z)] = E[-d^2 + z^2]$$

Since $d > z$ we have $E[-d^2 + z^2] < 0$ which is a negative measured covariance term indicating the stocks trend in opposite directions. But these two stocks move in exactly the same direction, namely, z.

It is also possible for two stocks to move in opposite directions, but have a positive covariance measure. For example, if $\bar{x} = z$ and $\bar{y} = -z$, $x = y = d$, and $d > z$, the covariance calculation is:

$$E[(x - \bar{x})(y - \bar{y})] = E[(d - z)(d - - z)] = E[d^2 - z^2]$$

Since $d > z$ we have $E[d^2 - z^2] > 0$, which is a positive measured covariance term indicating the stocks trend in the same direction. But these two stocks move in the exact opposite direction.

The most important finding from the previous example is that when we compute covariance and correlation on a stock-by-stock basis using historical returns and price data, it is possible that the calculated measure is opposite what is happening in the market. These "false positive" and/or "false negative" relationships may be due to the error term about the trend rather than the trend, or possibly due to too few data points in our sample.

Example 5.1: False Negative Signal Calculations

Table 5.1 contains the data for two stocks A & B that are moving in the same direction. Figure 5.1a illustrates this movement over 24 periods. But when we calculate the covariance between these stocks, we get a negative correlation, rho $= -0.71$. How can stocks that move in the same direction have a negative covariance term? The answer is due to the excess terms being on opposite sides of the price trend (Figure 5.1b). Notice that these excess returns are now on opposite sides of the trend, which results in a negative covariance measure. The excess returns are indeed negatively correlated, but the direction of trend is positively correlated.

Example 5.2: False Positive Signal Calculation

Table 5.2 contains the data for two stocks C & D that are moving in opposite directions. Figure 5.2a illustrates this movement over 24 periods. But when

Table 5.1 False Negative Signals

Period	Market Prices		Period Returns		Excess Returns	
	A	B	A	B	A	B
0	10.00	20.00				
1	11.42	22.17	13.3%	10.3%	7.0%	5.3%
2	11.12	25.48	−2.6%	13.9%	−8.8%	8.9%
3	12.60	28.62	12.5%	11.6%	6.3%	6.6%
4	12.96	33.56	2.8%	15.9%	−3.4%	10.9%
5	16.91	30.59	26.6%	−9.3%	20.4%	−14.3%
6	17.63	33.58	4.2%	9.3%	−2.0%	4.3%
7	17.78	37.86	0.8%	12.0%	−5.4%	7.0%
8	19.93	38.93	11.4%	2.8%	5.2%	−2.2%
9	23.13	38.94	14.9%	0.0%	8.7%	−5.0%
10	24.21	39.64	4.6%	1.8%	−1.6%	−3.2%
11	23.39	46.32	−3.5%	15.6%	−9.7%	10.6%
12	23.92	49.59	2.3%	6.8%	−3.9%	1.8%
13	25.50	51.45	6.4%	3.7%	0.2%	−1.3%
14	23.97	56.96	−6.2%	10.2%	−12.4%	5.2%
15	27.35	56.60	13.2%	−0.6%	7.0%	−5.6%
16	31.27	57.37	13.4%	1.3%	7.2%	−3.7%
17	30.03	61.26	−4.0%	6.6%	−10.2%	1.6%
18	36.04	61.02	18.2%	−0.4%	12.0%	−5.4%
19	32.01	67.66	−11.9%	10.3%	−18.1%	5.3%
20	33.16	69.90	3.5%	3.3%	−2.7%	−1.7%
21	37.32	66.33	11.8%	−5.2%	5.6%	−10.2%
22	34.71	73.60	−7.3%	10.4%	−13.5%	5.4%
23	39.08	71.58	11.9%	−2.8%	5.7%	−7.8%
24	44.33	66.43	12.6%	−7.5%	6.4%	−12.5%
Avg:			6.2%	5.0%	0.0%	0.0%
Correl:			−0.71		−0.71	

Source: Science of Algorithmic Trading (Kissell, 2013)

we calculate the covariance between these stocks, we get a negative correlation, rho = +0.90. How can stocks that move in the same direction have a negative covariance term? The answer is due to the excess terms being on the same side of the price trend. Figure 5.2b illustrates the excess return in each time period. Notice that these excess returns are now on opposite sides of the trend, which results in a negative covariance measure. The excess returns are indeed positively correlated, but the direction of trend is negatively correlated.

(A)

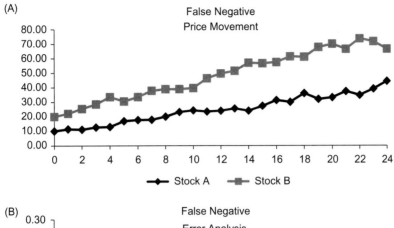

(B)

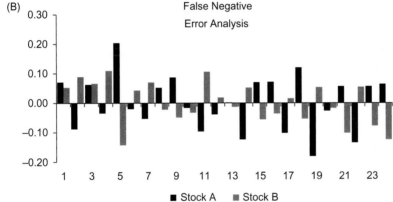

FIGURE 5.1 False Negative Signal

Empirical Evidence: False Signals

An interesting thing about financial theory is that many times in practice the empirical data does not conform to theory. Why is this so? There are many theories to explain why, and even these theories often break down. Many analysts' favorite saying to explain why things didn't happen the way they predicted is simply, "There was a regime shift." (I am still trying to figure out what that really means!). If regime shifts happen too often, it is more likely indicating issues with the risk-management practice or underlying data.

To determine if false positive relationships really occur in the market and how often they appear, we set out to test actual stock data. We compared computed covariance within a period to actual returns in the same period. It is important to note that we did not set out to test the accuracy of the covariance measure. We were much more conservative and only wanted to determine if the sign of the covariance measure was an indication of co-price movement. In other words, we

Table 5.2 False Positive Signals

Period	Market Prices		Period Returns		Excess Returns	
	C	D	C	D	C	D
0	60.00	50.00				
1	65.11	50.82	8.2%	1.6%	5.5%	5.1%
2	63.43	45.93	− 2.6%	− 10.1%	− 5.3%	− 6.6%
3	71.51	47.43	12.0%	3.2%	9.3%	6.7%
4	60.90	37.31	− 16.1%	− 24.0%	− 18.7%	− 20.5%
5	93.93	58.09	43.3%	44.3%	40.7%	47.8%
6	85.83	50.77	− 9.0%	− 13.5%	− 11.7%	− 10.0%
7	68.19	28.10	− 23.0%	− 59.2%	− 25.7%	− 55.7%
8	73.95	36.34	8.1%	25.7%	5.5%	29.2%
9	88.56	42.51	18.0%	15.7%	15.4%	19.2%
10	100.69	52.41	12.8%	20.9%	10.2%	24.4%
11	95.29	40.31	− 5.5%	− 26.3%	− 8.2%	− 22.8%
12	112.56	42.10	16.7%	4.3%	14.0%	7.8%
13	99.59	37.12	− 12.2%	− 12.6%	− 14.9%	− 9.1%
14	95.56	30.63	− 4.1%	− 19.2%	− 6.8%	− 15.7%
15	103.88	34.49	8.3%	11.9%	5.7%	15.4%
16	119.10	44.81	13.7%	26.2%	11.0%	29.7%
17	100.88	24.90	− 16.6%	− 58.7%	− 19.3%	− 55.3%
18	117.90	33.90	15.6%	30.9%	12.9%	34.3%
19	143.46	39.28	19.6%	14.7%	17.0%	18.2%
20	118.28	28.70	− 19.3%	− 31.4%	− 22.0%	− 27.9%
21	108.05	18.39	− 9.0%	− 44.5%	− 11.7%	− 41.0%
22	137.49	34.52	24.1%	63.0%	21.4%	66.5%
23	147.63	41.95	7.1%	19.5%	4.4%	23.0%
24	113.77	21.63	− 26.1%	− 66.2%	− 28.7%	− 62.7%
Avg:			2.7%	− 3.5%	0.0%	0.0%
Correl:			0.90		0.90	

Source: Science of Algorithmic Trading (Kissell, 2013)

wanted to test whether or not, if the sign of the covariance measure was positive, the stock prices would move in the same direction (e.g., both stocks are up or both stocks are down), and, if the sign of the covariance measure was negative, if the stock prices would move in opposite directions (e.g., one stock increases and one stock decreases). The analysis performed is as follows.

Sample Universe
Our sample universe consisted of all stocks for which we had complete data over the full analysis period.

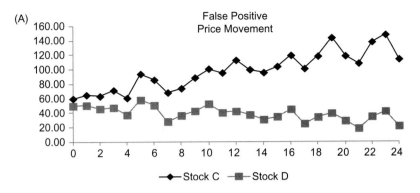

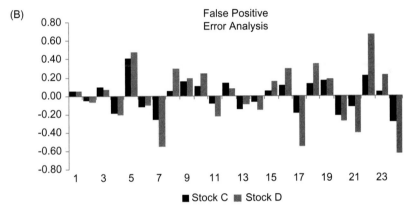

FIGURE 5.2 False Positive Signal

- SP500 Index (489 large-cap stocks)
- R2000 Index (1561 small-cap stocks

Date Period
Two years of data broken up over four six-month periods of data to determine stability of measures.

- January–June 2011
- July–December 2011
- January–June 2012
- July–December 2012

Calculation
- Covariance was computed using daily price change
- Return was computed as the total price movement over the period

Experiment

Our analysis consisted of computing the covariance across every pair of stock, and comparing whether the sign of the covariance metric was an indication of whether or not the stocks would move together in the same direction. Both metrics were computed from the same exact period and using the same exact data. For example, if the sign of the covariance between two stocks was positive, and the stocks both moved in the same direction, then the covariance metric provided a correct signal; but if the sign of the covariance measure was positive, and one stock was up and one stock was down, the covariance metric provided a false signal. The goal of the experiment was to determine how often we could get these negative signals.

Results

The results of our experiment were quite shocking. We found that using historical covariance computed from actual data would only provide a correct price movement signal for large-cap SP500 stocks 57% of the time (across all four periods). Thus, the historical covariance metric provided an incorrect signal 43% of time on average. And this is even using the same in-sample data! The results were very similar for small-cap R2000 stocks. The historical covariance metric only provided a correct price movement signal 54% of the time and provided an incorrect price movement signal 46% of the time! We leave it as an exercise for analysts to determine if these findings were specific for 2011–2012 and for our stock universe, or if they do indeed happen as often across different assets and time periods. We recommend analysts perform the same testing we performed previously for their specific financial instruments. Table 5.3 shows the actual price signal results for the SP500 and R2000 indexes for different periods of time.

Actual Stock Example

Figure 5.3 illustrates the previously experiment for two stocks ("A" and "ADM") over the period January 2011 through June 2011. The computed correlation of daily

Table 5.3 Actual Price Signal Results

Period	SP500 Correct	SP500 False	R2000 Correct	R2000 False
1/3/2011 – 6/30/2011	57%	43%	50%	50%
7/1/2011 – 12/30/2011	55%	45%	58%	42%
1/3/2012 – 6/29/2012	56%	44%	54%	46%
7/2/2012 – 6/30/2012	58%	42%	53%	47%
Avg	57%	43%	54%	46%

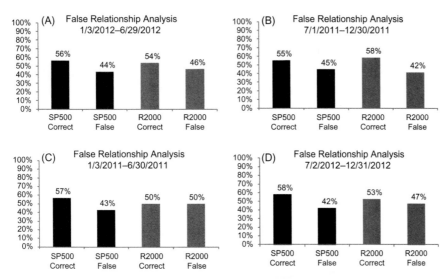

FIGURE 5.3 False Correlation Relationship Illustration for SP500 & R2000 Index

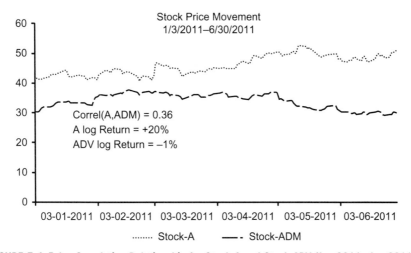

FIGURE 5.4 False Correlation Relationship for Stock A and Stock ADV (Jan 2011–Jun 2011)

log returns over this period was $\rho = 0.36$, which is often taken to be an indication that the stocks move up and down together. But the log return over the period for A was $+20\%$, and the log return for ADM over the period was -1%. Therefore, stock A and stock ADM moved in opposite directions over the period, but the calculated correlation was positive. Figure 5.4 illustrates price movement for each

9

stock. Notice that these prices begin to deviate and move in opposite directions starting around April 2011, but the computed correlation is still positive.

Conclusion

Our conclusion from this experiment is that relying on historical data alone, albeit daily price movement over a short horizon, has a very high likelihood of providing incorrect price movement signals. The mathematical theory previously discussed is not a rare event or a corner-case situation. This does indeed happen quite often. It is very important to further point out here that traders and portfolio managers are quite interested in short-term daily price movement, whether it be for stocks, bonds, FX, etc. Therefore, even relying on simple math formulas to determine a relationship between stocks is quite difficult.

To correct for covariance and correlation, it is advised to compare stock price movement based on a common trend (such as the market index) or a multi-factor model. Factor models are discussed further ahead.

Degrees of Freedom

A portfolio's covariance matrix consists of stock variances along the diagonal terms and covariance terms on the off diagonals. The covariance matrix is a symmetric matrix since the covariance between stock A and stock B is identical to the covariance between stock B and stock A.

If a portfolio consists of n-stocks, the covariance matrix will be $n \times n$ with n^2 total elements. The number of unique variance terms in the matrix is equal to the number of stocks n. The number of covariance terms is equal to $(n^2 - n)$, and the number of unique covariance terms is $(n^2 - n)/2 = n \cdot (n - 1)/2$.

The number of unique covariance parameters can also be determined from:

$$Unique\ Covariances = \binom{n}{2} = \frac{n(n-1)}{2} \tag{5.1}$$

The number of total unique elements "k" in the $n \times n$ covariance matrix is equal to the total number of variances plus the total number of unique covariances. This is:

$$k = n + \frac{n(n-1)}{2} = \frac{n \cdot (n+1)}{2} \tag{5.2}$$

In order to estimate these total parameters, we need a large enough set of data observations to ensure that the number of degrees of freedom is at least positive (as a starting point!). For example, consider a system of m-equations and k-variables. In order to determine a solution for each variable, we need to have m≥k or m-k≥0. If m < k, then the set of equations is underdetermined and no unique solution exists, meaning that we cannot solve the system of equations exactly.

The number of data points "d" that we have in our historical sample period of time is equal to d = n*t since we have one data point for each stock n. If there are t days in our historical period, we will have n*t data points. Therefore, we need to ensure that the total number of data points "d" is greater than or equal to the number of unique parameters "k" in order to be able to solve for all the parameters in our covariance matrix. This is:

$$d \geq k$$
$$n \cdot t \geq \frac{n \cdot (n+1)}{2}$$
$$t \geq \frac{(n+1)}{2}$$

Therefore, for a 500-stock portfolio there will be 125,250 unique parameters. Since there are 500 data points per day, we need just over one year of data (250 trading days per year) just to calculate each parameter in the covariance matrix.

However, now the determination of each entry in the covariance matrix is further amplified because we are not solving for a deterministic set of equations. We are seeking to estimate the value of each parameter. A general rule of thumb is that there need to be at least 20 observations for each parameter to have statistically meaningful results.

The number of data points required is then:

$$d \geq 20 \cdot k$$
$$n \cdot t \geq 20 \cdot \frac{n \cdot (n+1)}{2}$$
$$t \geq 10 \cdot (n+1)$$

Therefore, for a 500-stock portfolio (the size of the market index) we need 5010 days of observations, which is equivalent to over 20 years of data! Even if we require only 10 data points per parameter, this still results in over 10 years of data!

Figure 5.5a shows the number of unique elements in the covariance matrix for various numbers of assets. Figure 5.5b shows the number of days of data required for statistically significant estimation of covariance parameters based on different numbers of observations required per each parameter.

It has been suggested by some industry pundits that it is possible to estimate all unique parameters of the covariance matrix using the same number of observations as there are unique parameters. However, these pundits also state that in order for this methodology to be statistically correct, we need to compute the covariance terms across the entire universe of stocks and not just for a subset of stocks. But even if this is true, the relationship across companies in the methodology needs to be stable. The reasoning is that if we do use the entire universe of stocks with enough data points, we will uncover the true intrarelationship across all sub-groups of stocks and have accurate variance and covariance measures.

In the United States, there are over 7000 stocks and thus over 24.5 million parameters. This would require over 14 years of data history! We are pretty confident in the last 14 years that many companies have changed main lines of products (e.g., Apple) and changed their corporate strategy (e.g., IBM), and thus

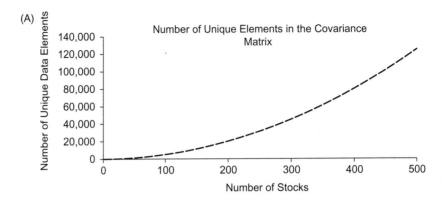

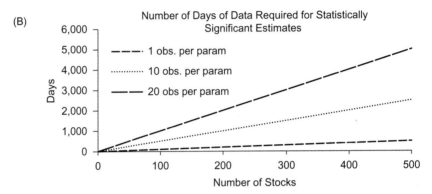

FIGURE 5.5 Data Requirements for Constructing a Statistically Significant Covariance Matrix

these relationships have changed. So even if we had enough data points, we know that companies do change, violating the requirements for this approach.

The last point to make is that for a global covariance matrix with a global universe of over 50,000 companies (at least 50,000!) there would be over 1.25 billion unique parameters and we would need a historical prices series of over 100 years! Think about how much has changed in just the last 10 years, let alone the last 100 years.

Mathematical Explanation

We can further illustrate this point mathematically using simple algebra. First, let us consider the following system of two equations and two unknowns (variables):

$$2x + 3y = 12$$
$$3x - 2y = 5$$

Here we can easily solve for our variables and we find $x = 3$ and $y = 2$. The reason we can solve for x and y is, first, that we have at least as many equations as variables, and, second, the columns are all independent. In matrix notation this is referred to as full rank. Now let us take a look at the following system of two equations with three unknowns:

$$x + y + z = 5$$
$$x - y + 2z = 6$$

Now the solution is not as simple; there is more than one solution. In fact, there are an infinite number of solutions for x, y, and z such that the system of equations previously shown will be correct.

In order to solve a system of equations, we need to have at least as many equations as variables. In finance, we need to have at least as many data points as we have parameters. The matrix needs to be full rank. Finance is no different in this respect than simple algebra.

Factor Models

Factor models address the two deficiencies we encountered when using historical market data to compute covariance and correlation. First, these models do not require the large quantity of historical observations that are needed for the sample covariance approach in order to provide accurate risk estimates. Second, factor models use a set of common explanatory factors across all stocks, and comparisons are made to these factors across all stocks. However, proper statistical analysis is still required to ensure accurate results. As with the previous sections, we follow the outline of risk models from *The Science of Algorithmic Trading and Portfolio Management* (Kissell, 2013) and enhance those explanations with empirical experiments and data analysis.

Factor models provide analysts with better insight into the overall covariance and correlation structure between stocks and across the market. Positive correlation means that the stocks will move in the same direction, and negative correlation means that stocks will move in opposite directions. A better way to word this is that factors models provide analysts with proper signals!

A factor model has the form:

$$r_t = \alpha_0 + f_{1t}b_1 + f_{2t}b_2 + \cdots + f_{kt}b_k + e_t \qquad (5.3)$$

where,

r_t = stock return in period t
α_0 = constant term
f_{kt} = factor k value in period t
b_k = exposure of stock i to factor k—this is also referred to as beta, sensitivity, or factor loadings
e_t = noise for stock i in period t—this is the return not explained by the model

Parameters of the model are determined via ordinary least squares (OLS) regression analysis. Some analysts apply a weighting scheme so more recent observations have a higher weight in the regression analysis. These weighting schemes are often assigned using a smoothing function and "half-life" parameter. Various different weighting schemes for regression analysis can be found in Green (2000).

To perform a statistically correct regression analysis, the regression model is required to have the following properties. See Green (2000), Kennedy (1998), Mittelhammer (2000), etc.

Regression properties:

1. $E(e_t) = 0$
2. $Var(e_t) = E(e'e) = \sigma_e^2$
3. $Var(f_k) = E[(f_k - \bar{f}_k)^2] = \sigma_{fk}^2$
4. $E(ef_k) = 0$
5. $E(f_{kt}, f_{lt}) = 0$
6. $E(e_t e_{t-j}) = 0$
7. $E(e_{it} e_{jt}) = 0$

Property 1 states that the error term has a mean of zero. This will always be true for a regression model that includes a constant term $\hat{b}_{0k}$ or for a model using excess returns $E(r_{it}) = 0$. Property 2 states that the variance of the error term for each stock is σ_{ei}^2. Properties 1–2 are direct byproducts of a properly specified regression model. Property 3 states that the variance of each factor is σ_{fk}^2 and is true by definition. Property 4 states that the error term (residual) and each factor are independent. Analysts need to test to ensure this property is satisfied. Property 5 states that the explanatory factors are independent. Analysts need to properly select factors that are independent, or make adjustments to ensure that they are independent. If the factors are not truly independent, the sensitivities to these factors will be suspect. Property 6 states that the error terms are independent for all lagged time periods, e.g., no serial correlation or correlation of any lags across the error terms. Property 7 states that the error terms across all stocks are independent, e.g., the series of all error terms are uncorrelated. Since the error term in a factor model indicates company-specific returns or noise that is not due to any particular market force, these terms need to be independent across companies. If there are stocks with statistically significant correlated error terms, then it is likely that there is some market force or some other explanatory variable that is driving returns that we have not accounted for in the model. In this case, although the sensitivities to the selected variables may be correct, some of our risk calculations may be suspect because we have not fully identified all sources of risk. For example, company-specific risk, covariance and correlation, and portfolio risk may be suspect due to an incomplete model and may provide incorrect correlation calculations.

When constructing factor models, analysts need to test and ensure that all properties are satisfied.

Matrix Notation

In matrix notation our single stock factor model is:

$$r_i = \alpha_i + Fb_i + e_i \qquad (5.4)$$

where,

$$r_i = \begin{bmatrix} r_{i1} \\ r_{i2} \\ \vdots \\ r_{in} \end{bmatrix}, \quad \alpha_i = \begin{bmatrix} \alpha_{i1} \\ \alpha_{i2} \\ \vdots \\ \alpha_{in} \end{bmatrix}, \quad F = \begin{bmatrix} f_{11} & f_{21} & \cdots & f_{k1} \\ f_{12} & f_{22} & \cdots & f_{k2} \\ \vdots & \vdots & \ddots & \vdots \\ f_{1n} & f_{2n} & \cdots & f_{kn} \end{bmatrix}, \quad b_k = \begin{bmatrix} b_{i1} \\ b_{i2} \\ \vdots \\ b_{ik} \end{bmatrix}, \quad e_i = \begin{bmatrix} e_{i1} \\ e_{i2} \\ \vdots \\ e_{in} \end{bmatrix}$$

r_i = vector of stock returns for stock i
r_{it} = return of stock i in period t
α_i = vector of the constant terms
F = column matrix of factor returns
f_{jt} = factor j in period t
b_i = vector of risk exposures
b_{ij} = risk sensitivity of stock i to factor j
e_i = vector of errors (unexplained return)
e_{it} = error term of stock i in period t
n = total number of time periods
m = total number of stocks
k = total number of factors

Constructing Factor Independence

Real-world data often results in factors that are not independent, which violates regression property 5. This makes it extremely difficult to determine accurate risk exposures to these factors. In these situations, analysts can transform the set of dependent original factors into a new set of factors that are linearly independent (Kennedy, 1988).

This process is described as follows:

Let, F, G, and H represent three explanatory factors that are correlated. First, sort the factors by explanatory power. Let F be the primary driver of risk and return, let G be the secondary driver, and let H be the tertiary driver. Second, remove the correlation between F and G. This is accomplished by regressing the secondary factor G on the primary factor F as follows:

$$G = \tilde{v}_0 + \tilde{v}_1 F + e_G$$

The error term in this regression e_G is the residual factor G that is not explained by the regression model, and by definition (P4) is independent of F. Then let that $\tilde{G}$ is simply e_G from the regression. That is:

$$\tilde{G} = G - \tilde{v}_0 - \tilde{v}_1 F$$

Third, remove the correlation between factor H and factor F and the new secondary factor $\tilde{G}$. This is accomplished by regressing H on F and $\tilde{G}$ as follows:

$$H = \hat{\gamma}_0 + \hat{\gamma}_1 F + \hat{\gamma}_2 \tilde{G} + e_H$$

The error term in this regression e_H is the residual factor H that is not explained by the regression model, and by definition (P4) is independent of F and G. This process can be repeated for as many factors as is present.

The factor model with uncorrelated factors is finally rewritten as:

$$r = \alpha_o + F b_f + \tilde{G} b_{\tilde{g}} + \tilde{H} b_{\tilde{h}} + \varepsilon \tag{5.5}$$

This representation now provides analysts with a methodology to calculate accurate risk exposures to a group of pre-defined factors which are now independent.

Estimating Covariance Using a Factor Model

A factor model across a universe of stocks can be written as:

$$R = \alpha + F\beta + \varepsilon \tag{5.6}$$

where

$$R = \begin{bmatrix} r_{11} & r_{21} & \cdots & r_{m1} \\ r_{12} & r_{22} & \cdots & r_{m2} \\ \vdots & \vdots & \ddots & \vdots \\ r_{1n} & r_{2n} & \cdots & r_{mn} \end{bmatrix} \quad F = \begin{bmatrix} f_{11} & f_{21} & \cdots & f_{k1} \\ f_{12} & f_{22} & \cdots & f_{k2} \\ \vdots & \vdots & \ddots & \vdots \\ f_{1n} & f_{2n} & \cdots & f_{kn} \end{bmatrix}, \quad \alpha' = \begin{bmatrix} \alpha_1 \\ \alpha_2 \\ \vdots \\ \alpha_n \end{bmatrix}$$

$$\beta = \begin{bmatrix} b_{11} & b_{21} & \cdots & b_{m1} \\ b_{12} & b_{22} & \cdots & b_{m2} \\ \vdots & \vdots & \ddots & \vdots \\ b_{1k} & b_{2k} & \cdots & b_{mk} \end{bmatrix} \quad \varepsilon = \begin{bmatrix} \varepsilon_{11} & \varepsilon_{21} & \cdots & \varepsilon_{m1} \\ \varepsilon_{12} & \varepsilon_{22} & \cdots & \varepsilon_{m2} \\ \vdots & \vdots & \ddots & \vdots \\ \varepsilon_{1n} & \varepsilon_{2n} & \cdots & \varepsilon_{mn} \end{bmatrix}$$

This formulation allows us to compute the covariance across all stock without the issues that come up when using historical market data. This process is described following Elton & Gruber (1995) as follows:

The covariance matrix of returns C is calculated as:

$$C = E[(R - E[R])'(R - E[R])]$$

From our factor model relationship we have

$$R = \alpha + F\beta + \varepsilon$$

The expected value of returns is:

$$E[R] = \alpha + \overline{F}\beta$$

Now we can determine the excess returns as:

$$R - E[R] = (F - \overline{F})\beta + \varepsilon$$

Now substituting in the previous result, we have:

$$
\begin{aligned}
C &= E[((F-\overline{F})^2\beta + \varepsilon)'((F-\overline{F})\beta + \varepsilon)] \\
&= E[\beta'(F-\overline{F})^2\beta + 2\beta'(F - \overline{F})\varepsilon + \varepsilon'\varepsilon] \\
&= \beta'E[(F-\overline{F})^2]\beta + 2\beta'E[(F - \overline{F})\varepsilon] + E[\varepsilon'\varepsilon]
\end{aligned}
$$

By property 4:

$$E[2\beta'(F - \overline{F})\varepsilon] = 0$$

By property 2 and property 7 we have

$$
E[\varepsilon'\varepsilon] =
\begin{bmatrix}
\sigma_{e1}^2 & 0 & \cdots & 0 \\
0 & \sigma_{e2}^2 & \cdots & 0 \\
\vdots & \vdots & \ddots & \vdots \\
0 & 0 & \cdots & \sigma_{en}^2
\end{bmatrix}
= \Lambda
$$

which is the idiosyncratic variance matrix and is a diagonal matrix consisting of the variance of the regression term for each stock.

By property 3 and property 5, the factor covariance matrix is:

$$
E[(F - \overline{F})^2] =
\begin{bmatrix}
\sigma_{f1}^2 & 0 & \cdots & 0 \\
0 & \sigma_{f2}^2 & \cdots & 0 \\
\vdots & \vdots & \ddots & \vdots \\
0 & 0 & \cdots & \sigma_{fk}^2
\end{bmatrix}
= \mathrm{cov}(F)
$$

The factor covariance matrix will be a diagonal matrix of factor variances. In certain situations there may be some correlation across factors. When this occurs, the off-diagonal entries will be the covariance between the factors. Additionally, the beta sensitivities may be suspect, meaning that we may not know the true exposures to each factor, and we will have some difficulty determining how much that particular factor contributes to returns. However, the covariance calculation will be correct, providing that we include the true factor covariance matrix.

Finally, we have our covariance matrix derived from the factor model:

$$C = \beta'\mathrm{cov}(F)\beta + \Lambda \tag{5.7}$$

This matrix can be decomposed into the systematic and idiosyncratic components. Systematic risk component refers to the risk and returns that is explained by the factors. It is also commonly called market risk or factor risk. The idiosyncratic risk component refers to the risk and returns that are not explained by the factors. This component is also commonly called stock-specific risk, company-specific risk, or diversifiable risk. This is shown as:

$$C = \underbrace{\beta' \text{cov}[F]\beta}_{\text{Systematic Risk}} + \underbrace{\Lambda}_{\text{Idiosyncratic Risk}} \qquad (5.8)$$

Types of Factor Models

Factor models can be divided into four categories of models: index models, macroeconomic models, cross-sectional or fundamental data models, and statistical factor models. These are described ahead.

Index Model

There are two forms of the index model commonly used in the industry: single-index and multi-index model. The single-index model is based on a single major market index such as the SP500. The same index is used as the input factor across all stocks. The multi-index model commonly incorporates the general market index, the stock's sector index, and additionally, the stock's industry index. The market index will be the same for all stocks, but the sector index and industry index will be different based on the company's economic grouping. All stocks in the same sector will use the same sector index, and all stocks in the same industry will use the same industry index.

Single-Index Model

The simplest of all the multi-factor models is the single-index model. This model formulates a relationship between stock returns and market movement. In most situations, the SP500 index or some other broad market index is used as a proxy for the whole market.

In matrix notation, the single factor model has the general form:

$$r_i = \alpha_i + \hat{b}_i R_m + e_i \qquad (5.9)$$

r_i = column vector of stock returns for stock i
R_m = column vector of market returns
e_i = column vector of random noise for stock i
$\hat{b}_i$ = stock return sensitivity to market returns

In the single-index model, we need to estimate the risk exposure $\hat{b}_i$ to the general index R_m. In situations where the index used in the single-index model is the broad market index and the constant term is the risk-free rate, the single-index model is known as the CAPM model (Sharpe, 1964), and the risk exposure $\hat{b}_i$ is the stock beta β.

Empirical Analysis

We analyzed daily stock returns as a function of the SP500 index returns for 2011 and 2012. We computed daily betas for stocks in the SP500 index and stocks in the R2000 index.

For SP500 stocks the average beta in 2011 was 1.12 (± 0.37), and in 2012 it was 1.10 (± 0.43). This is shown in Table 5.4, and Figure 5.6a shows the daily beta across stocks and over time. The question that naturally arises in these analyses is, why isn't the average beta equal to $B = 1$? There are a few reasons why. First, we are using an equal-weighted average of beta over time, rather than a market-cap-weight average as is used to compute the SP500 index returns. Larger stocks typically have betas closer to one. Second, our sample universe consists of stocks that were in the SP500 at the end of 2012 and for which we had complete data over the full period 1/2011 through 12/2012. Finally, and most importantly, the stocks in our sample were the stocks that were always in the index or were added to the index some time during the two year window. Stocks that were deleted from the index are not included in the index. Very often, stocks that are underperforming the index are removed from the index, while stocks that are outperforming the index are added into the index. This results in an equal-weighted beta greater than one.

We next investigated the predictability of beta from one year to the next. Quite often we see in publications that stock betas tend to revert to one over time. If this were true, we should see stocks with a beta greater than one decreasing and stocks with beta less than one increasing. Our regression analysis, however, did not find evidence of this relationship with large-cap stocks. The slope of the

Table 5.4 SP500 Index Stocks

Daily Beta Calculation Statistics

	2011	2012
Avg:	1.12	1.10
Stdev:	0.37	0.43

2012 Beta as function of 2011 Beta

	Value	Std Err	t-stat	t-stat2
Slope	1.04	0.03	40.14	1.57
Intercept	− 0.06	0.03	− 2.12	
R2	0.77			
SE	0.21			

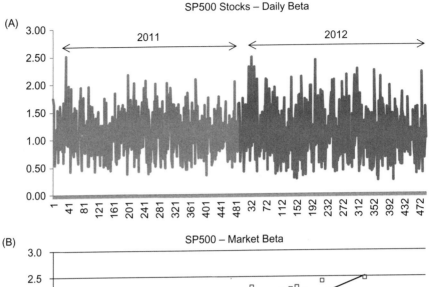

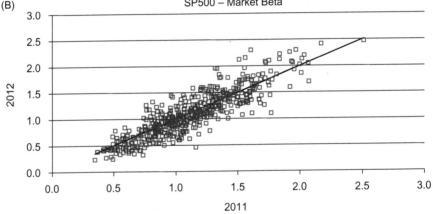

FIGURE 5.6 Evaluation of Market Beta for SP500 Index Stocks

regression line was 1.04, but this value was not significantly different from 1.0. Therefore, we conclude that large-cap stocks do not exhibit a mean reversion pattern (at least during 2011–2012). It could possibly be because these stocks are large-cap mature companies already. Figure 5.6b shows an x-y plot of 2012 beta as a function of 2011 beta.

For R2000 stocks, the average beta in 2011 was 1.40 (± 0.38), and in 2012 it was 1.26(± 0.46). Since small-cap stocks for the most part are more risky and have higher beta, it is interesting that these stocks had beta that moved closer to one in the second year (Table 5.5). There appears to be some evidence that beta reversion did occur for the small-cap stocks. Figure 5.7a plots small-cap stock betas over the period 1/2011 through 12/2012. Visual inspection of the data indicates that beta may be mean reverting. To test this hypothesis, we ran a regression of 2012 beta as a function of 2011 beta and found

Table 5.5 R2000 Index Stocks

Daily Beta Calculation Statistics

	2011	2012
Avg:	1.40	1.26
Stdev:	0.38	0.46

R2000 Stocks: 2012 beta as a function of 2011 beta

	Value	Std Err	t-stat	t-stat2
Slope	0.85	0.02	39.15	− 6.98
Intercept	0.07	0.03	2.14	
R2	0.50			
SE	0.33			

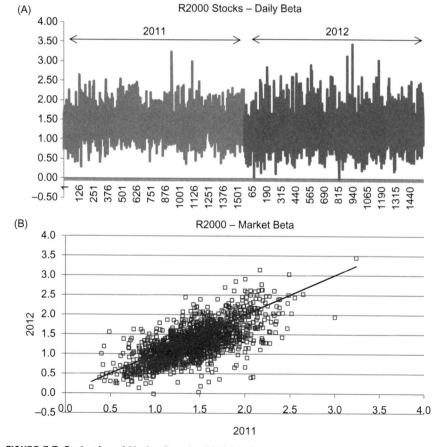

FIGURE 5.7 Evaluation of Market Beta for R2000 Index Stocks

statistical evidence (Table 5.5). The slope of this regression line was m = 0.85. Statistical tests show that this value is different from one. Hence, since small-cap stocks do tend to have beta > 1, there is statistical evidence suggesting beta mean reversion (at least for small-cap companies). Figure 5.7b is an x-y plot of 2012 beta as a function of 2011 beta. Notice that there is a higher concentration of data points below the y = x lines for stocks with a higher beta (e.g., beta >1).

Multi-Index Models

The multi-index factor model is an extension of the single-index model that captures additional relationships between price returns and corresponding sectors and industries. There have been numerous studies showing that the excess returns (error) from the single-index model are correlated across stocks in the same sector, and with further incremental correlation across stocks in the same industry (see Elton and Gruber, 1995).

Let R_m = market returns, S_k = the stock's sector returns, and I_k = the stock's industry return. Then the linear relationship is:

$$r_i = \alpha_i + b_{im}R_m + b_{ik}S_k + b_{il}I_i + e_i$$

where b_{im} is the stock's sensitivity to the general market movement, b_{ik} is the stock's sensitivity to its sector movement, and b_{il} is the stock's sensitivity to its industry movement.

There is a large degree of correlation, however, across the general market, sectors, and industry. These factors are not independent, and analysts need to make appropriate adjustment following the process outlined previously.

The general multi-index model after multicollinearity now has the form:

$$r_i = \alpha_i + \hat{b}_{im}R_m + \hat{b}^*_{isk}\tilde{S}_k + \hat{b}^*_{ill}\tilde{I}_l + \varepsilon \qquad (5.10)$$

Empirical Analysis

We analyzed daily stock returns and market risk using a variation of the multi-index model; but instead of using sector or industry returns, we incorporated a small-cap stock index (R2000 index). We incorporated the small-cap stock index to determine if there were any market forces specific to the small-cap universe that are driving stock returns.

The first step in the analysis is to construct small-cap index (R2000) returns that are uncorrelated with the main large-cap index (SP500) following procedures shown previously. The second step is to estimate daily stock returns based on these two indexes. The regression model we used is:

$$r_k = \hat{\alpha}_k + \hat{\beta}_{k1}R_m + \hat{\beta}_{k2}\tilde{I}_m + \varepsilon_k$$

where $\tilde{I}_m$ is the vector of small-cap index returns that are uncorrelated with SP500 index returns. The data period covered 2011–2012.

Following this model, risk can be decomposed into large-cap market risk, small-cap market risk, and idiosyncratic risk using the variance risk metric. These are:

$$LC\ market\ risk = \hat{\beta}_{k1}^2 \sigma_{Rm}^2$$

$$SC\ market\ risk = \hat{\beta}_{k2}^2 \sigma_{Im}^2$$

$$idiosyncratic = \sigma_{\varepsilon}^2$$

where total risk is:

$$\sigma_{rk}^2 = \hat{\beta}_{k1}^2 \sigma_{Rm}^2 + \hat{\beta}_{k2}^2 \sigma_{Im}^2 + \sigma_{\varepsilon}^2$$

The percentage of risk from each of these factors is simply the variance corresponding to those factors divided by the total variance for the stock. This is as follows:

$$LC\ market\ risk\ Pct = \frac{\hat{\beta}_{k1}^2 \sigma_{Rm}^2}{\sigma_{rk}^2}$$

$$SC\ market\ risk\ Pct = \frac{\hat{\beta}_{k2}^2 \sigma_{Im}^2}{\sigma_{rk}^2}$$

$$idiosyncratic = \frac{\sigma_{\varepsilon}^2}{\sigma_{rk}^2}$$

For our large-cap stock universe, we find that the market index represents 49% of total stock risk. The small-cap index only accounts for 1% of risk. Thus there is some small capitalization occurring in the market. Idiosyncratic market risk accounts for 50% of daily stock risk. Figure 5.8a shows risk decomposition across all of our stocks in the universe and Figure 5.8b shows the average quantity of risk corresponding to the indexes.

For our small-cap stock universe, we find that the market index represents 37% of total stock risk, which is much lower than observed for large-cap stocks. The small-cap index accounted for 5% of risk. While this is still small, it is still a much higher quantity than for large-cap stocks. Thus, further evidence of a small capitalization phenomenon effecting prices. Idiosyncratic market risk accounts for 59% of daily stock risk. Figure 5.9a shows risk decomposition across all of our stocks in the universe, and Figure 5.9b shows the average quantity of risk corresponding to the indexes.

The risk decomposition on a daily basis will often associate a higher percentage to idiosyncratic (company specific) risk. This is due primarily to actual company-specific risk, but it is also due to buying and selling pressure in the market. Over time, buying and selling pressure tends to net out.

(A)

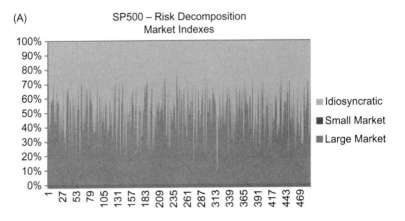

SP500 – Risk Decomposition
Market Indexes

(B)

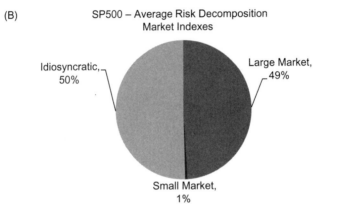

SP500 – Average Risk Decomposition
Market Indexes

FIGURE 5.8 Risk Decomposition for SP500 Index Stocks Using CAPM

Macroeconomic Factor Models

A macroeconomic multifactor model defines a relationship between stock returns and a set of macroeconomic variables such as GDP, inflation, industrial production, bond yields, etc. The appeal of using macroeconomic data as the explanatory factors in the returns model is that these variables are readily measurable and have real economic meaning.

While macroeconomic models offer key insight into the general state of the economy, they may not sufficiently capture the most accurate correlation structure of price movement across stocks. Additionally, macroeconomic models may not do a good job capturing the covariance of price movement across stocks in "new economies" or a "shifting regime," such as the sudden arrival of the financial crisis beginning in September 2008.

Chen, Roll, and Ross (1986) identified the following four macroeconomic factors as having significant explanatory power with stock return. These strong relationships still hold today and are:

- Unanticipated changes in inflation

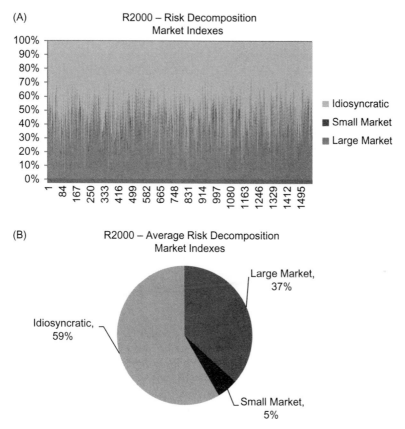

FIGURE 5.9 Risk Decomposition for R2000 Index Stocks Using CAPM

- Unanticipated changes in industrial production
- Unanticipated changes in the yield between high-grade and low-grade corporate bonds
- Unanticipated changes in the yield between long-term government bonds and t-bills; this is the slope of the term structure

Other macroeconomic factors have also been incorporated into these models, including change in interest rates, growth rates, GDP, capital investment, unemployment, oil prices, housing starts, exchange rates, etc. The parameters are determined via regression analysis using monthly data over a five-year period, e.g., 60 observations.

It is often assumed that the macroeconomic factors used in the model are uncorrelated, and analysts do not make any adjustment for correlation across returns. But improvements can be made to the model following the adjustment process described previously.

A k-factor macroeconomic model has the form:

$$r_i = \alpha_{i0} + \hat{b}_{i1}f_1 + \hat{b}_{i2}f_2 + \cdots + \hat{b}_{ik}f_k + e_i \qquad (5.11)$$

Analysts need to estimate the risk exposures $b'_{ik}s$ to these macroeconomic factors.

Cross-Sectional Multi-Factor Model

Cross-sectional models estimate stock returns from a set of variables that are specific to each company, rather than through factors that are common across all stocks. Cross-sectional models use stock-specific factors that are based on fundamental and technical data. The fundamental data consists of company characteristics and balance sheet information. The technical data (also called market-driven data) consists of trading activity metrics such as average daily trading volume, price momentum, size, etc.

Because of the reliance on fundamental data, many authors use the term "fundamental model" instead of cross-sectional model. The rationale behind the cross-sectional models is similar to the rationale behind the macroeconomic model. Since managers and decision makers incorporate fundamental and technical analysis into their stock selection process, it is only reasonable that these factors provide insight into the return and risk of those stocks. Otherwise, why would they be used?

Fama and French (1992) found that three factors consisting of 1) market returns, 2) company size (market capitalization), and 3) book-to-market ratio have considerable explanatory power. While the exact measure of these variables remains a topic of much discussion in academia, notice that the last two factors in the Fama-French model are company-specific fundamental data.

While many may find it intuitive to incorporate cross-sectional data into multi-factor models, these models have some limitations. First, data requirements are cumbersome, requiring analysts to develop models using company-specific data (each company has its own set of factors). Second, it is often difficult to find a consistent set of robust factors across stocks that provide strong explanatory power. Ross and Roll had difficulty determining a set of factors that provided more explanatory power than the macroeconomic models without introducing excessive multicollinearity into the data.

The cross-sectional model is derived from company-specific variables referred to as company factor loadings. The parameters are typically determined via regression analysis using monthly data over a longer period of time, e.g., a five-year period, with 60 monthly observations.

The cross-sectional model is written as:

$$r_{it} = x_{i1}^* \hat{f}_{1t} + x_{i2}^* \hat{f}_{2t} + \cdots + x_{ik}^* \hat{f}_{kt} + e_{it} \qquad (5.12)$$

where x_{ij}^* is the normalized factor loading of company i to factor j. For example,

$$x_{kl}^* = \frac{x_{kl} - E(x_k)}{\sigma(x_k)}$$

where $E(x_k)$ is the mean of x_k across all stocks, and $\sigma(x_k)$ is the standard deviation of x_k across all stocks.

And unlike the previous models in which the factors were known in advance, and we estimated the risk sensitivities, here we know the factor loadings (from company data) and we need to estimate the factors.

Empirical Evidence

We analyzed daily stock risk for our large-cap and small-cap indexes using the Fama-French factors[1]. We revised these factors so that each is independent, following approaches shown previously. The correlation matrix of factor is shown in Table 5.6.

The factors of this model are Mkt-Rf (market returns minus risk-free rate), SBM (small minus big), and HML (high book-to-market minus low book-to-market).

Surprisingly, the results of our risk decomposition were similar to our single-index and multi-index model approach. Figure 5.10a shows the percentage of risk corresponding to each of the Fama-French factors for large-cap stocks. Figure 5.10b shows the average values across all stocks for the large-cap universe. For large cap, the market is driving about 49% consistent with our multi-index model. HML is explaining 1% of risk, and we did not find SMB associated with any market risk. Therefore, idiosyncratic risk is 49%. Notice that this is slightly lower than for the multi-index model in which 50% of the risk was denoted as company specific.

Figure 5.11a shows the percentage of risk corresponding to each of the Fama-French factors for small-cap stocks. Figure 5.11b shows the average values across all stocks for the small-cap universe. For small-cap stocks, approximately 38% corresponds to the market (consistent with the multi-index model), HML corresponds to 1% of risk, SMB corresponds to 4% of market risk, and 58% of the risk is company specific.

Statistical Factor Models

Statistical factor models are also referred to as implicit factor models and principal component analysis (PCA). In these models, neither the explanatory factors

Table 5.6 Correlation across Fama-French Factors

	Mkt-Rf	SMB	HML
Mkt-Rf	1.000	− 0.001	− 0.003
SMB	− 0.001	1.000	− 0.001
HML	− 0.003	− 0.001	1.000

[1]Source: http://mba.tuck.dartmouth.edu/pages/faculty/ken.french/data_library.html.

(A)

SP500 – Risk Decomposition
Fama French Factors

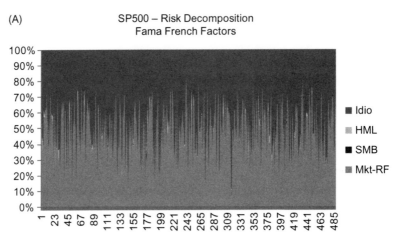

(B)

SP500 – Average Risk Decomposition
Fama French Factors

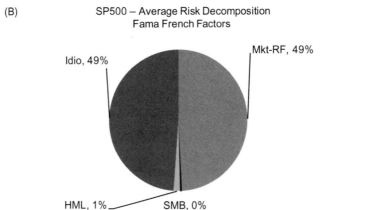

FIGURE 5.10 Risk Decomposition for SP500 Index Stocks Using Fama-French Factors

nor sensitivities to these factors are known in advance, and they are not readily observed in the market. However, both the statistical factors and sensitivities can be derived from historical data.

There are three common techniques used in statistical factor models: eigenvalue-eigenvector decomposition, singular value decomposition, and factor analysis. Eigenvalue-eigenvector is based on a factoring scheme of the sample covariance matrix, and singular value decomposition is based on a factoring scheme of the returns matrix of returns (see Pearson, 2002). Factor analysis (not to be confused with factor models) is based on a maximum likelihood estimate of the correlations across stocks. In this section we discuss the eigenvalue-eigenvector decomposition technique.

(A)

R2000 – Average Risk Decomposition
Fama French Factors

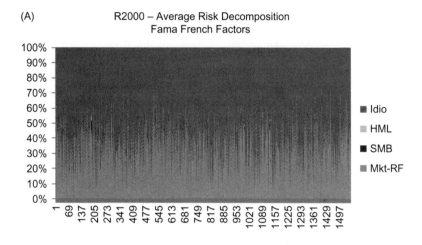

(B)

R2000 – Average Risk Decomposition
Fama French Factors

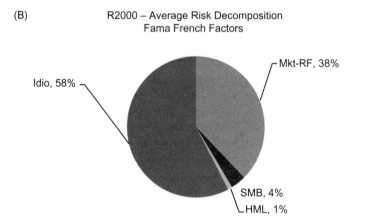

FIGURE 5.11 Risk Decomposition for R2000 Index Stocks Using Fama-French Factors

The statistical factor models differs from the previously mentioned models in that analysts estimate both the factors (F_ks) and the sensitivities to the factors (b_{ik}s) from a series of historical returns. This model does not make any prior assumptions regarding the appropriate set of explanatory factors or force any preconceived relationship into the model.

This approach is in contrast to the explicit modeling approaches in which analysts must specify either a set of explanatory factors or a set of company-specific factor loadings. In the explicit approaches, analysts begin with either a set of specified factors and estimate sensitivities to those factors (i.e., index models and macroeconomic factor model) or begin with the factor loadings (fundamental data) and estimate the set of explanatory factors (cross-sectional model).

The advantage of statistical factor models over the previously described explicit approaches is that it provides risk managers with a process to uncover accurate covariance and correlation relationships of returns without making any assumptions regarding what is driving the returns. Any preconceived bias is removed from the model. The disadvantage of these statistical approaches is that it does not provide portfolio managers with a set of factors to easily determine what is driving returns since the statistical factors do not have any real-world meaning.

To the extent that analysts are only interested in uncovering covariance and correlation relationships for risk management purposes, PCA has proven to be a viable alternative to the traditional explicit modeling approaches. Additionally, with the recent growth of exchange traded funds (ETFs), many managers have begun correlating their statistical factors to these ETFs in much the same way Ross and Roll did with economic data to better understand these statistical factors.

The process to derive the statistical model is as follows:

Step 1: Compute the sample covariance matrix by definition from historical data. This matrix will likely suffer from spurious relationships due the data limitations (not enough degrees of freedom and potential false relationships). But these will be resolved via principal component analysis.

Let $\overline{C}$ represent the sample covariance matrix.

Step 2: Factor the sample covariance matrix. We based the factorization scheme on eigenvalue-eigenvector decomposition. This is:

$$\overline{C} = VDV' \tag{5.13}$$

where D is the diagonal matrix of eigenvalues sorted from largest to smallest, $\lambda_1 > \lambda_2 > \cdots > \lambda_n$ and V is the corresponding matrix of eigenvectors and. These matrices are as follows:

$$D = \begin{bmatrix} \lambda_1 & 0 & \cdots & 0 \\ 0 & \lambda_2 & \cdots & 0 \\ \vdots & \vdots & \ddots & \vdots \\ 0 & 0 & \cdots & \lambda_n \end{bmatrix} \quad V = \begin{bmatrix} v_{11} & v_{21} & \cdots & v_{n1} \\ v_{12} & v_{22} & \cdots & v_{n2} \\ \vdots & \vdots & \ddots & \vdots \\ v_{1n} & v_{2n} & \cdots & v_{nn} \end{bmatrix}$$

Since D is a diagonal matrix we have $D = D^{1/2}D^{1/2}$, $D = D'$, and $D^{1/2} = (D^{1/2})'$

Then, our covariance matrix C can be written as:

$$\overline{C} = VDV' = VD^{1/2}D^{1/2}V' = VD^{1/2}(VD^{1/2})'$$

Step 3: Compute β in terms of the eigenvalues and eigenvectors:

$$\beta = (VD^{1/2})'$$

Then the full sample covariance matrix expressed in terms of β is:

$$\beta'\beta = VD^{1/2}(VD^{1/2})' \tag{5.14}$$

Step 4: Remove spurious relationships due to data limitation

To remove the potential spurious relationships, we only use the eigenvalues and eigenvectors with the strongest predictive power.

How many factors should be selected? In our eigenvalue-eigenvector decomposition, each eigenvalue λ_k of the sample covariance matrix explains exactly $\lambda_k / \sum \lambda$ percent of the total variance. Since the eigenvalues are sorted from highest to lowest, a plot of the percentage of variance explained will show how quickly the predictive power of the factors declines. If the covariance matrix is generated by, say, 10 factors, then the first 10 eigenvalues should explain the large majority of the total variance.

There are many ways to determine how many factors should be selected to model returns. For example, some analysts will select the minimum number of factors that explain a pre-specified amount of variance, and some will select the number of factors up to where there is a break-point or fall-off in explanatory power. Others may select factors so that the variance $> 1/n$, assuming that each factor should explain at least $1/n$ of the total. Readers can refer to Dowd (1998) for further techniques.

If it is determined that there are k-factors that sufficiently explain returns, the risk exposures are determined from the first k risk exposures for each stock since our eigenvalues are sorted from highest predictive power to lowest.

$$\beta = \begin{bmatrix} \beta_{11} & \beta_{21} & \cdots & \beta_{m1} \\ \beta_{12} & \beta_{22} & \cdots & \beta_{m2} \\ \vdots & \vdots & \ddots & \vdots \\ \beta_{1k} & \beta_{2k} & \cdots & \beta_{mk} \end{bmatrix}$$

The estimated covariance matrix is then:

$$C = \underset{n \times k \ k \times n}{\beta' \ \beta} + \underset{n \times n}{\Lambda} \tag{5.15}$$

In this case the idiosyncratic matrix Λ is the diagonal matrix consisting of the difference between the sample covariance matrix and $\beta'\beta$. That is,

$$\Lambda = diag(\overline{C} - \beta'\beta) \tag{5.16}$$

It is important to note that in the previous expression $\overline{C} - \beta'\beta$, the off-diagonal terms will often be nonzero. This difference is considered to be the spurious relationship caused by the data limitation and degrees of freedom issue stated previously. Selection of an appropriate number of factors determined via eigenvalue decomposition will help eliminate these false relationships.

Empirical Evidence

We performed an analysis of our sample covariance matrix for large-cap and small-cap stocks using eigenvalue-eigenvector decomposition over our historical period (2011−2012). Figure 5.12a depicts the explanatory power from the top 25 eigenvalues. Notice how quickly the explanatory power of the eigenvalues decreases after the first eigenvalue. Additionally, notice how the largest explanatory eigenvalue for large-cap stocks accounts for 48% of total variance, and for small-caps the first eigenvalue accounts for approximately 34% of total variance. These percentages are consistent with our findings using the multi-index and Fama French approaches. Figure 5.12b illustrates the cumulative explanatory power through the first 25 eigenvalues for both samples. The first 25 eigenvalues account for approximately 70% of total variance for large-cap stocks. This shows that there may be something else happening in the markets that is driving returns, perhaps a sector effect (see Elton and Gruber) or an industry effect (see Barra). The top 25 eigenvalues for small-cap stocks explain approximately 50% of total variance. This is consistent with the large-cap findings, especially after considering that small-cap stocks have a higher quantity of company-specific risk.

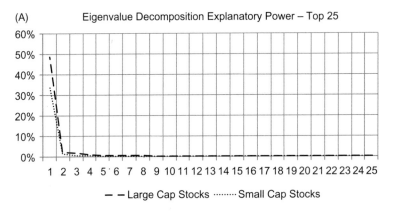

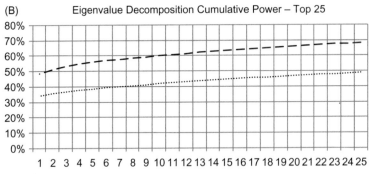

FIGURE 5.12 Eigenvalue Decomposition of Daily Stock Returns

Table 5.7 Eigenvalue Decomposition of Daily Stock Returns (2011–2012)

Rank	Explanatory Power		Cumulative Power	
	SP500	R2000	SP500	R2000
1	48.6%	34.2%	48.6%	34.2%
2	2.5%	1.7%	51.1%	35.8%
3	2.1%	1.0%	53.2%	36.8%
4	1.6%	0.8%	54.8%	37.7%
5	1.1%	0.8%	55.9%	38.5%
6	1.0%	0.8%	56.9%	39.2%
7	0.9%	0.7%	57.8%	39.9%
8	0.8%	0.7%	58.6%	40.6%
9	0.8%	0.6%	59.4%	41.3%
10	0.7%	0.6%	60.1%	41.9%
11	0.7%	0.6%	60.8%	42.5%
12	0.7%	0.6%	61.5%	43.1%
13	0.6%	0.5%	62.1%	43.6%
14	0.6%	0.5%	62.7%	44.2%
15	0.6%	0.5%	63.3%	44.7%
16	0.6%	0.5%	63.9%	45.1%
17	0.6%	0.5%	64.5%	45.6%
18	0.5%	0.5%	65.0%	46.1%
19	0.5%	0.4%	65.5%	46.5%
20	0.5%	0.4%	66.0%	46.9%
21	0.5%	0.4%	66.5%	47.4%
22	0.5%	0.4%	67.0%	47.8%
23	0.5%	0.4%	67.4%	48.2%
24	0.4%	0.4%	67.9%	48.6%
25	0.4%	0.4%	68.3%	49.0%

Table 5.7 illustrates the percentage of daily price variability explained by the primary eigenvalues over the period 2011 through 2012.

CONCLUSION

In this chapter, we provided readers with an overview of the different types of factor risk models, including single-index, multi-index, macroeconomic, cross-sectional, and statistical or principal component analysis (PCA) models. The chapter started with a discussion of why risk models are needed in the industry. Analysts who rely on historical data alone to compute covariance could get incorrect results due false relationships resulting from uncommon trend lines across the assets or data limitation issues in which there are not enough observations to compute statistically significant covariance across all the stocks.

We then performed a thorough analysis of the daily stocks returns for a large-cap sample (SP500 stocks) and a small-cap sample (R2000 stocks) over the period 2011−2012. Key findings of our analysis are that when relying on historical data as opposed to risk models, analysts may uncover false relationships that appear to occur about 40% of the time. Risk models are needed to better understand co-movement of asset returns. We also uncovered supporting evidence that shows beta tends towards one. Specifically, we found that stocks with a beta higher than one appeared to move closer to one in the following year. But we did not find as much supporting evidence for stocks with a beta much lower than one to increase towards one in the following year. Some of this may be explained by survivorship bias in our data. We concluded the chapter by decomposition risk for both the large-cap and small-cap universes using our multi-index modeling approach, the Fama-French factor model, and the eigenvalue-eigenvector statistical approach, with all the methodologies uncovering similar results. One of the biggest findings from these different models is that on a daily basis about 50% of stock risk (variance) is company-specific risk (e.g., risk that is not explained by any of the models). This is a larger percentage than many of the models find using a longer horizon such as weekly or monthly returns. However, it is essential that portfolio managers consider the high degree of idiosyncratic risk when developing a hedging strategy and when managers need to liquidate a position on a given day.

References

Chen, N., Roll, R., Ross, S., 1986. Economic Forces and the Stock Market. J. Bus. 59 (3), 383−403 (Jul., 1986).

Dowd, K., 1998. Beyond Value at Risk: The New Science of Risk Management. John Wiley & Sons.

Elton, E., Gruber, M., 1995. Modern Portfolio Theory, fifth ed. John Wiley & Sons, Inc, New York.

Fama, E., French, K., 1992. The cross section of variation in expected stock returns. J. Finance June 1992.

Greene, W., 2000. Econometric Analysis, fourth ed. Prentice-Hall, Inc.

Kennedy, P., 1998. A Guide to Econometrics, fourth ed. The MIT Press, Cambridge, Massachusetts.

Kissell, R., 2013. The Science of Algorithmic Trading and Portfolio Management. Elsevier, New York.

Mittelhammer, R., Judge, G., Miller, D., 2000. Econometrics Foundation. Cambridge University Press.

Roll, R., Ross, S., 1984. The arbitrage pricing theory approach to strategic portfolio planning. Financ. Analysts J. May-June 1984.

Equity Derivatives

6

INTRODUCTION

In this chapter we introduce readers to equity financial derivatives and provide an overview of options, forwards, futures, and swaps. The financial derivatives that are to be discussed in this chapter provide the building blocks and underlying foundation for many of the advanced and complex financial derivatives instruments. Our goal in the chapter is to provide readers with the necessary mathematics and conceptual understanding to be able to price and evaluate derivatives. The chapter is not intended to be a detailed comprehensive account or derivation of the complex instruments, but the chapter is intended to provide risk managers with a strong foundation to be able to evaluate the different derivative transactions in an objective and unbiased manner.[1]

The first section of this chapter provides an introduction to the options markets. We provide an overview of call and put options, and provide an introduction to different options pricing models including Black-Scholes and binomial trees. We discuss the various different derivative risks of delta, vega, theta, and gamma and give an overview of Volatility Smiles, volatility skew, Implied Volatility, and Implied Correlation. The second section provides readers with an overview of the futures markets. We give an introduction to the common cash-and-carry model and the reverse cash-and-carry model. We then expand on these formulations by incorporating transaction costs into the pricing of future prices. The third section of this chapter provides readers with an overview of the swaps market, in which investors agree to exchange series of cash flows over a period of time. The most common types of swaps are Interest Rate Swaps and Currency Swaps.

Readers interested in further background and a more detailed investigation into these financial instruments and derivatives are referred to endnotes [1−4]. We build on those sources throughout the chapter.

---

[1]We owe a special thanks to Diana Muzan for her contribution to the material and research contained in this chapter and for her help in proofreading the chapter and correcting the math in our examples.

Many of the definitions and examples provided in this chapter are based on those sources so as to provide readers easy access to additional information via the internet.

What are financial derivatives? Financial derivatives are financial instruments whose value is tied to a more elementary underlying financial instrument or asset such as a stock, bond, index, or commodity. Financial derivatives are used by money managers for various different investment purposes such as hedging, speculation, and financial risk management. More recently, many funds have begun using financial derivatives as an alternative to long-term buy-and-hold strategy. For example, some portfolio managers many choose to hold a portfolio of index futures as opposed to holding the actual underlying stocks that comprise the indexes.

The financial derivatives market allows investors to transfer various types of financial risk to other investors who are more willing to accept the incremental risk and are usually better able to manage the incremental risk. Of course, the transfer of this risk requires the seller of the risk to compensate the buyer of the risk. Much of the focus of this chapter will focus on determining the appropriate monetary value to assign to the transfer of the risk. In other words, how much does an investor need to pay another investor to accept the incremental risk units? This is what ultimately defines the price of the underlying derivative instrument.

Some of the more common types of financial derivatives include call and put options, futures, forwards, and swaps. These financial derivatives are defined as follows.

What are options? An options contract is a contract that gives the owner the right, but not the obligation, to buy or sell an underlying asset or financial instrument at a specified price (a "strike price") on or before a specified date.

What are futures? A Futures Contract is a financial obligation that requires the buyer to purchase an asset or financial instrument and/or a seller to sell an asset or financial instrument at a specified price and at a specified future date. The "Futures Contracts" define the underlying rules of the futures transaction. These contracts are standardized across all investors, and they trade on an exchange (e.g., futures exchange). The details of the contact could require actual physical delivery of the assets (such as oil, natural gas, commodities, etc.) or may call for the contract to be settled via cash.

What are forwards? A Forwards Contract is a non-standardized agreement between two parties to buy or sell an asset or financial instrument at a specified price and at a specified future date. It is similar to a Futures Contract, but the terms of the agreement are not standardized, and it does not trade on an exchange.

What are swaps? A swaps contract is a transaction between two counterparties (investors). In this type of transaction, each investor exchanges the cash flows from their financial instrument for the cash flow generated from the other party's financial instrument. The actual cash flow to be exchanged depends upon the type of financial instruments involved. For example, for a bond swap, the cash flow represents the periodic interest or coupon payments associated with the bond.

For an Interest Rate Swap, one party might agree to exchange their fixed interest rate payment on an investment with another party for their variable interest rate payment. The most common types of swaps are the Interest Rate Swap and the Currency Swap.

Option Contracts

As stated above, an options contract is a contract that gives the owner the right, but not the obligation, to transact an underlying asset or financial instrument at a specified price (e.g., the "strike price") on or before a specified time. The most basic options are the call option and the put option. An investor who bought an options contract is long the contract and an investor who sold the options contract is short the contract.

Notation. The options market has its own set of financial terminology and notation. This terminology consists of: stock price, strike price, expiration date, stock volatility, and risk-free interest rate. The notation used to price options is as follows:

- Stock price: S
- Exercise price: K
- Expiration date: T
- Stock volatility: σ
- Risk-free rate: r_f
- Call option price C
- Put option price P

Option Types. There are many different types of options that trade in the market. These include:

- European option: an option that can only be exercised on the expiration date
- American option: an option that can be exercised on or before the expiration date
- Asian option: an option whose payoff is determined by the average traded price over a specified time period
- Bermudan option: an option that can only be exercised only on a specified date before the expiration date

Call Option

A call option provides the owner of the contract the right, but not an obligation, to buy the stock at a specified price on or before a future point in time.

In a call option transaction, the buyer of the call option pays the seller the call option premium. If the stock is trading in the market on the expiration date at a price higher than the strike price, the owner of the call option will exercise the option. This allows them to buy the stock from the seller of the option at the lower strike price, and then sell the stock in the market at a higher price, thus earning a profit. If the stock is trading in the market on the expiration date at a price lower than the strike price of the contract, then the owner of the call option will not exercise the option. In this case the call option would expire, worthless.

The general profit functions for an investor who is long and short a call option are shown ahead.

Long Call Option: Profit Function

$$Profit\ at\ T = 0: \begin{cases} -C & S<K \\ S-K-C & S\geq K \end{cases}$$

The maximum loss for an investor who is long the call option is $-C$, which represents the cost of the option. The maximum gain for the investor who is long the call option is $+\infty$. For example, if the stock price decreases over the life of the options contract, the purchaser of the call is only out their initial investment of C. However, if the stock price keeps increasing in value over the life of the options contract, the purchaser of the call will be able to make an unlimited amount of profit. The call option provides the buyer with downside risk protection and provides unlimited earning potential.

Short Call Option: Profit Function

$$Profit\ at\ T = 0: \begin{cases} +C & S\leq K \\ S-K-C & S>K \end{cases}$$

The maximum loss for the investor who is short the call option is $-\infty$. For example, if the price continuously increases in value over the life of the contract, the owner of the call could call the stock from the seller of the .contract at the lower price and sell in the market at the much higher price. If the seller of the call contract does not own the stock, they will have to purchase it in the market at the much higher price, and sell it to the investor at the much lower price. And in theory, they could incur an unlimited loss. To protect oneself from an unlimited loss potential, sellers of call options will hold the underlying stock in their inventory. In this situation, they will just deliver the stock to the investor long the call contract. The maximum gain from selling a call option is $+C$.

Example 6.1

An investor purchases a call option for $C = \$5$ on a stock that is currently trading at $S = \$100$. If the strike price is $K = \$110$ and the length of the option is $t = 1$ year, what is the potential profit opportunity?

The profit function for an investor long this call option is determined by the equation

$$Profit\ at\ T = 1: \begin{cases} -\$5 & S \le \$110 \\ S - \$110 - \$5 & S > \$110 \end{cases}$$

Figure 6.1a illustrates this profit function graphically. If after one year (t = 1) the price of the stock is $S = \$110$ or less, the investor will incur a loss of $-\$5$, which is price of the call. If the stock price is above $S > \$110$, the investor will exercise the option, call the stock for $K = \$110$, and sell the stock in the market at the market price S. If the stock price is $S > \$115$, then the investor will incur a profit and recover the cost of the option. If the price is $\$110 \le S \le 115$, the investor will earn a profit on the sale of the stock, but will not recover the cost of the call option.

Figure 6.1b illustrates the profit function corresponding to this transaction for the market participant who sold the call option, e.g., for the investor who is short the call option. In this case, the participant receives $5 from the sale of the option. If the stock price falls over the year, the seller of the call will earn the price of the call. But if the price increases above $110, then they will begin to incur a loss. After the price increases above $S = \$115$, the seller of the call will incur a loss greater than the price received from the sale of the call. Theoretically, if the price increases indefinitely, the seller of the call could incur a loss of infinite value. To protect oneself from an infinite loss, the seller of a call option will usually hedge the position by purchasing the underlying shares of the stock.

Put Option

A put option provides the owner of the contract the right, but not an obligation, to put the stock into the market at a specified price on or before a future point in time.

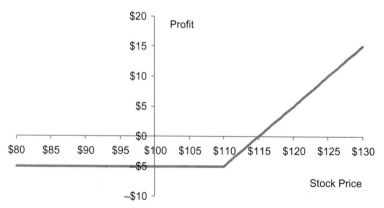

FIGURE 6.1A Profit Function — Long Call Option

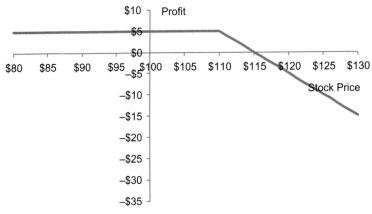

FIGURE 6.1B Profit Function – Short Call Option

In a put option transaction, the buyer of the put option pays the seller the put option premium. If the stock is trading in the market on the expiration date at a price higher than the strike price, the owner of the put will not exercise the contract since they could sell the stock in the market at a higher price. If the stock is trading in the market at a price lower than the strike price of the put option, then the investor will exercise the option and sell the shares to the participant short the put option at the higher price.

The general profit functions for an investor who is long and short a put option are shown ahead.

Long Put Option: Profit Function

$$\text{Profit at } T = 0: \begin{cases} -P & S \geq K \\ K - S - P & S < K \end{cases}$$

The maximum loss for an investor who is long the put option is $-\$P$, which represents the cost of the option. The maximum gain for the investor who is long the put option is $\$K - \$P$. For example, if the stock price falls to zero over the life of the contract, the investor could theoretically acquire the shares at $0\$$ and put them in the market at $\$K$. The net profit to the owner of a put contract is then $\$K - \$P$. However, if the stock price increases in value over the life of the contract, the holder of the put will not exercise the option and will only incur a loss of $\$P$. The put option provides the holder with downside risk protection and potential gains in times when the stock price falls.

Short Put Option: Profit Function

$$Profit\ at\ T = 0: \begin{cases} +P & S \geq K \\ S - K + P & S < K \end{cases}$$

The maximum loss for the investor who is short the call option is $-K + P$. For example, if the price falls to zero over the increases in value continuously over the life of the contract, the owner of the call could put the stock to the participant who is short the put contract at the strike price K. In this case, the participant purchased a stock for $\$E$ that is currently worth $\$0$. So this participant short the put option would have incurred a loss of $-\$E$, but still earned the put premium of $+\$K$.

The maximum gain the seller of the put option (the participant who is short the put) can have is equal to the price of the option $+\$P$. This would occur if the price of the stock increased over the life of the option contract.

Example 6.2

An investor purchases a put option for $P = \$5$ on a stock that is currently trading at $S = \$100$. If the strike price is $K = \$90$, and the length of the option contract is $t = 1$ year, what is the potential profit opportunity?

The profit function for the investor long this put option is determined by the equation

$$Profit\ at\ T = 1: \begin{cases} -\$5 & S \geq \$90 \\ \$90 - S - \$5 & S < \$90 \end{cases}$$

Figure 6.2a illustrates this profit function graphically. If after one year (t = 1) the price of the stock is $S = \$90$ or more, the investor will not exercise the put option and will incur a loss of $-\$5$ (which is price of the put). But if the stock price falls below $S < \$90$, the investor will exercise the put option and earn a profit of $\$90 - S - \$5$. In this case, the investor will not incur a positive profit until the stock price falls below $\$85$.

Figure 6.2b illustrates the profit function for this transaction for the market participant who sold the put option (e.g., for the participant who is short this put option). In this case, the participant receives $\$5$ from the sale of the option. If the stock price rises over the year, the seller of the put will earn the price of the put. But if the price falls below $\$85$, then they will begin to incur a loss. The maximum loss this participant might incur is if the price falls to $\$0$. In this case the total loss incurred would be $\$0 - 90 + \$5 = -\$85$.

Additional option terminology:

- *In-the-money option.* When the strike price is less than the market price for a call option, or when the strike price is greater than the market price for a put option.

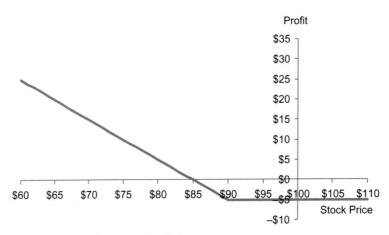

FIGURE 6.2A Profit Function - Long Put Option

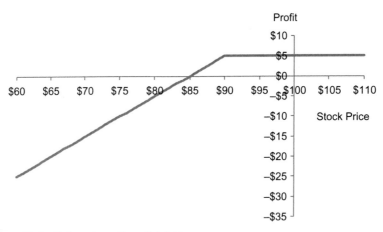

FIGURE 6.2B Profit Function - Short Put Option

- *Out-of-the-money option.* When the strike price is greater than the market price for a call option, or when the strike price is less than the market price for a put option.
- *At-the-money option (calls and puts).* When the stock price is trading at or near the strike price of the option contract.

Put-Call Parity

The put–call parity defines the relationship between the price of a call option and the price of a put option with identical strike prices and expiration dates. A detailed derivation of the Put-Call Parity can be found in Copeland and

Weston (1988). The relationship is based on a risk-free relationship in which an investor is indifferent to whether they hold a bond and call option or a stock and a put option. The Put-Call relationship determines the prices to make these two options equivalent.

The Put-Call Parity equation is stated as follows:

$$S - C + P = \frac{K}{(1+r_f)^t}$$

This states that the value of a portfolio consisting of the stock, a long call option, and short a put is equal to the strike price discounted at the risk-free rate.

Rearranging the terms in the equation above yields:

$$C + \frac{EK}{(1+R_f)^t} = S + P$$

Therefore, the Put-Call Parity defines the relationship between our factors.

Example 6.3

Determine the price of a put option if we have the following:

Call Price: $C = \$5$
Stock Price: $S = \$100$
Strike Price: $K = \$105$
Risk-Free: $R_f = 0.08/\text{year}$
Expiration Time: $t = 0.5$

Following the Put-Call Parity relationship we have:

$$C + \frac{K}{(1+R_f)^t} = S + P$$

$$5 + \frac{105}{(1+0.08)^{0.5}} = 100 + P$$

$$P = 5 + \frac{105}{(1+0.08)^{0.5}} - 100$$

$$P = \$6.03$$

Alternative Put-Call Parity Derivation

An alternative derivation of the Put-Call Parity equation is based on our continuous compounding formulation (see Chapter 7) and is as follows:

$$S - C(S, K, T) + P(S, K, T) = Ke^{-R_f T}$$

Notice the only difference here is with the treatment of the compounding of the interest rate. Continuous interest rate compounding provides analysts with appealing mathematical properties and will become useful working with the Black-Scholes option pricing model ahead.

Important note: Up until this point we have described the option profit function for a specified strike price over a year. It should not come as a surprise to readers that if the time to option expiration is longer, there is more opportunity for the price to move into the money. Additionally, if the stock has a higher volatility, there is more potential for the price to move into the money. In the sections ahead we discuss how to factor in both time to expiration and stock volatility to determine the option price.

Option Strategies

A large majority of the complex financial engineering products and risk management techniques are often based on simple plain vanilla option strategies. Analysts combine long and short call and put options at different strike prices (and often at different expiration dates) with the underlying stock asset (long or short) and also at times with risk-free bonds to create advanced derivative products and hedging strategies.

Investors use these different option strategies to hedge against various types of risk, and to better position the fund based on market expectations (e.g., bullish or bearish). While these techniques are often used to manage financial risk, they are also being used for market speculation, and recently for long-term investment objective. Some of the more common types of option combination strategies include the covered-call, straddle, and strangle.

The underlying premise behind pricing any derivatives instrument is based on a no arbitrage constraint. That is, investors are not able to realize a risk-free profit without any cash investment.

Covered call: An investment strategy in which the investor buys a stock (long) and sells (shorts) a call option. Recall that in the case in which the investor writes a call option, they are exposed to unlimited risk. If the stock price increases, the writer of the call is obligated to provide the buyer of the call the stock at the strike price. If the writer of the option does not have the stock in their inventory, they will need to purchase it in the market (which could be at an extremely high price) and deliver it to the buyer of the option at what could be a very low price (the strike price) and could potentially incur an extremely large loss. A covered call is a situation where the option writer has the stock in their inventory already and is then able to deliver the stock to the buyer of the option without having to go into the market; thus, they will not incur a potentially high loss. The covered call provides the option seller with protection if market prices increase.

Straddle: An investment strategy in which the investor simultaneously buys/sells both a call option and a put option at the same exercise price and at the same expiration date. In the case in which the investor is long the straddle (buys both put and call options), they will incur gain if the stock price moves in either direction. But if the price does not change or only changes a small amount, the investor will lose the cost of the buy and sell options. In the case where the investor is short the straddle (writes both put and call options), they will incur a gain if the market price does not change or if the market price only changes a small amount. But if the stock price changes a large amount in either direction, the writer of the straddle will incur a loss.

Strangle: An investment strategy (similar to the straddle) in which the investor simultaneously buys/sells both a call option and a put option with the same expiration date, but at different strike prices. A long strangle consists of the investor buying a call option and a sell option at different strike prices. The investor who is long the strangle position will realize a profit if there is a large price movement in either direction. The maximum cost to the investor long a strangle is the price of the call and put options. The advantage to the investor is unlimited upside potential. A short strangle position consists of writing a call option and writing a put option for the same expiration date, but for different strike prices. An investor who is short the strangle will realize a profit as long as there is not a large price movement in either direction. However, they are also subject to large losses in the event of a large price swing.

Figure 6.3 illustrates a straddle for a long position (Figure 6.3a) and a short position (Figure 6.3b). Figure 6.4 illustrates a strangle for a long position (Figure 6.4a) and a short position (Figure 6.4b).

Black-Scholes Options Pricing Model

The Black-Scholes options pricing model (OPM) was introduced by Fischer Black and Myron Scholes (1973). Robert Merton (1973) shortly thereafter expanded on the work of Black and Scholes and coined phrase the Black–Scholes options pricing model. Their breakthrough work earned Robert

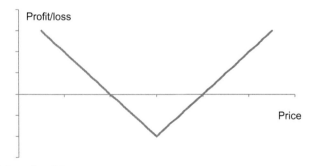

FIGURE 6.3A Long Straddle

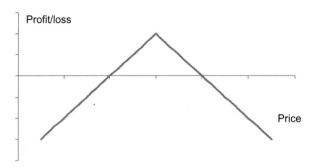

FIGURE 6.3B Short Straddle

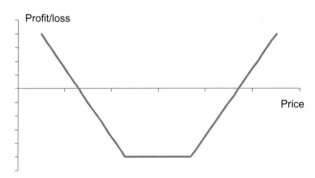

FIGURE 6.4A Long Strangle

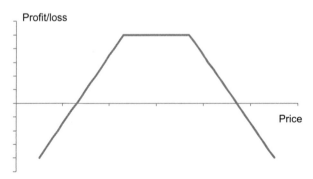

FIGURE 6.4B Short Strangle

Merton and Myron Scholes the 1997 Nobel Prize in Economics.[2] Fisher Black was not awarded the Nobel Prize due to his death in 1995, but he was cited as a key contributor.[3]

The Black-Scholes formulation is used to estimate the fair value cost of a call option under a given set of conditions. The general idea behind the model is that an investor could perfectly hedge all option risk by buying and selling options over time. This "no arbitrage" solution implies that there is only one fair value option price, hence the solution of the Black-Scholes option price.

In this section we provide the formulation of the Black-Scholes OPM. Readers interested in further details and the full derivation of the model are referred to Jarrow and Rudd (1983), Kolb (1993), and Hull (1997).

Model assumptions:

- European option
- No arbitrage
- Price evolution follows Weiner process (geometric random walk) with constant drift and variance
- No dividends
- Borrow and lend at the risk-free rate
- Buy, sell, and short any quantities or percentages
- No corresponding fees or costs
- No transaction costs (e.g., market impact is not incurred during trading)

While there are many variations and advancements of the Black-Scholes option pricing model, these approaches are based on these underlying assumptions, but some models allow for incorporation of transaction costs, dividends, and different interest rates for borrowing and lending (Chriss, 1997). The Black-Scholes model remains the workhorse options pricing model in the industry.

Model Notation:

- C = Call option price (what we are computing)
- P = Put option price (derived from the call price C based on Put-Call Parity described earlier)
- S = Stock price
- K = Strike price
- R_f = Risk-free rate
- σ = Instantaneous stock volatility
- T = Time to expiration
- $N(d)$ = cumulative standard normal distribution probability at d

---

[2]The Nobel Prize in Economics is actually the Sveriges Riksbank Prize in Economic Sciences. It is presented in memory of Alfred Nobel. Additionally, there is not a Nobel Prize for mathematics, but that is another story.

[3]The Nobel Prize is only awarded to living persons. The only exception is if the person dies after publically winning the award (Oct.), but before the actual awards ceremony (Dec.).

$$N(d) = \frac{1}{\sqrt{2\pi}} \int_{-\infty}^{d} e^{-\frac{z^2}{2}} dz$$

Black-Scholes formulation:

$$C(S, K, T) = S \cdot N(d_1) - Ke^{-rT} \cdot N(d_2)$$

where

$$d_1 = \frac{\ln\left(\frac{S}{K}\right) + \left(r + \frac{1}{2}\sigma^2\right)T}{\sigma\sqrt{T}}$$

$$d_2 = \frac{\ln\left(\frac{S}{K}\right) + \left(r - \frac{1}{2}\sigma^2\right)T}{\sigma\sqrt{T}} = d_1 - \sigma\sqrt{T}$$

Example 6.4: Determine the Price of a Call Option

What is the fair value call option price according to Black-Scholes option pricing model for the following situation?

- $S = \$100$
- $K = \$105$
- $\sigma = 30\%$
- $R_f = 5\%$ *annual*
- $T = 1$ *year*

Step 1: Compute $N(d_1)$:

$$d_1 = \frac{\ln\left(\frac{100}{110}\right) + \left(0.05 + \frac{1}{2}0.30^2\right) \cdot 1}{0.30 \cdot \sqrt{1}} = 0.1540$$

$$N(d_1) = N(0.1540) = 0.5612$$

Step 2: Compute $N(d_2)$:

$$d_2 = d_1 - \sigma\sqrt{T} = 0.1540 - 0.30 \cdot \sqrt{1} = -0.1460$$
$$N(d_2) = N(-0.1460) = 0.4420$$

Step 3: Compute the price of the call option:

$$C(S, K, T) = 100 \cdot 0.5612 - 105 \cdot e^{-0.05 \cdot 1} \cdot 0.4420$$
$$= 11.98$$

Example 6.5: Put Option Price Derivation

The price for the corresponding put option can also be computed using the put-call parity relationship and the Black-Scholes formulation. These steps are:

Step 1: Start with the Put-Call Parity equation:

$$S - C(S,K,T) + P(S,K,T) = Ke^{-R_f T}$$

Step 2: Rearranging the expressions yields:

$$P(S,K,T) = C(S,K,T) + Ke^{-R_f T} - S$$

Step 3: Recall the call price from Black-Scholes:

$$C(S,K,T) = S \cdot N(d_1) - Ke^{-R_f T} \cdot N(d_2)$$

Step 4: Substitute the call price (in step 2) with the Black-Scholes call option price (step 3). That is:

$$P(S,K,T) = \{S \cdot N(d_1) - Ke^{-R_f T} \cdot N(d_2)\} + Ke^{-R_f T} - S$$

Step 5: Rearranging the expressions yields:

$$P(S,K,T) = S \cdot (N(d_1) - 1) - Ke^{-R_f T}(N(d_2) + 1)$$

Example 6.6: Determine the Price of a Put

Using the information from Example 6.4 and Example 6.5, determine the price of the corresponding put option.

- $S = \$100$
- $K = \$105$
- $\sigma = 30\%$
- $R_f = 5\%$ *annual*
- $T = 1$ *year*

Solving for the call option price yields:

- $C(S,K,T) = 11.98$

Then the price of the put option is:

$$P(S,K,T) = 11.98 + 105 \cdot e^{-0.05 \cdot 1} - 100$$
$$= 11.86$$

Option Risk

The corresponding risks of an option are often referred to as the option "Greeks," in reference to mathematicians using Greek notation to represent the different risks. These calculations refer to how the value of an option will vary based on changing input variables (e.g., option factors). Therefore, we can think of our option risk as the sensitivity of the option value to the underlying factors. Option risk terms are of the utmost importance for portfolio managers when managing and evaluating financial risk.

The option risk terms are determined from the first-order derivatives and consist of *delta*, *vega*, *theta*, and *rho* and a second-order derivative of the value function, *gamma*.

To show these option risk terms mathematically, let us start by restating the Black-Scholes option pricing model:

$$C(S, K, T) = S \cdot N(d_1) - Ke^{-rT} \cdot N(d_2)$$

Where

$$d_1 = \frac{\ln\left(\frac{S}{K}\right) + \left(r + \frac{1}{2}\sigma^2\right)T}{\sigma\sqrt{T}}$$

$$d_2 = d_1 - \sigma\sqrt{T}$$

Notice that the call price is dependent upon:

- S = Stock price
- K = Strike price
- σ = Volatility
- T = Time to expiration
- R_f = Risk-free interest rate
- V = Value of the option (either call or put price)

It is important to point out that the option risk terms refer to the change in the option value due to changing factors. In the earlier formulation, the strike price variable is the only variable that will remain constant over the life of the option and thus does not typically have any risk assignment or a Greek notation. However, many managers evaluate how the call and put option prices will vary based on changing strike prices, and use this information as a comparison to the actual market prices for the different calls and put to determine if the market prices are over or undervalued. Additional information is provided by Chriss (1997) and Hull (1997).

The option risk terms include:

Delta: The measure of the option value's sensitivity to changing stock price. Most often, the value of delta is provided based on a $1 change in stock price. Mathematically, delta is determined as follows:

$$\Delta = \frac{\partial V}{\partial S}$$

Vega: The measure of the option value's sensitivity to changing volatility. Most often, the value of vega is based on a 1% change in volatility. Mathematically, vega is determined as follows:

$$\nu = \frac{\partial V}{\partial \sigma}$$

Theta: The measure of the option value's sensitivity to changing time. In this case, since we are holding the option the time variable is continuously decreasing as we move closer and closer to expiration date. Most often, the value provided is based on a one-day time change. Mathematically, theta is determined as follows:

$$\Theta = -\frac{\partial V}{\partial \tau}$$

Rho: The measure of the option value's sensitivity to changing risk-free interest rate. Most often, the value of rho is based on a 1% change in risk-free interest rate. Option value is usually the least sensitive to change in risk-free interest rate, and this is usually subject to the smallest number of changes over the life of the option. Mathematically, Rho is determined as follows:

$$\rho = \frac{\partial V}{\partial R_f}$$

Gamma: The measure of the sensitivity of the delta risk term with respect to changing stock price. The gamma risk is based on the second-order derivative and is most often provided on a $1 change in stock price. Mathematically, gamma is determined as follows:

$$\Gamma = \frac{\partial \Delta}{\partial S} = \frac{\partial^2 V}{\partial S^2}$$

Alternative Option Pricing Models
Binomial Model

The binomial option pricing model estimates the theoretical fair value of the call option based on a binomial tree and using discrete time intervals. It was introduced by Cox, Ross, and Rubinstein (1979). The approach consists of constructing a riskless portfolio consisting of a call option and a stock (similar to the approach used in Black-Scholes) and determining the option price at each node in the tree to satisfy the no-arbitrage condition. The process first determines the option value at the final node in the binomial tree and then, working backwards, determines the value for each node back to the starting position. In a Binomial Model, each future price can be either up or down. In a trinomial model, the stock price can be up, down, or unchanged. An advantage of a Binomial Model over other types of option pricing models is that it can incorporate dividend payments as well as a non-normal distribution. It is also more flexible with regards to pricing American and European options. Detailed analysis and derivation of the binomial option pricing model is provided by Chriss (1997).

Monte Carlo Model

A Monte Carlo option pricing model is determined from Monte Carlo simulation and estimates the fair value of an option through an averaging technique. It can be used to price various types of options including European, American, and Asian. For example, see Boyle (1977), Broadie and Glasserman (1996), and Longstaff and Schwartz (2001).

The Monte Carlo technique is as follows.[4] First, simulate several thousand option prices based on random as well as historically observed price trajectories. Second, compute the corresponding future payoff for the value of each price trajectory (following a risk-neutral valuation similar to Black-Scholes). Third, average the payoffs across all trajectories. Finally, discount the payoff value to the current time. An advantage of the Monte Carlo Model is that distribution of the data is not limited to a normal or log-normal distribution. We have the freedom to incorporate various different probability distribution functions including extreme value functions as well as incorporating economic shocks into the analysis. Monte Carlo methods provide analysts with tools to better perform advanced what-if and sensitivity analysis. It is one of the more important risk management analysis techniques.

Implied Volatility

When pricing option contracts, there are the known and observable factors (stock price, strike price, time to expiration, and risk-free rate) and the unknown and non-observable factor (expected forward-looking volatility). This forward-looking volatility term is often "implied" or inferred from the market-determined option prices. It could also be dramatically different from historical volatility, especially if the market believes that there has been a volatility regime shift (such as what we experienced during the financial crisis).

Implied Volatility is determined based on the general consensus of what the market believes is the fair value price for the underlying option price. For example, if the price of the call option is $5, then the Implied Volatility is the volatility value that will arrive at the $5 option price. In other words, we back into the volatility term using the actual market price and values of the observable factors (price, strike, risk-free, and time to expiration). Analysts will use the previously

---

[4]See: http://en.wikipedia.org/wiki/Monte_Carlo_methods_for_option_pricing; Lu, B. (2011), "Monte Carlo Simulations and Option Pricing;" and http://www.math.psu.edu/mazzucat/undergrad/bingqian MonteCarlo.pdf

described option pricing models (such as Black-Scholes, binomial tree, etc.) to determine the Implied Volatility of an asset.

Forward-looking volatility indicators include the VIX Index derived from a weighted average of options on the SP500 index, the VXN Index (derived from the NASDAQ 100 index futures), and IVX (derived from options on stocks and exchange-traded funds).

Implied Correlation

The Implied Correlation measure is similar to the Implied Volatility measure. It is the market's general consensus view of forward-looking stock correlation. It is computed as an average correlation across a sample of stocks. For example, if we have the Implied Volatility of a stock index such as the SP500 and the Implied Volatility for each of the underlying stocks, then the Implied Correlation is the average correlation value that will result in the Implied Volatility of the index.

Volatility Smile

A Volatility Smile is the graphical pattern for which in-the-money options and out-of-the-money options have higher implied volatilities as we move further away from the at-the-money option value. Plotting the implied volatilities as a function of the different strike prices reveals a pattern that depicts a smile. This pattern is believed to be based on different levels of risk aversion that require different payments (risk premiums) for different strike prices.

Futures Contracts

A Futures Contract is a financial obligation in which the buyer is required to purchase an asset, and the seller is required to sell the asset at a predetermined price on a predetermined date. The corresponding Futures Contract "asset" can be a physical good or commodity (such as gold, oil, natural gas, corn, wheat, etc.) or a financial instrument (such as a stock, bonds, indexes, etc.). The investors usually have the option to purchase or deliver the asset specified in the contract or settle the Futures Contract via a cash transaction.

The underlying Futures Contracts states the terms of the contract such as quantity of the underlying assets (such as gold) to transact along with the transaction price and transaction date. The Futures Contracts are standardized and trade on different exchanges.

The Futures Contract price is determined following a no-arbitrage pricing rule. The determinants of the futures price consist of:

- Spot price (cash price)
- Carrying charge

- Financing
- Storage
- Insurance
- Transportation
- Transaction Costs

Computing the fair value price of a Futures Contract can be determined following the "Cost-of-Carry Model" and the "Reverse Cost-of-Carry Model." In this section we provide a framework that can be used to compute the fair value futures price for various assets (both physical and financial). We provide an example for the futures price of gold following the examples provided by Kolb (1991, 1993). Readers can easily extend these formulations for the appropriate assets and trading characteristics.

In each of the following examples, we provide a cash flow analysis to show the profit or loss that an investor will incur by engaging in various transactions. We then show the bounds on these conditions required to eliminate a riskless arbitrage situation.

Example 6.7: Cost-of-Carry

In this example we demonstrate how the investor can earn a risk-free profit without any cash investment by purchasing the asset in the sport market via a loan and simultaneously selling a Futures Contract to lock in a profit. We follow the example shown in Kolb (1991, 1993). We make the additional assumption in this example that there are no corresponding storage, transportation, or transaction costs (Kolb, 1993).

Price scenario:

Spot price: S = $1000
Future price: F = $1100
Interest rate: Rf = 5%
Expiration: T = 1 year

Initial transaction:

Borrow $1000 at an interest rate of 5%: +$1000
Purchase Gold in the Cash Market at $1000: −$1000
Sell a Futures Contract for $1100: $0
Cash Outlay: $0

Expiration date transaction:

Deliver the Gold from Futures Contract: +$1100
Repay Loan ($1000 at 5%): −$1050
Cash Outlay: +$50
Profit = +$50

Under this pricing scenario the investor would earn a risk-free profit of $+\$50$ without any cash investment, which violates the no-arbitrage pricing rule. Thus, in order to adhere to our no-arbitrage pricing rule requirement, the futures price must adhere to the following constraint:

$$F \leq S(1 + R_f)$$

Example 6.8: Reverse Cost-of-Carry

In this example, we demonstrate how the investor can earn a risk-free profit without any cash investment by selling short an asset in the spot market and investing the proceeds of the sales at the risk-free rate, while simultaneously buying a Futures Contract. The position is then offset by accepting delivery of the asset and paying for the asset via proceeds from the loan. This is as follows from Kolb (1991, 1993). We make the additional assumption in this example that there are no corresponding storage, transportation, or transaction costs (Kolb, 1993).

Price scenario:

Spot Price: $S = \$1000$
Future Price: $F = \$1025$
Interest Rate: $Rf = 5\%$
Expiration: $T = 1$ year

Initial transaction:

Lend $1000 at an interest rate of 5%: −$1000
Short Gold in the Cash Market at $1000: +$1000
Buy Futures Contract for $1025: $0
Cash Outlay: $0

Expiration date transaction:

Receive Proceed from the Loan: +$1050
Purchase Gold from Futures Contract: −$1025
Offset the Short Position: +$0
Cash Outlay: +$25
Profit: +$25

In this example, the investor would earn a risk-free profit of +$25 without making any cash investment. Again, this violates our no-arbitrage pricing rule. In order to adhere to our no-arbitrage pricing rule requirement, the futures price must adhere to the following constraint:

$$F \geq S(1 + R_f)$$

In order to ensure that a risk-free arbitrage opportunity does not exist, the futures price must adhere to the following two conditions:

1. $F \leq S(1 + R_f)$
2. $F \geq S(1 + R_f)$

This, of course, yields:

$$F = S(1 + R_f)$$

Futures Price with Transaction Costs

In a futures transaction (over a time horizon of t), the relationship between the futures price, spot price, and determinants is bounded as follows:

$$S_0(1+C)^t(1 - TC) \leq F_t \leq S_0(1+C)^t(1 + TC)$$

where F_t represents the futures price at time t, S_0 is the sport price at time $t = 0$, C is the total carrying charge consisting of storage, transportation, and insurance, and t is the time to expiration of the contract. (see Kolb, 1993 and Hull, 1997).

Futures Price with Dividend Paying Instruments

In a financial transaction with transaction costs, the relationship between the futures price, spot price, and determinants is bounded as follows:

$$S_0(1+C)^t(1 - TC) - D(1+R_f)^{t-t1} \leq F_t \leq S_0(1+C)^t(1 + TC) - D(1+R_f)^{t-t1}$$

where F_t represents the futures price at time t, S_0 is the sport price at time $t = 0$, C is the total carrying charge consisting of storage, transportation, and insurance, t is the time to expiration of the contract, D is the dividend payment, and $t - t1$ is the time remaining to expiration.

Readers are encouraged to verify the above relationship (see Kolb, 1993 and Hull, 1997).

Forwards Contract

A Forwards Contract is a non-standardized contract between two participants. The participant buying the Forwards Contract becomes long the contract, and the participant selling the contract becomes short the contract. A Forwards Contract is similar to a Futures Contract in that the contract calls for an exchange of goods (physical or financial) at a specified price at a specified future date. But unlike a Futures Contract, a Forwards Contract is not traded on an exchange, and the

Forwards Contract is not subject to standardized contract terms. Pricing the Forwards Contract also follows the framework used to price a Futures Contract.

Comparison of Futures and Forwards

A Futures Contract and a Forwards Contract differ in several ways (see Salvatore 2001a, b):

- Futures trade on exchanges and have standardized contract terms.
- Forwards are traded over-the-counter and are customized between buyer and seller.
- Forward contracts are subject to counter-party risk.
- Futures Contracts are backed by the clearing house. Thus, futures are subject to less risk than a forward.
- To engage in a forward contract, an investor needs to find the counter-party to take the other side of the contract (which may or may not be easy).
- To engage in a Futures Contract, an investor only needs to interact with the futures exchange. They do not need to find the counter-party and negotiate all terms and conditions of the contract.

Swaps Contracts

A Swaps Contracts is an agreement between parties to exchange cash flows over a specified period of time. The parties involved in the swap agreement are known as the counterparties of the contract. An example of a swap agreement is as follows. Two counterparties, participant A and participant B, agree to swap interest rate over a specified period of time. Participant A agrees to pay participant B the fixed interest rate over the period, and participant B agrees to pay participant A the floating interest rate over the same three-year period. Another example of a swap agreement is where two parties A and B may agree to swap coupon payments from a bond over time. In situations where interest rates are the swap instrument, the cash flow to exchange is based on a contracted notional dollar amount such as one million USD.

The terms of a swap agreement are customized between the counterparties involved in the contract. The contract dictates the terms of the agreement such as the dates that the cash flows are to be exchanged and the underlying calculation metric. Often, one of the cash flows is based on a fixed rate, and the other cash flow is based on a variable or unknown rate. The swap contract is traded over-the-counter. They are facilitated by swap dealers who help to identify the counter-parties and terms of the swap agreement. Swaps are used in the financial industry to manage risk and hedge positions as well as for speculation. The most common types of swap contracts are the Interest Rate Swap and the Foreign Exchange Swap. We outline the process described by Kolb (1991, 1993), Chriss (1997), Hull (1997), and Salvatore (2001a, b).

Interest Rate Swap

An Interest Rate Swap consists of participant A paying a fixed rate to participant B, and participant B paying participant A the floating rate. The floating rate is commonly benchmarked to the LIBOR or EURIBOR rates. However, more recently, there have been industry discussions regarding moving the floating rate benchmark used for Interest Rate Swaps from the LIBOR to a weighted average index across various different interest rate benchmarks.

Example 6.9: Interest Rate Swap

Swap agreement terms:

- Counterparty A invests $1 million in a fixed bond paying 10% annually.
- Counterparty B invests $1 million in a variable financial instrument that pays LIBOR +2% annually.
- Counterparty A and counterparty B agree to exchange cash flows over the next years.
- The counterparties do not know in advance what the net cash flow will be because the LIBOR rate is subject to variability over the year. Thus, both parties are subject to interest rate risk in this swap contract.

If the LIBOR rate is 9% during the first year, what are the cash flow exchanges between the two counterparties?

After the first year, counterparty A is obligated to pay counterparty B $100,000 (10% of $1M), and counterparty B is obligated to pay counterparty A $110,000 (9% + 2% = 11% of $1M). The swap contract is then settled by counterparty B paying counterparty A the $10,000 difference between cash flows (Kolb, 1993 and Hull, 1997).

Currency Swap

A Currency Swap is a swap agreement between two counterparties to exchange one FX currency for another over a specified period of time. Currency Swap agreements are also over-the-counter products and are very similar to the Interest Rate Swaps described earlier. The main difference between a Currency Swap and an Interest Rate Swap is that the Currency Swap includes the exchange of principal value, whereas the Interest Rate Swap only involves the exchange of the difference in interest rate payments.

A plain vanilla Currency Swap is a transaction where one counterparty exchanges one currency for an equivalent value of a different currency. The plain vanilla Currency Swap agreement is as follows:

1. Both counterparties exchange equivalent values of the currencies. For example, a participant may exchange $100 million US dollars for the

equivalent of $100 million dollars in Euros. Both counterparties actually exchange the cash in this case.
2. Counterparties make interest rate payments to each other over the life of the swap.
3. At the expiration of the swap contract, both counterparties exchange their principal cash.

Example 6.10: Currency Swap

Counterparty A holds $100 million US dollars (USD) and wishes to engage in a Currency Swap with counterparty B for Euros (EU). What would the Currency Swap transaction look like based on the pricing data below?

Pricing data:

- The spot exchange rate between USD and EUR is 1.25. That is, it takes 1.25 USD to purchase 1.00 EUR.
- The swap agreement is for $100 million dollars.
- The US risk-free rate is 8%.
- The European risk-free rate is 12%.
- Duration = five years.
- Interest payments are made annually.

   Currency Swap details:

- Counterparty A exchanges $100 million USD for €80 million Euros with counterparty B.
- Counterparty A pays counterparty B an annual interest rate of €9.6 million Euros (12% of €80 MM Euros).
- Counterparty B pays counterparty A an annual interest rate of $8 million USD (8% of $100 MM USD).
- In actuality, the counterparties only transact the net difference in interest rate payments based on the spot rate at that time.
- Interest rate payments are made for the full five years.
- At the end of the swap agreement, counterparty A returns the €80 million Euros to counterparty B, and counterparty B returns the $100 million Euros to counterparty A.

   Source: Kolb (1993) and Hull (1997)

Alternative Types of Financial Swap

Volatility swap: A volatility swap is an over-the-counter swap contract on the future realized volatility of a financial instrument. This allows investors to trade and speculate on volatility levels in much the same manner that they would with regards to the underlying price movement of a performance index such as the SP500 index. They are also used to hedge the volatility risk of other financial positions and portfolios. The VIX index is often used as a proxy for the current market volatility level.

Correlation Swap: A Correlation Swap is an over-the-counter swap contract on the future realized correlation levels in the market. The correlation index is often based on an observed correlation measure across a collection of financial assets. This allows investors to trade and speculate on the underlying correlation levels in the market, similar to trading market volatility.

CONCLUSIONS

In this chapter we provided readers with an overview of the various different equity derivative products including options (call and puts), futures, and swap. We provided the basic foundations and building blocks for readers to be able to price the different derivative products as well as construct more complex products. As stated above, all of the derivative pricing is based on a "no-arbitrage" requirement. That is, an investor is not able to realize a risk-free profit. The chapter was enhanced with examples pertaining to plain vanilla pricing models. Readers looking to engage in more complex financial engineering analysis and risk management exercises can simply build and expand on these concepts.

Endnotes

[1] https://en.wikipedia.org/wiki/Derivative_(finance)
[2] http://en.wikipedia.org/wiki/Monte_Carlo_methods_for_option_pricing
[3] http://www.investopedia.com/terms/d/derivative.asp
[4] http://www.wilmott.com/

References

Black, F., Scholes, M., 1973. The pricing of options and corporate liabilities. J. Polit. Econ., 637–654.
Boyle, P., Ananthanarayanan, A., 1977. The impact of variance estimation in options valuation models. J. Financ. Econ. 5, 375–388.
Broadie, M., Glasserman, P., 1996. Estimating Security Price Derivatives Using Simulation. Manage. Sci. 42, 269–285.
Chriss, N., 1997. Black-Scholes and Beyond: Options Pricing Models. McGraw-Hill.
Copeland, T.E., Weston, J.F., 1988. Financial Theory and Corporate Policy, third ed. Addison-Wesley Publishing Company.
Cox, J.C., Ross, S.A., Rubinstein, M., 1979. Option pricing: a simplified approach. J. Financ. Econ. 7, 229–263.
Elton, E., Gruber, M., 1995. Modern Portfolio Theory, fifth ed. John Wiley & Sons, Inc, New York.

Hull, J., 1997. Options, Futures, and Other Derivatives, third ed. Prentice Hall.

Kolb, R., 1991. Options: An Introduction. Kolb Publishing, Miami.

Kolb, R., 1993. Financial Derivatives. New York Institute of Finance.

Jarrow, R.A., Rudd, A., 1983. Option Pricing. Irwin Press, Homewood, IL.

Longstaff, F.A., Schwartz, E.S., 2001. Valuing American Options by Simulation: A Simple Least Squares Approach. Rev. Financ. Stud. 14, 113–148.

Merton, R.C., 1973. Theory of Rational Pricing. Bell J. Econ. Manag. Sci., 141–183.

Lu, B., 2011. Monte Carlo Simulations and Option Pricing, <http://www.math.psu.edu/mazzucat/undergrad/bingqianMonteCarlo.pdf>.

Salvatore, D., 2001a. International Markets, seventh ed. John Wiley & Sons.

Salvatore, D., 2001b. Managerial Economics in a Global Economy, eighth ed. Harcourt College Publishers.

Foreign Exchange Market and Interest Rates

The foreign exchange market (FX market) is where participants come to buy and sell foreign currencies (e.g., foreign exchange rates, currencies, etc.). Foreign exchange trading occurs around the clock and throughout all global markets. It is the only truly continuous and nonstop trading market in the world, with participants trading day and night, weekday and weekend, and on holidays. It has also been described as the intersection of Wall Street and Main Street.

Participants trading on the foreign exchange include corporations, governments, central banks, investment banks, commercial banks, hedge funds, retail brokers, investors, and vacationers. One of the biggest differences between the FX markets and other financial markets is the overall activity from corporations to facilitate day-to-day business practices as well as to hedge longer-term risk. Corporations will engage in FX trading to facilitate necessary business transactions, to hedge against market risk, and, to a lesser extent, to facilitate longer-term investment needs.

Foreign exchange trading volumes from many of these global companies are dramatically larger than even the largest financial institutions, hedge funds, and some governments. Other financial markets (such as the markets) simply do not receive the same amount of interest from Main Street corporations because they do not meet their business needs of buying and selling goods in foreign countries.

The FX market is an over-the-counter market (OTC) in which prices are quoted by FX brokers (broker-dealers) and transactions are negotiated directly with the buyers and sellers (participants). The FX market is not a single exchange like the old New York Stock Exchange (NYSE). It is a global network of markets connected by computer systems (and even still by a phone network!) that more closely resembles the NASDAQ market structure. There are FX markets in all countries. The major FX markets are London, New York, Paris, Zurich, Frankfurt, Singapore, Hong Kong, and Tokyo. London is the largest.

In this chapter we provide an overview of the FX market and the important terms that need to be understood for proper risk-management practices. Readers interested in further background and a more detailed investigation into the foreign exchange market and interest rates are referred to endnotes [1—3]. We build on the framework and modeling methodology introduced in these sources throughout the chapters. Readers are encouraged to visit these sites for continuously updated references and modeling methodologies.

How Much Does the FX Market Trade?

The FX markets traded about $4—5 trillion dollars per day in 2012. This consists of value traded on the sport market and in forwards, futures, and swap transactions. The largest trading currencies in the world are the United States Dollar (42.5%), Euro (19.6%), Japanese Yen (9.5%), Pound Sterling (6.5%), and Australian Dollar (3.8%). Combined, these five currencies comprise more than 80% of the global currency value traded.

Many data sources (e.g., http://www.therichest.org/business/most-traded-currencies) use a 200% system to account for foreign exchange traded volume, since every currency trades in pairs. Table 7.1 shows the percentages of total FX value

Table 7.1 World's Most Traded Currencies

Rank	Region	Currency Name	Currency	Symbol	Pct Traded
1	United States	United States Dollar	USD	$	42.5%
2	European Union	Euro	EUR	€	19.6%
3	Japan	Japanese Yen	JPY	¥	9.5%
4	United Kingdom	Pound Sterling	GBP	£	6.5%
5	Australia	Australian Dollar	AUD	$	3.8%
6	Switzerland	Swiss Franc	CHF	Fr	3.2%
7	Canada	Canadian Dollar	CAD	$	2.7%
8	Hong Kong	Hong Kong Dollar	HKD	$	1.2%
9	Sweden	Swedish Krona	SEK	kr	1.1%
10	New Zealand	New Zealand Dollar	NZD	$	0.8%
11	South Korea	South Korean Won	KRW	₩	0.8%
12	Singapore	Singapore Dollar	SGD	$	0.7%
13	Norway	Norwegian Krone	NOK	kr	0.7%
14	Mexico	Mexican Peso	MXN	$	0.7%
15	India	Indian Rupee	INR	INR	0.5%
	other				6.1%
	Total				100.0%

Percentages have been divided by 2 to ensure a total value of 100%.
Source: http://www.therichest.org/business/most-traded-currencies/ (March 23, 2012)

Table 7.2 FX Broker Dealer Volumes

Rank	Bank	Pct
1	Deutsche	15.6%
2	Barclays	10.8%
3	UBS AG	10.6%
4	Citi	8.9%
5	JPMorgan	6.4%
6	HSBC	6.3%
7	RBS	6.2%
8	CreditSuisse	4.8%
9	Goldman	4.1%
10	MorganStanley	3.6%
	Total	77.3%

Source: www.therichest.org (March 23, 2012)

traded by the fifteen most-traded currencies. In this table, we divided the reported percentages by two in order to have a basis of 100%.

The FX currencies are traded throughout the world by foreign exchange brokers. The top fifteen brokers account for more than three-quarters of the total FX valued traded globally. This is shown in Table 7.1 and Table 7.2.

Foreign Exchange Markets

The foreign exchange markets include several different types of transactions (see Figure 7.1). These include:

Spot rate: The current exchange rate. It is the rate that is currently being charged. A transaction in the sport market requires an immediate cash settlement (e.g., either one or two days depending upon the currency). It is also referred to as the cash market.

Forward rate: A forward contract is an agreement between two parties to engage in a transaction for a specified FX rate and at a specified future point in time. Forward rates are negotiated between the two parties who engage in the contract. They trade in the over-the-counter market.

Future: A future contract is similar to the forward contract and trades on an exchange using a standardized set of rules. The length of time for the futures contact is most typically three months (although longer future contract time periods exist).

Swap: A swap is an agreement between two parties to exchange currencies for an agreed amount of time and then reverse the transaction at the end of the

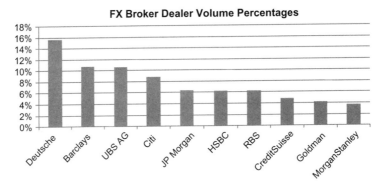

FIGURE 7.1 FX Broker Dealer Volumes

Source: http://www.therichest.org/business/most-traded-currencies/ (March 23, 2012)

time period. Swaps trade in the over the counter market and are negotiated between two parties.

Option: An option on a FX rate is similar to the options in the equity markets. Investors purchase the right to exchange one currency into another currency at an agreed upon point in time and at an agreed upon exchange rate at a future point in time.

Exchange Rate Determinates

There are many factors that will affect the foreign exchange rate. First, there are the economic factors such as government fiscal and monetary policies, interest rates, surplus and deficits, balance of payments and trade levels, inflation levels and trends, GDP, employment levels, retail sales, and production levels. Second, there are political factors such as how stable is the government, and is there going to be any change in policy (such as is always the question with a new president or prime minister). Third, there is market psychology and flight to quality as was experienced during the financial crisis. Fourth, exchange rates are also at least partially set by broker dealers based on real-time supply and demand and short-term momentum.

There are several academic theories intended to explain exchange rates (see Salvatore, Ch. 15, 2001). These theories include the relative Purchasing Power Parity, interest rate parity, domestic Fisher effect, international Fisher effect, balance of payments, and asset market model. These models, however, have not proven to be robust enough to explain exchange rate change over several time periods. These models are further described below.

Spot Market

The exchange rate, also known as the FX rate, is the rate at which a participant can exchange one currency for another currency. FX transactions occur in $100,000 lots, and prices are quoted to four decimals.

The exchange rate between US dollars (USD) and Euros (EUR) is represented as EUR/USD and denotes the number of US dollars required to purchase one Euro. For example, if the EUR/USD rate is 1.2990, it means that it will take 1.2990 USD to purchase 1 Euro.

On the surface, this expression may seem counter intuitive. It may seem to some readers that $EUR/USD = 1.2990$ means that it will take 1.2990 Euros to purchase one USD. But that is not the correct interpretation.

One sure way to not confuse the meaning of the expression is to write it out mathematically; then the meaning becomes straightforward. This is as follows.

Start with

$$\frac{EUR}{USD} = 1.2990$$

Multiply through to eliminate the fraction:

$$1.2990 \; USD = EUR$$

The equation now shows that it will take 1.2990 USD to purchase a EUR. The meaning from the mathematical expression is much more straightforward and is now intuitive!

This relationship can also be expressed to provide the number of EUR required to purchase a USD. It is determined in a similar way. Start with

$$\frac{EUR}{USD} = 1.2990$$

Multiply through to eliminate the fraction:

$$1.2990 \; USD = EUR$$

Divide each side by 1.2990 to obtain:

$$0.7698 \; EUR = USD$$

Therefore, it will take 0.7698 EUR to purchase one USD.

What happens if the exchange rate increases? For example, if the EUR/USD increases from 1.2990 to 1.3500, is the USD strengthening or weakening compared to the EUR? To determine, we again recommend using the mathematical representation. That is,

$$\frac{EUR}{USD} = 1.3500$$

$$\rightarrow 1.3500 \; USD = EUR$$

Therefore, it now takes 1.3500 USD to purchase a EUR. Since it takes more USD to purchase the same quantity of EUR we say that the USD value has depreciated compared to the EUR. We can also state that change as the USD weakened against the EUR.

When stating whether a currency has appreciated or depreciated in value, we always need to state the currency that we are using for comparison. It is quite possible that the USD appreciated against the EUR, but depreciated in value against another currency such as the JPY. Thus, stating that the USD has appreciated does not have a complete meaning.

The exchange rate between US dollars (USD) and Japanese yen (JPY) is expressed as USD/JPY. This ratio denotes the number of Japanese yen required to purchase one United States dollar. For example, if the USD/JPY rate is 94.46 it means that it will take 94.46 JPY to purchase one US dollar.

Again, to understand the meaning of this expression, it is helpful to express it mathematically. Start with

$$\frac{USD}{JPY} = 94.46$$

Multiply through to eliminate the fraction:

$$USD = 94.46 \; JPY$$

Therefore, this equation states that it will take 94.46 JPY to purchase one USD.

The number of USD required to purchase one JPY is found by dividing and isolating the JPY term. That is, we divide by 94.36.

$$USD = 94.46 \; JPY$$

$$\rightarrow \frac{1}{94.46} USD = JPY$$

$$\rightarrow 0.0106 \; USD = JPY$$

Therefore, it will take 0.0106 USD to purchase one JPY.

Now what if this value increases from 94.46 to 95.46? Has the USD grown stronger or weaker compared to the JPY? Let's take a look at this mathematically:

$$\frac{USD}{JPY} = 95.46$$

which can be expressed as

$$USD = 95.46 \; JPY$$

or equivalently,

$$\frac{1}{95.46} USD = JPY$$

$$\rightarrow 0.0105\ USD = JPY$$

Therefore, it will now take fewer USD to purchase one JPY, so the USD has strengthened compared to the JPY.

The FX market is a closed system. As one value increases another value has to decrease. Unlike stock prices, all FX rates cannot appreciate. This reminds me of a spy movie I saw a while ago. In the movie, the star character was seen reading the financial papers. Another character asked him how the markets were doing. The star character stated that all the currency markets are up, way up! The movie producers were no doubt trying to infer that in addition to the star character saving the earth from peril they also saved the earth from sure financial disaster! Perhaps the producers should have retained an economist to review their script for accuracy. Then we would not have to be mentioning this error!

Table 7.3 illustrates the USD ratios most commonly used when quoting the exchange rate. The ratio is specified as local/USD for EUR, GBP, and Australian dollars. For other countries, the USD ratios are most commonly quoted in terms of USD/local. Why isn't there any consistency across these metrics? The reason

Table 7.3 Exchange Rate Ratios

Country	Unit	Currency	Ratio	Type
European Union	Euro	EUR	EUR/USD	Free-Float
United Kingdom	Pound	GBP	GBP/USD	Free-Float
Australia	Dollar	AUD	AUD/USD	Free-Float
Canada	Dollar	CAD	USD/CAD	Free-Float
Japan	Yen	JPY	USD/JPY	Free-Float
China	Yuan	CNY	USD/CNY	Managed-Float
South Korea	Won	KRW	USD/KRW	Free-Float
India	Rupee	INR	USD/INR	Free-Float
Indonesia	Rupiah	IDR	USD/IDR	Free-Float
Russia	Rubles	RUB	USD/RUB	Free-Float
Turkey	Liras	TRY	USD/TRY	Free-Float
South Africa	Rand	ZAR	USD/ZAR	Free-Float
Mexico	Peso	MXN	USD/MXN	Free-Float
Argentina	Peso	ARS	USD/ARS	Managed-Float
Brazil	Real	BRL	USD/BRL	Free-Float
Saudi Arabia	Riyal	SAR	USD/SAR	Fixed

is that it is much easier to work with numbers greater than one rather than with numbers less than one.

The nomenclature used to represent exchange rates is extremely confusing to many professionals in the industry. But using the mathematical formulation shown previously will help both novice and seasoned analysts decompose the meaning of the FX rate. These rates get extremely confusing since they are not quoted in the same manner.

Tim Weithers, author of *Foreign Exchange: A Practical Guide to the FX Markets* (2006), provided a very interesting mathematical explanation of this reason. The story presented is as follows.

Every semester Professor Weithers asks his class who is good in math. He then asks the student who is good in math to sum the following series of numbers without using a calculator:

$$1 + \frac{1}{2} + \frac{1}{3} + \frac{1}{3} + \frac{1}{5} + \frac{1}{6} + \frac{1}{7}$$

The professor than selects another student (who is not good at math) and asks that student to sum the second series of numbers:

$$1 + 2 + 3 + 4 + 5 + 6 + 7$$

The second student has always been able to sum their series of numbers much quicker than the first student could sum their series of numbers, even though the first student is good at math and even had a head start in solving the problem. The moral of this story is that it is much easier to work with values greater than one than with values less than one. The same is true with dealing with FX rates. It is easier for us to work with exchange rates that are greater than one than less than one.

FX Quoting Conventions

Direct quotation, or price quotation, is when the FX quoting convention uses the home country's currency as the price currency. For example, in the United States the direct quotation of the United States Dollar (USD) in terms of the Great Britain Pound (GBP) would be GBP 0.656 = USD 1.00 (3/24/2013). In Great Britain the direct quotation would be written as USD 1.5230 USD = 1.00 GBP. The direct quotation system is always writing from the home country's perspective.

Quotes using a country's home currency as the unit currency (e.g., EUR 1.00 = USD 1.35991 in the Eurozone) are known as indirect quotation, or quantity quotation; these are used in British newspapers and are also common in Australia, New Zealand, and the Eurozone.

Using direct quotation, if the home currency is strengthening (i.e., appreciating, or becoming more valuable) then the exchange rate number decreases. Conversely, if the foreign currency is strengthening, the exchange rate number increases, and the home currency is depreciating.

Bid-Ask Spreads

FX quotes follow the same system of bids and asks as in the equity markets. The bid is the price at which the broker is willing to buy the currency from a market participant, and the ask is the price at which the broker is willing to sell the currency. The difference between the bid and ask is the dealer's compensation for the work involved in matching buyers and sellers and for the risk they incur for holding an inventory of currency.

The difference between the ask price and bid price is known as the pip, which stands for percentage in point. FX rates are quoted to the fourth decimal point in the markets. For example, the EUR/USD might be bid at 1.2990 and offered at 1.2995. Thus, the spread is five pips wide.

Arbitrage

Arbitrage refers to the process of buying a currency in one market at a lower rate and immediately selling it in another market at a higher rate. The difference between these two rates is the profit to the participant. For example, suppose that exchange rate between the Euro and US dollar is $EUR/USD = 1.2990$ in London and $EUR/USD = 1.2995$ in New York. Therefore, the participant could buy the Euro for \$1.2990 in London, immediately turn around and sell the Euro in NY for \$1.2995, and earn a profit of \$0.0005 (five pips). This seems like a very small profit for the transaction, but if the participant transacted \$100,000, it would result in a profit of \$50; if they transacted \$1,000,000, it would result in a profit of \$500. Now imagine if there were market participants with high-speed computers just waiting around observing the quotes, waiting for these mispricing opportunities to occur, and making these types of arbitrage trades several hundred times per day; the profit levels could really become a meaningful amount. This is exactly what the electronic high-frequency traders are doing. They are sitting back waiting for arbitrage opportunities to occur, and then they jump on the opportunity to earn even a small profit. In reality, the mispricing has to be large enough to offset any commission fee or costs incurred to execute two trades. Arbitrage of two currencies in two markets is known as two-point arbitrage.

Triangular Arbitrage

Triangular Arbitrage is also known as cross-currency arbitrage or three-point arbitrage. Since the FX markets are a closed system, all FX rates are governed by laws of mathematics and forces of economics. Triangular Arbitrage is the process of exploiting mispricing across three different currencies.

The forces of economics imply that all exchange rates need to be tied together. For example, in a three-currency example with the USD, EUR, and GBP, the relationship between rates is as follows. Let

$$\frac{EUR}{USD} = 1.2990$$

$$\frac{GBP}{USD} = 1.5230$$

Then the FX rate for GBP/EUR is determined as follows. Set each FX rate equal to one:

$$\frac{EUR}{USD} = 1.2990 \rightarrow \frac{EUR}{1.2990 \cdot USD} = 1$$

$$\frac{GBP}{USD} = 1.5230 \rightarrow \frac{GBP}{1.5230 \cdot USD} = 1$$

Then we can compute the relationship between GBP/EUR by setting these expanded formulations equal to each other. That is,

$$\frac{EUR}{1.2990 \cdot USD} = \frac{GBP}{1.5230 \cdot USD}$$

Solving we get

$$\frac{GBP}{EUR} = \frac{1.5230 \cdot USD}{1.2990 \cdot USD} = 1.1724$$

And

$$\frac{EUR}{GBP} = \frac{1.2990 \cdot USD}{1.5230 \cdot USD} = 0.8529$$

This relationship can also be defined as

$$\frac{GBP}{EUR} = \frac{GBP}{USD} \cdot \frac{USD}{EUR}$$

A Triangular Arbitrage strategy involves three offsetting transactions and three currencies. Suppose that we have three currencies: A, B, and C. The Triangular Arbitrage strategy would be:

1. Exchange currency A for currency B
2. Exchange currency B for currency C
3. Exchange currency C back to currency A

In general, the FX relationship between three currencies (A, B, and C) needs to adhere to the following:

$$\frac{A}{B} = \frac{A}{C} \cdot \frac{C}{B}$$

If we run into the situation where

$$\frac{A}{B} > \frac{A}{C} \cdot \frac{C}{B}$$

Or

$$\frac{A}{B} < \frac{A}{C} \cdot \frac{C}{B}$$

Then we have a Triangular Arbitrage opportunity. The difference, however, still needs to be greater than the transaction cost associated with the trades.

Example 7.1

Suppose that we have the following FX rates:

$$\frac{EUR}{USD} = 1.2990 \qquad \frac{GBP}{USD} = 1.5230 \qquad \frac{GBP}{EUR} = 1.2000$$

Then we have an arbitrage opportunity, because

$$\frac{GBP}{EUR} > \frac{GBP}{USD} \cdot \frac{USD}{EUR} \rightarrow 1.2000 > 1.5230 \cdot \frac{1}{1.2990}$$

This Triangular Arbitrage is as follows. Start with $1 USD.

1. 1 USD buys 0.6566 GBP
2. 0.6566 GBP buys 0.7879 EUR
3. 0.7879 EUR buys 1.0235 USD

Finish with $1.0235 USD.
Therefore, we just earned a profit of $0.0235.

Example 7.2

Suppose that we have the following FX rates:

$$\frac{EUR}{USD} = 1.2990 \qquad \frac{GBP}{USD} = 1.5230 \qquad \frac{GBP}{EUR} = 1.1600$$

Determine if we have a Triangular Arbitrage and, if we do, how would the market participant earn a profit?
We leave the math to the reader as an exercise.

Purchasing Power Parity (PPP)

Purchasing Power Parity is an economic model that postulates that the difference between the price level of a basket of goods in one country and the price level of an identical basket of goods in another country is due to the equilibrium FX rate between the two countries. The basket of goods chosen for comparison, however, needs to be a robust representative of the price level in that country. We can think of this price level for a basket of goods as a general price index that is comprised of various goods and services in the country. For example, the consumer price index (CPI) in the United States is a representative price level for a basket of goods.

There are two forms of the Purchasing Power Parity: absolute and relative.

Absolute Purchasing Power Parity: The equilibrium FX rate between two countries is equal to the ratio of the price levels in the two countries. Mathematically, the FX rate between the home and foreign country is

$$R = \frac{P}{P^*}$$

where R is the FX rate, P is the price level in the home country, and P^* is the price level in the foreign country.

Relative Purchasing Power Parity: The change in the equilibrium FX rate between two countries is proportional to the ratio of the change in price levels in the two countries. Mathematically, the FX rate between the home country and a foreign country is

$$R_1 = \frac{P_1/P_0}{P_1^*/P_0^*} \cdot R_0$$

where R_1 and R_0 are the exchange rates in period 1 and period 0 respectively, P_1 and P_0 are the price levels in the home country in period 1 and period 0 respectively, and P_1^* and P_0^* are the price levels in the foreign country in period 1 and period 0 respectively.

The PPP exchange rate model has some limitations due to the difficulty in constructing identical baskets of goods across both countries. The prices in one country compared to another may differ due to the country's natural resources, housing prices, and cultural differences (such as how much each country values entertainment prices or uses a certain good or service). People in different countries will typically consume different baskets of goods, and people in different countries will typically have different utility functions for identical baskets of goods. Thus, it is quite difficult to use these baskets as points of comparison for exchange rate reference. For the PPP theory to be able to provide a fair comparison of prices levels, we need to have identical basket of goods in each country, and the people of each country need to apply the same economic utility to these baskets of goods.

Law of One Price

The law of one price is a variation of Purchasing Power Parity that relates to a single commodity as opposed to a basket of goods. This theory postulates that the difference in prices for identical commodities in two countries is due to the FX rate between the two countries.

Two of the more quoted laws of one price commodities are the Big Mac Index and the Starbucks Index (both introduced by the Economist).

Big Mac Index

The Big Mac Index compares the price of a McDonald's Big Mac hamburger in different countries. The Big Mac mostly adheres to the requirements for a law of one price commodity. It is identical in all countries. It is made in the exact same manner with the exact same local ingredients (bread, beef, lettuce, tomatoes, cheese, pickles, special sauce), and utilizes identical local services (labor, advertising, real estate, etc.). The Big Mac Index may not adhere to the law of one price requirements in all countries due to the pricing of some ingredients and consumers' perceived value. For example, the cost of beef will vary across countries due to the abundance of cattle in some countries. Furthermore, consumers may place different economic utility on the value of a Big Mac since in some countries it is considered an inexpensive and quick meal, but in other countries it is considered a luxury commodity because it is relatively new to the market.

If the costs of all underlying ingredients for the Big Mac are the same in each country, then it is reasonable to expect the Big Mac to cost exactly the same amount in each country. The only difference in price should be due to the FX rate between the two countries. Therefore, the price of the Big Mac can be used as a proxy for exchange rate comparison. If after adjusting for the market exchange rate we find that the Big Mac is more expensive in the home country than in a foreign country, this would suggest that the home country currency is overvalued compared to the foreign country.

Starbucks Index

The Starbucks index compares the price for a Starbucks coffee across countries. Similar to the Big Mac, the Starbucks tall coffee is identical across different countries, and it is made in the same exact manner. Therefore, we would expect the cost of the Starbucks coffee to be exactly the same in each country. The only expected difference in price should be due to the FX rate between the two countries.

In theory, if currency markets function with complete efficiency, the price of an identical product, such as a Starbucks' coffee or a McDonald's Big Mac, should have an identical USD cost in every country. Therefore, if one of these commodities cost significantly less in one country than another, this suggests that the country's currency with the cheaper commodity price is undervalued compared to the country with the more expensive commodity price. We would expect in this situation for there to be an adjustment of FX rates if it is indeed true that the FX rates have moved away from equilibrium, or an adjustment in the price of the commodity.

If the price of a commodity was significantly lower in the US than in Canada in USD, it would be possible to purchase the commodity in the US and bring it into Canada for sale. The importer, however, would also incur all costs for transporting the commodity to Canada (e.g., transportation, labor, etc.), as well as any tariffs for the commodity. Thus, the difference in FX rate following the law of one price may fluctuate around a band equal to the cost of bringing the commodity from one country to another. This is similar the how the price of gold could also potentially vary from one country to another due to associated transaction costs such as transportation, storage, insurance, etc.

Balance of Payments Model

The balance of payments model postulates that a foreign exchange rate in equilibrium will remain in equilibrium, providing it maintains a stable account balance. The model is based on the expectation that foreign exchange rates are completely determined by the trade deficit (exports—imports).

A country with a trade deficit (e.g., the country is importing more goods than it is exporting) will experience a devaluation of its foreign exchange rate. A country with a trade surplus (e.g., the country is exporting more goods than it is importing) will experience a strengthening of its foreign exchange rate. When the country experiences a trade deficit, it also experiences a decrease in its foreign reserves. This results in a lower currency value making its goods, services, and products less expensive, which is likely to stimulate foreign purchases and exports and reduce imports because the foreign goods have become more expensive. In theory, this is expected to then balance the trade deficit and bring currency rates back to equilibrium. When the country experiences a trade surplus, it also experiences an increase in its foreign reserves. This results in a higher currency value, making its goods, services, and products more expensive, which is likely to reduce foreign demand due to higher prices, but will also stimulate imports since the foreign prices are now lower. In theory, this is expected to then balance the trade deficit and bring currency rates back to equilibrium.

The balance of payments model is similar to Purchasing Power Parity in that it focuses solely on goods, services, and commodities that are tradeable. It does not consider the effect of capital flows and financial assets (e.g., stocks and bonds) on the foreign exchange rates. These factors are considered in the asset market model.

Asset Market Model

The asset market model expands the traditional foreign exchange models that incorporate goods, services, and commodities by incorporating the trading of financial assets (e.g., stocks, bonds, and real estate) into the relationship between FX rates and money demand. Asset market model theory suggests that the cross-border trading of financial assets is as important a determinant of foreign exchange rates as the cross-border trading of goods and services, as well as traditional economic variables (GDP growth, inflation, productivity, imports and exports). Statistics now show that cross-border trading in financial assets has become dramatically larger than cross-border trading in goods and services.

The asset market model postulates that the country's foreign exchange rate is related to the inflow and outflow of foreign investment into the home country's financial markets. As foreign entities invest in the home country's financial markets, the assets are treated as exports, resulting in an increase in currency valuation (strengthening). In fact, the foreign entity is now demanding more of the home country's currency so that they can purchase the underlying assets. As foreign entities divest in the home country's financial markets (e.g., redemptions), the assets are treated as imports, resulting in a decrease in currency value (weakening). Here, the foreign entity is demanding less of the home country's currency.

The asset market model is based on the supply and demand of the home currency regardless of the reason behind the need for this currency, for example, to purchase goods or services, to invest in financial assets as well as selling goods or services, or to divest financial assets. An interesting aspect of the asset model is that the rates could in fact change even if there is no change in trade deficit or foreign investment into or out of foreign markets. Since the prices of the financial assets change, the potential investment or divestment quantities will change, thus affecting the FX rates.

Interest Rate Parity

Interest rate parity refers to a no-arbitrage state in which investors are indifferent regarding the interest rate in two different countries. That is, the investor could invest in either of the two countries and earn equivalent interest. In time, when this condition does not hold, then there is an arbitrage opportunity from which investors could potentially earn a riskless profit.

Interest Arbitrage

Interest arbitrage refers to the international flow of liquid capital from one country to another country in order to earn a higher return. This flow of capital is most often a short-term flow of capital. The interest arbitrage opportunity can be either covered or uncovered.

Uncovered Interest Arbitrage

An uncovered interest arbitrage transaction happens when one country has a higher interest rate than another country. Then investors could transfer funds from the country with the lower interest rate to the country with the higher interest rate to earn the higher interest. Then at the time of maturity, the investor could then transfer the earnings back to the original country currency. However, this transaction subjects the investor to currency risk. If the FX rate for the country where the funds were invested depreciated, then the investor could in fact earn a smaller return due to having less after transferring the currency back to the original units. If the FX rate for the country where the funds were invested appreciated, then the investor would in fact earn a return that is higher than the interest rate of the investment. Uncovered interest arbitrage is subject to FX risk.

Example 7.3

A US Government bond rate is 5%/year, and the interest rate for a UK Government bond is 7%/year. Then US investors could exchange USD for GBP and purchase UK Government bonds. This would yield a 7% interest rate, which is higher than the 5% that they could have earned had they purchased US Government bond. Thus investors would receive a 2% premium for investing in the UK bond. After maturity of the bond, the investor will need to exchange the GBP back to USD. If the USD strengthened, the investor would get back fewer dollars, and if the USD weakened, the investor would bet back more dollars. If the USD weakened by 3% over the period, the investor would receive a total premium of 2% from the higher bond return, plus 3% more dollars due to the change in exchange rate, for a total of +5%. If the USD strengthened by 3% instead the investor would receive a total of 2% premium minus 3% due to loss in USD due to the change in exchange rate for a total of −1%. In the latter situation, the investors would have been better off had they not invested in the UK Government bond. The investor is exposed to FX risk in an uncovered interest arbitrage transaction.

Uncovered interest arbitrage formula:

$$(1 + i_1) = \frac{E_t(S_{t+k})}{S_t}(1 + i_2)$$

where

$$i_1 = local\ exchange\ rate$$
$$i_2 = foreign\ exchange\ rate$$
$$S_t = FX\ spot\ rate$$
$$E_t(S_{t+k}) = expected\ FX\ rate\ at\ time\ t + k$$
$$E_t(\cdot) = time\ expectation$$

The calculation illustrates that the expected actual return in local currency will be equal to the return earned in the foreign currency multiplied by the change in the FX rate between the two currencies.

But even in this situation, the return is not locked in. Notice that the return is only an expectation. The actual return realized will be a function of the change in FX rates which could make the transaction more or less profitable.

Covered Interest Arbitrage

In order to avoid the FX risk incurred during an interest arbitrage transaction, investors will cover their FX risk. To achieve this, investors will engage a spot market transaction where they purchase the foreign currency to invest in the foreign country to earn the specified interest rate and a simultaneous forward contract to exchange the foreign currency plus interest earned back to local currency. In this case, the investor locks in the FX exchange rates and hedges all FX risk.

But quite often in these situations, the expected foreign currency for the country with the higher discount rate will be selling at a discount, and this discount will be equal to the difference in interest rates between the two countries. It is extremely difficult to achieve a free lunch.

Example 7.4

A US Government bond yield is 5%/year, and a UK Government bond yield is 7%/year. The GBP is currently selling at a 1% discount. Then US investors could exchange USD for GBP and purchase UK Government bonds and earn a higher interest rate of 2%, then exchange the GBP back to USD. To achieve a covered interest arbitrage, the US investor would exchange USD for GBP in the spot market and also engage in a forward contract to sell GBP to USD at a 1% discount. In this situation, the US investor would achieve an incremental return of 2% from the higher bond rates and incur a 1% loss due to the discounted forward contract. But in this case, the investor would earn an overall return premium of 1% (2% − 1% = 1%). The investor locks in the interest rate return and does not incur any FX risk.

Covered interest arbitrage formula:

$$(1 + i_1) = \frac{F_t}{S_t}(1 + i_2)$$

where

$$i_1 = local\ exchange\ rate$$
$$i_2 = foreign\ exchange\ rate$$
$$S_t = FX\ spot\ rate$$
$$F_t = Forward\ rate\ at\ time\ t$$

Notice that in this case we are not using time expectations since the investor locked in the future FX rate. It is important, however, that the investor engage in a forward contract that is equal to the initial principal value plus the interest that will be earned from the foreign investment. If the investor only engages in a forward contract equal to the initial principal value, they will incur FX risk on the interest earned.

Interest Rates

In this section we provide readers with an overview of interest rates and interest rate formulas. Proper understanding of interest rates is essential for risk management and international trade, as well as for pricing derivatives, futures, and options.

What is interest? Interest is the dollars paid by a borrower to a lender for use of funds over a specified period of time. It is usually expressed as a percentage of the principal borrowed per time period (e.g., monthly or annual rate). For example, a small business owner may borrow $100,000 from a bank at a rate of 10% annually for a one-year period. At the end of the one-year period, the business owner is required to pay the bank a total of $110,000, which consists of $100,000 principal plus $10,000 interest (10% of $100,000 = $10,000). Terms of the loan contract could also be on a monthly basis (e.g., equipment leases, credit card obligations, or foreign trade agreements) as well as for a time period that is longer than one year (e.g., mortgage loans).

The total interest rate component is referred to as the nominal interest rate. It consists of two components: real and inflation. The inflation component represents the overall increase in economic cost, and the real component represents the actual profit or gain received by the lender. For example, if a person deposits $100 in a bank account at an interest rate of 10% annually, after one year of time they will receive $10 interest and will have an account balance of $110. However, if the goods and services that could have been purchased with $100 one year ago now cost the investor $104, the real interest received is only $6. Therefore, while the nominal interest rate is 10%, the real interest is 6%, and inflation is 4%. Investors and lenders are often most interested in the real interest rate since this denotes the true profit margin. Since investors do know the real interest rate beforehand—they only know the nominal rate that is charged—they rely on the expected or forecasted inflation rate to help them derive estimates for the real interest rate.

Let's take a look at this relationship. Let

$$i = nominal\ interest\ rate$$

$$r = real\ interest\ rate$$

$$\pi = inflation\ rate$$

Then we have

$$(1 + i) = (1 + r)(1 + \pi)$$

That is, the nominal interest rate is comprised of the real interest rate and the rate of inflation.

Next, rearrange the expressions to isolate the real rate term. That is,

$$(1 + r) = \frac{(1 + i)}{(1 + \pi)}$$

Then solving for the real rate r, we have

$$r = \frac{(1 + i)}{(1 + \pi)} - 1$$

This is known as the Fisher equation.

Let's again consider our expression:

$$(1 + r) = \frac{(1 + i)}{(1 + \pi)}$$

But this time take a log-transformation of each side. Then we have

$$ln(1 + r) = ln\left(\frac{1 + i}{1 + \pi}\right)$$

This can be written as:

$$ln(1 + r) = ln(1 + i) - ln(1 + \pi)$$

Now, using the relationship $ln(1 + k) = k$ for small values of k we have

$$r \approx i - \pi$$

Therefore, our real interest rate is approximated by the nominal rate minus the inflation. This is a much easier calculation then earlier; we have $r = ((1 + i)/(1 + \pi)) - 1$ and this allows analysts to make quick and accurate, real interest rate calculations.

It is important, however, that analysts note that this is a close approximation and only holds for small interest rates. The approximation begins to breakdown at around 10% and has noticeable differences after 20%. This is shown in Figure 7.2.

Mathematically, we can show this discrepancy in terms of the nominal interest rate i as follows. Start with

$$(1 + i) = (1 + r)(1 + \pi)$$

Multiply through our terms and we have

$$1 + i = 1 + r + \pi + r\pi$$

Solving for the nominal interest rate i, we have

$$i = r + \pi + r\pi$$

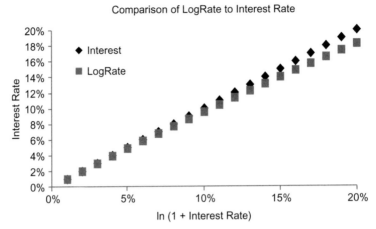

FIGURE 7.2 Comparison of LogRate to Percentage Rate

Compare this to our log-transformation approximation, for which we have

$$r \approx i - \pi$$

which can be written as

$$i \approx r + \pi$$

Notice that these two nominal interest rates differ by $r\pi$. This is calculated by taking the difference of the two nominal interest rate calculations:

$$i_1 = r + \pi + r\pi$$
$$i_2 = r + \pi$$
$$i_1 - i_2 = (r + \pi + r\pi) - (r + \pi) = r\pi$$

For small interest rates this product is extremely small. If inflation is $\pi = 3\%$ and the real rate is $r = 5\%$, the error term is $r\pi = 0.03 \cdot 0.05 = 0.0015 = 15bp$.

Types of Interest Rates

Interest rates can be either fixed or variable terms. A fixed interest rate is a rate that does not change over the life of the loan or investment regardless of the changing economic conditions. A variable interest rate is subject to change and is often pegged to an underlying index such as the one-year t-bill rate or, even more commonly, the LIBOR rate.

The advantage of a fixed interest rate is that the borrower will always know the amount that they will need to repay. Repayment will be exactly the same in each month over the life of the loan. This provides a high level of certainty with business planning. The disadvantage of a fixed interest rate is that if the markets rates drop dramatically, the borrower will be paying a significantly higher rate than they otherwise would.

The advantage of a variable interest rate is that it is often lower than a fixed interest rate at the time of the load. However, the loan is associated with more risk over time due to potential interest rate fluctuations, and these rates could be potentially much higher in the future. If rates increase too much going forward, the loan may become difficult for the borrower to repay, thus increasing potential for default.

Time Value of Money

In this section we provide an overview of the calculations required to determine the time value of money including cash flows and compounding effects. The formulas ahead will provide analysts with the necessary formulation required to solve numerous different cash flow problems such as present and future value, annuities and uniform payment streams, compounding and continuous compounding problems, and break-even analysis.

Future Value

The future value of an investment is equal to the investment value multiplied by the interest rate. This is:

$$F_t = P_0 \cdot (1+r)^t$$

where

$$P_0 = present\ value$$
$$F_t = future\ value\ of\ investment\ at\ time\ t$$
$$r = interest\ rate\ per\ period$$
$$t = number\ of\ periods$$

Example 7.5

An investment is paying 5% per year. An investment of $100 after one year will have a value of

$$F_{t=1} = 100 \cdot (1+0.05)^{t=1} = \$105$$

This investment after two years will be worth

$$F_2 = F_1 \cdot (1+r)^1 = \underbrace{P_0 \cdot (1+r)^1}_{F_1} \cdot (1+r)^1 = P_0 \cdot (1+r)^2$$

Thus, after two years, the $100 investment at 5% annual is

$$F_2 = 100 \cdot (1+0.05)^2 = \$110.25$$

Present Value

The present value determined from a future value is computed as the future value divided by the discount rate. Very often, the discount rate used to determine present value is the risk-free interest rate (e.g., US t-bill) or the internal rate of return (if evaluating a corporate investment option or alternative). This is

$$P_0 = \frac{F_t}{(1+r)^t}$$

Or alternatively,

$$P_0 = F_t \cdot (1+r)^{-t}$$

Compounding

A general formula for calculation of a future value based on a compounding effect is shown ahead. This is useful at times in which the interest will be paid at set intervals over the course of a year:

$$F_t = P_0 \cdot \left(1+\frac{r}{n}\right)^{-nt}$$

where

$F_t = $ *future value at time t*

$P_0 = $ *investment value at time t = 0*

$r = $ *interest rate*

$n = $ *number of times interest will be compounded per year*

$t = $ *number of years*

Example 7.6

An investment of $10,000 is deposited into a bank with annual interest of $r = 5\%$, and interest is paid quarterly. Find the future value of the investment after ten years.

$$F_t = \$10,000 \cdot \left(1+\frac{0.05}{4}\right)^{-4 \cdot 10} = \$16,436.19$$

Continuous Compounding

Suppose that the interest rate is compounded continuously. This is the same as if we take $n \to \infty$. Then our calculation is as follows:

$$F_t = \lim_{n \to \infty} P_0 \cdot \left(1 + \frac{r}{n}\right)^{-nt} = P_0 \cdot e^{rt}$$

Thus, future value and present value under continuous compounding is

$$F_t = P_0 \cdot e^{rt}$$

$$P_0 = P_0 \cdot e^{-rt}$$

This is the familiar formulation used in derivative pricing models.

Present Value Payment Stream

An investor is receiving a set dollar amount X each year for n years. An example of this type of transaction is winning the lottery, in which case the winner is given the option of being paid a fixed dollar amount for a specified number of years or being given a lump sum payment immediately. It would be helpful for the winner to determine the present value of the stream of payments based on their interest rate expectations and compare to the lump sum payment to determine which option is most beneficial.

If we use a constant interest rate discount factor r, the present value of this cash flow is determined as follows:

$$P_0 = \frac{X}{(1+r)^1} + \frac{X}{(1+r)^2} + \frac{X}{(1+r)^3} + \cdots + \frac{X}{(1+r)^n}$$

Rewrite the equation as follows:

$$P_0 = X(1+r)^{-1} + X(1+r)^{-2} + X(1+r)^{-3} + \cdots + X(1+r)^{-n}$$

Factor the equation:

$$P_0 = X((1+r)^{-1} + (1+r)^{-2} + (1+r)^{-3} + \cdots + (1+r)^{-n})$$

Let

$$A_n = (1+r)^{-1} + (1+r)^{-2} + (1+r)^{-3} + \cdots + (1+r)^{-n}$$

Then we have

$$P_0 = X \cdot A_n$$

Multiply A_n by $(1 + r)$, that is:

$$(1+r)A_n = 1 + (1+r)^{-1} + (1+r)^{-2} + \cdots + (1+r)^{-(n+1)}$$

Next compute $(1+r)A_n - A_n$:

$$(1+r)A_n - A_n = 1 + (1+r)^{-1} + (1+r)^{-2} + \ldots + (1+r)^{-(n+1)}$$
$$-(1+r)^{-1} + (1+r)^{-2} + (1+r)^{-3} + \ldots + (1+r)^{-n}$$
$$= 1 - (1+r)^{-n}$$

Therefore, we have

$$(1+r)A_n - A_n = 1 - (1+r)^{-n}$$

This reduces to

$$r \cdot A_n = \frac{(1+r)^n - 1}{(1+r)^n}$$

And finally, we have

$$A_n = \frac{(1+r)^n - 1}{r \cdot (1+r)^n}$$

Therefore, the present value of the annuity payment stream is

$$P_0 = X \cdot \frac{(1+r)^n - 1}{r \cdot (1+r)^n}$$

Example 7.7

A lottery winner has the option of receiving $100,000 per year for 10 years starting in one year or receiving a lump sum payment of $750,000 immediately. If the discount rate is $r = 0.05$, what is the best option for the winner?

The present value of the payment stream is

$$P_0 = \$100,000 \cdot \frac{(1+0.05)^{10} - 1}{0.05 \cdot (1+0.05)^{10}} = \$772,173.49$$

Therefore, the investor can either receive $750,000 immediately or an option with a present value worth of $772,173.49. This lottery winner would be better off receiving the payment stream, since it has a higher present value.

This illustration is used to show the calculation formulation to compute the present value of a stream of cash flows at a specified discount rate. It does not consider the uncertainty of the discount rate over the period. The lottery winner may still wish to select the lump sum payment due to a higher level of certainty. It does not include any interest rate risk.

Example 7.8

Now let us evaluate a cash flow in which the investor will receive n-payments of $X with each payment being made annually. For a constant payment value and a constant discount rate r, the present value P_0 calculation is as follows:

$$P_0 = X(1+r)^0 + X(1+r)^{-1} + X(1+r)^{-2} + \cdots + X(1+r)^{-(n-1)}$$

Notice that this differs from the previous example in that the calculation begins at the current point in time and has value of $X (since $X(1+r)^0 = X \cdot 1 = X$). Additionally, this payment stream only continues through year $n-1$ because at that point in time all n-payments would have been made (the first payment is at time period $t = 0$ and the last payment is made at time period $t = n-1$, for a total of n-payments).

We solve this problem as follows:

$$P_0 = X(1 + (1+r)^{-1} + (1+r)^{-2} + \cdots + (1+r)^{-(n-1)})$$

Define

$$A_n = 1 + (1+r)^{-1} + (1+r)^{-2} + \cdots + (1+r)^{-(n-1)}$$

$$(1+r) \cdot A_n = (1+r) + 1 + (1+r)^{-1} + (1+r)^{-2} + \cdots + (1+r)^{-(n-2)}$$

Then we can compute

$$(1+r) \cdot A_n - A_n = (1+r) + 1 + (1+r)^{-1} + (1+r)^{-2} + \cdots + (1+r)^{-(n-2)}$$

$$-(1 + (1+r)^{-1} + (1+r)^{-2} + \cdots + (1+r)^{-(n-1)})$$

$$= (1+r) - (1+r)^{-(n-1)}$$

Solving, we obtain

$$r \cdot A_n = (1+r) - (1+r)^{-(n-1)}$$

which is equal to

$$A_n = \frac{1}{r} \cdot \frac{(1+r)^n - 1}{(1+r)^{n-1}}$$

If the cash payment were to include $n = 10$ payments of $100,000 starting at the current time period and paid over the next nine years (at that time, all ten payments would have been made), and if the discount factor selected is $r = 0.05$, the present value of this payment stream is

$$P_0 = \$100,000 \cdot \frac{1}{0.05} \cdot \frac{(1+0.05)^{10} - 1}{(1+0.05)^9} = \$810,782.17$$

Notice that this amount is greater than in the previous example where payments began after the first year and continued into the tenth year. Determining the proper start and end year for the payment stream is an important point for these types of cash flow problems.

Example 7.9

If the cash flow payment treat is going to continue for an infinite number of periods, we can use the formulas above to determine the present value of these cash streams. The multiplier factor for an infinite series is computed simply by taking the limit as $n \to \infty$ as follows:

$$\lim n \to \infty \ of \ A_n = \frac{1}{r} \cdot \frac{(1+r)^n - 1}{(1+r)^{n-1}} = \frac{1+r}{r}$$

Therefore, if the lottery winner will receive \$100,000 per year starting in the first year, and this payment will continue forever, and using a discount factor of $r = 5\%$, the present value of the payment stream is

$$P_0 = \$100,000 \cdot \frac{1 + 0.05}{0.05} = \$2.1 \text{million}$$

Future Value Payment Stream:

The multiplier factors to provide the future value of a cash flow at time $t = n$ for a payment stream from $t = 0, \ldots, n - 1$ and $t = 1, \ldots, n$ are provided below. We leave it as an exercise for the reader to verify these formulas.

Next let us consider the future value at a time period $t = n$ for a constant cash flow stream with discount factor r from $t = 0$ through $t = n - 1$. Here there are n payments, and we are interested in the future value of the payment stream one year after the payments have ended.

$$F_n(t = 0, \ldots, n - 1) = \frac{(1+r)^{n+1} - (1 + r)}{r}$$

Now examine the future value at time $t = n$ for a constant cash flow stream with discount factor r from $t = 1$ through $t = n$. Here there are n payments, and we are interested in the future value of the payment stream at the time of the last payment.

$$F_n(t = 1, \ldots, n) = \frac{(1+r)^n - 1}{r}$$

Important note: In this section, we presented readers with the formulation for present and future values, compounding and continuous compounding formulation, and a process to compute the present value for a stream of payments. These formulas could be used to determine the multiplier factor for various streams of cash flows, annuity payments, and interest rate conversions. These are essential formulations for many different interest rate problems and concerns.

Market Observations and Analysis

As discussed earlier, many of our foreign exchange rate and interest rate problems require knowledge of the prevailing interest rate. Sensitivity analysis on these rates require some knowledge of the potential change of these rates and the magnitude of the potential change of these rates. For example, uncovered interest rate arbitrage and, to some extent covered interest rate arbitrage, as well as our cash flow calculations from earlier, all are accompanied by some level of uncertainty.

In order to understand the potential variability of these rates and ultimately manage the corresponding risk of these rates, analysts continuously investigate FX rates via market data. Two of the more common methodologies are 1) via historical volatility measures and 2) via strengthening or weakening of the currency value. These techniques are described ahead.

Figure 7.3 illustrates annualized volatility of USD FX rates for fifteen major currencies over the months of August 2012 and September 2012. Analysts measure realized volatility in order to determine if the FX rate uncertainty is stable (if similar volatility for two previous months) or whether there is some potential for change in volatility (if the two volatilities differ statistically). In Figure 7.3, the highest-volatility FX rates were for South Africa (ZAR) and Russia (RUB). The least volatile were China (CNY) and Argentina (ARS), which is no surprise since these FX rates are managed floating rates. Canada (CAD) and UK (GBP) also have FX rates with low volatility. The volatility in India (INR) and Indonesia (IDR) increased in September 2012 compared to August 2012, which is a market signal of more uncertainty, possibly due to political reasons or a change in economic policy. Currencies showing an increase in volatility should be monitored.

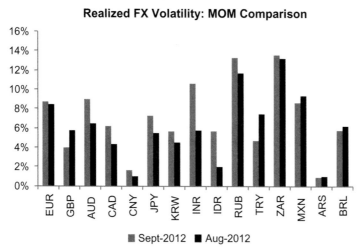

Realized FX Volatility: MOM Comparison

■ Sept-2012   ■ Aug-2012

FIGURE 7.3 Realized Volatility (Month over Month Comparison)

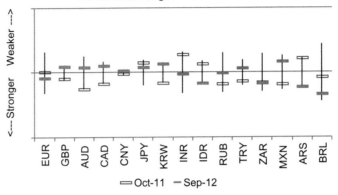

FIGURE 7.4 USD FX Rates (Normalized Ranges)

Figure 7.4 illustrates the change in the USD FX rates for fifteen major currencies. This figure shows the twelve-month range of the normalized FX rate measured in terms of USD to the foreign currency FX rate. In this case, the normalization basis is the same for all countries. The rates are shown as a variation of open-high-low-close stock price graphs. In this figure we show the high and low FX rates over the twelve month period September 2012 through October 2013 to present the trend in the strength of the USD compared to different countries. The FX rates across different countries as of March 24, 2013 is shown in Table 7.4. Since the denominator is the same across all currencies, a higher value is an indication that it takes more USD to purchase a unit of the foreign currency, and hence there is a weaker dollar. A lower value is an indication that it takes few USD to purchase a unit of the foreign currency, and hence there is a stronger dollar. Figure 7.4 shows the USD strengthening compared to the EUR, ARS, and BRL and weakening compared to the GBP, AUD, and MXN.

Forecasting Volatility

Volatility and FX rates are often forecasted via a generalized autoregressive conditional heteroscedastic GARCH model. This model is described in detail in Chapter 4, Price Volatility, and is restated ahead.

Let, X_t represent the FX rate at time t. Then our GARCH model is

$$X_t = \sigma_t \varepsilon_t$$

$$\sigma_t^2 = \omega_0 + \sum_{i=1}^{p} \alpha_i X_{t-i}^2 + \sum_{j=1}^{q} \beta_j \sigma_{t-j}^2$$

Table 7.4 Foreign Exchange Cross Rates: March 24, 2013

	USD	EUR	JPY	GBP	CHF	CAD	AUD	HKD
USD	–	1.2990	0.0106	1.5230	1.0629	0.9773	1.0444	0.1288
EUR	0.7698	–	0.0081	1.1727	0.8184	0.7524	0.8041	0.0992
JPY	94.4600	122.7300	–	142.8571	90.0901	92.5926	99.0099	12.1655
GBP	0.6566	0.8527	0.0070	–	0.6979	0.6418	0.6858	0.0846
CHF	0.9408	1.2219	0.0111	1.4329	–	0.9200	0.9825	0.1212
CAD	1.0232	1.3290	0.0108	1.5582	1.0869	–	1.0686	0.1318
AUD	0.9575	1.2437	0.0101	1.4581	1.0178	0.9358	–	0.1233
HKD	7.7639	10.0839	0.0822	11.8243	8.2524	7.5887	8.1083	–

where $\omega_0 > 0$, $\alpha_i \geq 0$, $\beta_j \geq 0$ are the model parameters that are to be estimated via maximum likelihood estimation (MLE) techniques, ε_t is a sequence of independent and identically distributed random variables with mean zero and variance one, and σ_t is the volatility in period t which we are seeking to forecast.

The GARCH model also has a bound on the parameters to ensure a stable model. This is:

$$0 \leq \sum_{i=1}^{p} \alpha_i + \sum_{j=1}^{q} \beta_j < 1$$

CONCLUSION

In this chapter we provided an overview of the FX market. Readers were introduced to the various different arbitrage opportunities such as Triangular Arbitrage and interest rate arbitrage (covered and uncovered). We presented an overview of different FX theories such as Purchasing Power Parity (absolute and relative), law of one price, balance of payments model, and the asset market model. We provided an overview of different interest rate formulations and an in-depth discussion of interest rate cash flows (present value, future value, and uniform payments), as well as the derivation of the corresponding multiplier factor. The formulation discussed in the above sections provides analysts with the necessary skillset to analyze and develop more advanced models. These formulations are the building blocks of many of the more complex models. The chapter concluded with an illustration of FX rate volatility for fifteen of our major currencies.

Endnotes

[1] http://en.wikipedia.org/wiki/
[2] http://www.investopedia.com
[3] http://www.wilmott.com/

References

Carbaugh, R., 2000. International Economics, seventh ed. South-Western College Publishing.

Nicholson, W., 2002. Microeconomic Theory: Basic Principles and Extensions, eighth ed. South-Western, Thomson Learning.

Salvatore, D., 2001. International Markets, seventh ed. John Wiley & Sons.

Salvatore, D., 2001. Managerial Economics in a Global Economy, eighth ed. Harcourt College Publishers.

Weithers, T., 2006. "Foreign Exchange: A Practical Guide to the FX Markets". John Wiley & Sons, Inc.

http://en.wikipedia.org/wiki/Foreign_exchange.

Algorithmic Trading Risk

8

INTRODUCTION

Algorithmic trading represents computerized execution of financial instruments. Currently, algorithms are being used to trade stocks, bonds, currencies, and a plethora of financial derivatives. The new era of algorithmic trading has provided investors with more efficient strategy implementation and lower transaction costs, resulting in improved portfolio performance. But in addition to these advantages and savings comes a new set of algorithmic risks. In this chapter we introduce readers to the algorithmic trading process and corresponding uncertainty. Readers interested in a more thorough examination of algorithms are referred to *The Science of Algorithmic Trading*, Kissell (2013). In this chapter, we follow the description previously outlined in *The Science of Algorithmic Trading*.

Investors trading via algorithms (also known as black box trading, robo-trading, high frequency trading, etc.) need to specify their investing and/or trading goals in terms of mathematical instructions. Dependent upon investors' needs, customized instructions range from simple and straightforward to highly complex and sophisticated.

Portfolio managers use algorithms in a variety of ways. Money management funds—mutual and index funds, pension plans, quantitative funds, and even hedge funds—use algorithms to implement investment decisions. In these cases, money managers use different stock selection and portfolio construction techniques to determine their preferred holdings, and then employ algorithms to implement those decisions. Algorithms determine the best way to slice orders and trade over time. They determine appropriate price, time, and quantity of shares (size) to enter the market. Often, these algorithms make decisions independent of any human interaction.

Similar to a more antiquated, manual market making approach, broker dealers and market makers now use automated algorithms to provide liquidity to the marketplace. As such, these parties are able to make markets in a broader spectrum of securities electronically rather than manually, cutting the costs of hiring additional traders.

Aside from improving liquidity to the marketplace, broker dealers are using algorithms to transact for investor clients. Once investment decisions are made, buy-side trading desks pass orders to their brokers for execution using algorithms. The buy-side may specify which broker algorithms to use to trade single or basket orders, or rely on the expertise of sell-side brokers to select the proper algorithms and algorithmic parameters. It is important for the sell-side to precisely communicate to the buy-side expectations regarding expected transaction costs (usually via pre-trade analysis) and potential issues that may arise during trading. The buy-side will need to ensure these implementation goals are consistent with the fund's investment objectives. Furthermore, it is crucial for the buy-side to determine future implementation decisions (usually via post trade analysis) to continuously evaluate broker performance and algorithms under various scenarios.

Quantitative, statistical arbitrage traders, sophisticated hedge funds, and the newly emerged class of investors known as high-frequency traders will also program buying/selling rules directly into the trading algorithm. The program rules allow algorithms to determine instruments and how they should be bought and sold. These types of algorithms are referred to as "black-box" or "profit and loss" algorithms.

While empirical evidence has shown that, when properly specified, algorithms result in lower transaction costs, the process necessitates that investors be more proactive during implementation than they were previously when utilizing manual execution. Algorithms must be able to manage price, size, and timing of the trades, while continuously reacting to market condition changes.

Advantages

Algorithmic trading provides investors with many benefits such as:

- *Lower commissions.* Commissions are usually lower than traditional commission fees since algorithmic trading only provides investors with execution and execution-related services (such as risk management and order management). Algorithmic commissions typically do not compensate brokers for research activities, although some funds pay a higher rate for research access.
- *Anonymity.* Orders are entered into the system and traded automatically by the computer across all execution venues. The buy-side trader either manages the order from within his firm or requests that the order is managed by the sell-side sales traders. Orders are not shopped across the trading floor as they once were.
- *Control.* Buy-side traders have full control over orders. Traders determine the venues (displayed/dark), order submission rules such as market/limit prices, share quantities, and wait and refresh times, as well as when to accelerate or decelerate trading based on the investment objective of the fund and actual market conditions. Traders can cancel the order or modify the trading instructions almost instantaneously.

- *Minimum information leakage.* Information leakage is minimized since the broker does not receive any information about the order or trading intentions of the investor. The buy-side trader is able to specify their trading instructions and investment needs simply by the selection of the algorithm and specifications of the algorithmic parameters.
- *Transparency.* Investors are provided with a higher degree of transparency surrounding how the order will be executed. Since the underlying execution rules for each algorithm is provided to investors in advance, investors will know exactly how the algorithm will execute shares in the market, as algorithms will do exactly what they are programmed to do.
- *Access.* Algorithms are able to provide fast and efficient access to the different markets and dark pool. They also provide co-location, low-latency connections, which provides the investor with the benefits of high-speed connections.
- *Competition.* The evolution of algorithmic trading has seen competition from various market participants such as independent vendors, order management and execution management software firms, exchanges, third-party providers, and in-house development teams (DMA) in addition to the traditional sell-side broker dealers. Investors have received the benefits of this increased competition in the form of better execution services and lower costs. Given the ease and flexibility of choosing and switching between providers, investors are not locked into any one selection. In turn, algo providers are required to be more proactive in continually improving their offerings and efficiencies.
- *Reduced transaction costs.* Computers are better equipped and faster to react to changing market conditions and unplanned events. They are better able to ensure consistency between the investment decision and trading instructions, which results in decreased market impact cost, less timing risk, and a higher percentage of completed orders (lower opportunity cost).

Disadvantages

Algorithmic trading has been around only since the early 2000s, and it is still evolving at an amazing rate. Unfortunately, algorithms are not the be-all and end-all for our trading needs. Deficiencies and limitations include:

- Users can become complacent and use the same algorithms regardless of the order characteristics and market conditions simply because they are familiar with the algorithm.
- Users need to continuously test and evaluate algorithms to ensure they are using the algorithms properly and that the algorithms are doing what they are advertised to do.
- Users need to measure and monitor performance across brokers, algorithms and market conditions to understand what algorithms are most appropriate given the type of market environment.

- Algorithms perform exactly as they are specified, which is nice when the trading environment is what has been expected. However, in the case that unplanned events occur, the algorithm may not be properly trained or programmed for that particular market, which may lead to subpar performance and higher costs.
- Users need to ensure consistency across the algorithm and their investment needs. Ensuring consistency is becoming increasingly difficult during times in which the actual algorithmic trading rule is not as transparent as it could be or the algorithms are given non-descriptive names that do not provide any insight into what they are trying to do.
- There are too many algos and too many names. VWAP, volume weighted average price, is an example of a fairly descriptive algorithmic name and is fairly consistent across brokers. However, an algorithm such as Tarzan is not descriptive and does not provide insights into how it will trade during the day. Investors may need to understand and differentiate between hundreds of algorithms, and keep track of the changes that occur in these codebases. For example, a large institution may use 20 different brokers with five to ten different algorithms each and with at least half of those having names that are non-descriptive.
- *Price Discovery*. The growth of algorithms and decline of traditional specialists and market marker roles has led to a more difficult price-discovery process at the open. While algorithms are well-versed at incorporating price information to determine the proper slicing strategy, they are not yet well-versed at quickly determining the fair market price for a security.

Direct market access or "DMA" is a term used in the financial industry to describe the situation in which the trader utilizes the broker's technology and infrastructure to connect to the various exchanges, trading venues, and dark pools. The buy-side trader is responsible for programming all algorithmic trading rules on their end when utilizing the broker for direct market access. Many times, funds combine DMA services with broker algorithms to have a larger number of execution options at their disposal.

Brokers typically provide DMA to their clients for a reduced commission rate, but do not provide the buy-side trader with any guidance on structuring the macro- or micro-level strategies (limit order strategies and smart order routing decisions). Investors utilizing DMA are required to specify all slicing and pricing schemes, as well as a selection of appropriate pools of liquidity on their own.

In the DMA arena, the buy-side investor is responsible for specifying:

1. *Macro trading rules.* Specify the optimal trading time and/or trading rate of the order.
2. *Adaptation tactics*. Rules to determine when to accelerate or decelerate trading, based on market prices, volume levels, realized costs, etc.
3. *Limit order strategies.* How should the order be sliced into small pieces and traded in the market, e.g., market or limit order, and, if limit order, at what price and how many shares?

4. *Smart order-routing logic.* Where should orders be posted, displayed or dark, how long should we wait before revising the price or changing destination, how to best take advantage of rebates?

The investor then takes advantage of the brokers' DMA connectivity to route the orders and child orders based on these sets of rules. Under DMA, the investor is in a way renting the brokers advanced trading platforms, exchange connectivity, and market gateways.

Many broker networks have been developed with the high-frequency trader in mind and are well equipped to handle large amounts of data, messages, and volume. The infrastructure is built on a flexible ultra-low latency platform. Some of these brokers also provide smart order-routing access as they are often better prepared to monitor and evaluate level II data, order book queues, and trade flows and executions by venue in real-time.

Advantages

- *Lower commissions.* Brokers are paid a fee by the fund to compensation them for their infrastructure and connectivity to exchanges, trading venues, dark pools, etc. This fee is usually lower than the standard commission fee, and the fund does not receive any additional benefit from the broker such as order management services, risk management controls, etc.
- *Anonymity.* Orders are entered into the system and managed by the trader. Brokers do not see or have access to the orders.
- *Control.* Traders have full control over the order. Traders determine the venues (displayed/dark), order submission rules such as market/limit prices, share quantities, and wait and refresh times, as well as when to accelerate or decelerate trading based on the investment objective of the fund and actual market conditions. Information leakage is minimized since the broker does not receive any information about the order or trading intentions of the investor.
- *Access.* There is access to the markets via the broker technology and infrastructure. This includes colocation, low-latency connections, etc.
- *Perfectly customized strategies.* Since the investor defines the exact algorithmic trading rules, they are positioned to ensure the strategy is exactly consistent with their underlying investment and alpha expectations. Funds rarely (if ever at all!) provide brokers with proprietary alpha estimates.

Disadvantages

- *Increased work.* Funds need to continuously test and evaluate their algorithms, write and rewrite codes, and develop their own limit order models and smart order routers.

- *Lack of economies of scale.* Most funds do not have access to the large number and breadth of orders entered by all customers. Therefore, they do not have as large of a data sample to test new and alternative algorithms. Brokers can invest substantial resources in an algorithmic undertaking since the investment cost will be recovered over numerous investors. Funds incur the entire development cost themselves.
- *Research requirements.* They need to continuously perform their own research to determine what works well under what types of market conditions.
- *Locked into existing systems.* It is difficult and time consuming to rewrite code and redefine algorithms rules for all the potential market conditions or whenever there is a structural change in the market or a trading venue. However, many traders who utilize DMA also have the option of utilizing broker suites of algorithms (for a higher commission rate). The main exception in this case is the high-frequency traders.
- *Monitor.* There is a need to continuously monitor market conditions, order book, prices, etc., which could be extremely data intensive.

Market Environment

Analysis of market volumes has found that, while visible liquidity at the best bid and ask may have decreased, actual traded volume has increased dramatically. Figure 8.1 shows the increase in volume for NYSE-listed securities from 2000 to 2012. Total consolidated volume peaked during the financial crisis in 2008–2009, at which time it was more than six times the average in 2000. Volume has succumbed since year 2000, but in 2012 it is still 3.3 times the 2000 average. While volumes increased in the market, the issue of fragmentation

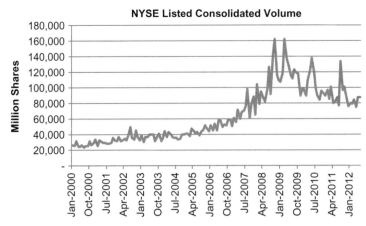

FIGURE 8.1 NYSE Listed Consolidated Volume

transpired. Traded volume in the NYSE was between 80%−90% on average for 2000 through 2005, but then started decreasing (partly due to Reg-NMS in 2007) through 2008/2009. Currently, the NYSE group accounts for only 33%, and the traditional NYSE floor exchange accounts for 20%−23% of total volume in NYSE-listed stocks. The NYSE group includes trades in NYSE, AMEX, and ARCA. This is illustrated in Figure 8.2.

Empirical evidence from the NYSE confirms that decimalization made trading more difficult by increasing the total number of transactions required to fill an order. Average trade size on the NYSE has decreased −82% since 2000, at which time the average trade size was 1222 shares, compared to only 222 shares in 2012. Investors with large positions now require more than five times the number of trades to complete the order than was required prior to decimalization. This does not even include the increase in quote revisions and cancellations for price discovery purposes (and fishing expeditions). Figure 8.3 shows the rapid decrease in trade size over the period 2000 through about 2005, with the decline continuing more gradually until about 2009. Since 2009, the average trade size has been just over 200 shares per trade. Figure 8.4 shows the decline in average trade size for the NYSE group. The difference in this analysis is that NYSE combined with AMEX and ARCA in 2004 started to include crossing session volumes, auctions, etc. into its reported volume statistics. As a result, higher volume values were reported on the NYSE group reports than to the consolidated public tape, and average trade sizes were much larger than the median or the average trade size, excluding auctions and crossing session volume. Even under this new definition we can see that the average trade sizes (computed by dividing the NYSE group reported volume by the total number of reported trades) dramatically declined. These average sizes show the different equity listings (NYSE, AMEX, ARCA, and NASDAQ), and exchange-traded funds (ETFs). In May and June of 2006,

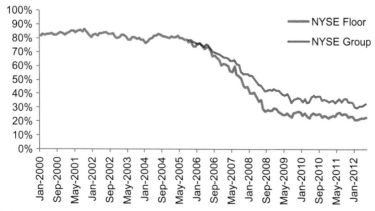

FIGURE 8.2 NYSE Exchange Percentage of Total Volume

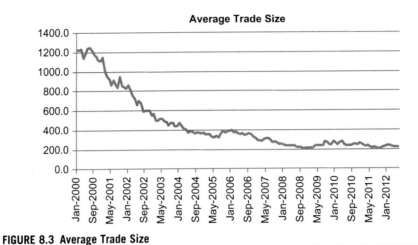

FIGURE 8.3 Average Trade Size

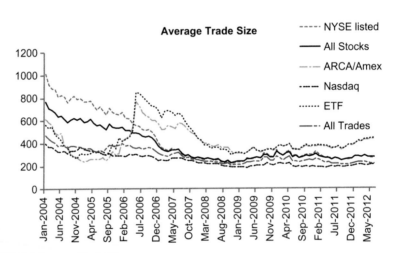

FIGURE 8.4 Average Trade Size

NYSE group started reporting all crossing session volumes in its ETF and Amex/ Arca volume statistics, resulting in what appears to be an increase in trade size, but the increase was due to the reporting data, not any increase in trade size. The most representative average trade size figures in this chart are the all-trades average (computed from market data) and the NYSE-reported NASDAQ values, since all NASDAQ trades and volume were reported to the tape. NYSE does not run any crossing or auctions for NASDAQ listed stocks. One interesting observation that follows is that the average ETF trade size (441 shares in 2012) is almost

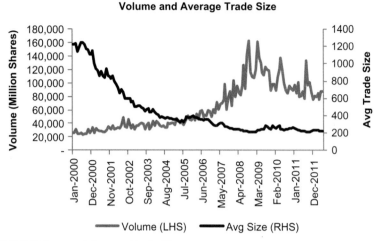

FIGURE 8.5 Volume and Average Trade Size

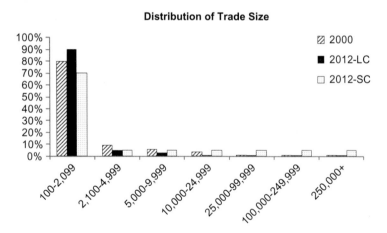

FIGURE 8.6 Distribution of Trade Size

double the average equity size (222 shares in 2012). A comparison of volume and trade size is shown in Figure 8.5. Notice the inverse relationship between the two. Whiles volumes have increased, average trade size has declined, thus causing a higher number of trades and more work to complete an order. A comparison of the distribution of trade sizes in 2000 and in 2012 is shown in Figure 8.6.

The quantity of block trading activity on NYSE has also decreased considerably (Figure 8.7). The decreased activity has greatly contributed to the smaller

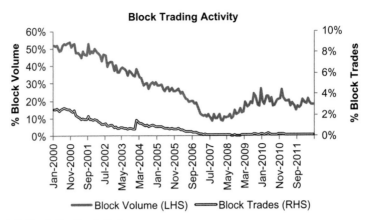

FIGURE 8.7 Block Trading Activity

trade sizes and to more difficulty in completing an order. However, much of the challenge can be attributed to algorithmic trading. The percentage of block volume (10,000 shares or more) has decreased dramatically from 52% of total volume in 2000 to fewer than 20% in 2012. The number of block transactions has decreased −95%, from about 2.6% of total trades to 0.1% of total trades in 2012. Clearly, trading has become more difficult, measuring from the number of transactions required to fill an order.

Our analysis period has seen a dramatic surge in program trading activity over 2000 through 2007. During this time, program trading increased from about 10% of total volume to almost 40%. Then in August 2007, there was a market correction that is believed to be due to a high correlation across different quantitative strategies that caused many quantitative funds to incur losses and lose assets under management. Subsequently, program trading activity declined through about September 2008. Moreover, due to the financial crisis, many funds turned to program trading to facilitate their trading needs from a risk-management perspective, which caused program trading to again increase through 2010, at which point it seems to have since leveled off, at about 30%−35% of total market volume (Figure 8.8).

It is easy to see that the increase in program trading has also helped open the door for algorithmic trading. Program trading is defined as trading a basket of 15 or more stocks with a total market value of $1 million dollars or more. Since 2000, program trading on the NYSE has increased 273%, from 10% in 2000 to 36% in 2012. This more than triple increase in program trading has been attributable to many factors. For example, institutional investors have shifted towards to embracing quantitative investment models (e.g., mean-variance optimization, long-short strategies, minimal tracking error portfolios, stock-ranking model, etc.) where the model results are a list of stocks and corresponding share

FIGURE 8.8 Program Trading Volume

quantities, compared to the more traditional fundamental analysis that only recommends whether a stock should be bought or sold without any insight into the number of shares to transact. The recent increase in program trading activity is also due to large broker-dealers offering program trading at lower commission rates than traditional block executions. Technological improvements (e.g., Super DOT on NYSE, Super Montage on NASDAQ, and in-house trading systems) have made it much easier for brokers to execute large lists of stocks more efficiently. Now, combine the large increase in program trading with the large reduction in block volume, and we begin to appreciate the recent difficultly in executing large positions and the need for more efficient implementation mechanisms. Execution and management of program trades have become much more efficient through the use of trading algorithms, and these program trading groups have pushed for the advancement and improvement of trading algorithms as a means to increase productivity.

Recent Growth in Algorithmic Trading

To best position themselves to address the changing market environment, investors have turned to algorithmic trading. Since computers are more efficient at digesting large quantities of information and data, more adept at performing complex calculations, and better able to react quickly to changing market conditions, they are extremely well-suited for real-time trading in today's challenging market climate. Algorithmic trading became popular in the early 2000s. By 2005, it accounted for about 25% of total volume. The industry faced an acceleration of algorithmic trading (as well as a proliferation of actual trading algorithms), and the volume increased threefold to 75% in 2009. The rapid increase in activity was largely due to the increased difficulty investors faced executing orders. During the financial crisis, it was not uncommon to see stock price swings of 5–10% during the day, as well as the changing market environment (discussed earlier). These trends are shown in Figure 8.9. Over the years, there have been various sources providing algorithmic trading estimates. For example, Tabb Group and Aite Group have published participation rates for buy-side algorithmic trading usage that are lower than the figures reported in this book. Our estimates include the execution's end product. So, even if the investor did not trade directly with an algorithm, but did in fact route the algorithm to a broker who ultimately transacted the shares with an algorithm, those shares are included with the algorithmic trading volume figures.

The decade 2000–2010 was also mirrored with changing market participants. We analyzed market participant order flow by several different categories of investors: traditional asset managers (including mutual funds, indexers, quantitative funds, and pension funds), retail investors, hedge funds (including statistical arbitrage and proprietary trading funds), market makers, and high-frequency traders. In our definition, the high-frequency traders only consisted of those investors considered liquid or rebate traders. We discuss the different types of high-frequency trading ahead.

In 2003–2004, market volumes were led by asset managers accounting for 40% of total volume. High-frequency traders had almost negligible percentages in 2003, but grew to about 10% of the total market volumes in 2006. During the financial crisis, high frequency/rebate traders accounted for about 33% of volume, followed by hedge funds (21%). The biggest change we have observed over 2000–2012 is the decrease in asset manager volumes from 40% (2003) to about 23% (2012) and the increase in high-frequency trading from 1–3% to about 30% of total volumes. Hedge fund trading volumes as a percentage of total decreased

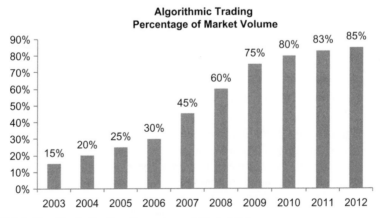

FIGURE 8.9 Algorithmic Trading. Percentage of Market Volume

slightly, but this is due to the increased competition across hedge funds, withdrawal of dollars, and a shift for some of these funds and managers from traditional hedge fund strategies into the ultra-short-term, high-frequency strategies. Hedge fund volume percentage has also increased slightly in 2012. These statistics are illustrated in Figure 8.10.

Opponents of high-frequency trading will often argue that it disadvantages institutional and retail investors because it is causing trading costs to spike and liquidity to dry up. We have always found it humorous that whenever someone is trying to make a point or affect change for something that will benefit them, they pull retail into the mix and imply that the current structure is harming particular retail investors, indicating that we must make changes in order to protect these mom and pop investors. Otherwise, these retail investors are almost entirely ignored. What is more likely in these situations is that the market has become increasingly competitive, and high-frequency traders have achieved higher levels of profitability than traditional investors. As such, they are pushing for change that will either favor their particular trading needs or investment style or help them (albeit in an indirect way) by taking an advantage away from a competitor.

For example, during the period of increased high-frequency trading activity (2006–2009) these funds were reported to be highly profitable. In contrast, over the same period the more traditional funds were not as profitable as they were previously (and especially in comparison to the high-frequency traders). As a result, the belief (either correct or not) is that high-frequency traders must be doing something that is harmful and detrimental to the general markets. Their trading must be toxic. A similar situation occurred back in the early 2000s when traditional hedge funds were highly profitable. They were greatly criticized at the time for being "fast money" and for causing price dislocations due to their buying and selling pressure, which wasn't good for—you guessed it—retail investors.

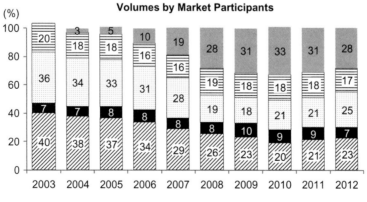

FIGURE 8.10 Volumes by Market Participants

As a follow-up to the high frequency criticism, many financial pundits are stating that high-frequency trading accounts for upwards of 50%–70% of total market volumes. These are very different values than what our research has found; we estimated high frequency trading to account for only 33% of total volume. What is behind these differences? It just so happens that this difference is due to the definition of "high-frequency" trader. These parties have grouped high-frequency trader (our rebate trader definition) with market maker participants and some hedge fund traditional statistical arbitrage traders (including pairs trading, index arbitrage, and market neutral strategies).

Figure 8.11 shows a plot of the percentage of market volume for high-frequency traders (HFT), market making (MM), and hedge funds (HF). Notice the increasing trend of HFT and the initial decrease in HF trading percentage, but with a recent increase. Market making (MM) appears to have been relatively steady, but has decreased from about 20% down to 17% of market volumes. Notice our maximum HFT market volume percentage of 33% in 2010. We additionally plot trends consisting of high-frequency trading and market makers (HFT + MM) and high-frequency trading, market makers, and hedge funds (HFT + MM + HF). Notice that in the peak of the financial crisis, 2008–2009, high-frequency trading was only about 33% of total market share: a large discrepancy from the widely reported 50%–70%. But the combination of HFT and MM percentage peaks at about 50% during the period and then tapers off in 2011–2012 when markets have become increasingly competitive, and some high-frequency traders have exited the business. Furthermore, as we add the hedge fund trader percentage to HFT and MM, we start approaching values of about 60–70%. Thus, the classification of the different types of traders is what accounts for the disparity in statistical figures.

An important issue to point out is that the actual market volume percentage of HFT + MM + HF has only increased slightly over 2003–2012 from 57% to 70%.

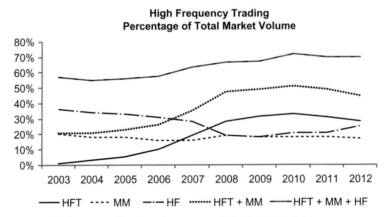

FIGURE 8.11 High Frequency Trading. Percentage of Total Market Volume

So, it is more likely that the more nimble market makers and hedge fund traders turned to high-frequency trading strategies than that this class of investors just appeared overnight (Figure 8.11).

Algorithmic trading is currently one of the hottest areas of capital expenditure for Wall Street firms (both buy-side and sell-side). There are numerous conferences and seminars dedicated to algorithmic trading throughout the United States, Europe, Asia, and Australia. Unfortunately, the amount of academic research has not kept pace with the surge in algorithmic trading. Most industry awareness regarding algorithmic trading has come from broker-dealers whose marketing information is mainly self-serving, with the main purpose being to increase order-flow and business. There is a strong need for unbiased academic research and a well-tested decision-making methodology. We seek to bridge the gap between academia and Wall Street.

Classifications of Algorithms

One of the more unfortunate events in the financial industry is the proliferation of the algorithmic nomenclature used to name trading algorithms. Brokers have used catchy names and phrases for the algorithms to have them stand out from competitors, rather than using naming conventions that provide insight into what it is that the algorithm is trying to accomplish. While some of the industry algorithms do have logical, descriptive names, such as "VWAP," "TWAP," "Arrival Price," and "Implementation Shortfall," there are many others such as "Tarzan," "Bomber," "Lock and Load," and, one of the all-time favorites, "The Goods" (although this name is soon to be replaced). None of these catchy names offer any insight into what it is that the algorithm is trying to accomplish or the actual underlying trading strategy.

As a way to shed some light on the naming convention used, we suggest classifying algorithms into one of three categories: hyper-aggressive, working order, and passive. These are as follows:

Aggressive: The aggressive family of algorithms (and sometimes hyper-aggressive strategies) are designed to complete the order with a high level of urgency and capture as much liquidity as possible at a specified price or better. These algorithms often use terminology such as "get me done," "sweep all at my price or better," "grab it," etc.

Working order: The working order algorithms are the group of algorithms that look to balance the trade-off between cost and risk, as well as management appropriate order placement strategies through appropriate usage of limit/market orders. These algorithms consist of VWAP/TWAP, POV, implementation shortfall (IS), arrival price, etc.

Passive: The passive family of algorithms are those algorithms that seek to make large usage of crossing systems and dark pools. These algorithms are mostly designed to interact with order flow without leaving a market footprint. They execute a majority of their orders in the dark pools and crossing networks.

Types of Algorithms

Single-stock algorithms: Single-stock algorithms interact with the market based on user-specified settings and will take advantage of favorable market conditions only when it is in the best interest of the order and the investor. Single-stock algorithms are independent of one another while trading in the market and make decisions based solely on how those decisions will affect the individual order.

VWAP: Volume weighted average price algorithms participate in proportion with the intraday volume curve. If 5% of the day's volume trade is in any specified period, then the VWAP algorithm will transact 5% of the order in that period. The intraday volume profile used to follow a U-shaped pattern with more volume traded at the open and close than mid-day. But recently, intraday volume profiles have become more back-loaded and resemble more of a J-shaped pattern than a U-shaped pattern. A VWAP strategy is a static strategy and will remain constant throughout the day.

TWAP: Time weighted average price algorithms execute orders following a constant participation rate through the entire day. A full day order will trade approximately 1/390 of the order in each one-minute bucket (there are 390 minutes in the trading day in the US). It is important to note that many TWAP algorithms do not participate with volume in the opening and closing auctions since there is no mathematical method to determine the quantity of shares to enter into these auctions. In *Optimal Trading Strategies*, the TWAP curve was referred to as the uniform distribution or uniform strategy and was used for comparison purposes. A TWAP strategy is a static strategy and will remain constant throughout the day.

Volume: These strategies are referred to as volume inline or percentage of volume (POV) of participation rate algorithms. These algorithms participate with market volume at a pre-specified rate such as 20% and will continue to trade until the entire order is completed. The algorithms will trade more shares in times of higher liquidity and fewer shares in times of lower liquidity, and thus react to market conditions (at least to changing volume profiles). One drawback to these volume strategies is that they do not guarantee completion of the order by the end of the time horizon. For example, if we are trading an order that comprises 20% of the day's volume at a POV = 20% rate, but the actual volume on the day is only half of its normal volume, the order would not complete by the end of the day. As a safety around potential uncompleted orders, some brokers have offered a parameter to ensure completion by the end of the period. This parameter serves as a minimum POV rate and adjusts in real-time to ensure order completion by the designated end time.

Arrival price: The arrival price algorithm has different meanings across different brokers and vendors, so it is important to speak with those parties to understand the exact specifications of these algorithms. But in general, the arrival price algorithm is a cost-minimization strategy that is determined from an optimization that balances the tradeoff between cost and risk (e.g., Almgren & Chriss, 1997). Users specify their level of risk aversion or trading urgency. The resulting solution to the optimization is known as the trade schedule or trade trajectory and is usually front-loaded. However, some parties solve this optimization based on a POV rate rather than a static schedule in order to take advantage of changing liquidity patterns.

Implementation shortfall: The implementation shortfall algorithm is similar to the arrival price algorithm in many ways. First, its meaning varies across the different brokers and different vendors, so it is important to speak with those parties to under their exact specifications. Second, we base the implementation shortfall algorithm on Perold's (1987) paper and seek to minimize cost through an optimization that balances the tradeoff between cost and risk at a user-specified level of risk aversion. In the early days of algorithm trading, the arrival price and implementation shortfall algorithms were identical across different brokers. Thus, to distinguish implementation shortfall from arrival price, brokers began to incorporate real-time adaptation tactics into the implementation shortfall logic. These rules specify how the initial solution will deviate from the optimally prescribed strategy in times of change market liquidity patterns and market prices. Thus, while arrival price and implementation shortfall still do not have a standard definition across the industry, the general consensus is that the arrival price algorithm is constant, while the implementation shortfall algorithm incorporates a second level of adaptation tactics based on market volumes and market prices.

Basket algorithms: Basket algorithms, also known as portfolio algorithms, manage the tradeoff between cost and total basket risk based on a user-specified level of risk aversion. These algorithms will manage risk throughout the trading day and adapt to the changing market conditions based on user specifics. The algorithms are usually based on a multi-trade period optimization process. They make real-time trading decisions based on how those decisions will affect the overall performance of the basket. For example, a basket algorithm may choose to not accelerate trading in an order even when faced with available liquidity and favorable prices if doing so would increase the residual risk of the basket. Furthermore, the basket algorithm may be more aggressive in an order even in times of illiquidity and adverse price movement if doing so would result in a significant reduction of residual basket risk. The biggest difference between single-stock and basket algorithms is that the basket algorithm will manage cost and total basket risk (correlation and covariance), whereas the single-stock algorithm will seek to manage the cost and individual risk of the stock. Important basket-trading constraints include cash balancing, self-financing, and minimum and maximum participation rate.

Risk-aversion parameter: The meaning of the risk-aversion parameter used across the different brokers will vary. First, the optimization technique is not constant. For example, some parties will optimize the tradeoff between cost and variance since it fits a straightforward quadratic optimization formulation. Others optimize based on the tradeoff between cost and standard deviation (square root of variance), which results in a nonlinear optimizations formulation. Second, the definition of the risk aversion parameter, usually denoted by λ, varies. Some brokers specify $\lambda = dCost/dRisk$ where $\lambda > 0$. Some map λ to be between 0 to 1 (0 = most passive and 1 = most aggressive), and still others map risk aversion to be between 1 to 3 or 1 to 10. Thus, selecting a value of $\lambda = 1$ could mean the most aggressive strategy, the most passive strategy, or somewhere in the middle. Still others use a qualitative measure such as passive, medium, aggressive, etc., rather than a specified value of λ. Investors need to discuss the meaning of the risk-aversion parameter with their providers in order to determine how it should be specified in the optimization process in order to ensure consistency across trading goals and investment objectives.

Black box algorithms The family of black box trading algorithms are commonly referred to as profit and loss algorithms and/or robo-trading algorithms. These include all algorithms that make investment decisions based on market signals and execute decisions in the marketplace. Unlike the implementation algorithms that are tasked with liquidating a pre-determined position within some specified guidelines or rules, the black box algorithms monitor market events, prices, trading quantities, etc., for a profiting opportunity search. Once profiting opportunity appears in the market, the algorithm instantaneously buy/sells the shares. Many black box algorithms have time horizons varying from seconds to minutes, and some longer time horizons run from hours to days. While many investors use black-box algorithms, they are still primarily tools of the quants, especially when it comes to high-frequency trading. Some black box trading algorithms are pairs trading, auto market making, and statistical arbitrage. Black box trading strategies and corresponding mathematics are discussed in detail in Chapter 13.

Algorithmic Trading Trends

Algorithmic usage patterns have also changed with the evolution of trading algorithms. In the beginning, algorithmic trading was mostly dominated by "VWAP/TWAP" trading that utilized a schedule to execute orders. The advantage was that investors acquired a sound performance benchmark, "VWAP," to use for comparison purposes. The improvement in algorithms, and their ability to source liquidity and manage micro order placement strategies more efficiently, led the way for price-based algorithms such as "Arrival Price," "Implementation Shortfall," and the "AIM" and "PIM" tactics. During the financial crisis, investors were more

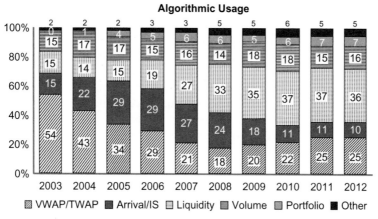

FIGURE 8.12 Algorithmic Usage

concerned with urgent trading and sourcing liquidity, and many turned to "Liquidity Seeking" algorithms to avoid the high market exposure present during these times. The financial crisis resulted in higher market fragmentation owing to numerous venues and pricing strategies and a proliferation of dark pools. However, the industry is highly resourceful and quick to adapt. Firms developed internal crossing networks to match orders before being exposed to markets, providing cost benefits to investors and incorporating much of the pricing logic and smart order capabilities into the "Liquidity Seeking" algorithms. Thus, usage of these algos has remained relatively constant. Currently, liquidity-seeking algorithms account for 36% of volume, VWAP/TWAP accounts for approximately 25%, Percentage of Volume algorithms accounts for approximately 16%, Arrival Price/IS algorithms accounts for approximately 10%, and Portfolio algorithms accounts for approximately 7%. This is shown in Figure 8.12.

Trading Venue Classification
Displayed Market

A displayed exchange is a trading venue that discloses order book information. This consists of bid and offer prices, share quantities, and depth of book. Investors transacting in a displayed venue are able to see exactly how many shares are available at each price increment. This allows investors to compute expected transaction prices for a specified number of shares and also calculate the expected wait time for a limit order to transact since they have knowledge where the order would sit in a queue and how many orders would need to transact ahead of them before their order will execute. Examples of displayed exchanges are NYSE, NASDAQ, Chicago, CBOE, etc.

Dark Pool

A dark pool is a crossing network or other type of matching system that does not display or disseminate order information such as bid and offers, depth of book, number of orders, buy/sell imbalances, etc. Customers enter buy or sell orders into the dark pool. The order is executed only if there is a match. Dark pools do have drawbacks, however. This includes no prior knowledge of order execution or where orders will sit in the order book queue. The dark pool's opaque/nontransparent nature makes it difficult for customers to determine if a market order or marketable limit order will execute at specified prices. In addition it is problematic to calculate the likelihood that a limit order will be executed at a specified price increment since the customer does not know where it will sit in the queue. An advantage of dark pool is that since order details are not disseminated there is no information leakage. Investors can enter large block orders without showing their hand to market participants. Dark pools also allow investors to cross at the mid-point of the bid-ask spread, and they are maintained by brokers and third-party vendors. Broker "internal dark pools" are used for matching internal and client orders away from the displayed exchanges. Third-party dark pools, such as Liquidnet, Bids Trading, and Level ATS provide investors with the opportunity to trade large block positions anonymously, thus reducing information leakage and market impact.

Grey Pools

The term grey pool denotes a displayed venue that allows investors to enter hidden orders and view displayed orders, prices, depth of book, etc., similar to the displayed exchanges. However, there may be another level of hidden orders on the order book transacting with incoming orders, providing there is a match. For example, an investor sending a market order to a "grey pool" may transact at a price better than the NBBO if there is a hidden order in the venue at a better price.

Dark Pool Controversies

Historically, there has been a large amount of debate surrounding dark pool executions, adverse selection, and toxic order flow. Adverse selection refers to situations when you use a dark pool and have the order executed fully (100%). Subsequent price movement is in your favor (e.g., buys become cheaper and sells become high), so you would have been better off waiting to make the trade. And when you do not execute in the dark pool or execute less than the full order (<100%), the subsequent price movement is away from your order (e.g., buys become more expensive and sells become lower in value). The belief is that there is either some information leakage occurring in the dark pool, or the interaction with high-frequency orders is toxic, meaning that the high-frequency traders are able to learn information about the order such as the urgency of the investor or the number of shares that still need to be executed. In turn, they adjust their prices based on leaked knowledge. However, we have not yet found evidence of adverse selection in dark pools to confirm these suspicions.

But let us evaluate the preceding situation from the order level. Suppose we have a buy order for 100,000 shares, and there is a seller with an order for 200,000 shares. Thus, there is a sell imbalance of $-100,000$ shares. If both parties enter the order into the crossing network (dark pool or other type of matching system), there will be 100,000 shares matched, with the buy order being 100% filled and the sell order being only 50% filled. The seller will then need to transact another 100,000 shares in the market, and the incrementing selling pressure will likely push the price down further due to the market impact cost of their order. So the downward price movement is caused by the market imbalance, not by the dark pool. Next, suppose that the seller only has 50,000 shares. Thus, there is a $+50,000$ buy imbalance. If these orders are entered into the crossing network on 50,000 shares, the buy order will match. The buyer will then need to transact those incremental 50,000 shares in the displayed market, where their buying pressure will likely push the price up further. Thus we can see that the adverse price movement is caused by the market imbalance and not the dark pool. This type of price movement is commonly observed in times of market imbalances.

To be fair, there was a time when dark pools and venues allowed flash orders to be entered into their systems. These flash orders would provide some market participants with a preview of whether there would be a match before the entire marketplace was involved. Many believed that this provided an unfair advantage to those privileged to these flash orders. Flash trading is no longer allowed in any of the market venues.

Types of Orders

The market allows numerous different types of orders such as market, limit, stop loss, etc. But the three most important order types for algorithmic trading are market, limit, and marketable-limit order.

Market order: A market order specifies to the algorithm to buy or sell at the best available market price. This order is most likely to be executed because there are no restrictions on its price and it will not be placed into an order book. The disadvantage is that in today's markets, prices can move away so quickly that the best ask or best bid could in effect be much higher or much lower than they were at the time the order was routed for execution. Market order will "take" liquidity.

Limit order: A limit order specifies to the algorithm to buy or sell at the specified limit price or better. In most cases, the limit order will be entered into the order book of the exchange or venue and is subject to the queue before it is eligible to be executed. For example, in price-time priority, existing orders at that price or better will need to transact before that order with an offsetting buyer. A limit order is not guaranteed to execute, but it provides some safety surrounding the execution price and ensures that the execution will not be worse than the pre-specified limit price. A limit order will "provide" liquidity and is also referred to as posting an order.

Marketable limit: A marketable-limit order is an order that specifies to the algorithm to buy or sell at a specified price or better. This order will be either executed in the market at the specified price or better or cancelled if there are no existing orders at that price or better in the market.

Rebates: Depending upon the exchange or venue, investors may receive a rebate for posting liquidity to their exchange, and others may provide a rebate for taking exchange from their exchange, as well as the more traditional model where both buyers and sellers pay a specified commission fee.

Algorithmic Decision-Making Process

Proper specification of algorithmic trading rules requires investors to make decisions on a macro and micro scale. The macro-level decisions are specified by users prior to trading and consist of selecting the appropriate optimal trading strategy. In addition, algorithms need to determine the appropriate mix of limit and market orders and determine the best venue to trade the order. These decisions are made in conjunction with limit order models and smart order routers.

Macro-Level Decisions

The macro-level strategy decision rules consist of specifying an appropriate optimal trading strategy (e.g., order slicing schedule or percentage of volume rate) and real-time adaptation tactics that will take advantage of real-time market conditions such as liquidity and prices when appropriate. This type of decision making process is consistent with the framework introduced by Kyle (1985), Bertsimas and Lo (1998), Almgren and Chriss (1999, 2000), Kissell and Glantz (2003), and Kissell, Glantz, and Malamut (2004). For investors, macro-level trading specifications consists of a two-step process.

Step 1: Choose Implementation Benchmark

The first step of the macro decision process is selection of the implementation price benchmark. The more common price benchmarks include implementation shortfall ("IS"), decision price, price at order entry ("inline"), opening price, prior night's close, future closing price, and VWAP. Another common implementation goal is to minimize tracking error compared to some benchmark index. It is essential that the implementation goal be consistent with the manager's investment decision. For example, a value manager may desire execution at their decision price (i.e., the price used in the portfolio construction phase), a mutual fund manager may desire execution at the closing price to coincide with valuation of the fund, and a indexer may desire execution that achieves VWAP (e.g., to minimize market impact) or one that minimizes tracking error to their benchmark index.

Step 2: Select Optimal Execution Strategy

The second step of the process consists of determining the appropriate optimal execution strategy. This step is most often based on transaction cost analysis. Investors typically spend enormous resources estimating stock alphas and consider these models proprietary. Market impact estimates, however, remain the holy grail of transaction cost analysis and are usually provided by brokers due to the large quantity of data required for robust estimation. Risk estimates, on the other hand, can be supplied by investors, brokers, or a third-party firm.

The selected optimal execution strategy could be defined in terms of a trade schedule (also referred to as slicing strategy, trade trajectory, or waves), a percentage of volume ("POV"), or other types of liquidity participation or price target strategies. For example, trade as much as possible at a specified price or better.

The more advanced investors will perform TCA optimization. This consists of running a cost-risk optimization where the cost component consists of price trend and market impact cost. That is,

$$Min \ (MI + Trend) + \lambda \cdot Risk$$

where λ is the investor's specified level of risk aversion. Investors who are more risk averse will set $\lambda > 1$ and investors who are less risk averse will set $\lambda < 1$. In situations where the trader does not have any expectations regarding price trend, our TCA optimization is written in terms of market impact cost and risk as follows:

$$Min \ MI + \lambda \cdot Risk$$

Depending upon expected price trend optimization may determine appropriate front- and/or back-loading algorithms to take advantage of better prices. For example, an algorithm may call for a 15% POV rate in the morning, increasing to a POV of 25% beginning mid-day (back-loading) to take advantage of expected better prices in the afternoon, while still balancing the tradeoff between market impact and timing risk. Furthermore, an algorithm may call for a POV of 30% in the morning, falling to 10% in the afternoon (front-loading) as a means to reduce risk and hedge the trade list.

Solving the optimization problem described previously for various levels of risk will result in numerous optimal trading strategies. Each has the lowest cost for the specified level of risk and the lowest risk for the specific amount of cost.

The set of all these optimal strategies comprises the efficient trading frontier ("ETF") first introduced by Almgren and Chriss (1999).

After computing the ETF, investors will determine the most appropriate "optimal" strategy for their implementation goal. For example, informed traders with expectations regarding future price movement are likely to select an aggressive strategy (e.g., POV = 30%) with higher cost but more certainty surrounding expected transaction prices. Indexers are likely to select a passive strategy (e.g., POV = 5%) or a risk-neutral strategy to reduce cost. Some investors may select a strategy that balances the tradeoff between cost and risk depending upon their level of risk aversion, and others may elect to participate with volume throughout the day (e.g., a VWAP strategy).

Micro-Level Decisions

Investors next specify how the algorithm is to adapt to changing market conditions. These decisions may include multiple types of adaptation tactics. Below we outline some common adaptation settings.

Volume-based: Adjust the trading schedule based on market liquidity. A POV/participation rate algorithm is an example of a volume-based adaptation tactic. While these are often constant volume rates, it results in faster trading in times of higher market volume and slower trading in times of lower market volume.

Price-based: Adjust the trading schedule based on market prices. Aggressive-in-the-money ("AIM") algorithms that trade faster in times of favorable prices and slower in times of adverse price movement and passive-in-the-money ("PIM") algorithms that trade slower in times of favorable prices and faster in times of adverse price movement are types of price-based scaling algorithms.

Time-based: The algorithm adjusts its trading rate to ensure executions by a specified time, such as no later than the close. This algorithm may well finish sooner than specified, but it will not finish any later.

Probabilistic: Determines the appropriate trading rate to always provide the best chances (highest likelihood) of achieving the investment objective, based on a non-linear optimization technique, such as maximizing Sharpe ratio or minimizing tracking error.

Optimization Technique: The trade schedule is continuously adjusted so that its expected finishing price will be within a specified tolerance. These types of algorithms will often be based on a variation of a z-score measure (see Chapter 9) and incorporate realized costs (past), sunk cost or savings (dependent upon prices increase or decrease since commencement of trading), and expected future prices (based on actual market conditions and specified trading strategy).

Cash Balancing: In times of portfolio or basket trading, investors often select cash balancing adaptation techniques. The most common variations of cash balancing are risk management and self-financing. Risk management adaptation techniques will manage the unexecuted positions to keep the risk within a specified tolerance level. Self-financing adaptation techniques are used when the sells will be used to pay for the buys. Here we are managing the shares that have already traded and, depending upon market prices and movement, we may require the unexecuted buy shares to be revised (either increasing or decreasing).

Dark Pool Utilization: Investors may elect to use dark pools in a different manner than the displayed venues. For example, investors may choose to try to maximize trading in dark pools, but keep trading in the displayed markets at a different rate. Furthermore, the participation in dark and displayed venues may also be determined by stock prices or market movement.

The goal of the micro-level scheme is three-fold. First, ensure the executions follow the optimally prescribed strategy entered by the user. Second, ensure that the algorithms deviate from the optimally prescribed strategy only when it is in the best interest of and defined by the investor. Third, achieve fair and reasonable prices without incurring unnecessary market impact cost. In situations where the fixed costs and exchange costs are high, optimizing, crossing, and micromanagement on each exchange can also lead to substantial cost savings.

It is essential that the micro-pricing strategy ensure consistency with the macro-level objective and ensure that transactions adhere to the specified implementation goal. For example, it would not be in the best interest of the fund to execute an aggressive strategy (e.g., POV = 40%) using solely limit orders, because execution with limit orders is not guaranteed execution and there is a high likelihood that this type of strategy may fall behind the targeted rate. But it would be appropriate to transact a passive macro strategy (e.g., POV = 5%) utilizing a larger number of limit orders to avoid crossing the bid-ask spread, since there is ample time for these limit orders to be lifted in the market.

In most situations it will be appropriate to use a combination of limit, market, floats, and reserve orders. For example, suppose the specified macro-level optimal strategy is a POV rate of 15%. Here, a micro-level algorithm may submit limit orders to the market for execution better than the mid-quote as long as the actual POV rate is consistent with 15% of market volume, but once the algorithm starts lagging behind the specified rate or some specified tolerance level it would submit appropriately sized and spaced market orders to be more aggressive and adhere to the 15% rate. A reserve order could also be used to automatically replenish limit orders at favorable prices. Some of the more advanced micro-pricing strategies utilize real-time data, prices and quotes, order book information, and recent trading activity to forecast very short-term price trends and provide probabilistic estimates surrounding the likelihood that a limit order will execute within a certain period of time.

Limit Order Models

Limit order models determine the appropriate mix of limit and market orders to best adhere to the higher-level macro goals. The limit order model is a probabilistic model that takes into account current market conditions, price momentum, order book information, macro goals, and timing. Traditionally, limit order models will determine the probability that an order will execute in the market at a stated price and within a stated amount of time. The limit order model here is a modified limit order model, with the output being a mix of prices and share quantities to ensure completion (or at least a sufficiently high likelihood of completion) by the end of the time period, rather than a probability estimate of executing at a specified price point.

For example, if the optimal trading rate specified in the macro-level decision for a buy order is POV = 10%, and we forecast 10,000 shares will be traded in the next one minute, then we will need to execute 1,000 shares in the next one minute to adhere to our 10% POV rate. If the current market is $30.00–$30.10, the limit order model may determine that the most cost-effective mix of prices, order types, and shares quantities to trade these 1000 shares in the next one minute is:

- Limit order, 200 shares at $29.95
- Limit order, 300 shares at $30.00
- Limit order, 300 shares at $30.05
- Market order, 200 shares at $30.10

Smart Order Routers

The smart order router (SOR) is responsible for routing the child orders to the different exchanges, venues, and dark pools. The SOR will collect, monitor, and maintain trading activity data at the different venues and dark pools throughout the day using market/public data and in-house transactions. The SOR determines the likelihood of executing an order at each of the different venues based on frequency of trading and where the order would reside in the order book queue at that price. If the trading frequency and all else is equal across two venues, the SOR will route the limit order to the venue, where it will sit highest in the queue. If one venue has 10,000 shares at the desired price, and another venue has 5,000 shares at the desired price, the SOR will route the shares to the venue with only 5,000 shares since it is more likely to execute at that location quicker. The SOR determines on an expected value basis the likelihood of trading, so it may route the order to a venue where it initially sits lower in queue if that venue has higher trading activity, or it may route the order to a venue that does not trade as frequently as others if it sits higher in the queue. For the most part, this is an expected value calculation.

Revisiting our example above, where we are tasked with trading 1000 shares in the next one minute with the best mix of limit and market prices being 200 at $29.95, 300 at $39.00, $30 at $30.05, and 200 at $30.10 (the offer), the SOR may decide to enter 200 shares in a dark pool at the mid-point of the bid-ask spread ($30.05) and 300 shares at the primary exchange at the best bid price of $30.00. Furthermore, 200 shares may be entered into a non-traditional exchange at

$29.95, where it sits first in the queue and may perhaps even have to pay a rebate for posting (inverted pricing model).

Finally, the SOR may determine that to avoid potentially falling behind the schedule and having to possibly trade 200 shares at the market at the end of the one minute period where the price may move away (increase for the buy order), it would be best to trade 100 shares at the market immediately and 100 shares after perhaps 30–45 seconds, thus increasing likelihood that they will not fall behind and will have to trade in an aggressive and costly manner to catch-up.

One reason why someone might decide to pay to post an order is to ensure that they will be the first 200 shares to trade at that price (if the market falls). Rational investors would route an order to a venue where they will receive a rebate to trade over a venue where they have to pay to trade. Here the savings achieved by transacting at the better price will more than make up for the rebate that has to be paid for posting liquidity. Another reason why someone may pay a rebate to post is that rather than have to increment the bid price to be first in queue (at a 1 cent increment), the investor may decide to enter the order to an exchange where they pay to post (inverted pricing model), to almost ensure themselves the top of the queue because the counter party would rather transact with their order and receive a rebate than transact with another order on a different venue and pay a fee. Here, the rebate cost of posting the order will be lower than the 1 cent that they would need to increment the bid even after accounting for any rebate they may receive.

In times of NYSE and NASDAQ (well, really ARCA and INET for algorithms) order routing was a much easier problem. But now with multiple destinations, venues, dark pools, etc., this is a much more complex problem.

In addition to maintaining order-routing data across the various exchanges and computing the probabilities of executions, the SOR is also responsible for all order submission rules. The more common pricing rules as mentioned are market, limit, marketable limit, and floating prices that are pegged to a reference price such as the bid, ask, or midpoint and that change with the reference price, etc. Varying these order types allows the algorithm to adhere to the optimally prescribed strategy by executing aggressively (i.e., market orders) and/or passively (i.e., limit orders) when needed. Order sizes are set in quantities that can be easily absorbed by the market. The order type variation disguises the actual trading intentions (i.e., limit orders) and minimizes potential adverse price impact (i.e., market orders). A reserve (iceberg) order is another technique commonly used in micro-pricing strategies, and it refers to a continuously replenishing order at a stated size. For example, a 10,000 share order could be entered as a 1,000 share reserve book order in which 1,000 shares would be displayed and immediately replenished each time it transacts until the order is filled. Finally, the SOR maintains, randomizes, and varies wait and cancellation times to help disguise trading intentions. Some orders may remain in the market for longer periods of time, while other orders remain on the book for a shorter period of time before cancellation. Additionally, randomizing the time between orders and waves helps hide trading intentions, minimizes information leakage, and helps improve the likelihood of achieving more favorable prices.

An important note that is often overlooked in the algorithmic trading arena is that a smart order router should only be used as a smart order router. Many vendors have made the mistake of forcing the smart order router to provide a combination of services such as limit order model, macro strategy selection model, etc. These parties have tried to market these services as an all-in-one algorithmic smart order solution. Without understanding the macro-level needs of the investor or their trading goals, it is simply not possible to be able to provide this type of all-in-one solution. The best-in-class solutions to these algorithmic issues have followed our algorithmic decision making process—trading goal, adaptation tactic, limit order model, order submission rules—not the all-in-one type of solution.

High-Frequency Trading

High-frequency trading (HFT) is the usage of sophisticated mathematical techniques and high-speed computers to trade stocks, bonds, or options with the goal to earn a profit. This differs from the execution trading algorithms that are tasked with implementing an investment decision that has previously been determined. In other words, the HFT system makes both the investment and trading decisions simultaneously. High-frequency trading in this sense is also called "black box" and "robo" trading.

HFT strategies can be classified into three different styles: Auto Market Making (AMM), Quant Trading/Statistical Arbitrage, and Rebate/Liquidity Trading. Donefer (2010) provides a similar classification in "Algos Gone Wild." There is often some overlap across these styles as we point out ahead, but for the most part, each of these styles has completely different goals and objectives. In short, high-frequency trading has these features:

- *Automated trading.* Algorithms determine what to buy and what to sell, as well as the micro-order placement strategies such as price, size, and timing of the trade. These decisions are determined from actual real-time market data including price signals, momentum, index or sector movement, volatility, liquidity, and order book information. These decisions are made independent of human interaction.
- *No net investment.* HFT does not require a large cash inflow since the inventory imbalances are netted out by the close each day. HFT strategies take both long and short positions in different names and close these positions before the end of the day so that they do not take on any overnight risk. In cases where the HFT holds overnight positions, they will mostly likely use the proceeds from short sales to pay for the buys.
- *Short trading horizons.* Depending upon the strategies, HFT time horizons can vary from seconds to minutes, but also up to hours.

Auto Market Making

Auto market making (AMM) provides the financial community with the same services as the traditional market makers or specialists. The main difference, however, is that rather than employing human market makers, the AMM system uses advanced computer systems to enter quotes and facilitate traders. The registered AMM still has an obligation to maintain a fair and orderly market, provide liquidity when needed, and provide market quotes a specified percentage of the time.

AMM systems automatically enter bids and offers into the market. After the AMM system transacts with a market participant, they become either long or short shares, and they will seek to offset any acquired position through further usage of limit orders. The auto market making systems look to profit from buying at the bid, selling at the offer, and earning the full spread. And as an incremental incentive, registered auto market maker firms are often provided an incremental rebate for providing liquidity. Therefore, they can profit on the spread plus rebates provided by the exchange. This is also causing some difficulty for portfolio managers seeking to navigate the price discovery process and determine fair value market prices.

AMM black box trading models will also include an alpha model to help forecast short-term price movement and assist in determining the optimal holding period before being forced to liquidate an acquired position to avoid a loss. For example, suppose the bid-ask spread is $30.00 to $30.05, and the AMM system bought 10,000 shares of stock RLK at the bid price of $30.00. If the alpha forecast expects prices to rise, the AMM will offer the shares at the ask price of $30.05, or possibly higher in order to earn the full spread of $0.05/share or more. However, if the alpha forecast expects prices to fall, the AMM system may offer the shares at a lower price such as $30.04 to move to the top of the queue, or if the signal is very strong the AMM systems may cross the spread, sell the shares at $30.00, and thus not earn a profit—but not incur a loss either.

Most AMM traders prefer to net out all their positions by the end of the day so that they do not hold any overnight risk. But they are not under any obligation to do so. They may keep positions open (overnight) if they are properly managing the overall risk of their books or if they anticipate future offsetting trades/orders (e.g., they will maintain an inventory of stock for future trading). Traditional AMM participants continue to be concerned about transacting with an informed investor, as always, but it has become more problematic with electronic trading since it is more difficult to infer if the other side is informed (have strong alpha or directional view) or uninformed (e.g., they could be a passive indexer required to hold those number of shares), since the counterparties' identities are unknown.

Some of the largest differences between AMM and traditional MM is that the AMM maintains a much smaller inventory position, executes smaller sizes, and auto market makers are not committing capital for large trades as the traditional market makers once did.

Quantitative Trading/Statistical Arbitrage

Traditional statistical arbitrage trading is trying to profit from a mispricing in different markets, in indexes, or even ETFs. Additionally, statistical arbitrage trading strategies in the high-frequency sense will try to determine profiting opportunities from stocks that are expected to increase or decrease in value, or at least increase or decrease in value compared to another stock or group of stocks (e.g., relative returns). To use short timeframe "long-short" strategies relies on real-time market data and quote information, as well as other statistical models (such as PCA, probit and logit models, etc.). These traders do not necessarily seek to close out all positions by the end of the day in order to limit overnight risk, because they are based on alpha expectations, and the profit and loss is expected to be derived from the alpha strategies, not entirely from the bid-offer spread. These are the traditional statistical arbitrage strategies of the past, but the time horizon could be much shorter now due to potential opportunity, better real-time data, and faster connectivity and computational speeds. This category of trading could also include technical analysis-based strategies, as well as quant models (pairs, cointegration). These types of trading strategies have traditionally been considered as short-term or medium-term strategies, but due to algorithmic and electronic trading and access to an abundance of real-time data and faster computers, these strategies have become much more short-term, reduced to hours or minutes, and are now also considered to be HFT strategies. However, they do not necessarily need to be that short of time or HFT strategies. These participants are less constrained by the holding period of the positions (time), and most concerned by the expected alpha of the strategy.

Rebate/Liquidity Trading

This is the type of trading strategy that relies primarily on market order flow information and other information that can be inferred or perceived from market order flow and real-time pricing including trades, quotes, depth of book, etc. These strategies include "pinging" and/or "flash" orders, and a strong utilization of dark pools and crossing venues (e.g., non-traditional trading venues). Many of these non-traditional trading venues have structures (such as the usage of flash orders) that may allow certain parties to have access to some information before other parties. These traders seek to infer buying and selling pressure in the market based on expected order flow and hope to profit from this information. The liquidity trading strategies can be summarized as those strategies that seek to profit through inefficient market information. What is meant by this is that the information that can be inferred, retrieved, processed, computed, compiled, etc., from market data to generate a buy or sell signal, through the use of quick systems and better computers, infrastructure, location of servers, etc., is colocation, pinging, indication of interests (IOI's), and flash orders. The "liquidity trading" HFT is often the category of HFT that is gaining the most scrutiny and questions in the market. Market participants are worried that these strategies have an unfair advantage through the colocation, available order types, ability to decipher signals, etc. These participants counter argue that they adhere to the same market rules and have an advantage due to their programming skills or mathematical skills, better computers, connectivity (e.g., super computers), and colocation of servers, all of which is available to all market participants (albeit for a cost).

Another variation of the rebate trader is an opportunistic AMM. This is again similar to the AMM and the traditional market-making role, but the opportunistic trader is not under any obligations to provide liquidity or maintain a fair and orderly market. These market participants will provide or take liquidity at their determined price levels, as they are not required to continuously post bids and offers, or maintain an orderly market. Since they are not registered or under any obligations to provide liquidity, these parties do not receive any special rebates that are made available to the registered AMM. This party tends to employ alpha models to determine the best price for the stocks (e.g., theoretical fair-value models) and corresponding bids and offers to take advantage of market prices; they only tend to provide quotes when it is in their best interest to do so and when there is sufficient opportunity to achieve a profit. If prices are moving away from them, they may no longer keep a market quote. As a result, they may only have a quote on one side of the market, or will quickly close the position via a market order to avoid potential adverse price movement. These parties expect to profit via the bid-ask spread (similar to the tradition AMM participants) as well as via market rebates and alpha signals. But unlike traditional AMM participants, the rebates and alpha signals are a primary P/L opportunity. They only perform the AMM function when these signals are in their favor, and they do not have any obligation to continuously provide market quotes. The opportunistic AMM participants are more likely to net and close their positions by the end of the day because they do not want to hold any overnight risk even if they are well-hedged. Furthermore, the opportunistic AMM participants are not willing to hold any inventory of stock in anticipation of future order flow. But they will hold an inventory (usually small) of stock (either long or short) based on their alpha signal, which is usually very short term (before the end of the day). They often close or net their positions through market orders, and do so especially when they can lock in a profit. Additionally, some of the opportunistic AMM may continuously net positions throughout the day so that they keep very little cash exposure. These parties also try to profit via rebates, and utilize limit order models (and other statistical models relying on real-time data) to infer buying and selling pressure and their preferred prices.

The New Equity Exchange Environment

The landscape of trading exchanges has changed dramatically since the early days of the NYSE and NASDAQ. There are four exchange groups operating ten exchanges, with an additional three independent venues and dark pools. These groups are:

- NYSE/Euronext: NYSE, Arca, AMEX
- NASDAQ/OMX: NASDAQ, BSX, PSX
- BATS: BYX, BZX
- Direct Edge: EDGA, EDGX
- Independents: NSX, CBOE, CBSX
- FINRA: TRF (trade reporting facilities)

In this section we examine the underlying trading volumes across market groups learn how to best utilize this information when developing algorithms and specifying trading strategies. The data analysis period is 1Q-2012.

Trading Volumes

Market Share

The equity markets are dominated by four major regional and crossing exchange groups. Of these, NYSE has the largest market share with 24.5% of total share volume. NASDAQ is second with 21.6% of total share. BATS and Direct Edge are third and fourth, respectively. For the period analyzed we found BATS with 10.4% and Direct Edge with 9.3% of stock share volume. Direct Edge and BATS have been pretty consistent, with each having about 9%−10% of total market share. The regional exchanges, surprisingly, only account for about 1.3% of total share volume. FINRA TRF's volume consists of the dark pools and crossing network matches, including both third-party networks and internal broker dealings crossing systems. These trades account for about 33% of total share volume traded in the market.

Large- and Small-Cap Trading

NYSE-listed large stocks account for a much larger percentage of market shares than NYSE-listed small-cap stocks. NYSE LC stocks account for 77% of market volumes, and NYSE SC stocks account for about 23% of market volumes. The breakdown of NASDAQ market share is not as skewed for large-cap as it is for NYSE stocks. NASDAQ large-cap stocks account for 52% of the market volume, and NASDAQ small-cap stocks account for 48% of the market volume. It is important to point out that there is not a difference across exchanges. NYSE trades more volume in large cap compared to small cap, and vice-versa for NASDAQ. Historically, the smaller, less-established companies would list on the NASDAQ exchange initially, but would often migrate to the NYSE exchange as they grew and matured. This trend, however, is beginning to change, as we see some large-cap NYSE-listed companies moving to the NASDAQ exchange. For example, Texas Instruments (Dec 2011) and Kraft (Jun 2012) moved from NYSE to NASDAQ.

Do Stocks Trade Differently Across The Exchanges and Venues?

We next analyzed volumes across all trading venues. Stocks were segmented by exchange listing and then by market cap to determine if there is any material difference to how they trade.

For NYSE stocks we found very little difference between large- and small-cap stocks. Small-cap stocks did trade slightly more in the NYSE/AMEX market (specialist/DMM model) and in the crossing networks (FINRA-TRF). Large caps traded a little more in the alternative exchanges, NASDAQ, and ARCA. For NASDAQ stocks, we once again found similar trading activity across large- and small-cap stocks. Large-cap stocks traded a little more on NASDAQ and ARCA, and small-cap stocks traded slightly more in the crossing networks.

We next analyzed the difference across market-cap stocks and how they traded in the different venues over the two year period 2011−2012. We found that the listed large-cap stocks traded much more on the NYSE/AMEX venue as expected, since these are primarily the stocks that are listed on the NYSE exchange, and the NASDAQ large-cap stocks traded more in the NASDAQ venue as well as in the alternatives exchanges and ARCA. Similar results were found for small-cap stocks. Listed small-cap stocks traded a larger percentage in NYSE/AMEX, and NASDAQ small-cap stocks traded a larger percentage in NASDAQ. The trading volume across the different alternative exchanges were similar, but with NASDAQ small-caps trading slightly more in the alternative exchanges and in the dark pools.

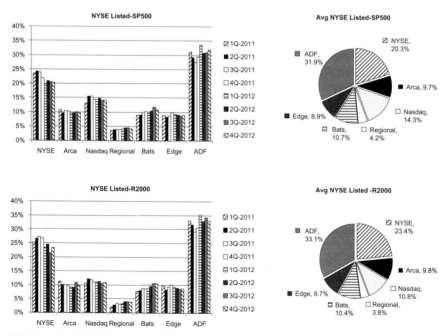

FIGURE 8.13 NYSE Listed Stock Volumes by Trading Venue

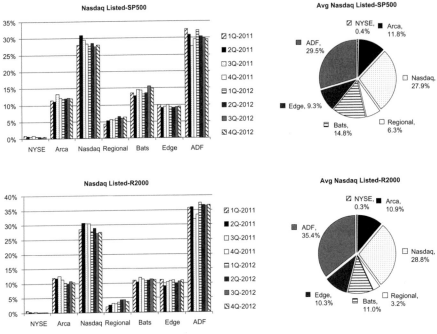

FIGURE 8.14 Nasdaq Listed Stock Volumes by Trading Venue

Volume Distribution Statistics

Investigation into stock trading patterns uncovered some interesting volume distribution properties. Namely, the difference in trading volume across market capitalization. As expected, large-cap stocks trade a much higher number of shares than small-cap stocks. Large-cap stocks traded an average of 6.1 million shares per day, and small-cap stocks traded an average of 496 thousand shares per day. NASDAQ large-cap stocks (7.4 million) trade more daily volume than NYSE-listed large-cap stocks (5.8 million). NYSE-listed small-cap stocks (639 thousand) trade more daily volume than NASDAQ-listed small-cap stocks (400 thousand).

The difference across trading volume by large cap is likely to be driven by sector and information content. First, NASDAQ is more dominated by large-cap technology and internet stocks than NYSE. These companies are also more likely to be growth companies or companies with a high return potential, thus making them attractive to those seeking higher returns. Since NASDAQ stocks are traded more via market makers, there is some double counting in the names. Additionally, the NASDAQ technology and internet stocks are becoming a favorite of retail investors, since they are known names and it is sexier to trade technology and internet stocks than, say, utilities. NYSE small-cap stocks are believed to trade more volume than NASDAQ small-cap stocks because these are the more established companies with a history of earnings and company-specific fundamentals. Furthermore, NASDAQ small-cap stocks are usually larger than NASDAQ small stocks. Finally, it is the designated market maker model with lower spreads that result in lower trading costs and hence make NYSE small cap stocks a more attractive investment opportunity than NASDAQ small-cap stocks. Another interesting daily volume property is that the median daily volume is much lower than the average daily volume measure. The ratio of median volume to average volume is NYSE-LC = 0.48, NASDAQ-LC = 0.38, NYSE-SC = 0.40, and NASDAQ-SC = 0.37. This is an indication that NYSE stocks have much more stable day-to-day patterns than NASDAQ stocks. Analysis of the skewness of absolute daily volumes finds NYSE = 4.33 and NASDAQ = 5.59, and large cap = 3.23 and small cap = 5.43. This shows that daily volumes are very positively skewed for all stocks (NYSE and NASDAQ, and large- and small-cap stocks). High kurtosis is also an indication of peaked means and fat tails, or in this case, an indication of outliers. Non-normal distribution patterns for asset returns and their repercussion on risk and return have been greatly researched and published. But the non-normal volume profiles and its repercussion on daily trading costs and ultimately portfolio returns has not been given the same level of attention as with asset prices. But it is just as important.

Another aspect of daily volume distribution and the use of "average" over "median" is that the positive skewness of the distribution causes the "average" volume metric to overestimate actual volumes the majority of times. Since volumes are highly skewed by positive outliers, it results in a value that could be much higher than the middle point of the distribution. In our data, the average is approximately in the 60%–65% percentile, thus leading to an overestimation of daily volume 60–65% of the time. We have found (as we show in later chapters) that the median is a much more accurate predictor of daily volume than average. Why is this so? The reason is simple. When there are earnings announcements, company news, or macro events, there will be more volume traded than on a normal day. Stock volume is highly skewed. As a fix, many practitioners compute the average by taking out the highest and lowest one or two data points, which results in a much more accurate measure. Interestingly, practitioners can compute a more accurate adjusted average by taking out the highest one or two data points since they are the most skewed outliers.

Table 8.1 Daily Volume Distribution Statistics

	Avg ADV	Avg Median	Avg Stdev	Avg Skew	Avg Kurt	Avg CoV
Exchange						
Nyse	2,450,075	592,194	1,360,792	4.33	38.98	74%
Nasdaq	991,463	177,048	689,431	5.59	58.01	99%
Market Cap						
LC	6,160,167	2,785,869	3,186,060	3.31	23.65	55%

(Continued)

Table 8.1 (Continued)

	Avg ADV	Avg Median	Avg Stdev	Avg Skew	Avg Kurt	Avg CoV
SC	495,593	187,777	429,620	5.43	55.60	95%
NYSE						
LC	5,836,089	2,785,869	2,986,093	3.23	22.77	54%
SC	639,273	255,871	491,600	4.92	47.65	85%
Nasdaq						
LC	7,405,640	2,753,902	3,954,560	3.61	27.04	59%
SC	400,455	148,711	388,579	5.77	60.86	102%
Large Cap						
NYSE	5,836,089	2,785,869	2,986,093	3.23	22.77	54%
Nasdaq	7,405,640	2,753,902	3,954,560	3.61	27.04	59%
Small Cap						
NYSE	639,273	255,871	491,600	4.92	47.65	85%
Nasdaq	400,455	148,711	388,579	5.77	60.86	102%

Period: 1Q-2012
Source: The Science of Algorithmic Trading (Kissell, 2013)

Day-of-Week Effect

Historically there has always been a day-of-week pattern associated with market volumes. Stocks would trade the least amount on Monday, increasing on Tuesday and Wednesday, and then decreasing on Thursday and Friday. Examination of large-cap trading volume in 2012 found similar patterns. Mondays were the least active trading day, with volume increasing on Tuesday-Thursday and falling slightly on Friday. We found similar patterns across NYSE- and NASDAQ-listed large-cap stocks. Analysis of small-cap stocks found a different pattern. Volumes were the lowest on Monday as expected, but highest on Tuesday and Friday. Similar patterns for small-cap stocks were found for NYSE- and NASDAQ-listed stocks.

We next examined the day-of-week effect for large- and small-cap stocks across time to see if the Friday effect for small-cap stocks is relatively new or due to randomness. We evaluated volumes by day over 2009–2012 to address this question. For large-cap stocks we found similar weekly patterns for each of the years except for 2010, during which volumes increased on Friday. For small-cap stocks we found that the current weekly pattern has existed since at

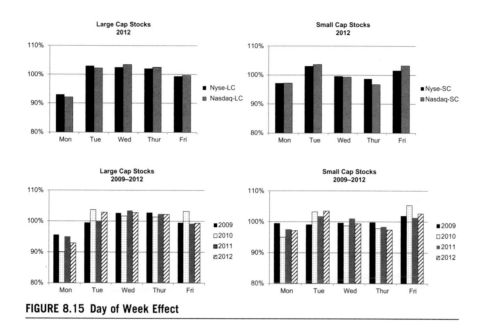

FIGURE 8.15 Day of Week Effect

least 2009. One of the common beliefs for why Friday volumes have increased for small-cap stocks is that portfolio managers do not want to hold weekend risk for stocks with a large amount of company-specific risk. Thus, where managers may have been willing to hold open positions over the weekend at one point in time, they may be less willing to hold open positions in these names in today's trading environment. In 2010, large-cap stocks exhibited similar patterns with Friday volumes increasing. A belief by market participants is that this was the result of a hangover effect in which managers were not willing to hold open positions for large- as well as small-cap stocks due to market environment and uncertainty at that point in time. Managers are still haunted by the overnight collapse of many large-cap companies during the financial crisis.

Intraday Trading Profiles

We examined the intraday trading patterns for spreads, volume, volatility, and intraday trading stability. Historically, each of these measures followed a U-shaped pattern. For example, volume and volatility were both high at the open, decreasing into midday, and then increasing again into the close. Spreads also followed a similar U-shaped intraday trading pattern. Examination of the same profiles in today's market found a distinctly different trading pattern. There were also distinct differences across market capitalization (LC/SC) and exchange listings (NYSE/NASDAQ). Our analysis period was 1Q-2012.

Spreads:

- Intraday spreads were measured as the average bid-ask spread in each fifteen minute trading period.
- Spreads are higher at the open than at midday, but do not spike at the close. Spreads in fact decrease slightly into the close.
- Spreads decrease and level out after about the first 15–30 minutes for large-cap stocks and after about 30–60 minutes for small-cap stocks. The amount of time spreads persist at the higher values is longer than it was historically, when both large- and small-cap spreads used to decline rather quickly, often within 15 minutes for both.
- Small-cap spreads persists longer than large-cap spreads.
- Small-cap spreads are higher than large-cap spreads due to the higher risk of each company, less trading frequency, and higher potential for transacting with an informed investor.
- NYSE stocks have slightly lower spreads than NASDAQ stocks even after adjusting for market capitalization.

Analysis of intraday spreads found three observations worth noting. First, spreads are much higher in the beginning of trading, and these higher spreads persist longer due to a difficult price discovery process. Specialists and market makers used to provide a very valuable service to the financial markets in terms of price discovery and determining the fair starting price for the stock at the market open. Now, the price discovery is often left to trading algorithms transacting a couple hundred shares of stock at a time. While algorithms have greatly improved, they are still not as well equipped as the specialists and market makers in assisting price discovery. For example, specialists used to have access to the full order book and investor orders prior to the market open, so they could easily establish a fair-value opening price by balancing these orders and customer preferences. Market makers also had a large inventory of positions and customer orders which allowed them to provide reasonable opening prices. The current electronic trading arena in which investors only have access to their individual orders does not allow for an efficient price discovery process. Second, NASDAQ spreads are lower than NYSE spreads even after adjusting for market cap. This is likely due to the NYSE designated market maker (DMM) system that has been established to encourage the DMM participants to participate in the process by providing liquidity when necessary. Third, spreads now decrease going into the close rather than increasing. This is likely due to greater transparency surrounding closing imbalances and investors' ability to offset any closing auction imbalance.

Intraday Volumes:

- Intraday volume is measured as the percentage of the day's volume that is traded in each fifteen trading period.

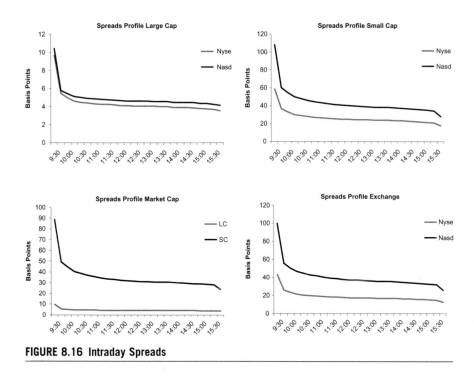

FIGURE 8.16 Intraday Spreads

- Intraday volume profiles are not following the traditional U-shaped trading patterns.
- Intraday profiles are now more "J-shaped," with only slightly more volume traded at the open, then decreasing, then increasing significantly into the close.
- NYSE-listed companies trade a little less at the open and a little less at the close than NASDAQ-listed companies
- Small-cap stocks trade more at the open and close than large caps.

There are five likely reasons why intraday trading patterns have shifted from a U-shaped trading pattern to a J-shaped pattern. First, similar to an increase in Friday daily volumes, where managers are less inclined to hold open positions over the weekend, trades are less inclined to hold open positions overnight and not make a more conscious effort to complete those positions before the market close. Second, there are currently fewer active investment strategies in today's markets than previously. Active managers typically trade at the open at known and preferred prices, rather than wait to near the end of the day when prices are not known. Third, there are more index funds and closet index funds today than previously. These are the managers who more often trade at and into the close than in the morning hours. This is done in order to transact as close to the closing price as possible and to minimize tracking error compared to the closing price, since the fund will be valued based on the day's closing price. Fourth, there has been a dramatic increase in exchange-traded funds (ETFs). ETFs are used for many different reasons. For example, ETFs are used to gain certain market exposures or to hedge very short-term risk. And very often investors who were hedging short-term market risk net out those positions at the end of the day, resulting in increased trading volume. ETF trading has also caused an increase in trading volume towards the end of the day due to the creation and redemption of these ETFs. While we have not found evidence suggesting correlation between overall ETF and stock volume, we have found a statistically significant relationship between the shift in intraday volume trading and ETF volume. Thus, ETF trading has played a part in shifting the stock's intraday volume profile towards the close and away from the open. Fifth, the increase in closing imbalance data and the investor's ability to offset end-of-day imbalances (as well as easy and direct access to this information) has helped improve the price discovery process. This, coupled with less end-of-day price volatility, allows funds an easier time to achieve market prices at the close than previously occurred, and hence there is more trading at the close. Finally, over the last few years there has been a decrease in quantitative investment strategies. Quant managers have reduced leverage of their portfolios, and the general economic climate has not provided these managers with as much profiting opportunity as in years past. Since quant managers do not currently have a strong need to achieve particular market prices, they are able to utilize a more passive execution style such as VWAP rather than utilizing a front-loading execution style such as IS or arrival price.

To the extent that there is another shift away from index and ETF trading back to active management and quantitative styles, we are likely to see a corresponding shift in intraday volume profiles with more volume trading at the open and less dramatic spiking towards the close. Portfolio manager investment styles have a dramatic effect on when volumes occur throughout the day.

Volatility:

- Measured as the average high-low percentage price range in each fifteen-minute trading period.
- Does not currently follow its historical U-shaped profile. Intraday volatility is higher at the open than midday and only increases slightly into the close.
- Higher at the open due to a more difficult price discovery process, and the higher levels persist for a longer period of time than historically.
- Does not increase into the close to the same extent that it did historically.
- Slightly lower volatility at the NYSE-listed stocks than NASDAQ-listed stocks.
- Small-cap intraday volatility is much higher than large-cap volatility, as expected.

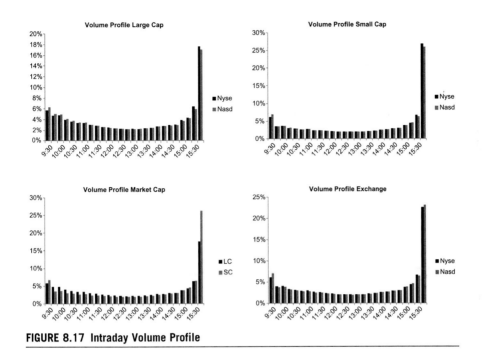

FIGURE 8.17 Intraday Volume Profile

As mentioned, the old specialist and market maker system provided valuable price discovery. Today's market algorithms, however, are left to determine the fair-value price by trading a couple hundred shares at a time. It is not uncommon to look at the tape and see a price change of $0.50/share at the open with only a few hundred shares trading in the interval. Leaving algorithms to determine fair market prices by trading relatively small amounts causes opening period volatility to be higher than it was previously as well as to persist longer than it has before. It appears that the NYSE DMM system is providing value in terms of lower opening spreads and volatility levels. The decrease in end-of-day volatility is due to an improved and more transparent closing auction process.

Intraday Trading Stability—Coefficient of Variation:

- Measured as the average standard deviation of interval volume.
- High variation in volumes at the open. Leveling off midday and then decreasing into the close.
- Small-cap volume variation is about two times the large-cap variation.
- No difference in volume variation across NYSE- and NASDAQ-listed stocks after adjusting for market cap.

Coefficient of variation is a rarely used risk statistic in the industry. As any trader will confirm, intraday liquidity risk is one of the most important aspects of

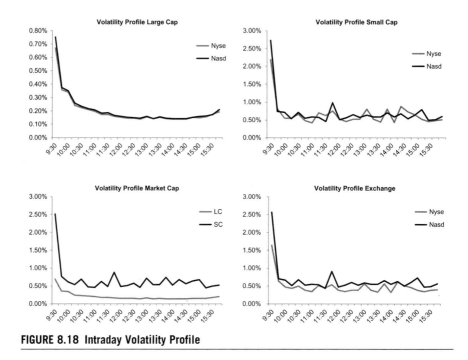

FIGURE 8.18 Intraday Volatility Profile

trading and will be one of the primary reasons for a trader to deviate from a pre-scribed strategy, change the algorithm, or adjust the algorithmic parameters and settings. The intraday coefficient of variation, when computed and used properly, will serve as a valuable liquidity risk measure and provide information that allows traders to improve overall performance. Additionally, as we show in later chapters, the coefficient of variation is a large determinant of stock-specific trading cost and could be a valuable component of any market impact model.

Trading Cost Equations

Our market impact and timing risk equations expressed in terms of percentage of trading volume (*POV*) are:

$$I_{bp}^{*} = \hat{a}_1 \cdot \left(\frac{X}{ADV} \right)^{\hat{a}_2} \cdot \sigma^{\hat{a}_3} \tag{8.1}$$

$$MI_{bp} = \hat{b}_1 \cdot I^{*} \cdot POV^{\hat{a}_4} + (1 - \hat{b}_1) \cdot I^{*} \tag{8.2}$$

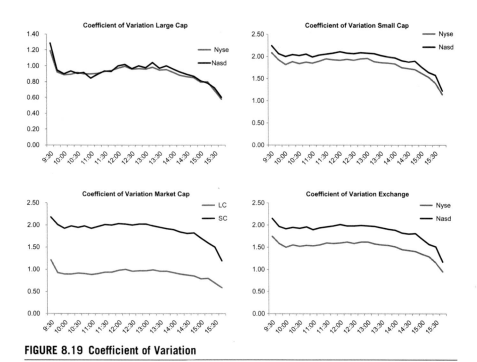

FIGURE 8.19 Coefficient of Variation

$$TR_{bp} = \sigma \cdot \sqrt{\frac{1}{3} \cdot \frac{1}{250} \cdot \frac{X}{ADV} \cdot \frac{1 - POV}{POV}} \cdot 10^4 \ bp \qquad (8.3)$$

where

X = total shares to trade

ADV = average daily volume

σ = annualized volatility (expressed as a decimal, e.g., 0.20)

$POV = X/X + V_t$ = percentage of trading volume rate

V_t = expected market volume during trading period (excluding the order shares X)

$\hat{a}_1, \hat{a}_2, \hat{a}_3, \hat{a}_4, \hat{b}_1$ = model parameters estimated via non-linear estimation techniques

The trading cost equations for a basket of stock are as follows:

$$I_{\$i}^* = \hat{a}_1 \cdot \left(\frac{X_i}{ADV_i} \right)^{\hat{a}_2} \cdot \sigma_i^{\hat{a}_3} \cdot P_{i0} \qquad (8.4)$$

$$MI_\$(x_k) = \sum_{i=1}^{m} \left(\sum_{t=1}^{n} \hat{b}_1 \cdot I_i^* \cdot \frac{x_{it}^2}{X_i(x_{it} + v_{it})} \right) + (1 - \hat{b}_1) \cdot I_i^* \qquad (8.5)$$

$$TR_\$(x_k) = \sigma \cdot \sqrt{\sum_{k=1}^{n} r_k' \tilde{C} r_k} \qquad (8.6)$$

where,

r_k = column vector of unexecuted shares at the beginning of the period k

$$r_k = \begin{pmatrix} r_{1k} \\ r_{2k} \\ \vdots \\ r_{mk} \end{pmatrix}$$

r_{ik} = unexecuted shares of stock i at the beginning of period k
$\tilde{C}$ = covariance matrix expressed in terms of \$/share^2 and scaled for a trading period.

To express the timing risk for the basket of stock in terms of basis points we simply divide the timing risk dollar amount by the initial value of the trade list: $V_\$ = \sum X_i \cdot P_{i0} \cdot 10^4$.

Trading Risk Components

The timing risk (*TR*) measure is a proxy for the total uncertainty surrounding the cost estimate. In other words, it is the standard error of our forecast. This uncertainty is comprised of three components: price uncertainty, volume variance, and parameter estimation error. These are further described as follows:

Price volatility: Price volatility refers to the uncertainty surrounding price movement over the trading period. It will cause trading cost (ex-post) to be either higher or lower depending upon the movement and side of the order. For example, if the price moves up \$0.50/share, this movement results in a higher cost for buy orders, but a lower cost (savings) for sell orders. For a basket of stock, price volatility also includes the covariance or correlation across all names in the basket. Price volatility is the most commonly quoted standard error for market impact analysis. It is also very often the only standard error component.

Volume variance: Volume variance refers to the uncertainty in volumes and volume profiles over the trading horizon, which could be less than, equal to, or more than a day. For example, if an investor trades an order over the full day, the cost will be different if total volume is 1,000,000 shares, 5,000,000 shares, or only 200,000 shares.

Parameter estimation error: Parameter estimation error is the standard error component from our non-linear regression models. As is the case with all regression models there is always some degree of uncertainty surrounding the parameters which will affect parameter estimates and analysts need to perform proper statistical analysis to verify the results within a defined level of confidence. For simplicity, we define the timing risk measure to only include the price volatility term when quoting the standard error of the market impact estimate, but analysts conducting advanced sensitivity analysis may want to incorporate these additional components into the timing risk estimate. We have found the easiest way to determine the overall uncertainty is via Monte Carlo simulation in which volumes, intraday profile, price movement, and parameter values are sampled from historical observations and their estimated distribution. Investors performing this type of analysis may find that corresponding market impact uncertainty is much larger than simply the standard deviation of price movement.

Volume Forecasting Techniques
Monthly Volumes

In this section we describe a process to forecast average monthly volume levels. This process could also be extended to estimate annual volume levels. Having a forward-looking ADV estimate can be very helpful for the portfolio manager who is looking to rebalance his/her portfolio at some future point in time when volumes may look much different than they do now.

Methodology:

Period: Ten (10) years of data, Jan. 2002 through Dec. 2011.
Universe: Average daily volumes for large-cap (SP500) and small-cap (R2000) stocks by month.
Definitions
$V(t)$ = average daily volume across all stocks per day in corresponding market cap category
$\sigma(t)$ = average stock volatility in the month.
SPX = SP500 index value on last day in month.
$\Delta V(t)$ = log change in daily volume (MOM)

$$\Delta V(t) = ln\{V(t)\} - ln\{V(t-1)\}$$

$\Delta V(t-1)$ = previous month's log change in daily volume (MOM) to incorporate an auto-regressive term. This is also a proxy for momentum.

$$\Delta V(t-1) = ln\{V(t-1)\} - ln\{V(t-2)\}$$

$\Delta V(t-12)$ = log change in daily volume (MOM) one year ago to incorporate a monthly pattern.

$$\Delta V(t - 12) = \ln\{V(t - 12)\} - \ln\{V(t - 13)\}$$

$\Delta\sigma_{large}(t) = $ log change in large cap volatility (MOM).

$$\Delta\sigma_{large}(t) = \ln\{\sigma_{large}(t)\} - \ln\{\sigma_{large}(t - 1)\}$$

$\Delta\sigma_{small}(t) = $ log change in small cap volatility (MOM).

$$\Delta\sigma_{small}(t) = \ln\{\sigma_{small}(t)\} - \ln\{\sigma_{small}(t - 1)\}$$

$\Delta Spx(t) = $ log change in SP500 index value (MOM). We used the change in SP500 index values for both large cap and small cap forecasts.

$$\Delta Spx(t) = \ln\{spx(t)\} - \ln\{spx(t - 1)\}$$

Monthly Volume Forecasting Model:

$$\Delta V(t) = b_0 + b_1 \cdot \Delta V(t - 1) + b_2 \cdot \Delta V(t - 12) + b_3 \cdot \Delta\sigma + b_4 \cdot \Delta Spx$$

Figure 8.20 shows the average daily volume per stock in each month for large-cap and small-cap stocks over the period January 2002 through December 2011 (10 years of monthly data). For example, in June 2011 the average daily volume for a large-cap stock was 5,766,850 per day, and the average daily volume for a small-cap stock was 555,530 per day. It is important to note that historical volume levels will change based on stock splits and corporate actions.

Analysis:

The monthly volume forecasting analysis is to determine an appropriate relationship to predict the expected change in monthly volume levels. Since the number of trading days will differ in each month due to weekdays, holidays, etc., it is important that we adjust for the number of trading days in order to make a fair comparison across time. Our analysis included one and twelve month autoregressive terms, the change in monthly volatility levels for each market-cap category, and the MOM change in SP500 index for both large- and small-cap stocks.

We estimated our regression coefficients for large and small cap stocks using a 10-year horizon. We further defined three periods to evaluate the stability of these relationships. These periods are:

Ten Years: 1/2002–12/2011
Five Years: 1/2007–12/2011
Five Years: 1/2002–12/2006

Regression Results:

The result of our regression study is shown in Table 7.4. In total, there are six scenarios that were analyzed: three for LC and three for SC. The results show the estimated betas, corresponding standard errors and t-stat, and the R2 statistic. Overall our regression model had a very strong fit. The model did explain a larger percentage of the variation for large-cap stocks than for small-

(A)

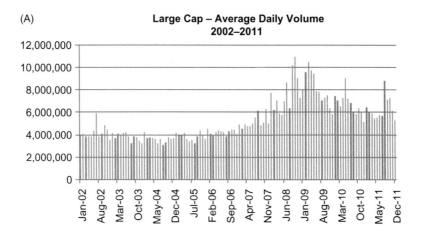

(B)

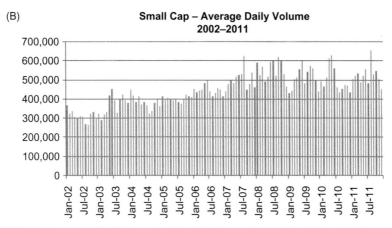

FIGURE 8.20 Average Daily Volumes by Month for Large Cap and Small Cap Stocks

cap stocks (as is expected due to the trading stability of the smaller companies). The R2 using 10 years of data was $R2 = 0.70$ for large-cap stocks and $R2 = 0.39$ for small-cap stocks. Overall, our formulation is a very statistically sound model.

Our monthly volume forecasting models for large- and small-cap stocks are:

$$\text{Large Cap:} \quad \Delta V(t) = 0.0056 - 0.2990 \cdot \Delta V(t-1) + 0.1354 \cdot \Delta V(t-12) \\ + 0.5461 \cdot \Delta \sigma_{large}(t) - 0.1877 \cdot \Delta Spx \tag{8.7}$$

$$\text{Small Cap:} \quad \Delta V(t) = 0.0029 - 0.2212 \cdot \Delta V(t-1) + 0.2385 \cdot \Delta V(t-12) \\ + 0.3569 \cdot \Delta \sigma_{small}(t) + 0.3437 \cdot \Delta Spx \tag{8.8}$$

Table 8.2 Monthly Volume Forecasts: Average Daily Volume per Stock

Large Cap Stocks (SP500)

Ten Years: 2002–2010

	const	ΔV(−1)	ΔV(−12)	Δσ	ΔSpx
beta	0.0056	−0.2990	0.1354	0.5461	−0.1877
se	0.0064	0.0435	0.0461	0.0328	0.1466
t-stat	0.8806	−6.8785	2.9352	16.6699	−1.2798
R2	0.79				

Recent Five Years: 2007–2010

	const	ΔV(−1)	ΔV(−12)	Δσ	ΔSpx
beta	−0.001	−0.313	0.088	0.529	−0.432
se	0.009	0.060	0.061	0.042	0.196
t-stat	−0.072	−5.245	1.461	12.601	−2.201
R2	0.83				

Previous Five Years: 2002–2006

	const	ΔV(−1)	ΔV(−12)	Δσ	ΔSpx
beta	0.010	−0.366	0.211	0.550	0.379
se	0.008	0.071	0.074	0.057	0.253
t-stat	1.216	−5.132	2.862	9.601	1.499
R2	0.76				

Small Cap Stocks (SP500)

Ten Years: 2002–2010

	const	ΔV(−1)	ΔV(−12)	Δσ	ΔSpx
beta	0.0029	−0.2212	0.2385	0.3569	0.3437
se	0.0077	0.0732	0.0784	0.0475	0.1717
t-stat	0.3773	−3.0216	3.0423	7.5084	2.0016
R2	0.39				

Recent Five Years: 2007–2010

	const	ΔV(−1)	ΔV(−12)	Δσ	ΔSpx
beta	−0.001	−0.225	0.143	0.362	0.140
se	0.012	0.100	0.109	0.058	0.222
t-stat	−0.103	−2.254	1.310	6.259	0.629
R2	0.49				

Previous Five Years: 2002–2006

	const	ΔV(−1)	ΔV(−12)	Δσ	ΔSpx
beta	0.004	−0.225	0.367	0.271	0.744
se	0.010	0.119	0.114	0.101	0.300
t-stat	0.372	−1.889	3.215	2.696	2.478
R2	0.32				

Forecasting Model: Monthly(t) = b0 + b1*Monthly(t−1) + b2*Month(−12) + b3*Volt_Chg + b4*Chg_SPX
Source: The Science of Algorithmic Trading (Kissell, 2013)

Main Observations:

- Monthly volumes exhibit trend reversion. The sign of the $\Delta V(t-12)$ variable was negative across both large- and small-cap stocks in each of the scenarios. If volume levels were up in one month, they were more likely to be down in the following month. If volume levels were down in one month, they were more likely to be up in the following month. This relationship is more significant for large cap than small cap stocks. Monthly volumes exhibit a positive seasonal trend. The sign of the $\Delta V(t-12)$ variable was positive and significant in most cases, indicating a monthly pattern exists, although monthly volume levels vary. For example, December and August are consistently the lowest-volume months during the year. October and January are the two highest-volume months of the year (measured over our 10 year period). The relationship is stronger for small-cap than for large-cap stocks.
- Volumes are positively correlated with volatility. One way of thinking about this is that volume causes the volatility. Another explanation is that portfolio managers have a better opportunity to differentiate themselves and earn a higher return in times of increasing volatility. Hence they trade and rebalance their portfolios more often. The relationship here is slightly stronger for large-cap stocks.
- The connection between volume and price level (SPX index) is the only factor that produces different relationships for large- and small-cap stocks. Small-cap volume has always been positively related to price level. As the market increases, volume in small-cap stocks increases, likely due to high investor sentiment during times of increasing market levels. Investors will put more in small-cap stocks in a rising market hoping to earn higher returns, but will trade small stocks less often in a decreasing market. The strength of this relationship has declined between the 2002–2006 and 2007–2011 periods. During 2002–2006, large-cap stock volumes were also positively related to market price levels. But that relationship has reversed during 2007–2011.
- Currently, large-cap stock volume is inversely related to prices. The relationship could be due to the current investor sentiment (since the financial crises). Investors are very wary of the market and fear further sharp declines. A cash investment of a fixed dollar amount will purchase fewer shares in a rising market, but more shares in a falling market. Redemption of a fixed dollar amount will require fewer shares to be traded in a rising market and more shares to be traded in a declining market. We expect that this trend will stay constant and may additionally become negative for small-cap volumes until investor sentiment and overall market confidence increases.
- Our analysis did not uncover any relationships between volume levels and correlation. However, correlation still remains a favorite indicator for portfolio managers. We suggest readers experiment with alternative correlation measures such as log change and actual level. This may improve the accuracy of our volume forecast model.

Daily Volumes

Our daily volume forecasting approach is based on an autoregressive moving average (ARMA) technique. Our research finds daily volumes to be dependent upon: 1) either a moving average (ADV) or a moving median (MDV) daily volume, 2) a historical look-back period of 10 days, 3) a day-of-week effect, or 4) a lagged daily volume term. Additional adjustments can also be made to the volume forecasts on special event days such as earnings, index reconstitution, triple and quadruple witching day, fed day, etc. (see Chapter 2, Market Microstructure in *The Science of Algorithmic Trading* (Kissell, 2013)).

Our daily volume forecasting analysis is as follows:

Definitions:

Historical Look-Back Period. The number of days (data points) to use in the forecasts. For example, should the measure be based on 66 days, 30 days, 20 days, 10 days, or 5 days of data?

Average Daily Volume (ADV). Average daily volume computed over a historical period. We will use a rolling average in our forecast.

Median Daily Volume (MDV). Median daily volume computed over a historical period. We use a rolling median in our forecast.

Day of Week. A measure of the weekly cyclical patterns of trading volumes. Stocks tend to trade different percentages per days. This cyclical effect has varied over time and differs across market-cap categories.

Lagged Daily Volume Term. We found some evidence of persistence in market volume. Many times, both high and low volume can persist for days. However, the persistence is more often associated with high volume days due to the effect of trading large orders over multiple days to minimize price impact. Thus, when an institution is transacting a multi-day order, there is likely to be excess volume.

Authors' note: It is important to differentiate between the ADV measure used to normalize order size in the market impact estimate and the ADV or MDV measure used to predict daily volume. The ADV used in the former model needs to be consistent with the definition used by traders to quantify size. For example, if traders are using a 30 day ADV measure as a reference point for size, the market impact model should use the same metric. It is essential that the ADV measure that is used to quote order size by the trader be the exact measure that is used to calibrate the market impact parameters in the estimation stage. The daily volume forecast, however, is used to determine costs for the underlying trading strategy, whether it be a trade schedule, a POV-based strategy, or a trading rate-based strategy. An order for 100,000 shares or 10% ADV will have different expected costs if the volume on the day is 1,000,000 shares or 2,000,000 shares. In this case, a more accurate daily volume estimate will increase precision in cost estimate and lead to improved trading performance.

Daily Forecasting Analysis—Methodology:

Time Period: Jan. 1, 2011 through Dec. 31, 2011.
Sample Universe: S&P 500 (large cap) and R2000 (small cap) indexes on Dec. 31, 2011. We only included stocks where we had complete trading history over the period Nov. 10, 2010 through Dec. 31, 2011. The days from Nov. 11, 2010 to Dec. 31, 2010 were used to calculate the starting point for the historical average daily volume (ADV) and historical median daily volume (MDV) on Jan. 1, 2011.

Variable Notation:

$V(t)$ = actual volume on day t
$\hat{V}(t)$ = forecasted volume for day t
$MDV(n)$ = median daily volume computed using previous n-trading days
$ADV(n)$ = Average daily volume computed using previous n-trading days
$DayOfWeek(t)$ = The percentage of weekly volume that typically trades on the given weekday
$\hat{\beta}$ = Auto-regressive sensitivity parameter, estimated via OLS regression analysis
$e(t)$ = forecast error on day t

ARMA Daily Forecasting Model:

$$\hat{V}(t) = \overline{V}_t(n) \cdot DayOfWeek(t) + \hat{\beta} \cdot e(t-1) \qquad (8.9)$$

where $\overline{V}_t(n)$ is either the n-day moving ADV or n-day moving MDV, and $e(t-1)$ is the previous day's volume forecast error (actual minus estimate). That is,

$$e(t-1) = V(t-1) - (\overline{V}_{t-1}(n) \cdot DayOfWeek(t-1)) \qquad (8.10)$$

The previously shown error term is calculated as the difference between actual volume on the day and estimated volume only using the day-of-week adjustment factor. The theoretical ARMA model will cause persistence of the error term as it includes the previous day's error in the forecast, e.g., $e(t-2)$. However, our analysis has found that we could achieve more accurate estimates defining the error term only as shown previously. Additionally, computation of daily volume estimates is also made easier since we do not need to maintain a series of forecast errors.

Analysis Goal:

The goal of our daily volume forecasting analysis is to determine:

- Which is better: ADV or MDV?
- What is the appropriate number of historical days?
- Day-of-week adjustment factor
- Autoregressive volume term

The preferred form of the ARMA model is determined via a three-step process; the forecasting model should be re-examined at least on a monthly basis and recalibrated when necessary.

Step 1:

Determine which is more appropriate, ADV or MDV, and the historical look-back number of days.

- Compute the ADV and MDV simple forecast measure for various look-back periods. E.g., let the historical look-back period range from t = 1 to 30.
- Compute the percentage error between the actual volume on the day and simple forecast measure. That is:

$$\varepsilon(t) = ln(V(t)/\overline{V}(n))$$

- The percentage error is used to allow us to compare error terms across stocks with different liquidity.
- Calculate the standard deviation of the error term for each stock over the sample period.
- Calculate the average standard deviation across all stocks in the sample.
- Repeat the analysis for look-back periods from 1 to 30 days.
- Plot the average standard deviation across stocks for each day (from 1 to 30).

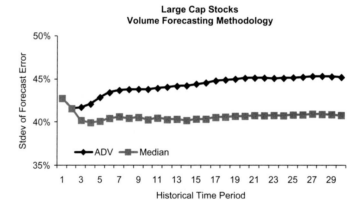

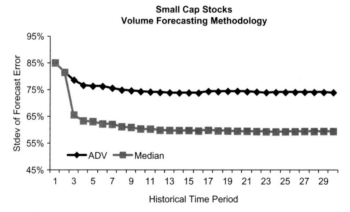

FIGURE 8.21 Daily Volume Forecast

A plot of our forecast error analysis for each measure is shown in Figure 8.21a for large-cap stocks and in Figure 8.21b for small-cap stocks. Notice that for both large- and small-cap stocks the MDV measure has a lower error than the ADV. This is primarily due to the positive skews of daily volume which causes the corresponding ADV measure to be higher. Next, notice that the error term for both market-cap categories follows a convex shape with a minimum error point. For large-cap stocks, the minimum error is around 5−10 days, and for small-cap stocks, the minimum error is close to 10 days.

Conclusion 1:

We conclude that the median daily volume using a historical period of 10 days, e.g., MDV(10), has the lowest forecast error across stocks and market cap during our analysis period.

Authors' note: As shown previously, the ADV measure will more often be higher than the actual volume due to the positive skew of the volume distribution. Volume distributions tend to be more above average than below average outliers. This will result in actual costs being higher than the predicted costs. For example, if we trade 200,000 shares out of a total ADV of 1,000,000 shares, we may be tempted to state that a full-day strategy corresponds to a trading rate of 20%. However, if the actual volume on the day is only 800,000 shares, the actual trading rate will be 25%, resulting in higher than predicted costs. The market impact forecasting error will be biased (to the high side) when using the ADV measure to predict daily volume. In our sample, we found the ADV to be higher than the actual volume on the day 65% of the time.

Step 2:

Estimate the ***DayOfWeek(t)*** parameter.

We analyzed whether or not there is a cyclical trading pattern during the week. To avoid bias that may be caused by special event days such as FOMC, triple witching, index reconstitution, earnings, month end, etc., we adjusted for these days in our analysis. It is important to note that if month end is not excluded from the data, there may be a strong bias suggesting that Friday is the heaviest trading day of the week, since three out of seven month ends occur on Fridays (due to weekends). Many investors trade more often on the last day of the month.

Our day-of-week process is as follows:

- For each stock, compute the percentage of actual volume traded on the day compared to the average volume in the week.
- Exclude the special event days that are historically associated with higher traded volume.
- Compute the average percentage traded on each day across all stocks in the sample.
- It is important to use a large enough sample in the analysis. We used one full year as a trading period to compute the day-of-week effect.

The result of our day-of-week analysis is shown in Figure 8.15. Monday is consistently the lowest-volume day in the week for large- and small-cap stocks.

After adjusting for month-end volume, we found that small-cap volume increases on Fridays, but large-cap volume decreases. The effect may be due to investors not willing to hold an open position in small-cap stocks over the weekend for fear there is too much market exposure for small-cap stocks; they may elect to pay higher market impact before the weekend to ensure completion.

Step 3:

Estimate the autoregressive parameter $\hat{\beta}$.

The autoregressive parameter is used to correct for persistence of volume over consecutive days. We found above-average volume days were more likely to be followed by above-average volume days, and below-average volume days are more likely to be followed by below-average volume days. But the relationship was much more significant for above-average volume days than for the below-average volume days. This process is as follows:

- Estimate volume for the day based on the 10 day median plus the day-of-week adjustment.
- Compute the forecast error term as the difference between the actual volume on the day and the estimated volume. This difference is:

$$\varepsilon(t) = V(t) - Median(t) \cdot DayOfWeek(t)$$

- Run a regression of the error term on its one-day lagged term, that is,

$$\varepsilon(t) = \alpha + \beta \cdot \varepsilon(t-1)$$

- Compute the slope term β for large- and small-cap stocks.

Large-cap stocks had a much larger degree of autocorrelation than small-cap stocks. The average correlation of errors was $\beta_{large} = 0.452$ for large-cap stocks and $\beta_{small} = 0.284$ for small-cap stocks. After correcting for autocorrelation, there was still a very slight amount of autocorrelation present, negligible to the effect on our forecasts due to the constant term in our regression model.

Forecast improvements:

We next compared the results from our preferred ARMA model (shown earlier) to a simple thirty-day ADV measure (e.g., ADV 30) to determine the extent of the forecasting improvement. The preferred ARMA model reduced forecast error -17% for large-cap stocks and -21% for small-cap stocks.

Daily Volume Forecasting Model:

Our daily volume forecasting models for large- and small-cap stocks can finally be formulated as:

$$\text{Large Cap} \quad \hat{V}(t) = MDV(10) \cdot DayOfWeek(t) + 0.450 \cdot e(t-1) \qquad (8.11)$$

$$\text{Small Cap} \quad \hat{V}(t) = MDV(10) \cdot DayOfWeek(t) + 0.283 \cdot e(t-1) \qquad (8.12)$$

Conclusion 2:

- There is statistical evidence that there is persistence of volume trading.
- Forecasts can be improved through incorporation of an autoregressive term.

Table 8.3 One-Period Lag: Error Correlation

Category	Beta	Correlation Before Adj.	Correlation After Adj.	Net Chg Improvement
LC	0.450	0.452	− 0.015	− 0.437
SC	0.283	0.284	− 0.008	− 0.276
All	0.319	0.320	− 0.010	− 0.311

Table 8.4 ARMA Improvement over ADV30 Forecasting Methodology

Mkt Cap	ADV30	ARMA	Net Change Improvement	Percent Improvement
LC	40.9%	33.9%	− 7.0%	− 17.1%
SC	56.0%	44.3%	− 11.7%	− 20.9%
All	53.2%	42.8%	− 10.4%	− 19.5%

Forecasting Model: $Y(t) = Median(10)*DOW + AR*Y(t-1)$
Source: The Science of Algorithmic Trading (Kissell, 2013)

Author's notes:

- In theory, the beta term in an ARMA model is often shown to be forecasted without the constant term alpha, but since we are using a moving median it is not guaranteed that the mean error will be zero, and thus a constant term is needed.
- The ARMA forecast with the "beta" autoregressive terms can be computed both with and without special event days. Since it is important that this technique be continuous, unlike the day-of-week adjustment, we need to include all days. As an adjustment, we can 1) treat the special event day and day after the special event as any other day and include an adjustment for the previous day's forecasted error, 2) define the forecast error to be zero on a special event day (this way it will not be included in the next day's forecast), or 3) use a dummy variable for special event days.
- Our analysis calculated an autoregressive term across all stocks in each market-cap category. Users may also prefer to use a stock-specific autoregressive term instead. We did not find statistical evidence that a stock-specific beta is more accurate for large-cap stocks, but there was some evidence supporting the need for a stock-specific beta for small-cap stocks. Readers are encouraged to experiment with stock-specific forecasts to determine what works best for their specific needs.

Trading Risk: Covariance Matrix

In this section we discuss a technique to construct a short-term risk model based on our price volatility forecasting model and multifactor model to estimate covariance. In Kissell and Glantz (2003), we provide a detailed process to construct a short-term trading risk model based on a principal component risk model and a GARCH volatility estimate. In this section we provide a more general process that can incorporate any risk model combined with any volatility estimate (e.g., the HMA-VIX approach).

This process is as follows. Let

$\overline{C}$ = covariance matrix constructed from our multifactor model
D = diagonal matrix of historical volatilities (from risk model)
$\hat{D}$ = diagonal matrix of forecasted volatilities (e.g., HMA-VIX, Garch, etc.)
P = diagonal matrix of current prices
Step 1: Convert the covariance matrix C to a correlation matrix Rho by dividing by the corresponding volatility terms.

$$Rho = D^{-1}CD^{-1}$$

Step 2: Incorporate the forecasted volatility from the preferred forecasting model, e.g., HMA-VIX, GARCH, EWMA, etc., into the new covariance matrix $\hat{C}$:

$$\hat{C} = \hat{D}(Rho)\hat{D} = \hat{D}D^{-1}CD^{-1}\hat{D}$$

This covariance matrix will now be scaled to the same time period as the price volatility term. For example, if the volatility forecast is a one-day forecast, then the covariance matrix $\hat{C}$ is also a one-day estimate. If we are interested in a time period that is different than the time scale of the price volatility estimate, we simply divide by that appropriate value. For example, if we break the day into n-trading periods, the covariance matrix for the time horizon is

$$\hat{C} = \frac{1}{n} \cdot \hat{D}(Rho)\hat{D} = \frac{1}{n} \cdot \hat{D}D^{-1}CD^{-1}\hat{D}$$

Step 3: Convert the covariance matrix expressed in returns^2 into ($/share)^2. Here we simply multiply by our diagonal price matrix from P (shown previously):

$$\tilde{C} = P\hat{C}P = \frac{1}{n} \cdot P\hat{D}D^{-1}CD^{-1}\hat{D}P$$

This covariance matrix is now scaled for the appropriate length of time for our trading period and is expressed in ($/share)^2 for our trade schedule timing risk calculations. This matrix will also be extremely important for portfolio optimization.

The general form of our trading risk model is

$$\tilde{C} = \frac{1}{n} \cdot P\hat{D}D^{-1}CD^{-1}\hat{D}P \qquad (8.13)$$

Table 8.5 Market Impact Parameters by Trade Strategy Definition

Technique	a1	a2	a3	a4	b1	non-R^2
POV	708	0.55	0.71	0.50	0.98	0.41
SE	28	0.15	0.08	0.17	0.01	
Trade Rate	534	0.57	0.71	0.35	0.96	0.41
SE	47	0.18	0.06	0.11	0.01	
Trade Schedule	656	0.48	0.45	1	0.90	0.38
SE	38	0.16	0.08		0.04	

Source: The Science of Algorithmic Trading *(Kissell, 2013)*

Many times investors will need the covariance matrix to be adjusted for a one-sided portfolio. In this case, we adjust the entries in the covariance matrix based on the side of the order. For example,

$$c_{ij}^{*} = side(i) \cdot side(j) \cdot c_{ij} \tag{8.14}$$

where c_{ij} is the computed covariance scaled for the length of the trading period and in ($/share)^2. The full-side adjusted covariance is computed via matrix multiplication following techniques shown earlier as follows:

$$\tilde{C} = \frac{1}{n} \cdot (Side)P\hat{D}D^{-1}CD^{-1}\hat{D}P(Side) \tag{8.15}$$

where $(Side)$ is a diagonal matrix consisting of either a 1 if a buy order or -1 if a sell order.

Estimation Error

One of the most often overlooked components of algorithmic trading risk is the estimation error surrounding the model parameters. These models are often calibrated via nonlinear regression techniques such as nonlinear least squares (NLS) or maximum likelihood estimation (MLE), or computed using nonlinear optimization. The limitation of many of these types of canned mathematical procedures is that the library functions may not include the standard error calculation. This is due to the complexity surrounding these and also because many of these functions are written in a generic form that can be used for any formulation, and the standard error calculation is not included.

Estimates from our trading cost model including standard errors are shown ahead in Table 8.5.

CONCLUSION

Algorithmic trading has provided the industry with many benefits. These include efficiency, lower transaction costs, and better portfolio performance. However, for investors to achieve maximum levels of performance, they need to become more proactive in the algorithmic decision-making process. In order to accomplish this, these investors need to understand all sources of algorithmic trading risk. These include price volatility, short-term covariance, daily volume forecasts, monthly volumes, intraday trading patterns (spreads, volume pattern, volatility, etc.), and, just as important, parameter estimation error surrounding the market impact model. Additionally, the new trading environment now has numerous trading venues and dark pools. It no longer consists of the specialist- and market maker-driven models. This introduces another layer of transaction uncertainty when utilizing limit order models and smart order routers. Funds that are properly positioned to manage all these new sources of trading risk during asset acquisition and liquidation will surely achieve better execution performance.

References

Almgren, R., Chriss, N., 1999. Value under liquidation. Risk. Dec. 1999.

Almgren, R., Chriss, N., 2000. Optimal execution of portfolio transactions. Risk. 3, 5−39.

Bertsimas, D., Lo, A., 1998. Optimal control of liquidation costs. J. Financ. Markets 1, 1−50.

Chan, N.H., 2002. Time Series: Application to Finance. Wiley-Interscience.

Chiang, A., 1984. Fundamental Methods of Mathematical Economics, third ed. McGraw-Hill.

Donefer, B., 2010. Algos Gone Wild: Risk in the World of Automated Trading Strategies. J. Trading 5 (2), 31−34, Spring 2010.

Enders, W., 1995. Applied Econometric Time Series. John Wiley & Sons.

Harvey, A., 1999. The Econometric Analysis of Time Series, second ed. The MIT Press.

Johnson, J., DiNardo, J., 1997. Econometric Methods, fourth ed. McGraw-Hill.

Kissell, R., 2013. The Science of Algorithmic Trading and Portfolio Management. Elsevier, New York.

Kissell, R., Glantz, M., 2003. Optimal Trading Strategies. AMACOM, Inc, New York.

Kissell, R., Glantz, M., Malamut, R., 2004. A Practical Framework for Estimating Market Impact and Achieving Best Execution. Elsevier, Finance Research Letters 1.

Konishi, Makimoto, 2001. Optimal slice of a block trade. J. Risk 3 (4), 33−51.

Kyle, A., 1985. Continuous auctions and insider trading. Econometrica. 53, 1315−1335.

Tsay, R., 2002. Analysis of Financial Time Series. John Wiley & Sons.

Pemberton, M., Rau, N., 2001. Mathematics for Economists: An Introductory Textbook. Manchester University Press.

Risk-Hedging Techniques

9

INTRODUCTION

In this chapter we introduce readers to the necessary mathematics behind some of the more advanced portfolio-hedging techniques. In particular, we discuss the derivation of the hedge ratio and its usage in finance to determine the optimal manner to hedge a held portfolio. We examine the hedge ratio in terms of various pricing models, such as CAPM and APT, and discuss in terms of portfolio dollars and weights. The chapter concludes with a general solution to the optimal hedging ratio problem that can be used across asset classes and investment instruments.

In many of the traditional courses on risk management, the main focus of risk management and hedging incorporates futures and/or derivatives to limit potential losses. In these situations, investors pay a premium for downside protection if their portfolio decreases in value. One of the more common hedging techniques is in the form of a futures contract. In this arrangement, two parties agree to buy and sell an asset at a specific time in the future and at a specific price. The advantage of a futures contract is that both parties offset the risk of the asset becoming more or less expensive. The futures contract allows both parties to minimize price variability of the instrument. Futures contracts are very common in the commodities markets, where there will be a delivery of real goods at a future point in time. Futures contracts are also common in the financial industry, using index futures such as the S&P500 futures. Another common hedging technique is through derivatives such as call and put options. For these contracts, investors will gain protection from a decrease in value or have the opportunity to gain in a falling market. Straddles and strangles are more complex option hedging strategies that allow investors to profit in either a rising or falling market environment. However, they will incur a loss if the markets remain at or close to current levels. These advanced straddle and strangle strategies are simply the combination of the more vanilla call and put options. As with many of the advanced or exotic hedging techniques, many are simply the combination of the simple approaches. Readers interested in hedging strategies using futures and derivations are referred to Hull (1997).

The difficulty in using a specified financial instrument to hedge, however, is that often the selected instrument will not provide the maximum level of risk reduction.[1] In these situations, investors could benefit dramatically from a customized risk-reducing portfolio. This practice has been growing on Wall Street in the recent years in the form of Delta One trading desks. These Delta One desks are tasked with developing customized hedging strategies for specific portfolios. Investors are now using these desks for a variety of reasons, including risk hedging, a means to gain exposure to a specified instrument or factor that is outside of the mandate of the firm, and speculation. These are described as follows.

Hedging: Reducing portfolio risk through the introduction of holding additional assets or financial instruments in the portfolio. Investors may seek to lock in their returns for a specified period of time, without liquidating portfolios. This may occur near year end if the manager wishes to lock in returns and manager performance profit. Additionally, managers may wish to minimize portfolio risk at times of a major economic event or announcement, such as fiscal or monetary policy, tax rate change, government bond auction, etc.

Factor exposure: At times, portfolio managers may wish to mimic the returns of an alternative asset class without holding instruments in that asset class. For example, a fund with a mandate to only hold equities may wish to construct a portfolio that will earn a return following a bond index yield or commodities or energy exposure. Since the manager can only hold equities, they will develop a portfolio that minimizes tracking error to the bond index. Alternatively, managers may wish to match factor exposure to a specified designation such as a growth or value index, a macroeconomic indicator, or a stated fundamental exposure.

Speculation: At times, managers may wish to allocate fund dollars to a specified factor or sector because they have a short-term belief that that particular area has exceptional earning activities. Additionally, managers may seek to mimic the return stream of a particular sector if they have a strong view that the sector as a whole will have strong earnings announcements. In these situations, rather than liquidate their current portfolio and invest in the preferred portfolio, which could be very expensive from a trading cost perspective, these managers will manage portfolio risk and factor exposure to mirror the factor exposure of the preferred portfolio.

In the remainder of this chapter we discuss the necessary mathematics behind many of the more complex hedging and risk management techniques. These are approaches have been recently integrated into many of the risk and Delta One trading desks at Wall Street institutions. Unfortunately, brokers still tend to keep most of their calculations and risk-modeling processes as a black box hidden from investors. We believe that the reason for this is primarily to continue to charge investors higher commissions and fees and above fair-value risk premiums. Our goal is to shed light on the risk management-process and provide investors with a cost-effective framework that they can implement themselves to manage risk.

---

[1] An exception to this statement is when the futures or options contract is written for the underlying instrument, such as gold, silver, S&P 500 index, or an individual stock.

Important chapter notes:

- The derivation process presented ahead provides insight into various hedging techniques. These techniques can be easily applied to risk management across the various asset classes, and can also be applied for hedging a single financial instrument or asset as well as portfolios.
- We provide techniques to determine the optimal dollar value to invest into a pre-specified hedged portfolio to minimize overall risk. We provide a framework for both unconstrained and constrained problems.
- In theory, idiosyncratic risk refers to company-specific risk. In actuality, this is the risk that is unaccounted for by the model. It may come as a surprise to many investors that when we hedge a held portfolio using a custom basket or custom portfolio with at least some portion of idiosyncratic risk, the overall or total risk of the combined portfolios decreases due to reducing total market exposure, but the idiosyncratic risk portion actually increases. Idiosyncratic risk is an additive factor and will always increase when we increase the absolute dollar value of the portfolio. The only time that this does not hold true is when we decrease the value of the held portfolio. Portfolio managers will achieve a decrease in idiosyncratic risk by increasing the number of stocks in the portfolio and diversifying stock-specific risk. But if the dollar value increases, as it does with the combined portfolio consisting of the original portfolio and the hedge portfolio, then overall stock-specific risk will increase in dollar value by the dollar value of the stock-specific risk in the newly created hedging portfolio. It does not decrease.
- Using a pre-specified hedging portfolio may not necessarily be the best way to reduce overall risk. Investors should investigate alternative hedging portfolios, weights, and dollar values when evaluating risk-reduction possibilities.
- The mathematical formulations discussed in this chapter are based on techniques and formulations used in Trademetrics © and those published in *Credit Derivatives*, (Banks, Glantz, and Siegel, 2007), and "Managing Trading Risk" (working paper, Kissell, 2003).
- The techniques in this chapter can be applied to a large array of financial instruments including equities, futures, exchange-traded funds (ETFs), bonds, real estate, long-short portfolios, and numerous alternative investment vehicles.
- Minimizing portfolio risk with regards to the hedge ratio or hedge value usually refers to determining the optimal dollar value to invest in the pre-specified hedging portfolio to in order to reduce combined portfolio risk. Thus, the dollar values of the held portfolio and hedging portfolio are most often different quantities.
- Minimizing tracking error (in a risk-management sense) usually refers to determining the optimal weighting for stocks in a pre-specified hedging portfolio using the same dollar value as in the held portfolio or for a specified dollar value. Minimizing tracking error (in an investment-process sense) often

refers to determining the subset of stocks and optimal weighting in a target portfolio that best tracks a benchmark portfolio (such as a stock index). This is the same as determining the weightings and subset of stock that minimizes overall risk between the target portfolio and benchmark portfolio (such as S&P 500 or R2000).

- A more complete and beneficial risk management exercise, however, entails determining the instruments to comprise the optimal portfolio, their corresponding weights in the optimal portfolio, and the optimal dollar value to invest in that optimal portfolio in order to minimize overall risk. This technique is not discussed ahead.

Definitions

The "hedge ratio" is defined to be the ratio of dollars in the hedged portfolio to the dollar value of the original held portfolio. That is:

$$h = \frac{Hedge\ Portfolio\ Value}{Current\ Porfolio\ Value}$$

The "hedge ratio" for the held portfolio X to the hedging portfolio Y can be computed directly from the covariance between the held portfolio and the hedging portfolio and the variance of the hedging portfolio. This is as follows:

$$h_{xy} = -\frac{cov(y, y)}{var(x)}$$

An interesting property that will be further discussed ahead is that the hedge ratio between two portfolios is not symmetric. That is:

$$h_{xy} \neq \frac{1}{h_{yx}}$$

This reason why this inverse does not hold is as follows.
Starting with

$$h_{xy} = -\frac{cov(x, y)}{var(x)}; h_{yx} = -\frac{cov(x, y)}{var(y)}$$

we have

$$-\frac{cov(x, y)}{var(x)} = -\frac{cov(x, y)}{var(y)} \cdot \frac{var(y)}{var(x)}$$

which yields

$$h_{xy} = h_{yx} \cdot \frac{var(y)}{var(x)}$$

The reason the inverse does not hold true is due to the idiosyncratic risk of each portfolio.

The "dollar hedge value" to invest in the hedging portfolio Y is determined directly from the "hedge ratio" and dollar value of the held portfolio X as follows:

$$Y_\$ = h_{xy} \cdot X_\$$$

Or in general terms,

$$Y_\$ = \frac{-\text{cov}(x, y)}{\text{var}(y)} \cdot X_\$$$

The dollar hedge value can also be found via minimizing overall risk for a joint portfolio consisting of the original held portfolio X and the pre-specified hedging portfolio Y.

Hedge Ratio

As stated, the hedge ratio of a portfolio is defined as the value invested into the hedged position compared to the value of the original portfolio. For example, if the current portfolio has a value of $100 million and the manager hedges the portfolio using $50 million of a futures index, the hedge ratio is calculated as:

$$h = \$50 \ million / \$100 \ million = 1/2.$$

Notice that in this calculation the ratio is not the hedged position divided by total dollar value invested by the manager of $150 million (e.g., $100 million invested in the portfolio plus a $50 million value invested in the futures index equals $150 million). That is, the hedge ratio is not $50 million/$150 million = 1/3.

It is important to distinguish the difference in the hedge ratio calculations to ensure proper hedging values and weighting schemes. Different authors and different practitioners may denote the hedge ratio using different denominators. That is, depending upon the context of the study, the hedge ratio from the previous example may be stated as h = 1/2 or h = 1/3. While the definition we provided is the true and universally accepted definition, this, unfortunately, is not used consistently throughout the industry. Analysts are always encouraged to verify the definition being used by the researcher.

The optimal hedge ratio h is defined as the proportion of portfolio dollars to invest into the hedge portfolio in order to best minimize total portfolio risk. For example, a hedge ratio of h = 2 indicates that the dollar value of the hedge portfolio must be two times the dollar value of the held portfolio, and a hedge ratio of h = 1/2 indicates that the dollar value of the hedge portfolio must be one-half times the dollar value of the held portfolio.

Mathematically, the optimal hedge ratio is equal to the negative covariance between the held portfolio and the hedging portfolio divided by the variance of the hedging portfolio. That is:

$$h_{xy} = -\frac{\sigma_{xy}}{\sigma_x^2}$$

Incorporating the negative sign in this formulation ensures that a negative hedge value will denote a short hedge position, and a positive value will ensure a long hedge position.

Dollar Hedge Value

Unconstrained

The dollar hedge value $Y_\$$ is computed by multiplying the dollar value of the portfolio $X_\$$ by the hedge ratio h_{xy}. That is,

$$Y_\$ = h_{xy} \cdot X_\$$$

For example, if the portfolio value is $X_\$ = \$100$ million dollars and the optimal hedge ratio using portfolio Y is $h_{xy} = 1/2$, the dollar value to invest into portfolio Y is:

$$Y_\$ = 1/2 \cdot \$100 \; M = \$50 \; M$$

That is, the portfolio manager needs to be long (buy) $50 million of portfolio Y.

If the optimal hedge ratio using portfolio Y is $h_{xy} = -1/2$, the dollar value to invest into portfolio Y is:

$$Y_\$ = -1/2 \cdot \$100 \; M = -\$50 \; M$$

That is, the portfolio manager needs to short (sell) $50 million of portfolio Y.

Constrained

Let us next suppose that the portfolio manager has portfolio X with $100 million dollars. If the manager wishes to hedge using hedging portfolio Y and the hedge ratio is $h_{xy} = +1/4$, the manager will need to buy $25 million of portfolio Y to achieve the preferred hedge. But what if the manager does not have the cash on hand to purchase $25 million of portfolio Y? In this case, the manager will need to sell off portfolio X to raise cash to purchase portfolio Y.

In this case we determine the optimal holding amounts in each portfolio as follows. Let

$X_\$^* = $ *new value to hold in portfolio X*
$Y_\$^* = $ *new value to hold in hedging portfolio Y*
$h_{xh} = +1/4$
$V_\$ = \$100$ *million*

Then we solve the following system of equations:

$$h_{xh} = \frac{Y_\$^*}{X_\$^*}$$

$$X_\$^* + Y_\$^* = V_\$$$

Notice that solving for these equations ensures that total value on hand by the manager and the hedge ratio remains constant. Substituting in our values for $h_{xy} = +1/4$ and $V_\$ = \$100\ M$ yields

$$\frac{1}{4} = \frac{Y_\$^*}{X_\$^*}$$

$$X_\$^* + Y_\$^* = \$100\ M$$

Solving for $X_\$^*$ and $Y_\$^*$ yields

$$X_\$^* = \$80\ M$$

$$Y_\$^* = \$20\ M$$

Readers can confirm that these values for $X_\$^*$ and $Y_\$^*$ and h_{xy} remain unchanged from the original values.

Optimal Hedge Ratio

The prior sections showed how to compute the hedging portfolio and dollar value based on a specified "hedge ratio" and hedging portfolio. But how is a manager to determine the optimal hedging ratio? In this section we provide the process to compute the optimal hedge ratio between two portfolios denoted as X (current portfolio) and Y (hedging portfolio). Going forward, we will use the terms hedge ratio and hedging ratio interchangeably.

This value is determined via a minimization process. We explain the process for the two situations described previously. In the first scenario, the portfolio manager can acquire the hedging portfolio by either buying the instruments or selling (shorting) the instruments, and thus is able to keep their current portfolio constant. In the second scenario, the manager may need to reallocate dollars from the current portfolio into the hedge portfolio. The scenario is essential for a manager who does not have additional cash to acquire shares in the hedge portfolio or who may be constrained on the value that they are allowed to be short.

Unconstrained Optimal Hedge

The process to determine the optimal hedging ratio is as follows.
Let,

$X = Portfolio\ Value$
$Y = Hedging\ Portfolio\ Value$

$\sigma_x^2 = variance\ of\ portfolio\ X$
$\sigma_y^2 = variance\ of\ portfolio\ Y$
$\sigma_{xy} = Covariance\ between\ X\ and\ Y$

Then the total risk for the combined position consisting of portfolio X and hedging portfolio Y is:

$$Risk = X^2\sigma_x^2 + Y^2\sigma_y^2 + 2XY\sigma_{xy}$$

The value of Y that minimizes this equation is found by solving for Y in $dRisk/dY = 0$. This is:

$$\frac{dRisk}{dY} = 2Y\sigma_y^2 + 2X\sigma_{xy} = 0$$

Solving for Y we obtain

$$Y = -X \cdot \frac{\sigma_{xy}}{\sigma_y^2}$$

Finally, since the hedge ratio is defined to be the ratio of the value of the hedge portfolio Y to the value of the current portfolio X, we have

$$h_{xy} = \frac{Y}{X} = -\frac{\sigma_{xy}}{\sigma_y^2}$$

Notice that this is exactly what we defined the hedged ratio as previously.

Constrained Optimal Hedge

Let us next determine the solution for the optimal hedge for a situation where the starting value needs to remain constant. For example, if the portfolio manager holds a $100 million portfolio and wishes to hedge, they may not have any additional cash to purchase the hedge, so they will need to reallocate value from the current portfolio to the hedged portfolio.

This solution is solved via a constrained optimization problem that can be easily solved via the use of Lagrange multipliers. The process is as follows:

Let,

$V = Current\ portfolio\ (needs\ to\ remain\ constant)$
$X^* = New\ portfolio\ value\ (after\ allocating\ to\ the\ hedge)$
$Y^* = Value\ of\ the\ hedged\ portfolio$

Next, minimize risk in the following set of equations:

$$Min\quad X^{*2}\sigma_x^2 + Y^{*2}\sigma_y^2 + 2X^*Y^*\sigma_{xy}$$
$$s.t.\quad X^* + Y^* = V$$

Minimum risk given our value constraint is found by solving the following.

Step 1:

Rewrite our risk equation in terms of the Lagrangian multiplier λ:

$$Min \quad R = X^{*2}\sigma_x^2 + Y^{*2}\sigma_y^2 + 2X^*Y^*\sigma_{xy} + \lambda \cdot (V - X^* - Y^*)$$

Step 2:

Differentiate with respect to X, Y, and γ as follows:

$$\frac{dR}{dX} = 2X^*\sigma_x^2 + 2Y^*\sigma_{xy} - \lambda = 0$$

$$\frac{dR}{dY} = 2Y^*\sigma_Y^2 + 2X^*\sigma_{xy} - \lambda = 0$$

$$\frac{dR}{d\gamma} = V - X^* - Y^* = 0$$

This yields

$$X^* = V \cdot \left[\frac{\sigma_y^2 - \sigma_{xy}}{\sigma_x^2 - 2\sigma_{xy} + \sigma_y^2} \right]$$

$$Y^* = V \cdot \left[\frac{\sigma_x^2 - \sigma_{xy}}{\sigma_x^2 - 2\sigma_{xy} + \sigma_y^2} \right]$$

$$\lambda = 2V \cdot \left[\frac{\sigma_x^2\sigma_y^2 - (\sigma_{xy})^2}{\sigma_x^2 - 2\sigma_{xy} + \sigma_y^2} \right]$$

Readers can also follow this formulation to determine the optimal hedge ratio for an inequality constrained optimization problem. Final optimization solutions incorporating inequality constraints, however, need to satisfy the Kuhn-Tucker conditions (see Bradley, Hax, and Magnanti (1977), Chiang (1984), or Pemberton and Rau (2001)).

CAPM Dollar Value Hedging Technique

In this section we derive the optimal "dollar hedge value" and "hedge ratio" using the capital asset pricing model (CAPM). These calculations are dependent upon variance and beta to the underlying index.

In general, the pre-specified hedging portfolio could be a single-stock position, a basket of stocks, an index (such as the S&P 500), futures, ETF, etc. Specifically, we derive the "optimal dollar value" to invest in the pre-specified hedging portfolio and the corresponding "hedge ratio." The hedge ratio h provides the investor with the ratio of hedging portfolio value to current portfolio value that minimizes the investor's overall portfolio risk.

Furthermore, readers could also use any type of factor model (CAPM, APT, statistical, etc.) or defined data relationship (variance, covariance, and correlation). We provide this derivation in the section titled "General Solution" below.

Step 1:

Start with CAPM Model for stocks or a portfolio of assets.

The CAPM model for either a stock or portfolio is written as follows:

$$r_x = r_f + B_x(R_m - r_f) + \varepsilon_x$$

where,

r_x = return for portfolio/stock x
r_f = risk-free rate of return
B_x = portfolio/stock beta to the market index
R_m = return of market index
ε_x = portfolio/stock idiosyncratic risk (company specific risk)

In practice, the S&P 500 index is most often used as a proxy for the market index.

Step 2:

Convert returns into dollar units.

Since we are interested in the dollar value required to hedge the total dollar risk of the held portfolio, we convert our CAPM equation into dollar returns as follows:

$$X_\$ = X \cdot r_x = X(r_f + B_x(R_m - r_f) + \varepsilon_x)$$
$$= X \cdot r_f + X \cdot B_x(R_m - r_f) + X \cdot \varepsilon_x$$

where $X_\$$ is the current dollar value return formulation of portfolio X.

Thus, our dollar value CAPM formulation is:

$$X_\$ = X_\$ \cdot r_f + X_\$ \cdot B_x(R_m - rf) + X_\$ \cdot \varepsilon_x$$

For simplicity, we drop the $ subscript going forward.

Step 3:

Define the problem.

Suppose we have two portfolios X and Y. These portfolios can consist of a single stock, a basket of stocks, or a specified index or ETF, etc. Then, the dollar value CAPM return model for each portfolio is

$$X = X \cdot r_f + X \cdot B_x(R_m - r_f) + X \cdot \varepsilon_x$$
$$Y = Y \cdot r_f + Y \cdot B_y(R_m - r_f) + Y \cdot \varepsilon_y$$

Now, construct a new portfolio L consisting of X and Y. That is

$$L = X + Y$$

Written in CAPM dollar formulation, we have

$$L = (X \cdot r_f + X \cdot B_x(R_m - r_f) + X \cdot \varepsilon_x) + (Y \cdot r_f + Y \cdot B_y(R_m - r_f) + Y \cdot \varepsilon_y)$$

which simplifies to

$$L = (X + Y) \cdot r_f + X \cdot B_x(R_m - r_f) + Y \cdot B_y(R_m - r_f) + X \cdot \varepsilon_x + Y \cdot \varepsilon_y$$

The total risk (described as variance) of this combined position is

$$Var\{L\} = Var\{(X + Y) \cdot r_f + (X \cdot B_x + Y \cdot B_y)(R_m - r_f) + X \cdot \varepsilon_x + Y \cdot \varepsilon_y\}$$

which can be further simplified as

$$\sigma_L^2 = (X \cdot B_x + Y \cdot B_y)^2 \sigma_m^2 + X^2 \xi_x^2 + Y^2 \xi_y^2$$

where,

σ_L^2 = total risk (variance) of combined position L
σ_m^2 = market risk (variance of market portfolio)
ξ_x^2 = idiosyncratic risk (variance) for portfolio X
ξ_x^2 = idiosyncratic risk (variance) for portfolio Y

Step 4:
Calculating the dollar hedge value and hedge ratio.
Our goal now is to determine the dollar value to invest in the pre-specified hedge portfolio Y that minimizes total risk. This is determined by solving for $\partial \sigma_L^2 / \partial Y = 0$ and holding $X_\$$ constant. These steps are:
Step 4.1:
Start with the combined total risk equation:

$$\sigma_L^2 = (X \cdot B_x + Y \cdot B_y)^2 \sigma_m^2 + X^2 \xi_x^2 + Y^2 \xi_y^2$$

Step 4.2:
Compute $\partial \sigma_L^2 / \partial Y$:

$$\frac{\partial \sigma_L^2}{\partial Y} = 2 \cdot B_y \cdot (X \cdot B_x + Y \cdot B_y) \sigma_m^2 + 2 \cdot Y \cdot \xi_y^2 = 0$$

Step 4.3:
Solve for Y in $\partial \sigma_L^2 / \partial Y = 0$.

$$2 \cdot B_y \cdot (X \cdot B_x + Y \cdot B_y) \sigma_m^2 + 2 \cdot Y \cdot \xi_y^2 = 0$$
$$2 \cdot X \cdot B_x \cdot B_y \cdot \sigma_m^2 + 2 \cdot Y \cdot B_y^2 \cdot \sigma_m^2 + 2 \cdot Y \cdot \xi_y^2 = 0$$
$$Y(B_y^2 \cdot \sigma_m^2 + \xi_y^2) = - X \cdot B_x \cdot B_y \cdot \sigma_m^2$$

From CAPM, we have

$$(B_y^2 \cdot \sigma_m^2 + \xi_y^2) = \sigma_y^2$$

Thus,

$$Y \cdot \sigma_y^2 = - X \cdot B_x \cdot B_y \cdot \sigma_m^2$$

And the optimal dollar hedge value to hold in the pre-specified hedging portfolio Y is

$$Y_\$ = \frac{-X_\$ \cdot B_x \cdot B_y \cdot \sigma_m^2}{\sigma_y^2}$$

Step 4.4:
The hedge ratio of portfolio Y to X is

$$h_{xy} = \frac{Y}{X} = -\frac{B_x \cdot B_y \cdot \sigma_m^2}{\sigma_y^2}$$

Now, from CAPM we have $\sigma_{xy} = -B_x \cdot B_y \cdot \sigma_m^2$. Therefore the hedge ratio h_{yx} is simply the covariance of the hedging portfolio to the held portfolio divided by the variance of the hedging portfolio. That is:

$$h_{yx} = -\frac{\sigma_{xy}}{\sigma_y^2}$$

Interested readers can easily confirm that if we start with $Y_\$$ in the hedging portfolio and compute the "optimal hedging ratio" to portfolio X, we find:

$$h_{xy} = -\frac{\sigma_{xy}}{\sigma_x^2}$$

This implies that the hedge ratio for one portfolio is not the inverse of the hedge ratio of the other portfolio. That is

$$h_{yx} \neq h_{xy}$$

This is an important property that should not be overlooked in the risk-management process.

Examples
Example 9.1: Hedge a Portfolio X with the Market Index

An investor holds $100 million in portfolio X and wishes to hedge using the market index Y (e.g., S&P 500 index). The market index has a volatility of 10%. Portfolio X has a beta to the index of $B_x = 2$ and volatility of $\sigma_x = 25\%$. Therefore, its idiosyncratic risk is $\xi_x = 15\%$.

The investor wishes to hedge their portfolio using the S&P 500 index. Compute the optimal dollar value to invest in the S&P 500 index to minimize overall risk and the corresponding hedge ratio.

Step 1:
Start with the total risk equation:

$$\sigma_L^2 = (X \cdot B_x + Y \cdot B_y)^2 \sigma_m^2 + X^2 \xi_x^2 + Y^2 \xi_y^2$$

Step 2:
Since Y is the market portfolio, by definition it has $B_y = 1$ and ξ_y^2. Therefore, our combined risk equation is

$$\sigma_L^2 = (X \cdot B_x + Y)^2 \sigma_m^2 + X^2 \xi_x^2$$

Step 3:
Solve for $\partial \sigma_L^2 / \partial Y = 0$.

$$\frac{\partial \sigma_L^2}{\partial Y} = 2(X \cdot B_x + Y)\sigma_m^2 = 0$$

$$Y = -X \cdot B_x$$

This yields dollar value

$$Y_\$ = -B_x \cdot X_\$$$
$$Y_\$ = -2 \cdot \$100 \; Million$$
$$Y_\$ = -\$200 \; Million$$

The investor should short $200 million of the S&P 500 index in order to minimize overall risk.

Step 4:
The optimal hedge ratio is

$$h_{xy} = \frac{Y}{X} = -\beta$$

Or,

$$h_{xy} = -2$$

So finally, if we own portfolio X with $100 million, the best way to hedge using the market index would be to short $200 million in the market index.

Figure 9.1 further illustrates this example. The graph shows the risk of the combined portfolios (y-axis) for various dollar values invested into the hedged portfolio (on x-axis). Here we are using the market index as the hedging portfolio. The original portfolio with $100 million has a risk of $25 million. But as we invest into the hedged portfolio (as a short position) the overall risk begins to decrease. The combined risk curve with $100 million of the original portfolio and various amounts of the hedged portfolio (from $0 through $400 million) has a convex shape with a minimum risk value of $15 million at $200 million invested into the hedged position (albeit short). Thus, risk is decreasing as we invest up to $200 million into the hedged portfolio, and then begins to increase again as we invest more than $200 million into the hedged portfolio. This figure illustrates how combined risk evolves for various hedging portfolio values.

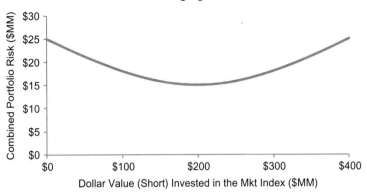

Hedging Portfolio X using the Market Index Portfolio as the Hedging Portfolio

FIGURE 9.1 Hedging Portfolio X using the Market Index Portfolio

Example 9.2: Hedge the Market Index with a Portfolio X

Now let us evaluate the same example but from the perspective of holding the market portfolio Y and hedging with portfolio X. Here the manager owns a $200 million market portfolio (i.e., $Y =$ S&P 500 index) and wishes to hedge risk using the pre-specified hedging portfolio X. Determine the optimal dollar value to invest in portfolio X to minimize risk and the corresponding hedge ratio.

Step 1:
Start with the total risk equation:

$$\sigma_L^2 = (X \cdot B_x + Y \cdot B_y)^2 \sigma_m^2 + X^2 \xi_x^2 + Y^2 \xi_y^2$$

Step 2:
Since Y is the market portfolio, we have $B_y = 1$ and $\xi_y^2 = 0$ (the market portfolio does not contain any risk or excess return in relation to itself). The total risk equation reduces to

$$\sigma_L^2 = (X \cdot B_x + Y)^2 \sigma_m^2 + X^2 \xi_x^2$$

Step 3:
Now since we own portfolio Y and are looking to hedge using portfolio X, we need to solve for $\partial \sigma_L^2 / \partial X = 0$. This is as follows:

$$\frac{\partial \sigma_L^2}{\partial X} = 2 \cdot (X \cdot B_x + Y) \cdot B_x \cdot \sigma_m^2 + 2 \cdot X \cdot \xi_x^2 = 0$$

$$X(B_x^2 \sigma^2 + \xi_x^2) = - Y \cdot B_x \cdot \sigma_m^2$$

Since by CAPM, $\sigma_x^2 = B_x^2 \sigma^2 + \xi_x^2$, we have

$$X \cdot \sigma_x^2 = -Y \cdot B_x \cdot \sigma_m^2$$

$$X = -Y \cdot B_x \cdot \frac{\sigma_m^2}{\sigma_x^2}$$

Thus, for $Y_\$ = \$200$ million, $B_x = 2$, $\sigma_x = 25\%$, the optimal hedging dollar amount is:

$$X_\$ = -\$200 \; Million \cdot 2 \cdot \frac{(0.10)^2}{(0.25)^2}$$

$$X_\$ = -\$64 \; Million$$

Notice that the dollar value is different from Example 9.1, where $X_\$ = \$100$ million with the exact same statistics. The reason is due to the treatment of idiosyncratic risk in the process and the fact that the investor had could not change the holdings in portfolio X (e.g., $X_\$\$100$ million).

Step 4:

The hedge ratio in this example is

$$h = \frac{X}{Y} = -B_x \cdot \frac{\sigma_m^2}{\sigma_m^2}$$

$$h = -2 \cdot \frac{(0.10)^2}{(0.25)^2}$$

$$h = -0.32$$

That is, invest 32% of the current portfolio value Y in the hedge portfolio X. Notice that this is different than the hedge ratio earlier where its inverse $X/Y = 1/2 = 0.5$. This further shows the importance of understanding idiosyncratic portfolio risk.

Why is there a difference in these two solutions? If we start with $100 million in portfolio X, the best way to hedge is with $-$ $200 million in portfolio Y (market portfolio). But if we start with $200 million in portfolio Y, the best way to hedge is to invest $-$ $64 million in portfolio X. The answer is pretty straightforward, and also often overlooked in the industry and in analysis. In the first example, we held the value of portfolio X constant and varied the value of portfolio Y. The total absolute holding in this situation was $300 million and a net value of $-$ $100 million. In the second example, we held the value of the market portfolio constant and varied the value of the hedge portfolio. The total absolute holding value of this solution was $264 million and a net value of $136 million.

Figure 9.2 provides additional insight into this issue. The figure shows the risk of the combined portfolio (y-axis) consisting of $200 million of the market

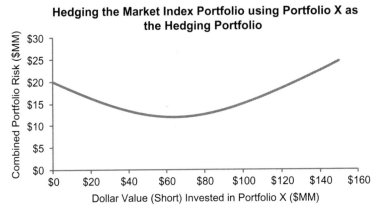

FIGURE 9.2 Hedging the Market Index Portfolio using Portfolio X

portfolio Y and various dollar amounts invested into the hedging portfolio X (x-axis) as a short position (e.g., $50 million in the hedging portfolio indicates a short position). When there are no dollars invested into the hedging portfolio, the combined portfolio consists of only the market portfolio, and the overall risk is $20 million (the volatility of the market portfolio in this example is 10%). As with the previous example, this combined risk curve is a convex shape in which risk decreases to a minimum value of $12 million when there is $64 million invested in the hedging portfolio (short), and then risk begins to increase if there are more dollars invested into the hedged position. The risk minimizing strategy calls for a $64 million investment into the hedging portfolio.

Example 9.3: Hedge Portfolio X with Portfolio Y

An investor has portfolio X with $100 million and wishes to hedge risk using portfolio Z. What is the best allocation of the $100 million if the investor needs to hold the total notional value of the combined portfolio constant? That is, the total dollar amount invested in both portfolios needs to equal exactly $100 million.

This is an example of a constrained hedging portfolio optimization problem. It is appropriate for managers who do not have any additional cash on hand to invest in the risk-reducing portfolio. Therefore, they need to sell shares form the current portfolio to finance the investment in the hedging portfolio.

This process to determine the appropriate portfolio mix is as follows:

Step 1:
Calculate the risk characteristics for the two portfolios.

Table 9.1 Portfolio Risk Statistics

Portfolio	Volatility	Beta	IdioRisk
X	25%	2.00	15.0%
Z	35%	−2.50	24.5%
Mkt Index	10%	1	
Covar(X,Z)	−0.050		
X0_$:	$100		

Step 2:

Determine the appropriate mix of assets across portfolio X and portfolio Z that minimizes risk, holding the total investment value at $100 million.

This is determined by minimizing combined portfolio variance using the formulation from earlier:

$$\sigma_p^2 = (X \cdot B_x + Z \cdot B_z)^2 \cdot \sigma_m^2 + X^2 \xi_x^2 + Z^2 \xi_z^2$$
$$s.t. \quad X + Y = \$100$$

Solving for X and Z, we find that the minimum risk is $13.45 million with $61 million invested in portfolio Z and $39 million invested in portfolio Z. Therefore, the portfolio manager will need to sell $39 million of the existing portfolio X and invest this amount in portfolio Z to best hedge portfolio risk.

The example is further illustrated in Figure 9.3. The figure shows the overall risk of the combined portfolios (y2-axis) for the dollar values allocated across the original portfolio Y and the hedging portfolio Z. Once again we see the familiar convex-shaped total risk curve. The minimum risk position is $13.45 million and

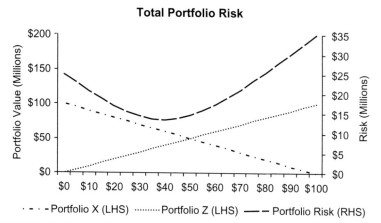

Total Portfolio Risk

· - · - Portfolio X (LHS) ········ Portfolio Z (LHS) —— Portfolio Risk (RHS)

FIGURE 9.3 Minimizing Portfolio Risk with Dollar Value held Constant

occurs when there is $61 million invested in the original portfolio (long) and $39 million invested in the hedging portfolio (long). Here we have a total of $100 million invested in two long portfolios. The reason that we do not have to short either portfolio to minimize risk is because of the negative beta for portfolio Z. Since the betas of the two portfolios have opposite signs, we can hold both portfolios long and achieve the necessary risk reduction.

Example 9.4: Idiosyncratic Risk

We have been emphasizing throughout the chapter the importance of idiosyncratic risk and its effect on the overall risk-management processes. Mismanagement of the idiosyncratic risk term could have dire consequences on the risk of the combined portfolios.

For example, suppose an investor holds $200 million in the S&P 500 index ($Y_\$ = \$200\ M$), and wishes to hedge the position using a portfolio X with beta $B_x = 2$. If the investor ignores idiosyncratic risk in the risk management process and simply hedges based on the inverse of the hedge ratio $h = -1/B_x = -1/2$, they would sell (short) $100 million of portfolio X.

This results in an erroneous risk-management process. In this case, overall risk is determined using the risk equation

$$\sigma_p^2 = (X \cdot B_x + Y \cdot B_y)^2 \cdot \sigma_m^2 + X^2 \xi_x^2 + Y^2 \xi_y^2$$

Using our values, we have

$$\sigma^2(L_1) = (100 \cdot 2 - 200 \cdot 1)^2 \cdot (0.10)^2 + 100^2 \cdot (0.15)^2 + 200^2 \cdot 0 = \$225$$

(recall that the market index has a beta of $B = 1$ and it does not have any idiosyncratic risk).

Now consider the scenario where the investor properly computes the hedge ratio and optimal dollar hedge value using the techniques shown previously and finds $h = -0.32$ and $X_\$ = -\$64$ million. That is, the manager would only short $64 million of portfolio X.

Then the overall risk of the combined position is

$$\sigma^2(L_2) = (64 \cdot 2 - 200 \cdot 1)^2 \cdot (0.10)^2 + 64^2 \cdot (0.15)^2 + 200^2 \cdot 0 = \$144$$

In this scenario, erogenous risk management could lead the fund to incur 25% more risk than necessary! This is computed as follows:

$$Risk\ Ratio = \sqrt{\frac{\sigma^2(L_1)}{\sigma^2(L_2)}} = \sqrt{\frac{225}{144}} = 1.25$$

Incredibly, by not properly managing the idiosyncratic risk piece in the process, the desk incurs 25% more risk than necessary in this example! This is not a "black swan event," but rather a misunderstanding of risk computations.

Example 9.5: Hedge Portfolio X with Portfolio Y

An investor with portfolio $X = \$100$ million wishes to hedge risk using portfolio Y. The risk statistics of the two portfolios are:

Table 9.2 Portfolio Risk Statistics

Portfolio	Beta	Volatility	Idio Risk
X	2.00	25%	15.0%
Y	1.50	35%	31.6%
Mkt Index	1	10%	
Covar(X < Y)	0.030		

Determine the optimal dollar value and hedge ratio.

Step 1:

Start with the total risk equation:

$$\sigma_p^2 = (X \cdot B_x + Y \cdot B_y)^2 \cdot \sigma_m^2 + X^2 \xi_x^2 + Y^2 \xi_y^2$$

Step 2:

Since Y is an arbitrary portfolio in this example (e.g., not the market portfolio as was used in the previous example) the prior equation cannot be simplified. Since we are hedging with pre-specified portfolio Y, we solve for $\partial \sigma_L^2 / \partial Y = 0$:

$$\frac{\partial \sigma_L^2}{\partial Y} = 2(XB_x + YB_y)\sigma_m^2 B_y + 2Y\xi_y^2 = 0$$

$$= Y(B_y^2 \sigma_m^2 + \xi_y^2) = -XB_x B_y \sigma_m^2$$

$$= Y\sigma_y^2 = -XB_x B_y \sigma_m^2$$

$$Y = -XB_x B_y \cdot \frac{\sigma_m^2}{\sigma_y^2}$$

Note that this can also be written as

$$Y = -X\frac{\sigma_{xy}}{\sigma_y^2}$$

Therefore, with the previous statistics, the optimal hedge dollar value is:

$$Y = -XB_x B_y \cdot \frac{\sigma_m^2}{\sigma_y^2}$$

$$= -100 \cdot 2 \cdot 0.75 \cdot \frac{(0.10)^2}{(0.35)^2}$$

$$= -24.49$$

Therefore, the optimal dollar amount to invest in pre-specified portfolio is $Y = -\$24.49$ million.

Step 4:

The optimal hedge ratio is

$$h = -\frac{Y}{X} = \frac{-24.49}{100} = -0.249$$

Example 9.6 General Solution using a Preselected Hedging Basket

In the preceding examples, we derived the optimal dollar hedge value and hedge ratio based on CAPM. These values can also be easily derived using any model such as APT, a statistical factor model, or by strictly using variances, covariance, and correlations. In this section we compute the optimal dollar value and hedging ratios using a general modeling framework.

In general, the variance of any portfolio written in matrix notation is:

$$\sigma_p^2 = Z^T C Z$$

where Z is the vector of holdings and C is the variance-covariance matrix.

Suppose that Z is a portfolio comprised of two different portfolios X and Y. Let portfolio X be the current portfolio and let portfolio Y be the portfolio that was selected to hedge overall risk. In this case, the manager is not able to change the weightings of the stocks that comprise portfolio Y, but can change the dollar value invested in this portfolio. In the next example we discuss a situation where the manager has full flexibility regarding the dollar values invested in each individual stock within the selected portfolio. As we will show, the solution to that problem is identical to this problem.

The risk statistics of our two portfolios X and Y are:

Variance of portfolio X is σ_x^2
Variance of portfolio Y is σ_y^2
Covariance of X and Y is $\sigma_{xy} = \rho_{xy}\sigma_x\sigma_y$
Current value of portfolio X is $X_\$$

Then the risk equation formulated in matrix notation is

$$\sigma_p^2 = \begin{pmatrix} X_\$ & Y_\$ \end{pmatrix} \begin{pmatrix} \sigma_X^2 & \rho_{xy}\sigma_x\sigma_y \\ \rho_{xy}\sigma_x\sigma_y & \sigma_y^2 \end{pmatrix} \begin{pmatrix} X_\$ \\ Y_\$ \end{pmatrix}$$

Expanding the matrix risk equation notation we get

$$\sigma_p^2 = X_\$\sigma_X^2 + 2X_\$ Y_\$ \rho_{xy}\sigma_x\sigma_y + Y_\$^2\sigma_y^2$$

The optimal dollar value hedge for portfolio Y is computed by solving

$$\frac{\partial \sigma_p^2}{\partial Y} = 0$$

This is

$$\frac{\partial \sigma_p^2}{\partial Y} = 2X_\$ \rho_{xy} \sigma_x \sigma_y + 2Y_\$ \sigma_y^2 = 0$$

Solving, we get

$$Y = -X \frac{\rho_{xy} \sigma_x \sigma_y}{\sigma_y^2}$$

Or alternatively,

$$Y = -X \frac{\sigma_{xy}}{\sigma_y^2} = -X \frac{Cov(X, Y)}{Var(Y)}$$

The hedge ratio is thus

$$h_{yx} = \frac{Y}{X} = -\frac{Cov(X, Y)}{Var(Y)}$$

Thus we have the general equations for optimal dollar hedge value and optimal hedging ratio for two arbitrary portfolios. Optimal hedging statistics can be determined directly from the variance of the hedging portfolio and the variance of the held portfolio.

Example 9.7: General Solution using Preselected Stocks, but not Weightings

In this example, we show how investors can develop a customized hedging portfolio for a specified hedging universe in which the actual dollar weights in the hedging portfolio are unknown. The hedging universe can consist of any combination of stocks, ETFs, or financial assets. The only requirement is for the analyst to have volatility and covariances for each asset in the hedging universe.

Suppose the current portfolio is X with n-stocks and the selected hedging universe is Y with m-stocks. That is,

$$X = \begin{pmatrix} x_1 \\ x_2 \\ \vdots \\ x_n \end{pmatrix} \quad Y = \begin{pmatrix} y_1 \\ y_2 \\ \vdots \\ y_m \end{pmatrix}$$

Let Z be the combined portfolio consisting of $n + m$ total stocks:

$$Z = \begin{pmatrix} z_1 \\ z_2 \\ \vdots \\ z_n \\ z_{n+1} \\ z_{n+2} \\ \vdots \\ z_{n+m} \end{pmatrix} = \begin{pmatrix} x_1 \\ x_2 \\ \vdots \\ x_n \\ y_1 \\ y_2 \\ \vdots \\ y_m \end{pmatrix}$$

Here, $z_1, \ldots z_n$ represents the current portfolio (original n-stocks) and $z_{n+1}, \ldots, z_{n+m}$ represents the dollar value in the m-hedging stocks. Our goal now is to determine the optimal dollar value to invest in each hedging stock: $z_{n+1}, z_{n+2}, \ldots, z_{n+m}$.

The optimal dollar value to invest in each of the m-hedging stocks is found by minimizing the following equation:

$$Min \ L = Z^T C Z$$

Algebraically, this solution is found by differentiating L for each of the hedging stocks, and solving the set of m-differential equations.

The derivative $\partial z_k / \partial L$ is

$$\frac{\partial z_k}{\partial L} = \sum_{i=1}^{n+m} z_i \sigma_{ik} = 0$$

where $\sigma_{jj} = \sigma_j^2$.

Then our set of m-equations are

$$\sum_{i=1}^{n+m} z_i \sigma_{in+1} = 0$$

$$\sum_{i=1}^{n+m} z_i \sigma_{in+2} = 0$$

$$\vdots$$

$$\sum_{i=1}^{n+m} z_i \sigma_{in+m} = 0$$

Since the values of the first n-stocks remain constant, this reduces to

$$\sum_{i=n+1}^{n+m} z_i \sigma_{in+1} = \sum_{i=1}^{n} z_i \sigma_{in+1}$$

$$\sum_{i=n+1}^{n+m} z_i \sigma_{in+2} = \sum_{i=1}^{n} z_i \sigma_{in+2}$$

$$\vdots$$

$$\sum_{i=n+1}^{n+m} z_i \sigma_{in+m} = \sum_{i=1}^{n} z_i \sigma_{in+m}$$

Where the LHS represents the m-variables that we are looking to determine, and the RHS consists of a constant value. Notice that this set of simultaneous equations has the form

$$Ax = b$$

If the investor is not able to invest additional dollar amounts into the portfolio to acquire the hedging stocks, they determine the optimal hedging portfolio by minimizing risk in the following equations:

$$Min \quad L = Z^T C Z$$
$$s.t. \quad \sum_{k=1}^{n+m} z_k = V^*$$

where V^* is the current portfolio value. This is determined via the use of Lagrange multipliers and a modified objective function L_2 as follows:

$$Min\ L = Z^T C Z + \lambda \left(V^* - \left(\sum_{k=1}^{n+m} z_k \right) \right)$$

The solution is found now by differentiating across all $n + m$ stocks and solving the set of $n + m + 1$ simultaneous equations with $n + m + 1$ values. Please note that the inclusion of the Lagrange multiplier introduces an additional equation and an additional unknown. These equations are

$$\sum_{i=1}^{n+m} z_i \sigma_{i1} = \lambda$$
$$\sum_{i=1}^{n+m} z_i \sigma_{i2} = \lambda$$
$$\vdots$$
$$\sum_{i=1}^{n+m} z_i \sigma_{in+m} = \lambda$$
$$\sum_{i=1}^{n+m} z_i = V^*$$

There may be occasions where analysts wish to hedge the portfolio, but need to keep the value of the portfolio constant and can only hedge using a specified dollar value V'. The optimal portfolio is found by minimizing the following:

$$Min \quad L = Z^T C Z$$
$$s.t. \quad \sum_{k=n+1}^{n+m} z_k = V^*$$

Its solution is found via the modified objective function and usage of Lagrangian multipliers as follows:

$$Min\ L = Z^T C Z + \lambda \left(V' - \left(\sum_{k=n+1}^{n+m} z_k \right) \right)$$

We leave it as an exercise for the reader to derive the set of simultaneous equations to solve for this scenario.

The last point worth mentioning here is that the previous solutions could be either long or short positions. If the analyst needs to only be long a position or can only short a position, they will need to furnish an additional set of inequality constraints. This solution requires the use of a mathematical optimization process. Finally, at times analysts may have a constraint to keep the absolute value of the notional dollars invested in the hedging position less than or greater than some specified value V. This solution requires more advanced optimization processes. The constraint is written as

$$\sum_{k=n+1}^{n+m} |z_k| \le V$$

Example 9.8: Specify the Number of Assets to Include

We next discuss a process for analysts to use to determine the optimal portfolio size for a specified number of stocks (or other financial assets) to hold in the hedging portfolio. In this case, analysts need to pre-specify the hedging universe and the number of stocks to include in the hedge. The pre-specified hedging universes could consist of equities, exchange-traded funds, or any combination of these instruments.

If the analyst chooses to use the S&P 500 index as the hedging universe, but only wishes to use 50 stocks in the hedged portfolio, they will need to determine the most appropriate 50 stocks to manage overall risk. In general, if we chose "k" stocks from a total of "n" stocks, the total number of possibilities is

$$\binom{n}{k} = \frac{n!}{k!(n-k)!}$$

In our example, the total number of combinations of selecting 50 from 500 is:

$$\binom{500}{50} = \frac{500!}{50!(500-50)!} = 2.3 \cdot 10^{69}$$

Wow! There are $2.3 \cdot 10^{69}$ total combinations to form a 50-stock portfolio from a 500-stock universe. And if we were to use the Russell 2000 stock universe as the basis to select our 50 stocks, there are $1.99 \cdot 10^{100}$ possible 50-stock portfolios from a 2000-stocks universe.[2] This number of possibilities is beginning to approach a googolplex! This is a very unmanageable number for analysts. Luckily, mathematicians have techniques that will solve these types of problems. The optimization

[2]The Russell 2000 index may have less than 2000 stocks due to mergers, bankruptcies, and other corporate actions that may occur during the quarter. See http://www.russell.com/indexes/data/us_equity/russell_us_indexes_methodology.asp for full details of the Russell reconstitution methodology.

techniques are called mixed-integer problems and will determine both the appropriate dollar value for each hedging stock and select the specified number of stock to include in the portfolio. Hence, mixed-integer optimization problems will provide us with our optimal solution hedging portfolio. The only problem, however, is that even with today's computational power and resources it could still take hours, days, weeks, or even longer to solve for the optimized solution. This is surely an unreasonable amount of time for any financial analyses.

To resolve this issue, analysts need to use some numerical approximation methodologies to reduce the universe of 500 stocks to the most appealing 50 stocks for the hedged portfolio. While there are many techniques being used, each has its own advantages and disadvantages, and, unfortunately, these advantages and disadvantages will vary for the different hedging reasons. Analysts need to determine the best approach for these exact needs.

It is important to note that the initial optimization to determine the appropriate weightings for a selected hedging universe is straightforward. And in the case where the analyst is not putting any constraints on the side of the order (e.g., it could be long or short in the hedging portfolio), analysts can determine a direct analytical solution using Lagrange multipliers as described earlier. This means that the analysts does not even have to invoke any optimization process, and the solution is almost instantaneous. But issues do arise when analysts place constraints on the number of stocks and/or on the side of the position that can be held in the portfolio.

We highlight three of the more common stock-reduction methodologies being used in practice.

Weightings: Start by determining the best hedge using all stocks in the universe. This optimization solution often has a direct analytical solution, so we will have the solution almost instantaneously. Stocks are then deleted from the universe starting with the smallest dollar value or weight. The optimal hedging portfolio is then recalculated using the smaller number of stocks in the universe. This process is continued until the hedging portfolio contains the number of stocks specified by the analyst. Depending on the size of the hedging universe, analysts may elect to eliminate more than one stock from the universe each iteration to improve the solution speed.

Risk contribution: Start by determining the best hedge using all stocks in the universe. Then compute the risk contribution of each stock in the hedging portfolio. This is calculated as the difference in risk of the combined portfolio (original portfolio plus hedged portfolio) and the combined portfolio without the stock. For example, the risk contribution of stock k is computed as follows:

$$Z_1 = \begin{pmatrix} z_1 \\ \vdots \\ z_k \\ \vdots \\ z_n \end{pmatrix} \quad Z_2 = \begin{pmatrix} z_1 \\ \vdots \\ z_k = 0 \\ \vdots \\ z_n \end{pmatrix}$$

$$RC(z_k) = Z_1^T CZ_1 - Z_2^T CZ_2$$

Stocks are then deleted from the hedging universe starting with the stocks that have the highest risk contribution to the portfolio.

Marginal contribution to risk: Start by determining the best hedge using all stocks in the universe. Then compute the marginal contribution to risk for each stock in the hedging portfolio. Mathematically, marginal contribution to risk is defined as:

$$MCR(z_k) = \frac{\partial z_k}{\partial Risk} \cdot side(z_k) \cdot - 1$$

The expression *side*(z_k) is used to denote the direction where $1 = $ long and $-1 = $ short. The derivative of an equation always gives the change corresponding with increasing the value of the variable. For risk management in the process in which we are eliminating stocks from the hedging universe, we are always interested in the value corresponding to moving the position size towards zero. This adjustment ensures we determine the proper marginal contribution to risk for each stock in the portfolio.

Another process that is used to compute the marginal contribution to risk for each hedging stock is to simply decrease the value of the stock by 10%. Then the calculation is similar to the risk contribution shown earlier. This is

$$Z_1 = \begin{pmatrix} z_1 \\ \vdots \\ z_k \\ \vdots \\ z_n \end{pmatrix} \qquad Z_2 = \begin{pmatrix} z_1 \\ \vdots \\ z_k \cdot 0.90 \\ \vdots \\ z_n \end{pmatrix}$$

$$MCR(z_k) = Z_1^T CZ_1 - Z_2^T CZ_2$$

Stocks are then deleted from the hedging universe starting with those stocks that have the highest marginal contribution to risk.

It is important to note that risk contribution is an all-or-none calculation, and the marginal contribution to risk decreases the value in the holding. Therefore, it is possible for the values from these two metrics to be opposite. An interpretation of this type of result could imply that there are some shares of the stock that are decreasing in risk, but if we remove too much of the value of the stock the risk will begin to increase.

There are some processes being used to evaluate both contribution to risk and marginal contribution to risk that start by eliminating the stocks that show up as the least advantageous to risk management from both metrics.

Single-side holding: As stated previously, there are times when the investor can only hold a long or short hedging position. That is, all stocks in the hedging portfolio have to be long or short. In the unconstrained optimization, the final solution could contain stocks with values that are both positive (long) and negative (short). Therefore, the process to reduce the number of stocks form the hedging universe would remove those stocks where the solution places them on the wrong side of the hedge, e.g., these are stocks that have negative values for a long-only portfolio or positive values for a short-only portfolio.

Alternative techniques: The techniques previously discussed included a process to reduce stocks form the hedging portfolio. Another solution being used to develop optimal hedging portfolios is to determine the stocks that provide the most risk-reduction benefit, and then add those stocks to the hedged portfolio based on the earlier techniques. In this process, the analysts will add stocks into the hedged portfolio one by one until they arrive at the specified number of stocks.

Unfortunately, the final solutions determined from our reduction methodology and our addition methodology may not yield the same results due to cross correlation terms in the portfolios. We encourage analysts to evaluate all methodologies to determine the approach that best suits their needs.

Idiosyncratic risk: In many of these situations, the number of specified stocks to include in the hedged portfolio is more than the number of stocks required to offset market risk, and the only term contributing to overall portfolio risk is the idiosyncratic risk term. Therefore, some of the processes being used in practice will filter out the stocks with highest amount of idiosyncratic risk at the beginning to help speed up the solution process. For example, eliminate the bottom quartile of stocks ranked from least amount to highest amount of idiosyncratic risk. This approach would reduce the S&P 500 universe down to 375 stocks. Additionally, we may wish to include only the top quartile of lowest-idiosyncratic risk stocks of the hedging universe in the potential solution space. So we will be starting with a much smaller potential universe from the beginning. This approach would reduce the S&P 500 universe to 125 stocks.

Important note: Since all stocks are correlated with every stock in the portfolio, our techniques of either eliminating stocks from the hedged portfolio or adding stocks to the original portfolio may not completely measure the overall risk reduction of all subsets of stocks. These techniques provide some insight into how industry analysts are overcoming the time issue to solve these often complex problems.

Example 9.9: How Many Assets to Hedge All Systematic Risk of the Portfolio

It is important to note that if the covariance matrix was derived using a k-factor risk model, then the analyst can completely hedge all market risk using any random k-stock hedging portfolio. The reason is that the current portfolio will have k-sensitivities: one sensitivity to each risk factor. Then we can determine a weighting scheme to negate each of the k-sensitivities using any k-stocks.

Many times analysts will use dummy variables to designate sectors or industries, to force the optimization procedure to use stocks from the same sectors or industries to hedge the portfolio risk. In this manner, the analyst would not completely hedge all market risk using a random k-stock portfolio. They would need to at least include stocks from the same sectors and industries.

This eliminates some of the randomness issues. This will also help address the errors surrounding the covariance calculations.

If the covariance was developed using a 10-factor model, the optimal hedging portfolio would include the ten stocks with the least amount of idiosyncratic risk. Since the optimization can eliminate all market risk using any 10-stock portfolio (since the covariance matrix was constructed using a 10-factor model), the optimization will seek to minimize idiosyncratic risk. Since idiosyncratic risk is an additive risk term (for the reasons stated previously), the best solution should consist of those stocks with the least amount of idiosyncratic risk. Due to the weightings across the stocks to manage market risk, the final stocks may not be the 10 lowest in idiosyncratic risk, but they will consist of the stocks on the lower side of the idiosyncratic risk spectrum.

Example 9.10: Factor Exposure

Investors are often tasked with constructing a portfolio to achieve a desired factor exposure. Often the factor exposure is to the general market such as the S&P 500 index, or possibly to a size factor (e.g., Fama-French exposure), growth or value stocks, country or region exposure, or to achieve a desired level of sensitivity to a macroeconomic indicator such as interest rates, GDP, etc.

Achieving risk exposure in this sense is equivalent to hedging a portfolio to a portfolio that is comprised of underlying factor exposure.

Minimize tracking error: In a situation in which the underlying factor exposure can be expressed directly as a stock portfolio such as the market index, a small-cap index, or possibly a growth or value index, the factor exposure portfolio Y can be computed by minimizing the tracking error to the specified factor exposure portfolio X. This process is as follows.

Let X represent the factor exposure portfolio. Let Y represent the portfolio that will achieve the desired factor exposure. This portfolio can consist of the same names as in the underlying portfolio as well as additional names. We join the elements of the two portfolios so that the first n stocks are the stocks in the underlying factor exposure portfolio and the stocks from $n + 1$ to $n + m$ represent the m-stocks that are not in the underlying factor exposure portfolios. Therefore, portfolio X will have weights for stocks 1 to n, and zeros for stocks $n + 1$ to $n + m$. Portfolio Y will contain the holdings or weightings in these stocks to minimize tracking error to the underlying portfolio. These portfolios are:

$$x = \begin{pmatrix} x_1 \\ x_2 \\ \vdots \\ x_n \\ 0 \\ \vdots \\ 0 \end{pmatrix} \quad y = \begin{pmatrix} y_1 \\ y_2 \\ \vdots \\ y_n \\ y_{n+1} \\ \vdots \\ y_{n+m} \end{pmatrix}$$

If the potential tracking portfolio Y is not able to hold a stock that is in portfolio X such as stock k, we simply set that particular value to zero in our optimization constraint. That is, $y_k = 0$. The optimal tracking portfolio is then constructed by solving the following optimization problem:

$$Min_y \quad (x-y)^T C(x-y)$$
$$s.t. \quad constraints$$

The constraints will be defined by the investors and can include the maximum number of names to hold in portfolio Y (e.g., the number of non-zero Y entries), as well as a constraint on the maximum or minimum weighting, etc. If the investor cannot hold the same names in the tracking portfolio as in the factor exposure portfolio, we would set these constraints to be zero for those stocks, e.g., $y_1 = 0, y_2 = 0, \ldots, y_n = 0$. The portfolio that minimizes tracking error is the portfolio that achieves the desired factor exposure.

Minimize factor sensitivities: Let us suppose that the desired factor exposure cannot be represented as an underlying stock portfolio, such as exposure to GDP, interest rates, bond yields, or currency rates. In this case, the investor can estimate sensitivities to the same factors used in the stock covariance factor model. Suppose the risk factor model consists of k-factors. This model can be expressed based on any of the techniques described in Chapter 4. Additionally, the PCA model provides a great means for developing factors used to construct factor exposure portfolios because the factors are ensured to be independent. The process is outlined as follows:

Step 1:

Estimate the beta sensitivities factor exposure observations as a function of the risk factor model.

Investors will need to determine the appropriate series of data to define the desired factor. But in most cases, the selection is easy such as GDP, interest rates, currency rates, etc. This is determined via ordinary least squares regression analysis as follows:

$$R_{Factor} = b_0 + b_1 F_1 + b_2 F_2 + \ldots + b_k F_k + \varepsilon$$

Suppose that the sensitivities are found to be:

$$\bar{b}_0, \bar{b}_1, \bar{b}_2, \ldots, \bar{b}_k$$

Step 2:

Determine the sensitivities to each risk factor k based on the underlying stocks in the portfolio. This is as follows:

Let the weightings of each stock in the portfolio P be $w_1, w_2, \ldots, w_n$
Let the sensitivities of each stock i to the risk factors be $b_{i0}, b_{i1}, \ldots b_{ik}$
Then the portfolio exposure to each factor k is computed as follows:

$$b_{pk} = \sum_{i=1}^{n} w_i b_{ik}$$

Step 3:

Determine the optimal stock portfolio to achieve factor exposure.

Analysts can now determine the portfolio that minimizes tracking error to a single-asset portfolio following the previous steps in which we compute the covariance matrix across all assets and solve. Another approach, however, is to minimize the sum of square errors as in the following:

$$Min \quad L = (b_{p0} - \bar{b}_0)^2 + (b_{p1} - \bar{b}_1)^2 + \ldots + (b_{pk} - \bar{b}_k)^2 + (\varepsilon_p^2 + \bar{\varepsilon}^2)^2$$

where

$$b_{pk} = \sum w_i b_{ik}$$

and $\bar{\varepsilon}^2$ denotes idiosyncratic risk (variance).

In fact, analysts familiar with optimization will notice that these two approaches are identical.

One improvement to the preceding procedure, and one that cannot be easily accomplished via the minimize tracking error procedure, is to use a weighted minimization scheme as follows:

$$Min \quad L = \gamma_0(b_{p0} - \bar{b}_0)^2 + \gamma_1(b_{p1} - \bar{b}_1)^2 + \ldots + \gamma_k(b_{pk} - \bar{b}_k)^2 + \gamma_\varepsilon(\varepsilon_p^2 + \bar{\varepsilon}^2)^2$$

An approach that has been used to minimize tracking error is to base the weighting scheme on the risk premium of each factor as determined via arbitrage pricing theory (APT). (For example, see Ross (1976), Roll and Ross (1984), and Chen, Roll, and Ross (1986)). This is:

$$Min \quad L = \lambda_0(b_{p0} - \bar{b}_0)^2 + \lambda_1(b_{p1} - \bar{b}_1)^2 + \ldots + \lambda_k(b_{pk} - \bar{b}_k)^2 + \lambda_\varepsilon(\varepsilon_p^2 + \bar{\varepsilon}^2)^2$$

where λ_k is the risk premium for factor k. Investors need to determine the proper weighting for the idiosyncratic variance term. Depending on the APT process used, the approach may provide a risk premium for company-specific variance. We do, however, suggest using some weighting for idiosyncratic variance to ensure that the tracking portfolio provides the same proportion of risk decomposition as for the factor exposure matrix.

CONCLUSIONS

In this chapter we provided the derivation of the optimal hedge dollar value to invest in a pre-specified hedging portfolio and the corresponding hedge ratio. We showed that the hedge ratio reduces to the negative of the covariance between the held portfolio and the hedging portfolio divided by the variance of the hedging portfolio. That is,

$$h_{yx} = -\frac{\text{cov}(X, Y)}{\text{var}(Y)}$$

Most importantly, we show that the relationship between hedging ratios is not symmetric due to the idiosyncratic risk component of the portfolios. Thus,

$$h_{yx} \neq \frac{1}{h_{xy}}$$

The chapter also provided techniques to determine appropriate dollar value hedges using a specified index portfolio (S&P 500) and an arbitrary portfolio.

In many cases, the time required to solve the risk reduction optimization problem could take hours, days, weeks, or longer, especially if we need to specify a predetermined number of stocks to hold in the hedging portfolio. To reduce the solution time into a time in which it is reasonable for investors to make decisions, we introduced various techniques such as the weighting scheme, risk contribution, and marginal contribution to risk. The chapter concluded with a discussion of achieving factor exposure following the same techniques we use to minimize risk and develop optimal hedging portfolios.

The last important note is that the approaches provided here can be applied to any asset class or set of financial instruments.

References

Banks, E., Glantz, M., Siegel, P., 2006. Credit Derivatives: Techniques to Manage Credit Risk for Financial Professionals. McGraw-Hill.

Banks, E., Glantz, M., Siegel, P., 2007. Credit Derivatives: Techniques to Manage Credit Risk for Financial Professionals. McGraw-Hill.

Bradley, S., Hax, A., Magnanti, T., 1977. Applied Mathematical Programming. Addison Wesley.

Chen, N., Roll, R., Ross, S., 1986. Economic forces and the stock market. J. Bus. July 1986.

Chiang, A., 1984. Fundamental Methods of Mathematical Economics. McGraw-Hill, Inc.

Hull, J., 2012. Options, Futures, and Other Derivatives, eighth ed. Prentice Hall.

Kissell, R., 2003. Managing trading risk. Working Paper, <www.kissellresearch.com>.

Kuhn, H.W., Tucker, A.W., 1951. Nonlinear programming. Proceedings of Second Berkeley Symposium. Berkeley: University of California Press, pp. 481−492. MR47303.

Markowitz, H.M., 1952. Portfolio Selection. J. Finance 7 (1), 77−91.

Markowitz, H.M., 1956. The Optimization of a Quadratic Function Subject to Linear Constraints. Naval Research Logistics Quarterly 3, 111−133.

Markowitz, H.M., 1959. Portfolio Selection: Efficient Diversification of Investments. John Wiley & Sons, New York.

Pemberton, M., Rau, N., 2001. Mathematics for Economists. Manchester University Press.

Roll, R., Ross, S., 2001. The arbitrage pricing theory approach to strategic portfolio planning. Financ. Analysts J. May-June 1984.

Roll, R., Ross, S., 1984. The arbitrage pricing theory approach to strategic portfolio planning. Financ. Analysts J. May-June 1984.

Ross, S., 1976. The Arbitrage Theory of Asset Pricing. J. Econ. Theory. 13 (3), 341−360.

Sharpe, W.F., 1964. Capital Asset Prices: A Theory of Market Equilibrium. J. Finance 19 (3), 425−442.

Rating Credit Risk: Current Practices, Model Design, and Applications

The credit crisis of 2008−2009 was in many ways a credit-rating crisis. The financial crisis might not have happened without credit-rating agencies issuing stellar ratings on toxic mortgage securities. The Securities and Exchange Commission has been investigating possible wrongdoing at one of the largest credit-rating agencies, accusing the firm of inflating ratings of mortgage investments and setting them up for a crash when the financial crisis struck. Furthermore, doubts about credit-rating agencies arose due to numerous conflicts of interest and the backward-looking nature of the analytical process, which seemed not to predict well. Structured finance products, such as mortgage-backed securities, accounted for over $11 trillion of outstanding US debt. The lion's share of these securities was highly rated. For example, more than half of structured finance securities rated by Moody's carried AAA ratings, the highest credit rating, typically reserved for near-riskless securities. The point: Banks should build industry- and deal-specific internal risk models. Internal ratings, because they are based on "know thy customer," provide a potent framework for assessing multi-asset portfolios. The internal risk models discussed ahead understand client fundamentals.

External Ratings

Rating agencies generate ratings after assessing and interpreting information received from issuers and other available sources. Ratings express opinions about the ability and willingness of an issuer, such as a corporation or state or city government, to meet its financial obligations in accordance with the terms of those obligations. Credit ratings are opinions about the credit quality of an issue, such as a bond or other debt obligation, and the relative likelihood that it may default. Investors use ratings to help assess credit risk and compare different issuers and debt issues in the process of making investment decisions and managing portfolios. Individual investors, for example, may use credit ratings in evaluating the purchase of a municipal or corporate bond from a risk-tolerance perspective.

Multi-Asset Risk Modeling.
© 2014 Elsevier Inc. All rights reserved.

Rating methodologies typically involve analysts, the use of mathematical models, or a combination of the two.

- *Model-driven ratings*: A small number of credit rating agencies focus almost exclusively on quantitative data, which they incorporate into a mathematical model. For example, an agency using this approach might evaluate an entity's asset quality, funding, and profitability based on data from the institution's public financial statements and regulatory filings.
- *Analyst-driven ratings*: In rating a corporation or municipality, agencies using the analyst-driven approach generally assign an analyst, often in conjunction with a team of specialists, to take the lead in evaluating the entity's creditworthiness. Typically, analysts obtain information from published reports, as well as from interviews and discussions with the issuer's management. They use that information to assess the entity's financial condition, operating performance, policies, and risk-management strategies.

Standard and Poor's Credit Scoring Models

Standard and Poor's two central credit scoring/credit models[1]:

- *CreditModel* helps clients evaluate credit quality by creating quantitatively derived estimates of creditworthiness ("credit scores") for thousands of public and private firms. CM contains migration and recovery statistics.
- *CreditPro*® offers a database that provides a strong statistical foundation to assess ratings migration and default and recovery rates across geographies, regions, industries and sectors. The data goes back to 1981 for more than 15,000 issuers, 130,000 securities, 150,000 structured finance tranches, and 140 sovereigns.

Table 10.1 shows Standard & Poor's Ratings Services-McGraw Hill Financial. The ratings represent Standard & Poor's opinion on the general creditworthiness of an obligor, or the creditworthiness of an obligor with respect to a particular debt security or other financial obligation. Table 10.2, as indicated, is a representation of Standard & Poor's risk factors associated with corporate ratings.

Table 10.1 S&P Credit Ratings

Investment/ Speculative Grade	Rating	
		Ratings from "AA" to "CCC" may be modified by the addition of a plus (+) or minus (−) sign to show relative standing within the major rating categories.
Investment Grade	AAA	Extremely strong capacity to meet financial commitments. Highest rating.
Investment Grade	AA	Very strong capacity to meet financial commitments.

(Continued)

---

[1]S&P Guide to Credit Rating Essentials, 2012.

Table 10.1 (Continued)

Investment Grade	A	Strong capacity to meet financial commitments, but somewhat susceptible to adverse economic conditions and changes in circumstances.
Investment Grade	BBB	Adequate capacity to meet financial commitments, but more subject to adverse economic conditions.
Investment Grade	BBB−	Considered the lowest investment grade by market participants.
Speculative Grade	BB+	Considered highest speculative grade by market participants.
Speculative Grade	BB	Less vulnerable in the near term, but faces major ongoing uncertainties to adverse business, financial, and economic conditions.
Speculative Grade	B	More vulnerable to adverse business, financial, and economic conditions, but currently has the capacity to meet financial commitments.
Speculative Grade	CCC	Currently vulnerable and dependent on favorable business, financial, and economic conditions to meet financial commitments.
	CC	Currently highly vulnerable.
	C	A bankruptcy petition has been filed or similar action taken, but payments of financial commitments are continued.
	D	Payments in default on financial commitments.

Table 10.2 S&P Risk Factors for Corporate Ratings[2]

Risk Factors	Business Risk Or Financial Risk Business Risk + Financial Risk = Rating
Country Risk	Business Risk
Industry Characteristics	Business Risk
Company Position	Business Risk
Profitability, Peer Group Comparison	Business Risk
Accounting	Financial Risk
Governance, Risk Tolerance, Financial Policy	Financial Risk
Cash Flow Adequacy	Financial Risk
Capital Structure	Financial Risk
Liquidity, Short-Term Factors	Financial Risk

---

[2]S&P Guide to Credit Rating Essentials, 2012.

Moody's — KMV Quantitative Risk Assessment Models[3]

- *RiskCalc*™ is a Web-based statistical network of empirically validated and locally calibrated Probability of Default (PD) models. Models used in the credit evaluation of private corporate borrowers. They provide default probabilities that help financial institutions with measuring, monitoring, and managing portfolio credit risk.
- *CreditEdge*™ is a Web-based tool used to measure the probability of default. CreditEdge includes Moody's KMV expected default frequency (EDF) credit measure of over 25,000 publically-traded firms globally, updated each day with the firm's latest stock price. CreditEdge is designed for those actively transacting in the credit markets that make buy and sell decisions quickly and often.
- *LossCalc*™ predicts recovery rates for defaulted debt instruments. Investors accurately model the overall expected losses associated with defaulted debt instruments by incorporating both default rates using RiskCalc and recovery rates using LossCalc.
- *CRDViewer*™ is a reporting tool for displaying middle-market credit risk benchmarks from the Moody's KMV proprietary Credit Research Database™ (CRD). Covering the United States and Canada, CRDViewer combines historical financial statements, Moody's RiskCalc™ probabilities of default (PDs), company descriptors, and obligation details into a single, customizable view.
- *Default Reports* allows clients to receive monthly default reports via e-mail, and the data underlying report charts and graphs are available.
- *The Corporate Bond Default Database* makes a key portion of Moody's proprietary credit history database publicly available for the first time. It allows credit risk professionals to employ Moody's ratings and credit history experience to better measure and manage credit risk, to price credit risk, to identify industry and geographic concentrations, and to measure the impact of the prospective purchase or sale of debt within a portfolio context.

Internal Ratings

One objective of the Basel III accords is to reduce bank over-reliance on external credit ratings, i.e., ratings issued by credit-rating agencies. This goal is attainable by (1) encouraging banks to make informed investment decisions supported by appropriate internal systems, and (2) by banks with a material number of exposures in a given portfolio developing internal ratings for that portfolio instead of relying on external ratings for the calculation of their capital requirements.

---

[3]Source: Moody's Analytics 2012.

If the debt crisis taught one lesson, it is that external ratings alone should not be the defining factor in risk decision-making, but should instead be a check on internal due diligence (which is this chapter's argument).

The Basel Committee has issued important papers on credit risk including internal ratings, credit risk modeling, and credit risk management.[4] Regulators call for the use of sound and prudent credit risk assessment, valuation policies, and practices by banks. *A significant cause of bank failures is poor credit quality and credit risk assessment. Failure to identify and recognize deterioration in credit quality in a timely manner can aggravate and prolong the problem. Thus, inadequate credit risk assessment policies and procedures, which may lead to inadequate and untimely recognition and measurement of loan losses, undermine the usefulness of capital requirements and hamper proper assessment and control of a bank's credit risk exposure.*

- Principle 9: Banks must have in place a system for monitoring the condition of individual credits, including determining the adequacy of provisions and reserves.
- Principle 10: Banks are encouraged to develop and utilize an internal risk rating system in managing credit risk.
- Principle 11: Banks must have information systems and analytical techniques that enable management to measure the credit risk inherent in all on- and off-balance sheet activities.
- Principle 12: Banks must have in place a system for monitoring the overall composition and quality of the credit portfolio.
- Principle 13: Banks should take into consideration potential future changes in economic conditions when assessing individual credits and their credit portfolios, and should assess their credit risk exposures under stressful conditions.

The reason internal ratings are crucial components in any banker's decision toolbox is that they encompass a fundamental assessment of credit approvals. Bankers who fail to grasp the essentials of a client's business or carry out a fundamental credit analysis may be severely constrained by insufficient statistical data on historical performance of loans and other modeled variables. We note that difficulties in estimating key parameters in non-fundamental approaches are further impaired by long time horizons used in statistical credit risk models, suggesting that many years of data, spanning multiple credit cycles may be required to estimate default probabilities. Even if we model individual default probabilities precisely, the process of combining these for a portfolio might still be hampered by the scarcity of correlation data.

---

[4]Basel Committee on Banking Supervision Sound credit risk assessment and valuation for loans, June 2006.

Data limitations also encourage the use of various simplifying assumptions, for example:

- Determinants of credit loss are assumed to be independent from one another.
- Certain variables, such as the level of loss given default in some models, are treated as non-random variables, while estimated parameters and structural model assumptions are treated as if they were "true" (i.e., known with certainty).

Fundamental analysis is all about real-world dynamics. For example, within the context of risk-rating modeling, we evaluate quality, magnitude and trend of cash flow, debt capacity, management quality, contingencies, and effect of strategies for introducing new products or for diversifying into diverse businesses or geographical locations. Analysts carrying out fundamental credit analysis can employ stochastic forecasting tools and adapt their analyses in response to rapidly changing market conditions or to unforeseen events. Fundamental analysis is better suited to evaluate mergers and acquisitions, changing industry demographics, and macroeconomic stress better than quantitative credit models. Another positive feature of fundamental credit analysis is that it provides rational and insight behind its end results, meaning credit analysis are able to offer reasoning behind conclusions, not simply "black box" output.

Fundamental analysis incorporates stress testing and scenario analysis. Stress testing and scenario analysis are properly viewed as aspects of fundamental analysis because qualitative judgment informed by historical experience—i.e., fundamental analysis—provides the basis for defining stress scenarios and processing scenarios through various forecasting techniques ranging from modified percentage of sales to advanced stochastic optimization analysis.

Fundamental credit risk model benefits:

1. The use of credit risk models offers banks a framework for examining this risk in a timely manner, centralizing data on global exposures, and analyzing marginal and absolute contributions to risk. These properties of models may contribute to an improvement in a bank's overall ability to identify, measure, and manage risk.
2. Credit risk models may provide estimates of credit risk (such as unexpected loss) which reflect individual portfolio composition; hence, they may provide a better reflection of concentration risk compared to non-portfolio approaches.
3. By design, models may be both influenced by, and be responsive to, shifts in business lines, credit quality, market variables, and the economic environment. Consequently, modeling methodology holds out the possibility of providing a more responsive and informative tool for risk management.
4. Models offer: (a) the incentive to improve systems and data collection efforts; (b) a more informed setting of limits and reserves; (c) more accurate risk- and performance-based pricing, which may contribute to a more transparent decision-making process; and (d) a more consistent basis for economic capital allocation.

Computerized models absent of "know thy customer" experienced hands cannot deliver wide-ranging solutions that meet all needs and cover all situations. They are often black boxes that assume the real world is simpler as and more orderly than it really is. To get around this problem, professional analysts employ quantitative credit models, harnessing the models' advantages while retaining a sound fundamental approach in the overall risk-measuring process.

Chapter 10 models fall into three sections: (1) modeling corporate credit risk, (2) modeling specialized exposure risk, and (3) modeling financial institution risk.

Modeling Corporate Credit Risk

Illustrative Example: Corporate Credit Rating Model
File Name: Risk Analysis—Corporate Risk Rating System
Location:
Models are available on the Elsevier Website, at http://booksite.elsevier.com/ 9780124016903.
Brief Description: General corporate risk rating system adaptable to industry specific or deal specific
Requirements: Our corporate rating system includes three workbooks: (1) new rating, (2) update current rating, and (3) start tutorial rating. Examine the tutorial rating first.

Corporate risk rating is central to the credit management process, providing bankers with a systematic methodology for uniformly analyzing risk across their portfolios. The principles underlying a corporate risk rating system represent a common framework for assessing risk with a high degree of uniformity and providing a way to distinguish between levels of risk. In connection with the supervisory assessment of credit risk, the Federal Reserve reviews internal management reports describing the institution's credit exposure by internal risk grade. Since the supervisory assessment of these reports began, Federal Reserve staff has been engaged in a detailed analysis of internal credit risk rating systems and exposures at large institutions, with the near-term goal of identifying sound practices in their use, and the long-term goal of encouraging broader adoption of such practices as well as further innovation and enhancements.

Credit ratings form the basis for a continuous loan review process, under which large corporate credits are reviewed and re-graded at least annually to focus attention on deteriorating credits so they can be classified in of advance of reaching the point of no return. In addition, just as importantly, credit grades form the basis upon which capital and loan provisions are calculated, developed, and assessed, allowing for determination of exposures through risk-adjusted returns on equity and other key bank benchmarks. These measurements serve as guides for resource allocation and active portfolio management and planning.

Corporate credit grading is important in pricing transactions, aiding bankers, and setting rates and/or fees commensurate with risk levels. Internal rating systems form an important part of the loan approval process used by banks identify problem loans, allocate capital, price deals, contribute to profitability analysis, and to help determine loan loss reserves. In addition, ratings aid in determining the level of service and monitoring required. Grades indicating high-risk levels encourage managerial and accounting follow-up action.

The principles underlying a risk rating system are to:

1. Establish a common framework for assessing risk.
2. Establish uniformity throughout the bank's units, divisions, and affiliates.
3. Establish compatibility to regulatory definitions, which distinguish various levels of "poor" credit risk.
4. Distinguish various levels of "satisfactory" credit risk.
5. Promote common training through expanded definitions and risk-rating guides.
6. Initiate and maintain ratings on a continuous basis.
7. Set criteria for review of ratings by the bank's auditing department to verify accuracy, consistency, and timeliness.
8. Institute a systematic methodology for uniformly analyzing risk across the loan portfolio.

A corporate rating scale should be established to effectively distinguish gradations of risk within the institution's portfolio so that there is clear linkage to loan quality (and/or loss characteristics), rather than simply serving an administrative function. We design the system so that it can address the range of risks typically encountered in the underlying businesses of the institutions enabling banks to evaluate and track risk on individual transactions and relationships on a continuous basis. In addition, of course, it allows the bank to track and manage risk within the portfolio as a whole.

We define risk as the probability that an exposure loss will be sustained. Credit risk ratings reflect not only the likelihood or severity of loss, but also the variability of loss over time, particularly as this relates to the effect of the business cycle. Commercial loans expose banks to two types of risk: obligor risk and facility (or transaction) risk. Obligor risk is associated with economic and industry risks, industry structure risks, customer-specific risks, and the ever-present operating risks inherent in the lending business. Facility risks are risks inherent in an instrument or facility. If a bank feels that combined risk levels are unacceptable, it might sell the exposure or acquire other deals that are less exposed to these forces, thus reducing the risk of the portfolio.

A rating begins with the risk of the obligor, and then adds risks associated with the particular transaction, variables that increase or decrease risk: collateral, guarantees, terms, tenor, and portfolio impact. The risk rating is the "key" rating, as it is the risk of the facility or transaction. A single borrower would have only one obligor rating, but might have several different facilities with different facility ratings, depending on terms, collateral, etc.

The Structure of a Corporate Risk-Grading System

There are two major classifications of risk in any transaction. The first is risk associated with the borrower, *obligor grade*, and the second is risk associated with the facility, *facility grade*. The obligor grade and facility grade combine to form the final risk grade. The final grade determines loss given default (LGD). Obligor and facility grade requisites are included in Chapter 10, Appendix. Table 10.3 is typical of profiling appropriate links between (1) grades 1 through 10 (assuming a 10-point system), (2) respective bond or debt rating, and (3) dynamic default probabilities (Banks update default data by subscribing to rating services or suitable vendors).

Table 10.3 Comparing the Credit Grade to the Bond Rating and Expected Default Frequency[5]

Credit Grade	Bond Rating	Key Words	EDF High in bp	EDF Mean in bp	EDF Low in bp
1	AAA to AA−	World Class Organization	0.02	0.02	0.02
2	AA to A−	Excellent Access To Capital Markets	0.13	0.02	0.02
3	A+ to BBB+	Cash Flow Trends Generally Positive	0.27	0.06	0.03
4	BBB+ to BBB	Leverage, Coverage Somewhat Below Industry Average	0.87	0.16	0.08
5	BBB to BBB−	Lower Tier Competitor; Limited Access To Public Debt Markets	1.62	0.25	0.24
6	BBB− to BB−	Narrow Margins; Fully Leveraged; Variable Cash Flow	2.65	0.52	0.24
7	B	Cash Flow Vulnerable To Downturns; Strained Liquidity; Poor Coverage	5.44	1.89	0.64
8	C	Special Mention (1)	19.06	2.89	2.85
9	D	Substandard (2)			
10	D	Doubtful (3)			

[5]These ratings and default frequency listings serve as examples only. They should be updated and made industry specific.

Table 10.4 Definitions of Poor Credit Grades by the Authorities

Definitions Issued by the Regulatory Bodies	Comptroller of the Currency Federal Deposit Insurance Corporation Federal Reserve Board Office of Thrift Supervision
Special Mention	A special mention asset has potential weaknesses that deserve management's close attention. If left uncorrected, these potential weaknesses may result in deterioration of the repayment prospects for the asset or in the institution's credit position at some future date. Special mention assets are not adversely classified and do not expose an institution to sufficient risk to warrant adverse classification.
Substandard Assets	A substandard asset is inadequately protected by the current sound worth and paying capacity of the obligor or of the collateral pledged, if any. Assets so classified must have a well-defined weakness or weaknesses that jeopardize the liquidation of the debt. They are characterized by the distinct possibility that the firm will sustain some loss if the deficiencies are not corrected.
Doubtful Assets	An asset classified doubtful has all the weaknesses inherent in one classified substandard, with the added characteristic that the weaknesses make collection or liquidation in full, on the basis of currently existing facts, conditions, and values, highly questionable and improbable.
Loss Assets	Assets classified as loss are considered uncollectible and of such little value that their continuance as viable assets is not warranted. This classification does not mean that the asset has absolutely no recovery or salvage value, but rather it is not practical or desirable to defer writing off this worthless asset even though partial recovery may be affected in the future.

Obligor Risk Grade Key Inputs: Details[6]

Obligor Financial Measures:

- Earnings and operating cash flow
- Debt capacity and financial flexibility
- Balance sheet quality and structure
- Corporate valuation
- Contingencies
- Financial reporting
- Management and controls

---

[6]Appendix reviews the essentials of corporate risk rating.

Remaining Obligor Measures:

- Recent developments
- Industry risk
  - Industry segment
  - Industry position
- Country Risk

Facility Risk Grade Key Inputs:

A. Documentation
B. Guarantees
C. Collateral
D. Loan purpose
E. Loan tenor
F. Portfolio

The corporate model is generic and illustrative, but is transformable to meet industry-specific, deal-specific and local environment requirements.

- Algorithm processes included in the macro worksheet drop and add industry-specific pages.
- Develop industry-specific primary financial measures and industry worksheets. Modify algorithms to drop/include these worksheets.

Specialized Lending Risk Models

In October 2001, the Basel Committee's Models Task Force first proposed to treat specialized lending differently from other corporate loans under the internal ratings-based (IRB) approach. In its "Working Paper on the Internal Ratings Based Approach to Specialized Lending Exposures," the Task Force defined specialized lending (SL) products as including project finance loans, income-producing real estate loans, object finance (e.g., vessels, aircraft, and rolling stock), and commodities finance transactions. In this chapter, we deal specifically with the risk ratings of these SL products in context with Basel II Accord Section 249.[7]

---

[7]The authors acknowledge that much of the information in this chapter is drawn from the Basel Committee on Banking Supervision guidelines on *The Internal Ratings-Based Approach to Specialized Lending Exposures and Bank for International Settlements*. The risk-rating systems themselves, "Supervisory Slotting Criteria for Specialized Lending," were presented in hard text and set in Excel by the authors so models could be applied in practice. Since SL risk ratings are acknowledged as a fundamental capital issue with regulators, much of the important source text remains in its original form with the proper acknowledgement to the true experts/authors at the Bank for International Settlement and the Basel Committee on Banking Supervision.

The regulations specify that capital assigned against SL exposures is computed using one of three approaches:

1. *Standardized approach*: Banks must allocate exposures into buckets of credit quality, and a capital percentage is assigned to each bucket.
2. *Foundation internal ratings-based (IRB) approach*: Lenders are able to use their own models to determine their regulatory capital requirement. Under the foundation IRB approach, lenders estimate a probability of default (PD), while the supervisor provides set values for loss given default (LGD), exposure at default (EAD), and maturity of exposure (M). These values are plugged into the lender's appropriate risk weight function to provide a risk weighting for each exposure or type of exposure.
3. *Advanced IRB approach*: Lenders with the most advanced risk management and risk modeling skills are able to move to the advanced IRB approach, under which the lender estimates PD, LGD, EAD, and M. In the case of retail portfolios, only estimates of PD, LGD, and EAD are required, and the approach is known as *retail IRB*.

Banks that do not meet the requirements for the estimation of probability of default (PD) under the foundation approach for their specialized lending assets are *required to use the standardized approach and map their internal risk grades to five supervisory categories, each of which is associated with a specific risk weight.*[8]

The characteristics that define the supervisory categories, and the probabilities of defaults associated with each category, have been developed to express the same degree of default risk across the four SL product lines: project, object, commodity finance, and real estate. As such, project finance (PF) exposure slotted in the "strong" PF supervisory category would be associated with the same PD as a real estate exposure that is slotted into the "strong" category. The supervisory default probabilities estimates are set out ahead. We base values on industry consultation on the comparable riskiness of different specialized lending exposure types, anecdotal and empirical evidence on the quality distribution of banks' specialized lending portfolios, and analysis of default data from banks and external rating agencies. Table 10.5 depicts

Table 10.5 Preliminary Bank for International Settlements Supervisory Slotting Class

Supervisory Slotting Class	1-Year Default Probability	Approximate Correspondence to External Debt Rating
Strong	0.5%	BBB− or better
Fair	2.5%	B+ to BB+
Weak	12.5%	B or worse
Default	100%	D

[8]Basel II Accord Sections 244 to 269. The five supervisory categories associated with a specific risk weight are "Strong," "Good," "High Satisfactory," "Low Satisfactory," and "Weak."

the Basel Committee's Models Task Force historically significant *preliminary* recommendations regarding specialized lending supervisory default probability estimates. Readers may refer to The Basel Committee on Banking Supervision, Working Paper on the Internal Ratings-Based Approach to Specialized Lending Exposures October 2001, Page 11.

Specialized lending encompasses exposures whereby the obligor's primary repayment source depends on the cash flow generated by financed assets rather than the financial strength of a business. Such exposures are embedded with special characteristics:

- Loans are directed to special purpose vehicles or entities created specifically to operate or finance physical assets.
- The borrowing entity has little, if any, material assets or does not conduct any other business activity, and thus has no independent cash flow or other sources of payment except the specific assets financed; that is, the cash flow generated by the collateral is the loan's sole or almost exclusive source of repayment.
- The primary determinant of credit risk is the variability of the cash flow generated by the collateral rather than the independent capacity of a broader commercial enterprise.
- The loan represents a significant liability in the borrower's capital structure.
- Financing terms provide lenders with complete asset control and domination over the flow of funds the asset generates.

We generally express corporate exposures as the debt obligations of corporations, partnerships, or single-entity businesses (proprietorships).

Specialized lending internal credit ratings play an important role not only as a "first step" in the credit risk measurement process, but also as an important stand-alone risk management tool. Credit ratings are a basis for regular risk reports to senior management and boards of directors. Internal rating systems are also the basis for a continuous loan review process, under which large corporate credits generally are reviewed and regarded at least annually in order to focus attention on deteriorating credits well before they become "criticized" by examiners or external auditors.

Project Finance

Illustrative Example: Project Finance Risk Rating System
Location:
Models are available on the Elsevier Website, at http://booksite.elsevier.com/9780124016903.
Brief Description: Supervisory slotting BIS risk rating system developed in Excel by the authors from primary financial measures to security modules, Moody's KMV, S&P default rates, project EDF, and loan loss provisions.

Project finance is defined by the International Project Finance Association (IPFA) as the financing of long-term infrastructure, industrial projects, and public services based on a nonrecourse or limited recourse financial structure in which project debt and equity used to finance the project are paid back from the cash flow generated by the project. This type of financing is usually for large, complex, and expensive installations that might include, for example, power plants, chemical processing plants, mines, transportation infrastructure, environment, and telecommunications infrastructure. Usually, a project financing structure involves a number of equity investors, known as sponsors, as well as a syndicate of banks that provide loans to the operation. In such transactions, the lender is usually paid solely or almost exclusively out of the funds generated by the contracts for the facility's output, such as the electricity sold by a power plant. The borrower is usually a special purpose entity (SPE) that is not permitted to perform any function other than developing, owning, and operating the installation. Project lenders are given a lien on all of these assets, and are able to assume control of a project if the project company has difficulties complying with the loan terms.

Generally, we can create a special purpose entity for each project, thereby shielding other assets owned by a project sponsor from the detrimental effects of a project failure. As a special purpose entity, the project company has no assets other than the project. Capital contribution commitments by the owners of the project company are sometimes necessary to ensure that the project is financially sound. Project finance is often more complicated than alternative financing methods. Traditionally, project financing has been most commonly used in the mining, transportation, telecommunication, and public utility industries. More recently, particularly in Europe, project-financing principles have been applied to public infrastructure under public–private partnerships (PPP) or, in the UK, Private Finance Initiative (PFI) transactions.

Risk identification and allocation is a key component of project finance. A project may be subject to a number of technical, environmental, economic, and political risks, particularly in developing countries and emerging markets. Financial institutions and project sponsors may conclude that the risks inherent in project development and operation are unacceptable. To cope with these risks, project sponsors in these industries (such as power plants or railway lines) are generally made up of a number of specialist companies operating in a contractual network with each other that allocates risk in a way that allows financing to take place. The various patterns of implementation are sometimes referred to as "project delivery methods." The financing of these projects must also be distributed among multiple parties, to distribute the risk associated with the project while simultaneously ensuring profits for each party involved.

Example[9]:

A bank finances a special purpose vehicle that will build and operate a project. If the bank is exposed to the key risks in the project—construction risk (the risk that the project will not be completed in a timely and/or cost effective manner), operational/technology risk (the risk that the project will not operate up to specifications), or market/price risk (the risk that the demand and the price of the output will fall and/or that the margin between output prices and input prices and

---

[9]Basel Committee on Banking Supervision, Working Paper on the Internal Ratings-Based Approach to Specialized Lending Exposures, October 2001, pg. 2.

production costs will deteriorate)—then the project should be classified as SL. In addition, if a circular relationship exists between the end user's and the project's financial strength, the project should be classified as SL. This would be the case when an end user has limited resources or capacity to generate revenues apart from those generated by the project being financed, so that the end user's ability to honor its off-take contract depends primarily on the performance of the project.

Criteria:

- *Market conditions*: It is important that the bank consider whether the project has a durable advantage in location, the cost, if there are few competing suppliers, and if demand is strong and growing.
- *Financial ratios*: Banks must determine and interpret financial measures considering the level of project risk. Project financial ratios include cash available for debt service; debt service reserve account; earnings before interest and taxes plus depreciation and amortization; free cash flow; cost of debt; interest and debt service coverage ratios; minimum and average debt service coverage ratio; loan life coverage ratio; cost-to-market price; loan-to-value ratio.
- *Stressed conditions*: Unexpected macroeconomic shocks can easily undermine a project. Banks must determine if the project can meet its financial obligations under the most severely stressed conditions.
- *Financial structure*: If the useful life of the project falls significantly below the tenure of the loan, risks may be significant.
- *Currency risk*: There may be risk of devaluation and/or inconvertibility of local currency into another currency. Banks consider the risk that local currency will depreciate, revenue and cost streams will become mismatched, or substantial currency risk will occur.
- *Political risk*: This includes transfer risk.
- *Government support*: In some countries, a key question is what is a project's importance for the particular country over the long term? Lenders should verify that the project is of strategic importance (preferably export oriented) and enjoys strong support from the government.
- *Legal and regulatory environment*: The bank must carefully evaluate the legal and regulatory environment and risk of frequent changes in the law. Current or future regulatory issues may affect the project.
- *Support acquisition*: This means acquisition of all necessary supports and approvals for relief from local content laws.
- *Contract enforceability*: The bank must assure that contracts are enforceable—particularly contracts governing collateral and security—and the necessary permits are obtained. If there are major unresolved issues dealing with enforcement of contracts, they must be cleared.
- *Design and technology risk*: Unproven technology and design pose a significant project risk. We must make an effort to obtain the appropriate report or studies.
- *Construction risk*: Permits need to be obtained and the bank should verify that no adverse conditions are attached. If some permits are still outstanding, their receipt should, at the least, be very likely.

- *Completion guarantees*: Completion should be assured and substantial liquidated damages paid, supported by the financial substance of the sponsor. The bank should verify the sponsor's financial standing and record of accomplishment.
- *Operating risk*: Operating and maintenance contracts should be strong and long term, backed by the operator's expertise, record of accomplishment, and financial strength. The contracts should provide incentives and/or reserves. Banks should determine if the local operator is dependent on local authorities.
- *Off-take risk*: An off-taker is the purchaser of a project's output, while in an off-take agreement, the off-taker agrees to purchase all or a substantial part of the product produced by a project, which typically provides the revenue stream for a project's financing. Two possibilities exist: (1) if there is a take-or-pay or fixed-price off-take contract (the off-taker is the purchaser of a project's output) and (2) if there is no take-or-pay or fixed-price off-take contract (the take-or-pay contract requires the buyer to take and pay for the good or service only if it is delivered). If condition (1) applies, the bank should determine the creditworthiness of the off-taker, whether strong termination clauses exist, and if the tenure of the contract comfortably exceeds the maturity of the debt. If off-take risk (2) exists, the bank should verify that the project produces essential services or offers a commodity sold widely on a world market whereby the output can easily be absorbed at projected prices or, conservatively, even at lower-than-historic market growth rates.
- *Supply risk*: The bank should ensure that the supply contract is not short term. A long-term supply contract should not be completed with a financially weak supplier. Also, check if the degree of price risk definitely remains and if the project relies to some extent on potential and undeveloped reserves.
- *Assignment of contracts and accounts and pledge of assets*: The assignment of contracts should be fully comprehensive. The bank should check to see if they have obtained first (perfected) security interest in all project assets, contracts, permits, and accounts necessary to run the project.
- *Lender's control over cash flow*: A lender may improve control over cash flow by the use of independent escrow accounts and cash sweeps. An *independent escrow account* involves the right to hold funds in escrow, that is, a deposit held in trust by a third party to be turned over to the grantee on specified conditions. In project finance, an escrow account is often used to channel funds needed to pay debt service. During a *cash sweep*, the entire cash flow available for debt service is used to repay principal and interest. Stand-alone cash sweep analysis is used to calculate the amount of time it takes to repay the project debt in full.
- *Strength of the covenant package*: The bank must have a sound process to monitor mandatory prepayments, payment deferrals, and payment cascade and dividend restrictions. The covenant package should be strong for the project because the project may issue unlimited additional debt to secure the bank's position.
- *Reserve funds*: It is imperative that the bank employ robust procedures to control debt service, operating and maintenance, renewal and replacement, and

unforeseen events. Shorter-than-average coverage periods should be watched as well as reserve funds funded from operating cash flows.

Object Finance

Illustrative Example: Object Finance Risk Rating System
Location:
Models are available on the Elsevier Website, at http://booksite.elsevier.com/ 9780124016903.
Brief Description: Supervisory slotting object finance BIS risk rating system developed in Excel by the authors from primary financial measures to security package, suggested EDF, and loan loss provisions.

Object finance refers to a method of funding the acquisition of physical assets (e.g., ships, aircraft, satellites, and railcars) in which the repayment of the exposure is dependent on the cash flows generated by the specific assets that have been financed and pledged or assigned to the lender. A primary source of these cash flows might be rental or lease contracts with one or several third parties. In contrast, if the exposure is to a borrower whose financial condition and debt-servicing capacity enables it to repay the debt without undue reliance on the specifically pledged assets, the exposure should be treated as a collateralized corporate exposure. As a matter of principle, LGDs should reflect a bank's own loss experience, tempered with some conservatism.

Examples[10]:

1. A charter airline with an established business plan, many aircraft, and diversified service routes finances the purchase of additional aircraft to be used in its own operations. The airline establishes a special purpose vehicle (SPV) to own the subject aircraft. The bank lends to the SPV and takes a security interest in the aircraft. The SPV enters into a long-term lease with the airline. The lease's term exceeds the term of the underlying loan. The lease cannot be terminated under any condition. This exposure would be placed in the corporate exposure class. Loan repayments depend on the overall operations of the airline, and are not unduly dependent upon the specific aircraft as the primary source of repayment.
2. Same example as the preceding, except that (a) the lease term can be cancelled by the airline without penalty at some time before the end of the loan term, or (b) even if the lease is noncancellable, the lease payments do not fully cover the aggregate loan payments over the life of the loan. This loan should be classified as object finance, given that the airline/lessee is not fully committed to a lease sufficient to repay the loan, so pass-through treatment is inappropriate.

Rating components consist of a comprehensive set of building blocks that determines LGD, the asset's risk grade, and the appropriate loan loss reserve.

---

[10]Basel Committee on Banking Supervision, Working Paper on the Internal Ratings-Based Approach to Specialized Lending Exposures, October 2001, pg. 4.

Basic Structure:

1. Asset credit assessment using estimated default statistics.
2. Individual and cumulative grades within each rating module. The cumulative grades are determined by a weighting system and weights assigned by bankers evaluating the financing.
3. Modules include: *Object Financial Measures* (market conditions, financial ratios, stress analysis, financial structure); *Political and Legal Environment* (political risk, legal and regulatory risk); *Transaction Characteristics* (financial terms compared to the economic life of the asset); *Operating Risk* (permits licensing, scope, and nature of O and M contract, operator's financial strength); *Asset Characteristics* (configuration, size, design, and maintenance; resale value; sensitivity of the asset value and liquidity to economic cycle); *Strength of Sponsor* (operator's financial strength, sponsor's track record and financial strength); *Security Package* (asset control, rights and means at the lender's disposal to monitor, insurance against damages); and *Composite* (as with the project finance system, each module's composite rating, final asset grade before/after overrides, estimated LGD, dollar exposure risk, and reserve for asset write-off).

Criteria:

- *Market conditions*: The bank should ascertain that demand is strong and growing for the asset financed, and whether there exist strong entry barriers, low sensitivity to changes in technology, and a strong economic outlook for the asset.
- *Financial ratios*: Ratios are significant determinates of the asset's financial potential and include debt service coverage ratio and loan-to-value ratios. Financial ratios should be evaluated in context of the level of project risk.
- *Stress analysis*: A viable asset will enjoy stable long-term revenues capable of withstanding severely stressed conditions through an economic cycle.
- *Financial structure*: Asset liquidity should be evaluated as residual value provides lenders with degree of protection in the event cash flow is insufficient to retire loans.
- *Political risk, including transfer risk*: Banks should watch excessive exposures with no or weak mitigation instruments.
- *Legal and regulatory risks*: In the event the asset's debt service fails, banks will need to enforce contracts. Thus, jurisdiction is favorable to repossession and enforcement of contracts.
- *Transaction characteristics*: Financing tenure should be shorter than the economic life of the asset.
- *Asset characteristics*: The configuration, size, design, maintenance, and age (plane or boat, e.g.) should be checked against other assets in the same market. The criteria include strong advantage in design and maintenance, and that the object meets a liquid market.

- *Resale value*: The bank should ensure resale value does not fall below debt value.
- *Sensitivity of the asset value and liquidity to economic cycles*: Asset value and liquidity are relatively insensitive to economic cycles.
- *Asset control*: Legal documentation provides the lender effective control (e.g., a first perfected security interest, or a leasing structure including such security) on the asset, or on the company owning it.
- *Rights and means at the lender's disposal to monitor location and condition of the asset*: The lender is able to monitor the location and condition of the asset, at any time and place (regular reports, possibility to lead inspections).
- *Insurance against damages*: Insurance to cover collateral damages using top-quality insurance companies.

Commodities Finance

Illustrative Example: Commodities Finance Risk Rating System
Location:
Models are available on the Elsevier Website, at http://booksite.elsevier.com/9780124016903.
Brief Description: Supervisory slotting commodities finance BIS risk rating system developed in Excel by the authors from primary financial measures to security package, suggested EDF, and loan loss provisions.

The structured nature of the commodities finance is designed to compensate for the weak credit quality of the borrower. The exposure's rating reflects the self-liquidating nature of the transaction and the lender's skill in structuring the transaction rather than going through a traditional credit analysis. Commodities finance is defined as short-term financing for the acquisition of readily marketable commodities that are to be resold and the proceeds applied to loan repayment. Commodities finance deals with structured short-term lending to finance reserves, inventories, or receivables of exchange-traded commodities, such as crude oil, metals, and crops, whereby exposures are repaid from the proceeds of the sale of the commodity and the obligor operates no other activities, owns no other material assets, and thus has no independent means to satisfy the obligation.

Examples[11]:

1. The bank extends short-term documentary trade credit to a small independent trading company that acts as an intermediary between producers and their customers. The trader specializes in a single commodity and a single region. Each commodity shipment handled by the trader is financed and secured separately. Credit is extended upon delivery of the commodity to the trader, who has already contracted for the resale of the commodity shipment. A trustworthy third party controls the shipment of the commodity, and the bank

---

[11]Basel Committee on Banking Supervision, Working Paper on the Internal Ratings-Based Approach to Specialized Lending Exposures, October 2001, pg. 7.

controls payment by the customer. This loan would be classified as a commodity finance exposure in the SL exposure class, since repayment depends primarily on the proceeds of the sale of the commodity.

2. The bank extends short-term documentary trade credit to a small trader. The circumstances are the same as in the preceding case, except that the trader has not yet contracted for the resale of the commodity. This loan would be classified as a corporate exposure since it may not be self-liquidating, given that the trader has not hedged the transaction's market risk. The bank's credit exposure is primarily to the nonhedged trader that is long the commodity.

3. The bank provides an unsecured nontransactional working capital loan to a small trader, either separately or as part of a transactional credit facility. Such an unsecured loan would be classified as a corporate exposure, since its repayment depends on the trader rather than on the revenues generated by the sale of any specific commodity shipment being financed.

Basic Structure:

1. Asset credit assessment using estimated default statistics.
2. Individual and cumulative grades within each rating module. The cumulative grades are determined by a weighting system and weights assigned by bankers evaluating the financing.
3. Modules include: *Financial Measures* (degree of over-collateralization); *Political and Legal Environment* (country risk, mitigation of country risks); *Asset Characteristics* (liquidity and susceptibility to damage); *Strength of Sponsor* (financial strength of trader, track record, including ability to manage the logistic process, trading controls and hedging policies, quality of financial disclosure); and *Security Package* (asset control, insurance against damages).

Criteria:

• *Degree of overcollateralization*: Should be strong. Loan value of collateral must be no greater than the current fair market value of the collateral at the time of drawing. Commodity collateral should be marked to market frequently and promptly whenever there is any indication of material depreciation in value or any default by the borrower. In the case of material depreciation of value, the commodity collateral must be revalued by a professional appraiser and not assessed by references to statistical methods only. These procedures must be fully reflected in the underlying loan agreement.
  • There must be liquid markets for the collateral to facilitate disposal and existence of publicly available market prices.
  • Periodic valuation and revaluation processes must include physical inspection of the collateral.
• *Country risk*: Strong exposure to country risk (in particular, inland reserves in an emerging country).
• *Mitigation of country risks*: Very strong mitigation, strong offshore mechanisms, strategic commodity, first-class buyer.

- *Legal enforceability of physical collateral*: Banks must confirm enforceability and priority under all applicable laws with respect to the bank's security over the commodity collateral. In addition, bankers must confirm security interests are properly and timely perfected and, in line with this, the bank must continuously monitor existence of priority liens, particularly governmental liens associated with unpaid taxes, wage withholding taxes, or social security claims.
- *Asset control*: The agreement must assure the bank can take command of collateral soon after default.
- *Asset characteristics*: Commodity is quoted and can be hedged through futures or OTC instruments. Commodity is not susceptible to damage.
  Financial strength of trader: Very strong, relative to trading philosophy and risks.
- *Track record, including ability to manage the logistic process*: Extensive experience with the type of transaction in question. Strong record of operating success and cost efficiency.
- *Trading controls and hedging policies*: Watch if trader has experienced significant losses on past deals.
- *Quality of financial disclosure*: All documentation related to credit risk mitigation must be supported by legal opinions in all relevant jurisdictions in addition to documentation pertaining to the security interests themselves.
- *Asset control*: First perfected security interest provides the lender the legal control of the assets at any time if needed.
- *Insurance against damages*: The bank must assure that the collateral is adequately insured against loss or deterioration, in that it has strong insurance coverage including collateral damages with top-quality insurance companies.
  Income-Producing Real Estate, High-Volatility Commercial Real Estate Exposures, and Real Estate Projects under Construction Models are available on the Elsevier Website, at www.ElsevierDirect.com.
  Illustrative Examples: Risk Rating Complete Stabilized Property; Risk Rating Property under Construction
  Location:
  Models are available on the Elsevier Website, at http://booksite.elsevier.com/9780124016903.
  Brief Description: Supervisory slotting income producing real estate developed in Excel by the authors.

Income-Producing Real Estate

Income-producing real estate refers to a method of providing funding to real estate (such as office buildings to let, retail space, multifamily residential buildings, industrial or warehouse space, office parks, supermarkets, shopping centers, and hotels) where the prospects for repayment and recovery on the exposure depend primarily on the cash flows generated by the asset. The primary source of these cash flows would generally be lease or rental payments or the sale of the asset. The borrower may be, but is not required to be, a special purpose entity, an operating company focused on real estate construction or holdings, or an operating company with sources of revenue other than real estate. The distinguishing characteristic of income-producing real estate versus other collateralized corporate exposures is a strong positive correlation between the prospects for repayment of the exposure and the prospects for recovery in the event of default, with both depending primarily on the cash flows generated by a property.

Examples[12]:

1. A bank makes a loan to an SPV to finance the construction of an office building that will be rented to tenants. The SPV has essentially no other assets and has been created just to manage this office building. The office building is pledged as collateral on the loan. This loan should be classified in the income-producing real estate (IPRE) product line of SL, given that the prospects for repayment and recovery depend primarily on the cash flow generated by the asset.

2. A bank makes a loan to a large, well-diversified operating company to finance the construction of an office building that will be primarily occupied by the company. The office building is pledged as collateral on the loan, and the loan is a general obligation of the company. The loan is small relative to the overall assets and debt service capacity of the company. This loan should be classified as a corporate exposure since repayment depends primarily on the overall condition of the operating company, which does not, in turn, depend significantly on the cash flow generated by the asset.

3. A bank makes a loan to an operating company to finance the construction or acquisition of an office building that will be let to tenants. The office building is pledged as collateral on the loan, and the loan is a general obligation of the company. The company has essentially no other assets. The bank underwrites the loan using its corporate procedures. Despite the fact that the borrower is an operating company and the bank uses its corporate underwriting procedures, this loan should be classified in the IPRE product line of SL. The motivation is that the prospects for repayment and recovery both depend primarily on the cash flow generated by the asset. Although there is legal recourse to the project sponsor, which is an operating company, the overall condition of the project sponsor depends primarily on the cash flow generated by the asset. Therefore, in the event of project failure, the sponsor will have essentially no ability to meet its general obligations.

4. Same as Example 3, except that the loan is unsecured. Again, the loan should be classified as IPRE. The fact that the office building is not pledged as collateral on the loan does not override the fact that the loan shares the risk characteristics common to IPRE loans in the SL portfolio.

5. A bank makes a loan to an SPV to finance the acquisition of an office building that will be primarily leased to a large, well-diversified operating

---

[12]Basel Committee on Banking Supervision, Working Paper on the Internal Ratings-Based Approach to Specialized Lending Exposures, October 2001, pg. 3, 4.

company under a long-term lease. The SPV has essentially no other assets and has been created just to manage this office building. The lease is at least as long as the loan term and is noncancellable, and the lease payments completely cover the cash flow needs of the borrower (debt service, capital expenditures, operating expenses, etc.). The loan is amortized fully over the term of the lease with no bullet or balloon payment at maturity. In classifying this loan, the bank may look through the SPV to the long-term tenant, treating it as a corporate loan. This is because the prospects for repayment and recovery depend primarily on the overall condition of the long-term tenant, which will determine the cash flow generated by the asset.

6. Same as Example 5, except that (1) the lease term can be cancelled at some time before the end of the loan term or (2) even if the lease is noncancellable, the lease payments do not fully cover the aggregate loan payments over the life of the loan. This loan should be classified in the IPRE product line of SL because the tenant is not fully committed to the lease sufficient to repay the loan, so pass-through treatment is inappropriate.

High-Volatility Commercial Real Estate

Illustrative Examples: Risk Rating Complete, but Unstabilized Property
Location: Models are available on the Elsevier Website, at http://booksite.elsevier.com/9780124016903.
Brief Description: Supervisory slotting high volatility commercial real estate developed in Excel by the authors.

Lending in the category of high-volatility commercial real estate (HVCRE) represents the financing of commercial real estate that exhibits higher loss rate volatility (i.e., higher asset correlation) compared to other types of specialized lending. Transactions involving HVCRE include the following characteristics:

- Commercial real estate exposures secured by properties of types that are categorized by the national supervisor as sharing higher volatilities in portfolio default rates.
- Loans financing any of the land acquisition, development, and construction phases for properties of those types in such jurisdictions.
- Loans financing any other properties where the source of repayment at origination of the exposure is either the future uncertain sale of the property or cash flows whose source of repayment is substantially uncertain (e.g., the property has not yet been leased to the occupancy rate prevailing in that geographic market for that type of commercial real estate), unless the borrower has substantial equity at risk.

Rating components consist of a comprehensive set of building blocks that determines loss given default, the real estate financing risk grade, and the appropriate loan loss reserve.

Basic Structure:

1. Individual and cumulative grades within each rating module. The cumulative grades are determined by a weighting system and weights assigned by project bankers and project managers in analysis.
2. Modules include: *Real Estate Financial Measures* (market conditions' financial ratios; stress analysis; cash flow predictability for complete and stabilized property, for complete but not stabilized property, and for construction phase[13]); *Asset Characteristics* (location, design and condition, property is under construction [if applicable]); *Strength of Sponsor/Developer* (financial capacity and willingness to support the property, reputation and track record with similar properties, relationship with relevant real estate actors); *Security Package* (nature of lien, assignment of rents for projects leased to long-term tenants, quality of the insurance coverage); and *Composite* (each module's composite rating, final project grade before and after overrides, LGD, dollar exposure risk, estimated 20-year average of 3-year cumulative default risk, and reserve for real estate project write-off).

Criteria:

- *Management experience*: The bank should verify that management is experienced and the sponsors' quality is high and beyond reproach.
- *Management reputation*: Management should have a solid reputation and a lengthy, successful record with similar properties.
- *Competitive properties*: Competitive properties coming to market should be lower than demand.
- *Ratios*: Lenders should ensure the property's debt service coverage ratio is strong (not relevant for the construction phase), while loan-to-value ratio is low given its property type.
  - The loan-to-value is the ratio of the fair market value of an asset to the value of the loan that will finance the purchase. Loan-to-value tells the lender if potential losses due to nonpayment may be recouped by selling the asset.
  - The ratio between an asset's indebtedness and its market value is a strong predictor of its level of credit risk. An asset's loan-to-value is closely related to its debt service coverage ratio.
  - Due to the relationship between a project's debt service coverage ratio and its loan-to-value, these two assessments should work together in identifying property cash flows that are deteriorating and improving. The debt service coverage ratio (DSCR) represents the relationship between an asset's cash flow and its debt service requirement and is a strong predictor of financial capacity.
- *Stress testing should be undertaken*: Stress testing will generally show how a project's cash flows and debt coverage ratios respond to an extreme scenario.

---

[13]Income-producing real estate and HVCRE are similar except for cash flow predictability.

The stress-testing process is important for real estate projects, particularly high-volatility projects as it looks at the "what if" scenarios to flag vulnerabilities.

- Regulators globally are increasingly encouraging the use of stress testing to evaluate capital adequacy. There have also been calls for improved stress testing and scenario analysis, particularly in the wake of the 2008 banking crisis when it quickly became clear that something had gone badly wrong with the banks' stress-testing regimes.
- The property's leases should be long term with creditworthy tenants and maturity dates scattered. The bank should ensure the property has a track record of tenant retention on lease expiration and that the vacancy rate is low. In addition, if expenses (maintenance, insurance, security, and property taxes) are predictable, project risk is more manageable.
- If the property is under construction, lenders should check to see if the property is entirely pre-leased through the tenure of the loan or presold to an investment-grade tenant or buyer, or the bank has a binding commitment for take-out financing from an investment-grade lender.
- Property location should desirable and convenient to services tenants desire. The bank should also ensure the property is appropriate in terms of its design, configuration, and maintenance and is competitive with new properties.
- If the property is under construction, the bank should confirm that contractors are qualified and the construction budget they submit is conservative, while technical hazards are limited.
- If the sponsor/developer made a substantial cash contribution to the construction or purchase of the property and has substantial resources combined with limited direct and contingent liabilities, the bank may consider reducing the project's loan loss reserves. Lenders should also check whether the sponsor/developer's properties are spread out geographically and diversified by property type.
- Property and casualty insurance is necessary, and banks should check policies carefully to ensure that the quality of insurance coverage is appropriate. Insurance protects lenders by providing coverage not only against fire damage (bank has lien on property), but protects cash flow coverage by offering protection for all business-related tangible and intangible assets including money, accounting records, inventory, furniture, and other related supplies.

Camels Bank Rating System

Illustrative Examples: CAMELS Risk Rating Model
Location:
Models are available on the Elsevier Website, at http://booksite.elsevier.com/9780124016903.
Brief Description: Factors by which regulators determine banks' riskiness developed in Excel by the authors.

Under the Uniform Financial Institutions Rating System, the regulatory agencies evaluate and rate financial condition, operational controls, and compliance in six areas. Camels rating is a United States supervisory rating of the bank's overall condition used to classify the nation banks. This rating is based on bank financial statements and on-site examination by regulators such as the Federal Reserve, the Office of the Comptroller of the Currency, and the Federal Deposit Insurance Corporation. The scale is from one to five, with one being strongest and five being weakest.

Capital
Asset quality
Management
Earnings
Liquidity
Sensitivity to market risk

Ratings Key Points
Capital:

- Bank capital fosters public confidence and provides a buffer for contingencies involving large losses, thus protecting depositors from failure.
- Capital funds provide time to recover so losses can be absorbed out of future earnings rather than capital funds, winding down operations without disrupting other businesses and ensuring public confidence that the bank has positioned itself to withstand new hardships placed on it.
- Banks are generally considered solvent as long as capital is unimpaired, asset values are at least equal to adjusted liabilities, and bank assets are diligently appraised, marked-to-market, and cushioned to a high degree against unexpected risks (risk adjusted).
- Bank wide risks falling under protective capital:
  - Credit risk, the potential that a borrower or counterparty will fail to perform on an obligation.
  - Because most earning assets are in the form of loans, poor loan quality is the major cause of bank failure.
  - Market risk arises from adverse movements in market price or rate, for example, interest rates, foreign exchange rates, or equity prices.
  - Liquidity risk is the possibility that an institution will be unable to meet obligations when due because assets cannot be liquidated and required funding is unavailable (referred to as "funding liquidity risk"). Specific exposures cannot be unwound without significantly lowering market prices because of weak market depth or market disruptions ("market liquidity risk").
  - Operational risk is risk that inadequate information systems, operational problems, breaches in internal controls, fraud, or unforeseen catastrophes will result in unexpected losses frequently. Operating risks account for a substantial fraction (20% or more) of large banks' total risk.

- Legal risk is the potential that unenforceable contracts, lawsuits, or adverse judgments can disrupt or otherwise negatively affect the operations or condition of a banking organization.
- Reputation risk is the potential that negative publicity regarding an institution's business practices, whether true or not, will cause a decline in the customer base, costly litigation, or revenue reductions.

Asset Quality:

- Asset quality refers to the amount of risk or probable loss in assets, and the strength of management processes to control credit risk.
- Where losses are judged small and management processes are strong, asset quality is considered good.
- Where losses appear large and management processes are weak, asset quality is poor.
- Monitor level and trend in loan quality at the bank to judge the effectiveness of policies in safeguarding asset quality.
- Use ratios to judge asset quality and reserve adequacy.

Management:

- Quality and character of individuals that guide and supervise the bank, encompassing:
  - Knowledge, experience, and technical expertise (leadership).
  - Organizational and administrative skills.
  - Ability to plan and adapt to changing circumstances.
  - Honesty and integrity.
  - Long-term planning.
  - Adequate plans and back-up procedures in place to address operational contingencies, such as destruction of its building or failure of its automated systems.
  - Set out clear policies and monitor bank's operations for compliance.
  - Bank directors must be active in supervising the implementation of policies, monitoring compliance with them, and reviewing their overall adequacy.
  - Studies of failed banks show that many were governed by inattentive, uninformed, or passive directorates; as a result, many signs of trouble went unrecognized until it was too late and the banks failed.

Earnings:

- Earnings quality refers to composition, level, trend, and stability of bank profits.
- Earnings quality represents a financial report card on how well a bank is doing.
- When earnings quality is good, the bank has sufficient profits to support operations, provide for asset growth, and build capital.

- Profits should grow over time and show little variability.
- Depositors are given an extra margin of protection, and shareholders receive a competitive return on their investment.
  - When earnings quality is poor, a bank may not be able to adequately serve the credit needs of the community, provide for losses, or build capital.
  - Depositors may be at greater risk, and shareholder returns may be inadequate.

Liquidity:

- Bank liquidity refers to the ability of a bank to quickly raise cash at a reasonable cost.
- Banks must have adequate liquidity to serve customers and operate efficiently.
- Those with adequate liquidity are able to pay creditors, meet unforeseen deposit runoffs, satisfy periodic changes in loan demand, and fund loan growth without making costly balance sheet adjustments.
- Banks with poor liquidity may not be able to meet these funding demands and, in extreme cases, may be closed.
- Providing for a bank's liquidity needs can present many practical challenges
  - One reason is that funding demands may change suddenly and unexpectedly in response to economic and other events.

Sensitivity to market risk:

Sensitivity ratings represent examiners' attempts to rate a bank's sensitivity to market risk. This means sensitivity to interest rate risk. For agricultural banks, it may also mean sensitivity to commodity prices, farm prices, or other changes in the future that could adversely affect the institution's earnings or economic capital.

- The sensitivity rating is one of the building blocks in the regulators' drive toward "forward-looking" supervision.
- The sensitivity component will look at sensitivity to market risk today, but by default, is required to consider sensitivity to market risk in the future as well.
- Regulators evaluate management and the board's ability to identify, measure, monitor, and control market risk with respect to a bank's size, complexity, capital, and earnings adequacy in relation to its market risk exposure.

Corporate Risk Rating: Obligor and Facility Grade Requisites

Obligor Risk Grade Key Inputs: Details

Obligor Financial Measures

- Earnings and operating cash flow
- Debt capacity and financial flexibility
- Balance sheet quality and structure
- Corporate valuation
- Contingencies
- Financial reporting
- Management and controls

Remaining Obligor Measures

- Recent developments
- Industry risk
  - Industry segment
  - Industry position
- Country Risk

Facility Risk Grade Key Inputs

A. Documentation
B. Guarantees
C. Collateral
D. Loan purpose
E. Loan tenor
F. Portfolio

Earnings and Operating Cash Flow

Cash flow grades are key drivers of obligor risk. Cash flow is literally the cash that flows through a company during the course of a quarter or the year after adjusting for non-cash, non-operating events. Lenders rely on cash flow statements because cash flows reveal both the degree by which historical and future cash flows cover debt service and borrowers' chances for survival. Cash flow is the firm's lifeblood. The greater and more certain the cash flows, the lower the default probabilities. Volatile cash flow is associated with weak bond ratings, higher yields-to-maturity ratios, and marginal support of the borrower's client bases as its sources of supply.

- Are earnings stable, growing, and of high quality?
- Are margins solid compared to the industry?
- Is cash flow magnitude sufficient to fund growth internally?
- Is operating cash flow strong in relation to present and anticipated debt?
- Is *Net Cash Flow from Operations* sufficient to cover most non-discretionary outlays?

Generic Points

- Cash flow statements retrace all financing and investment activities of a firm for a given period of time.
- Today, more and more lenders rely on the statement of cash flows as a measure of corporate performance because it "images" the probability distribution of future cash flows in relation to debt capacity.
- The greater and more certain the cash flows, the greater the debt capacity of the firm.
- SFAS 95 mandates segregating the borrower's business activities into three classifications: operating, financing, and investing activities. The operating activities section may be presented using either a direct or indirect presentation.
- The direct method focuses on cash and the impact of cash on the financial condition of the business.
- Investing activities involve making and collecting loans and acquiring and disposing of debt or equity instruments and property, plant, and equipment and other productive assets—that is, assets held for or used in the production of goods or services by the enterprise.
- Cash flows from unconsolidated subsidiaries include dividends from subsidiaries, advances and repayments, and the acquisition or sale of securities of subsidiaries. Noncash transactions include equity earnings, translation gains and losses, and consolidations.
- Prudent bankers must obtain a full disclosure concerning the project's future cash flows since construction projects may report noncash earnings— construction accounting or equity earnings.
- Investing activities involve obtaining resources from owners and providing them with a return on, and return of, their investment; borrowing money and repaying amounts borrowed or otherwise settling the obligation; and obtaining and paying for other resources obtained from creditors on long-term credit.

- Operating activities include all transactions and other events that are not defined as investing or financing activities. Operating activities generally involve producing and delivering goods and providing services. Cash flows from operating activities are generally the cash effects of transactions and other events that enter into the determination of income.
- Gross operating cash flow is often the most important line in the cash flow statement, representing net income plus all noncash charges less all noncash credits, plus or minus all nonoperating transactions.
- Cash generated from nonrecurring items may artificially inflate earnings for a period, but it cannot be depended on to provide cash flow to support long-term financing.
- Net income must be the predominant source of a firm's funds in the end.
- For the most part, current assets represent more than half the total assets of many businesses. With such a large, relatively volatile cash investment connected to optimizing shareholder value, current assets are deserving of financial management's undivided attention.
- Net operating cash flow denotes the cash available from gross operating cash flow to internally finance a firm's future growth after working capital demands have been satisfied.
- Sources of cash include decreases in assets, increases in liabilities, and increases in equity. Uses of cash include increases in assets, decreases in liabilities, and decreases in equity.
- The control sheet shows that the change in the cash account is always equal to the difference between sources and uses of cash.
- Sources and uses of cash are usually net changes, meaning the result of many different transactions. Thus, reconciliations lie at the core of cash flow analysis.
- The quality, magnitude, and trend of operating cash flow must be examined carefully since it should contribute a reasonable amount to financing. These features are readily determined by the composition of the gross operating cash flow.
- When depreciation expenses consistently exceed capital expenditures over time, this occurrence is an indication of a business in decline. Eventually, it will lead to a reduction in earnings and profitability.
- If investment in unconsolidated subsidiaries represents a large item on the balance sheet, lenders should ask for financial statements of the unconsolidated subsidiary—or at least a full financial summary.

Debt Capacity and Financial Flexibility

A borrower's ability to "tolerate" debt depends on the availability and volatility of future operating cash flows. Borrowers with relatively stable internal cash streams are less likely to become cash inadequate, debt burdened, or just flat insolvent. Firms with risky (volatile) and uncertain inflow streams are far less able to assume the fixed charges related to debt. Financial risk is not solely a product of debt alone: management's fiduciary responsibility lies in debt management with as discerning an eye as they use to they manage assets. Debt capacity comes down to us in five shades: asset quality, cash flow coverage, product visibility and market strength, wide breath of financial alternatives, and of course an established repayment record of accomplishment.

- Do leverage and coverage ratios fall within the first or second quartile of the industry peer group?
- What alternative sources of debt and capital exist?
- Does the obligor have acceptable investment grade ratings?
- Can the obligor weather economic downturn?
- Are debt maturities manageable?

Balance Sheet Quality and Structure

- Is asset quality acceptable and valued?
- Does the liability structure match the asset structure?
- Do assets show concentration of location or use?
- Are liquidity margins narrow?
- Have asset turnover ratios been evaluated, and are they acceptable?

Corporate Valuation

Management's goal is to facilitate higher levels of value by maintaining parity between operating cash flow, working capital, investments, dividend policy, and financial strategies. Hax and Majluf[14] suggest that firms destroy value if the discounted value of cash flow reaches a critically low mass such that corporate resources are tied up that could be better served elsewhere. Businesses of this sort are "cash traps" and have a permanent negative cash flow that diminishes the contribution of other operating segments having positive cash flows. Under such conditions, asset write-downs and divestiture might be logical choices.

Corporate value is a function of the firm's future cash flow potential and the risks (threats) of those future cash flows. In addition, it is these perceived risks or threats that help define the discounting factor used to measure cash flows in present value terms. Cash flow depends on the industry and the economic outlook for the business' products, current and future competition, sustainable competitive advantage, projected changes in demand, and the business' capacity to grow in

---

[14]*Strategic Management: An Integrative Perspective*, Arnoldo C. Hax and Nicolas Majluf, Prentice Hall; June, 1984.

light of its past financial and operational performance. Risk factors include the business' financial condition (profitability, cash flows, the magnitude of financial and operational leverage, and ability to pay debt), management's ability to sustain operations and profitability, market and industry trends and outlook, competitive forces, the economic environment, legal and regulatory issues, and contingent liabilities. It is for these reasons that the valuation column acts as "fail safe" verification of cash flow performance. Thus, entering a cash flow grade of two, for example, would be inconsistent with grade eight entered in the valuation column.

- Do you develop a shareholder valuation from client projections?
- Is there a healthy spread between the obligor's asset values and the market value of debt?
- What is the spread between the obligor's operating profit margin and the threshold margin? The threshold margin is the minimum profit margin required to increase shareholder value.
- Does the obligor have hidden liabilities that may result in a significant erosion of shareholder value?
- What are probabilities that shareholder value will fall below zero?
- Is the liquidation value of the borrower's assets below the shareholder value?

Contingencies

Understanding the nature of contingencies is important in any effort to complete a fundamental credit analysis. Many potential losses fail to appear on financial reports because they are considered remote. Litigation, guarantees of indebtedness, guarantees to repurchase receivables or property sold or otherwise assigned, and warranty/product liability are obligations. Environmental laws are becoming increasingly complex, with considerable governmental emphasis on compliance. Noncompliance can result in costly cleanups, fines, and penalties, turning a creditworthy company into a financially distressed write-off. Key questions include:

- Are contingencies limited and easily controlled?
- Is potential impact on tangible net worth negligible?
- Is the expected value of contingencies certain?
- Have you determined the amount to accrue for a loss contingency involving litigation?
- Have you checked the nature and amount of large guarantees?
- What are the borrower's obligations related to product liabilities, warranties, and catastrophic losses?
- Have you assessed the probability that other parties will be able to pay their share of any apportioned liability?
- Did you discount any long-term contingent liabilities net of related recoveries?
- Did the borrower fail to record the costs of rectifying environmental problems?

Financial Reporting: General Audits

Bankers should fully understand financial statements, budgets, projections, and other documents supporting loan exposures. They also have a responsibility to insure the audits the bank depends on are representational, faithful, verifiable, neutral, and consistent. Financial statements should not confuse; rather, they should form a comprehensive, cohesive, and coherent body of financial disclosure that spells out the truthful story. In the words of SEC Chairman Arthur Levitt: *"Transparent financial reporting must reign supreme—not only in the US—but around the world."*

- Does a reputable firm regularly complete an audit?
- Are financial reports issued punctually?
- Are statements accurate and complete?
- Have you analyzed business segments having a significant impact on the consolidated entity?
- Did you verify the reliability of information in business reporting?
- Did you check the accountant's file and can confirm that past audits received passed the test of reliability and comparability?
- How does the company and/or its auditors assess whether significant estimates and assumptions are based on the best information available?
- Does the company use independent specialists or sophisticated quantitative techniques to validate or develop key estimates and assumptions?
- What negative events or unsatisfactory outcomes occurred during the year, and how are those presented in the financial statements?
- How do the company's accounting policies, disclosures, format of financial statements, and other financial communications compare to the company's competitors?
- What changes, if any, have there been in the company's accounting policies or in management's application of the policies and the use of estimates and judgments?
- Does the audit contain significant disclaimers or an adverse opinion?
- Is the timeliness of statements problematic?
- Did you review the borrower's business plan carefully in terms of consistency with independent audits?

Financial Reporting: Industry Specific

In financial reporting, a segment is a part of the business that has separate financial information and a separate management strategy. Segments may be geographic, line of business, or departmental. Public companies are required to report by segment in the notes of financial statements. Bankers should understand the unique financial reporting practices of industries they lend to; segment information is germane to assessing the risks and returns of a diversified or multi-locational enterprise. The International Accounting Standard IAS 14 (Revised 1997) published by the International Accounting Board (IASB) is the pronouncement on "Segment Reporting." Bankers should fully understand segment financial reporting practices of firms before they interview the client or finalize risk rating. An example of mining industry financial reporting illustrates this important point. The mining industry includes thousands of companies engaged in mining an array of products including precious metals, base metals, coal, uranium, and other industrial minerals.

- Accounting for and disclosure of mineral reserves
  - How should the costs of acquiring mineral rights or properties be accounted for given these acquisitions may take the form of taking title to properties, obtaining mineral and mining rights, leases, patents, and so on?
  - How should generally accepted principles for determination of the impairment of such costs capitalized be determined?
  - What financial information should be disclosed to investors that will provide relevant, comparable, and transparent disclosures of mineral reserves?
- Accounting for costs associated with exploration and development activities
  - Clarify that costs incurred in exploring for minerals may not be capitalized.
  - Provide definitions of exploration activities (related costs are expensed) versus mine development activities (related costs are capitalized).
- Accounting for development activities performed contemporaneous to production
  - Specify that costs incurred at an operating mine, excluding costs included in inventory, should not be deferred.
  - Provide guidance as to when a mine is under construction versus in production.
  - Due to the nature of the business, specify which, if any, mine development costs incurred prior or subsequent to commercial production commencing should be capitalized.
- Accounting for operating activities
  - Define when it would be appropriate for inventories of precious and base metals to be recorded at other than cost.
  - Provide guidance about common revenue recognition matters unique to the industry.

Management and Controls

Poor management lacks the driving commitment to maximize shareholder value. Management in the lower-risk categories lack adaptability; they are not responsive and innovative in their approach to changing. Management's lack of alertness to changes dealing with measuring and implementing economic, competitive, technological, and financial factors can become extremely detrimental for sustained growth and profitability and will affect default probabilities. High management ratings reflect, on the other hand, management's ability to capture the essence of strategy formulation; that is, to organize the combined disciplines of risk and valuation and to guide the corporation into a winning future.

As you consider the grade, consider how well management responds to changes in the external environment and how they creatively deploy internal resources to improve the firm's competitive position. The key to success is to be able to quantify these factors and integrate them into strategic planning and formulation.

- Is management capable and tried and tested, now and for the near future?
- Are strong operating and financial controls in place?
- Does management have broad industry experience, good continuity, and depth?
- Do senior managers keep changing?
- Is there a succession plan in place?
- In the case of a closely held firm, is there a buy/sell agreement to facilitate ownership transfer upon the death of a principal?
- Have the owners and managers taken salary cuts during difficult times?
- Is management meeting customer or marketplace expectations?
- How efficiently is management running the firm's operations?
- Does management set goals and provide a context for achieving them?

Industry Segment and Position Key Points

- Cyclicality
- Seasonality
- Regulatory issues
- Environmental issues
- Product liability
- Barriers to entry
- Technical obsolescence
- Industry lifecycle
- Does the borrower rank in the first tier of the industry? Is the borrower industry "focused," enjoying a meaningful market share?
- Are performance ratios generally better than industry peers?
- Is the obligor a significant factor in the industry or market?

Bank Regulators and Examiners generally categorize industry analysis on five levels: identification of loans by industry, (2) analysis of industry fundamentals, (3) reporting industry concentrations, (4) quantifying industry risk, and (5) incorporating industry analysis into the loan portfolio.

- *Level 1, Identify Loans by Industry*: (a) attach an industry code to every loan, (b) define industry groups, (c) assign a credit risk rating to every loan,

(d) distinguish between credit rating for borrower versus credit rating for a loan transaction.

- *Level 2, Analyze Industry Fundamentals*: (a) prepare industry studies for loan officers and credit committees (b) evaluate credit risk exposure in relation to industry, (c) identify borrowers by industry, (d) analyze individual bank credits by industry, (e) analyze individual bank credits by industry, (f) perform comparative analysis of industries; analyze financial ratios, (g) compare operating characteristics, (h) understand financial and operating risks, (i) establish industry credit standards (loan structure, collateral coverage, documentation requirements).

- *Level 3, Report Industry Concentrations*: (a) aggregate industry concentrations; use weighted average or percentiles of credit ratings aggregated by industry, (b) analyze risk of portfolio by industry, (c) establish an *industry credit policy committee*, (d) analyze concentrations in relation to capital or loans, (e) set loan limits, (f) use for strategic planning purposes, (g) identify growth industries and problem industries.

- *Level 4, Quantify Industry Risk*: (a) develop industry risk ratings for industry analysis, (b) use an external model from an outside vendor, (c) develop an internal model, (d) utilize economic or industry data, (e) use financial or bond market data as indicators of industry risk, (f) compare industry risk ratings with the weighted average credit rating of the bank's exposure by industry, (g) run scenarios to determine the sensitivity of the loan portfolio to outside shocks, (h) determine covariance of industries or interrelationships among industries.

- *Level 5, Incorporate Industry Analysis Into the Loan Portfolio*: (a) diversify the loan portfolio to reduce industry risk and industry concentrations, (b) distinguish between decision to originate loan and the decision to retain it for the portfolio, (c) use loan sales to reduce concentrations in the portfolio, (d) use industry risk systems to influence loan pricing develop risk adjusted rates of return measures, and (e) assign capital or loan loss reserves.

Country Risk

Cross border risks usually include but are not restricted to:

- *Economic risk*: The significant change in the economic structure or growth rate that produces a major change in the expected return of an investment.
- *Transfer risk*: The risk arising from a decision by a foreign government to restrict capital movements. Restrictions could make it difficult to repatriate profits, dividends, or capital.
- *Exchange risk*: An unexpected adverse movement in the exchange rate. Exchange risk includes an unexpected change in currency regime such as a change from a fixed to a floating exchange rate.

- *Location risk*: The spillover effects caused by problems in a region, in a country's trading partner, or in countries with similar perceived characteristics
- *Sovereign risk*: Deals with whether a government will be unwilling or unable to meet its loan obligations, or is likely to renege on loans it guarantees. Sovereign risk can relate to transfer risk in that a government may run out of foreign exchange due to unfavorable developments in its balance of payments.
- *Political risk*: Risk of a change in political institutions stemming from a change in government control, social fabric, or other noneconomic factors. This category covers the potential for internal and external conflicts, expropriation risk, and traditional political analysis.

Facility Grade Details

Facility risk refers to risks inherent in an individual facility, commitment, or loan: the credit product, the tenor/maturity (long versus short), collateral and support, guarantees, purpose of facility, documentation quality and verification, and portfolio. Attentiveness to all aspects of the loan's structure, particularly the deal's structure, can significantly reduce possibilities of loan downgrades or write-offs. For example, a bank approves a revolving credit to a US subsidiary of a German company secured by a borrowing base (75% receivables, 60% inventory). The bank relies on monthly borrowing base reports from the company. While the borrower is profitable, its financial flexibility is limited by modest debt capacity. Ultimate repayment lies in the ability of the German parent to provide financing. Because of the facility's structure, you suggest a −1 improvement in the grade.

Downgrades to obligor risk ratings are exceptions. However, you might decide to downgrade if the facility calls for unusual tenor, if documentation is weak, if the loan's marketability has deteriorated, or the purpose of the loan is inappropriate.

A. Documentation

Disasters are usually in the cards for bankers who fail to review loan documentation. This means reviewing covenants and recent compliance or violations, checking and updating subordination agreements and corporate resolutions, and, as we saw earlier, making sure that collateral requirements and documents are up to date. A fail-safe rule to follow: risk rating is not finalized until the banker reviews loan documentation under his or her jurisdiction.

B. Guarantees Classification Standards

A guarantee is a written contract, agreement, or undertaking involving three parties. The first party, the Guarantor, agrees to see that the performance of the second party, the Guarantee, is fulfilled according to the terms of the contract, agreement, or undertaking. The third party is the Creditor, or the party to benefit by the performance. For example, party B makes a loan through his bank. The bank desires a guarantor for this loan in case of default by B. B asks A to act as guarantor for his loan. A agrees and signs a Guaranty Agreement. A is the Guarantor, B is the Guarantee, and the bank is the creditor.

For partial guarantees, the worksheet calculates a weighted risk rating. The weighted risk rating depends on: a) prorate credit responsibility and b) the expected default frequency for the obligor and guarantor. Guarantees need to be unconditional and uncontested to be acceptable at full value. At full value, the bank will consider substituting the guarantor's credit grade for obligor's. Coverage may include a few conditions, may include several conditions, may be very conditional, or may be of such limited value that grade improvement is not possible. Guarantees are only as good supporting documents and should be reviewed by legal counsel.

C. Collateral Classification Standards

Collateral represents property pledged as security for the satisfaction of a debt or other obligation. The credit grade assigned to secured loans will depend upon, among other things, the degree of coverage, the economic lifecycle of the collateral versus the term of the loan, possible constraints of liquidating the collateral, and the bank's ability to skillfully and economically monitor and liquidate collateral.

- What is its value compared to credit exposure?
- What is its liquidity, or how quickly may its value be realized and with what certainty?
- Is negotiable collateral held under joint custody?
- Has the customer obtained and filed for released collateral sign receipts?
- Are securities and commodities valued and margin requirements reviewed at least monthly?
- When the support rests on the cash surrender value of insurance policies, is a periodic accounting received from the insurance company and maintained with the policy?
- Is a record maintained of entry to the collateral vault?
- Has the bank instituted a system that ensures that security agreements are filed, collateral mortgages are properly recorded, title searches and property appraisals are performed in connection with collateral mortgages, and insurance coverage (including loss payee clause) is in effect on property covered by collateral mortgages?
- In mortgage warehouse financing, does the bank hold the original mortgage note, trust deed, or other critical document, releasing only against payment?
- Have standards been set for determining percentage advance to be made against acceptable receivables?
- Are acceptable receivables defined?

- Has the bank established minimum requirements for verification of borrower's accounts receivable and established minimum standards for documentation?
- Have accounts receivable financing policies been reviewed at least annually to determine if they are compatible with changing market conditions?
- Have loan statements, delinquent accounts, collection requests, and past due notices been checked to the trial balances that are used in reconciling subsidiary records of accounts receivable financing loans with general ledger accounts?
- Were payments from customers scrutinized for differences in invoice dates, numbers, terms, etc.?
- Does bank record show, on a timely basis, a first lien on the assigned receivables for each borrower?
- Do loans granted on the security of the receivables also have an assignment of the inventory?
- Does the bank verify the borrower's accounts receivable or require independent verification on a periodic basis?
- Does the bank require the borrower to provide aged accounts receivable schedules on a periodic basis?

D. Loan Purpose Classification Standards

- Facility is appropriate for business
- Match funding appropriate
- Financing strategy not appropriate for obligor
- Obligor borrowing short term to finance capital requirements
- Facility used to finance excessive dividends
- Unsecured facility while other lenders have the best collateral
- Bank is subordinated lender
- Poor loan structure

E. Tenor

Ratings Migration Risk

The likelihood of a customer migrating from its current rating category to any other category within the time horizon is frequently expressed in terms of a rating transition matrix similar to that depicted in Exhibit 10A.1. Given the customer's current credit rating (delineated by each row), the probability of migrating to another grade (delineated by the columns) is shown within the intersecting cell. Thus, in the exhibit, the likelihood of a BBB-rated loan migrating to single B within one year would be 0.32%. Since under the DM paradigm only rating migrations into the default state lead to changes in the values of loans, only the last column of this matrix would be relevant. Within the MTM paradigm (discussed ahead), however, the other columns of the transition matrix also play a critical role.

Exhibit 10A.1 Sample credit rating transitions matrix (Probability of migrating to another rating within one year as a percentage)

Credit rating one year in the future

Current credit rating		AAA	AA	A	BBB	BB	B	CCC	Default
	AAA	87.74	10.93	0.45	0.63	0.12	0.10	0.02	0.02
	AA	0.84	88.23	7.47	2.16	1.11	0.13	0.05	0.02
	A	0.27	1.59	89.05	7.40	1.48	0.13	0.06	0.03
	BBB	1.84	1.89	5.00	84.21	6.51	0.32	0.16	0.07
	BB	0.08	2.91	3.29	5.53	74.68	8.05	4.14	1.32
	B	0.21	0.36	9.25	8.29	2.31	63.89	10.13	5.58
	CCC	0.06	0.25	1.85	2.06	12.34	24.86	39.97	18.60

Note: The credit rating transition matrix is based on the historical migration frequencies of publicly rated corporate bonds.
Source: Greg M. Gupton, Christopher C. Finger and Micky Bhatia, CrediMetrics—Technical Document, Morgan Guaranty Trust Co., New York, April 1997, p.76.

F. Portfolio Risk and Investment Factors

The two main points of this section are (1) will the facility have a neutral effect on the bank's portfolio and (2) will the facility provide adequate opportunities in the secondary market? These are important questions. Small banks and banks located in industry/economic pockets (the agriculture Midwest belt, for example) may not have acknowledged credit concentrations within specific industries. A concentration of credit generally consists of direct or indirect (1) extensions of credit and (2) contingent obligations exceeding 25% of the bank's capital structure (tier 1 plus loan loss reserves). This definition does not simply refer to loans, but includes the aggregate of all types of exposures: loans and discounts, overdrafts, cash items, securities purchased outright or under resale agreements, sale of federal funds, suspense assets, leases, acceptances, letters of credit, placements, loans endorsed, guaranteed, or subject to repurchase agreements, and any other actual or contingent liability.

Limitations imposed by bank management and regulators are intended to prevent a client from borrowing an undue amount of the bank's resources, increasing risk by reducing the loan spread among a relatively large number of firms engaged in different businesses. Bankers should recognize the various types of concentrations identified in a loan portfolio before completing the worksheet:

- Loans dependent upon a particular agricultural crop or livestock herd. Banking institutions located in farming, dairying, or livestock areas may grant substantially all their loans to individuals or concerns engaged in and dependent on the agricultural industry. A concentration of this type is commonplace and may be necessary if the bank is to perform the function for which it was chartered.
- The aggregate amount of interim construction loans that do not have firm permanent takeout commitments. In the event that permanent financing is not obtainable, the bank will have to continue financing the project. This longer-term financing subjects the bank to additional liquidity and possibly interest rate risks as well as those risks associated with the real estate itself.
- Loans to groups of borrowers who handle the product from the same industry. Although the borrowers may appear to be independent from one another, their financial conditions may act in similar ways if there is a situation that results in a slowdown of that economic sector.
- Concentrations located in towns economically dominated by one or a few business enterprises. Such banks may extend a substantial amount of credit to the company and to a large percentage of the company's employees.

If exposure concentrations are material, the appropriateness of concentrations should be verified before or during the risk-grading process. Concentrations that involve excessive or undue risks should be examined and reduced over a reasonable period.

References

Gupton, G.M., Christopher, F.C., Bhatia, M., 1997. CreditMetrics—Technical Document. Morgan Guaranty Trust Co., New York, p. 76.

Hax, A.C., Majluf, N., 1984. Strategic Management: An Integrative Perspective. Prentice Hall.

A Basic Credit Default Swap Model

The CDS model functions similarly to an insurance policy, with the swap buyer paying the swap seller a premium to protect against losses resulting from a defined credit event such as bankruptcy, reorganization, moratorium, payment default, or repudiation. The swap purchaser (i.e., the beneficiary) "swaps" the credit risk with the provider of the swap (i.e., the insurer or guarantor), receiving a compensatory benefit if the credit event is triggered. Since the transaction is unilateral (i.e., the purchaser expects the seller to perform if the credit event occurs), it does not take the form of a standard OTC swap contract, which is always bilateral. In fact, the CDS can more properly be considered a credit default put option, giving the purchaser the economics of a long put position on a credit-risky bond price. If the defined credit event occurs, the CDS seller must either accept delivery of the reference asset and pay par value (for an asset that is likely to be trading at a deep discount) through a process known as physical settlement, or compensate the buyer for the difference between par and the post-default price through a process known as cash (or financial) settlement.

The premium (or fee) payable on a CDS can be paid upfront or over the life of the transaction. In practice it is generally set as a basis point spread over LIBOR times the notional amount of the contract. The premium is a function of various factors including time to maturity, probability of reference credit default, expected recovery rate given default, credit rating of the CDS counterparty, and possible correlation between the counterparty and the reference credit; these factors are summarized in Table 11.1.

Valuing credit derivatives is a complex process that requires certain assumptions to be made prior to implementation; indeed, selection of any of the approaches summarized earlier implies that an institution is making assumptions about which valuation process/drivers it believes are most suitable. Model specification is thus an involved project. However, the essence of a credit derivative pricing process can be simplified in order to illustrate the salient points. Our goal in this section is to introduce a basic CDS model to demonstrate the development of a workable framework. Though the model is based on generalizations, it

Table 11.1 Premium Impact Factors

Factor	Pricing Impact
Time to maturity	The longer the maturity, the greater the likelihood of default, the higher the premium
Probability reference credit will default	The higher the probability of default, the higher the premium
Credit rating of CDS counterparty (as seller)	The lower the credit rating of the CDS counterparty, the lower the premium
Correlation between CDS seller and reference credit	The higher the correlation between the seller and reference, the lower the premium
Expected recovery rate	The higher the recovery rate, the lower the premium

provides a starting point related to default probability and recovery rates, and how these can impact credit derivative prices.

We know that a standard CDS provides the protection buyer with a compensatory payment if a reference asset is impacted by a credit event. CDS pricing is typically based on a reference asset's credit spread over a floating rate benchmark (e.g., LIBOR or EURIBOR); the spread reflects the market's assessment of default probability, when default might occur, and what amount is likely to be recovered on the outstanding debt after the company's assets have been liquidated.

The pricing approach can be considered in two ways:

- Establishing the current probability that the reference credit will default during the chosen exposure period; the default probability will vary by tenor, i.e., the longer the tenor, the greater the default probability.
- Hypothesizing that the market price of the CDS reflects the true price of the reference entity's credit and that the default probability implied in this price is correct.

An estimate of the recovery rate is required in either case. If we find that the credit derivative market is truly arbitrage-free, however, the two approaches should yield the same result.

Determining Probability of Default from Market Spreads

In order to develop the pricing model, we need to determine the credit spread over the risk-free rate for a risky bond. The spread compensates the investor for accepting the probability that the credit may default; the higher the perceived probability of default, the higher the compensation demanded by the investor, and the higher the resulting spread. We can extract this implied probability of default from the quoted market spread.

The future value (FV) of a continuously compounded return on a risk-free investment over time can be expressed as:

$$e^{rate*time}$$

where e is the natural logarithm.

For example, the FV of $1 invested for five years at a continuously compounded rate of 3% is:

$$= \exp\{0.03^*5\} = \$1.1618$$

The present value (PV) of a cash flow can be computed by using the negative exponential. For instance, the PV of $1 to be received in five years at a 3% continuously compounded rate is:

$$= \exp\{-0.03^*5\} = \$0.8607.$$

We know that the return for a risky bond must also include the credit spread, so we expand the equation as follows:

$$e^{(rate+spread)*time}$$

Assuming that the credit spread over the risk-free rate for this bond is 75 bps (i.e., 0.0075), the FV is:

$$= \exp\{(0.03 + 0.0075)^*5)\} = \$1.2062$$

If the spread of 75 bps truly compensates the investor for accepting the associated probability of default, then the return on the risk-free bond should equal the return on the risky bond, adjusted for the probability of default (PD), in a no-arbitrage market. We can express this as follows:

$$e^{rate*time} = e^{(rate+spread)*time}*(1 - PD)$$

If this equation holds true, then we can rearrange terms and solve for the probability of default, PD:

$$PD = (1 - e^{(-spread*time)})$$

Using our previous example, the cumulative three-year probability of default for a reference with a credit spread of 75 bps is:

$$PD(Yr = 3) = 1 - e^{(-0.0075^*3)} = 2.225\%$$

This calculation can be performed for all maturity combinations. For example, the cumulative default probability in year two (using 75 bps) is 0.995%. This is computed as follows:

$$PD(Yr = 2) = 1 - e^{(-0.0075^*2)} = 1.489\%$$

Similarly, the default probability from year two to three is the difference between the two cumulative probabilities as follows:

$$PD(\text{Yr 2 to Yr 3}) = PD(Yr = 3) - PD(Yr = 3)$$
$$= 2.225\% - 1.489\%$$
$$= 0.736\%$$

When calculating these figures, we must remember that there exists a term structure of credit spreads. For most reference credits, the further out in time we go the greater the probability of default and the greater the credit spread; the term structure is said to be positive. There is, however, one exception to this rule; CCC-rated credits tend to feature a negative term structure, as there is a perception that while such credits may default in the near term, they may actually survive for the long-term if they overcome short-term difficulties (such as a liquidity crisis). Table 11.2 illustrates this phenomenon.

Figure 11.1 illustrates the difference in term structure across these different credit ratings. Notice how the rates increase with time for all ratings except for the CCC-rated credits, which are decreasing with time. Additionally, notice how the terms structures are higher for the lesser rated credits.

We have described how the probability of default can be determined, but our calculations have not yet considered recovery rates. We therefore return to our original equation and consider how recoveries can impact value.

Probability of Default and Recoveries

When a credit defaults, we know that there is a strong likelihood that creditors will receive some recovery value after the defaulting company's assets are liquidated; only in the most severe insolvencies, based on extreme asset overvaluation, might recoveries be close to zero. Our original equation assumes no recoveries, meaning that any capital invested would be completely lost in the event of default; this assumption must therefore be adjusted to reflect greater market consistency. By incorporating the recovery rate RR, any loss can be described as (1-RR). The adjusted formula indicates that the probability of default is the PV of the credit spread, extended to reflect recoveries:

$$PD = \frac{(1 - e^{(-spread^* time)})}{1 - RR}$$

We illustrate how this formula works by using a three-year spread of 75 bps and an assumed recovery rate of 55%:

$$PD = \frac{(1 - e^{(-0.0075^*3)})}{1 - 0.55} = \frac{2.225}{0.45} = 4.944\%$$

Table 11.2 Credit Interest Rate Term Structure (%)

Yr.	Risk-free Rate	AAA Rates	AAA Spread	A Rates	A Spread	BBB Rates	BBB Spread	CCC Rates	CCC Spread
1	3.00	3.25	0.25	3.45	0.45	3.70	0.70	11.00	8.00
2	3.35	3.70	0.35	3.90	0.55	4.15	0.80	10.35	7.00
3	3.65	3.95	0.30	4.30	0.65	4.55	0.90	9.65	6.00
4	3.95	4.25	0.30	4.65	0.70	4.90	0.95	8.95	5.00
5	4.20	4.55	0.35	4.95	0.75	5.20	1.00	8.70	4.50
6	4.50	5.00	0.50	5.25	0.75	5.50	1.00	8.50	4.00
7	4.75	5.25	0.50	5.55	0.80	5.80	1.05	8.25	3.50
8	5.00	5.50	0.50	5.90	0.90	6.15	1.15	7.50	2.50
9	5.20	5.75	0.55	6.20	1.00	6.45	1.25	7.20	2.00
10	5.35	5.95	0.60	6.45	1.10	6.70	1.35	7.10	1.75

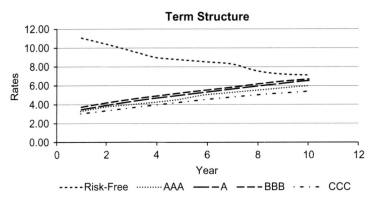

FIGURE 11.1 Interest Rates Term Structure

The formula generates an adjusted three-year cumulative probability of default of 4.944%, which is higher than the 2.225% calculated earlier when recoveries were assumed to be zero. Note that if we had used a credit spread of 50 basis points and a recovery rate of 50%, we would again have generated a 1.489% probability of default. Thus, if using a 50% recovery rate still requires a 50 bp spread to compensate for the default risk, it follows that the probability of default must be higher. This simple example shows the close relationship between market credit spreads, default probabilities, and recovery rates.

Default and Survival Probabilities

We noted earlier that the probabilities of survival and default for a particular period must always equal 1. There is, however, a conditional aspect in credit derivatives pricing that must be considered. The probability of default in some future period exists only if the credit has not defaulted by the end of the previous period. This means that the probability of survival up to a particular future point *plus* the sum of the probability of defaults to that point must equal 1. We extend Table 12.3 by including a total for the probability of default column; this yields the results in Table 12.5. Looking at the 10-year period, we note that if we sum the default probabilities we obtain a total of 0.2989. Adding this to the 10-year probability of survival (0.7011) yields a total of 1. The probability of survival to a specific point is a key factor in assessing the value of the CDS premium.

Table 11.3 Assume Yield Curve and BBB Default and Survival Probabilities

Period	Years	Futures/swap prices	BBB Spread	Discount Factors	Probability of Default	Cumul Prob of Default	Probability of Survival
1	0.5	3.00	0.70	0.9851	0.0035	0.0035	0.9965
2	1.0	3.35	0.80	0.9671	0.0080	0.0115	0.9885
3	1.5	3.65	0.90	0.9467	0.0134	0.0249	0.9751
4	2.0	3.95	0.95	0.9240	0.0188	0.0437	0.9563
5	2.5	4.20	1.00	0.9003	0.0247	0.0684	0.9316
6	3.0	4.50	1.00	0.8737	0.0296	0.0979	0.9021
7	3.5	4.75	1.05	0.8468	0.0361	0.1340	0.8660
8	4.0	5.00	1.15	0.8187	0.0450	0.1790	0.8210
9	4.5	5.20	1.25	0.7914	0.0547	0.2337	0.7663
10	5.0	5.35	1.35	0.7653	0.0653	0.2989	0.7011
						Total = 0.2989	

Present Value of the CDS Premiums

Our next step is to calculate the present value of the CDS premium stream to assess whether compensation for default risk is adequate. The PV of the spread for the first period is given as:

= CDS Spread*Discount Factor*Probability of Survival to end of period 1

*(actual days/basis for period 1)

We are attempting to determine the PV of the CDS spread which, when calculated, will be the same for all periods in a given maturity. The discount factor is simply the zero-coupon interest rate required to bring the future cash flow to today's value. The probability of survival is applied to the future period, as this indicates the probability of actually receiving the premium in the future. The day count for the period in question is applied to adjust the value. To simplify this process, we assume that each semi-annual period is exactly half a year (i.e., 0.5 years instead of actual/basis); the formula can, of course, be made more general.

Returning to our continuing example, the first period yields:

PV of CDS Payment, period 1 = CDS Spread*0.9851*0.9965*0.5 years

The same calculation for period two is:

PV of CDS payment, period 2 = CDS Spread*0.9671*0.9885*0.5 years

We can repeat this process for all 10 periods.

Using S to denote the CDS spread, the sum of the PVs of spread payments over k periods is calculated as:

$$PV_{spread,k} = S\sum_{i=1}^{k} DF_i{}^*PS_i{}^*0.5$$

This produces the PV of all of the CDS spreads received or paid during the life of the transaction, assuming no default, and represents the denominator in the CDS pricing formula described ahead.

We next consider how to evaluate the PV of the cash flow stream, assuming that default occurs.

Present Value of a Default Payment

If a default occurs at the beginning or end of a period, the CDS protection seller is only entitled to the CDS premiums up to that point. However, the seller of protection is entitled to receive the recovery value of the underlying asset. We can capture the PV of default payments in period 1 as:

PV of Default Payment = (1 − Recovery)*Discount Factor for period 1*

Probability of Default in Period 1.

Assuming default and a recovery rate of 40%, the PV of the loss in period 1 is thus:

$$PV \text{ of Default Payment} = (1 - 0.40)^*0.9851^*0.0035$$

Using the discount factor and probability of default for period 2 yields:

$$PV \text{ of Default Payment} = (1 - 0.40)^*0.9671^*0.0080$$

Summing these gives us the PV of the possible default payments. Using RR as the assumed recovery rate, we can summarize the process in general over k periods as follows:

$$PV_{default,k} = (1 - RR) \sum_{i=1}^{k} F_i{}^* PD_i$$

This equation forms the numerator in the total pricing equation ahead.

Calculating the CDS Spread Premium

We now have an equation that computes the PV of the CDS spread premiums and an equation that gives us the PV of any possible default payment. The value of a CDS at inception is based on equal pay/receive flows between the two counterparties; this is consistent with standard swap convention. The two equations developed previously should, therefore, be equal to one another if the transaction is priced fairly:

$$PV_{spread,k} = PV_{default,k}$$

or

$$S \sum_{i=1}^{k} DF_i{}^* PS_i{}^*0.5 = (1 - RR) \sum_{i=1}^{k} DF_i{}^* PD_i$$

This equation can now be simplified and rearranged in order to solve for the CDS spread S:

$$S = \frac{(1 - RR) \sum_{i=1}^{k} DF_i{}^* PD_i}{\sum_{i=1}^{k} DF_i{}^* PS_i{}^*0.5}$$

The calculation can be performed for each period. We can then add the PVs to determine the CDS premium for this transaction; the results are given in Table 11.4.

The formula we have developed gives us calculated CDS premiums for different maturities. Given the parameters and assumptions, a six-month CDS would

Table 11.4 Complete CDS Premium Pricing

Period	Years	Futures/ Swap Prices	BBB Spread	Discount Factors	Prob of Default	Prob of Survival	Denominator (Eq 6.4)	Numerator (Eq 6.5)	CDS Price
1	0.5	3.00	0.70	0.9851	0.0035	0.9965	0.4908	0.0024	0.0049
2	1	3.35	0.80	0.9671	0.0080	0.9885	0.9688	0.0078	0.0081
3	1.5	3.65	0.90	0.9467	0.0134	0.9751	1.4304	0.0167	0.0117
4	2	3.95	0.95	0.9240	0.0188	0.9563	1.8722	0.0289	0.0154
5	2.5	4.20	1.00	0.9003	0.0247	0.9316	2.2916	0.0444	0.0194
6	3	4.50	1.00	0.8737	0.0296	0.9021	2.6857	0.0625	0.0233
7	3.5	4.75	1.05	0.8468	0.0361	0.8660	3.0524	0.0839	0.0275
8	4	5.00	1.15	0.8187	0.0450	0.8210	3.3885	0.1097	0.0324
9	4.5	5.20	1.25	0.7914	0.0547	0.7663	3.6917	0.1400	0.0379
10	5	5.35	1.35	0.7653	0.0653	0.7011	3.9599	0.1749	0.0442

feature a premium of 0.49%, while a five-year CDS would command a premium of 4.42%.

Let us next examine the three-year (six-period) CDS price in more detail. First, the period 4 (year two) denominator is calculated:

$$= (0.8737^*0.9021^*0.5)$$
$$+ 2.6857 \text{ (the sum of the calculations to period 3)} = 3.0798$$

Next, the period 4 numerator is computed:

$$= ((1 - 0.30)^*0.9021^*0.0296)$$
$$+ 0.0625 \text{ (the sum of the calculations to period 3)} = 0.0187$$

Finally, the CDS premium S is obtained:

$$= 0.0187/3.0798 = 0.61\%$$

This corresponds to the result contained in the table.

Other Considerations

The process described previously gives us a straightforward way of calculating CDS premiums from default probabilities. The calculation relies heavily on data input, and we have already discussed the difficulty of accurately forecasting default probabilities and recovery rates; these are sensitive assumptions that can impact significantly on model accuracy. The CDS premiums quoted in the market reflect assumptions, and the bid-offer spread for a particular entity and maturity reflects the market's current evaluation of the assumptions. It is possible, of course, to use market CDS prices and adjust the probabilities to reflect the market's actual CDS premiums; doing so assumes that the recovery rate used by the market is the same as the one used in the model.

An institution believing that its proprietary assessments of recovery rates and default probabilities are more accurate than those contained in the market can take a position based on that belief. Higher expected recovery rates or lower default probabilities would encourage the institution to sell protection at a higher market rate than might otherwise be justifiable. Similarly, an assessment that the market has underestimated the probability of default or overestimated the recovery rate would encourage the purchase of protection at the lower market rate. Commercial products such as CreditMetrics and CreditRisk supply market participants with ready-made applications to manage the pricing factors discussed above. However, it appears that the application of products such as these has been somewhat limited, and the main driver of CDS premiums is still derived from the pricing of bonds in the capital markets.

To reiterate, any method used to price a CDS premium is only as good as the assessment of the probability of default over a specific period and the accuracy of the recovery rate. Most efforts by market makers to improve their pricing process concentrate on refining these two factors.

References

Duffy, G., 1999. An Introduction to Credit Derivatives. J. Risk Finance.

Glantz, M., Banks, E., Siegel, P., 2007. Creit Derivatives. Techniques to Manage Credit Risk for Financial Professionals. McGraw-Hill.

Geoff, C., April, 2010. Credit Derivatives: Trading, Investing, and Risk Management (The Wiley Finance Series).

He, J., Credit Derivatives and Commercial Banks' Risk Management, Acad. J. Article Can. Soc. Sci., 6: 4.

Schönbucher, P., June 2003. Credit Derivatives Pricing Models: Models, Pricing and Implementation (The Wiley Finance Series).

Tavakoli, J., 2001. Credit Derivatives & Synthetic Structures: A Guide to Instruments and Applications, second ed. John Wiley.

Vasudev, P., January 2013. Credit derivatives and the Dodd–Frank Act: Is the regulatory response appropriate? Journal of Banking Regulation advance online publication 23.

Multi-Asset Corporate Restructurings and Valuations[1]

12

This chapter focuses on corporate restructuring, value creating, and decision making under uncertainty. We discuss optimal funding allocation, corporate restructuring, risk budgeting, and stress testing. We present techniques based on real-world indicators to construct a multi-asset corporate portfolio and offer ways to minimize risk. This chapter integrates Monte Carlo simulations with stochastic optimization as a means to realize shareholder value and uncover unacceptable outcomes such as high volatility and low margins.

"The sum of the parts equals the whole"; similarly, the sum of operating subsidiaries (synergy adjusted) forms a consolidated corporate entity. We measure divisional contributions under conditions of uncertainty first, and from there we can decide on consolidated corporate and equity values using a valuation model like the McKinsey valuation model or Real Options Valuation's model (ROV/ Modeling Toolkit/Valuation/Valuation Model; consolidated analysis is beyond the scope of this chapter). Our goal will be to advance a debt financed divisional stochastic portfolio optimization model.

The essence of shareholder wealth and strategy formulation is to organize the combined disciplines of risk and valuation and to guide the corporation into a new and better future. The key to effective strategic planning, then, has to deal with two relevant dimensions: (1) responding to changes in the external environment and (2) creatively deploying internal resources to improve the competitive position of the firm. Lack of alertness to changes dealing with measuring and implementing economic, competitive, technological, and financial factors can become detrimental for sustained growth and profitability. The key to success is to be able to quantify these factors and integrate them into corporate and shareholder valuation and strategic planning and formulation. Most importantly, a technical planning process must be responsive to individual talents and capabilities that reside within the corporation.

Indeed, valuations are blueprints for long-term planning; short-term events like today's stock price are only loosely tied to intrinsic value. Management may be

---

[1]Software screenshots are the property of Real Options Valuation, and are reproduced with permission.

under significant pressure to deliver value to stockholders whether or not short-term numbers support it. Some companies have even played an earnings game to jump the stock price. With executive compensation tied to options, the so-called positive spin (on stock prices) can be tempting, particularly post debt crisis. A tactic for the less forthright is to publicize one set of results in a quarterly (news) release, then file a different (less positive) earnings report with regulators weeks later. We leave random walks and spins and turn to old-fashioned intrinsic valuations, the likes of which embrace well-designed strategic planning, growth potential, and, of course, key free cash flow components and value drivers that deliver the cash.

Before we separate our corporate entity into operating subsidiaries and measure individual intrinsic values, let us see what discounted free cash flow valuation is all about. The discounted cash flow method is a powerful tool to analyze complex situations. However, the DCF method is subject to substantial assumption bias. Even slight changes in underlying assumptions can drastically alter valuation results. In order to reduce the possibility of assumption bias, we require (1) a vigilant divisional and corporate historical cash flow analysis and (2) seed input, that is, a stochastic value-driver forecast.

Corporate value is a function of the firm's future cash flow potential and the risks (threats) of those future cash flows (remember the key point: value drivers deliver valuation). In addition, it is these perceived risks or threats that help define the discounting factor used to measure cash flows in present value terms. Both divisional and corporate cash flow depend on industry factors and the economic outlook for the business' products, current and future competition, sustainable competitive advantage, projected changes in demand, and capacity (measured in this chapter by divisional contributions) to grow in light of its past financial and operational performance. Risk factors include the business' financial condition (profitability, cash flows, the magnitude of financial and operational leverage, and ability to pay back debt), management's ability to sustain operations and profitability, market and industry trends and outlook, competitive forces, the economic environment, legal and regulatory issues, and contingent liabilities—all under uncertainty conditions. Indeed, while stochastic shareholder valuations deal in data—plenty of it—valuations and risk assessments entail good old-fashioned intuition and creativity; it calls for a special kind of due-diligence, one that builds on stochastic technology, structure, and purpose.

Building Blocks of Valuation

We determine corporate worth by estimating the following three "building blocks" of value:

1. Cash flow from operations
2. Long-term horizon
3. Risk and time value of money

Cash Flow from Operations

By concentrating on an entity's operating cash flow forecast, we can make a distinction between operating and financing decisions. Once we estimate cash flow, we consider risk by discounting those cash flows by the cost of capital. A good place to start is due diligence with respect to gross operating cash flow, a commanding valuation component since gross operating cash flow turns income to cash. Gross operating cash flow equals net income adjusted for noncash charges, noncash credits, and non-operating events. We then factor in operating cash needs relative to operating current assets and operating cash sources relative to operating current liabilities. Finally, we consider investment activities to arrive at free cash flow that is discounted back to present value by the cost of capital.

The estimation of cash flow involves the employment of forecast techniques that try to include the best possible information. When estimating company cash flow, it is not practical to estimate discrete cash flow to infinity for a going concern. Therefore, a simplifying assumption must be made to estimate the value of cash flow generated after a discrete time horizon (or "forecast period"). Instead of considering value equal to the present value of a single stream of cash flow, think of it as the sum of the present value of cash flow from a discrete forecast horizon plus the present value of a "residual" value estimate.

This presents us with the necessity of having to develop both an estimate of how long we forecast discrete cash flow for a divisional operation or the corporation itself (i.e., forecast horizon) and to make a simplifying assumption regarding the value of cash flow generated after the end of the forecast horizon (i.e., the residual value).

Choosing the Length of the Forecast Horizon

The length of the forecast horizon is not simply a "convenient" period of time in which management feels comfortable in estimating financial performance (i.e., the typical long-range planning period is three years), but a period based on the economics of the company and industry. As a result, we refer to this time horizon as a company's value growth duration (VGD). As will be demonstrated in the next section on driver analysis, the VGD is as an important measure as any of the key "value drivers" (i.e., sales growth, operating margin, etc.).

As Porter (1980) has emphasized, in a competitive market with free entry firms cannot earn returns substantially greater than the cost of capital (hurdle rate) for long because that would encourage other firms to enter and drive down prices and thus returns. Normal accounting profits will be just enough to pay for the cost of capital and compensate the owners for any unique inputs to production (e.g., management expertise) that they provide.

On the road to profits are barriers to entry such as patents, economies of scale, research costs, product differentiation, or preferential access to scarce

Table 12.1 Factors that can Affect VGD	
Existence of:	**Effect on VGD**
Proprietary Technologies	Lengthen
Patented Products	Lengthen
Limited Product Life Cycle	Shorten
Established Brands	Lengthen
Extensive Distribution Channels	Lengthen
Industry-Wide Price Competition	Shorten

resources. Hence, the main assumption regarding the length of the forecast period is that it should be equal to the period management expects the rate of return on its new investments to exceed the required rate of return (cost of capital) for the company or investment. In addition, when estimating the appropriate VGD, management considers the industry dynamics that will affect the firm's competitive position on both divisional and corporate levels. Table 12.1 contains a short list of potential factors that can affect that position and the relevant effect on its VGD.

Residual Value

Residual value signifies the value of cash flow reasonably expected to extend beyond the forecast horizon. We determine this value, also known as the terminal value, by multiplying the cash flow at the end of the forecast horizon (the first day of the residual period is the last day of the forecast horizon) by a multiple. Selected multiples commonly use the median multiple of total invested capital to EBITDA of the firm or comparable companies. The selected multiple may be discounted to reflect company performance or size characteristics relative to comparable companies. This is quite similar to dividing the cash flow by the weighted average cost of capital and including a growth factor.

Once we estimate the discrete forecast horizon cash flow, a simplifying assumption can be made regarding the cash flow generated after the forecast period. Investment rate of return for new investments during the VGD greater than the cost of capital creates value during the forecast horizon. However, beyond the forecast horizon—that is, during the *residual period*—a simplifying assumption is generally made whereby the average rate of return on new investments will equal the cost of capital. Understand that this is not necessarily a no-growth state; rather, the implication is that any post forecast period growth is not expected to increase shareholder value since the rate of return on these new investments equals the discount rate (i.e., cost of capital). In any way of speaking, this is the same as a no-growth state.

Incorporated in our discounted cash flow analysis, we will use the last forecast year's taxable operating profit (after-tax) as a proxy for continuing cash flow in the residual period (perpetuity).

The assumptions supporting the use of operating profit (after-tax) as the perpetuity cash flow instead of operating cash flow is as follows:

1. In growing capital-intensive firms, capital expenditures in any given year will be greater than depreciation expense.
2. Incremental fixed capital investment (the amount above depreciation expense necessary for new growth) and incremental working capital investment have already been determined to return only the cost of capital and therefore would not have any effect on the NPV of the firm if included. Therefore, they are excluded to simplify the calculation.

We employ the perpetuity method of calculating residual value as it provides a methodology consistent with the shareholder value approach during the discrete forecast period. Of course, there may be instances where a more aggressive assumption regarding the value impact from new investments is appropriate. Variations of the perpetuity method can be made to accommodate these alternate situations.

Market Signals Analysis

In order to estimate what the specific VGD should be for a given company (instead of speaking in relative terms), it is useful to gain insight into what the stock market is estimating the length of the horizon to be. Using market signals analysis, we can gain that insight. Having a reasonable handle on a company's forecasted cash flow and risk (i.e., cost of capital), we can "solve" for the known stock price. If our discrete period cash flow forecast is earning rates of returns above the cost of capital, we know that our estimate of value will increase by extending the forecast horizon. This, in essence, delays the time when the residual value assumptions (new investments earning only the cost of capital) will kick in. This method obviously requires a publicly traded company for which to compare estimated value to stock market value. Privately held companies (or divisions of public companies, for that matter) can estimate their VGDs by performing similar analysis on publicly traded peer companies.

Value Driver Structure

Knowing what "value drivers" have the largest impact value gives management a basis to formulate strategies to maximize the value of the firm. The seven observable value drivers are:

1. Sales growth rate
2. Operating profit margin

3. Incremental working capital investment
4. Incremental fixed capital investment
5. Cash tax rate
6. Cost of capital
7. Value growth duration

Deterministic Value Drivers

Deterministic valuation spreadsheets capture uncertainty in one of three ways: point estimates, range estimates, and what-if scenarios (or classical worst, base, and optimistic cases). Point estimates occur when you use what you think are the most likely values (technically referred to as the modes) for the uncertain variables. These estimates are the easiest, but can return very misleading results. For example, try crossing a river with an average depth of three feet; or consider what happens if it takes you an average of 25 minutes to get to the airport and you leave 25 minutes before your flight. You will miss your plane 50% of the time.

Range estimates typically calculate three scenarios: the best case, the worst case, and the most likely case. While estimates show you the range of outcomes, probabilities are absent. What-if scenarios are usually based on range estimates involving only scenario combinations that you think of. What is the worst case? What if sales are best case, while expenses are the worst case? What if sales are averages, but expenses are best case? What if sales are average, expenses average, but next month sales are flat? Deterministic analysis is time consuming and data substantial, but cannot deliver probabilities.

A model is a spreadsheet that has taken the leap from being a data organizer to an analysis tool. A model represents a process with combinations of data, formulas, and functions. As you add cells that help you better understand and analyze your data, your data spreadsheet becomes a spreadsheet model.

Stochastic Analysis of Multi-Asset Restructuring: A Banker's Perspective

The broad array of restructuring initiatives has fostered extensive academic literature on the impact of restructuring. Although many studies have reported that restructuring improves performance, some report no or even negative effects. The diversity in outcomes is to be expected because the rubric of restructuring includes a diverse array of company actions, from selling old lines of business to acquiring new lines, from eliminating debt to repurchasing stock, and from introducing business units to downsizing work forces.

Portfolio restructuring is associated with significant changes in the mix of a firm's assets or the lines of business in which a firm operates, including liquidations, divestitures, asset sales, and spin-offs. A company may restructure its business portfolio for several reasons. To refocus, it can dispose of a unit peripheral to the core business. Companies may restructure their product mix to boost sales and profits or to survive when the corporate structure becomes impaired. In successful restructurings, management not only actualizes lucrative new projects, but abandons existing projects when they no longer yield sufficient returns, thereby channeling resources to more value-creating uses.

Corporate restructuring has become a staple of management life over the long term. Numerous firms have reorganized divisions, streamlined operations, and spun-off their divisions. As in most strategic decisions, the common driver has been the assumption that such actions spur company performance. For supportive experience, company executives often turn to publicized accounts of restructurings elsewhere that have worked well. They then take their own actions in the name of enhancing productivity, reducing costs, or enlarging shareholder wealth.

On one level, restructuring can be viewed as changes in financing structures and management. At another level, restructuring may be operational, in response to production overhauls, market trends, technology, and industry or macroeconomic disturbances. It is often the essence of strategy formulation—that is, management's response to changes in the environment—to improve the firm's competitive position by creatively deploying internal resources. Indeed, changing operating and financial structures in pursuit of a long-run strategy is a key corporate goal and the most direct path to shareholder value.

For banks called on to finance multi-asset corporate restructurings, things are a bit different. For example, most loans provide a fixed return over fixed periods that are dependent on interest rates and the borrower's ability to pay. A good loan will be repaid on time and in full. Hopefully the bank's cost of funds will be low, with the deal providing attractive risk-adjusted returns. If the borrower's business excels, the bank will not participate in upside corporate values (except for a vicarious pleasure in the firm's success). However, if a borrower ends up financially distressed, lenders share much, perhaps most, of the pain.

Two disparate goals—controlling default (credit) risk, the bank's objective, and value maximization, a traditional corporate aspiration—are often at odds, particularly if borrowers want term money to finance excessively aggressive projects. In the vast majority of cases of traditional credit analysis, in which the spotlight focuses on deterministically drawn projections, hidden risks are often exceedingly difficult to uncover. Devoid of viable projections, bankers will repeatedly fail to bridge gaps between their agendas and client aspirations.

Bankers have a duty to advance both their analytics and communication skills; senior bank officials and clients alike need to "get the deal done" and insure risk/reward agendas are set in equilibrium. As we pointed out earlier, the most efficient way to achieve results is to take a stochastic view of strategic plans rather than falling back on old-fashioned deterministic base case/conservative forecast scenarios. Let us start with the following fundamentals:

- Stochastically driven optimization models allow bankers to more realistically represent the flow of random variables.

- In negotiating restructuring loans, borrowers (and bankers) can determine under stochastic assumptions optimal amounts to invest in and/or borrow to finance projects.
- McKinsey and Company, Inc.[2] suggests that business units should be defined and separated into lines of business. Business units should be broken down into the smallest components and analyzed at the base level first.
- Consolidating financials, rather than consolidated reports, should be used to perform business-unit valuations.
- In this post-crisis age, bankers will likely think twice before failing to look beyond consolidated financials to get restructuring or project finance deals done; above all, they will note if the credit grade is weak.
- Knowing the market value and volatility of the borrower's assets is crucial in determining the probability of default.
- A firm's leverage has the effect of magnifying its underlying asset volatility. As a result, industries with low asset volatility can take on larger amounts of leverage, while industries with high asset volatility tend to take on less.
- After restructuring is optimized at the unit stage, unit level valuations are linked to the borrower's consolidated worksheet to process corporate valuations.

Mini Case

Consider the data in Excel spreadsheets depicted in Tables 12.2 and 12.3 and Figure 12.1. The worksheets depict the management's original restructuring plan, and the model can be found in http://booksite.elsevier.com\9780124016903 ABC

Table 12.2 Product Line Assumptions			
	Distribution	**Operating Profit Margin Range**	**Operating Profit Margin Most Likely**
All-Weather Resin Wicker Sets	Triangular	0.085–0.115	0.097
Commuter Mobile Office Furniture	Triangular	0.066–0.086	0.076
Specialty Furniture	Normal	Mean = 0.035	SD = 0.0035
Custom-Built Furniture	Uniform	0.045–0.055	None

[2]Valuation (Third Edition), McKinsey & Company, Inc., Tom Copeland et al, John Wiley & Sons, 2000.

Bank is asked to approve a $3,410,000 loan facility for the hypothetical firm RI Furniture Manufacturing LTD. Management wants to restructure four of its operating subsidiaries. In support of the facility, the firm supplied the bank with deterministic base case and conservative consolidating and consolidated projections: income statement, balance sheet, and cash flows.

The deterministic or static forecasts tendered the bank limited the variability of outcomes. From a banker's perspective, it is often difficult to single out which of a series of strategic options the borrower should pursue if the bank fails to understand differences in the range and distribution shape of possible outcomes and the most likely result associated with each option. Indeed, an overly aggressive restructuring program might reduce the firm's credit grade and increase default probabilities. We will not let this happen. Undeniably, this deal deserves stochastic analytics rather than a breadbasket consisting of passé deterministic tools.

From (deterministic) consolidating projections, bankers developed a stochastic spreadsheet depicted in Figure 12.1. This spreadsheet included maximum/

Table 12.3 Investment Boundaries

Product Line	Lower Bound	Upper Bound
All-Weather Resin Wicker Sets	1,000,000	1,250,000
Commuter Mobile Office Furniture	600,000	1,000,000
Specialty Furniture	570,000	1,100,000
Custom-Built Furniture	400,000	900,000

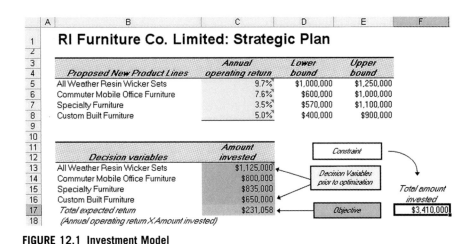

FIGURE 12.1 Investment Model

minimum investment ranges supporting restructuring in each of four product lines. Using ROV Risk Simulator, the firm's bankers came up with a stochastic solution. On a unit level, they developed a probability distribution assigned to each uncertain element in the forecast, established an optimal funding array for the various business combinations, and held cash flow volatility to acceptable levels, preserving the credit grade (again at the unit level). Finally, the last optimization (worksheet) was linked to the consolidating/consolidated DCF valuation worksheet(s). The firm bankers then determined post-restructuring equity values, specific confidence levels, and probabilities that asset values will fall below debt values.

Business History:

RI Furniture started operations in 1986. The firm manufactures a full line of indoor/outdoor furniture. Operating subsidiaries targeted for restructuring, depicted ahead, represent approximately 65% of consolidated operations.

All-Weather Resin Wicker Sets:

This furniture comes with a complete aluminum frame with hand-woven polypropylene resin produced to resist weather. Operating profit margin distributions and investment ranges for each subsidiary are shown in Tables 12.2 and 12.3, and Figure 12.1.

Commuter Mobile Office Furniture:

The commuter rolls from its storage location to any work area, and sets up in minutes. It integrates computer peripherals (monitor, CPU tower, keyboard, and printer) in a compact, secure mobile unit.

Specialty Furniture:

After restructuring, this business segment will include production of hotel reception furniture, café furniture, canteen furniture, restaurant seating, and banqueting furniture.

Custom-Built Furniture:

Furniture will be custom built in the firm's own workshop or sourced from a host of reputable manufacturers both at home and abroad.

In the first optimization run (Run 1), a constraint is placed on the $3,410,000 investment; that is, the bank's facility cannot exceed $3,410,000. Later, we place an additional constraint: the forecast variable's risk (measured in terms of volatility).

Risk Simulator Optimization Procedures

The model is already set up with optimization and simulation assumptions, and can be run by simply clicking on the *Risk Simulator | Optimization | Run Optimization*. For the sake of completeness, the following illustrates the procedures in setting up the optimization model from scratch:

1. Create a new profile by starting the model and clicking on *Risk Simulator | New Profile*, and give it a name. By creating a new profile, you can now set

up different simulation assumptions and optimization parameters in the same Excel model, without having to create multiple models.

Note: In this example write-up, we selected the "Specify a random number sequence" seed value of 123456.

2. Select cell C5 and click on *Risk Simulator | Set Input Assumption*, and enter in the relevant assumptions (Figure 12.2 illustrates an assumption):

All Weather Resin Wicker Sets (C5):
Triangular Distribution: Min 8.5%, Most Likely 9.7% and Max 11.5%
Commuter Mobile Office Furniture (C6):
Triangular Distribution: Min 6.6%, Most Likely 7.6% and Max 8.6%
Specialty Furniture (C7):
Normal Distribution: Mean 3.5%, Standard Deviation 0.35%
Custom Built Furniture (C8):
Uniform Distribution: Min 4.5% and Max 5.5%

3. Set the Objective of the optimization. Select cell C17 and click on *Risk Simulator | Run Optimization | Set Objective* (or click on the "O" icon in the Risk Simulator toolbar), and select MAX (see Figure 12.3).

4. Set the Decision Variables. Select cell C13 and click on *Risk Simulator | Optimization | Set Decision Variable* (or click on the "D" icon in the Risk Simulator toolbar). Then, select Continuous as the decision type, and you can either enter in the lower and upper bound values (1000000 and 1250000) or

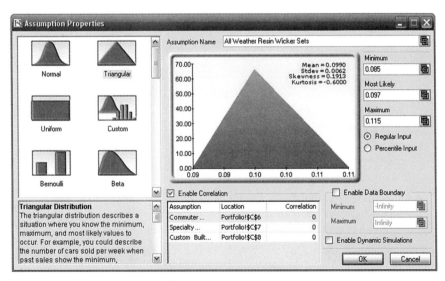

FIGURE 12.2 Setting Input Assumptions

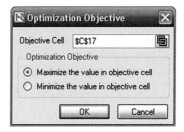

FIGURE 12.3 Setting the Optimization Objective

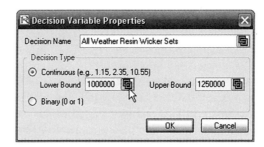

FIGURE 12.4 Optimization's Decision Variables

simply click on the link icon and link it to the relevant cells (D5 and E5) as shown in Figure 12.4. Repeat for cells C14 to C16 with the relevant upper and lower bounds:

	Lower Bound	Upper Bound
All-Weather Resin Wicker Sets	$1,000,000	$1,250,000
Commuter Mobile Office Furniture	$600,000	$1,000,000
Specialty Furniture	$570,000	$1,100,000
Custom-Built Furniture	$400,000	$900,000

Note: clicking on the link icon (Figure 12.4) will allow you to link the lower and upper bounds to specific cells instead of typing it in. The benefit of linking is that you can do a simple Risk Simulator Copy/Paste to replicate the decision variables on other cells.

5. Set the Constraint. Click on *Risk Simulator | Optimization | Set Constraint* (or click on the "C" icon in the Risk Simulator toolbar) and click ADD to add a constraint. Then, click on the link icon to link it to cell F17 and set it to be <= (less than or equal to) 3410000 (Figure 12.5).

FIGURE 12.5 Setting a Constraint

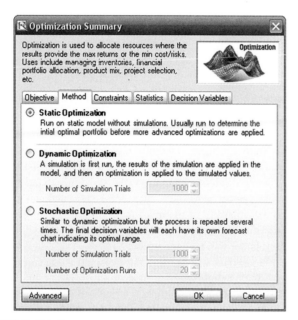

FIGURE 12.6 Optimization Summary

6. Run the Optimization. Click on *Risk Simulator | Optimization | Run Optimization* or click on the Run Optimization icon. You may now click on OK to run the optimization, or review the model setup by reviewing all the tabs (Figure 12.6).

7. Interpret the results. Notice that after the optimization, the Total Expected Return has increased from $231,058 to $246,072, creating a higher level of expected total returns. In both cases, the total amount invested remains the same at $3,410,000 (Figure 12.7).

8. You may now run a simulation both on submitted and optimized portfolios (simply click on *Risk Simulator | Run Simulation*). The results are shown in Figures 12.8 and 12.9. Note that the expected value increased for the

Before Optimization	Decision variables	Amount invested
	All Weather Resin Wicker Sets	$1,125,000
	Commuter Mobile Office Furniture	$800,000
	Specialty Furniture	$835,000
	Custom Built Furniture	$650,000
	Total expected return	$231,058
	(Annual operating return X Amount invested)	

After Optimization	Decision variables	Amount invested
	All Weather Resin Wicker Sets	$1,250,000
	Commuter Mobile Office Furniture	$1,000,000
	Specialty Furniture	$570,000
	Custom Built Furniture	$590,000
	Total expected return	$246,072
	(Annual operating return X Amount invested)	

FIGURE 12.7 Results of Optimization: Before (top) and After (bottom)

optimized portfolio, but there is slightly higher risk, as measured by the standard deviation. However, the proportional increase in risk is minimal as measured by the coefficient of variation (the standard deviation divided by mean), which is a measure of the return-to-risk ratio and can also can be interpreted as the volatility of the investment returns. Therefore, the optimized portfolio is significantly better by returning over $15,000 without much change to the relative risk-to-returns ratio.

Analytical Note: You will see that the expected value (mean) from the simulation may be slightly different than the single-point estimates in the model (cell C17). This is because the simulated forecast results are based on thousands of scenarios as well as based on the input assumptions set in the model. If asymmetrical assumptions are set, the results may be slightly different from the single point results.

Risk Simulator Optimization Procedures Volatility and Optimization

Client's Agenda	Banker's Agenda
Maximize Shareholder Value (Goal: Profit Maximization)	Prevent client's risk rating (debt rating) from migrating beyond a predetermined value (Goal: Risk Reduction)
Minimize Cost of Capital	

Volatility of operating results affects the volatility of assets. This point is crucial in the banking business. Suppose we determine the market value of a corporation's assets along with the volatility of that value using Risk Simulator.

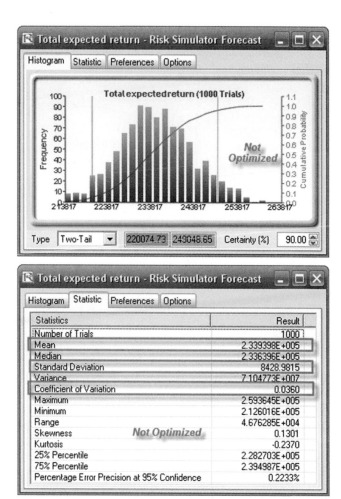

FIGURE 12.8 Not-Optimized Simulation Results

Volatility measures the propensity of asset values to change within a given time period. For example, Moody's KMV demonstrates that volatility correlates to default probabilities. For instance, assume corporate asset market value is $150 million, and $75 million debt is due in one year. If asset volatility causes current asset market value to fall below $75 million, default will occur.

Thus, as a prudent next step, bankers discuss the first optimization run with management on three levels: (1) maximum expected return, (2) optimal investments/loan facility, and (3) volatility of expected return. If volatility is unacceptable, the standard deviation must be reduced to preserve credit-grade integrity.

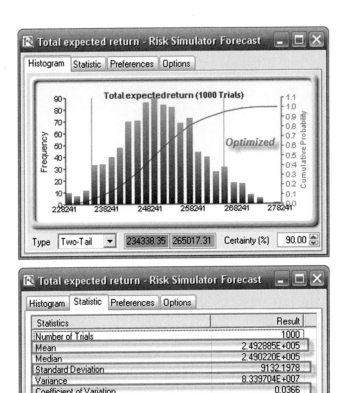

FIGURE 12.9 Optimized Simulation Results

The model we use in Figure 12.10 is Part B of the Furniture Optimization model found in the Modeling Toolkit (*Modeling Toolkit | Optimization | Capital Investments—Part B*). To get started, please first review Part A of the model before attempting to run this follow-up model. This follow-up model looks at a twist at the optimization procedures performed in Part A by now incorporating risk and the return-to-risk ratio (Sharpe Ratio, a Nobel Prize winning concept). Notice some updated information in this model, complete with risk measures (volatilities of cash flow returns) as well as other added results from the Markowitz Efficient Frontier.

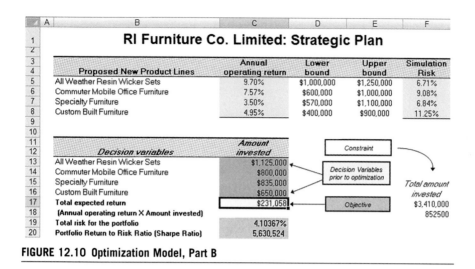

FIGURE 12.10 Optimization Model, Part B

Table 12.4 Sample Optimization Results

	Original	Opt Run 1	Opt Run 2
All Weather Resin Wicker Sets	$1,125,000	$1,250,000	$1,250,000
Commuter Mobile Office Furniture	$800,000	$1,000,000	$924,636
Specialty Furniture	$835,000	$570,000	$570,000
Custom Built Furniture	$650,000	$590,000	$665,364
Objective to Maximize		**Returns**	**Returns/ Risk**
Total expected return	$231,058	$246,072	$238,816
Total risk for the portfolio	4.104%	4.270%	4.055%
Portfolio Return to Risk Ratio (Sharpe Ratio)	5630524	5762758	5889030

In this model, instead of simply maximizing returns in the portfolio (Opt. Run 1 in the Part A model), which will by definition create a potentially higher risk portfolio (high risk equals high return), we may also want to maximize the Sharpe Ratio (portfolio returns-to-risk ratio), which will in turn provide the maximum levels of return subject to the least risk or for the same risk, provide the highest returns, yielding an optimal point on the Markowitz Efficient Frontier for this portfolio (Opt. Run 2 in the Part B model).

As can be seen in the optimization results in Table 12.4, Opt. Run 1 provides the highest returns ($246,072), as opposed to the original value of $231,058. Nonetheless, in Opt. Run 2, in which we maximize the Sharpe Ratio instead, we

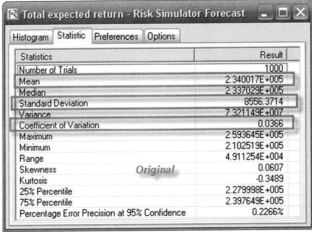

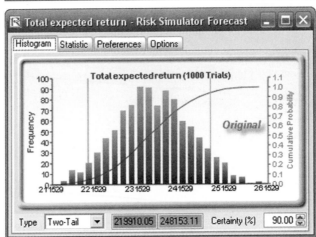

FIGURE 12.11 Simulation Results of Original Investment Values

get a slightly lower return ($238,816), but the total risk for the entire portfolio is reduced to 4.055% instead of 4.270%. This illustrates the concepts most professionals believe in; high risk may yield high return.

A simulation is run on the original investment allocation, Opt. Run 1, and Opt. Run 2, and the results are shown in Figures 12.11 to 12.13. Here, we clearly see that the slightly lower returns provide a reduced level of risk, which is good for the bank.

To run this predefined optimization model, simply click on *Risk Simulator | Optimization | Run Optimization* and click OK. To change the objective from Maximizing Returns to Risk, to Maximizing Returns, simply click on the

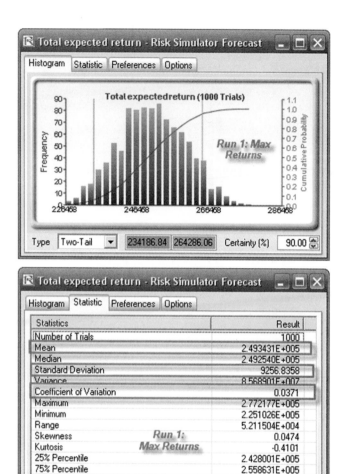

FIGURE 12.12 Simulation Results of Optimization Run 1

Objective "O" icon in the Risk Simulator toolbar or click on *Risk Simulator | Optimization | Set Objective* and link it to either cell C20 for Sharpe Ratio or C17 for Returns, and then run the optimization.

To set up the optimization from scratch, please refer to the instructions for Model A or Part I of this exercise.

In addition, the total investment budget allowed can be changed to analyze what happens to the returns and risk of the portfolio. For instance, Figure 12.14 illustrates the results from such an analysis and the resulting expected risk and return values. In order to better understand each point's risk structure, an optimization is carried out and a simulation is run. Figures 12.15 and 12.16 show two

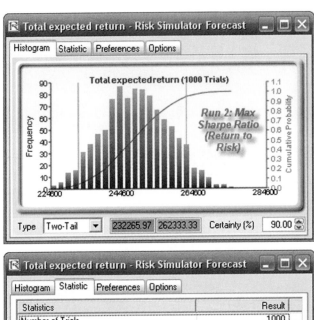

FIGURE 12.13 Simulation Results of Optimization Run 2

sample extreme cases where $2.91M versus $3.61M is advanced. From the results, one can see that the higher the risk (higher range of outcomes), the higher the returns (expected values are higher, and the probability of beating the original expected value is higher). Such analyses will allow the bank to better analyze the risk-return characteristics of the deal.

Many additional analyses can be applied in this model. For instance, we can apply the probability of default computations of implied asset value and implied volatility to obtain the cumulative default probability so that the bank can understand the risk of this deal and decide (based on the portfolio of deals) what the threshold of lending should be. For instance, if the bank does not want anything

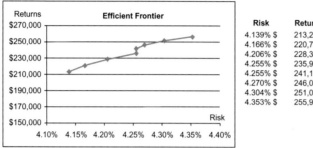

Maximizing Returns with Different Budget Constraints:

Risk	Returns	Budget
4.139%	$ 213,210	$ 2,910,000
4.166%	$ 220,777	$ 3,010,000
4.206%	$ 228,343	$ 3,110,000
4.255%	$ 235,910	$ 3,210,000
4.255%	$ 241,122	$ 3,310,000
4.270%	$ 246,072	$ 3,410,000
4.304%	$ 251,022	$ 3,510,000
4.353%	$ 255,972	$ 3,610,000

FIGURE 12.14 Efficient Frontier of Lending

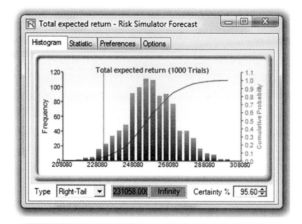

FIGURE 12.15 Sample Simulation Results with a Budget of $3.61 M

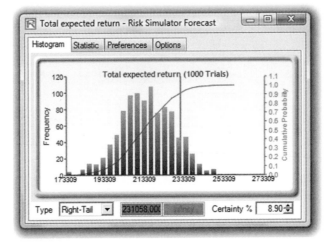

FIGURE 12.16 Sample Simulation Results with a Budget of $2.91 M

above a 3.5% probability of default for a five-year cumulative loan, then $3.41 M is the appropriate loan value threshold. Table 12.5 illustrates this situation.

In addition, value-at-risk for a portfolio of loans (Table 12.6) can also be determined for before and after this new loan, for the bank to decide if absorbing this new loan is possible and to figure out the effects on the entire portfolio's VaR valuation and capital adequacy. Table 12.6 shows some existing loans (grouped by tranches and types) and the new loan request. It is up to management to decide if the additional hit to capital requirements is reasonable.

The story does not end here; our analysis up to now was restricted to the unit level, that is, to business segments involved in the restructuring. While the model shown worked its stochastic wonders, it must now link to consolidating and consolidated DCF valuation worksheets.

Table 12.5 Probability of Default Tied into the Lending Threshold

Probability of Default Analysis to Determine Lending Threshold			
Total Investment/Loan Required ($000)	$3,410	$2,910	$3,610
Other Liabilities and Debt ($000)	$3,512	$3,512	$3,512
Total Equity Value ($000)	$1,200	$1,200	$1,200
Equity Volatility	20.00%	20.00%	20.00%
Maturity of New Debt	5	5	5
Riskfree Rate	5.00%	5.00%	5.00%
Implied Asset Value	$6,583.56	$6.196.20	$6,738.31
Implied Asset Volatility	4.75%	4.82%	4.73%
Probability of Default	3.3649%	2.6577%	3.6890%

Consolidated discounted cash flow valuations provide a "going concern" value: the value driven by a company's future economic strength. RI Furniture Ltd.'s value is determined by the present value of future cash flows for a specific forecast horizon (projection period) plus the present value of cash flows *beyond* the forecast horizon (residual or terminal value). In other words, the firm's value depends on cash flow potential and the risks (threats) of those future cash flows. It is these perceived risks or threats that help define the discounting factor used to measure cash flows in present value terms. Cash flow depends on the industry and the economic outlook for RI Furniture's products, current and future competition, sustainable competitive advantage, and projected changes in demand and the borrower's capacity to grow in light of its past financial and operating performance. Risk factors the firm's bankers will examine carefully include their borrower's financial condition, quality, and magnitude and volatility of cash flows, financial and operating leverage, and management's capacity to sustain operations on a profitable basis. These primary attributes cannot be ignored when bankers determine distributions associated with assumption variables.

Risk Simulator embedded into powerful valuation models provides an intuitive advantage; it is a decidedly efficient and precise way to get deals analyzed, done, and sold.

In summary, here are a few suggestions:

1. Use consolidating financials to determine valuation building blocks intrinsic in operating segments you are analyzing. Consolidated statements alone do not provide sufficient answers.
2. Employ the Risk Simulator and Basel II Modeling Toolkit software programs (specifically, use the Corporate Valuation model included in the toolkit). The model contains preformatted financial statements and analytical reports for evaluating performance and valuing projected performance using both the Enterprise DCF and Economic Profit approaches.
3. Enter the borrower's most likely projections, adding residual period and cost of capital assumptions.

Table 12.6 New Loan's Effect on Value-at-Risk

Value at Risk Contribution Analysis to the Bank's Portfolio of Holdings

	Daily Volatilities	Amounts
Existing Loan (Tranche 1)	0.1254%	$5,410,000
Existing Loan (Tranche 2)	0.3255%	$4,450,000
Existing Loan (Tranche 3)	0.1444%	$3,410,000
Existing Loan (Tranche 4)	0.1854%	$3,410,000
Existing Loan (Tranche 5)	0.2654%	$3,410,000
New Loan Addition	0.2163%	$3,410,000

Correlation Matrix	Existing Loan (Tranche 1)	Existing Loan (Tranche 2)	Existing Loan (Tranche 3)	Existing Loan (Tranche 4)	Existing Loan (Tranche 5)	New Loan Addition
Existing Loan (Tranche 1)	1.0000	0.2500	−0.1510	0.0250	0.0140	0.0200
Existing Loan (Tranche 2)	0.0000	1.0000	−0.1335	0.0020	0.1500	−0.1200
Existing Loan (Tranche 3)	0.0000	0.0000	1.0000	0.0255	0.0480	−0.1700
Existing Loan (Tranche 4)	0.0000	0.0000	0.0000	1.0000	0.0560	−0.2600
Existing Loan (Tranche 5)	0.0000	0.0000	0.0000	0.0000	1.0000	0.2500
New Loan Addition	0.0000	0.0000	0.0000	0.0000	0.0000	1.0000
Holding Days	365					
Percentile	99.95%					
Value at Risk of Portfolio Before New Loan	$1,318,330					
Value at Risk of Portfolio After New Loan	$1,378,376					

4. Open Risk Simulator and determine value drivers (assumption variables) and distributions first on the unit level, then use results to refine consolidating/ consolidated valuations.

5. On the consolidated valuation, select a forecast cell: *Equity Value, Operating Value,* or *Enterprise Value.*

6. Run a simulation. Determine the forecast variable's value within a confidence level. Then find probabilities for which the equity value falls below zero. The last step is quite illuminating since within the universe and/or constraints of your valuation model, this is the expected default probability.
7. Run a report. Finally, if borrowers or colleagues are unfamiliar with Risk Simulator report statistics, take the time to explain the key numbers.

A Banker's Guide: Valuation Appraisal of Business Clients

INTRODUCTION

Valuation appraisals help bankers understand whether borrowers are creditworthy. Appraisals are used for many reasons: to determine acquisition prices of consolidated businesses made up of numerous, separate units; for bankruptcy liquidations/restructurings; to establish values of standalone businesses; for cost studies; for estate planning; to comprehend borrowers' strategic plans; for insurance loss settlement; for finance mergers and acquisitions; and to help settle taxation issues.

Bank Loans and Other Financing
When applying for a commercial loan, it is common for loan officers to ask for valuation appraisals, mainly from new clients. A methodical, competent valuation can be the difference between obtaining a loan or not.

Financing Acquisitions, Divestures and Restructurings
Bankers rely on valuation appraisals to establish a reasonable asking or offering price. Business units are valued as standalone entities, then valued as if combined using anticipated synergies from acquisitions and restructurings. Valuation appraisals help bankers determine financing and fair market price.

Partnership/Shareholder Agreements (Buy/Sell)
Buy/sell agreements should be founded on business appraisals. Valuations are finalized when shareholders buy into or exit businesses.

Financing Employee Stock Ownership Plans (ESOPs)
Employee stock ownership plans (ESOPs) are created to transfer a portion or all of the ownership of a business to employees. When dealing with an ESOP, stock must be valued by independent business appraisers annually.

Litigation Issues Involving Economic/Financial Reparations
These cases often require valuation appraisals to decide economic damages. Usually businesses are valued twice: before and after the actions that initiated damages. The spread between before and after typically represents economic damages.

Estate Planning
> Bankers serving high net worth clients who have interests in closely held businesses are often called upon to oversee estate planning. Valuation appraisals are normally required and must be included in gift or estate tax returns. Since these business valuation reports are closely examined by tax authorities, it is important to retain a highly qualified business appraiser to prepare the needed company valuation. Bankers should have contact or be familiar with estate-planning appraisers.

Liquidation vs. Restructuring Decisions
> Management's decision to divest a business unit is quantified by spreads between market value and liquidation value. Why is a low ratio significant? It means a firm is likely to have more value liquidating than by trying to stay in business to preserve "cash traps." "Cash traps" are associated with sustainable negative cash flow that siphons cash from successful operating units.

S Corporation Elections
> Some firms find they can reduce tax burdens by changing from a C corporation to a subchapter S corporation. This election often eliminates corporate income taxes paid at the business level. When the election is made, appraisals may be required if assets are sold.

Eminent Domain Actions
> Governments frequently invoke eminent domain laws that require sale or relocation of businesses. If banks are asked to help with financing, it is essential to work with competent valuations to establish fair prices.

Intangible Assets and Goodwill Impairment (SFAS 141 and 142)
> Statement of financial accounting standard (SFAS) 141 on business combinations requires intangible assets must be valued and recorded on a borrower's financial statement. SFAS 142 states that goodwill must be balance sheet recorded and tested at least annually for impairment.

Incentive or Employee Stock Options (ISOs and ESOs)
> Incentive stock options are an important component of employee, board, investor, or advisor compensation. Rule 409 A changed the rules for issuing incentive stock options.

Strategic Planning
> Far-sighted financial, operational, and strategic management requires knowledge of the business and the valuation methodology. A firms' value rises and declines over discrete time horizons for a number of reasons, including management actions and changes in economic or industry conditions. With these changes, optimal strategies will make course corrections.

Valuation Appraisals: Documents and Information

A. Financial statements (for up to the last five fiscal years if available).
- **1.** Primary financial statements (statements should cover a *relevant period*, that is, a period over which the statements represent the company's general operations, leading up to and including the valuation date).
  - **i.** Balance sheets.
    - **a.** If the company significantly changed its operations a few years before the valuation date, only the last three or four years' statements may be relevant to the valuation. But if the business has a long history and some or all recent years were abnormal in some way (such as during a cyclical peak or trough in the company's industry), statements for the past seven, ten, or more years may constitute a relevant period for valuing it.
  - **ii.** Income statements.
  - **iii.** Cash flows.
  - **iv.** Statement of stockholders' equity or partners' capital accounts.
- **2.** Income tax returns for the same years.
  - **i.** A convenient summary of differences between tax return and income statement reporting is found in Schedule M1, "Reconciliation of Income per Books with Income per Return." In general, the statements that most closely conform to industry practices would most fairly represent the company's financial position and earning power. The financial data and ratios derived from tax return data normally would not be relied on when comparing the company to the price/earnings or price/book value ratios derived from publicly traded comparatives.
- **3.** Latest interim statements if valuation date is three months or more beyond the end of last fiscal year, and interim statement for the comparable period the year before.
- **4.** List of subsidiaries and/or financial interest in other companies with relevant financial statements.
- **5.** Off balance sheet assets or liabilities.
  - **i.** As we saw in Chapter Two, financial events (contingencies) may significantly affect an obligor firm's value; events that do not appear as line items on the balance sheet. Lawsuits, for example.
  - **ii.** An important category of off balance sheet liabilities is the potential cost of compliance with environmental or other government requirements.
  - **iii.** Product liability and liability for warranties are other significant items.
- **6.** Fiscal projections (five years).
- **7.** Short term cash budgets.

B. Other financial data.
   1. Equipment list and depreciation schedules.
      i. Lists of property owned should include the acquisition date, a description adequate for identifying each piece or group, the original cost, the depreciation method and life used, and the net depreciated value. The totals of such schedules should reconcile with line items in the financial statements. For real estate, the schedule should show the size (acres of land and dimensions and square feet of floor space of buildings), with a brief description of the construction and any special features. It should also indicate the dates and costs of additions and remodeling.
   2. Lease agreements.
      i. Leases may be favorable or unfavorable. A long-term lease costing the company less than the current market value adds to value; being saddled with a long-term lease on inadequate quarters for which the company cannot find an alternative tenant is anything but favorable. Lease renewal terms about to expire are important considerations as well, especially if the lease is not renewable or is renewable only at a significantly increased cost. For companies that have many leased outlets, such as retail chains, we may want to prepare a list of leases with a summary of their provisions.
   3. Real and personal property tax assessments.
      i. Tax assessments may not be the best yardstick of asset values, but they are almost always readily available. Most tax assessed values are lower than replacement costs, although they may be well above liquidating value, especially those for personal property.
      ii. We usually can obtain local information on the broad relationship between tax-assessed values and market values for a particular jurisdiction. In many jurisdictions, the tax-assessed value purports to represent not market value, but some fixed percentage of market value, such as 30%. Of course, in those instances we need to adjust the figures upward to the market value directly implied by the tax-assessed value before making further adjustments, if any, for whatever systematic biases are perceived as prevailing in the particular jurisdiction.
   4. Insurance appraisals.
      i. Unlike tax appraisals, insurance appraisals have some tendency to overvalue property, primarily to ensure that the insurance will be adequate to cover any potential loss.
   5. Independent appraisal reports
      i. An independent appraisal by a qualified practitioner, if available, usually is a more reliable guide to asset value than either a tax assessment or insurance appraisal. Such appraisals generally specify the approach taken, the assumptions made, and some guidance for appropriate interpretation and use of the appraisal. A replacement cost

or depreciated replacement cost appraisal, for example, normally will differ significantly from a liquidation value appraisal, and none of those may be appropriate for appraising assets being used in a specific ongoing business situation.

6. Capital requirements.
   i. Capital requirements can arise from many sources, including catching up on deferred maintenance (a common need in small- and medium-sized companies), increasing working capital needs, or making capital expenditures.

7. Aged accounts receivable list.
   i. The *aged receivables list* (aged list) can yield insight into the company's profitability and even viability. The statement lists the accounts alphabetically, sometimes categorized into customer groups. The spreadsheet is laid out with columns for the total amount due, the current portion, and the portions over 30 days, over 60 days, over 90 days, and over 120 days past due. Unusual circumstances regarding a specific account should be noted somewhere on the statement, perhaps as footnotes. Any notes or other receivables besides normal trade receivables should be listed separately, with enough detail to permit evaluation. The statement date should be as of the latest annual or interim financial statement so that the total on the balance sheet will reconcile with the amount on the aged list.

8. Customer base.
   i. The fewer customers the company relies on for its market, the more important an analysis of the customer base becomes. A convenient way to compile the customer base information is in simple tabular form. We list, in order of size of billings, the 10 to 20 largest customers in the latest year or fiscal period and the dollar amounts of billings and the percentage of total billings for each. This information should be shown for several periods in the past as well as for the latest period. The columns for the past years should also show any customers that accounted for a significant proportion of the billings at that time, even if they are not current customers. A budgeted figure for each customer for the current or forthcoming year is helpful if available.

9. Customer contracts.
   i. Customer contracts are significant items for some companies, such as a manufacturer whose customers lease rather than buy its equipment. Contracts to obtain key raw materials may be significant for some firms. An analysis of the terms and strengths of such contracts can be an important consideration in valuing the business.

10. Aged accounts payable list.
11. List of prepaid expenses.

12. Inventory list with any necessary information on inventory accounting policies (including work in process, if applicable). Raw material inventory replacement costs, i.e., cotton.

   i. The amount of detail desired in the inventory list will vary greatly from one appraisal to another, depending on the inventory's importance in the valuation and the extent to which inventory accounting methods tend to differ within the particular industry. In any case, the total should be reconcilable with the inventory as shown on the financial statements, using whatever adjustments conform to the company's method of inventory valuation.

13. Order backlog.

   i. If the company's order backlog is significant, we should compare the backlog on the valuation date with that on one or more past dates. Such comparison, especially with the backlog a year prior to the valuation date, is one indication of the company's future prospects that is solidly based on its past record.

14. Supplier list

   i. Like the customer base, the *supplier list* becomes more important with fewer suppliers. It also becomes more important if the future availability of certain supplies is uncertain enough to increase the company's risk. If future sources of supply are a critical factor, the appraiser should compile a list of sources other than those currently being used. The supplier list could take the same format as the customer base.

15. Any other existing contracts (employment agreements, covenants not to compete, supplier and franchise agreements, customer agreements, royalty agreements, equipment lease or rental contracts, loan agreements, labor contracts, employee benefits plans, etc.).

16. Loan agreements.

   i. Most loan agreements contain various requirements and restrictive covenants. One reason for reading the loan agreements is to check whether the company is in danger of defaulting on any requirement. Another consideration is the effect of any loan agreement restrictions on the company's ability to pay dividends and/or transfer stock ownership.

17. List of stockholders or partners, with number of shares owned by each or percentage of each partner's interest in earnings and capital.

   i. The *stockholder list* should include each stockholder's name and number of shares held. If there is more than one class of stock, it should show the stockholders' holdings in each class. It should also identify any family or other relationships among the stockholders. This list will be examined by the IRS and the courts if they are involved.

18. Compensation schedule for owners, including all benefits and personal expenses (we should compare this information to the RMA industry average *officer's salaries/sales ratio*).
    i. An *officers' and directors' compensation schedule* usually should be prepared for the same number of years as the financial statements. It may provide a basis for adjustments to the income statements, offering evidence of the company's earning capacity.
    ii. These benefits would include: base salary; bonuses or commissions; amount paid into pension, profit sharing, or other employee benefit funds; and other employee benefits. It also should include compensation other than cash, such as stock or options, company cars, or other property used, and any significant expenses paid or reimbursed for business activities performed by the employee.
    iii. We should be aware of the fact that the IRS sometimes attempts to depict compensation to owners of closely held businesses as excessive so as to get dividend tax treatment for a portion of it.
19. Dividend schedule.
    i. The *dividend schedule* normally should cover the same time period that the financial statements do. It should show the date of each dividend payment and the per-share amount for each class of stock.
    ii. Dividend paying capacity, one criterion of the value of a business interest, represents a competing use of capital, and each company must decide whether to retain cash with which to carry out needed purchases or distribute its earnings to stockholders.
20. Schedule of "key man" insurance in force.
    i. In many closely held companies, the loss of a single key individual can have a significant impact on the company's operations. It is always desirable to know how much of this risk is covered by life insurance. This insurance may have to be considered as part of the company's value.
C. Company and other documents relating to rights of owners.
    1. Articles of incorporation, bylaws, any amendments to either, and corporate minutes.
        i. The official documents of a corporation or partnership often hold facts that significantly affect the entity's valuation. The articles of incorporation, along with any amendments, and documents specifying rights attaching to each class of stock outstanding provide information that is particularly important for companies with more than one class of stock. There may be other information in the articles or bylaws relevant to the value. Certain items in the board of directors' and stockholders' minute books may be important, especially if transactions with parties related to the company have occurred. In a partnership, the partners' rights and obligations should be contained in the articles of partnership.

2. Any existing buy-sell agreements, options to purchase stock, or other documents affecting the ownership rights of the interest being valued.

   i. To the extent that past transactions in the stock were at arm's length, they provide objective evidence of value. Even if not accepted, a bona fide offer, particularly if submitted in writing, can at least corroborate the value. In preparing the record of past transactions or offers, it is important to list any relationships among the parties in order to determine whether each transaction was at arm's length. The transaction record usually should go as far back as the number of years of financial statements used. On this basis, past transaction prices can be compared with the current book values, earnings, or other relevant variables.

   ii. Buy-sell or repurchase agreements with major stockholders may contain provisions that can affect the company's shares to which they apply and, in many cases, all the outstanding stock as well. Provisions in such agreements may address the question of value directly or may impose restrictions on transferability, which may bear on the value of the affected shares. If the company has an employee stock ownership plan (ESOP), the terms of the buyback provisions have a major bearing on the marketability of the shares involved and thus must be considered when valuing ESOP shares.

3. Employment and *non-compete* agreements.

   i. Employment agreements with key personnel may affect the company's value, as may important agreements not to compete. These agreements could have either a positive or negative effect on value depending on the relationship between the cost and the value to the company.

D. Other information.

1. Brief history, including length of time in business and details of any changes in ownership and/or bona-fide offers received.

   i. We need to set the stage for placing the company in the context of its industry, especially its competition, as well as in the general economy. A relatively brief history will suffice in most cases. The history should indicate how long the company has been in business and some chronology of major changes, such as form of organization, controlling ownership, location of operations, and lines of business. Sometimes predecessor companies are a relevant part of the background. Some companies have relatively complex histories, requiring detailed explanations of transactions that have fundamentally contributed to the company's composition as of the valuation date.

2. Brief description of the business, including position relative to competition and any factors that make the business unique.

3. Organization chart.

4. Information on related party transactions.

5. Marketing literature (catalogs, brochures, advertisements, etc.).

    i. It is helpful to receive a set of the firm's sales materials, such as brochures, catalogs, and price lists. These items make it easier to become familiar with the company's products, services, and pricing and to evaluate the written sales materials.

6. List of locations where company operates, with size and whether owned or leased.

7. List of states in which licensed to do business.

8. List of competitors, with location, relative size, and other relevant factors.

9. Resumes of, or list of, key personnel with age, position, compensation, length of service, education, and prior experience (much of this can be obtained from a D&B report).

10. Relevant trade or government publications.

11. Trade associations and industry sources.

    i. It is helpful to obtain a list of trade associations to which the company belongs, or is eligible to belong, along with the name and address of the executive director of each. If necessary, you can then contact the trade association for industry information. Many industries have other trade sources, such as trade journals or sources of composite data. The company may be able to furnish a list of such sources and often can supply copies of relevant publications.

12. Any existing indicators of asset values, including latest property tax assessments and any appraisals that have been done.

13. List of patents, copyrights, trademarks, and other intangible assets.

    i. A list of patents, copyrights, and trademarks should include the items covered and relevant issue and/or expiration dates. It should have at least a brief description and enough information to permit understanding of the items. The importance of these items and the degree of detail necessary vary greatly from one situation to another.

14. Contractual agreements and obligations.

    i. We should evaluate all significant contractual obligations for their potential positive or negative effect on the company's value. Contracts that may be significant for the value of a business or business interest can cover a wide variety of subjects.

15. Any filings or correspondence with regulatory agencies.

> If the standard of value is derived from a statute or regulation, the exact source of the governing standard of value needs to be referenced. For example, we need to include the eight factors listed in revenue ruling 59-60 if the valuation is for gift or estate taxes, an ESOP, or some other tax-related matter.

> The introduction is brief and may cover any or all of half a dozen key points in summary form.

> The scope and organization of the appraisal report must be tailored to the purpose of the valuation. Formats or variations will differ depending on purpose.

> The scope and content of the valuation report can vary considerably depending on the size and complexity of the firm and the use or uses to which the report will be put.

Valuation Appraisal Outline

Purpose of the valuation report.
- **A.** Taxes; estate tax purposes.
  - **1.** Address factors enumerated in revenue ruling 50–60.
- **B.** ESOP.
  - **1.** Department of Labor regulations.
- **C.** Lawsuit.
  - **1.** Issues raised in relevant case law precedents.
- **D.** Strategic planning.
  - **1.** Maximize shareholder value.
  - **2.** Understand the mechanics of wealth creation.
  - **3.** Identify and sell off unprofitable business units.
    - **i.** Liquidation vs. cash flow value.
  - **4.** Purchase business.
- **E.** Respond to offer to buy business.
- **F.** Bank loan facilities.

Scope and content of the valuation report.
- **A.** Audience.
  - **1.** Prospective parties at interest and their beneficiaries.
    - **i.** Internal use by officers and directors.
      - **a.** Description of the company may be unnecessary or may allude only to certain salient points that directly affect the valuation of the firm.
      - **b.** If audience is financially sophisticated, we can assume some knowledge of finance and accounting.
  - **2.** Representatives of any regulatory authorities involved.
  - **3.** Judge and jury if there is existing or potential litigation.

Organization.
- **A.** Introduction.
  - **1.** Description of the assignment.
    - **i.** Who was retained by whom to do the appraisal?
      - **a.** Appraiser's statement of qualifications.
      - **b.** Reviewer's judgments; for example, "have I adequately and convincingly supported the use of each discount rate,

capitalization rate and multiple used in the valuation? Is the conclusion consistent with the economic, industry, and financial statement analysis presented? Is the analysis and conclusion consistent with the stated purpose of the appraisal and standard of value, including any statutory, regulatory, or other legal requirements"?

   ii. Definition of the property being valued.
   iii. Effective date of the appraisal.
   iv. Purpose of the valuation.

2. Summary description of the company.
   i. For the readers' convenience, it us useful to include in the introduction a brief statement of Robinson Textiles' business, its location, some idea of its size, and possibly one or two salient or unique aspects of the company.

3. Capitalization and ownership.
   i. Class or classes of stock and the distribution of ownership.

4. Applicable standard of value (if appropriate).
   i. Internal Revenue Service Ruling 59–60 outlines the valuation of closely held stocks and includes the following:
      a. Nature of business and history of enterprise.
      b. Economic outlook and outlook of the specific industry.
      c. Book value and financial condition.
      d. Earning capacity.
      e. Dividend-paying capacity.
      f. Intangibles, including goodwill.
      g. Stock sales and size of the block to be valued.
      h. Market price of publicly traded stock in same or similar lines of business.
   ii. Statutes governing dissolution or dissenting stockholder actions (if any).
      a. Statement to that effect, or summary statement of interpretation of the case law from a financial analysis point of view.

5. Sources of information used in the appraisal.
   i. List of financial statements and supporting schedules that were examined, including the years studied for each statement.
      a. Statement as to accountant's opinion.
   ii. Corporate tax returns (if appropriate).
   iii. Internally prepared budgets for the next six-to-twelve months.
   iv. Facilities visited.
   v. Equipment list and depreciation schedule (if appropriate).
   vi. Inventory lists and receivables aging (if appropriate).
   vii. Stockholders' list as of December 31, 1993.
   viii. Schedule of total owners' compensation (if appropriate).
   ix. Copies of leases.
   x. Articles of incorporation and bylaws.

        xi. Industry information and periodicals.

       xii. Information on comparative publicly traded companies from S&P corporation records and SEC 10-Ks. Various brokers reports on these companies.

    6. Valuation approach and conclusion.

      i. Broad criterion or criteria used in reaching the valuation conclusion.

      ii. Brief statement of the conclusion.

B. Description of the company.

    1. Background.

    2. Physical facilities.

    3. Product and/or services.

    4. Distribution channels.

    5. Sources of supply.

    6. Labor/capital intensive; operating leverage.

    7. Management.

    8. Capitalization and ownership.

    9. Seasonality (if any).

C. Industry data.

    1. Size of firm relative to competitors.

    2. Specialized segments of the market the firm serves.

    3. Competitive strengths and weaknesses.

    4. Technology and production.

    5. Regulation.

    6. Industry Phase.

      i. Mature phase: Product technology well established, markets saturated, long term growth in line with general economy. Companies compete for market share on price basis.

      ii. Price earnings ratio is down, therefore the equity market is less attractive to the company. Generally reduced need for financing.

    7. Cyclicality.

      i. Should be compared to a benchmark such as real GDP growth, and should consider both industry-specific cycles and economic cycles.

    8. Entry barriers.

      i. Economies of scale and other cost advantages, capital requirements, intensity, product differentiation, access to distribution channels, and regulations.

    9. Cost structure.

      i. Labor cost, material cost, capital intensity, economies of scale, technological advantages/disadvantages, operating leverage.

D. Economic data.

    1. Aspects of economic conditions that may have a bearing on the firm's prospects.

      i. Identify clearly macroeconomic variables that affect the firm's sales and gross profit margin.

E. Financial analysis.
1. Analysis of the latest fiscal year.
   i. Income statement, balance sheet, cash flow and ratios.
   ii. Industry comparatives.
2. Deterministic projections and analysis.
   i. Most likely projections—ratio, cash flow, financial needs, and debt-capacity analysis—will show the firm has financial resources available and is viable.
   ii. Conservative (worse case) projection highlights.
      a. Sales growth and gross margin pegged to historical five-year lows. Average collection and holding periods set at historical five-year highs.
      b. Analysis reinforces firm's viability given worst-case scenario.
3. Stochastic projection and analysis.

F. Valuation analysis.
1. Approaches.
   i. Price: revenue multiples.
   ii. Capitalization of five year average earnings.
   iii. Capitalization of projected earnings.
   iv. Market capitalization: book capitalization multiples.
   v. Price earnings and price book.
   vi. Transaction multiple approach.
   vii. Liquidation value.
   viii. Dividend model.
   ix. Cash flow (while we will construct a weighted average, discounted free cash flow model will carry a substantial weight).
   x. The forecast horizon.
      a. Points we need to discuss to determine this extremely important valuation determinant.
      b. Proprietary technologies.
      c. Limited product lifecycle.
      d. Distribution channels.
      e. Industry-wide price competition.
2. Residual value.
   i. Once the discrete forecast horizon cash flows have been estimated, we can make a simplifying assumption regarding the cash flow generated after the forecast period.
3. Cost of capital.
   i. Textiles had a beta last year of 1.16.
   ii. We need to discuss the cost of debt, applying the cost of debt to the firm's tax rate.
4. Value driver analysis.
   i. Sales growth rate.
   ii. Incremental working capital investment.

        iii. Incremental fixed capital investment.

        iv. Cash tax rate.

        v. Cost of capital.

    5. Relative impact of key variables on shareholder value.

    6. Analysis of valuation ratios.

        a. Market value/book value.

        b. Liquidation value/market value.

G. Simulations: "Proving the valuation is right on target."

    1. Define assumptions.

        i. Understanding and working with value drivers.

        ii. Selecting the right distribution to fit data.

            a. Fitting distributions to data.

        iii. Correlations between independent variables and/or between independent variable (s) and the forecast variable.

            a. Responding to problems with correlated assumptions.

    2. Define forecast.

        i. Determining the certainty level.

            a. Finding the probability that valuation falls within specific ranges.

    3. Developing a sensitivity check and working with sensitivity charts.

    4. Creating reports.

H. Strategic planning: optimizing the company's value.

    1. Setting up and optimizing the linear programming model (Risk Simulator).

        i. Defining decision variables and selecting decision variables to optimize.

        ii. Specifying constraints (value driver(s) limitations).

        iii. Selecting the forecast objective: maximize shareholder value by linear programming changes to value drivers.

        iv. Perform sensitivity analysis.

Conclusion.

Summary of the valuation appraisal and recommendations.

Generalized list of the sources of information used. The degree of detail that is appropriate depends on the purpose and audience.

This section should be descriptive and analytical, allowing one to understand the firm and make qualitative judgments on the positive and negative aspects of the company that bear on its value.

Industry growth rate may be measured using any indicator relevant to the industry, including revenues, units shipped or produced, and assets. Appropriate benchmarks include real GDP growth, PCE (consumer spending), and S&P 500 growth.

> Stochastic projections: likely projections should be supported by simulations set at 5000 trials and a 95% certainty level. *Risk Simulator and Real Options Super Lattice Solver Software.*

> The length of the forecast horizon is not simply a convenient period of time in estimating financial performance, but a period based on the economics of the company and its industry.

Valuation Appraisal Toolkit

In the Modeling Toolkit software, there are several valuation models that can be used to perform valuation appraisals of clients. For instance, under *Modeling Toolkit | Valuation | Valuation Appraisal Model*, you will see the valuation appraisal model. The cells in boxes are the required inputs and the results are displayed throughout various worksheets in the model.

Figure 12A.1 is the *Corporate Valuation Model*, used for developing financial statements as well as for enterprise valuation and computing the total enterprise

Assumptions

Base Year (Valuation Year)	2008					
Start of Forecast Year	2008					
Years to Forecast	5					

Discounting — Discrete End-of-Year Discounting

Forecast Year	0	1	2	3	4	5
Year	2008	2009	2010	2011	2012	2013
Weighted Average Cost of Capital	15.00%	15.00%	15.00%	15.00%	15.00%	15.00%

Currency Units (e.g., in $000's)	1000
Equity Starting Value	129567
Marginal Tax Rate	35%
Return on Invested Capital	10%
Assumed Terminal WACC	10.00%
Assumed Terminal Growth Rate	5.00%
Current Stock Price	10.00

This is the Corporate Valuation Model used for developing financial statements as well as for enterprise valuation, and computing the total enterprise value, earnings per share, economic profit, and other financial metrics. The inputs are the boxed cells. You can extend the model to additional years by first entering the Years to Forecast (cell E7) and typing in the various required values in these future years (the boxes will automatically appear).

Revenues	678023	711924	747520	784896	824141	865348
Revenue: % Growth		5.00%	5.00%	5.00%	5.00%	5.00%
Other Operating Revenues	14554	17465	20958	25149	30179	36215
Other Operating Revenues: % Growth		20.00%	20.00%	20.00%	20.00%	20.00%
Cost of Goods Sold	180054	194458	210015	226816	244961	264558
Cost of Goods Sold: % Growth		8.00%	8.00%	8.00%	8.00%	8.00%
Selling, Gen & Admin Expenses	385447	393156	401019	409039	417220	425565
Selling, Gen & Admin Expenses: % Growth		2.00%	2.00%	2.00%	2.00%	2.00%
Non-Operating Income	7345	8080	8887	9776	10754	11829
Non-Operating Income: % Growth		10.00%	10.00%	10.00%	10.00%	10.00%
Interest Expense	23190	24350	25567	26845	28188	29597
Interest Expense: % Growth		5.00%	5.00%	5.00%	5.00%	5.00%
Cash	12826	14109	15519	17071	18779	20656
Cash: % Growth		10.00%	10.00%	10.00%	10.00%	10.00%
Accounts Receivable	24611	27072	29779	32757	36033	39636
Accounts Receivable: % Growth		10.00%	10.00%	10.00%	10.00%	10.00%
Inventories	16080	17688	19457	21402	23543	25897
Inventories: % Growth		10.00%	10.00%	10.00%	10.00%	10.00%

FIGURE 12A.1 Corporate Valuation Model

NOPLAT

EBITA	85755.00	69007.08	75352.45	82897.22	91753.69	119875.66
Adjustments (Operating Leases, Retirement Liabilities, Ongoing Provisions)	2672.00	0.00	0.00	0.00	0.00	0.00
Adjusted EBITA	**88427.00**	**69007.08**	**75352.45**	**82897.22**	**91753.69**	**119875.66**
Tax on EBT	24676.00	22743.41	25834.11	29233.67	33136.98	37675.09
Tax Shield on Interest Exp	0.00	0.00	0.00	0.00	0.00	0.00
Tax Shield on Operating Lease Interest	0.00	0.00	0.00	0.00	0.00	0.00
Tax Shield on Retirement Rel. Liab.	0.00	0.00	0.00	0.00	0.00	0.00
Tax on Interest Income	0.00	0.00	0.00	0.00	0.00	0.00
Tax on Non-operating Income	0.00	0.00	0.00	0.00	0.00	0.00
Change in Deferred Taxes	0.00	0.00	0.00	0.00	0.00	0.00
Taxes on EBITA	24676.00	22743.41	25834.11	29233.67	33136.98	37675.09
NOPLAT	63751.00	46263.66	49518.34	53663.55	58616.71	82200.57

FREE CASH FLOW

NOPLAT	63751.00	46263.66	49518.34	53663.55	58616.71	82200.57
Depreciation	41321.00	38268.45	40028.18	41523.96	42795.36	43876.06
Gross Cash Flow	105072.00	84532.11	89546.52	95187.51	101412.07	126076.62
Change in Capital Expenditures	56011.00	50000.00	50000.00	50000.00	50000.00	50000.00
Change in Investment of Working Capital	13585.00	-6205.52	711.92	747.52	784.90	824.14
Change in Other Operating Assets/Liabilities	23402.00	4000.00	4000.00	4000.00	4000.00	4000.00
Operating Leases	0.00	0.00	0.00	0.00	0.00	0.00
Total Investments on Working Capital	36987.00	-2205.52	4711.92	4747.52	4784.90	4824.14
Gross Investments	92998.00	47794.48	54711.92	54747.52	54784.90	54824.14
Free Cash Flow Excl. Goodwill	12074.00	36737.63	34834.60	40439.99	46627.18	71252.48
Investment in Goodwill and Intangibles	0.00	0.00	0.00	0.00	0.00	0.00
Free Cash Flow Incl. Goodwill	12074.00	36737.63	34834.60	40439.99	46627.18	71252.48
Interest Income (After Tax)	0.00	0.00	0.00	334.16	1868.21	3726.46
Decreases in Excess Marketable Securities	0.00	0.00	0.00	0.00	0.00	0.00
Foreign Exchange Translation Effects	0.00	0.00	0.00	0.00	0.00	0.00
Non-Operating Cash Flow	0.00	0.00	0.00	0.00	0.00	0.00
Extraordinary Items	1003.00	0.00	0.00	0.00	0.00	0.00
Cash Flow Available to Investors	13077.00	36737.63	34834.60	40774.14	48495.39	74978.94

ECONOMIC PROFIT

Operating Working Capital	-23008.00	-16802.48	-17514.41	-18261.93	-19046.82	-19870.97
Net Property Plant and Equipment	255123.00	266854.55	276826.37	285302.41	292507.05	298630.99
Other Assets Net of Other Liabilities	5553.00	9553.00	13553.00	17553.00	21553.00	25553.00
Value of Operating Leases	0.00	0.00	0.00	0.00	0.00	0.00
Total Invested Capital	237668.00	259605.07	272864.96	284593.48	295013.23	304313.03
Return on Invested Capital	26.82%	17.82%	18.15%	18.86%	19.87%	27.01%
Weighted Average Cost of Capital	15.00%	15.00%	15.00%	15.00%	15.00%	15.00%
Spread	11.82%	2.82%	3.15%	3.86%	4.87%	12.01%
Economic Profit (Before Goodwill)	28100.80	7322.90	8588.60	10974.53	14364.73	36553.61

FIGURE 12A.2 NOPLAT Valuation Output

value, earnings per share, economic profit, and other financial metrics. The inputs are the boxed cells. You can extend the model to additional years by first entering the Years to Forecast and typing in the various required values in these future years (the boxes will automatically appear). The model returns a set of financial statements such as the balance sheet, income statement or statement of cash flows, as well as the resulting computations of NOPLAT (net operating profits less adjusted taxes) (Figure 12A.2), which is then used in the computation of free cash flows to the firm and the resulting economic profit analysis and the valuation of the company. In addition, the market approach ratios analysis is also included in the model, as a way of calibrating the valuation results.

Note that this model uses a growth rate approach in which starting values are entered, the subsequent annualized growth rates of the variables are entered, and the model computes the future values of these variables. You can override any of the assumption cells above by simply typing over the values (changing growth

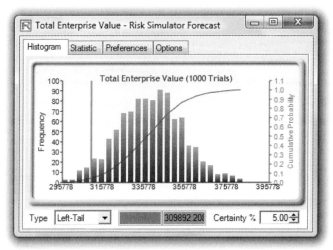

FIGURE 12A.3 Two Forecast Results: Projected Stock Price and Total Enterprise Value

rates over time or using actual values rather than growth rates). In addition, some sample input assumptions have been set up (cells in green) and an example simulation was run. Figure 12A.3 illustrates the same results from the simulation, indicating that there is a 12.90% chance that the stock price at the end of five years will fall below $23 per share (Figure 12A.3, top), and the total enterprise value at the worst-case scenario (5th percentile) Value-at-Risk is $309,892,000 (Figure 12A.3, bottom). You may override these input assumptions as required to create your own valuation model.

References

Glantz, M., Mun J. The Bankers Handbook on Credit Risk, Elsevier (AP), Chapter 11, p 245.

Mun, J. CEO of Real Options Valuation, Inc., premier software, training, and consulting firm located in California <www.realoptionsvaluation.com>. The software applications presented herein includes Risk Simulator, Modeling Toolkit, and others from the company.

Porter, M.E., 1980. Competitive Strategy: Techniques for Analyzing Industries and Competitors. Free Press, New York.

Valuation (Third Edition), 2000., McKinsey & Company, Inc., Tom Copeland et al., John Wiley & Sons.

Extreme Value Theory and Application to Market Shocks for Stress Testing and Extreme Value at Risk

13

This chapter presents extreme value functions and the role these functions play in extreme risk management in the financial services industry. We show how quantitative finance methodologies and internal risk modeling based on value at risk's normality assumption and historical statistical relationships failed to capture recent extreme events. We apply extreme theory and application to market shocks for stress testing and extreme value at risk, employing a model developed by Dr. Johnathan Mun, chairman, founder, and CEO of Real Options Valuation, Inc.

Recent history tells us it is unwise to discount the possibility of extreme events. Tail risk is real, and the real world does not fit neatly into a bell curve. If credit portfolio losses were bell shaped, we could specify the likelihood of large losses by defining portfolio expected and unexpected loss. The problem is that individual debt assets have very "skewed" loss probabilities. For instance, AAA debt assets enjoy a near-zero standard deviation, while a B-rated debt asset may have a five standard deviation within its distribution. In most cases, the obligor does not default and the loss is zero, but when default occurs, the loss could be substantial. Given the positive correlation between defaults, this unevenness of loss never fully resolves. There is always a large probability of relatively small losses, and a small probability of substantial losses.[1] Tail-event analysis includes two modeling functions: *value at risk* (VaR) and *extreme value* ("black swan"). VaR is based on normality, and linked to historical statistical relationships. Extreme value is usually associated with systemic catastrophic events such as the stock market crash of October 1987, the breakdown of the European Monetary System in September 1992, the turmoil in the bond market in February 1994, and the 2008 debt crisis.

Value at Risk and Systemic Shocks

Despite its many uses, VaR, like any statistical aggregate, is subject to the risk of misinterpretation and misapplication. Few deterministic, structural VaR models

---

[1]Dr. Jeffrey R. Bohn, *Managing Bank Risk*, Ch 13: Portfolio Management of Default Risk, Elsevier.

are successful at capturing event risk such as unexpected macroeconomic shocks. One problem with VaR stems from simplifying assumptions within a structural world that make it easier to arrive at the calculation, for example, the assumption of normality. While bank regulators have historically allowed banks to use internal VaR models for capital allocation, they recognized that few VaR models accurately capture event risk. It is mainly for this reason that regulators mandated special treatment for VaR components not determined by market-wide shocks. This component is "specific risk." Specific risk includes idiosyncratic risk (for example, price fluctuations not correlated with systemic shocks) and event risk. The higher multiplier on specific risk shows that VaR models typically underestimate specific risk *because they fail to incorporate event risk.*

Recent economic events made it abundantly clear that quantitative finance methodologies and internal risk-modeling techniques based on normality assumptions and historical (statistical) relationships fail to capture extreme events occurring in periods of systemic stress. Backward-looking assumptions about correlations, volatility, and market liquidity embedded in banks' VaR and other risk models did not hold up. Historical relationships do not constitute an end-all basis for forecasting grave risks. It stands that under the normality assumption, the probability of large market movements is largely underestimated and, more specifically, the probability of any deviation beyond 4 sigma is basically zero. Unfortunately, in the real world, 4-sigma events do occur, and they certainly occur more than once every 125 years, which is the supposed frequency of a 4-sigma event (at a 99.995% confidence level) under the normal distribution. Even worse, the 20-sigma event corresponding to the 1987 stock crash is supposed to happen not even once in trillions of years.[2]

Because they are systemic, and their magnitude is so difficult to predict, left-tail "black swan" events can have a devastating impact on credit-related portfolios. VaR failures led the Basel Committee to encourage banks to concentrate on rigorous stress testing that captures extreme tail events and integrate an appropriate risk dimension in banks' risk management policies and capital allocation. For example, the Basel III framework affords a bigger role for stress testing governing capital buffers. In fact, a 20-sigma event, under the normal distribution, would occur once every "googol," which is a 1 with 100 zeroes after it. In 1996, the Basel Committee had already imposed a multiplier of four to deal with model error. The essential non-normality of real financial market events suggests that such a multiplier is not enough. Following this, regulators have said VaR-based models contributed to complacency, citing the inability of advanced risk-management techniques to capture tail events.

Hervé Hannoun, deputy general manager at the Bank for International Settlements, reported that during the crisis, VaR models *"severely"*

---

[2]The Basel III Capital Framework: a decisive breakthrough, Hervé Hannoun, Deputy General Manager, Bank for International Settlements, BoJ-BIS High Level Seminar on Financial Regulatory Reform: Implications for Asia and the Pacific Hong Kong SAR, 22 November 2010.

underestimated the tail events and the high loss correlations under systemic stress. The VaR model has been the pillar for assessing risk in normal markets, but it has not fared well in extreme stress situations. *"Systemic events occur far more frequently and the losses incurred during such events have been far heavier than VaR estimates have implied. At the 99% confidence level, for example, you would multiply sigma by a factor of 2.33."*

The following analytical case study was authored by Dr. Johnathan Mun, chairman, founder, and CEO of Real Options Valuation, Inc., a premier software, training, and consulting firm located in California (www.realoptionsvaluation.com). The software applications presented herein include Risk Simulator, Modeling Toolkit, and others from the company. You can download free models, case studies, whitepapers, and trial software from the company's website. Dr. Mun holds professorships at multiple universities globally and has authored 12 books, some of which were co-authored with Morton Glantz.

Extreme Value Theory and Application to Market Shocks for Stress Testing and Extreme Value at Risk

Economic capital is highly critical to banks (as well as central bankers and financial regulators who monitor banks), as it links a bank's earnings and returns on investment tied to risks that are specific to an investment portfolio, business line, or business opportunity. In addition, these measurements of economic capital can be aggregated into a portfolio of holdings. To model and measure economic capital, the concept of value at risk (VaR) is typically used to try to understand how the entire financial organization is affected by the various risks of each holding as aggregated into a portfolio, after accounting for pairwise cross-correlations among various holdings. VaR measures the maximum possible loss given some predefined probability level (e.g., 99.90%) over some holding period or time horizon (e.g., 10 days). Senior management and decision makers at the bank usually select the probability or confidence interval, which reflects the board's risk appetite, or it can be based on Basel III capital requirements. Stated another way, we can define the probability level as the bank's desired probability of surviving per year. In addition, the holding period usually is chosen such that it coincides with the time period it takes to liquidate a loss position.

VaR can be computed several ways. Two main families of approaches exist: *structural closed-form models* and *Monte Carlo risk simulation* approaches. We showcase both methods later in this chapter, starting with the structural models. The second and much more powerful of the two approaches is the use of Monte Carlo risk simulation. Instead of simply correlating individual business lines or assets in the structural models, entire probability distributions can be correlated using more advanced mathematical copulas and simulation algorithms in Monte Carlo risk simulation methods by using the Risk Simulator software. In addition, tens to hundreds of thousands of scenarios can be generated using simulation, providing a very powerful stress testing mechanism for valuing VaR. Distributional fitting methods are applied to reduce the thousands of historical data into their appropriate probability distributions, allowing their modeling to be handled with greater ease.

While a normal distribution is usable for a multitude of applications, including its use in computing the standard VaR where the normal distribution might be a good model near its mean or central location, it might not be a good fit to real data in the tails (extreme highs and extreme lows), and a more complex model and distribution might be needed to describe the full range of the data. If the extreme tail values (from either end of the tails) that exceed a certain threshold are collected, you can fit these extremes to a separate probability distribution. There are several probability distributions capable of modeling these extreme cases, including the Gumbel distribution (also known as the extreme value distribution type I), the generalized Pareto distribution, and the Weibull Distribution. These models usually provide a good fit to extremes of complicated data.

Figure 13.1 illustrates the shape of these distributions. Notice that the Gumbel max (extreme value distribution type I, right skew), Weibull 3, and generalized

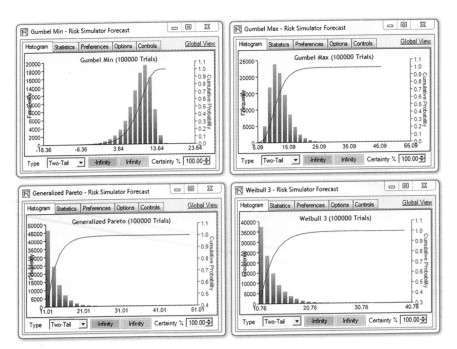

FIGURE 13.1 Sample Probability Distribution Function Shapes of the Common Extreme Value Distributions

Pareto all have a similar shape, with a right or positive skew (higher probability of a lower value, and a lower probability of a higher value). Typically, we would have potential losses listed as positive values (a potential loss of ten million dollars, for instance, would be listed as $10,000,000 *losses* instead of $-$ $10,000,000 in *returns*) as these distributions are unidirectional. The Gumbel min (extreme value distribution type I, left skew), however, would require negative values for losses (e.g., a potential loss of ten million dollars would be listed as $-$$10,000,000 instead of $10,000,000). See Figure 13.4 for an example dataset of extreme losses. This small but highly critical way of entering the data to be analyzed will determine which distributions you can and should use.

The probability distributions and techniques shown in this chapter can be used on a variety of datasets. For instance, you can use extreme value analysis on stock prices (Figure 13.2) or any other macroeconomic data such as interest rates or price of oil, and so forth (Figure 13.3 illustrates historical data on US Treasury rates and global crude oil Prices for the past 10 years). Typically, macroeconomic shocks (extreme shocks) can be modeled using a combination of such variables. For illustration purposes, we have selected Google's historical stock price to model. The same approach can be applied to any time-series macroeconomic data.

Macroeconomic shocks can sometimes be seen on time-series charts. For instance, in Figures 13.2 and 13.3, we see the latest US recession at or around January 2008 to June 2009 on all three charts (highlighted vertical region).

Therefore, the first step in extreme value analysis is to download the relevant time-series data on the selected macroeconomic variable. The second step is to determine the threshold—data above and beyond this threshold is deemed as extreme values (tail ends of the distribution)—for which these data will be analyzed separately.

Figure 13.4 shows the basic statistics and confidence intervals of Google stock's historical returns. As an initial test, we select the 5th percentile (-6.61%) as the threshold. That is, all stock returns at or below this -6.00% (rounded) threshold are considered potentially extreme and significant. Other approaches can also be used such as (i) running a GARCH model, in which this generalized autoregressive conditional heteroskedasticity model (and its many variations) is used to model and forecast volatility of the stock returns, thereby smoothing and filtering the data to account for any autocorrelation effects; (ii) creating Q-Q quantile plots of various distributions (e.g., Gumbel, generalized Poisson, or Weibull) and visually identifying at what point the plot asymptotically converges to the horizontal; and (iii) testing various thresholds to see at what point these extreme value distributions provide the best fit. Because the last two methods are related, we only illustrate the first and third approaches.

Figure 13.4 shows the filtered data where losses exceed the desired test threshold. Losses are listed as both negative values as well as positive (absolute) values. Figure 13.5 shows the distributional fitting results using Risk Simulator's distributional fitting routines applying the Kolmogorov-Smirnov test.

	A	B	C	D	E	F	G	H	I	J	K	L
1	HISTORICAL STOCK PRICES (WEEKLY) FOR GOOGLE											
2	Date	Open	High	Low	Close	Volume	Adj Close		Absolute	Relative	LN Relative	GARCH (1,1)
3	8/19/2004	100.00	109.08	95.96	108.31	16890200	108.31		Returns %	Returns	Returns	Volatility
4	8/23/2004	110.75	113.48	103.57	106.15	5605400	106.15		-1.99%	0.9801	-0.0201	
5	8/30/2004	105.28	105.49	98.94	100.01	3956300	100.01		-5.78%	0.9422	-0.0596	32.54%
6	9/7/2004	101.01	106.56	99.61	105.33	2952100	105.33		5.32%	1.0532	0.0518	33.93%
7	9/13/2004	106.63	117.49	106.46	117.49	4817300	117.49		11.54%	1.1154	0.1093	34.33%
8	9/20/2004	116.95	124.10	116.77	119.83	4314100	119.83		1.99%	1.0199	0.0197	41.64%
9	9/27/2004	119.56	135.02	117.80	132.58	8347800	132.58		10.64%	1.1064	0.1011	39.19%
10	10/4/2004	135.25	139.88	132.24	137.73	6662800	137.73		3.88%	1.0388	0.0381	43.99%
11	10/11/2004	137.00	145.50	133.40	144.11	6560600	144.11		4.63%	1.0463	0.0453	42.01%
12	10/18/2004	143.20	180.17	139.60	172.43	15788600	172.43		19.65%	1.1965	0.1794	40.71%
13	10/25/2004	176.40	199.95	172.55	190.64	20887400	190.64		10.56%	1.1056	0.1004	57.45%
14	11/1/2004	193.55	201.60	168.55	169.35	14340500	169.35		-11.17%	0.8883	-0.1184	58.37%
15	11/8/2004	170.93	189.80	165.27	182.00	12926300	182.00		7.47%	1.0747	0.0720	61.01%
16	11/15/2004	180.45	188.32	165.73	169.40	15270100	169.40		-6.92%	0.9308	-0.0717	58.99%
17	11/22/2004	164.47	180.03	161.31	179.39	11635600	179.39		5.90%	1.0590	0.0573	57.21%
18	11/29/2004	180.36	183.00	177.51	180.40	7672100	180.40		0.56%	1.0056	0.0056	54.70%
19	12/6/2004	179.13	180.70	168.47	171.65	6527500	171.65		-4.85%	0.9515	-0.0497	50.69%
20	12/13/2004	172.17	180.69	169.45	180.08	8667400	180.08		4.91%	1.0491	0.0479	48.54%
21	12/20/2004	182.00	188.60	181.87	187.90	5718100	187.90		4.34%	1.0434	0.0425	46.55%
22	12/27/2004	189.15	199.88	189.10	192.79	5300100	192.79		2.60%	1.0260	0.0257	44.50%
23	1/3/2005	197.40	203.64	187.72	193.85	11577300	193.85		0.55%	1.0055	0.0055	41.92%
24	1/10/2005	194.50	200.01	190.50	199.97	7833100	199.97		3.16%	1.0316	0.0311	39.17%
25	1/18/2005	200.97	205.30	188.12	188.28	10672500	188.28		-5.85%	0.9415	-0.0602	37.43%

Google Stock Price

FIGURE 13.2 Google's Historical Stock Prices, Returns, GARCH (1,1) Volatility Estimates, and Time-Series Chart

We see in Figure 13.5 that the negative losses fit the Gumbel minimum distribution the best, whereas the absolute positive losses fit the Gumbel maximum distribution the best. These two probability distributions are mirror images of each other, and therefore using either distribution in your model would be fine. Figure 13.6 shows two additional sets of distributional fits on data with 4% and 7% loss thresholds, respectively. We see that the best-fitting dataset for the extreme value is at the 7% loss threshold (a higher p-value means a better fit, and

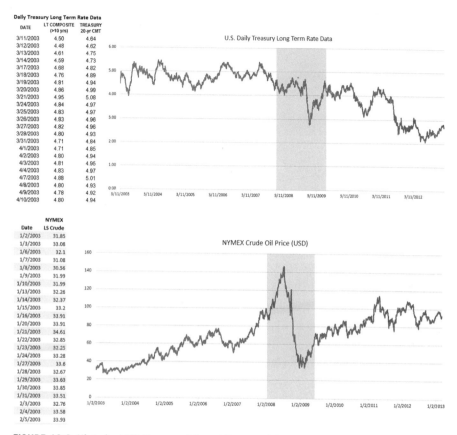

Daily Treasury Long Term Rate Data

DATE	LT COMPOSITE (>10 yrs)	TREASURY 20-yr CMT
3/11/2003	4.50	4.64
3/12/2003	4.48	4.62
3/13/2003	4.61	4.75
3/14/2003	4.59	4.73
3/17/2003	4.68	4.82
3/18/2003	4.76	4.89
3/19/2003	4.81	4.94
3/20/2003	4.86	4.99
3/21/2003	4.95	5.08
3/24/2003	4.84	4.97
3/25/2003	4.83	4.97
3/26/2003	4.83	4.96
3/27/2003	4.82	4.96
3/28/2003	4.80	4.93
3/31/2003	4.71	4.84
4/1/2003	4.71	4.85
4/2/2003	4.80	4.94
4/3/2003	4.81	4.95
4/4/2003	4.83	4.97
4/7/2003	4.88	5.01
4/8/2003	4.80	4.93
4/9/2003	4.78	4.92
4/10/2003	4.80	4.94

Date	NYMEX LS Crude
1/2/2003	31.85
1/3/2003	33.08
1/6/2003	32.1
1/7/2003	31.08
1/8/2003	30.56
1/9/2003	31.99
1/10/2003	31.99
1/13/2003	32.26
1/14/2003	32.37
1/15/2003	33.2
1/16/2003	33.91
1/20/2003	33.91
1/21/2003	34.61
1/22/2003	32.85
1/23/2003	32.25
1/24/2003	33.28
1/27/2003	33.6
1/28/2003	32.67
1/29/2003	33.63
1/30/2003	33.85
1/31/2003	33.51
2/3/2003	32.76
2/4/2003	33.58
2/5/2003	33.93

FIGURE 13.3 Historical US Treasury Interest Rates and Global Crude Oil Prices

a p-value of 93.71% on the 7% threshold data returns the best fit among the three).[3]

We recommend using the Kolmogorov-Smirnov method, as it is a nonparametric test and would be best suited for fitting extreme value tail events. You can also try the other fitting methods available in Risk Simulator's BizStats module, including Anderson-Darling, Akaike information criterion, Schwartz/Bayes criterion, Kuiper's statistics, and so forth.

---

[3]The null hypothesis tested is that the theoretically fitted distribution is the correct distribution, or that the error between the theoretical distribution tested and the empirical distribution of the data is zero, indicating a good fit. Therefore, a high p-value would allow us to not reject this null hypothesis and accept that the distribution tested is the correct distribution (any fitting errors are statistically insignificant).

Absolute Returns %	Relative Returns	LN Relative Returns	GARCH (1,1) Volatility
-1.99%	0.9801	-0.0201	
-5.78%	0.9422	-0.0596	32.54%
5.32%	1.0532	0.0518	33.93%
11.54%	1.1154	0.1093	34.33%
1.99%	1.0199	0.0197	41.64%
10.64%	1.1064	0.1011	39.19%
3.88%	1.0388	0.0381	43.99%
4.63%	1.0463	0.0453	42.01%
19.65%	1.1965	0.1794	40.71%
10.56%	1.1056	0.1004	57.45%
-11.17%	0.8883	-0.1184	58.37%
7.47%	1.0747	0.0720	61.01%

	Absolute Returns %	Relative Returns	GARCH (1,1) Volatility
Average	0.57%	1.0057	33.25%
Stdev	4.76%	0.0476	8.39%
1% Percentile	-11.62%	0.8838	23.71%
5% Percentile	-6.61%	0.9339	24.32%
50% Percentile	0.68%	1.0068	30.52%
95% Percentile	8.18%	1.0818	51.29%
99% Percentile	13.68%	1.1368	59.18%
Minimum	-15.35%	0.8465	22.69%
Maximum	19.65%	1.1965	63.73%
Threshold	-6.00%		

Returns >Threshold	Returns >Threshold
-15.35%	15.35%
-14.32%	14.32%
-14.19%	14.19%
-12.92%	12.92%
-11.98%	11.98%
-11.17%	11.17%
-10.76%	10.76%
-10.24%	10.24%
-9.83%	9.83%
-8.93%	8.93%
-8.92%	8.92%
-8.70%	8.70%
-8.45%	8.45%
-8.30%	8.30%
-8.21%	8.21%
-8.03%	8.03%
-7.85%	7.85%
-7.64%	7.64%
-7.21%	7.21%
-6.99%	6.99%
-6.92%	6.92%
-6.79%	6.79%
-6.65%	6.65%
-6.48%	6.48%
-6.38%	6.38%
-6.24%	6.24%
-6.19%	6.19%
-6.11%	6.11%
-6.10%	6.10%

FIGURE 13.4 Extreme Losses (Negative Returns) Statistics and their Values Above a Threshold

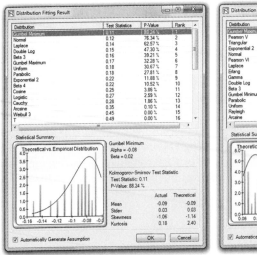
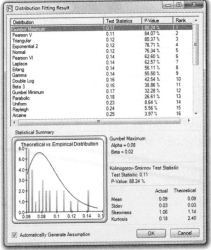

FIGURE 13.5 Distributional Fitting on Negative and Positive Absolute Values of Losses (6% loss threshold)

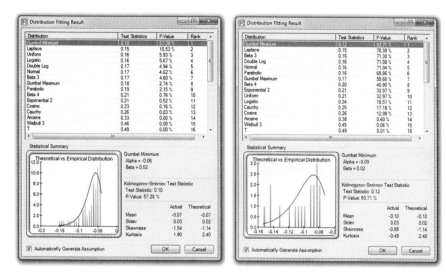

FIGURE 13.6 Distributional Fitting on 4% and 7% Loss Thresholds

To illustrate another method of data filtering, Figure 13.7 shows how a GARCH model can be run on the historical macroeconomic data. See the technical section later in this chapter for the various GARCH model specifications (e.g., GARCH, GARCH-M, TGARCH, EGARCH, GJR-GARCH, etc.). In most situations, we recommend using either GARCH or EGARCH for extreme value situations. The generated GARCH volatility results can also be charted, and we can visually inspect the periods of extreme fluctuations and refer back to the data to determine what those losses are. The volatilities can also be plotted as Control Charts in the Risk Simulator's BizStats module (Figure 13.8) in order to determine at what point the volatilities are deemed statistically *out of control*, that is, deemed to be extreme events.

Figure 13.9 shows the distributional fitting report from Risk Simulator. If we run a simulation for 100,000 trials on both the Gumbel minimum and Gumbel maximum distributions, we obtain the results shown in Figure 13.10. The VaR at 99% is computed to be a loss of −16.75% (averaged and rounded, taking into account both simulated distributions' results). Compare this −16.75% value, which accounts for extreme shocks on the losses, to, say, the empirical historical value of a −11.62% loss (Figure 13.4) only accounting for a small window of actual historical returns, which may or may not include any extreme loss events. The VaR at 99.9% is computed as −21.35% (Figure 13.10).

Further, as a comparison, if we assumed and used only a normal distribution to compute the VaR, the results would be significantly below what the extreme value stressed results should be. Figure 10.11 shows the results from the normal distribution

HISTORICAL STOCK PRICES (WEEKLY) FOR GOOGLE

Date	Open	High	Low	Close	Volume	Adj Close
8/19/2004	100.00	109.08	95.96	108.31	16890200	108.31
8/23/2004	110.75	113.48	103.57	106.15	5605400	106.15
8/30/2004	105.28	105.49	98.94	100.01	3956300	100.01
9/7/2004	101.01	106.56	99.61	105.33	2952100	105.33
9/13/2004	106.63	117.49	106.46	117.49	4817300	117.49
9/20/2004	116.95	124.10	116.77	119.83	4314100	119.83
9/27/2004	119.56	135.02	117.80	132.58	8347800	132.58
10/4/2004	135.25	139.88	132.24	137.73	6662800	137.73
10/11/2004	137.00	145.50	133.40	144.11	6560600	144.11
10/18/2004	143.20	180.17	139.60	172.43	15788600	172.43
10/25/2004	176.40	199.95	172.55	190.64	20887400	190.64
11/1/2004	193.55	201.60	168.55	169.35	14340500	169.35
11/8/2004	170.93	189.80	165.27	182.00	12926300	182.00
11/15/2004	180.45	188.32	165.73	169.40	15270100	169.40
11/22/2004	164.47	180.03	161.31	179.39	11635600	179.39
11/29/2004	180.36	183.00	177.51	180.40	7672100	180.40
12/6/2004	179.13	180.70	168.47	171.65	6527500	171.65
12/13/2004	172.17	180.69	169.45	180.08	8667400	180.08
12/20/2004	182.00	188.60	181.87	187.90	5718100	187.90
12/27/2004	189.15	199.88	189.10	192.79	5300100	192.79
1/3/2005	197.40	203.64	187.72	193.85	11577300	193.85
1/10/2005	194.50	200.01	190.50	199.97	7833100	199.97

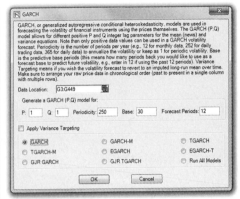

GARCH: Generalized Autoregressive Conditional Heteroskedasticity (Volatility Forecast)

GARCH models are used mainly for computing the volatility on liquid and tradable assets such as stocks in financial options; this model is sometimes used for other traded assets such as price of oil and price of electricity. The drawback is that a lot of data is required, advanced econometric modeling expertise is required, and this approach is highly susceptible to user manipulation. The benefit is that rigorous statistical analysis is performed to find the best-fitting volatility curve, providing different volatility estimates over time. GARCH is a term that incorporates a family of models that can take on a variety of forms, known as GARCH (P,Q), where P and Q are positive integers that define the resulting GARCH model and its forecasts. In most cases for financial instruments, a GARCH (1,1) is sufficient and is most generally used.

GARCH Model (P, Q)	1,1	Periodicity (Periods/Year)	52
Optimized Alpha	0.1107	Predictive Base	12
Optimized Beta	0.8386	Forecast Periods	12
Optimized Omega	0.0001	Variance Targeting	FALSE

	Period	Data	Volatility
8/19/2004	0	108.31	
8/23/2004	1	106.15	
8/30/2004	2	100.01	32.54%
9/7/2004	3	105.33	33.93%
9/13/2004	4	117.49	34.33%
9/20/2004	5	119.83	41.64%
9/27/2004	6	132.58	39.19%
10/4/2004	7	137.73	43.99%
10/11/2004	8	144.11	42.01%
10/18/2004	9	172.43	40.71%
10/25/2004	10	190.64	57.45%
11/1/2004	11	169.35	58.37%
11/8/2004	12	182.00	61.01%
11/15/2004	13	169.40	58.99%
11/22/2004	14	179.39	57.21%
11/29/2004	15	180.40	54.70%
12/6/2004	16	171.65	50.69%
12/13/2004	17	180.08	48.54%
12/20/2004	18	187.90	46.55%
12/27/2004	19	192.79	44.50%
1/3/2005	20	193.85	41.92%
1/10/2005	21	199.97	39.17%
1/18/2005	22	188.28	37.43%
1/24/2005	23	190.34	37.99%

GARCH or generalized autoregressive conditional heteroskedasticity models are used in forecasting the volatility of financial instruments, using the prices themselves. The GARCH (P,Q) model allows for different positive P and Q integer lag parameters for the mean (news) and variance equations. Note than only positive data values can be used in a GARCH volatility forecast. Periodicity is the number of periods per year (e.g., 12 for monthly data, 252 for daily trading data, 365 for daily data) to annualize the volatility or keep as 1 for periodic volatility. Base is the predictive base periods (this means how many periods back you would like to use as a forecast base to predict future volatility, and is typically between 1 and 12). Variance Targeting means if you wish the volatility forecast to revert to an imputed long-run mean over time. Make sure to arrange your raw price data in chronological order (past to present in a single column with multiple rows).

GARCH Volatility

FIGURE 13.7 Generalized Autoregressive Conditional Heteroscedasticity (GARCH) Model Results

VaR, where the 99% and 99.9% VaR show a loss of -8.99% and -11.99%, respectively, a far cry from the extreme values of -16.75% and -21.35%.

Another approach to predict, model, and stress-test extreme value events is to use a jump-diffusion stochastic process with a Poisson jump probability. Such a

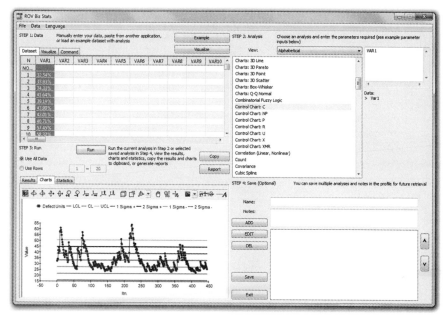

FIGURE 13.8 Time-Series Control Charts on GARCH Volatility Estimates

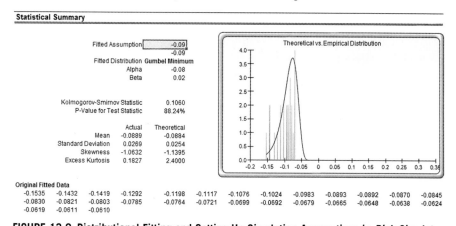

FIGURE 13.9 Distributional Fitting and Setting Up Simulation Assumptions in *Risk Simulator*.

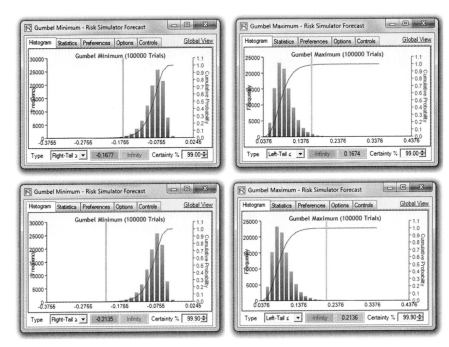

FIGURE 13.10 Gumbel Minimum and Gumbel Maximum Sample Simulated Results

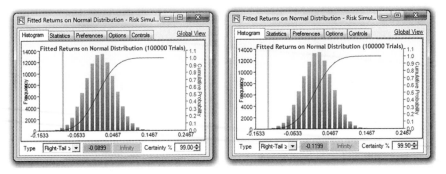

FIGURE 13.11 Similar Distributional Shapes of Gumbel, Generalized Pareto, and Weibull Distributions

model will require historical macroeconomic data to calibrate its inputs. For instance, using Risk Simulator's Statistical Analysis module, the historical Google stock returns were subjected to various tests and the stochastic parameters were calibrated as seen in Figure 13.12. Stock returns were used, as the

Stochastic Process - Parameter Estimations

Statistical Summary

A stochastic process is a sequence of events or paths generated by probabilistic laws. That is, random events can occur over time but are governed by specific statistical and probabilistic rules. The main stochastic processes include Random Walk or Brownian Motion, Mean-Reversion, and Jump-Diffusion. These processes can be used to forecast a multitude of variables that seemingly follow random trends but yet are restricted by probabilistic laws. The process-generating equation is known in advance but the actual results generated is unknown.

The Random Walk Brownian Motion process can be used to forecast stock prices, prices of commodities, and other stochastic time-series data given a drift or growth rate and a volatility around the drift path. The Mean-Reversion process can be used to reduce the fluctuations of the Random Walk process by allowing the path to target a long-term value, making it useful for forecasting time-series variables that have a long-term rate such as interest rates and inflation rates (these are long-term target rates by regulatory authorities or the market). The Jump-Diffusion process is useful for forecasting time-series data when the variable can occasionally exhibit random jumps, such as oil prices or price of electricity (discrete exogenous event shocks can make prices jump up or down). Finally, these three stochastic processes can be mixed and matched as required.

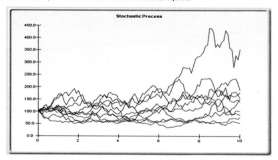

Statistical Summary

The following are the estimated parameters for a stochastic process given the data provided. It is up to you to determine if the probability of fit (similar to a goodness-of-fit computation) is sufficient to warrant the use of a stochastic process forecast, and if so, whether it is a random walk, mean-reversion, or a jump-diffusion model, or combinations thereof. In choosing the right stochastic process model, you will have to rely on past experiences and a priori economic and financial expectations of what the underlying data set is best represented by. These parameters can be entered into a stochastic process forecast (**Risk Simulator | Forecasting | Stochastic Processes**).

(Annualized)

Drift Rate*	0.60%		Reversion Rate**	N/A		Jump Rate**	12.13%
Volatility*	48.79%		Long-Term Value**	1.01		Jump Size**	0.07

Probability of stochastic model fit: 50.99%

*Values are annualized

FIGURE 13.12 **Stochastic Process Parameter Estimates from Raw Returns**

first-differencing creates added stationarity for the data. The calibrated model has a 50.99% fit (small probabilities of fit are to be expected because we are dealing with real-life non-stationary data with high unpredictability). The inputs were then modeled in the *Risk Simulator | Forecast | Stochastic Processes* module (Figure 13.13). The results generated by Risk Simulator are shown in Figure 13.14. As an example, if we use the end of Year 1's results and set an assumption, in this case, a normal distribution with whatever mean and standard deviation is computed in the results report (Figure 13.14), and a Monte Carlo risk simulation is run, the forecast results are shown in Figure 13.15, indicating that the VaR at 99% for this holding period is a loss of -11.33%. Notice that this result is consistent with Figure 13.4's 1% percentile (left 1% is the same as right tail 99%) of -11.62%. In normal circumstances, this stochastic process approach is valid and sufficient, but when extreme values are to be analyzed for the purposes of extreme stress testing, the underlying requirement of a normal distribution in stochastic process forecasting would be insufficient in estimating and

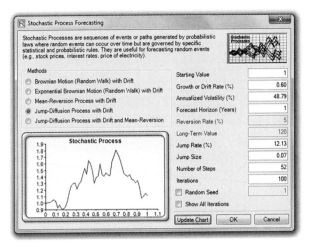

FIGURE 13.13 Modeling a Jump-Diffusion Stochastic Process

modeling these extreme shocks. And simply fitting and calibrating a stochastic process based only on extreme values would also not work as well as using, say, the extreme value Gumbel or generalized Poisson distributions.

Extreme co-movement of multiple variables does occur in the real world. For example, if the US S&P 500 index is down 25% today, we can be fairly confident that the Canadian market suffered a relatively large decline as well. If we modeled and simulated both market indices with a regular normal copula to account for their correlations, this extreme co-movement would not be adequately captured. The most extreme events for the individual indices in a normal copula require that they be independent of each other (iid random). The T-copula, in contrast, includes a degrees-of-freedom input parameter to model the co-tendency for extreme events that can and do occur jointly. The T-copula enables the modeling of a co-dependency structure of the portfolio of multiple individual indices. The T-copula also allows for better modeling of fatter-tail extreme events, as opposed to the traditional assumption of jointly normal portfolio returns of multiple variables.

The approach to run such a model is fairly simple. Analyze each of the independent variables using the methods described above, and when these are inputted into a portfolio, compute the pairwise correlation coefficients, and then apply the T-copula in Risk Simulator, available through the *Risk Simulator | Options* menu (Figure 13.16). The T-copula method employs a correlation matrix you enter, computes the correlation's Cholesky-decomposed matrix on the inverse of the T Distribution, and simulates the random variable based on the selected distribution (e.g., Gumbel max, Weibull 3, or generalized Pareto distribution).

Stochastic Process Forecasting: Jump Diffusion with Poisson Process

Statistical Summary

A stochastic process is a sequence of events or paths generated by probabilistic laws. That is, random events can occur over time but are governed by specific statistical and probabilistic rules. The main stochastic processes include Random Walk or Brownian Motion, Mean-Reversion, and Jump-Diffusion. These processes can be used to forecast a multitude of variables that seemingly follow random trends but yet are restricted by probabilistic laws.

The Random Walk Brownian Motion process can be used to forecast stock prices, prices of commodities, and other stochastic time-series data given a drift or growth rate and a volatility around the drift path. The Mean-Reversion process can be used to reduce the fluctuations of the Random Walk process by allowing the path to target a long-term value, making it useful for forecasting time-series variables that have a long-term rate such as interest rates and inflation rates (these are long-term target rates by regulatory authorities or the market). The Jump-Diffusion process is useful for forecasting time-series data when the variable can occasionally exhibit random jumps, such as oil prices or price of electricity (discrete exogenous event shocks can make prices jump up or down). Finally, these three stochastic processes can be mixed and matched as required.

The results on the right indicate the mean and standard deviation of all the iterations generated at each time step. If the Show All Iterations option is selected, each iteration pathway will be shown in a separate worksheet. The graph generated below shows a sample set of the iteration pathways.

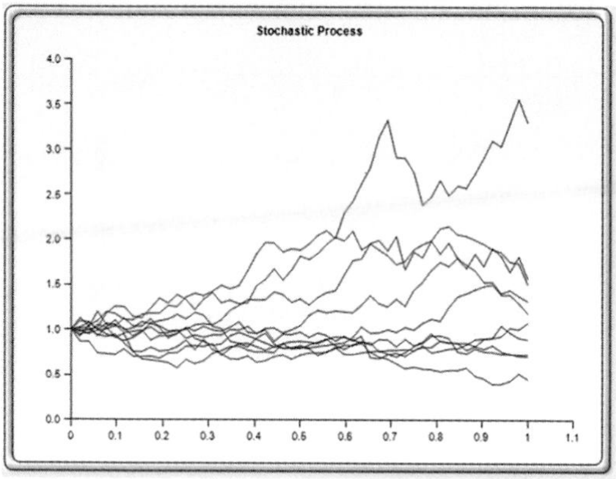

Time	Mean	Stdev
0.0000	1.0000	0.0000
0.0192	1.0069	0.0684
0.0385	1.0135	0.0845
0.0577	1.0194	0.1166
0.0769	1.0049	0.1300
0.0962	1.0080	0.1587
0.1154	1.0142	0.1738
0.1346	1.0134	0.1828
0.1538	1.0209	0.1962
0.1731	1.0281	0.2056
0.1923	1.0364	0.2151
0.2115	1.0291	0.2204
0.2308	1.0300	0.2400
0.2500	1.0325	0.2363
0.2692	1.0205	0.2442
0.2885	1.0353	0.2626
0.3077	1.0293	0.2743
0.3269	1.0387	0.2808
0.3462	1.0388	0.2843
0.3654	1.0430	0.2864
0.3846	1.0552	0.3048
0.4038	1.0501	0.3062
0.4231	1.0668	0.3368
0.4423	1.0624	0.3357
0.4615	1.0622	0.3428
0.4808	1.0592	0.3453
0.5000	1.0657	0.3576
0.5192	1.0729	0.3713
0.5385	1.0782	0.3874
0.5577	1.0917	0.4084
0.5769	1.0993	0.4151
0.5962	1.1051	0.4194
0.6154	1.1071	0.4311
0.6346	1.0942	0.4353
0.6538	1.0990	0.4516
0.6731	1.0988	0.4688
0.6923	1.1024	0.4815
0.7115	1.0870	0.4707
0.7308	1.0930	0.4704
0.7500	1.0971	0.4663
0.7692	1.0984	0.4653
0.7885	1.1056	0.4671
0.8077	1.1118	0.4788
0.8269	1.1121	0.4836

Stochastic Process: Jump-Diffusion Process with Drift

Start Value	1	Steps	52.00	Jump Rate	12.13%	
Drift Rate	0.60%	Iterations	100.00	Jump Size	0.07	
Volatility	48.79%	Reversion Rate	N/A	Random Seed	1091287598	
Horizon	1	Long-Term Value	N/A			

FIGURE 13.14 Stochastic Process Time-Series Forecasts for a Jump-Diffusion Model with a Poisson Process

Technical Details
Extreme Value Distribution or Gumbel Distribution

The extreme value distribution (type 1) is commonly used to describe the largest value of a response over a period of time, for example, in flood flows, rainfall, and earthquakes. Other applications include the breaking strengths of materials, construction design, and aircraft loads and tolerances. The extreme value distribution is also known as the Gumbel distribution.

The mathematical constructs for the extreme value distribution are as follows:

$$f(x) = \frac{1}{\beta} z e^{-z} \text{ where } z = e^{\frac{x-\alpha}{\beta}} \text{ for } \beta > 0; \text{ and any value of } x \text{ and } \alpha$$

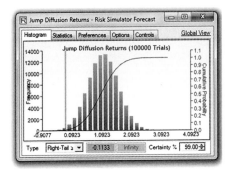

FIGURE 13.15 Risk Simulated Results from the Jump-Diffusion Stochastic Process Joint Dependence and T-copula for Correlated Portfolios

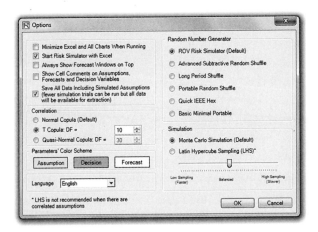

FIGURE 13.16 T-copula

$$Mean = \alpha + 0.577215\ \beta$$

$$\text{Standard Deviation} = \sqrt{\frac{1}{6}\pi^2\beta^2}$$

$$Skewness = \frac{12\sqrt{6}(1.2020569)}{\pi^3} = 1.13955 \text{ (this applies for all values of mode}$$

and scale)

$$Excess\ Kurtosis = 5.4 \text{ (this applies for all values of mode and scale)}$$

Mode (α) and scale (β) are the distributional parameters.

Calculating Parameters

There are two standard parameters for the extreme value distribution: mode and scale. The mode parameter is the most likely value for the variable (the highest point on the probability distribution). After you select the mode parameter, you can estimate the scale parameter. The scale parameter is a number greater than 0. The larger the scale parameter, the greater the variance.

The Gumbel maximum distribution has a symmetrical counterpart, the Gumbel minimum distribution. Both are available in Risk Simulator. These two distributions are mirror images of each other in that their respective standard deviations and kurtosis are identical, but the Gumbel maximum is skewed to the right (positive skew, with a higher probability on the left and lower probability on the right), as compared to the Gumbel minimum, in which the distribution is skewed to the left (negative skew). Their respective first moments are also mirror images of each other along the scale (β) parameter. Extreme Value Distributions shown in figures 13.17–13.24 include Gumbel, Pareto and Weibull distributions. The three distributions were created in stochastic mode by Johnathan Mun, Real Options Valuation Inc. and are available in Risk Simulator.

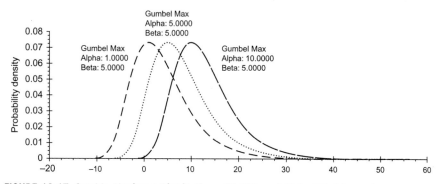

FIGURE 13.17 Gumble Maximum Distribution with Different Alpha (Mode)

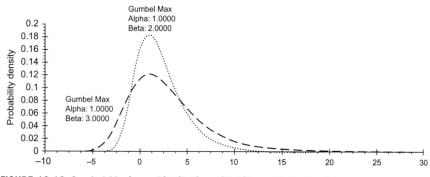

FIGURE 13.18 Gumbel Maximum Distribution with Different Beta (Scale)

Input requirements:

Mode alpha can be any value.
Scale beta > 0.

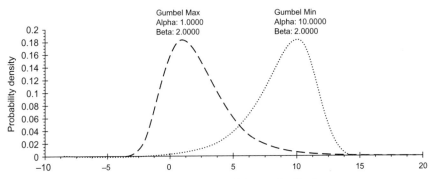

FIGURE 13.19 Gumbel Maximum versus Gumbel Minimum Distributions

ROV PROBABILITY DISTRIBUTIONS										

Distributions | Charts and Tables

This tool lists all the probability distributions available in Real Options Valuation, Inc.'s suite of products.

Apply Global Inputs

Minimum	10	Alpha	2	Location	10	Percentile	0.5	Mean	10
Maximum	20	Beta	5	Probability	0.5	DF	10	Stdev	2
MostLikely	15	Lambda	1.2	Factor	2	Trials	20	Successes	5

Alpha 1	5	DF Numerator	10
Alpha 2	5	DF Denominator	20
Population	100	Pop Success	50

Gamma		Geometric		Gumbel Max		Gumbel Min		Hypergeometric	
Alpha	2	Probability	0.5	Alpha	1	Alpha	1	Population	100
Beta	5			Beta	2	Beta	2	Trials	20
								Pop Success	50
Random X	14	Random X	2	Random X	14	Random X	-5	Random X	14
Percentile	0.5	Percentile	0.5	Percentile	0.5	Percentile	0.5	Percentile	0.5
PDF	0.0341	PDF	0.2500	PDF	0.0008	PDF	0.0237	PDF	0.0278
CDF	0.7689	CDF	0.7500	CDF	0.9985	CDF	0.0486	CDF	0.9886
ICDF	8.3917	ICDF	2.0000	ICDF	1.7330	ICDF	0.2670	ICDF	10.0000
Mean	10.0000	Mean	1.0000	Mean	2.1544	Mean	-0.1544	Mean	10.0000
Stdev	7.0711	Stdev	1.4142	Stdev	2.5651	Stdev	2.5651	Stdev	2.0101
Skew	1.4142	Skew	2.1213	Skew	1.1395	Skew	-1.1395	Skew	0.0000
Kurtosis	3.0000	Kurtosis	6.5000	Kurtosis	2.4000	Kurtosis	2.4000	Kurtosis	-0.0657

Laplace		Logistic		Lognormal (Log)		Lognormal (Arit...		Lognormal 3 (Log)	
Alpha	2	Alpha	2	Mean	5	Mean	168.17	Mean	5
Beta	5	Beta	5	Stdev	0.5	Stdev	89.63	Stdev	0.5
								Location	10
Random X	14	Random X	14	Random X	100	Random X	100	Random X	110
Percentile	0.5	Percentile	0.5	Percentile	0.5	Percentile	0.5	Percentile	0.5
PDF	0.0091	PDF	0.0153	PDF	0.0058	PDF	0.0058	PDF	0.0058
CDF	0.9546	CDF	0.9168	CDF	0.2149	CDF	0.2149	CDF	0.2149
ICDF	2.0000	ICDF	2.0000	ICDF	148.4132	ICDF	148.4075	ICDF	158.4132
Mean	2.0000	Mean	2.0000	Mean	168.1741	Mean	168.1700	Mean	178.1741
Stdev	7.0711	Stdev	9.0690	Stdev	89.6268	Stdev	89.6300	Stdev	89.6268
Skew	0.0000	Skew	0.0000	Skew	1.7502	Skew	1.7503	Skew	1.7502
Kurtosis	3.0000	Kurtosis	1.2000	Kurtosis	5.8984	Kurtosis	5.8993	Kurtosis	5.8984

Decimals: 4 | Language: English | | Run | Close

FIGURE 13.20 Gumbel Maximum versus Gumbel Minimum Distributions' Statistics and Moments

Generalized Pareto Distribution

The generalized Pareto distribution is often used to model the tails of another distribution.

The mathematical constructs for the extreme value distribution are as follows:

$$f(x) = \frac{1}{\sigma}\left[1 + \frac{\varepsilon(x-\mu)}{\sigma}\right]\exp\left(-\frac{1}{\varepsilon}-1\right) \text{ for all nonzero } \varepsilon \text{ else } f(x) = \frac{1}{\sigma}\exp\left(\frac{-(x-\mu)}{\sigma}\right)$$

$$\text{Mean} = \mu + \frac{\sigma}{1-\varepsilon} \text{ if } \varepsilon < 1$$

$$\text{Standard Deviation} = \sqrt{\frac{\sigma^2}{(1-\varepsilon)^2(1-2\varepsilon)}} \text{ if } \varepsilon < 0.5$$

Location (μ), scale (σ), and shape (ε) are the distributional parameters.
Input requirements:

Location mu can be any value.
Scale sigma > 0.

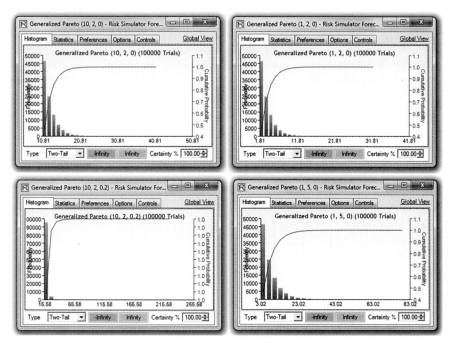

FIGURE 13.21 Generalized Pareto Distributions with Different Parameters

Shape epsilon can be any value. $\varepsilon < 0$ would create a long-tailed distribution with no upper limit, whereas $\varepsilon > 0$ would generate a short-tailed distribution with a smaller variance and thicker right tail, in which $\mu \le x < \infty$. If shape epsilon and location mu are both zero, then the distribution reverts to the exponential distribution. If the shape epsilon is positive and location Mu is exactly the ratio of scale sigma to shape epsilon, we have the regular Pareto distribution. The location mu is sometimes also known as the threshold parameter.

Distributions whose tails decrease exponentially, such as the normal distribution, lead to a generalized Pareto distribution's shape epsilon parameter of zero. Distributions whose tails decrease as a polynomial, such as Student's T-distribution, lead to a positive shape epsilon parameter. Finally, distributions whose tails are finite, such as the beta distribution, lead to a negative shape epsilon parameter.

Weibull Distribution (Rayleigh Distribution)

The Weibull distribution describes data resulting from life and fatigue tests. It is commonly used to describe failure time in reliability studies as well as the breaking strengths of materials in reliability and quality control tests. Weibull Distributions are also used to represent various physical quantities, such as wind speed.

The Weibull distribution is a family of distributions that can assume the properties of several other distributions. For example, depending on the shape parameter you define, the Weibull distribution can be used to model the exponential and Rayleigh distributions, among others. The Weibull distribution is very flexible. When the Weibull shape parameter is equal to 1.0, the Weibull distribution is identical to the exponential distribution. The Weibull location parameter lets you set up an exponential distribution to start at a location other than 0.0. When the shape parameter is less than 1.0, the Weibull distribution becomes a steeply declining curve. A manufacturer might find this effect useful in describing part failures during a burn-in period.

The mathematical constructs for the Weibull distribution are as follows:

$$f(x) = \frac{\alpha}{\beta} \left[\frac{x}{\beta}\right]^{\alpha-1} e^{-\left(\frac{x}{\beta}\right)^{\alpha}}$$

$$\text{Mean} = \beta\, \Gamma(1 + \alpha^{-1})$$

$$\text{Standard Deviation} = \beta^2[\Gamma(1 + 2\alpha^{-1}) - \Gamma^2(1 + \alpha^{-1})]$$

$$Skewness = \frac{2\Gamma^3(1 + \beta^{-1}) - 3\Gamma(1 + \beta^{-1})\Gamma(1 + 2\beta^{-1}) + \Gamma(1 + 3\beta^{-1})}{[\Gamma(1 + 2\beta^{-1}) - \Gamma^2(1 + \beta^{-1})]^{3/2}}$$

$$Excess\ Kurtosis \doteq \frac{-6\Gamma^4(1 + \beta^{-1}) + 12\Gamma^2(1 + \beta^{-1})\Gamma(1 + 2\beta^{-1}) - 3\Gamma^2(1 + 2\beta^{-1}) - 4\Gamma(1 + \beta^{-1})\Gamma(1 + 3\beta^{-1}) + \Gamma(1 + 4\beta^{-1})}{[\Gamma(1 + 2\beta^{-1}) - \Gamma^2(1 + \beta^{-1})]^2}$$

Shape (α) and central location scale (β) are the distributional parameters, and Γ is the gamma function.

Input requirements:

Shape alpha ≥ 0.05.
Scale beta > 0 and can be any positive value.

The Weibull 3 distribution uses the same constructs as the original Weibull distribution, but it adds a location (or shift) parameter. The Weibull distribution starts from a minimum value of 0, whereas the Weibull 3 (or shifted Weibull) distribution shifts the starting location to any other value.

Alpha, beta, and location or shift are the distributional parameters.

Input requirements:

Alpha (shape) ≥ 0.05.
Beta (central location scale) > 0 and can be any positive value.
Location can be any positive or negative value including zero.

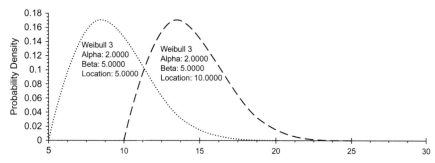

FIGURE 13.22 Weibull Distribution with Different Location Parameter

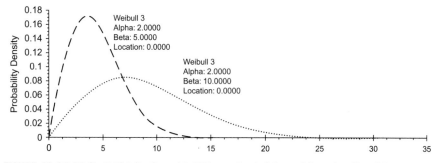

FIGURE 13.23 Weibull Distribution with Different Scaled Central Location (Beta) Parameter

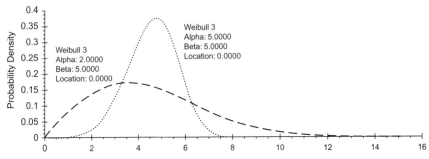

FIGURE 13.24 Weibull Distribution with Different Shape (Alpha) Parameter

GARCH Model: Generalized Autoregressive Conditional Heteroskedasticity

The generalized autoregressive conditional heteroskedasticity (GARCH) model is used to model historical and forecast future volatility levels of a marketable security (e.g., stock prices, commodity prices, oil prices, etc.). The dataset has to be a time series of raw price levels. GARCH will first convert the prices into relative returns and then run an internal optimization to fit the historical data to a mean-reverting volatility term structure, while assuming that the volatility is heteroskedastic in nature (changes over time according to some econometric characteristics). The theoretical specifics of a GARCH model are outside the purview of this chapter.

Procedure:

- Start Excel, open the example file *Advanced Forecasting Model*, go to the *GARCH* worksheet, and select *Risk Simulator | Forecasting | GARCH*.
- Click on the link icon, select the *Data Location*, and enter the required input assumptions (see Figure 13.25), and click *OK* to run the model and report.

Notes:

The typical volatility forecast situation requires $P = 1$, $Q = 1$; Periodicity = number of periods per year (12 for monthly data, 52 for weekly data, 252 or 365 for daily data); Base = minimum of 1 and up to the periodicity value; and Forecast Periods = number of annualized volatility forecasts you wish to obtain. There are several GARCH models available in Risk Simulator, including EGARCH, EGARCH-T, GARCH-M, GJR-GARCH, GJR-GARCH-T, IGARCH, and T-GARCH.

GARCH models are used mainly in analyzing financial time-series data to ascertain their conditional variances and volatilities. These volatilities are then

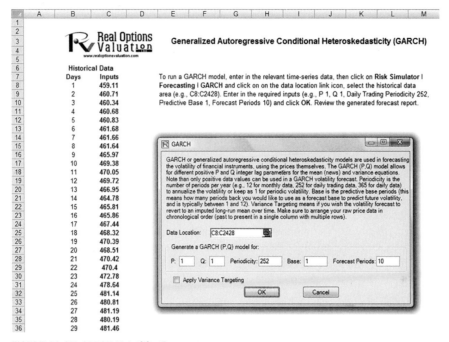

	A	B	C	D	E	F	G	H	I	J	K	L	M
6		Historical Data											
7		Days	Inputs										
8		1	459.11										
9		2	460.71										
10		3	460.34										
11		4	460.68										
12		5	460.83										
13		6	461.68										
14		7	461.66										
15		8	461.64										
16		9	465.97										
17		10	469.38										
18		11	470.05										
19		12	469.72										
20		13	466.95										
21		14	464.78										
22		15	465.81										
23		16	465.86										
24		17	467.44										
25		18	468.32										
26		19	470.39										
27		20	468.51										
28		21	470.42										
29		22	470.4										
30		23	472.78										
31		24	478.64										
32		25	481.14										
33		26	480.81										
34		27	481.19										
35		28	480.19										
36		29	481.46										

FIGURE 13.25 GARCH Volatility Forecast

used to value the options as usual, but the amount of historical data necessary for a good volatility estimate remains significant. Usually, several dozen—and even up to hundreds—of data points are required to obtain good GARCH estimates. GARCH is a term that incorporates a family of models that can take on a variety of forms, known as GARCH(p,q), where p and q are positive integers that define the resulting GARCH model and its forecasts. In most cases for financial instruments, a GARCH(1,1) is sufficient and is most generally used. For instance, a GARCH (1,1) model takes the form of:

$$y_t = x_t \gamma + \varepsilon_t$$
$$\sigma_t^2 = \omega + \alpha \varepsilon_{t-1}^2 + \beta \sigma_{t-1}^2$$

where the first equation's dependent variable (y_t) is a function of exogenous variables (x_t) with an error term (ε_τ). The second equation estimates the variance (squared volatility σ_τ^2) at time t, which depends on a historical mean (ω), news about volatility from the previous period, measured as a lag of the squared residual from the mean equation $(\varepsilon_{\tau-1}^2)$, and volatility from the previous period $(\sigma_{\tau-1}^2)$. The exact modeling specification of a GARCH model is beyond the scope of this chapter. Suffice it to say that detailed knowledge of econometric modeling (model specification tests, structural breaks, and error estimation) is required to run a GARCH model, making it less accessible to the general analyst. Another problem with GARCH models is that the model usually does not provide a good statistical fit. That is, it is impossible to predict the stock market and, of course, equally hard if not harder to predict a stock's volatility over time. Note that the GARCH function has several inputs, as follows:

- *Time-series data:* The time series of data in chronological order (e.g., stock prices). Typically, dozens of data points are required for a decent volatility forecast.
- *Periodicity:* A positive integer indicating the number of periods per year (e.g., 12 for monthly data, 252 for daily trading data, etc.), assuming you wish to annualize the volatility. For getting periodic volatility, enter 1.
- *Predictive base:* The number of periods back (of the time-series data) to use as a base to forecast volatility. The higher this number, the longer the historical base used to forecast future volatility.
- *Forecast period*: A positive integer indicating how many future periods beyond the historical stock prices you wish to forecast.
- *Variance targeting:* This variable is set as false by default (even if you do not enter anything here), but it can be set as true. False means the omega variable is automatically optimized and computed. The suggestion is to leave this variable empty. If you wish to create mean-reverting volatility with variance targeting, set this variable as true.
- *P*: The number of previous lags on the mean equation.
- *Q*: The number of previous lags on the variance equation.

Table 13.1 lists some of the GARCH specifications used in Risk Simulator, with two underlying distributional assumptions: one for normal distribution and the other for the T-distribution.

For the GARCH-M models, the conditional variance equations are the same in the six variations, but the mean questions are different and the assumption on z_t can be either normal distribution or T-distribution. The estimated parameters for GARCH-M with normal distribution are those five parameters in the mean and conditional variance equations. The estimated parameters for GARCH-M with the T-distribution are those five parameters in the mean and conditional variance equations plus another parameter, the degrees of freedom for the T-distribution. In contrast, for the GJR models, the mean equations are the same in the six variations, and the differences are that the conditional variance equations and the assumption on z_t can be either a normal distribution or T-distribution. The estimated parameters for EGARCH and GJR-GARCH with normal distribution are those four parameters in the conditional variance equation. The estimated parameters for GARCH, EARCH, and GJR-GARCH with T-distribution are those parameters in the conditional variance equation plus the degrees of freedom for the T-distribution.

Table 13.1 GARCH Specifications used in Risk Simulator

	$z_t \sim$ **Normal Distribution**	$z_t \sim$ **T-Distribution**
GARCH-M Variance in Mean Equation	$y_t = c + \lambda\sigma_t^2 + \varepsilon_t$ $\varepsilon_t = \sigma_t z_t$ $\sigma_t^2 = \omega + \alpha\varepsilon_{t-1}^2 + \beta\sigma_{t-1}^2$	$y_t = c + \lambda\sigma_t^2 + \varepsilon_t$ $\varepsilon_t = \sigma_t z_t$ $\sigma_t^2 = \omega + \alpha\varepsilon_{t-1}^2 + \beta\sigma_{t-1}^2$
GARCH-M Standard Deviation in Mean Equation	$y_t = c + \lambda\sigma_t + \varepsilon_t$ $\varepsilon_t = \sigma_t z_t$ $\sigma_t^2 = \omega + \alpha\varepsilon_{t-1}^2 + \beta\sigma_{t-1}^2$	$y_t = c + \lambda\sigma_t + \varepsilon_t$ $\varepsilon_t = \sigma_t z_t$ $\sigma_t^2 = \omega + \alpha\varepsilon_{t-1}^2 + \beta\sigma_{t-1}^2$
GARCH-M Log Variance in Mean Equation	$y_t = c + \lambda\ln(\sigma_t^2) + \varepsilon_t$ $\varepsilon_t = \sigma_t z_t$ $\sigma_t^2 = \omega + \alpha\varepsilon_{t-1}^2 + \beta\sigma_{t-1}^2$	$y_t = c + \lambda\ln(\sigma_t^2) + \varepsilon_t$ $\varepsilon_t = \sigma_t z_t$ $\sigma_t^2 = \omega + \alpha\varepsilon_{t-1}^2 + \beta\sigma_{t-1}^2$
GARCH	$y_t = x_t\gamma + \varepsilon_t$ $\sigma_t^2 = \omega + \alpha\varepsilon_{t-1}^2 + \beta\sigma_{t-1}^2$	$y_t = \varepsilon_t$ $\varepsilon_t = \sigma_t z_t$ $\sigma_t^2 = \omega + \alpha\varepsilon_{t-1}^2 + \beta\sigma_{t-1}^2$
EGARCH	$y_t = \varepsilon_t$ $\varepsilon_t = \sigma_t z_t$ $\ln(\sigma_t^2) = \omega + \beta\cdot\ln(\sigma_{t-1}^2) + \alpha\left[\left\lvert\dfrac{\varepsilon_{t-1}}{\sigma_{t-1}}\right\rvert - E(\lvert\varepsilon_t\rvert)\right] + r\dfrac{\varepsilon_{t-1}}{\sigma_{t-1}}$ $E(\lvert\varepsilon_t\rvert) = \sqrt{\dfrac{2}{\pi}}$	$y_t = \varepsilon_t$ $\varepsilon_t = \sigma_t z_t$ $\ln(\sigma_t^2) = \omega + \beta\cdot\ln(\sigma_{t-1}^2) + \alpha\left[\left\lvert\dfrac{\varepsilon_{t-1}}{\sigma_{t-1}}\right\rvert - E(\lvert\varepsilon_t\rvert)\right] + r\dfrac{\varepsilon_{t-1}}{\sigma_{t-1}}$ $E(\lvert\varepsilon_t\rvert) = \dfrac{2\sqrt{\nu - 2}\,\Gamma((\nu+1)/2)}{(\nu-1)\Gamma(\nu/2)\sqrt{\pi}}$

(Continued)

Table 13.1 (Continued)

	$z_t \sim$ **Normal Distribution**	$z_t \sim$ **T-Distribution**
GJR-GARCH	$y_t = \varepsilon_t$	$y_t = \varepsilon_t$
	$\varepsilon_t = \sigma_t z_t$	$\varepsilon_t = \sigma_t z_t$
	$\sigma_t^2 = \omega + \alpha \varepsilon_{t-1}^2 +$	$\sigma_t^2 = \omega + \alpha \varepsilon_{t-1}^2 +$
	$\quad r\varepsilon_{t-1}^2 d_{t-1} + \beta \sigma_{t-1}^2$	$\quad r\varepsilon_{t-1}^2 d_{t-1} + \beta \sigma_{t-1}^2$
	$d_{t-1} = \begin{cases} 1 & \text{if } \varepsilon_{t-1} < 0 \\ 0 & \text{otherwise} \end{cases}$	$d_{t-1} = \begin{cases} 1 & \text{if } \varepsilon_{t-1} < 0 \\ 0 & \text{otherwise} \end{cases}$

Economic Capital and Value at Risk Illustrations
Structural VaR Models

The first VaR example model shown is the *Value at Risk—Static Covariance Method*, accessible through *Modeling Toolkit | Value at Risk | Static Covariance Method.* This model is used to compute the portfolio's VaR at a given percentile for a specific holding period, after accounting for the cross-correlation effects between the assets (Figure 13.26). The daily volatility is the annualized volatility divided by the square root of trading days per year. Typically, positive correlations tend to carry a higher VaR compared to zero-correlation asset mixes, whereas negative correlations reduce the total risk of the portfolio through the diversification effect (Figures 13.26 and 13.27). The approach used is a portfolio VaR with correlated inputs, where the portfolio has multiple asset holdings with different amounts and volatilities. Assets are also correlated to each other. The covariance or correlation structural model is used to compute the VaR given a holding period or horizon and a percentile value (typically 10 days at 99% confidence). Of course, the example illustrates only a few assets or business or credit lines for simplicity's sake. Nonetheless, using the VaR functions in Modeling Toolkit (*B2VaRCorrelationMethod*), many more lines, assets, or businesses can be modeled.

VALUE AT RISK (VARIANCE-COVARIANCE METHOD)

Asset Allocation	Amount	Daily Volatility
Asset A	$1,000,000.00	1.20%
Asset B	$2,000,000.00	2.00%
Asset C	$3,000,000.00	1.89%
Asset D	$4,000,000.00	3.25%
Asset E	$5,000,000.00	4.20%

Correlation Matrix	Asset A	Asset B	Asset C	Asset D	Asset E
Asset A	1.0000	0.1000	0.1000	0.1000	0.1000
Asset B	0.1000	1.0000	0.1000	0.1000	0.1000
Asset C	0.1000	0.1000	1.0000	0.1000	0.1000
Asset D	0.1000	0.1000	0.1000	1.0000	0.1000
Asset E	0.1000	0.1000	0.1000	0.1000	1.0000

Horizon (Days)	10
Percentile	99.00%

Value at Risk (Daily)	$655,915.30
Value at Risk (Horizon)	$2,074,186.30

Daily Value at Risk (Positive Correlations)	$2,074,186.30
Daily Value at Risk (Zero Correlations)	$1,889,345.26
Daily Value at Risk (Negative Correlations)	$1,684,340.28

FIGURE 13.26 Computing VaR using the Structural Covariance Method

Correlation Matrix	Asset A	Asset B	Asset C	Asset D	Asset E
Asset A	1.0000	0.1000	0.1000	0.1000	0.1000
Asset B	0.1000	1.0000	0.1000	0.1000	0.1000
Asset C	0.1000	0.1000	1.0000	0.1000	0.1000
Asset D	0.1000	0.1000	0.1000	1.0000	0.1000
Asset E	0.1000	0.1000	0.1000	0.1000	1.0000

Correlation Matrix	Asset A	Asset B	Asset C	Asset D	Asset E
Asset A	1.0000	0.0000	0.0000	0.0000	0.0000
Asset B	0.0000	1.0000	0.0000	0.0000	0.0000
Asset C	0.0000	0.0000	1.0000	0.0000	0.0000
Asset D	0.0000	0.0000	0.0000	1.0000	0.0000
Asset E	0.0000	0.0000	0.0000	0.0000	1.0000

Correlation Matrix	Asset A	Asset B	Asset C	Asset D	Asset E
Asset A	1.0000	-0.1000	-0.1000	-0.1000	-0.1000
Asset B	-0.1000	1.0000	-0.1000	-0.1000	-0.1000
Asset C	-0.1000	-0.1000	1.0000	-0.1000	-0.1000
Asset D	-0.1000	-0.1000	-0.1000	1.0000	-0.1000
Asset E	-0.1000	-0.1000	-0.1000	-0.1000	1.0000

FIGURE 13.27 Different Correlation Levels

VaR Models using Monte Carlo Risk Simulation

The model used is *Value at Risk—Portfolio Operational and Capital Adequacy* and is accessible through *Modeling Toolkit | Value at Risk | Portfolio Operational and Capital Adequacy*. This model shows how operational risk and credit risk parameters are fitted to statistical distributions, and it shows their resulting distributions modeled in a portfolio of liabilities to determine the VaR (99.50th percentile certainty) for the capital requirement under Basel II requirements. It is assumed that the historical data of the operational risk impacts (*Historical Data worksheet*) are obtained through econometric modeling of the key risk indicators.

The *Distributional Fitting Report* worksheet is a result of running a distributional fitting routine in Risk Simulator to obtain the appropriate distribution for the operational risk parameters. Using the resulting distributional parameter, we model each liability's capital requirements within an entire portfolio. Correlations can also be inputted, if required, between pairs of liabilities or business units. The resulting Monte Carlo simulation results show the VaR capital requirements.

Note that an appropriate empirically based historical VaR cannot be obtained if distributional fitting and risk-based simulations were not first run. The VaR will be obtained only by running simulations. To perform distributional fitting, follow the steps ahead:

1. In the *Historical Data* worksheet (Figure 13.28), select the data area (cells *C5:L104*), and click on *Risk Simulator | Tools | Distributional Fitting (Single Variable)*.

Basel II - Credit Risk and Capital Requirement (Portfolio-Based)

This model applies the Basel II requirements on capital adequacy and modeling the operational risk of probability of default on 100 loans as well as the loss given default. These values are fitted based on the bank's historical loss data (Historical Data and Distributional Fitting Report sheets) using Risk Simulator. Then, the relevant historical simulation assumptions are set in this model (Credit Risk sheet) and a Monte Carlo risk-based simulation was run in Risk Simulator to determine the expected capital required and 99.50% Value at Risk (VaR). A simulation has to be run in order to determine the VaR.

Market Factor	2.000	Rating level	P (Default) - Long term
		1	0.5%
		2	1.0%
		3	1.5%
Weighting:		4	2.0%
Macro	50%	5	2.5%
Micro	50%	6	3.0%
		7	5.0%
Correlation	100%		

	Static	Stochastic with Risk-Simulation
Expected Value of Total Capital	$11,734.54	$11,112.81
VaR 99.50% of Total Capital	$30,888.34	$25,959.60

Without running historical simulations, the 99.50% VaR cannot be obtained directly. The only recourse is to apply a theoretical distributional analysis using the fitted distributions' empirical parameters and estimating the theoretical cumulative density function value at 99.50%, and computing the relevant theoretical confidence level. This approach is at best an overestimation of the required capital (thereby requiring too much capital) and at worst, wrong.

| | | | | Sum | $11,734.54 | $ - |
| | | | | Static 99.50% | $30,888.34 | |

Bank loan	Size of loan	Rating grade	P (Default) - Long term	Operational Risk Factor	P (Default) - Now	Default?	Loss Given Default (LGD%)		Losses	
							Static	Stochastic	Static	Stochastic
1	$ 13,274.73	5	2.5%	2.000	5.00%	0	30.0%	30.0%	$ 199.12	$ -
2	$ 14,215.77	6	3.0%	2.000	6.00%	0	30.0%	30.0%	$ 255.88	$ -
3	$ 9,003.59	1	0.5%	2.000	1.00%	0	30.0%	30.0%	$ 27.01	$ -
4	$ 1,324.27	3	1.5%	2.000	3.00%	0	30.0%	30.0%	$ 11.92	$ -
5	$ 11,203.14	1	0.5%	2.000	1.00%	0	30.0%	30.0%	$ 33.61	$ -
6	$ 5,480.61	4	2.0%	2.000	4.00%	0	30.0%	30.0%	$ 65.77	$ -
7	$ 9,853.12	5	2.5%	2.000	5.00%	0	30.0%	30.0%	$ 147.80	$ -
8	$ 12,356.22	3	1.5%	2.000	3.00%	0	30.0%	30.0%	$ 111.21	$ -
9	$ 8,255.80	4	2.0%	2.000	4.00%	0	30.0%	30.0%	$ 99.07	$ -
10	$ 1,662.99	2	1.0%	2.000	2.00%	0	30.0%	30.0%	$ 9.98	$ -
11	$ 7,175.82	3	1.5%	2.000	3.00%	0	30.0%	30.0%	$ 64.58	$ -

FIGURE 13.28 Sample Historical Bank Loans

2. Browse through the fitted distributions, and select the best-fitting distribution (in this case, the exponential distribution in Figure 13.29) and click *OK*.

3. You may now set the assumptions on the *Operational Risk Factors* with the Exponential Distribution (fitted results show *Lambda* = 1) in the *Credit Risk* worksheet. Note that the assumptions have already been set for you in advance. You may set the assumption by going to cell *F27* and clicking on *Risk Simulator | Set Input Assumption*, selecting *Exponential Distribution*, and entering *1* for the *Lambda* value and clicking *OK*. Continue this process for the remaining cells in column F, or simply perform a *Risk Simulator Copy* and *Risk Simulator Paste* on the remaining cells.

   a. Note that since the cells in column F have assumptions set, you will first have to clear them if you wish to reset and copy/paste parameters. You

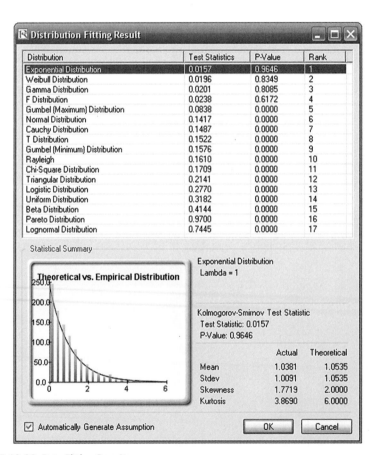

FIGURE 13.29 Data Fitting Results

can do so by first selecting cells *F28:F126* and clicking on the *Remove Parameter* icon or select *Risk Simulator | Remove Parameter*.

   b. Then select cell *F27*, click on the *Risk Simulator Copy* icon or select *Risk Simulator | Copy Parameter*, and then select cells *F28:F126* and click on the *Risk Simulator Paste* icon or select *Risk Simulator | Paste Parameter*.

4. Next, you can set additional assumptions, such as the probability of default using the Bernoulli distribution (column H) and *Loss Given Default* (column J). Repeat the procedure in Step 3 if you wish to reset the assumptions.

5. Run the simulation by clicking on the *Run* icon or clicking on *Risk Simulator | Run Simulation*.

6. Obtain the value at risk by going to the forecast chart once the simulation is done running, selecting *Left-Tail*, and typing in *99.50*. Hit *Tab* on the keyboard to enter the confidence value and obtain the VaR of $25,959 (Figure 13.30).

Another example on VaR computation is shown next, where the model *Value at Risk—Right Tail Capital Requirements* is used, available through *Modeling Toolkit | Value at Risk | Right Tail Capital Requirements*.

This model shows the capital requirements per Basel II requirements (99.95th percentile capital adequacy based on a specific holding period's value at risk). Without running risk-based historical and Monte Carlo simulations using Risk Simulator, the required capital is $37.01M (Figure 13.31), as compared to only $14.00M required using a correlated simulation (Figure 13.32). This is due to the cross-correlations between assets and business lines, and can be modeled only using Risk Simulator. This lower VaR is preferred, as banks can now be required to hold less required capital and can reinvest the remaining capital in various profitable ventures, thereby generating higher profits.

1. To run the model, click on *Risk Simulator | Run Simulation* (if you had other models open, make sure you first click on *Risk Simulator | Change Simulation | Profile*, and select the *Tail VaR* profile before starting).

FIGURE 13.30 Simulated Forecast Results and the 99.50% VaR Value

TAIL VALUE AT RISK MODEL (BASEL II REQUIREMENT)

Correlation Matrix

Line of Business	Mean Required Capital	99.95th Percentile	Capital Required	Allocation Weights	Minimum Allowed	Maximum Allowed			1	2	3	4	5	6	7	8	9	10
Business 1	$10.50	$36.52	$26.01	10.00%	5.00%	15.00%	3.48	1										
Business 2	$11.12	$47.52	$36.39	10.00%	5.00%	15.00%	4.27	2	-0.20									
Business 3	$11.77	$48.99	$37.22	10.00%	5.00%	15.00%	4.16	3	-0.13	0.35								
Business 4	$10.77	$37.34	$26.56	10.00%	5.00%	15.00%	3.47	4	-0.05	0.01	0.00							
Business 5	$13.49	$49.52	$36.03	10.00%	5.00%	15.00%	3.67	5	0.23	0.50	0.15	0.00						
Business 6	$14.24	$55.59	$41.35	10.00%	5.00%	15.00%	3.91	6	0.00	0.00	-0.15	0.00	0.03					
Business 7	$15.60	$60.24	$44.64	10.00%	5.00%	15.00%	3.86	7	0.25	0.00	-0.26	0.01	0.10	-0.10				
Business 8	$14.95	$64.69	$49.74	10.00%	5.00%	15.00%	4.33	8	0.36	-0.25	-0.60	-0.30	0.00	0.00	-0.15			
Business 9	$14.15	$61.02	$46.87	10.00%	5.00%	15.00%	4.31	9	-0.01	-0.20	0.16	0.04	-0.01	0.01	0.00	0.00		
Business 10	$10.08	$35.37	$25.29	10.00%	5.00%	15.00%	3.51											
Portfolio Total	$12.67	$49.68	$37.01	100.00%														
Total Capital Required			$14.00															

FIGURE 13.31 Right-Tail VaR Model

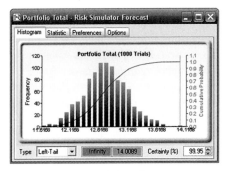

FIGURE 13.32 Simulated Results of the Portfolio VaR

2. When the simulation run is complete, select *Left-Tail* in the forecast chart, enter *99.95* in the *Certainty* box, and hit *TAB* on the keyboard to obtain the value of $14.00M value at risk for this correlated simulation.

3. Note that the assumptions have already been set for you in advance in the model in cells *C6:C15*. However, you may set them again by going to cell *C6* and clicking on *Risk Simulator | Set Input Assumption*, selecting your distribution of choice or using the default *Normal Distribution* or performing a distributional fitting on historical data, then clicking *OK*. Continue this process for the remaining cells in column C. You may also decide to first *Remove Parameters* of these cells in column C and then set your own distributions. Further, correlations can be set manually when assumptions are set (Figure 13.31) or by going to *Risk Simulator | Edit Correlations* (Figure 13.32) after all the assumptions are set.

If risk simulation was not run, the VaR or economic capital required would have been $37M, as opposed to only $14M. All cross-correlations between

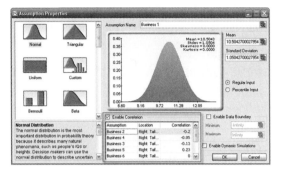

FIGURE 13.33 Setting Correlations One at a Time

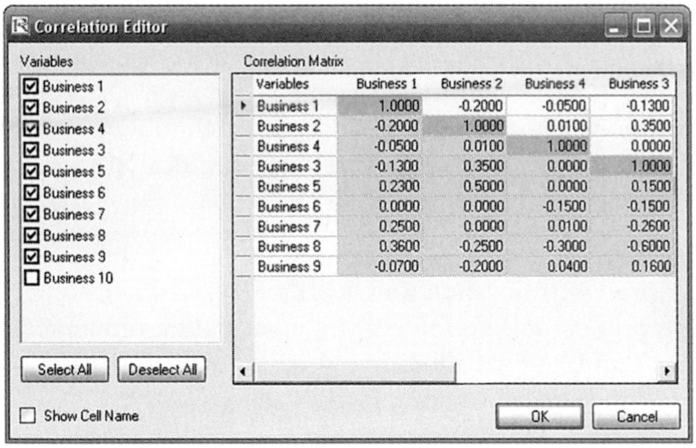

FIGURE 13.34 Setting Correlations using the Correlation Matrix Routine

business lines have been modeled, as are stress and scenario tests, and thousands and thousands of possible iterations are run (Figure 13.33). Individual risks are now aggregated into a cumulative portfolio-level VaR (Figure 13.34).

Efficient Portfolio Allocation and Economic Capital VaR

As a side note, by performing portfolio optimization, a portfolio's VaR can actually be reduced. We start by first introducing the concept of stochastic portfolio optimization through an illustrative hands-on example. Then, using this portfolio optimization technique, we apply it to four business lines or assets to compute the VaR for a non-optimized versus an optimized portfolio of assets, and see the

difference in computed VaR. You will note that at the end, the optimized portfolio bears less risk and has a lower required economic capital.

Stochastic Portfolio Optimization

The optimization model used to illustrate the concepts of stochastic portfolio optimization is *Optimization—Stochastic Portfolio Allocation*, and it can be accessed
via *Modeling Toolkit | Optimization | Stochastic Portfolio Allocation*. This model
shows four asset classes with different risk and return characteristics. The idea
here is to find the best portfolio allocation such that the portfolio's bang for the
buck or returns-to-risk ratio is maximized. That is, in order to allocate 100% of
an individual's investment among several different asset classes (e.g., different
types of mutual funds or investment styles such as growth, value, aggressive
growth, income, global, index, contrarian, momentum, and so forth), optimization
is used. This model is different from others in that there exist several simulation
assumptions (risk and return values for each asset), as seen in Figure 13.35. That
is, a simulation is run, then optimization is executed, and the entire process is
repeated multiple times to obtain distributions of each decision variable. The
entire analysis can be automated using stochastic optimization.

In order to run an optimization, several key specifications on the model have
to first be identified:

Objective: Maximize return-to-risk ratio (C12)
Decision Variables: Allocation weights (E6:E9)
Restrictions on Decision Variables: Minimum and maximum required (F6:G9)
Constraints: Portfolio total allocation weights 100% (E11 is set to 100%)
Simulation Assumptions: Return and risk values (C6:D9)

The model shows the various asset classes. Each asset class has its own set of
annualized returns and annualized volatilities. These return and risk measures are

	A	B	C	D	E	F	G	H

ASSET ALLOCATION OPTIMIZATION MODEL

Asset Class Description	Annualized Returns	Volatility Risk	Allocation Weights	Required Minimum Allocation	Required Maximum Allocation	Return to Risk Ratio
Asset 1	10.60%	12.41%	25.00%	10.00%	40.00%	0.8544
Asset 2	11.21%	16.16%	25.00%	10.00%	40.00%	0.6937
Asset 3	10.61%	15.93%	25.00%	10.00%	40.00%	0.6660
Asset 4	10.52%	12.40%	25.00%	10.00%	40.00%	0.8480
Portfolio Total	10.7356%	7.17%	100.00%			
Return to Risk Ratio	1.4970					

FIGURE 13.35 Asset Allocation Model Ready for Stochastic Optimisation

annualized values such that they can be compared consistently across different asset classes. Returns are computed using the geometric average of the relative returns, and the risks are computed using the logarithmic relative stock returns approach.

Column E, *Allocation Weights*, holds the decision variables, which are the variables that need to be tweaked and tested such that the total weight is constrained at 100% (cell *E11*). Typically, to start the optimization, we will set these cells to a uniform value; in this case, cells *E6* to *E9* are set at 25% each. In addition, each decision variable may have specific restrictions in its allowed range. In this example, the lower and upper allocations allowed are 10% and 40%, as seen in columns F and G. This setting means that each asset class can have its own allocation boundaries.

Next, column H shows the return-to-risk ratio, which is simply the return percentage divided by the risk percentage; the higher this value, the higher the bang for the buck. The remaining sections of the model show the individual asset class rankings by returns, risk, return-to-risk ratio, and allocation. In other words, these rankings show at a glance which asset class has the lowest risk, the highest return, and so forth.

Running an Optimization

To run this model, simply click on *Risk Simulator | Optimization | Run Optimization*. Alternatively, and for practice, you can set up the model using the following approach:

1. Start a new profile (*Risk Simulator | New Profile*).
2. For stochastic optimization, set distributional assumptions on the risk and returns for each asset class. That is, select cell C6 and set an assumption (*Risk Simulator | Set Input Assumption*) and make your own assumption as required. Repeat for cells C7 to D9.
3. Select cell E6, and define the decision variable (*Risk Simulator | Optimization | Decision Variables* or click on the Define Decision icon); make it a continuous variable, and then link the decision variable's name and the minimum/maximum required to the relevant cells (B6, F6, G6).
4. Then use the Risk Simulator Copy on cell E6, select cells E7 to E9, and use Risk Simulator's Copy (*Risk Simulator | Copy Parameter*) and Risk Simulator's Paste parameter, or use the copy and paste icons.
5. Next, set up the optimization's constraints by selecting *Risk Simulator | Optimization | Constraints*, selecting ADD, and selecting the cell E11, and making it equal 100% (total allocation, and do not forget the % sign).
6. Select cell C12, the objective to be maximized, and make it the objective: *Risk Simulator | Optimization | Set Objective*, or click on the "O" icon.
7. Run the simulation by going to *Risk Simulator | Optimization | Run Optimization*. Review the different tabs to make sure that all the required inputs in Steps 2 and 3 above are correct. Select *Stochastic Optimization*, and let it run for 500 trials repeated 20 times (Figure 13.36 illustrates these setup steps).

FIGURE 13.36 Setting Up the Stochastic Optimization Problem

You may also try other optimization routines, such as the following:

Discrete optimization is an optimization that is run on a discrete or static model, where no simulations are run. This optimization type is applicable when the model is assumed to be known and no uncertainties exist. Also, a discrete optimization can be run first to determine the optimal portfolio and its corresponding optimal allocation of decision variables before more advanced optimization procedures are applied. For instance, before running a stochastic optimization problem, a discrete optimization is run first to determine if there exist solutions to the optimization problem before a more protracted analysis is performed.

Dynamic optimization is applied when Monte Carlo simulation is used together with optimization. Another name for such a procedure is *simulation-optimization*. In other words, a simulation is run for N trials, and then an optimization process is run for M iterations, until the optimal results are obtained or an infeasible set is found. That is, using Risk Simulator's optimization module, you can choose which forecast and assumption statistics to use and replace in the model after the simulation is run. Then, these forecast statistics can be applied in the optimization process. This approach is useful when you have a large model with many interacting assumptions and forecasts, and when some of the forecast statistics are required in the optimization.

Stochastic optimization is similar to the dynamic optimization procedure, except that the entire dynamic optimization process is repeated T times. The results will be a forecast chart of each decision variable with T values. In other words, a simulation is run, and the forecast or assumption statistics are used in the optimization model to find the optimal allocation of decision variables. Then another simulation is run, generating different forecast statistics, and these new updated values are then optimized, and so forth. Hence, each of the final decision variables will have its own forecast chart, indicating the range of the optimal decision variables. For instance, instead of obtaining single-point estimates in the dynamic optimization procedure, you can now obtain a distribution of the decision variables and, hence, a range of optimal values for each decision variable, also known as a stochastic optimization.

Viewing and Interpreting Forecast Results

Stochastic optimization is performed when a simulation is first run, and then the optimization is run. Then the whole analysis is repeated multiple times. The result is a distribution of each decision variable, rather than a single point estimate (Figure 13.37). This distribution means that instead of saying you should invest 30.57% in Asset 1, the optimal decision is to invest between 30.10% and 30.99%, as long as the total portfolio sums to 100%. This way, the optimization results provide management or decision makers a range of flexibility in the optimal decisions.

Portfolio Optimization and Portfolio VaR

Now that we understand the concepts of optimized portfolios, let us see what the effects are on computed economic capital through the use of a correlated portfolio VaR. This model uses Monte Carlo simulation and optimization routines in Risk Simulator to minimize the VaR of a portfolio of assets (Figure 13.38). The file used is *Value at Risk—Optimized and Simulated Portfolio VaR*, which is

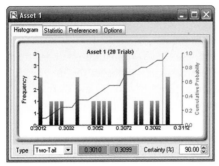 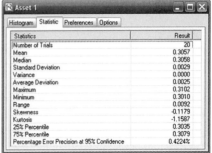

FIGURE 13.37 Simulated Results from the Stochastic Optimization Approach

VALUE AT RISK WITH ASSET ALLOCATION OPTIMIZATION MODEL

Asset Class Description	Annualized Returns	Volatility Risk	Allocation Weights	Required Minimum Allocation	Required Maximum Allocation
S&P 500	7.10%	9.80%	10.00%	10.00%	40.00%
Small Cap	9.51%	14.35%	27.30%	10.00%	40.00%
High Yield	15.90%	22.50%	22.70%	10.00%	40.00%
Govt Bonds	4.50%	7.25%	40.00%	10.00%	40.00%
		Total Weight:	**100.00%**		

Correlation Matrix	S&P 500	Small Cap	High Yield	Govt Bonds
S&P 500	1.0000	0.7400	0.6500	0.5500
Small Cap	0.7400	1.0000	0.4200	0.3100
High Yield	0.6500	0.4200	1.0000	0.2300
Govt Bonds	0.5500	0.3100	0.2300	1.0000

Covariance Matrix	S&P 500	Small Cap	High Yield	Govt Bonds
S&P 500	0.0096	0.0104	0.0143	0.0039
Small Cap	0.0104	0.0206	0.0136	0.0032
High Yield	0.0143	0.0136	0.0506	0.0038
Govt Bonds	0.0039	0.0032	0.0038	0.0053

Starting Value	$1,000,000.00
Term (Years)	5.00

Annualized Return	8.72%	**Profit/Loss**	$87,151.94
Portfolio Risk	9.84%	**Return to Risk Ratio**	88.59%
Ending Value	$1,087,151.94		

Specifications of the optimization model:

Objective:	*Maximize Return to Risk Ratio (E28)*
Decision Variables:	*Allocation Weights (E6:E9)*
Restrictions on Decision Variables:	*Minimum and Maximum Required (F6:G9)*
Constraints:	*Portfolio Total Allocation Weights 100% (E10 is set to 100%)*

FIGURE 13.38 Computing Value at Risk (VaR) with Simulation

accessible via *Modeling Toolkit | Value at Risk | Optimized and Simulated Portfolio VaR*. In this example, we intentionally used only four asset classes to illustrate the effects of an optimized portfolio. In real life, we can extend this process to cover a multitude of asset classes and business lines. Here we now illustrate the use of a left-tail VaR instead of a right-tail VaR, but the concepts are similar. First, simulation is used to determine the 90% left-tail VaR. The 90% left-tail probability means that there is a 10% chance that losses will exceed this VaR for a specified holding period. With an equal allocation of 25% across the four asset classes, the VaR is determined using simulation (Figure 13.39). The annualized returns are uncertain and are therefore simulated. The VaR is then read off the forecast chart. Then, optimization is run to find the best portfolio subject to the 100% allocation across the four projects that will maximize the portfolio's bang for the buck (returns-to-risk ratio). The resulting optimized portfolio is then simulated once again, and the new VaR is obtained (Figure 13.40). The VaR of this optimized portfolio is a lot less than the not-optimized portfolio. That

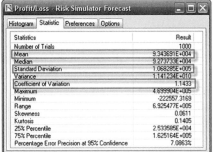

FIGURE 13.39 **Non-Optimized Value at Risk**

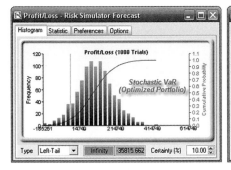

FIGURE 13.40 **Optimal Portfolio's Value at Risk through Optimization and Simulation**

is, the expected loss is $35.8M instead of $42.2M, which means that the bank will have a lower required economic capital if the portfolio of holdings is first optimized.

CONCLUSION

The fundamental cause of the 2008 financial crisis was accumulation of substantial quantities of tail risks in the financial sector, leaving financial institutions unprepared to mitigate the impact when tail risk events struck. Risk management activities under normality fail to distinguish between tail risk and normal risk. However, recall that tail risk has a dissimilar landscape, systemic drivers, and a huge magnitude of impact (sometimes cataclysmic), which is why an independent approach to tail risk is crucial if financial institutions are to survive systemic shocks. The name of the game is preparation: sustainability management, the theme of our next chapter. Consequently, new capital requirements proposed by regulators may not prevent future meltdowns unless survival fundamentals are properly addressed and strategically charted. In Chapter 14, Ensuring Sustainability of an Institution as a Going Concern: An Approach to Dealing with Black Swan or Tail Risk, we will examine the underlying causes of the 2008 crisis, the unique nature of tail risk, and key lines of defense available to financial firms to effectively mitigate and manage a future tail risk crisis. We will see that tail risk exposure can mount up and threaten survival. Implementation of robust tail risk sustainability is vital to continued existence, not only for a single financial institution, but for stability of the worldwide financial sector.

References

Hannoun, H., 22 November 2010. Deputy General Manager, Bank for International Settlements. The Basel III Capital Framework: a decisive breakthrough, BoJ-BIS High Level Seminar on Financial Regulatory Reform: Implications for Asia and the Pacific Hong Kong SAR.

Dr. Jeffrey R.B., Managing Bank Risk, Ch 13: Portfolio Management of Default Risk, Elsevier.

Mun, J., CEO of Real Options Valuation, Inc., premier software, training, and consulting firm located in California <www.realoptionsvaluation.com>. The software applications presented herein includes Risk Simulator, Modeling Toolkit, and others from the company.

Ensuring Sustainability of an Institution as a Going Concern: An Approach to Dealing with Black Swan or Tail Risk

14

Karamjeet Paul[1]

Tail risk is the bane of a financial institution's revenue model ... always has been.
Karamjeet Paul

Despite rigorous models and risk management controls, multi-asset financial institution exposure from tail risk can accumulate. For highly leveraged financial institutions, cumulative exposure from tail risk may threaten survival in a stressed environment. While traditional models normally work well in risk portfolios, they do not address certain critical issues related to policies, governance, limits, strategies, and guidelines to manage the *total* risk of a financial institution. What should be the goal of tail-risk management? How much tail risk does the institution have? How do you manage tail risk proactively? Let us begin with a short story entitled "A Crisis Can Materialize Quickly and Out of Nowhere."

> ***6:45am*** *As he walks to his trading desk, Rupert cannot help feeling the conflict. Ten days ago, based upon the announcement by South Korea to curb the appreciation of the won against the US dollar, he had committed the bank to a large, complex position in Asian and British pound currencies. He is excited, as the position (although within his allotted limit) is the largest bet in his seven-year career at the bank. He feels comfortable holding it until next Tuesday or Wednesday ... and so far, so good, but the thought of leaving his desk with such a large open position for about four hours during the prime hours of the pound trading later in the day is making him somewhat uncomfortable. Anything can happen!*
>
> *At the same time, he is looking forward to seeing Ian, who was his 9th floor roommate at Hughes-Parry Hall while attending the University College of London ten years ago. It has been four years since they last had a few pints together at Ian's bachelor party at Packies in Kenmare, Ireland.*

---

[1]The provided material is and will remain the intellectual property of Karamjeet Paul.

Ian is in London today for barely 11 hours on very short notice for a client meeting in the morning. He cannot stay overnight as his wife is expecting their first child any day now. So they settled on an old tradition from their UCL days. A chicken tikka masala lunch at Motijheel Restaurant on Marchmont Street, followed by a few pints of lager at Mabel's Tavern, down the street from their old residence hall at Cartwright Gardens, before Ian takes the Piccadilly line to Heathrow for an early evening British Airways flight back to Dublin.

8:30am *Global financial markets are operating without signs of anything extraordinary. Rupert chuckles and thinks to himself "probably riding on the wrong side of the road," as he reads a big story from the G-8 Summit about President George W. Bush colliding with a British police officer during a bike ride. The officer had to be hospitalized.*

9:03am *Rupert stops by Stewart's office. The head of the foreign exchange trading desk reminds him to keep a close watch on his large position, which already has a £785,000 paper profit. Rupert confirms his plan to close it by no later than next Wednesday, following some announcements he expects at the end of the G-8 Summit this weekend.*

9:16am *Glancing at the Reuter screen, Rupert notices a newsflash about a possible explosion in London.*

9:22am *Another newsflash says that there may have been explosions on three different Underground lines. Should he take whatever profits he can capture and get out? "Aw, there is probably nothing very significant about any explosions, if indeed they happened," he thinks.*

10:15am *There is confirmation of bombs on three Underground trains, and a newsflash about another explosion on a bus in Central London.*

11:18am *London Metropolitan Police Commissioner Ian Blair confirms six explosions on a bus and at Underground stations and calls the situation confusing. Stock markets are chaotic. FTSE 100 index is down 200 points. Foreign exchange markets have a lot of activity without any signs of a panic. But Rupert is very nervous ... his position is down to a paper loss of £327,000 ... his first large bet ... Will it become a blot on his career? Should he take the loss and get out now?*

11:38am *Rupert is still trying to absorb the potential impact of the news when his thoughts are interrupted by the booming voice of Stewart over the intercom: "Listen up, everybody. We've been asked to evacuate the building. No time for any trading, as we have only about ten minutes. But before you leave your desks, I want everyone to close out your net positions by transferring them to the bank's desk in Paris or the early morning desk in New York. So let's get on with it, boys! And one more thing: Take the stairs. No lifts."*

12:05pm *As the last trader is leaving his desk, an image of Prime Minister Tony Blair flashes on the TV screen with a statement regarding a "series of terrorist attacks in London" and his plans for an immediate return from the G-8 Summit in Gleneagles, Scotland.*

Leaving the building, Rupert cannot avoid a sinking feeling ... His first big bet and he can't do much about it now! Mabel's Tavern and pints of lager are the farthest things from his thoughts.

Quick Effective Solutions Can Mitigate A Disaster

In the following days, the bank realized no major negative impact from leaving the London trading desk unattended because of Stewart's directive to transfer all net positions to Paris and New York desks, where they were managed without any significant problem. Had he not done so, the operational interruption at the trading desk's location with the marketplace in turmoil would have cost the bank millions of pounds. Rupert's position netted a profit of £3,732,000 by the time he closed it the following Wednesday.

Quick thinking by Stewart? Or a set of preplanned actions by the bank to blunt the impact of an extreme operational event?

A historical, fictional account of 7/7: London, July 7, 2005

Sustainability Management is Critical to Weather a Crisis
Disciplined Emphasis on Protection From Extreme Tail Risk

Following the experiences of 7/7 and 9/11, financial institutions cannot afford to be without pre-planned actions or business continuity plans (BCPs) to mitigate the impact of extreme exposure from major business interruptions, and they have invested hundreds of millions of dollars in them. In fact, it is a regulatory requirement. As a result, exposure from an extended interruption at a major location is not considered life threatening. As we saw in Chapter 10, Introduction to Extreme Risk Management in the Financial Services Industry, exposure from a more dire risk threatens financial institutions as going concerns—extreme tail financial risk. However, financial institutions often do not have a set of preplanned operating or corporate activities (similar to BCPs) to blunt such exposure. Unlike BCPs in which no known details are left to chance, predefined activities (if they exist) to stem the impact of tail financial risk do not include elaborate and specifically defined plans. Nor, unless explicitly planned, can plans be readily implemented.

It is not that institutions fail to consider tail risk or extreme exposure. As we saw in Chapter 10, Introduction to Extreme Risk Management in the Financial Services Industry, there are several probability distributions capable of modeling extreme cases, including the Gumbel distribution (also known as the extreme value distribution type I), the generalized Pareto distribution, and the Weibull distribution. These models usually provide a good fit to extremes of complicated data. However, it is human nature that unless something is defined and quantified in real terms, people leave it in the abstract. As discussed in Chapter 10, during the last crisis, models such as value at risk severely underestimated the tail events and the high loss correlations under systemic stress.[2] Without an objective

---

[2]The Basel III Capital Framework: a decisive breakthrough, Hervé Hannoun, Deputy General Manager, Bank for International Settlements, BoJ-BIS High Level Seminar on Financial Regulatory Reform: Implications for Asia and the Pacific Hong Kong SAR, 22 November 2010.

definition and quantification, it is difficult to develop explicit policies clearly stating what is acceptable, what specific preplanned actions may be initiated in case of an extreme event, or who is authorized to trigger such actions. It is even more difficult to define explicitly what would trigger preplanned actions because without quantifications there are no obvious objective parameters.

Operational risks deal with physical events, leaving no doubt when to invoke contingency plans. In the fictional account outlined earlier, it was clear to Stewart that there was an interruption in their operational activities, which called for an immediate need to do something about it—or else! How do you establish an objective trigger for an extreme tail financial risk event? Should a financial institution have triggered counter actions in 2006 ... or in 2007 ... or even in early 2008? Yet triggers are essential if contingency or backup defensive plans are to be meaningful.

Do regulatory requirements address effective tail-risk management? In the financial services industry, regulatory advances often become the impetus for new safeguards. Sometimes they can also lead institutions into thinking—mistakenly, perhaps—that by meeting regulatory requirements, they are managing extreme tail risk adequately. Three recent developments have drawn attention in relation to extreme financial risk and going-concern sustainability. None of these developments addresses effective tail-risk management effectively.

Stress Testing

Recall from earlier chapters that following the crisis of 2008, major financial institutions are required to stress-test exposures. While a step in the right direction, stress tests do not go far enough in managing institutional sustainability as going concerns for two reasons: (i) stress testing is based upon subjective scenarios, and (ii) stress testing is designed to meet regulatory objectives, which may not necessarily meet objectives needed to maintain going-concern integrity of institutions.

Stress testing reveals how an institution would fare under certain subjective scenarios. Such scenarios may seem quite stressful compared to normal circumstances, but they *are not representative of the most extreme events*. As the crisis of 2008 showed, no one can be certain of the extreme events institutions may face.

Planning grounded in subjective scenarios is like having a BCP that provides for counteractions only for interruptions from specified events, rather than providing for counteractions for a major interruption regardless of its cause. Most disastrous results, including business failures brought on by financial crises, arise because of unpreparedness: a failure of imagination and extreme tail-risk planning. After every major disaster, from the rout of Napoleon's army in Russia and the sinking of Titanic, to 9/11, 7/7, Katrina, and Fukushima, to name a few, people have said, "Who would have thought that ...!" Therefore, planning for survival in crisis based on subjective scenarios is imprudent and constitutes a fundamental shortcoming of the stress-testing approach to tail risk.

In addition, stress testing addresses regulatory objectives, which are not necessarily going-concern objectives. Regulatory objectives relate to the preservation of the financial system, prevention of systemic problems, and minimizing taxpayer cost; going-concern objectives, on the other hand, must address the ongoing integrity of an institution. There is a significant gap between these objectives. For example, orderly liquidation may accomplish regulatory objectives, as happened with many distressed financial institutions, such as Bear Stearns, Wachovia, or Washington Mutual. In each event, investors incurred losses because the institution stopped operating as a going concern. Because of this gap between regulatory objectives and going-concern objectives, scenario-based stress testing fails to go far enough to address extreme tail risk and going-concern sustainability.

Living Will Provision

Living will provision is another recent regulatory requirement. By outlining how a failed institution's business would be liquidated in an orderly manner, regulators ensure systemic risk is alleviated *after* an institution no longer operates as a going concern. While useful in limiting contagious systemic impact, living wills do not preserve going-concern sustainability.

Liquidity Reserves

Maintaining adequate liquidity reserves is another regulatory requirement. It is useful if the marketplace freezes and liquidity dries up for a limited period, as happened in late 2008. However, liquidity reserves fail to address the real going-concern issue. The financial institution model, driven by market confidence, is based upon the illiquidity of borrowing short and lending long. Illiquidity built into its business model means that a financial institution can never maintain adequate liquidity reserves if market confidence dissipates.

A crisis can quickly turn confidence-based liquidity models into illiquid institutions. By the time an institution needs to tap liquidity reserves to allay confidence problems, it is often too late. The marketplace begins to funnel remaining liquidity from the institution. Bear Stearns, Lehman Brothers, and MF Global had liquidity crises before their collapse because the marketplace lost confidence in their sustainability as going concerns. If a confidence problem develops, no amount of additional liquidity reserves can help preserve a going concern. In fact, it is the other way around. Marketplace confidence brings about sufficient liquidity.

To maintain marketplace confidence, institutions must be perceived as capable of surviving a financial crisis. Survival calls for disciplined preplanned activities or an effective sustainability management plan that prevents extreme events from turning into a life-threatening liquidity crisis, just as the BCPs are designed to prevent extreme events from becoming very expensive or life-threatening operational interruptions.

Tail Risk and Sustainability Management Need Explicit Focus

Tail risk has always been the bane of a financial institution's revenue model. However, tail risk did not receive much attention until recently. Prior to 2008, extreme crises were rare, lacking the depth and the scale of what we have come to think of as extreme crises. The events of 2008—and the perception that they could happen again—have underscored the need to manage tail risk proactively. A new approach to tail risk, distinct from traditional risk management and capital management, is a vital component of total risk management. The suggestion of a distinct approach departs pointedly from how the industry traditionally has addressed risk. A little background surrounding this point is useful.

SUSTAINABILITY MANAGEMENT OBJECTIVE

A financial institution should never be in a position where tail risk can adversely impact the sustainability of the institution as a going concern and thus turn into a crisis of confidence. This is the purpose of effective sustainability management or tail-risk management.

Revenue models require managing risk prudently. However, for leveraged financial institutions, where financial risk primarily drives revenues, managing risk has life-and-death implications. Banking has always been about deriving the risk premium needed to cover expected loss in addition to expenses and a profit margin. Therefore, financial institutions invest only where a required risk premium can be derived and priced into transactions. However, uncertainty requires focus beyond pricing because actual returns are determined by how events and market conditions unfold.

If conditions turn out favorable relative to expected loss values, there are larger profits than expected; if they turn out to be unfavorable, there is an erosion of expected profits or even a net loss that must be offset by profits from other transactions. However, conditions may turn out to be so unfavorable that large losses exceed profits from other transactions and erode capital; in an extreme case, catastrophic losses may arise that exceed capital and thus threaten going-concern sustainability. Therefore, despite sophisticated models, how uncertainty with its two components is managed determines financial results.

RISK ARISES FROM TWO COMPONENTS OF UNCERTAINTY
- Quantifiable uncertainty
- Unquantifiable uncertainty

Quantifiable Uncertainty

Quantifiable uncertainty drives a financial institution's model. Using historical data, quantifiable uncertainty is expressed in expected loss values and required risk premiums. Therefore, bankers structure revenue models to earn adequate risk premiums or revenues over time to absorb expected losses. In addition, if risk premium falls short, then other operational means may be used to mitigate the shortfall to yield required profit targets. This means that exposure from quantifiable uncertainty can be mitigated and/or priced in the normal course of running a business.

This makes risk premium the primary loss-absorbing agent, or the driver of protection against expected losses. As a result, *structuring* (through the risk-reward relationship), *preserving* (through subsequent business actions), and *protecting* (through controls) revenues and profits from risk to generate adequate risk premium can cover exposure from quantifiable uncertainty. This is the objective of traditional risk management, with a goal to leverage the uncertainty to maximize revenues, while mitigating and absorbing expected losses. With prudent guidelines and limits, accompanied by proper controls, this goal drives the revenue engine most of the time. However, because of unquantifiable uncertainty, not all events can be predicted or priced. The unfolding of events from unquantifiable uncertainty can disrupt an otherwise smoothly driven risk-management model, and in extreme situations it can threaten going concerns.

Unquantifiable Uncertainty

There is a small segment of the risk/exposure spectrum where uncertainty cannot be defined and quantified, and can give rise to unexpected losses. In addition to being unexpected, such losses can also be so huge as to be catastrophic in extreme situations, and so large they cannot be priced into transactions. The combination of their unexpected nature and the potential enormity makes it difficult, if not impossible, to mitigate such losses in the normal course of business. Unless management takes specific steps, the only defense against unexpected losses is capital. This is the defined purpose of capital and why regulators place strong emphasis on its adequacy. In extreme scenarios, unexpected losses can exceed capital and threaten an institution's survival. In such cases, survival depends on how well capital has been protected and preserved.

This makes capital the primary driver of defense against unexpected losses from unquantifiable uncertainty. Therefore, *preserving and protecting capital from risk* must be a high priority to cover or mitigate exposure from unquantifiable uncertainty. This is the objective of sustainability management (also referred to here as tail-risk management), with a goal to leverage resources to maintain adequate capital that is protected from unexpected losses. With prudent guidelines, limits, and proper controls, this goal can drive the going-concern sustainability.

A comparison of the impact of quantifiable uncertainty and unquantifiable uncertainty is summarized in Figure 14.1.

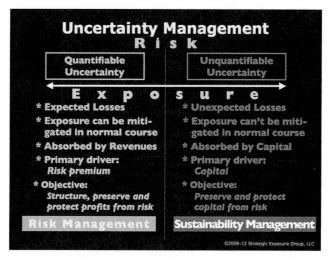

FIGURE 14.1 Uncertainty Management: Quantifiable and Unquantifiable Uncertainty

MANAGING SUSTAINABILITY VIA A TRADITIONAL RISK-MANAGEMENT APPROACH IS IMPRUDENT

Let us assume that you own a roofing business. In addition, you know from experience that there is a 1 in 10,000 chance of a fatal defect in your product. Based upon historical data, you also know that the expected loss value of the 1 in 10,000 defect in your product is $1 million. Your experience tells you that you can never completely eliminate the chance of a fatal defect, but you can reduce it to 1 in 1,000,000 by investing $10 million in product improvement. Would you accept the risk represented by the 1 in 10,000 chance? Alternatively, would you reject the risk and invest $10 million to mitigate it?

If these statistics were the only considerations, most people would accept this risk. After all, why would you spend $10 million in product improvements to offset a $1 million expected loss value! This is risk management in a traditional sense, where cost-benefit comparisons and profit motivations drive decisions.

Now, let us assume that you and your spouse need to add a room to your house for your newborn baby. We will assume that, since you own a roofing company, your business will install the roof on the new room.

Should you say this to your spouse? "Honey, we are going to have a nice room for our baby. But I want you to know that there is a 1 in 10,000 chance that the roof could come down and possibly kill our baby. I think we should live with this risk, as it costs too much money to alleviate it." What do you think your spouse's reaction will be? In addition, if the reaction is not to your liking, should you add this? "But Honey, we do this at the office all the time!"

Most people would agree that it is dysfunctional to think of your child's life in terms of a monetary cost-benefit tradeoff. In fact, most people would do everything they can so that their child's life is not at risk because of cost-benefit or other financial factors. This is sustainability management, in which existential motivations drive decisions.

Similarly, to think of sustainability of a going concern in terms of probabilities, expected values, cost-benefit tradeoff, etc. is not just dysfunctional; it is also imprudent. No responsible, prudent individual wants to leave survival to probabilities.

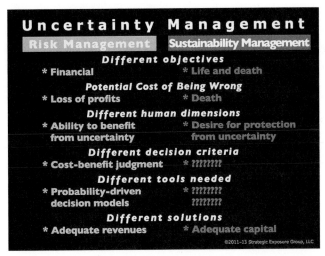

FIGURE 14.2 Uncertainty Management: Risk and Sustainability Management Compared

As summarized in Figure 14.2 and illustrated through the roofing example in the sidebar, risk management and sustainability management have such different objectives and motivations driving their decisions that one cannot be extended to manage the other. Risk management drives the revenue engine, while sustainability management preserves the going concern. Each discipline requires its own unique management process. Relying on risk management to manage sustainability can lead to disastrous results, as shown by the events of 2008. Similarly, extending sustainability management to manage the entire spectrum of risk will keep an institution from maximizing financial returns associated with its revenue model. Instead, simultaneous but distinct effective management is imperative to capture the full growth potential of business models aggressively and prudently.

Issues related to risk management dealing with quantifiable uncertainty and sustainability management dealing with unquantifiable uncertainty are starkly different.

- Risk management has a *financial* objective, while sustainability management is about *life or death*.
  - Risk management miscalculations may *compromise profits*, but poor sustainability management could *end survival*.
- Risk management denotes the *ability to benefit from uncertainty*; sustainability management relates to the *desire for protection from uncertainty*.
- Risk management employs *cost-benefit judgment* for decision criteria; what should be the decision criteria for sustainability management of a going concern?
- Risk management employs *probability-driven models*; what tools should be used for sustainability management?

FIGURE 14.3 The Three Legs Of Risk Governance

- Risk management solutions are driven by the *adequacy of revenues* (risk premium); sustainability management solutions must be driven by the need to *maintain adequate capital.*

   In addition to a distinct focus, sustainability management requires a distinct parameter as becomes clear by a review of uncertainty in terms of known and unknown elements. The known-unknown analysis divides the world into four parts, as shown in Figure 14.3: known-knowns, unknown-knowns, known-unknowns, and unknown-unknowns. Separating parts of uncertainty along these lines yields the following results for financial institutions.

- Known-knowns do not involve uncertainty. Therefore, we put this aside.
- Unknown-knowns deal with specific outcomes that are *unknown*, but expected losses are quantifiable and thus are *known*. Therefore, one can derive risk premiums and manage this part of uncertainty. *This is traditional risk management.*
- Known-unknowns relate to the *known* scenarios we can create to gauge their impact. However, their occurrences are *unknown* and cannot be defined. *This is traditional capital management,* where stress testing focuses on known scenarios.
- Unknown-unknowns relate to *unknown* scenarios that cannot be envisioned, and thus their occurrence is also *unknown*. Unknown-unknowns are the lessons we talk about after an extreme crisis in terms of "Who would have thought that . . .!" So how should we deal with unknown-unknowns? *Sustainability management* must cover this.

   Risk management, capital management, and sustainability management constitute three distinct areas of risk governance. There are well-defined parameters for risk management and capital management. How should the sustainability management parameters be defined and quantified?

Measurement is a Prerequisite to Effective Management

Unless there is a definition and quantification of a driving measure, it is nearly impossible to implement an effective management process. For example, it is difficult to manage profitability if there is no way to define, quantify, and measure profits. Similarly, earnings from risk management cannot be maximized effectively if there is no way to define and quantify expected loss values. Along the same lines, it is difficult, if not impossible, to manage the going-concern sustainability and protect against tail risk if there is no measure to drive this process.

AN EFFECTIVE MANAGEMENT PROCESS REQUIRES THREE SOUND COMPONENTS

- Definition and quantification criteria
- Judgment on limits
- Management controls

Currently, there is no such measure. Therefore, the key challenge today is to define a measure that can be used to develop metrics related to going-concern sustainability of institutions. Moreover, it is critical the measure is simple and objective, as otherwise complexity can add a new element of risk. Over the last 20 years, financial institution revenue models have become progressively more complex. As a result, it has become more complex to get a handle on exposure from risk. This is particularly more difficult in relation to tail risk, as no quantitative measures exist.

The risk management-driven models of Lehman Brothers and Bear Stearns were too complex to understand easily. To make matters worse, there were no simple tail risk measures to describe the growing vulnerability of these institutions. While elaborate mechanisms were in place to project and track the profitability of each incremental transaction, no such company-wide mechanism existed to gauge the institution's exposure from extreme tail risk. As a result, no alarms provided warnings as the institutions moved closer to the abyss.

A COMPLEX MEASURE CAN ADD ANOTHER ELEMENT OF RISK

Responding to complexity with complex metrics often adds another risk element, as the complexity and subjective assumptions underlying the metrics can hide the real risk. Therefore, what is needed is often the opposite; that is, more complex models require simpler measures to ensure that critical vulnerabilities can be easily and transparently spotted and monitored.

Probable Maximum Loss

Using established practices in several industries, a "Probable Maximum Loss" can be defined and quantified as a measure of extreme tail risk.

Probable maximum loss, or PML, is the maximum possible loss, mitigated by reliable, predefined, and structural actions and safeguards to reduce, prevent, or offset the loss. An institution's PML is the sum of PMLs from all off- and on-balance sheet items as well as PMLs of exposure from all of its operations. It represents a measure of maximum exposure from extreme tail risk.

AN EXAMPLE OF PML DEFINITION

PML of a $10 million loan portfolio or a $10 million of notional amount of credit default protection sold is $10 million. However, if there are collaterals, backstops, guarantees or safeguards that are designed to trigger automatically a set of reliable and predefined actions to reduce the maximum loss by $3 million, then the PML of the portfolio is $7 million ($10 million of maximum unmitigated exposure less $3 million of structural safeguards/backstops).

Quantifying PML is a broad task requiring a detailed review of data and records. Figure 14.4 shows a financial institution's assets totaling $200 billion. We need to add off-balance sheet items that can create exposure from uncertainty. To keep things simple, we add two items: the notional amount of credit derivatives and guarantees sold by the institution. This gives us a total of assets and equivalent items of $250 billion.

Assets & Equivalent Items

	Book Value in $Billions
ASSETS:	
Cash & Deposits	6
Fed Funds	3
Investments	44
Loans, net of Reserves	120
Intangibles & Deferred Tax	14
Other Assets	13
TOTAL ASSETS	200
OFF-BALANCE SHEET ITEMS:	
Credit Derivatives, Notional Amount	48
Guarantees	2
TOTAL	250

©2009–13 Strategic Exposure Group, LLC

FIGURE 14.4 Book Value of Asset and Equivalent Items

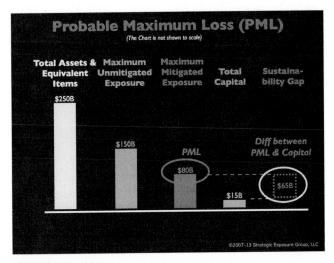

FIGURE 14.5 Probable Maximum Loss

The PML computation results of our example are summarized in Figure 14.5. The bar on the far left represents total assets and equivalent items amounting to $250 billion. The first step is to calculate the maximum amount of potential loss from each item on and off the balance sheet. This is the maximum loss in extreme unfavorable conditions, assuming the institution did not take any actions to mitigate the loss. It is the total amount of maximum loss structurally built into various portfolios of the institution. The total sum of these potential losses, referred to as the "Maximum Unmitigated Exposure" and represented by the second bar from the left in Figure 14.5, is $150 billion. One can think of this as the maximum amount of the total loss in the event of a most unfavorable scenario and as if there were no personnel or managers to take counteractions to prevent or mitigate the loss. The reason it is not the full value of total assets and equivalent items of $250 billion is that certain items, such as cash and US Government securities, are assigned zero-loss values in this example, while cash or cash-equivalent collaterals may reduce maximum losses for other items.

Institutions have managers not just to structure and price products, but to also protect revenues in extreme unfavorable conditions. This is called mitigation. In quantifying PML, only mitigations from specific plans and processes to backstop loss if things go awry should be included. Such mitigation plans and processes must be explicitly defined, credible, and realistic contingency actions that include disciplined guidelines to stop the portfolio from deteriorating further. This amount of mitigation is subtracted from the maximum unmitigated exposure to arrive at the "Maximum Mitigated Exposure" or PML, which is represented by the third bar from the left in Figure 14.5. In our example, the maximum unmitigated exposure amount of $150 billion is partially offset by a total amount of mitigation of

$70 billion, yielding the maximum mitigated exposure or PML of $80 billion. This represents the maximum loss given the most extreme catastrophic event, assuming an institution takes all steps necessary to mitigate potential maximum loss.

In our example, against an $80 billion PML we have $15 billion of institutional capital (represented by the fourth bar from the left in Figure 14.5) to provide protection from unexpected losses. The difference between PML and capital is designated the "Sustainability Gap." The institution in our example has a $65 billion sustainability gap. By itself, neither PML nor sustainability gap is a predictor of survival or failure.

The objective of sustainability management is not to close the sustainability gap, because this gap represents the key constituent of revenue model. Instead, by quantifying PML and the sustainability gap, we have defined the challenges involved in managing sustainability of a going concern. Strength or vulnerability in an extreme crisis will be determined by how well sustainability management preserves and protects capital.

Use of PML has Several Advantages

A common Scale

PML can be used to measure the exposure from extreme credit risk, market risk, and certain operational risks. While calculations may differ due to the uniqueness of each item's specific characteristics, all PML calculations lead to the measure of potential extreme loss, thus providing for a relative comparison of all items on a common scale.

> **PML PROVIDES**
> - A common scale across varied businesses and revenue models
> - A simple measure for complex models
> - The third dimension to provide a complete 3-D view of the risk-reward equation

A Simple Measure for Complex Models

The most significant advantage of PML comes from simple answers to simple questions. "What's the institution's exposure to extreme tail risk?" No complex answers; no need for prerequisites requiring knowledge of complex revenue models; no anxiety about the range of assumptions; no hard-to-understand black-box printouts.

One often hears that in 2008 senior managers at some institutions did not have an answer to *"How bad can it get?"* Such queries were met either with silence or with answers such as *"No one really knows."* Using PML, such queries are answerable and supported by objective data because PML is not a forecast of what will happen, but rather a measure of *what can happen*. The combination of simplicity and common scale across business segments elevates PML to commanding heights.

The Third Dimension Completing a 3-D View of the Risk-Reward Equation

Imagine a world where expected loss value measures are nonexistent and all we have is a single-dimension revenue measure. Risk-reward relationships cannot be optimized, nor can profitability be maximized. If we add a second dimension, we can quantify uncertainty through expected loss values. We can perceive risk and discriminate among transactions to maximize profits. This is traditional risk management, driven by a measure to optimize the risk-reward relationship, albeit only for risk from quantifiable uncertainty.

Now imagine two transactions A and B, both with identical revenue values of R and identical expected loss values of V. (For the moment, we will leave out extreme variances.) How do we discriminate for unquantifiable uncertainty between transactions A and B in order to maximize profitability? On a two-dimensional risk-reward scale, they are identical transactions.

Now let us add a third dimension, extreme tail-risk measure (as shown in Figure 14.6). The two transactions indicate extreme tail-risk values of T_A and T_B. That extreme tail-risk measure T_B is higher than T_A should lead us to prefer transaction A over B.

By adding a third dimension, we can discriminate for risk from unquantifiable uncertainty to maximize profitability. Therefore, PML enables us to turn a two-dimensional partial view of the risk-reward relationship into a complete three-dimensional risk profile that extends risk profiling from both quantifiable and

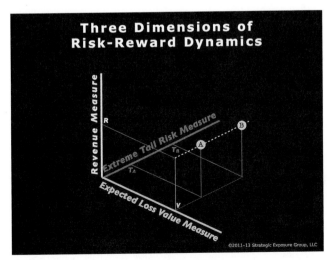

FIGURE 14.6 Risk-Reward Dynamics in Three Dimensions

unquantifiable uncertainty. We can now optimize three independent variables—revenues, expected loss value, and PML—to maximize financial profitability.

Expected losses from quantifiable uncertainty and extreme exposure from unquantifiable uncertainty are independent variables. Therefore, an institution may be efficient in managing traditional risk-reward dynamics regardless of how vulnerable it may be in the PML dimension. That an institution has proficient risk management policies and procedures and a history of impressive profits does not automatically mean it is immune to, nor better at managing, a sudden extreme financial crisis. Conversely, if an institution manages extreme tail risk effectively, it may well survive the next debt crisis regardless of its profitability or risk-management record. Revenues, expected loss value, and PML—three independent variables—taken together enable us to view risk in 3-D to drive revenue models and to protect and preserve capital.

PML: A Powerful Tool for the Effective Management of Tail Risk

- PML, when used properly, is *the most complete measure* of extreme exposure, as it is designed to cover all sources that give rise to tail risk, whether on or off the balance sheet. Unlike leverage ratios, PML takes aim beyond the balance sheet and what we understand as traditional financial risk.
- It is *the most objective quantification*, as it is based upon structural factors that constitute the business model, rather than being driven by subjective scenarios.
- It is *simple to communicate and understand*, as it relates to extreme tail-risk loss.
- PML provides *transparent answers* without black-box algorithms or complex equations.
- PML provides a *common scale*, enabling us to compare independent business lines with no common operational characteristics, as it translates exposure from all sources into a common measurement across all categories of risk.
- It is a *superior management tool* to establish targets, limits, and guidelines because of operating managers' ability to control items that contribute to it.

Proactive Sustainability Management

At the core of sustainability management are two important questions. How well has an institution formulated and implemented policies to prevent from getting too close to the abyss while maximizing its business model potential? How effective are the programs at keeping the institution from going over the edge if it finds itself being pulled too close? Among factors impacting how effectively these questions are addressed is how clearly and objectively the parameters have been defined to drive the process and develop proactive and effective solutions.

Proactive Quantification

The value of using PML goes beyond quantifying total extreme exposure. Simply knowing the total PML is neither useful nor meaningful for three reasons:

1. PML is not a forecast of what *will* happen. It is a quantification of what *can* happen in the extreme. So simulating the impact of an action on total PML by itself does not say anything about how the institution may weather a crisis. The next crisis may not necessarily be the most extreme, but it may be extreme enough to threaten the going concern.
2. A leveraged financial institution's PML for the most part is so substantial that it is nearly impossible to tackle it in its entirety.
3. An institution cannot eliminate total PML or a sustainability gap and expect to maintain a risk-management-based revenue model.

Yet the challenge to manage PML proactively is still there. Understanding what constitutes total PML is crucial and gaining a handle on extreme exposure through PML-based analyses can be leveraged into a number of sustainability management initiatives. For example:

- Fragmenting total PML into defined actionable components can lead to the formulation of sustainability management policies, strategies and limits.
- Analyzing the PML of each portfolio can provide for discrimination among business segments (along the lines of the conceptual illustration in Figure 14.6).
- Internalizing the impact of each component of PML can guide the development of defensive sustainability enhancement programs akin to BCPs.
- Effective implementation of defensive programs can provide cushions to preserve and extend the protective value of capital.
- Simple and transparent PML analyses, objectively showing strengths and vulnerabilities to tail risk, can be used for proactive dialogs with external audiences, such as regulators and the marketplace.

The first step in implementing any management process is to define its objective and formulate policies and strategies to achieve the objective. Let us examine an example of how we might fragment the total PML to develop sustainability management policies.

PML: ONLY A USEFUL TOOL, NOT A REPLACEMENT FOR SOUND JUDGMENT

PML turns abstract extreme exposure into actionable quantification. However, it should not replace sound judgment on limits, targets, and values that must guide risk governance.

We continue with data from our example used earlier. One way to fragment total PML is by designating the qualitative likelihood of the PML materializing. By adding the dimension of human judgment, we break down total PML into

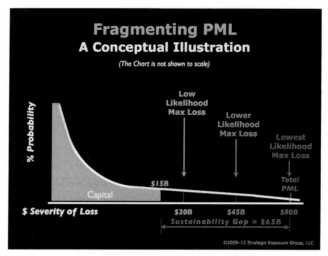

FIGURE 14.7 Fragmenting PML: A Conceptual Illustration

three fragments: low-likelihood PML, lower-likelihood PML, and lowest-likelihood PML.

Figure 14.7 depicts a conceptual example of the tail end of the exposure distribution curve, with the severity of loss on the horizontal axis and the probability of the loss on the vertical axis. The vertical axis is shown only for conceptual purposes and is not required to fragment total PML. The illustration shows that our financial institution has a low-likelihood PML of $20 billion and a lower-likelihood PML of $25 billon to yield a combined low- and lower-likelihood PML of $45 billion; it also has a lowest-likelihood PML of $35 billion to give the total low-, lower- and lowest-likelihood PML of $80 billion mentioned earlier. These translate into a low-likelihood sustainability gap of $5 billion (low-likelihood PML of $20 billion minus capital of $15 billion), a combined low- and lower-likelihood sustainability gap of $30 billion, and the total low-, lower-, and lowest-likelihood sustainability gap of $65 billion.

Fragmenting the total PML of $80 billion and sustainability gap of $65 billion this way paves the way for a proactive approach. For an institution of the size in our example, it is difficult, if not impossible, to manage a monolithic $65 billion sustainability gap. By fragmenting it into three smaller components, we now have manageable components. The kinds of actions required to manage the first $5 billion sustainability gap (with low-likelihood) will be quite different from actions one might employ to manage the next $25 billion sustainability gap (with lower-likelihood). For example, there may be some items with relatively higher likelihood of maximum loss. Based upon a 3-D discriminatory view of the risk-reward relationship, there may be candidates for removal or restructuring to reduce the amount of the low-likelihood gap, while other items with a lower likelihood of maximum loss may be better covered if management implements disciplined contingency programs. Therefore, there may be a Plan A to address the low-likelihood sustainability gap of $5 billion and a Plan B to address the next lower-likelihood sustainability gap of $25 billion. PML-based analyses can thus become the foundation for several critical initiatives that supplement risk- and capital-management processes. Some initiatives are summarized ahead.

PML: A DISCIPLINE TO ENHANCE RISK GOVERNANCE
PML supplements—and does not replace—risk management and capital management.

Effective Tail Risk Management
Objective Formulation of Policies, Limits, and Guidelines

What should be the objective of the sustainability management process? What size of extreme exposure is acceptable? How much protection should be provided? What guidelines should drive programs to protect against tail risk? What should be the extreme exposure limit for each business segment? Addressing questions and issues like these leads to tail-risk-management policies.

Currently such issues are addressed by employing proxies that do not objectively represent the real exposure from extreme tail risk. These proxies range from qualitative gut feeling opinions to quantitative measures that may bear little relationship to extreme exposure. A PML-based metric, by focusing on real exposure from extreme tail risk, enables transparent policy formulation and allows senior managers to exercise the judgment to balance sustainability-policy options with revenue and risk management objectives. Similarly, a PML-based approach optimizes resources by allocating limits among business segments and taking into account the three-dimensional view of the risk-reward relationship.

Enhanced Going-Concern Sustainability

Implementing policies and strategies in specific programs enhances the going-concern sustainability of institutions by enabling program decisions based upon objective analyses. For example, implementing a policy that limits the size and characteristics of the sustainability gap through PML-based discrimination will result in a reduction of the institution's tail risk.

Let us assume that the institution in our example adopts a policy to cap the low-likelihood PML at 10% below the amount of capital. This establishes a goal for managers to reduce low-likelihood extreme exposure by $6.5 billion to $13.5 billion (90% of the capital amount of $15 billion). This policy ensures that the going concern will be maintained through the maximum exposure from the

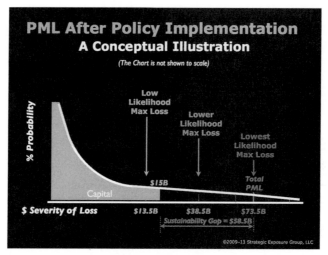

FIGURE 14.8 PML after Policy Implementation: A Conceptual Illustration

low-likelihood tail risk, as shown in Figure 14.8. In order to accomplish this goal, managers can target items on the risk-reward matrix as best candidates for restructuring, develop defensive operating programs that reduce the PML, or a combination of both. Effective implementation of such programs will enhance the going-concern sustainability to the tune of at least $5 billion (the reduction in the low-likelihood sustainability gap).

Proactive Continuous Monitoring of Extreme Exposure

An effective process needs more than sound policies and guidelines. It requires continuous monitoring to ensure no surprises. This is even more critical today, as progressively more complex revenue models have become increasingly dependent on fast-paced developments in global financial markets. As demonstrated by recent events, transactional complexities and a lack of measure make continuous monitoring of extreme exposure opaque and unavailable. Therefore, maintaining transparent continuous monitoring is imperative.

A PML-based sustainability-management process responds to this critical need via two features. First, it translates complex transactions into a simple measure by responding to complexity with simplicity. Second, because PML is based upon structural factors, not external conditions, it provides a measure of extreme tail risk at all times regardless of marketplace conditions. Establishing PML-based monitoring of extreme exposure, therefore, contributes to a significant element of an effective tail-risk-management process.

Protection of Capital

The banking industry has a paradoxical capital problem. Traditionally, financial institutions along with regulators address tail risk indirectly through capital adequacy models that suggest a preference for bigger capital cushions to absorb large unexpected shocks. The change in risk perception following 2008 has dramatically increased the intensity of calls for more capital. Actually, such calls are not new. There has always been tension between regulators and bankers concerning capital adequacy. Each crisis simply renews calls for more capital; the bigger the crisis, the louder the calls.

Post 2008, based upon regulatory and Basel III developments, several reputable forecasts have projected the industry's global need for additional capital in hundreds of billions of dollars. The need for a bigger shock-absorbing cushion is real because (i) market risk plays a significantly greater role in financial institutions' revenue models today than it did years ago and (ii) financial markets around the world have been growing increasingly more volatile, thus changing the risk profile of financial institutions. During the same period, the capital needed to absorb shocks from such growing activities has not kept pace with the increase in exposure from extreme tail risk. The net effect has been that although the risk that drives revenue models has changed fundamentally, the approach to dealing with exposure from extreme tail risk has changed only relatively marginally. However, simply looking to increased capital without addressing the factors that drive the need for greater shock-absorbing cushions is neither sustainable nor realistic.

Not Sustainable

If an institution adds capital, then it needs to generate higher earnings to cover the cost of incremental capital. The quest for higher earnings increases risk, as earnings are derived primarily from a risk-management-driven revenue model. In turn, higher risk creates the need for more capital. This is the paradox: Adding capital actually increases the need for more capital. Therefore, the industry's dependency on increased capital to maintain the current revenue engine is not sustainable.

Not Realistic

Given the high cost of capital, it is questionable if the industry can access the enormous amount of capital needed to support the continued growth in risk-based revenue models. Attracting large amounts of capital is difficult in normal times. Uncertainty makes it more challenging. The near-term forecast for uncertain economic environment increases this challenge exponentially. Recent developments in postponing the implementation of some elements of Basel III may be an indication of this difficulty.

Therefore, fundamentals must change, or the financial services industry, given its crucial role of liquidity provider, will remain increasingly capital-constrained and inhibit economic growth. New solutions are needed. This is where sustainability management comes in. Sustainability management does not add capital. However, managing tail risk effectively by preserving and protecting capital from unexpected losses can make capital go further.

There are two options to enhance sustainability via capital. One is by *increasing capital*, which, as outlined previously, is not a good option. The other is to allow current capital to go farther through well-structured defensive programs that *preserve and protect capital*. This requires a fundamental change from the current practice of employing capital as the first and only line of defense into employing capital as the last defense. This point is a crucial ingredient of sustainability management deserving additional discussion.

Capital as Last Defense Versus First Defense

The difference between capital as the first and the only defense versus the last defense may sound subtle, but it has far-reaching implications for capital adequacy as well as for revenue models. In the banking industry, it is often mentioned that quality of earnings, quality of management, effectiveness of the management process, and so on are first defenses against loss, which is true. However, these are all intangibles and do not provide the same measurable and objective protection as well-defined, tangible programs. For example, no risk management professional would recommend, nor senior managers would accept, an intangible like the quality of personnel/managers as a portfolio hedge instead of explicit tangible programs that define limits and controls. So why should capital protection programs be dependent on intangibles? Such intangibles are sound practices and they should be encouraged, but they are not a substitute for tangible defenses, thus leaving capital as the first and only tangible defense against risk.

Because of high cost, most industries do not use capital as the primary source of protection against losses from unquantifiable uncertainty. Most industries go out of their way to develop, implement, and monitor specific preventive and defensive programs to ensure that such initiatives meet their objective to preserve and protect capital.

OBJECTIVE OF SUSTAINABILITY MANAGEMENT
To preserve and protect capital from risk.

More and Stronger Defenses Mean Less Pressure on Capital

Identifying and structuring defensive programs, when implemented in a disciplined, credible manner (akin to BCPs), can provide the first tangible defense against unexpected losses and thus protect capital by reducing shocks to the institution's capital in a crisis.

Each institution must balance the need to drive revenues aggressively and maintain going-concern sustainability. Therefore, in order to allow risk to continue to drive the revenue engine in normal times and yet protect the institution from tail risk, sustainability enhancement programs can be developed and implemented as contingency programs. This allows an institution to capture the full potential of the revenue model aggressively, while protecting the capital prudently.

Contingency Defensive Programs

Everyone knows that the time to plan for and install smoke detectors is not when the building is on fire, but well ahead of time. The way to deal with defenses and protective programs to sustain a going-concern is well before an extreme financial crisis. Akin to smoke detectors, fire sprinklers, and BCPs, these programs should be implemented as contingency programs that are triggered by predefined criteria. The concept is not new; only its focus and how it may be applied are new.

From time to time, one hears of plans to supplement capital because of regulatory pressure. Some plans call for balance sheet restructuring; others call for asset sales to convert unrecorded gains into equity. Such programs are planned and implemented after capital has already taken a hit. Even if planning for such actions were to be completed ahead of time, because of the fast-paced marketplace, an institution in a crisis does not have the luxury of waiting weeks and months to implement them. Any counteraction needs to be quick and effective. The key difference between actions to convert unrecorded gains into equity and defensive programs is that effective sustainability management requires implementation as first defense rather than a response after capital is depleted. Another significant difference is that after-the-hit programs generally involve assets outside the operating functions with little or no impact on PMLs. Proactive sustainability management requires taking action in relation to operating assets and other items to reduce PML before the crisis and blunt the impact of unexpected losses on capital. Despite the disadvantages stated here, after-the-hit programs should continue to be a part of corporate plans.

Contingency-based defensive sustainability programs can be one of the most important parts of a sustainability management process. This is the frontline of the battle in a crisis, and the outcome of these programs could determine the going-concern sustainability of the institution. The effectiveness of contingency programs depends to a great degree upon how well and how carefully certain critical issues, such as those listed ahead, have been addressed upfront.

- What should be the objective and scope of contingency programs?
- How much protection should be provided?
- How far is an organization willing to go in a financial crisis to maintain going-concern sustainability?

- How much cost can be justified in developing, implementing, and maintaining contingency programs, and how much when they are triggered?
- When should they be triggered? What should be the mechanism to trigger them?
- How do you ensure, on an ongoing basis, that they can be counted upon to (i) trigger when they should, and (ii) reliably meet the stated objective and scope?

> ## THREE CRITICAL REQUIREMENTS OF CONTINGENCY PROGRAMS
> - Clearly established triggers
> - Effectiveness not dependent upon external factors
> - Timely implementation

While such issues require the collective wisdom of the senior-most management team, these judgments need to be based upon objective and clearly defined information. PML-based analyses, with a detailed and transparent description of the components of the total extreme exposure, provide solid foundation for addressing such critical issues.

The outcome of contingency programs does not provide additional capital. Such programs cannot substitute if an institution needs capital. However, capital planning and adequacy models should consider how such programs can effectively blunt the impact of unexpected shocks.

Such defensive programs, similar to BCPs, require upfront investments, and when triggered they will have significant costs and impact the institution's asset portfolio. Because of their impact on preserving and protecting capital, they represent the cheapest form of capital. Furthermore, developing and implementing effective shock-absorbing cushions, such as contingency programs, is a more effective way to relieve the pressure on capital, and far cheaper than adding capital to absorb shocks in an extreme crisis.

Reduction of Anxiety, Building Greater Confidence, and Adding Shareholder Value

Since the crisis of 2008, any mention of risk creates a high level of anxiety. This is because it is not possible for the market to gauge the strength and vulnerabilities of financial institutions given the possibilities of another extreme financial crisis. Revenue models and related risks are complex and not easily understandable. New regulations, while intended to avoid the systemic experience of 2008, have added confusion and complexity. Every financial institution is under pressure to show that significant progress has been made since 2008. Today, when inquiring about an institution's resiliency and ability to withstand and survive another crisis, one often hears:

> *It can't happen to us. We are well-diversified.*
> *Our equity ratios exceed regulatory requirements.*

We are ahead of Basel III implementation requirements.
We passed the stress test.
We have a fortress balance sheet.

Are these self-serving statements, or do they represent a false sense of security? On the other hand, are they comparable to similar claims that describe sentiments of the pre-2008 era? Can they be backed by an objective review of the issues that affect an institution's ability to handle exposure from extreme tail risk? How does one demonstrate the validity of these statements objectively, simply, and transparently?

All of these statements may be true, yet none captures an institution's going-concern strength in the face of a sudden financial crisis. There are no transparent, objective, and demonstrated links between the various steps taken by institutions and the needed enhancements in going-concern sustainability. Nor is there an objective way to gauge the relative effectiveness of various initiatives. This is the power of the PML-based approach! Since there are no black boxes or subjective assumptions, a PML-based sustainability management analysis can quantify the real exposure and show how an institution is managing it to ensure survival through a sudden financial crisis. For example, the impregnability of a fortress balance sheet can be demonstrated more effectively using an easy-to-understand and transparent PML-based analysis than through subjective anecdotal ratios or claims.

A transparent and simple dialog using a PML-based sustainability/tail risk analysis will help investors expand their understanding of not just how the institution's revenue model works, but also how it will fare through another crisis. Such an understanding will enable the investors to discriminate between institutions and thus (i) reduce the overall anxiety in the market place and (ii) reward the institutions that have a superior handle on tail risk.

Reduction of Systemic Risk

Effective sustainability management is in the public interest. Enhancing going concerns reduces systemic risk. Effective sustainability management has a higher going-concern threshold because of a fundamentally different focus. In addition to preserving the integrity of the financial system, regulators have an objective to protect depositors. Therefore, regulations may count certain non-common equity instruments as capital. However, if potential losses exceed common equity and reserves, then such non-common equity instruments cannot help to maintain the going concern. Sound sustainability management programs enhance the going-concern integrity. Therefore, the threshold for maintaining the going-concern integrity is higher than it is for regulatory purposes. As a result, effective sustainability management reduces the need for regulatory intervention in a crisis to protect the system.

In addition, by enabling a transparent discussion, a focus on extreme tail risk and going-concern sustainability can advance the too-big-to-fail public policy debate of the last four years more objectively.

PML-Based Sustainability Management has Large Rewards

A PML-based approach to sustainability/tail risk management:

- Leads to a simpler, easier-to-understand, and more transparent definition and management of exposure from extreme tail risk.
- Enhances the going-concern sustainability of institutions, which also reduces systemic risk.
- Encourages and helps build new cushions in front of capital, thus protecting and reducing pressures on capital.
- Adds shareholder value by improving the quality of earnings through proactive sustainability management steps.
- Enables and provides for a proactive and transparent dialog between institutions, regulators, and investors, thus alleviating the marketplace anxiety.

Sustaining a Going-Concern Through Tail-Risk Management

This discussion began with a glimpse of five hours around the desk of Rupert (a fictional character) amid the real events of July 7, 2005. The events clearly demonstrated the critical need for the proactive management of the operational risk of business interruption. Since the experiences of 9/11 and 7/7, significant and elaborate steps have been taken to reduce and minimize exposure from business-interruption risk. Business continuity plans represent one of the most significant steps in dealing with this operational risk.

This discussion concludes with a reference to the events of 2008. The experience clearly has demonstrated the critical need for proactive going-concern sustainability management in relation to tail risk. Implementation of clear sustainability-management policies and strategies and well-structured defensive programs must be the most important proactive step in relation to dealing with tail financial risk.

Just like many things in life, another major financial crisis is a sure bet. The only thing open to debate is its projected timing. Therefore, the sixty-four dollar question is: Will multi-asset financial institutions be better prepared to survive the next financial crisis?

For additional information, please contact:
Karamjeet Paul
kpaul@StrategicExposureGroup.com

References

Paul, K., Strategic Exposure Group is an advisory firm with an exclusive focus on extreme-exposure management of financial and business interruption risks. We leverage our expertise and experience to enable boards of large financial institutions to design top-down governance guidelines to ensure sustainability of the company as a going concern. For additional information, please contact: Karamjeet Paul, <kpaul@StrategicExposureGroup.com>.

The Basel III Capital Framework: a decisive breakthrough, Hervé Hannoun, Deputy General Manager, Bank for International Settlements, BoJ-BIS High Level Seminar on Financial Regulatory Reform: Implications for Asia and the Pacific Hong Kong SAR, 22 November 2010.

Index

Note: Page numbers followed by "*f*" and "*t*" refer to figures and tables, respectively.